Credit Derivatives

THE DEFINITIVE GUIDE

Credit Derivatives

THE DEFINITIVE GUIDE

Edited by Jon Gregory

Published by Risk Books, a division of Incisive Media plc.

Haymarket House
28–29 Haymarket
London SW1Y 4RX
Tel: +44 (0)20 7484 9700
Fax: +44 (0)20 7484 9800
E-mail: books@riskwaters.com
Sites: www.riskbooks.com
        www.riskwaters.com

Every effort has been made to secure the permission of individual copyright
holders for inclusion.

© Incisive Media Investments Ltd 2003

Reprinted 2004

ISBN 1 904 339 12 3

British Library Cataloguing in Publication Data
A catalogue record for this book is available from the British Library

Managing Editor: Sarah Jenkins
Editorial Assistant: Vasuki Balasubramaniam

Typeset by Mark Heslington, Scarborough, North Yorkshire

Printed and bound in Spain by Espacegrafic, Pamplona Navarra.

The challenges of a dynamic marketplace

Simon Greaves

Application Networks

The credit derivatives business is at a crossroads. This is a market that has enjoyed a phenomenal growth rate over the past five years or so. Historic credit events such as Enron and WorldCom have made it clear just how big the stakes are.

But the volatility of credit markets has also revealed a fundamental weakness in the way in which most financial firms manage their credit risk. Only a handful have developed systems that fully integrate their view of traditional bond and loan markets with their credit derivatives portfolios. And this weakness has contributed to mispricings and miscalculations of risk. The credit derivatives market has still to achieve efficiency.

The value of this book is that it is a thorough and balanced examination of the practical issues involved. This is not a dry academic text. As a practitioner at the sharp end of the business, the editor, Jon Gregory, has been able to commission expert contributors across the full range of those issues: from market practices, to quantitative analysis, regulatory, legal and control issues.

This book will help equip the reader for the new wave of credit derivative products that are revolutionising the way in which investors consider credit risk.

It is the greater liquidity in the credit derivative markets that is enabling the development of more sophisticated credit structures, such as complex collateralised debt obligations (CDOs), and options on credit default swaps (CDS). And it is this increased depth to the market that has prompted leading credit derivative players to develop credit derivative indices based on baskets of CDS. A third innovation in the market rests in the quest for "pure" credit risk transfer mechanisms. Indeed, the market is now developing a range of hybrid products that combine interest-rate, foreign-exchange or equity risk within a credit structure.

Increasingly, competitive advantage for derivatives dealers lies in the ability to develop, sell and trade these new instruments as quickly as possible.

But these second-generation credit derivatives are straining the technology infrastructure of dealing firms. Typically, research groups – working in tandem with sales teams and traders – can quickly construct and price new credit products to meet investor or end-user demand. Bottlenecks emerge, however, when the originating bank attempts to integrate the new product into its trade capture, trade processing, risk management and profit-and-loss systems. And this requires new approaches to software infrastructure, allowing the consolidation of risk across different assets. In the case of CDOs of CDOs, for example, the bank can be faced with extremely large underlying portfolios to track and risk-manage. Similarly, hybrid products require a cross-asset approach to risk management that, while firmly within the grasp of quants and front-office staff to price and manage, can pose significant problems in terms of their integration into middle- and back-office IT systems.

Traditional approaches to new product development are simply no longer adequate for both the rapid deployment of new products and their increasingly hybrid nature. The key drawback with the design of these legacy systems was that they were initially built with a single asset class in mind. This silo approach made them inflexible, cumbersome and difficult – in many cases almost impossible – to extend to new product lines.

One solution to the new product development problem is to decompose the pay-off features of new instruments into a series of "streams" or legs. Even the most complex structured products are composed of a number of distinct elementary economic pay-offs – whether credit, equity, FX or interest rates. These streams also allow users to describe processing aspects of the trade, such as how it resets and which credit events trigger default. Users can then package the new transaction by organising the different streams, using as many streams as necessary, and defining their relationship to one another.

This is not a new concept. The difficulty in the past has been a lack of the technology to allow for this implementation. Furthermore, this technology is now able to handle all asset classes – a vital requirement in a financial world that is becoming more cross-asset in orientation. This can be achieved by embracing a software design that is not tied to a particular asset class.

The development of the credit derivatives market offers leading banks a wealth of business possibilities – but it also raises significant questions over the handling of ever-more complex, and increasingly multi-asset, structures.

What is abundantly clear is that traditional approaches to IT infrastructure are simply not flexible enough to allow banks to move sufficiently quickly to meet investor expectations, and to exploit often short-lived windows of opportunity.

Just as investors are increasingly viewing the investment world in multi-asset terms, so too must banks. And at the heart of such a new approach to trading and risk management must be the IT infrastructure to support this new view of risk.

APPLICATION NETWORKS

Application Networks provides JRisk financial software for fast, flexible trading, trading support, and risk management solutions. JRisk´s new, innovative design supports activity across all financial products. It has been designed both with and for leading industry players to meet the most sophisticated functional requirements. JRisk is chosen by global invest-ment banks to allow the fast delivery of new business applications at a fraction of the cost. JRisk for Credit Derivatives is the solution of choice and is in production at the pioneers and leading players in the market.

Contents

SECTION 5: REGULATORY, DOCUMENTATION AND LEGAL ASPECTS

List of panels

CREDIT DERIVATIVES: KEY THEMES AND EXAMPLES

Throughout this book special panels introduce key themes and offer illustrative examples:

About the editor

Jon Gregory is global head of credit derivatives research analytics at BNP Paribas. His team has been instrumental in the growth of BNP Paribas global trading platform since the BNP and Paribas merger in 2000. Jon joined Paribas in 1997 and was responsible for the development of the internal model for analysing the economic capital of the fixed income division. In addition to his work on credit risk modelling he has worked on pricing and risk management issues in interest-rate and equity and insurance derivatives. His main interest lies in reconciling theoretical and practical approaches for pricing, hedging and managing credit risk. He worked in the Fixed Income division of Salomon Brothers (now part of Citigroup) prior to joining Paribas in 1997. In addition to publishing papers on the pricing of credit risk and related topics, he is co-author of the best selling book "Credit: The Complete Guide to Pricing, Hedging and Risk Management", short-listed for the Kulp-Wright Book Award for the most significant text in the field of risk management and insurance. Jon gained a BSc from the University of Bristol in 1993 and was awarded his PhD from Cambridge University in 1996.

List of contributors

Leif Andersen is currently co-head of the quantitative research group at Banc of America Securities. Prior to that, Leif spent 9 years at General Re Financial Products. Leif holds MSc's in electrical and mechanical engineering from the Technical University of Denmark, an MBA from the University of California at Berkeley, and a PhD in finance from Aarhus Business School.

Jesper Andreasen heads the product development team at Nordea Markets in Copenhagen, Denmark. The team is responsible for development and implementation of all derivatives models within Nordea, covering the areas of interest rates, credit, equities, foreign exchange, and hybrid derivatives. Prior to this, Jesper held positions in the quantitative research departments of General Re Financial Products and Bank of America in London. Jesper's current research interests include yield curve modelling, credit derivatives, volatility smiles, and numerical methods. In 2001 Jesper received *Risk* magazine's Quant of the Year award. Jesper holds a PhD in Mathematical Finance from Aarhus University, Denmark.

Alexander Batchvarov has served as Merrill Lynch's managing director of international structured credit research, since 1998. This team is based both in London and Tokyo. It provides research on the traditional asset backed securities (ABS) and mortgage backed securities (MBS), market developments and on new market segments such as alternative asset classes, CDOs, and CMBS synthetic securitisation in Europe and Asia. Previously, he worked as a structured finance analyst in the ABS Group, and as a sovereign analyst in the sovereign risk unit of Moody's Investors Service in London and New York. Alexander holds a PhD in international economics from the National Academy of Sciences in Bulgaria and an MBA in finance from the University of Alberta, Canada. He is a CFA charterholder and a member of AIMR and NYSSA.

Terry Benzschawel is a director in the quantitative credit modelling and analytics group in the fixed income research department of Citigroup Global Investments. Terry's responsibilities include supervision and construction of quantitative tools for the credit markets, including models of sovereign and corporate default, credit spreads, and cross-credit-sector asset allocation. Additionally, Terry builds neural network models for trading US Treasury and foreign currencies, and trades daily in those markets. He also coordinates post-graduate recruiting for the fixed income research department and chairs the department's modelling advisory group. Previously, Terry has worked at Salomon Brothers, where he built models for proprietary arbitrage trading in bonds, currencies and derivative securities for the emerging markets desk. Terry holds a PhD in experimental psychology from Indiana University and a BA (with distinction) from the University of Wisconsin. Terry has done post-doctoral fellowships in optometry at the University of California at Berkeley and in ophthalmology at the Johns Hopkins University School of Medicine.

Moorad Choudhry is head of Treasury at KBC Financial Products (UK) Ltd in London. At the time of writing, he was vice-president in structured finance services at JP Morgan Chase Bank in London. Previously he has worked as a government bond trader and money markets trader at ABN Amro Hoare Govett Sterling Bonds Ltd, and as a sterling proprietary trader at Hambros Bank Ltd. Moorad is a visiting professor at the department of economics, London Metropolitan University, and a senior fellow at the centre for mathematical trading and finance, CASS Business School, London. He has published widely in the field of fixed income and derivatives, and is the author of *The Bond and Money Markets: Strategy, Trading, Analysis*. Moorad holds an MA from the University of Reading, an MBA from Henley Management College, FRM from GarP, FSI(Dip) from Securities Institute, and a PhD from the University of London at Birkbeck.

Jenna Collins is vice president at Merrill Lynch's international structured credit research team. Since joining, she has had primary responsibility for commercial MBS, residential MBS, consumer ABS, small and medium-sized enterprise loan securitisations, and whole-business securitisations. She also covers the European CDO sector on a periodic basis and contributes regularly to the *International Structured Credit Weekly*. In addition, Jenna authors periodic sector and relative value reports. Prior to Merrill Lynch, Jenna was with Bank One's structured investment vehicle, White Pine Corporation Ltd, for two years to develop and enhance the quantitative models for the company. During this period, Jenna also managed the rating agency process to secure White Pine's senior and subordinated debt ratings as well as facilitated capital note placement with third party investors. Jenna has a BS from Georgetown University.

William Davies is the AVP for the international structured credit research team at, Merrill Lynch, London. He focuses on transactions, trends and developments in the European and Asian structured finance markets. The team is well known for in-depth analytics of the international ABS/MBS markets and regular publications: the *International Structured Credit Weekly*, annual reviews of the securitization markets in Europe and Asia, as well as detailed sector and asset specific publications. The Merrill Lynch structured credit research team has been consistently ranked as the best research provider in investor polls by *ISR, SRI, Euromoney, Credit Magazine, Institutional Investor*, etc. William holds a bachelors degree in medicine from the University of Nottingham, UK and is a chartered accountant and a CFA candidate.

Alla Gil is a managing director and the co-head of the strategic finance advisory group at Citigroup Global Markets in the US. In this role she is responsible for providing enterprise level finance advisory for clients worldwide. Her group develops innovative, theoretically sound and practical financial solutions by quantifying clients' exposures to different risk facets and identifying the most efficient risk mitigation strategies. Alla advises the senior management of major Citigroup clients on optimal capital structure, currency, interest rate, and credit risks as well as asset/liability, and economic capital management and optimisation. Prior to Citigroup, Alla spent three years at Goldman Sachs working on interest rate derivatives modelling, and two and a half years at CIBC developing credit derivatives models. Alla's background is in theoretical mathematics.

Simon Greaves is vice president of marketing at Application Networks. In his current role he leads the marketing group, bringing in-depth end-user expertise and perspective to the JRisk product. Before joining Application Networks, Simon was executive director of risk management for Sumitomo Finance in London. In this role he led the design and development of the VAR methodology and systems. He also directed the enhancement of risk analytics and the model creation and model validation group. Previously, Simon was based within the emerging markets group at CSFB. Simon holds an MA in Economics.

Greg M. Gupton is a director of quantitative research at Moody's KMV, a subsidiary of Moody's Corporation. His work is currently focused on LGD forecasting, EaD estimation, and refining asset volatility. Formerly, Greg was a leading force in building JP Morgan's internal credit risk methodologies. He developed pricing and risk models including credit derivatives modelling, designed risk management policy, and consulted on credit risk best practices for external clients. Greg is widely published on the topic of credit risk measurement and management and is the author of *CreditMetrics*. His CreditMetrics methodology (and its implementation, CreditManager) is the most widely applied credit value-at-risk tool worldwide. Greg holds a BA in accounting from the University of Washington, and a MS in industrial administration from Carnegie-Mellon University.

Paul Hawkins is a vice president in Merrill Lynch's securitisation group in London. His responsibilities include structuring, marketing and executing transactions for financial institutions, specialising in synthetic transactions and exotic asset classes. Prior to joining Merrill Lynch, Paul worked in a quantitative capacity with the credit derivatives group at Citibank, NA, and Salomon Smith Barney, structuring large portfolio transactions. Paul holds a PhD in quantitative finance from Imperial College, University of London, entitled *"Optimising Portfolios of Credit Risks by Maximising Expected Return on Economic Capital"*, and an MA in Mathematics from Cambridge University.

Erik Heitfield works as a staff economist for the board of governors of the Federal Reserve System, in the board's Monetary and Financial Studies Section, Erik conducts research and technical analysis in support of the Federal Reserve Board's bank supervision and regulation responsibilities. Erik has been actively involved in the Board's ongoing efforts to develop the New Basel Capital Accord (Basel II). His most recent research has focused on the measurement and management of credit risk in complex banking organisations. Erik received a PhD in economics from the University of California, Berkeley in 1998.

Viktor Hjort is an associate at Morgan Stanley in London. He primarily covers the areas of European credit strategy (IG) and credit derivatives strategy. He has three and a half years experience in credit strategy and credit derivatives trading. He was part of the team ranked first in credit strategy by *Credit Magazine* in 2001. In 2002 and 2003, his team was ranked first in *Institutional Investor's* all-Europe fixed income research team poll for investment grade strategy, and was in 2003 ranked second in high-grade credit strategy and third in credit derivatives strategy by *Euromoney* as well as first in high-grade credit strategy by *Credit Magazine*. Viktor holds an MSc in economics and a BSc in economics, both from the University of Lund.

Jouke Hottinga is risk manager at AEGON Netherlands. Prior to AEGON he worked at the quantitative research department of Robeco Asset Management where he was co-ordinator of the fixed income and asset allocation research. He graduated from the Erasmus University Rotterdam in 1995 with a master's degree in econometrics.

Monique Jeanblanc is a professor at Evry University, France. Her research fields are: stochastic control (existence of optimal control for degenerate diffusions, partial observation) and mathematical finance (optimisation, credit risk, jump-diffusion models). She is a co-author of *Financial Markets in Continuous Time, Valuation and Equilibrium* (with R.A. Dana) and *Mathematics Methods for Markets* (with M. Yor and M. Chesney). Monique is also a contributor to *Encyclopedia of Financial Engineering* and is the associate editor of *Finance and Stochastics, International Journal of Theoritical and Applied Finance*.

Monique teaches a training course on stochastic processes (HEC, France) and on credit risk (Ensae, France). She is an invited lecturer at Hong-Kong University, Spring School in Munich and Montréal University. Monique organises the Bachelier international conferences (selection of papers and invited speakers) and the Bachelier seminar in Paris.

Sean C. Keenan is currently a vice president in Citigroup's Risk Architecture Group. He is involved in the development of quantitative tools and methodologies for assessing credit risk including debt rating models for C&I lending, default prediction and early warning systems for large corporate obligors and risk assessment methodologies for a variety of asset-backed and structured loan products. Prior to joining Citigroup, Sean was with Moody's Risk Management Services, where was involved in the development and validation of quantitative credit scoring and default prediction and default-rate forecasting models. Sean holds a PhD in economics from New York University.

Maria Leibholz is a vice president and senior analyst in the derivatives group of Moody's Investors Service, where the principal focus of her work is the ongoing analysis of cash flow and synthetic CDOs, and structured note issuances as part of the initial rating and monitoring process. Prior to joining Moody's in 2002, Maria was an associate at Fried, Frank, Harris, Schriver and Jacobson, where her practice was concentrated on structured finance, primarily credit derivatives and collateralized debt obligations transactions. After receiving an MA in broadcast journalism from Moscow State University in 1991, she worked as a broadcast journalist for Central Television of Russia and earned a JD from Columbia University in 1998.

David X. Li is currently a director and New York head of the global credit derivative research group at Citigroup Global Markets Inc., where he leads model development to support global credit derivative trading business. Before joining CitiGroup he was a vice president of risk management at AXA Financial, where he was responsible for risk measurement for both assets and liabilities. He has also worked as a partner for The RiskMetrics Group where he initiated and developed the first commercial CDO model, CDO Manager. Previously, David worked at CIBC financial products group as a desk quant for credit derivative business. David is widely credited with introducing copula functions into credit portfolio modelling as well as for writing the first paper on credit curve construction. David has a PhD in statistics and master's degrees in economics, finance and actuarial science. He is also an associate of the Society of Actuaries.

Douglas Lucas is a director at UBS and head of CDO strategy. He is responsible for the monthly *CDO Insight* publication. Prior to joining UBS in 2001, Douglas was head of CDO research at JP Morgan. Before that he was co-CEO of Salomon Swapco for six years and had credit control positions with two boutique swap dealers. Douglas was at Moody's Investors Service from 1987 to 1993 where he wrote the rating agency's first default and rating transition studies. He also developed Moody's rating methodology for collateralized debt obligations and triple-A special purpose derivatives dealers. He is known for his work in default correlation. Douglas has a BA magna cum laude in economics from UCLA and an MBA with honours from the University of Chicago.

Louise Marshall is the policy director and head of communications for the International Swaps and Derivatives Association, Inc (ISDA). She works on a wide range of policy issues, including trading practice, credit derivatives and equity derivatives. Prior to joining ISDA, Louise spent the majority of her career as a financial journalist, specialising in derivatives and risk management. She worked as an editor for several of *Thomson Financial Networks'* online news services, and subsequently for *IFR Magazine, Financial Products,* and the *FOW* suite of publications.

Roy Mashal is an associate with the quantitative credit research group at Lehman Brothers Inc, New York. His main research interests are pricing and risk management of multi-name credit products such as CDOs, credit default baskets, and the modelling of counterparty exposure. Roy is an expert in specification and estimation of copula-based financial models. He holds a BSc and an MSc from Tel Aviv University and is a PhD candidate at the Columbia Business School.

Eileen Murphy is the global head of CDOs for Barclays Capital. She was recruited to establish the Barclays agency CDO group and assist Barclays in developing its CDO market strategy. The agency CDO group has responsibility for origination and structuring of arbitrage and balance sheet transactions for third-party clients. Prior to joining Barclays, Eileen worked at Chase Securities as global head of the collateralised debt obligations group. Here she was responsible for a global group of 23 professionals involved in the origination, structuring, distribution and trading of CDOs backed by bonds, loans and structured products. Eileen's previous position was at Moody's Investor Services, where she was managing director and co-head of the structured derivative products group. Prior to Moody's, Eileen worked as a bankruptcy and corporate finance attorney for Seward and Kissel in New York. She graduated with a Juris Doctor from the University of North Carolina at Chapel Hill.

Marco Naldi is senior vice president and head of US quantitative credit research at Lehman Brothers. He is responsible for the development of the new Lehman Brothers Risk Model, a tool for the risk management of benchmarked portfolios. His current research focuses on portfolio default risk, counterparty risk, capital structure arbitrage, and the valuation and risk management of multi-name credit derivatives such as basket default swaps, loss tranches and CDOs. Marco received his PhD in finance from Columbia Business School, where he also taught as an adjunct professor. He had previously earned a PhD in economics from the University of Bologna (Italy). His academic interests focused on fields such as market microstructure, corporate finance and empirical asset pricing.

Robert Reoch currently runs an independent consultancy, Reoch Consulting, which he set up in 2001. He has been closely involved with the credit derivatives market since 1994. Prior to this, Robert worked at the Bank of America as global head of credit derivatives, with responsibility for building a global credit derivatives business. Previously, he was the head of credit derivatives at Nomura International, where he was made with a mandate for rolling out the global business. He took on a pioneering role when he set up JP Morgan's European credit derivative business and was influential in the growth and development of the global credit derivatives market. Robert was an active spokesperson and contributed to the development of the legal and regulatory framework of the market. Robert has a BA and MA in law and in chinese studies from Cambridge University.

Alex Reyfman is a credit derivatives strategist in the US investment grade research group at Goldman Sachs. He focuses on the single name credit default swap (CDS) market. Alex joined Goldman Sachs in September 2000 from Lehman Brothers. At Lehman Brothers he worked in the structured credit strategies and fixed income quantitative research groups. Alex received a PhD in economics from the University of Chicago in 1997 and a BA from Columbia College.

Marek Rutkowski is Professor of mathematical finance at the Warsaw University of Technology (Politechnika Warszawska). He is the author of several research papers on stochastic processes and financial mathematics, which have appeared in numerous journals including *Mathematical Finance, Finance and Stochastics* and *Applied Mathematical Finance*. His recent fields of interest include modelling of the defaultable term structure, valuation of credit derivatives, and modelling of implied volatilities. He is a co-author, with Marek Musiela, of the monograph *Martingale Methods in Financial Modelling* published by Springer-Verlag in 1997. His joint monograph, with Tom Bielecki, entitled *Credit Risk: Modeling, Valuation and Hedging* was published in 2002. He is also a co-editor of *Finance and Stochastics* and *Mathematical Finance*. Marek gained his PhD degree in mathematics in 1981, and his DSc degree in financial mathematics in 1998. He has also taught for several years at the School of Mathematics, University of New South Wales, Sydney.

Jure Skarabot is an associate in the global credit derivative research group at Citigroup Global Markets Inc. In addition to credit derivatives research and quantitative modelling, his emphasis is on client research and analytical support in the area of single-name credit derivative products and synthetic credit portfolios. He joined Citigroup after completing his PhD in finance at Haas School of Business, University of California at Berkeley. His dissertation work was based on structural models of credit risk and he has presented his research at several conferences. He also holds a PhD in mathematics from the University of Wisconsin at Madison in the area of harmonic analysis.

Darren Smith is a director of the credit derivatives and securitisation group with Dresdner Kleinwort Wasserstein in London. Prior to this, Darren was responsible for UBS Warburg's CDO effort in Europe, which he joined as part of the merger with PaineWebber in 2000. Darren has broad experience in structuring CDOs, including cashflow and synthetics on assets as diverse as leverage loans, emerging markets, high yield and CDOs of CDOs.

Jorge Sobehart is a vice president / senior analyst at Citigroup Risk Architecture. He is currently involved in the probabilistic assessment of credit risk for portfolio risk management. Previously, he was a member of Moody's standing committee on quantitative tools and vice president / senior analyst in Moody's risk management services, where he developed and validated two credit risk models: RiskCalc for public firms, and RiskScore. During his career, he has worked and acted as a scientific consultant for several prestigious companies and institutions, and also acted as a referee for professional journals. In addition to publishing technical reports in many different fields, he has contributed to conferences. Jorge has advanced degrees in physics and has postdoctoral experience at the Los Alamos National Laboratory.

Alberto Thomas is an executive director and senior structurer within the global credit derivatives group at UBS. Alberto joined UBS in June 1997. Since then he has been involved in the structuring of credit derivatives transactions for institutional clients and private investors. His experience embraces different repackaging techniques covering several asset classes: from CDOs to credit derivatives to alternative investments repackaging. Alberto has two years previous experience in the structured products area at Credit Lyonnais Americas, New York. Alberto completed his education obtaining two financial engineering degrees from Politecnico di Torino and Ecole Centrale des Arts et Manufactures in Paris.

Klaus Toft heads the credit derivatives sales strategies group at Goldman Sachs. Prior to his current role, Klaus was responsible for Goldman's credit derivatives quantitative modelling and system developments. Klaus was on the faculty at the Graduate School of Business, University of Texas at Austin from 1994 to 1997, where he taught derivatives pricing and investment theory. His applied and academic research on credit derivatives, option pricing, second generation derivative securities, and optimal capital structure theory has appeared in *Derivatives Week, Futures and Options World, Journal of Derivatives, Journal of Finance, Journal of Financial and Quantitative Analysis, Journal of Financial Engineering, Review of Financial Studies*, and in *Risk Magazine*. Klaus received his MS and PhD in Finance from the University of California at Berkeley.

Rodanthy Tzani is an assistant vice president and analyst in the derivatives group of Moody's Investors Service where she focuses on the quantitative analysis of arbitrage cash flow and synthetic CDOs, as well as other more exotic types of CBOs and structured derivatives instruments. Whilst at Moody's, Rodanthy wrote a number of *New Issue Reports* and she is also working on research questions related to Moody's rating methodology. Prior to joining Moodys, she was a systems engineer with Ericsson Radio Systems AB, Sweden, where she worked on developing new features for wireless phone and data systems. She has 18 refereed publications. Rodanthy has held a number of research and teaching positions with various universities in Europe and the US, after receiving her PhD in theoretical physics from the City University of New York in 1989.

Assaf Zeevi is an assistant Professor of decision risk and operations in the Graduate School of Business at Columbia University, New York. His main research interests are in the areas of finance and risk management, and include financial econometrics, statistical estimation and simulation methods with applications to modelling, calibration and analysis of credit derivatives and credit risk. Assaf received his BSc and MSc from the Technion, Israel and subsequently his PhD from Stanford University, California.

Machiel Zwanenburg is a risk manager at Robeco. Currently, he is responsible for the implementation of Robeco's market risk methodology. Previously he has been a quantitative researcher responsible for, among other things, the development and implementation of risk management systems for credit portfolios, including collateralised debt obligations. He graduated with a master's degree in econometrics from the Erasmus University Rotterdam in 1998 and an MSc in economics from the London School of Economics and Political Science in 1999.

Introduction

Jon Gregory

BNP Paribas*

Financial derivatives and especially credit derivatives have experienced tremendous growth in recent years. Derivatives play an important role in improving the growth and efficiency of the global economy but can have potentially enormous risks, as highlighted by the 2001 collapse of the energy giant Enron. Warren Buffet, the legendary investor, has recently labelled derivatives "financial weapons of mass destruction", a remark that has received much attention in the markets and media. Mr Buffet's concerns extend to credit derivatives, specifically that there are large amounts of credit risk concentration. Alan Greenspan, chairman of the Federal Reserve, has taken an almost diametrically opposite view by stating that credit derivatives have helped make the economy shock-resistant and potentially diffuse losses arising from a major default such as Enron.

It is clear that there are hurdles to the development of the credit derivatives market, which can be compared, for example, to the OTC interest-rate derivatives market of around 15 years ago. The measurement and management of credit risk is much more complicated than that of market risk as parameters are hard to obtain and correlation effects hard to assess. There needs to be an increased transparency, especially as the instruments and risks involved are quite complex. Legal and documentation procedures need to be continually updated and the expanded role of rating agencies in rating portfolio credit transactions needs to be understood. Rapid advancements in quantitative research are required and new IT infrastructure needs to be developed.

This book is not purely focused on models, products or regulatory aspects but rather tries to cover the whole spectrum of issues. This text is

* All opinions expressed herein are those of the author and do not necessarily reflect those of his employers, past or present.

divided into five sections. The first covers the CDS market, including a short overview, and then focuses on some key issues: the factors driving credit spreads, basis effects, the restructuring debate and the equity-credit linkage. The second section introduces portfolio credit risk and describes the phenomena of default correlation and then describes various credit portfolio models such as the well-known CreditMetrics and KMV approaches, and finally shows how models can be built to facilitate dynamic management of a credit portfolio. Next, in Section 3, we look at structured credit derivatives, which have formed a large part of this market, looking at all the possible types such as cash/synthetic, balance-sheet/arbitrage, single-tranche, managed and so on. Section 4 is concerned purely with the modelling side and covers issues such as how to price a synthetic CDO tranche or credit spread option. Finally, in Section 5 we cover the regulatory, documentation and legal aspects.

When putting together the different chapters, I have tried to avoid any unnecessary overlap or repetition while allowing differing views on subjects to be expressed. This book can be read in order with concepts and ideas introduced successively so that the reader can build up a detailed understanding of the main practical and theoretical issues. However, it equally well can be used as a resource for dipping into particular topics of interest, as the chapters can generally be read as stand-alone pieces.

I am grateful for discussions with my colleagues at BNP Paribas, in particular Charles Donald, Steven Hutt and Jean-Paul Laurent, and to Sarah Jenkins of Risk Books for working so hard to coordinate the whole project. Finally, my thanks go to the authors, who have produced excellent chapters and adapted them to fit together in a cohesive way and therefore represent more than just a series of articles. Hopefully, we have been able to provide a comprehensive and unbiased view of the key topics in the credit derivatives market.

Jon Gregory
London, August 2003

Section 1

The Default Swap Market

Introduction

Jon Gregory
BNP Paribas

Financial markets have historically had a tendency to decompose risks from one another, allowing products to be tailor-made for particular investors. The development of the CDS market has partially arisen from the need to isolate credit risk compared with other components (funding, interest-rate), one such application being loan portfolio management. For example, banks have tended to have excessive credit exposure to particular individuals or to strongly correlated groups of borrowers and this lack of diversification of lending is hard to avoid (the banker's paradox). However, a CDS allows protection buyers to hedge such risks anonymously, freeing credit lines and removing exposure concentrations while maintaining borrower relationships and even potentially diversifying risk beyond their customer base by selling protection on other names. As such, the development of the CDS market gives the potential to facilitate a more efficient allocation of credit risk in the economy. Currently, this occurs mainly through regulatory arbitrage, but Basel II should align regulatory capital requirement more with economic risk and provide more incentive for credit risk management based on real underlying credit quality.

It is helpful to begin with a general overview of the credit derivatives market, including its development, the products and a look to the future. **Robert Reoch** of **Reoch Consulting** has been involved in the credit derivatives business for the last decade and has headed credit derivatives desks at JP Morgan, Nomura International and Bank of America. He is in a good position to contribute what I hope is a relatively impartial overview of the credit derivatives market as it is today and also provide an insight into where it may be tomorrow. This chapter covers products and applications, describes the new players in a market formally more the domain of banks and looks at developmental issues.

In the next chapter, **Jouke Hottinga** of **Aegon** and **Machiel Zwanenburg** of **Robeco Asset Management** analyse the determinants of credit spread returns. This could be of interest, for example, in a perfor-mance-measurement context in allocating credit assets over other sectors. The analysis is necessarily focused on bonds rather than CDSs since the synthetic market does not have data spanning enough names or sufficient history, while bond data allow a cross-sectional statistical study going back several years and including global events such as the 1998 Russian crisis. It is well known that there exists a risk premium, and expected default accounts for only a small part of a credit spread, especially for investment-grade corporates. This study finds that systematic risk explains around two-fifths of the credit spread returns for investment-grade corporates; the remaining components would obviously come from idiosyncratic or specific risks and also other factors not accounting for in the analysis, such as equity volatility. In terms of the explained spread changes, a general market movement has the largest influence with secto-rial effects also being important. Interestingly, there is little dependence on rating (except for high-yield bonds), which is not surprising since it is generally acknowledged that ratings lag spreads and not vice versa. The study also considers the importance of systematic factors for investment-grade compared with high-yield portfolios. The chapter concludes with a discussion of the basis between CDS and bonds, a topic taken up in more detail by **Viktor Hjort** of **Morgan Stanley**, who examines each of the components in turn, describing whether they have a positive or negative impact on the basis. Basis effects can be divided into contract components (deliverables, counterparty risk, funding, coupon effects) and market effects (repo effects, funding, asymmetries between protection buyers and sellers). The author argues that these components can sometimes reinforce one another, giving the CDS market a sort of "high-beta" character compared with the cash market.

A major component of the CDS-bond basis is the cheapest-to-deliver option, which is the subject of the next chapter by **Alex Reyfman** and **Klaus Toft** of **Goldman Sachs**. This has been a hot topic recently in the market, not least as a result of the Conseco restructuring, which led to calls for restructuring to be removed as a credit event from CDS contracts. Protection sellers would obviously be keen on this, worried perhaps about moral hazard in that lenders who are long protection have an incentive to restructure the loan. On the other hand, protection buyers may have an incomplete hedge if restructuring is not included and not get the reduction in regulatory capital they desire (a point to be addressed by Basel II). The authors extend a standard default swap pricing model to include both hard and soft credit events, allowing consistent pricing between the four types of contracts with different restructuring definitions that currently exist. The main model inputs are the probability of the soft credit event (restructuring) compared with the hard credit events and the assumed credit spread and maturity extension after a restructuring. The fact that in the future a company may issue more debt makes modelling the value of a cheapest-to-deliver option rather difficult. However, without such a model it is hard to estimate the relative differences between contracts with different deliverables and to understand how these differences would be impacted by effects such as maturity and spread level.

In the final chapter in this first section, we are introduced to the linkage between the credit and equity markets. This is an important area to explore fully since many of the ways in which credit risk is modelling both at a single-name and portfolio level is based on this. According to the well-known work of Merton (1974) – preceded to some degree by the Modigliani-Miller theorem (1958) and Black-Scholes (1973) option pricing model – corporate risk can be priced via a theoretical relationship between the equity (assets) and debt (liabilities) of a company. Of course, it is well known that such a theoretical relationship does not always persist, such as when the equity of a company with distressed debt is not priced close to zero or when there is weak correlation between bond prices and equities. We may observe significant changes in the equity market (such as an increase in volatility), leaving corporate bond spreads unchanged, or even a move such as after the terrorist attacks of 11 September 2001, when equity markets plummeted but a flight-to-quality meant that the bond market rallied. These deviations can be attributed to many factors, such as the behaviour of credit analysts or capital structure arbitrageurs; or that the no-arbitrage assumptions necessarily made by Merton do not hold. This subject is discussed by **Sean Keenan**, **Jorge Sobehart** and **Terry Benzschawel** of **Citigroup**. The authors describe the linkage between equity and debt markets and examine the fundamental reasons why the connection can break down. They also show how to extend the Merton framework to explicitly account for uncertainty in the equity and debt markets. Only recently have commercial Merton-type models become available, via KMV in the nineties, for estimating default probabilities, and then CreditGrades in 2002 as a transparent model for credit pricing. However, as **Jean-Pierre Lardy** of **JP Morgan** explains in Panel 1 of Chapter 5, traders have for longer than this been hedging debt exposures with equity positions and capital-structure arbitrage has been a common practice by a number of banks and hedge funds. This short piece gives a flavour of how structural Merton-type models can be valuable if the potential shortcomings are understood.

BIBLIOGRAPHY

Basel Committee on Banking Supervision, 2003, "Third consultative paper", http://www.bis.org/bcbs/bcbscp3.htm

Black, F., and M. Scholes, 1973, "The Pricing of Options and Corporate Liabilities", *Journal of Political Economy*, 81, pp 637–59.

Merton, R. C., 1974, "On the Pricing of Corporate Debt: The Risk Structure of Interest Rates", *Journal of Finance*, 29, pp 449–70.

Modigliani, F. and M. H. Miller, 1958, "The Cost of Capital, Corporate Finance and the Theory of Investment", *American Economic Review*, 48(63), pp. 261–97.

Tolk, S. J., 2001, "Understanding the Risks in Credit Default Swaps", Moody's Special Report.

1

Credit derivatives: the past, the present and the future

Robert Reoch

Reoch Consulting

A BRIEF HISTORY

The credit derivative market saw its earliest trades in 1993, when CSFB and the then Bankers Trust were transacting basket structures to lighten up credit exposures to the banking and sovereign sector. A few other banks followed suit in 1994, driven by, among other things, the desire to hedge sovereign credit exposures resulting from long-dated cross-currency swaps on the back of sizeable sovereign borrowings. With hindsight, it seems ironic that the market was kicked off by the hedging of swap-related credit exposures using first-to-default structures – two products that are still considered complex in today's market.

While the products of then and now may look the same, beneath the surface things are very different. The pricing, trading, booking, valuation and reporting of credit derivatives has changed beyond recognition. Hundreds of trades can now be executed in one day (rather than one trade taking hundreds of days), and the breadth of application goes way beyond the ad hoc hedging needs of the early nineties.

The change in end users has been more obvious as entire new sectors of the financial markets join the rapidly growing credit derivatives market. While the core group of significant players has looked the same over the years, this new group of "other participants" bears little resemblance to the early days. This market is no longer the exclusive domain of banks and securities houses: perhaps not surprisingly, it is spreading to all areas where credit risk is a component of doing business.

As with any new product or new market, the development of the credit derivatives market has been peppered with obstacles and disputes. Since bad news generally makes better press than good news, it has been the failings of the credit derivatives market that have been well reported and, hence, that tend to colour the memories of observers and commentators. Less well reported have been two main successes: an increasing percentage of robust contracts that perform as advertised and an ongoing review and modification process that ensures that holes in the market are plugged. By most performance measures the market is improving.

The rest of this introduction looks at these three categories – products, players and performance – in more detail.

PRODUCTS AND APPLICATIONS

The product set of the credit derivatives market falls into three categories: the credit default swap (CDS), portfolio products and other. The first two are by far the most prevalent, resulting in what looks like a rather polarised market: single-name trading at one end, portfolio trading at the other. The other category would include products such as hybrids and volatility products.

The CDS has established itself as the main instrument for transferring credit risk and hence dominates the market for single-name trading. Much attention has been given to addressing issues with its documentation, and the market has worked on standardising and simplifying the way that it trades. As a result, more than 1,000 credits are now being traded in the CDS market and, of these, more than 300 are considered to be as liquid as, if not more liquid than, their underlying bonds.

The term "portfolio product" covers a number of different structures with a common theme that the risk of multiple credits is contained within the structure. Hence, a cash or synthetic CDO would fall into this category, but so would a first-to-default structure. The former may reference hundreds of credits against the latter's half a dozen but in both cases the investor is exposed to nth loss or nth to default risk of multiple credits. The market is currently dominated by so-called single-tranche deals, where a dealer creates just one tranche of risk (for example, the second 5% of loss) to suit the needs of an investor and retains the residual risk position (the first 5% and the last 90% in the example) for its own book. The growth in this sector is due to a combination of investor demand for specific tranches and the relative ease of transacting such single-tranche deals. The necessary hedging that accompanies these transactions has led to significant growth in exotic trading books, now generally referred to as correlation trading.

As with other derivative markets, a number of hybrid products have emerged combining the transfer of credit risk with other risks such as market risk or equity risk. Hence a CDS, where the notional is equal to the value of an interest-rate swap and would allow a user to hedge the credit risk of the interest rate swap. A CDS where the trigger for payout is a fall in equity price (EDS) is one example of a number of applications that enable debt to be traded against equity, so-called "capital structure arbitrage".

Credit derivatives continue to trade as OTC products and the trading strategies employed by the market become ever more sophisticated. The sort of language that once was the domain of the interest-rate or bond world is now being used by the credit derivatives trading. Hence, the well-established directional trading and risk management activities are now accompanied by basis, curve and correlation trades and more esoteric activities such as capital structure arbitrage.

The structure of the market has evolved with the products and hence, broadly speaking, the trading of plain vanilla (single-name) and complex (correlation) products is managed and risk-managed by different groups. However, since many of the hedging strategies used by correlation trading require the use of the single-name market, there will be a close working relationship between the two groups.

Much of the single-name market and a small but growing section of the complex market are traded in the broker market. The brokers not only bring the dealers together in an efficient manner but also provide a quick outlet for hedging increasingly low-margin product and, above all provide a risk manager with much-sought-after confidentiality.

THE PLAYERS

Perhaps not surprisingly, banks and securities houses still dominate activity in the credit derivatives market and there is significant trading within the top 30 or so institutions. To the extent that credit risk is traded outside of this group, and informal discussions would suggest that this now represents at least half of market activity, the end-user group is broad. Other banks and the insurance sector have a significant role to play, each representing more than one quarter of end users; and another quarter is taken up by funds both leveraged (hedge funds) and so-called real-money accounts – the latter moving from almost zero to 7% (*Risk* Survey, February 2003) in just two years.

It is this last group of institutional investors that represents the most significant development for end users in the credit derivatives market because for a long time they shunned the credit derivatives market as an unacceptable new asset class. This lack of acceptance was due to a number of factors, including the bad name gained by being associated with the misselling of structured product in the mid-nineties. With the passage of time and the emergence of an environment of low interest rates and volatile equity markets, many institutions are now accepting the credit derivatives market and this important development is bound to have a positive impact on the market.

The insurance sector has already made its impact on the market with monolines, reinsurance companies and other insurance companies becoming investors at the mezzanine and senior levels of portfolio products. Their involvement may have wavered a bit in 2003 but is unlikely to go away, and will certainly increase with the advent of Basel II, which enables insurance companies to be acceptable counterparties for regulatory capital relief (something that only OECD banks can do today).

The involvement by corporates continues to disappoint the market and it seems increasingly likely that the slow cultural change that brought corporates around to the benefits of managing market risk may be just as slow or even slower for the management of credit risk.

MARKET PERFORMANCE AND DEVELOPMENTAL ISSUES

Documentation has been and is likely to continue to be at the forefront of market performance and developmental issues. Many of the market's failings to date have centred on a shortcoming in the documentation due not to poor drafting but to a failure to anticipate the vagaries, inefficiencies and lack of standardisation of the credit markets.

As the credit derivatives market continues to mature and as more and more underlying asset types are "derivatised", further revisions will be necessary. It is interesting to note that within days of the implementation of the long-awaited 2003 credit derivative Definitions, the market was already using a supplement.

One documentation stumbling block that cannot be fixed by creative legal drafting relates to market practice: not only do credit instruments vary considerably but how they are used and assessed for risk purposes also varies by user group. Hence, because of a differing approach to restructuring as a credit event in the US, Europe and Asia, the market now has a number of standards for restructuring as users differ in their acceptance of limiting the maximum maturity of deliverable obligations following a restructuring credit event or of limiting whether restructuring can be called for multi-holder or bilateral obligations. One of the choices favoured by a growing percentage of users is to remove restructuring altogether. It will be interesting to see where this debate leads – few can deny that the multiple standards are harming the market.

In the last year the question of infrastructure and technology has become more topical, and accounting has entered the limelight in the form of EIFT02/03 and IAS39, which have put a large question mark against Day One p&l for structured product. In true derivatives style, the market has taken this head on and embarked on a number of initiatives to resolve this problem. One likely outcome will be an improvement in the quality and quantity of credit pricing data (spreads, volatilities, correlation) and this will have knock-on benefits beyond the needs of the accounting world.

Technology enjoys a more prominent position in the credit derivatives market as ever-evolving products push out the modelling envelope. Not only are the computations becoming more complex but, due to the rapid evolution of the market, they are also constantly changing. No sooner has an institution rolled out its latest credit derivatives suite than a new product is born that has to be "shoe-horned" into the new system. There is a limit to how long a control environment will tolerate much shoe-horning, so of course the technology has to be modified. This process normally takes weeks or even months – plenty of time for another new product to come along.

From an infrastructure perspective, "straight-through processing" is becoming a buzz phrase in the credit derivatives market and in the last few months there has been much discussion of electronic confirmation clearing. For a growing number of institutions, a reduction or removal of the process of manually generating and sending out confirmations will have a material impact on the efficiency and resource needs of the credit derivative support function. There are two systems set to go live during the second half of 2003

The computation and management of counterparty risk has dogged the market since its outset and still creates problems today. From a quantitative perspective it is complex, given that in many cases Credit A is hedged by Credit B, which has posted Credit C as collateral. The model necessary to compute this risk is only as good as the data that feed it and herein lies the second complexity – correlation data, not readily available in today's market. Even if it were and the risks positions could be calculated, how could they be managed, since the exposure to a counterparty is changing from day to day? The market for hedging dynamic exposure is not well developed.

THE FUTURE

When all parties to a market seem to benefit differently but equally from that market's growth and development, it would appear to bode well for the future. On the supply side, banks are reaping the benefits of being able to hedge credit risk and, more importantly, of being able to separate the historical tie of binding client franchise to credit risk. On the buy side, investors are demanding and getting credit products structured very closely to their specific needs with a heightened level of transparency and the option of having a third-party asset manager.

The significant volumes generated by activity in the portfolio sector are having a knock-on effect in terms of producing both better data (credit spread and correlation) and an increased desire for new products (credit spread options and index products). The market would appear to have achieved the necessary critical mass whereby, as it grows, more problems are being solved than created. This phenomenon is also being helped by the move towards integrated credit as more and more banks are placing cash and derivatives trading of credit in the same unit.

Predictions about the future of the credit derivatives market tend to focus on how big it is going to be: how its apparent notional size of US$2 trillion will multiply over the next few years. More relevant perhaps than guestimates of size is whether the necessary components for growth are in place. There can be little doubt that the number and types of users are increasing; the number of underlying credits being traded is growing; and the mindset necessary to trade credit synthetically is also moving in the right direction. The regulatory environment is probably changing to incentivise and reward the hedging of credit risk, and within senior management of financial institutions there is a necessary cultural change under way that accepts the need for a portfolio approach to managing credit risk.

As was seen in the interest-rate swap market, this combination of improving infrastructure and external motivation is vital for a market's growth. Whether the credit derivatives market will follow the direction of its interest-rate cousin remains to be seen, but it is worth noting that the former is still a few percentage points of the size of its underlying cash market (bonds and loans), whereas the latter is a multiple of its underlying cash market (government bonds). Even a slight move in the right direction could make the number US$2 trillion look very small.

2

The determinants of credit spread returns

Jouke Hottinga and Machiel Zwanenburg*

Aegon and Robeco

In this chapter, we will consider the determinants of credit spread return, which is driven by both the level of and changes to the credit spread. This is important because if the credit spread of a bond increases, the yield of the bond will increase, resulting in a decrease in the bond's market value. Information on the factors that drive the credit market can be used in different situations. Possible applications are the forecasting of the return on credit bonds, the measurement (and attribution) of the risk of credit portfolios and the attribution of portfolio returns in a performance measurement context. Although we restrict ourselves in this document to the determinants of credit spread returns on credit bonds, we briefly describe to what extent our results are applicable to credit derivatives.

Figure 1 depicts the development of credit spreads over the last 14 years. We notice that there is a high level of variation in the credit spread, particularly during the most recent years. For example, for bonds rated Baa, the average spread was about 90 basis points (bps) at the end of 1997, whereas the average spread in the beginning of 2003 was around 250 bps.

We commence by discussing the determinants of the level of the credit spread. Drawing on these factors, we then look at changes that occur in the credit spreads. We also investigate the relative importance of systematic and specific risk factors for individual credit bonds as well as for credit portfolios. Furthermore, we examine the difference between investment grade and high-yield bonds regarding the importance of systematic risk factors. We conclude with a comparison of credit spreads on the spot market with credit spreads of credit default swaps (CDS).

* Jouke Hottinga is a risk manager at Aegon (NL). At the time of writing Machiel Zwanenburg was a quantitative researcher at Robeco Asset Management. He has been a risk manager at Robeco since July 2003.

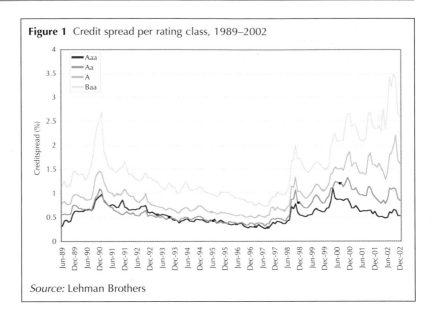

Figure 1 Credit spread per rating class, 1989–2002

Source: Lehman Brothers

CREDIT SPREADS

In this section, we address two classical approaches to explaining the level of the credit spread. We start with the approach initiated by Merton (1974) that considers corporate bonds in an option-pricing framework. We then consider reduced-form models, before discussing the risk premium part of the credit spread based on some empirical investigations of the credit spread.

Option approach to corporate bonds

Merton (1974) initiated the modern analysis of corporate debt by pointing out that the holders of risky corporate bonds can be thought of as owners of risk-free bonds who have issued put options to the holders of the firm's equity.[1] Models based on this approach are generally referred to as structural models and are covered in more detail in later parts of this book, most notably Chapters 5 and 18. The equity can be considered a call option on the asset value of the firm with a strike price equal to the value of the liabilities. The value of the corporate debt can therefore be calculated as the default risk-free value of the debt minus the value of the default option. In other words, next to the risk-free rate, an investor in corporate bonds also demands a credit spread to compensate for the written call option. The strike price of this option equals the face value of the debt and reflects the limited liability of equity holders in the event of bankruptcy.

From this viewpoint, the value of the default option and thus the credit spread depends on both the *asset value* and the *asset volatility*. The market value of the asset is just the sum of the equity value and the debt value. This depicts the direct link between equity returns and corporate bond returns. Negative equity returns imply a decrease in the market value of the asset. If we let the market value of debt consist of a default risk-free component and (a short position in) a default option, the decrease in the asset market value increases the value of the default option and thus decreases the value of the debt.

Another parameter that influences the value of the default option in this framework is the asset volatility, which is closely related to the equity volatility. A firm with more volatile equity is more likely to reach the boundary condition for default. Investors, recognising this risk, should require additional compensation in the form of a higher yield spread over the risk-free rate.

Equity volatility and asset volatility are dissimilar, although closely related. Their relationship is dependent on the leverage of the firm. The higher the leverage, the more volatile the equity vis-à-vis the asset. Therefore, the leverage of the firm is an important factor determining the credit spread.

The option approach to corporate bonds clearly shows that the value of the equity and the corporate debt are closely related. However, there are several reasons why the prices of corporate bonds might diverge from the prices of corporate equities.

❏ Stock prices will increase if investors become more optimistic about future corporate profits. Optimistic expectations benefit stock prices far more than bond prices, since stockholders receive all residual profits while corporate bondholders receive no more than the promised payments of principal and interest. The upside potential for bond-holders is thus limited.

❏ The spread of a corporate bond is not only a compensation for the default and market risk, but also includes a liquidity premium. An increase in the liquidity premium on corporate bonds relative to Treasury bonds might drive down corporate bond prices without any effect on equity prices.

❏ Volatility has opposite effects on stock and bond prices. Given expected profits, volatility of firm value hurts bondholders because it increases the probability of default (PD); it has a corresponding positive effect for equity holders (since they are long a call option). Thus, volatility should drive up the yields on corporate bonds.

The volatility that is relevant for option value, and thus for corporate debt, is total firm volatility; this includes both idiosyncratic volatility and systematic or market-wide volatility. Campbell and Taksler (2002) explore the effect of equity volatility on corporate bond yields, finding that for the late 1990s, idiosyncratic firm-level volatility can explain as much cross-sectional variation in yields as credit ratings can. In Merton's framework, volatility is linked to the spread level, as it influences the PD. This is true even if default risk is idiosyncratic. The importance of idiosyncratic volatility, together with the upward trend in idiosyncratic equity volatility documented by Campbell et al (2001), helps to explain recent increases in corporate bond yields.

Reduced form approach

An alternative approach to valuing corporate debt is the reduced form approach.[2] Reduced-form models assume exogenous stochastic processes for the default probability and the recovery rate. If we assume that the only reason a corporate bond sells for less than a similar Treasury bond is the possibility of default, it follows that the value of a corporate bond is equal to the value of a comparable Treasury bond, minus the present value of the cost of defaults. The latter depends on the PD and the loss in the case of default. By using this relationship to calculate the present value of the cost of defaults on a range of different bonds issued by the reference entity, and making an assumption about recovery rates, we can estimate the probability of the corporation defaulting at different future times.

From this relationship, we can distil the factors that determine credit spreads – ie, those that drive the PD of a company and those that drive the recovery rate. Both may be market-wide factors, such as the economic cycle or interest rates, as well as firm-specific factors such as the firm's financial situation.

Risk premium

A large amount of literature on the pricing of corporate bonds exists. We limit ourselves here to a brief discussion of two recent articles on the explanation of credit spreads that introduce a risk premium into the credit spread.

Elton et al (2001) argue that expected default can account for only a small part of the yield spread for investment-grade corporate over Treasury bonds, while state taxes (which are payable on corporate interest but not on Treasury interest) are relatively much more important.[3] The remaining portion of the spread is closely related to the factors that we commonly accept as explaining risk premiums for common stocks. In the case of 10-year corporate bonds, only 17.8% of the rate spread over treasuries is explained by the expected loss (EL) of default, 36.1% by local taxes, and 46.7% by systematic factors. Both time series and cross-sectional tests support the existence of a risk premium on corporate bonds. Huang and Huang (2003) reach a similar conclusion.

King et al (2002) find that differences in leverage and stock-return volatility are significant determinants of the cross-section of yield spreads.

Their results suggest that bond sensitivities to equity market systematic factors provide limited explanatory power to the cross-sectional variation in yield spread beyond firm and issue characteristics. They further identify two aggregate bond-market factors – debt ratio and asset volatility factors – as important determinants of time series variation in yield spreads. They decompose the yield to maturity of a risky bond into three components:

1. the default-free yield to maturity;
2. the risk premium, which is the difference between the expected and default-free yield to maturity; and
3. the default premium, which is the difference between the promised yield to maturity and the expected yield to maturity.

Their results suggest that cross-sectional differences in yield spreads at a given point in time are largely due to differences in default premium portion of the yield spread. On the other hand, time-variation in yield spreads is largely due to differences in the risk premium portion of the yield spread. This suggests that the risk premium is quite constant over issuers, but does fluctuate considerably through time. An investor interested in the asset allocation decision, that is, the percentage of assets to invest in credits, should focus on forecasting (factors driving) the risk premium. The centre of attention for an investor interested in selecting the best credits should lie with (factors driving) the default premium.

Note that part of the risk premium is attributable to liquidity problems.[4] Liquidity shortages occur frequently in bond trading. What is more, combined with the observation that corporate bonds are usually traded in small quantities with large notionals, rather than in large quantities and small notionals (such as shares), liquidity problems indicate that the assumption that arbitrageurs exist and constantly adjust prices to their accurate level is doubtful.

Both of the above studies conclude that the credit spreads consist of two components: a compensation for EL that is determined by the expected default and recovery rate, and a risk premium. Let us now return to the credit spread picture in Figure 1. There are two possible reasons why spread levels have risen over the last few years.

1. The market might expect higher default rates and/or lower recovery rates in the future. The higher spread is more than merely a compensation for the higher EL due to higher defaults and/or lower recovery values.
2. Credit investors might be more risk averse now, and consequently, be demanding a higher risk premium for the same amount of risk.

Figure 2 shows the historic annual one-year default rates of investment grade and high-yield bonds. We show both because investment-grade corporate bonds very rarely default within a period of one year.

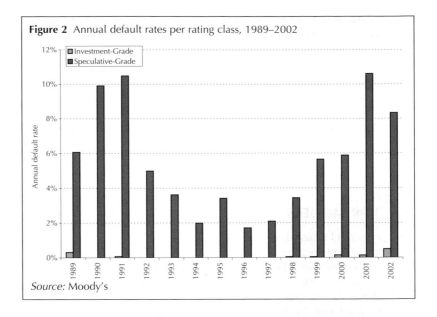

Figure 2 Annual default rates per rating class, 1989–2002

Source: Moody's

When we compare Figures 1 and 2, we notice strong similarities between the two graphs: the years with peaks and troughs in annual default rates and spread levels coincide. An explanation might be that when credit investors are confronted with higher default rates, they extrapolate these to higher expected default rates in the future. Furthermore, they might become more risk averse at such times. Both explanations result in higher demanded spreads.

CREDIT SPREAD CHANGES*

We have already encountered a lot of factors that influence the *level* of the credit spread, so we now look at the driving factors of credit spread *changes*. Factors that make up the credit spread also determine credit spread returns (although not necessarily in the same amount). For instance, we have seen that equity volatility is one of the key ingredients to the height of the credit spread. An increase in the volatility will, all else kept equal, result in an increase in the credit spread, due to a higher PD. Recent papers, some of which we discuss at the end of this chapter, have studied factors that are correlated with corporate bond yields cross-sectionally and over time.

First, we illustrate the relative importance of several factors in explaining credit spread changes by analysing them with a factor model.

* We are indebted to Jan Willem Wychmans for extensive help in the empirical research presented in this chapter.

We also discuss the importance of systematic *versus* bond specific factors. We conclude with a discussion of some other studies on driving factors of credit spread changes.

Factor model

A factor model is a regression model in which the return on a security is explained by a collection of factors. The part that cannot be explained is the part of the return that pertains to that particular security and is not

---

Panel 1
FACTOR MODELS

A factor model is based on the notion that the return (*the risk*) on a security can be explained by a collection of common factors (*the systematic risk*) plus an idiosyncratic element that pertains to that particular security (*the specific risk*).

So how do we split the risk into the different risk elements? The answer produced by Sharpe, Lintner and Treynor is known as the capital asset pricing model (CAPM). In the CAPM model, the systematic risk is purely driven by one factor: the volatility of market movements and the sensitivity of the portfolio to these market movements. A second alternative is the Arbitrage Pricing Theory (APT). The APT states that each security's expected excess return is determined by the security's exposures. For each factor there is a weight (called a factor forecast) such that the stock's expected excess return is the sum over all the factors of the security's factor exposures times the factor forecasts. The theory doesn't say what the factors are, how to calculate a security's exposures to the factors, or what the weights should be in the linear combination.

The APT postulates a multiple-factor model of excess returns. It assumes that there are K factors such that the excess returns can be expressed as:

$$r_t = \sum_{k=1}^{K} B_{i,k} \times f_k + e_i$$

$B_{i,k}$ is the exposure of security i to factor k. The exposures are frequently called factor loadings.

f_k is the factor return for factor k. These factor returns are either attributed to the factors at the end of the period or are observed during the period.

e_i is security i's specific return, the return that cannot be explained by the factors.

There are a great many ways to build an APT model. We describe two types of models briefly.

Fundamental factor model

Factor sensitivities are exogenously determined. The factors are predominantly observable security attributes. Factor returns are empirically determined (using cross-sectional regressions) random returns associated with these sensitivities.

Macro economic factor model

In this model, the factor returns are given. For example, take the factor returns as inflation, the percentage change in industrial production, etc. The exposures of the securities to the different factors are determined by regressing the excess returns on the returns of the factors, through the use of time-series regressions.

The different factor models can be used to link the return on credits (or, alternatively, credit spread changes) to external factors. We need to search for appropriate factors, that is, factors that help explain the return on the securities.

The return on a bond can be split in two elements: the systematic return and the remaining bond-specific return. Factor models centre on the first element. In our fundamental factor model, we perform a cross-sectional regression every month that relates the excess return – ie, the return on a corporate bond over the return on a comparable Treasury bond – of the bonds to the fundamental factors. This regression has the following form (based on the APT model given at a previous point in this panel):

$$R_{i,t} = \sum_{k=1}^{K} B_{i,t-1,k} \times f_{t,k} + e_{i,t}$$

The unknowns in this regression are the factor returns $f_{t,k}$ and the specific return $e_{i,t}$. The first term depicts the systematic return of the bond, whereas the second term, $e_{i,t}$, denotes the bond-specific return.

To present a concrete example, we now focus on the factor spread. If we assume that the height of the spread drives the return on a corporate bond, the height of the spread can be treated as the exposure B. Running the regression on all bonds over a specific time period then gives us, for that time period:

1. the return per unit of exposure spread f; and
2. the bond specific return for each bond, that is, the return that cannot be explained due to the spread.

The factor contribution, $B \times f$, gives the return per bond due to the exposure to the spread factor. The volatility of this factor contribution as a ratio of the overall volatility gives us the relative importance of that specific factor.

There are different ways to specify the factor loading of the variables. For instance, the dummies could be loaded with 1 if an issue is in that particular sector or rating, and by 0 if it is not. This gives an indication of the expectation we have about the impact of the factor return, namely that the factor returns are equally likely on each issue. However, this equal impact on each individual issue might not be true and may differ for issues that have a different duration.

In government-bond investment practice, the following first-order approximation for the relative price change of an (option-free) bond is often used:

$$\frac{\delta P}{P} = - MD \times \delta y,$$

where P is the price of the bond, MD is the modified duration of the bond and Dy the absolute yield change. This formula illustrates why we expect the impact of factor returns to differ over issues with a different duration; for bonds with a high duration, the change in price or return will be considerably larger than the change in price for low-duration bonds when the yield curve shifts.

If the fundamental factors drive spread changes, the first-order approximation outlined above tells us that all factor sensitivities should be multiplied with the duration of the securities. The alternative – ie, factor – sensitivities that are not adjusted for duration implies that factors drive prices. We expect high yield bonds to be "price-driven" due to the larger probability of default. For bonds with a high default probability, price is mostly driven by the recovery rate. This recovery rate is independent of the duration of the security.

relevant for other securities. Panel 1 contains a more detailed (mathematical) description of factor models.

With the factor model we try to explain the change in the spread of investment grade and high-yield bonds. There are many factors that can be included in the model to explain credit spread changes, but we limit ourselves to eight factors, which we explain below.

Rating

The rating of a bond issuer can be viewed as an estimate by the rating agency of the default probability of a company; the lower the rating, the higher the PD. In our analysis of the importance of rating in explaining spread changes, we distinguish six rating categories: Aaa/Aa, A, Baa, Ba, B and Ccc and lower. The rating we use originates from the rating agency Moody's.

Market

The market in general is believed to be a very important driver of individual credit spreads. A large part of the change of the spread of an individual company is due to the overall market movement. This same phenomenon can be seen in stock markets where the movement of the market as a whole is a strong driver of the return on an individual stock. We verify the importance of the market factor for the credit market by the constant in the factor model that is the same for all credits.

Sector

Besides the market as a whole, the sector of the bond issuer is generally believed to be a driver of credit spread changes. This means that bonds within the same sector tend to move together against the market. Put differently, the average correlation between spread movements of bonds in an identical sector is higher than the correlation between spread movements of bonds in different sectors. In our factor model, we distinguish the following sectors: agency, energy, banking, finance, basic industry, non-cyclical, communications, non-US, cyclical and utility.

Spread

At first sight, it may seem a bit strange to take the spread itself as a factor when explaining spread changes. However, the spread can be seen as an alternative to rating, since the current spread of the bond encompasses the market estimate of the default probability of a bond. In this sense, it seems likely that bonds with the same spread tend to move in the same way.

Price

This factor can be seen as an alternative to the spread factor, especially for high-yield bonds, which are generally considered to be more price-driven than spread-driven. For investment grade bonds, this factor is of less interest, since the price of an investment grade bond is strongly influenced by both spread and interest rate.

Time to maturity

Literature on the effect of maturity suggests that credit spread usually differs with maturity. Sarig and Warga (1989) give empirical evidence that credit spread is upward-sloping in maturity for investment grade bonds, yet downward-sloping for high-yield bonds. This effect is thought to occur due to the rating the bonds receive when they are issued. An investment grade issue starts off with a relatively high rating; this implies a low PD. So, in the course of life, the possibility of a downgrade is higher than the possibility of an upgrade. The PD will therefore have the tendency to increase through time. Long-term maturity bonds are more sensitive to this effect than short-term maturity bonds and thus have a higher credit spread. For high-yield bonds, the effect is opposite. As such a bond ages and still persists, the PD (and thus the credit spread) decreases.

Coupon

The coupon of a bond may influence changes in the spread. Due to tax advantages that may differ over time, market practitioners may prefer bonds with either a high or a low coupon.

Market capitalisation

This factor can be seen as a liquidity indicator. A large market capitalisation makes it easier to trade a specific bond. Issues with a lower market value usually pay a liquidity premium as compensation.

The factors *spread, time-to-maturity, price, coupon* and *market capitalisation* are measured relative to the average within a rating/sector category. All the variables are bond-specific and require no information on the issuing company. The data that we have at our disposal is on an issue level. Although we would ideally want to include company – or stock – factors, this is currently not possible.

The data is obtained from the Lehman Live website for the US aggregate credit and US high-yield indices. We use data on a monthly basis over the period April 1990 to May 2002. We exclude bonds with missing characteristics. Additionally, we eliminate all zero-coupon bonds.[4]

Relative importance

Using a cross-sectional regression, we are able to link the exposures to the different factors and the spread changes. This results in the contribution of each factor on the credit return on an individual issue on a monthly basis. The regression model does not give us an indication of the relative importance of the different factors, as the size of the various components of return does not give the actual effect on the return. The variance of these estimates over time indicates the true importance: the higher the variance of a particular factor, the more influence it has on an issue's return.

Figures 3 and 4 show the relative importance of the factors for investment grade and high-yield bonds. This is measured by taking the ratio of the volatility of each systematic factor return to the total volatility over five-year periods for the average issue. The graphs show the relative importance over a moving window of five years, starting with the period 1991–1995 and ending with 1998–2002.

We note that in determining the relative importance of each factor, only the part of the bond return that can be explained by the factors is considered. There still remains a large part of the return that cannot be explained by the above factors; we will consider this in the next paragraph.

Note that Figure 3 presents the relative importance of the factors driving (investment grade) *spread changes*, whereas Figure 4 presents the importance of the factors driving (high-yield) *credit returns*. The cause for the difference will become clear in the next paragraph.

The graphs show that there are large differences between investment grade and high-yield bonds. For investment grade bonds, the general market movement has the largest influence on spread changes. Other factors have a smaller influence, with sector and spread being the most important. Rating seems to have a small impact on spread change, but we note that the rating is largely covered with the spread factor, as both indicate the credit worthiness of the issuer of the bond. Note the sharp increase in the relative importance of the market factor after the Russia crisis in 1998.

For high-yield bonds, the relative importance is more evenly distributed. The factor spread appears to be most important; market, price, rating and sector are all more or less equally important. Note that the importance of the different factors varies considerably through time. It is worth noting the dominance of the spread factor during 1999 and 2000, when both the overall high-yield spread and the dispersion in spreads increases.

Explanatory power
We have considered the relative importance of the factors that were included in the factor model. However, the factor model was unable to explain all the spread variation, meaning a large part of the spread change remains unexplained.

We measure the explanatory power of the model by examining the systematic factors' ability to explain the credit spread changes for each

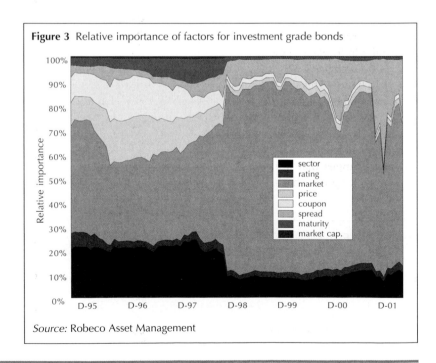

Figure 3 Relative importance of factors for investment grade bonds

Source: Robeco Asset Management

individual bond. Table 1 presents the average R^2 of this regression for both investment grade and high yield. We see that the explanatory power of the model is 38% for investment grade bonds and 28% for high-yield bonds. This means that the larger part of the credit return is unexplained by the systematic factors. The systematic factors are better capable of explaining, cross-sectionally, the return on investment grade issues than on high-yield issues.

Furthermore, the table shows the results for two different types of regression, from which we can infer some other interesting conclusions. Firstly, the table shows the results when we try to explain spread changes with the factor model. Secondly, the table shows the results when we try to explain credit returns with the factor model. The difference between a spread change and the induced credit return is determined by the spread duration (see Panel 1 for a more elaborate explanation). In theory, a higher spread duration results in a higher credit return at the same spread change. If this is the case, a model that explains spread changes should work better than a model that explains credit returns, wherein we ignore the spread duration.

However, in Table 1, we can see that for high-yield bonds, the model that explains credit returns works better. This means that the spread duration is of less importance for the high-yield market. This is contrary to the investment grade results that suggest that the spread duration is of importance.

Specific return

The results in Table 1 show that a large part of the variation in spread remains unexplained: 62% of the variation for investment and 72% for high-yield bonds. This might be due to the fact that we miss some important factors such as equity volatility, or simply that the larger part of the spread change of an individual bond is specific to that bond and has no relation with the spread change of other bonds. It is likely that it is caused by a combination of both.

Spread changes that are particular to a bond, without being related (correlated) to spread changes of other bonds, can be diversified away in a

Table 1.	Explanatory power of the factor model			
	Investment grade		High-yield	
Measure	Spread changes	Credit returns	Spread changes	Credit returns
R^2	38%	34%	24%	28%
Source: Robeco Asset Management				

portfolio of bonds. Consequently, the specific return will have very little influence on the total return on a well-diversified portfolio.

Let us now return to Table 1. Suppose that the unexplained part of the spread variation is caused solely by specific spread changes. In this case, we can see that for a single investment-grade bond, nearly 40% of the spread variation can be explained by the systematic factors in our factor model. However, if we have a portfolio of two bonds, 50% of the spread variation can be explained by the systematic factors. This is because the specific parts of two bonds' respective spread variations are uncorrelated and (partly) cancel each other out. The idea is that the systematic risk of a portfolio is independent of the number of issues present. Specific risk, or idiosyncratic risk, is specific to a given bond. By increasing the number of bonds in the portfolio, one is able to diversify and thus decrease the specific risk present in the portfolio. This effect is also present in equity portfolios: in general one stock is more volatile than a stock index. Figures 5 and 6 show the explanatory power of the systematic factors for investment-grade and high-yield portfolios as a function of the number of bonds.

Of course, we make some fairly unrealistic simplifying assumptions. Yet the general idea is that the specific risk factors affecting individual bonds can be diversified away in a portfolio of bonds, meaning that the credit return of the portfolio is mainly influenced by systematic factors, like the general market movement.

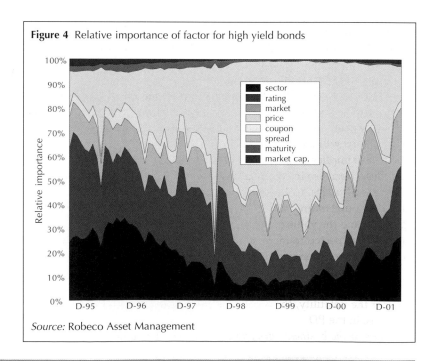

Figure 4 Relative importance of factor for high yield bonds

Source: Robeco Asset Management

In the above analysis, we have assumed that the specific volatility of each issue is identical. Empirical results point in a different direction. The height of the specific volatility can be partly explained by a range of factors. For example, we know that, in general, the specific volatility depends on the rating of the issue. The higher the creditworthiness of the issuing company, the lower the specific volatility of the issue. Specific volatility can also be shown to depend on other factors such as the sector, duration and age of the issue.

Other factors driving spread changes

As we have stated, there are likely to be other factors driving spread changes that we do not include in our factor model. Numerous studies have tested the explanatory power of a multitude of factors in explaining spread changes. Next, we briefly discuss two studies containing additional factors to the ones we have already covered.

Collin-Dufresne *et al* (2001) investigate the determinants of credit spread changes using a macro-economic factor model. They start with a Merton-like structural framework, where equity possesses characteristics similar to a call option, while the debt claim exhibits features analogous to those of a portfolio that has a claim to firm value, but which is short an option (as discussed earlier). On the basis of this model, they suggest factors that influence the value of the option (and thus the credit spread on the debt claim).

1. *Changes in the spot rate.* Option theory tells us that the *rho* – the rate of change of the value of a put option with respect to the interest rate – is negative. A higher spot rate reduces the incidence of default, and, in turn, reduces the credit spreads.
2. *Changes in the slope of the yield curve.* A decrease in the yield curve slope may imply a weakening economy and thus depress the expected recovery rate. As a result, theory predicts that an increase in the yield curve slope will create a decrease in credit spreads. An increase in the slope also implies an increase in the expected future short rate, and thus implies a decrease in credit spreads.
3. *Change in leverage.* Collin-Dufresne *et al* define leverage as the ratio of the debt outstanding and the value of the firm. The closer the value of the debt and the value of the firm, the higher the PD. Credit spreads are therefore expected to increase with leverage; this introduces a negative correlation between equity returns and credit spread changes.
4. *Changes in volatility.* Option theory tells us that *vega*, the rate of change of the value of a put option with respect to volatility, is positive. The higher the volatility, the higher the credit spread should be due to the increase in the PD.
5. *Changes in the business climate/business cycle.* The state of the economy

has an effect on the default probability of companies as well as on the expected recovery rates. A weakening economy is expected to depress recovery rates and increase default probabilities, thereby pushing up credit spreads from two sides.

Colin–Dufresne run a time-series regression for individual bonds, relating the observed credit-spread change to proxies for the above factors. They find that the variables only have limited explanatory power (adjusted R^2 ranging from 19% to 25%). Adding additional explanatory variables such as measures of changes in liquidity to the regression has a marginal effect on the explanatory power of the model.

Huang and Kong (2003) approach the problem from a different perspective. They do not examine credit spread changes of individual bonds, but instead use index credit spreads data per rating/maturity. They consider five sets of explanatory variables that characterise different aspects of credit risk.

1. *Changes in realised default rates.* If historical default rates predict future default risk in the corporate bond market, we would expect a close positive relationship between changes in realised default rates and changes in credit spreads.
2. *Changes in interest rate level, slope and volatility.* This variable is explained in the description of the Colin-Dufresne model, above.
3. *Equity market returns, volatility and risk premium.* These variables result from the Merton framework.
4. *Changes in supply/demand from corporate bond mutual funds.* The net new cashflow of corporate bond mutual funds is an indirect measure of the net demand for corporate bonds from investors. Higher net new cashflows indicate a higher demand and would push down credit spreads.
5. *Changes in macro-economic indicators.* Just as equity returns are driven by the position in the economic cycle, credit returns react to a changing economic situation. During periods of economic downturn, credit spreads are expected to increase as investors become more risk-averse and firms have lower asset returns.

Huang and Kong find that credit spread changes, especially for high-yield bond indices, are significantly explained by:

❏ the interest-rate historical volatility;
❏ the Russell 2000 index historical-return volatility;
❏ the Conference Board leading; and
❏ coincident economic indices.

Furthermore, more than 40% of credit spread changes in five out of nine rating/maturity indices are explained by these four variables, plus:

❏ the interest rate level;
❏ the yield curve slope;
❏ the Russell 2000 index return; and
❏ the Fama-French (1996) high-minus-low factor return.

Use of factor models as credit risk models

In this chapter, we have used a factor model to illustrate the relative importance of some factors in explaining credit spread changes. The same type of model can also be used as the basis of ex-ante risk modelling and ex-post performance attribution.[5] Two well-known factor model examples used in portfolio risk-estimation are the Lehman Brothers Multi-factor Risk model and the Barra Cosmos system.[6,7]

Lehman distinguishes the following factors.

❏ *Term-structure risk*: a set of risk factors designed to capture yield curve risk.
❏ *Sector risk*: a set of risk factors capturing the exposure to movements of sector spreads.
❏ *Quality risk (rating)*: a set of risk factors captures the exposure to movements of credit quality spreads.
❏ *Optionality risk*: a set of risk factors that compare the extent of optionality from several different angles.
❏ *Coupon risk*: the coupon level of a particular bond, relative to the rest of the market, that makes it more or less attractive to investors. This occurs to the extent that the value placed on coupon level responds to changes in tax codes, accounting standards, etc; this effect represents an additional source of risk.
❏ *Treasury-specific risk*: factors that capture the risk related to the Treasury market.
❏ *Various mortgage-backed security factors*: factors that reflect the fact that changes in prepayment speeds, volatilities and spreads, with a corresponding impact on risk.

These models combine the current exposures to the different factors, historical volatilities, and correlations between the different factor returns to calculate ex-ante risk measures. The same factor returns, now combined with historical observed exposures, makes it possible to attribute the total portfolio performance to the different factors.

CREDIT DEFAULT SWAP SPREADS

So far, we have focused on spread levels and spread changes on cash bonds. In theory, the spread on a credit default swap (CDS) is the same as the spread on the cash bond of the same issuer. For both types of instruments, the spread is a remuneration for the (default) risk present.

Therefore, the factors that drive the level and the change of CDS spreads are the same factors that drive the spreads on the cash market.

However, there are some practical reasons why the spreads on CDS and cash bonds differ. The difference between the CDS spread and that of the spread on a (*par floater*) cash bond is known as the default swap basis. Note that the basis can be both positive and negative, although a positive basis is typical. There are, therefore, additional factors that drive the spread on the CDS market.[8] This topic is the subject of the next chapter but we will briefly discuss the following factors here:

1. counterparty risk;
2. funding rate;
3. technical default;
4. coupon and accrued interest; and
5. delivery option.

These are surely not the only reasons for divergence; the above factors all result from the definition of a CDS contract. Other factors are more related to differences in the nature of the CDS market on the one hand and the cash market on the other.

Note that it is difficult to quantify the importance of the different factors. It is important to recognise that movements in CDS spreads and the spreads on the reference cash bond can differ quite substantially. This is apparent in Figures 7 and 8, which show the development through time of

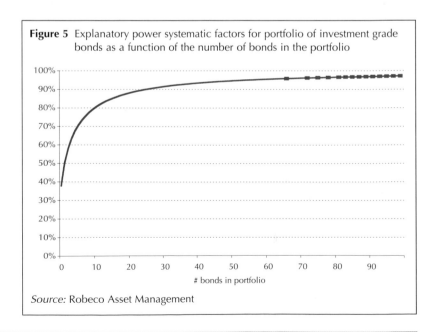

Figure 5 Explanatory power systematic factors for portfolio of investment grade bonds as a function of the number of bonds in the portfolio

Source: Robeco Asset Management

the CDS spread and the spread on the reference cash bond for Merrill Lynch and General Motors.

Counterparty risk

When you buy a bond on the cash market, the spread is a compensation for the credit risk on the issuer of the bonds. Note that there is an extra source of credit risk in a CDS transaction: counterparty risk. Since the CDS is an over-the-counter (OTC) contract with a single counterparty, protection buyers will generally pay a lower spread, since they are taking the risk that the protection seller will be unable to pay the compensation in case the underlying issuer of the CDS defaults. The presence of counterparty risk reduces the default swap basis. This means that along with the credit-worthiness of the underlying issuer, the credit-worthiness of the protection seller in a CDS transaction also determines the CDS spread.

Funding rate

A CDS is an unfunded transaction in the sense that it does not involve an initial investment. This means that investors can create credit exposure without any funding. Since the pricing of a CDS is based on Libor, it follows that they fund themselves at the Libor rate.

When investors create exposure to credit risk in the cash market, they have to fund their investments at their funding rate. Generally this funding rate is higher than Libor, as most investors have a credit quality less than AA. Since investing in credit, though CDS is very advantageous

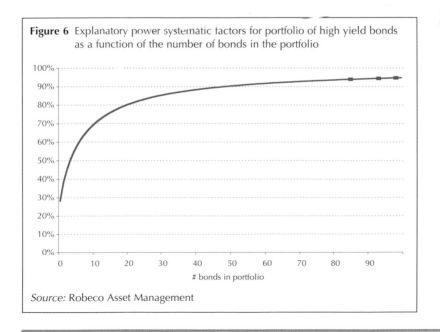

Figure 6 Explanatory power systematic factors for portfolio of high yield bonds as a function of the number of bonds in the portfolio

bonds in portfolio

Source: Robeco Asset Management

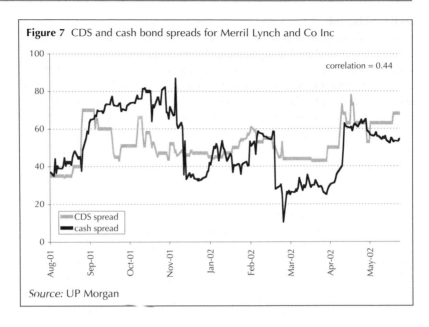

Figure 7 CDS and cash bond spreads for Merril Lynch and Co Inc

correlation = 0.44

Source: UP Morgan

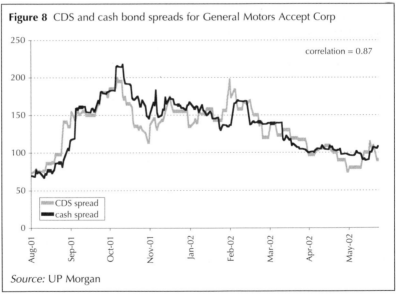

Figure 8 CDS and cash bond spreads for General Motors Accept Corp

correlation = 0.87

Source: UP Morgan

in this case, the protection sellers in a CDS can generally settle for a lower spread than on the cash market, thereby reducing the default swap basis. The average credit funding cost of the protection sellers on the CDS market is, therefore, another factor in determining the spread on the CDS.

Technical default

The risk of technical default means that the default situation according to the conditions in the CDS agreement differs from the default situation of the cash bonds. In general, the conditions in the CDS agreement are less binding, resulting in a widening of the default swap basis. Default swaps are traded within the framework of the International Swaps and Derivatives Association (ISDA) Master Agreement. While the aim within these agreements is to shadow as closely as possible the effective default of the bond, circumstances may arise in which the credit events included in the ISDA framework will actually trigger a CDS even when a material deterioration in the credit has not actually occurred.

Coupon and accrued interest

The underlying bond in a CDS is a par bond. In case of a default, the loss that is compensated for is the loss against par value. When you invest in a cash bond, generally the bond value is not equal to the par value, due to differences between the coupon of the bond, the market yield at that moment, and the accrued interest. Therefore, the loss on a cash bond and the loss defined in a CDS need not be identical. When the dirty price of the cash bond is above par, the loss of the cash bonds is correspondingly larger than the loss in a CDS. This means that the spread on the cash bond should be higher than the CDS spread when the dirty price of the bonds is above par. The opposite conditions are true if the cash bond's dirty price is below par. Coupon and accrued interest will therefore influence the spread on the cash bond, whereas they have no influence on the spread on the CDS. Note that the height of the coupon also influences the spread on the cash bonds due to tax-effects, as described earlier.

Delivery option

In the case of a default, an investor in a cash bond is left with the bond's recovery value. This recovery value need not be identical to the value of the asset in the settlement of a CDS. The protection buyer can generally choose an asset to deliver out of a basket of deliverables. Depending on the credit event, the investor might prefer to deliver an asset that differs from the cash bond, and thus has the potential to differ in price. This delivery option increases the default swap basis.

---

1   Other classic papers in this area are Black and Scholes (1973) and Ingersoll (1977).
2   Classic papers on the reduced-form approach are Duffie and Singleton (1999) and Jarrow and Turnbull (1995).
3   Note that this does not automatically imply that changes in expected default do not to a large extent drive changes in corporate yield spreads. If we assume that of all the factors influencing the absolute value of the corporate yield spread only expected default fluctuate through time, this will then be the only factor influencing changes in the spreads.

4   See Houweling *et al* (2003) for a discussion of liquidity premia.

5   We note that usually these factor models are built to measure risk and performance due to both interest rate and credit spread movements, while we have only focussed on credit spread movements, and have therefore discarded the return due to interest rate changes.

6   For more details about the Lehman Brothers model refer to Dynkin, Hyman and Wu (2002).

7   Refer to Cheyette (2002).

8   For a more extensive treatment of this subject, please see O'Kane and McAdie (2001 and 2003).

BIBLIOGRAPHY

Black, F. and M. Scholes, 1973, "The Pricing of Options and Corporate Liabilities", *Journal of Political Economy*, 81, pp. 637–54.

Campbell, J., M. Letter, B.G. Malkiel, and Y. Xu, 2001, "Have individual stocks become more volatile? An empirical explanation of idiosyncratic risk", *Journal of Finance*, 56, pp. 1–43.

Campbell, J.Y. and G.B. Taksler, 2002, "Equity Volatility and Corporate Bond Yields", working paper.

Cheyenne, O., 2002, "Global Credit Risk Modelling", BARRA Research Insights, http://www.barra.com/products/pdfs/GlobalCredit.pdf

Collin-Dufresne, P., R.S. Goldstein and J. Spencer Martin, 2001, "The Determinants of Credit Spread Changes", *Journal of Finance*, 56, pp. 2177–2207.

Duffie, D., and K. Singleton, 1999, "Modelling the Term Structure of Defaultable Bonds", *Review of Financials Studies*, 12, pp. 2225–41.

Dynkin, L., J. Hyman, and W. Wu, 2002, "The Lehman Brothers Multi-Factor Risk Model", The Theory and Practice of Investment Management, ed. Fabozzi, F. and H. Markowitz, John Wiley & Sons .

Elton, E.J., M.J. Gruber, D. Agrawal and C. Mann, 2001, "Explaining the Rate Spread on Corporate Bonds", *Journal of Finance*, 56, pp 247–77.

Fama, E.F. and K.R. French, 1996, "Multifactor Explanations of Asset Pricing Anomalies", *Journal of Finance*, 51, pp. 55–84.

Houweling, P., Mentink, A. and T. Vorst, 2003, How to measure Corporate Bond Liquidity?, Tinbergen Institute Discussion Paper, TI 2003-030/2.

Huang, J. and M. Huang, 2003, How Much of the Corporate-Treasury Yield Spread is Due to Credit Risk?, working paper.

Huang, J. and W. Kong, 2003, Explaining Credit Spread Changes: Some New Evidence from Option-Adjusted Spreads of Bond Indices, working paper.

Jarrow, R., and S. Turnbull, 1995, "Pricing Derivatives on Financial Securities Subject to Default Risk", *Journal of Finance*, 50, pp. 53–86.

Merton, Robert C., 1974, "In the pricing of corporate debt: The risk structure of interest rates", *Journal of Finance*, 29, pp. 449–70.

O'Kane, D. and R. McAdie, 2001, "Explaining the Basis: Cash versus Default Swaps", *Structured Credit Research*, May, Lehman Brothers.

O'Kane, D. and R. McAdie, 2003, "Trading the Default Swap Basis", *Fixed Income European Credit Strategies*, March, Lehman Brothers.

Sarig, O. and A. Warga, 1989, "Some Empirical Estimates of the Risk Structure of Interest rates", *Journal of Finance*, 44, pp. 1351–60.

Sharpe, W.F., 1964, "Capital Asset Prices: A Theory of Market Equilibrium Under Conditions of Risk", *Journal of Finance*, 19, pp. 425–42.

3

What's driving the default swap basis?

Viktor Hjort

Morgan Stanley

INTRODUCTION

The significant growth seen in the credit default swap (CDS) market has been driven to a great extent by its role as a proxy for the bond and loan market. Although the default swap market adds value for many investors by providing access to credits not readily available in the cash markets, its main importance is as an instrument that allows investors to isolate *credit* risk from interest and funding risk.

This assumes that the exposure achieved through a default swap position replicates that of a similar position in the cash market, but stripped of interest rate and funding risk. However, in the market we frequently observe divergence, often significant, between the premium paid on a default swap and that paid on a cash instrument of the same credit and maturity. Here, we present an overview of the factors driving this basis and also analyse the relationship between the cash and derivatives markets at the market, sector and individual credit levels.

The default swap market is often perceived as driven primarily by technical factors, particular to this market only. We find little evidence to support this view. Instead, the nature of the markets argues for a close correlation. It also argues for the default swap market effectively being a high-beta version of the underlying cash market.

A SIMPLIFIED WORLD: THE ARBITRAGE-FREE RELATIONSHIP

In order to explore the reasons why cash and default swap markets can trade at different levels, we must first establish the relationship between the two markets. This can be illustrated by a theoretically risk-free trade:

❑ The investor buys a par–par asset swap, paying a coupon of Libor plus a spread of S. The position is funded on balance sheet at a cost of Libor flat.

❏ The investor buys credit protection with identical maturity on the notional amount, at a default swap premium of D.

No default: In the absence of any default, the asset swap will redeem at par at the maturity of the trade, and the redemption amount will be used to pay off the funding. The default swap will simply terminate at that time.

Default event: In the event of a default, the investor will deliver the defaulted asset to the protection seller, and receive par in return. The par amount will be used to pay off the funding, and the default swap will then terminate.

Under both scenarios, the investor is fully hedged and has no exposure to the default of the asset – the trade is credit risk-neutral.[1] The *default swap basis* (D-S) in this theoretical arbitrage-free framework must therefore be zero. If it is positive, ie, the default swap premium is greater than the spread earned on the asset, the basis can be exploited by selling the asset and selling protection. If it is negative, the investor can buy the asset swap and buy protection. Both strategies would yield a positive margin for assuming no credit risk.[2]

The framework above does, however, require a number of assumptions, and these may not hold in the marketplace, hence causing a non-zero basis to exist. These factors may be of technical or fundamental nature. At any given point in time, the basis may be positive or negative, but most of the time it will be affected by more than one factor. Below, I discuss each of the factors in turn. Several factors, although listed as a driver of either positive or negative basis, can also work in the other direction if the opposite circumstance occurs. Coupon step-ups, for instance, will drive the basis in a positive direction, while coupon step-downs will drive it in a negative manner.

POSITIVE BASIS
The cheapest-to-deliver option
A physically settled default swap contract entitles the protection buyer to deliver any of a potentially large number of assets into the contract upon the occurrence of a credit event. This option can potentially have material value, depending on the number of assets available and, to some extent, the type of credit event, as it allows the protection holder to switch out of one asset into a cheaper one. The possibility of being delivered a less valuable asset should make protection sellers demand a higher premium than that of a comparable asset swap. If not, arbitrageurs would buy bonds and protection and get a free option.

In theory, the option should have little value, as all *pari passu*-ranked assets should trade on their recovery value following a default. In practice, however, this is not always the case. More structured assets may trade cheaper than more vanilla-type assets and less liquid assets cheaper than more liquid ones. In addition, loans should trade higher than bonds, as they have historically yielded better recovery values than bonds of the same seniority, due to covenants that often offer creditors better protection

Importantly, the type of credit event matters. A "soft" credit event, which does not immediately cause default, may allow the assets to continue to trade with price differentials. The rapid development of the standard default swap contract has significantly reduced the scope for contracts to be triggered by soft credit events, but some issues, notably the restructuring credit event, still leave that possibility open.

The most famous example of a soft credit event triggering a default swap contract was Conseco's debt restructuring in 2000. Conseco renegotiated an extension of the maturity of some of its outstanding loans by three months, but simultaneously increased the coupon and enhanced the covenant protection. The net effect of the changes was roughly credit-neutral and Moody's, for instance, did not consider it a "diminished financial obligation". The maturity extension, however, was clearly captured by the ISDA restructuring definition, and loss payments were triggered under default swap contracts. However, given that no "hard" default had occurred, there were major price differentials among Conseco debt-assets, and many protection buyers, rather than deliver the restructured loans (which were actually trading up in the market due to the credit-improving features) delivered cheaper, long-dated bonds.

The 2003 credit derivatives definitions result in four (!) different restructuring options:

❏ OldR: the Asian market standard;
❏ Modified restructuring (ModR): the US market standard, albeit nowadays increasingly often alongside no restructuring at all;
❏ Modified modified restructuring (MMR): the European market standard; and
❏ No restructuring (NoR): often used in the US market.

The restructuring supplement of 2001 (containing the ModR definition) attempted to deal partly with exposure to soft credit events by limiting and clarifying which restructuring events would trigger contracts. Above all, however, it limited the *economic exposure* to restructuring events by limiting the maximum maturity of the obligations that can be delivered.

MMR is a change compared with OldR in that it:

1. specifies different maturity limitation dates for the deliverable obligation following a restructuring event; and
2. provides mechanisms for the transfer of certain obligations. In particular, the definition:

❑ specifies that the deliverable obligation must not have a maturity longer than the "Modified restructuring maturity limitation date", which is the latest of:
1. 60 months following the restructuring date for the restructured obligation;
2. 30 months following the restructuring date for all other obligations; and
3. the scheduled termination date of the swap;
❑ specifies that the deliverable obligation must be conditionally transferable to all "modified eligible transferees", ie, consent for transfer cannot be "unreasonably" withheld or delayed to certain persons, in which case alternative delivery mechanisms (such as third-party delivery designate) kick in;
❑ applies only to physically settled transactions; and
❑ applies only to contracts triggered by the protection buyer.

In addition, Section 4.09 specifies that restructuring of (among other things) a *bilateral loan* may not trigger a credit event, as it fails to qualify as multiple holder obligation meaning. Further, and again in line with what is provided by ModR, section 3.90 allows multiple exercises on restructuring, meaning that protection buyers may seek *partial* recovery under a default swap through multiple credit event notices. As obligations are delivered in these multiple transactions, the remaining recovery to the protection buyer is accordingly adjusted.

In effect, the cheapest-to-deliver option adds an additional spread layer on top of the pure compensation for the credit risk. To the extent that the option has any value, it should increase the closer to the strike price – ie, a potential credit event – the option gets. This has the potential not only to cause a positive basis *per se*, but also to cause the basis to widen and tighten with the overall direction of the market. The reverse would be true as credit quality improves.

This additional option premium creates a high-beta characteristic of the default swap in relation to the cash bond, an issue that will be explored later in this chapter.[3]

Coupon step-ups in corporate bonds

An increasing number of bonds carry clauses triggering the coupon to step up in the event of a ratings downgrade or similar protective covenants. The value of this embedded option is a function of the probability of the downgrade, but it can never be less than zero. Therefore, the existence of step-ups will add a layer of protection for bondholders that is not reflected in a similar default swap position, and the basis should be positive as a result.

A number of issues also have step-down clauses. This implies a higher risk in the bond position compared with the default swap position, and would be a force for a negative basis. Where both step-up and step-down clauses are present, the basis would be a function of the probability of ratings action in either direction.

Default swap premiums floored at zero

Default swap premiums must be positive, since they represent an insurance premium. Even for very highly rated reference entities, such as the German government or the World Bank, where the probability of default is very low, the premium for assuming the default risk must still be positive.

However, as Libor merely reflects the interbank lending risk (roughly AA), it is obviously possible for higher-rated entities to finance themselves at sub-Libor yields, and thus an AAA-rated issue will normally asset swap to a negative spread, causing the basis to be positive.

An interesting effect of the positive basis at the high end of the ratings spectrum is the so-called "basis smile". This represents the default swap-cash basis, which is positive for lower-rated credits, for example due to the cheapest-to-deliver option, roughly zero in the "belly" of the curve, and then positive again at the very high end, due to the zero floor for default swap premiums.

Bond price less than par

Bonds (fixed-rate) regularly trade at prices away from par and not infrequently significantly away from par. The equivalence of a cash bond and a default swap position, however, requires the bond to trade at par. If the price is below par, a bond investor is exposed to lower risk than the seller of protection, who is guaranteeing a par amount.

An investor who owns a defaulting bond at a cash price of 50 with a recovery value of 40 loses 10% of the par amount. A seller of default protection, however, loses 60%. In the same way, if the bond position is above par, the risk is greater than the default swap position. This implies that, where bonds are trading below par, the basis should be positive and vice-versa (another factor contributing to the "basis smile" being positive at the lower and deteriorating end of the credit curve).

NEGATIVE BASIS
Funding above Libor

The choice of strategy for an investor/hedger comparing the default swap and cash alternatives will be impacted by the funding cost. On balance, the greater the ratio of lower-rated/higher-rated market participants, the more negative the basis.

As demonstrated above, default swaps are unfunded transactions that effectively lock in a funding cost of Libor. Bond investors, however, would need to finance the investment amount or, alternatively, fund the position on repo, in which case the cost of funding would be the repo rate. The cost of funding, therefore, becomes crucial for the relative attractiveness of the alternative strategies. For example, an investor with a funding cost of Libor + 30 would be indifferent between buying an asset at Libor + 100 and selling default protection on the credit at 70 basis points (bps) (ignoring counterparty risk, which we will come to below). The difference between the funding cost and Libor determines how far through the asset swap spread the default swap premium should trade for the investor to be indifferent between the two strategies.

For higher-rated investors that are able to finance themselves at sub-Libor levels, the reverse is true. An AAA-rated insurance company, for example, that finances itself at Libor-10 would prefer to buy the asset, as long as the default swap premium was no more than 10 bps wider than the asset swap spread.

Counterparty risk

Unlike a bond trade, the two counterparties in a default swap transaction bear exposure to each other's ability to fulfil their respective obligations throughout the life of the trade. In particular, the protection buyer's exposure can be significant, as it relies on the seller to redeem a defaulted asset at par. To compensate for the additional risk, the protection buyer will expect to pay less than the cash spread.

The protection seller's counterparty risk is the mark-to-market (MTM) loss on the position should the protection buyer default following spread tightening. This risk, however, will generally be of a very different order of magnitude from that of the protection buyer. A long credit position at 100 bps with PV01 of 5 that tightens 50 bps will have 2.5 points of profit at risk, quite unlike the protection buyer, who may lose 60 points or more, depending on recovery value, should the counterparty default following a default by the reference entity.[4] The default of Enron highlights how important this exposure can be. It also highlights the importance of risk mitigation through collateral agreements, which protected many of Enron's counterparties as the energy (and credit derivatives) trader collapsed.

Counterparty risk also affects an asset swap position (but not a par-FRN). The buyer of a par asset swap faces the MTM risk of the interest rate swap in the package in the event of the asset defaulting. This may cause an investor to demand a higher spread on the asset swap relative to the default swap, and drive the basis in a negative direction.

New issues

The impact of new issuance on default swap premiums illustrates the convergence of credit risk in different asset classes into the default swap market: in order to accommodate new credit risk, bank loan departments, bond investors and convertible bond investors would all look to the default swap market to hedge their risk. In that sense, the default swap market is the alternative asset class, the "opportunity cost", for all three markets and the default swap premium will widen with any new issuance, loans, bonds or convertibles. To the extent that the investor base in the three cash markets is segmented, ie, does not trade across asset classes, spread widening in the default swap market should widen the basis relative to those markets where the new issuance did *not* take place.

For example, the announcement of a new convertible bond issue would widen default swap premiums as investors, mainly hedge funds, hedge out the credit risk. Traditional investors in straight bonds, however, would not normally be investing in convertibles and would not sell existing positions to make room for new credit exposure. Spreads in that market would then remain stable, causing a widening in the basis.

The difficulty of shorting cash assets

The relative difficulty of outright shorting of the cash market, loans or bonds, and the relative ease of doing it through the default swap market, tends to push the basis wider for deteriorating credits.

Investors who want to express a negative view on a credit by short-selling a bond will have to source the bond in an often very illiquid repo market, running the risk of being bought out. In addition, the funding is variable and affected by the specialness of the asset. This adds risk to short-selling. Buying credit protection, on the other hand, does not involve any asset, and also effectively locks in the cost of funding at execution, making it generally a more convenient and less risky way of going short.

The structured synthetic bid for credit

The rise of large, structured synthetic portfolio trades has added a new dimension to the investment-grade credit market. Investors taking on broad, diversified exposure to the credit market through investment-grade synthetic CDOs create a demand for credit as they sell protection. This demand is usually hedged by brokers in the single-name default swap market; this pushes the default swap premium tighter for those names that are included in the basket, and may create a negative basis.

CDOs pool and tranche credit risk and redistribute it to investors requiring different risk-return profiles. Investment-grade synthetic CDOs will get done when the underlying collateral trades cheap relative to the cost of liabilities used to fund the structures. That generally happens when valuations in the investment-grade market deviate significantly from the underlying default profile. When risk aversion runs high, as it did in September 2002, investors whose performances are judged on a MTM basis may stay away from the market due to high perceived risk. However, this situation can create significant opportunities for investors with a hold-to-maturity setup, who can view the market as a whole as an asset, rather than individual risks. The bid for credit this creates can, at times, create very strong pressure on the default swap premiums for credits included in the baskets

The impact on individual credits, however, varies widely. In order to achieve a public rating, a given "diversity score" needs to be achieved. That requires all credits in the basket to be equally weighted, which means that the spread impact of sourcing the credit risk will vary significantly:

❏ Less liquid names will be more impacted than more liquid ones.
❏ Credits with high risk of downgrade to non-investment-grade and/or outright default tend to get excluded and hence are less impacted.

Funding risk

Selling protection removes the risk of changes to the cost of funding. Removing this risk will make the default swap relatively more attractive than the cash alternative and will reduce the basis.

A default swap effectively locks in Libor flat as the funding rate until maturity. Buying an asset and funding it on repo, however, usually requires regularly rolling the repo rate over – an extra risk the investor needs to be compensated for.

THE DEFAULT SWAP BASIS IN PRACTICE

At any given point in time, the default swap basis will always be affected by more than one factor. Sometimes these factors neutralise each other. For example, valuable step-up coupons in a bond should, all things being equal, push the basis wider, but, if the credit frequently becomes included in synthetic baskets, the net effect may be neutral.

Often, however, several factors act to reinforce one and the same trend. Look, for instance, at the number of factors that conspire to drive the basis wider on a deteriorating credit:

❏ The cheapest-to-deliver option increases in value as it approaches the strike price, ie, the credit event.
❏ The cheapening up in cash terms as the credit trades down and starts trading below par and so changes the risk profile relative to the default swap contract.
❏ Any coupon step-ups in the bonds will start to become valuable as the risk of ratings downgrades increases.
❏ The difficulty of shorting the cash market will push investors who want to express their negative view on the credit to the default swap market.

The important thing here is that all these factors will work in tandem to reverse the trend once the credit starts improving again. The delivery

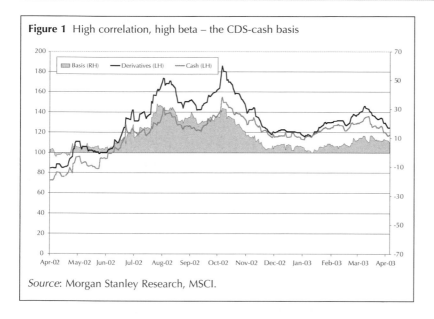

Figure 1 High correlation, high beta – the CDS-cash basis

Source: Morgan Stanley Research, MSCI.

option will lose value, the cash price will recover, step-ups will be increasingly ignored (and investors may start focusing on any step-downs instead), shorts will be covered and liquidity will improve.

The fact that all these factors work in tandem and reinforce each other gives the default swap market an important *high-beta character, vis-à-vis* the underlying cash market. In a widening environment, one would expect the default swap market to underperform the cash market, and vice versa, as demonstrated in Figure 1.

1   In the event of default, the investor will have exposure to the unwinding of the interest rate swap associated with the asset swap. If the asset is a par-floater, however, this will not be the case.

2   This arbitrage-free relationship will also hold in the event that the asset is funded on repo at Libor. It does not take into account any mark-to-market effect due to convexity differences between asset swap and default swap positions.

3   The cheapest-to-deliver option is only one of several factors contributing to the high-beta nature of the default swap. As explained later in this volume, a cash price less than par, bond coupon step-ups, difficulty of shorting the cash market and relative liquidity all add to this nature.

4   The degree of counterparty risk is also affected by the default correlation between the protection seller and the reference entity. For example, the value of credit protection on a Portuguese bank could be considerably lower if the main credit risk is systemic rather than idiosyncratic, ie, any potential risk would affect both banks at the same time.

4

What is the value of modified restructuring?

Alex Reyfman and Klaus Toft

Goldman Sachs

In this chapter, we present a framework for quantifying the value of modified restructuring (Mod R), modified modified restructuring (Mod Mod R), and old restructuring (Old R) in a credit default swap (CDS) contract, relative to a contract with only bankruptcy and failure to pay credit events (No R).[1] We find that for reasonable parameter values, the model produces a Mod R premium of 1–6% of the No R spread for a five-year 100 basis points (bps) CDS, which is at odds with the current market premium of 5–10% at the time of writing. This suggests that market participants may be overpaying for the cheapest-to-deliver option in Mod R contracts.

The value of the restructuring credit event in a CDS contract depends upon:

❏ the contractual maturity restrictions on deliverable obligations;
❏ the term of the CDS contract;
❏ the capital structure of the reference entity; and
❏ the likelihood of the restructuring credit event relative to bankruptcy or failure to pay.

The Mod R CDS contract places the most restrictions on the maturity of deliverable obligations, followed by the Mod Mod R variant, with Old R placing the least. For this reason, the value of the restructuring credit event is lowest in Mod R contracts, followed by Mod Mod R, and highest in Old R. The value of the cheapest-to-deliver option in CDS with restructuring declines with the term of the contract: The running spread premium in short-maturity CDS contracts is greater than in long ones. Not surprisingly, the more long-maturity or otherwise potentially low-priced liabilities the reference entity has outstanding, the higher is the value of restructuring. Finally, the greater the likelihood of the restructuring credit event relative to bankruptcy and failure to pay, the wider is the Mod R, Mod Mod R, and Old R CDS spread relative to No R.[2]

OVERVIEW

The question of restructuring as a credit event in standard CDS contracts has occupied market participants for the past several years.[3] Following the publication of the 1999 International Swaps and Derivatives Association (ISDA) credit derivatives Definitions, the market-standard set of credit events for corporate reference entities became:

❑ failure to pay;
❑ bankruptcy; and
❑ restructuring.[4]

To settle following a credit event, most CDS contracts allow the protection buyer to deliver a basket of debt that is equal to or greater in seniority relative to the contract's reference obligation, which is typically senior unsecured. This feature amounts to a cheapest-to-deliver option: the protection buyer can seek out the lowest-priced debt to settle the contract. If the protection buyer hedged a specific debt issue on its books, delivering lower-priced debt to settle the contract produces a gain.

The payoff of the cheapest-to-deliver option embedded in a CDS depends on the lowest-price obligation following a credit event. For example, if a reference entity has long-dated, foreign currency, or otherwise low-priced liabilities following a credit event, the payoff may be quite large. Alternatively, if all senior unsecured debt is trading at the same price following a credit event, the gain is minimal.

Unlike bankruptcy and failure to pay, which usually cause all debt at the same seniority level to trade roughly at the same recovery price, a restructuring often causes deliverable obligations to trade with a term structure. Longer-maturity obligations trade at higher spreads than short-term ones, reflecting the near-term liquidity improvement and continuing long-term uncertainty. The price dispersion of deliverable obligations increases the value of the cheapest-to-deliver option in contracts with restructuring.

To address market participants' concerns regarding the restructuring credit event, on May 11, 2001, ISDA issued the restructuring supplement to the 1999 ISDA credit derivatives Definitions. CDS market participants can include the Restructuring Supplement in CDS contracts. When incorporated into a CDS contract, with the restructuring Maturity Limitation marked applicable, this supplement limits the maturity of deliverable obligations used in settlement when:

❑ the protection buyer delivers the credit event notice; and
❑ restructuring is the sole credit event cited.

The restructuring Supplement provides the CDS market with contract language that limits the ability to deliver debt instruments that are often cheaper than the restructured instrument, while still offering hedgers protection from the restructuring credit event. Contracts that specify this limitation as applicable are referred to as "Mod R," while those that do not are called "Old R." CDS that list only failure to pay and bankruptcy as credit events are called No R contracts. Failure to pay and bankruptcy are called "hard" credit events by market participants, while restructuring is deemed a "soft" credit event.

By the middle of 2001, US dealers had adopted Mod R in the majority of investment-grade corporate CDS contracts. Protection sellers insisted on limiting the value of the cheapest-to-deliver option by switching to Mod R.

Panel 1
WHAT ARE RESTRUCTURING, MODIFIED RESTRUCTURING, AND MODIFIED MODIFIED RESTRUCTURING?

The 1999 ISDA credit derivatives Definitions define restructuring as one of the changes to the reference entity's obligations listed in Figure A.

Figure A. From Section 4.7.

(i) a reduction in the rate or amount of interest payable or the amount of scheduled interest accruals;

(ii) a reduction in the amount of principal or premium payable at maturity or at scheduled redemption dates;

(iii) a postponement or other deferral of a date or dates for either (A) the payment or accrual of interest or (B) the payment of principal or premium;

(iv) a change in the ranking in priority of payment of any obligation, causing the subordination of such obligation; or

(v) any change in the currency or composition of any payment of interest or principal

Source: The 1999 ISDA Credit Derivatives Definitions

The 2003 Definitions also clarify that the restructuring event must be binding on all holders of the restructured obligations. In practice, the most common change to the reference entity's debt terms that constitutes a credit event under restructuring but not under failure to pay is point (iii) (B) in Figure A – maturity extension. The analysis in the body of the report takes restructuring to mean debt maturity extension.

The restructuring Supplement to the 1999 ISDA credit derivatives Definitions limits the maturity of deliverable obligations. The purpose of introducing Mod R was to reduce the difference between:

1. the economic loss associated with holding the instrument suffering a restructuring; and
2. the economic loss associated with a written CDS.

Figure B presents the Supplement's Section 2.29, which contains the restructuring maturity limitation that is applied to deliverable obligations.[1]

Figure B. Modified restructuring definition

Section 2.29. Restructuring maturity limitation. If Physical settlement is specified in the related confirmation, restructuring is the only credit event specified in the credit event notice for which buyer is the notifying party, and "restructuring maturity limitation applicable" is specified in the related confirmation, then a deliverable obligation may be included in the portfolio only if it is a fully transferable obligation with a final maturity date not later than the restructuring maturity limitation date.

"Restructuring maturity limitation date" means the date that is the earlier of (x) 30 months following the restructuring date and (y) the latest final maturity date of any restructured bond or loan, provided, however, that under no circumstance shall the restructuring maturity limitation date be earlier than the scheduled termination date or later than 30 months following the scheduled termination date

---

Source: Restructuring Supplement To the 1999 ISDA Credit Derivatives Definitions

---

Simply, Section 2.29 states that if:

(1) the CDS contract settles with physical delivery;
(2) the protection buyer delivers a credit event notice; and
(3) restructuring maturity limitation is selected in the contract;

then the maturity of the deliverable obligations is limited to the restructuring maturity limitation date discussed in the next section. The definition of the restructuring maturity limitation date for Mod R contracts is most easily understood by referring to Figure C.

Figure C shows that there are three cases. The first case considers the situation wherein the scheduled termination date of the CDS, T_{CDS}, is after both the maturity date of the restructured obligation, T_{RM}, and the

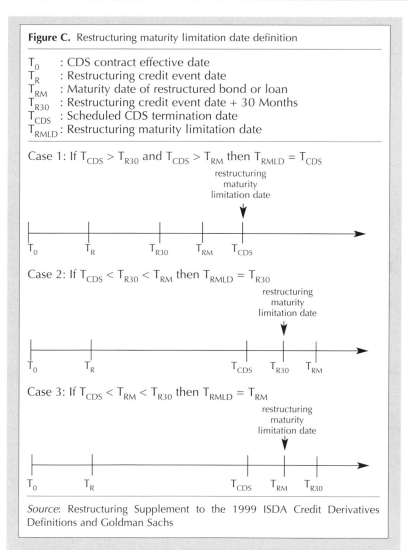

Figure C. Restructuring maturity limitation date definition

T_0 : CDS contract effective date
T_R : Restructuring credit event date
T_{RM} : Maturity date of restructured bond or loan
T_{R30} : Restructuring credit event date + 30 Months
T_{CDS} : Scheduled CDS termination date
T_{RMLD} : Restructuring maturity limitation date

Case 1: If $T_{CDS} > T_{R30}$ and $T_{CDS} > T_{RM}$ then $T_{RMLD} = T_{CDS}$

restructuring
maturity
limitation date

$T_0 \qquad T_R \qquad T_{R30} \qquad T_{RM} \quad T_{CDS}$

Case 2: If $T_{CDS} < T_{R30} < T_{RM}$ then $T_{RMLD} = T_{R30}$

restructuring
maturity
limitation date

$T_0 \qquad T_R \qquad T_{CDS} \quad T_{R30} \quad T_{RM}$

Case 3: If $T_{CDS} < T_{RM} < T_{R30}$ then $T_{RMLD} = T_{RM}$

restructuring
maturity
limitation date

$T_0 \qquad T_R \qquad T_{CDS} \quad T_{RM} \quad T_{R30}$

Source: Restructuring Supplement to the 1999 ISDA Credit Derivatives Definitions and Goldman Sachs

restructuring credit event date + 30 months, T_{R30}. In this case, the restructuring maturity limitation date equals the maturity of the CDS contract. The second case considers the situation wherein the scheduled termination date of the CDS, T_{CDS}, is after the restructuring credit event date + 30 months, T_{R30}, which in turn is before the maturity date of the restructured obligation, T_{RM}. In this case, the restructuring maturity limitation date equals the restructuring credit event date + 30 months.

Finally, the third case considers the situation where the scheduled termination date of the CDS, T_{CDS}, is before the maturity date of the restructured bond or loan, T_{RM}, which in turn is before the restructuring credit event date + 30 months, T_{R30}. In this situation, the restructuring maturity limitation date equals the maturity date of the restructured obligation. The restructuring Supplement has been incorporated into the 2003 credit derivatives Definitions as Section 2.32.

If the protection buyer exercises, Mod R restricts the maturity of the deliverable obligation significantly relatively to Old R. In no circumstances can the CDS contract be settled by delivering deliverable obligation with a scheduled maturity date of more than 30 months from the CDS maturity date, but it can always be settled with deliverable obligations with a maturity equal to or less than the maturity of the CDS contract.

Because deliverable obligations used to settle the CDS contracts can have maturities longer than the maturity of the CDS (up to 30 months), the delivery option is valuable if bonds and loans with different maturities can trade at different prices – a situation that may occur following a loan restructuring.

The Mod Mod R contract variant, described in section 2.33 of the 2003 Definitions, defines the modified restructuring maturity limitation date as the later of the scheduled termination date and 60 months following the restructuring date in the event the restructured bond or loan is delivered. When other obligations are delivered, the modified restructuring maturity limitation date is the latter of the scheduled termination date and 30 months following the restructuring date.

1 Section 2.30 of the restructuring Supplement also clarifies the definition of *Pari Passu* and subordination as applicable to restructuring, section 3.11 permits the notifying party to deliver multiple credit event notices in US$1 million increments when restructuring is the applicable credit event and section 4.10 limits the restructuring credit event to obligations held by multiple holders – ie, it explicitly excludes bilateral or closely held loans.

Currently, we estimate that fewer than 1% of all US investment-grade corporate contracts are executed with Old R, 92% with Mod R, and about 7% with No R. On high-yield trading desks (in both the US and Europe), Old R has been almost completely eliminated, with 2% of contracts executed with Mod R and the rest with No R.

Europe and Asia continued to trade with Old R, primarily because some bank hedgers were uncertain whether they would achieve regulatory capital relief with Mod R contracts. In Europe, 94% of CDS contracts are executed with Old R, 3% with Mod R, and 3% with No R. The latest news from the Basel II process suggests that bank regulators may provide regulatory capital credit for CDS hedges executed without restructuring, providing the hedger has veto power over the restructuring. However, at this time, the question of regulatory capital credit for No R contracts has not been fully resolved.

The restructuring Supplement has been incorporated into the ISDA 2003 credit derivatives Definitions, which are expected to become market practice in early Summer, 2003. The new Definitions (see Chapter 19) provide another modified restructuring option (referred to as Mod Mod R by the market), as has been requested by European market participants. This language allows a slightly larger set of deliverable obligations following restructuring than those specified under Mod R.[5]

In the US, the spread difference between five-year No R and Mod R CDS contracts has typically been in the range of 5–10% of the No R spread (Mod R contract spreads are 5–10% wider than otherwise identical No R ones), while the difference between Old R and No R is in the range of 10–20%. Evidence from synthetic TRACERS – a basket of 100 reference entities traded as one No R contract – implies a larger Mod R premium of nearly 10%. By contrast, our model results suggest that the premium between Mod R and No R contracts should be in the 1–6% range, while the premium between Old R and No R could be from 4% to over 30%, depending on the probability of restructuring relative to "hard" credit events. Since a market for Mod Mod R contracts does not yet exist, we cannot provide a spread estimate between No R and Mod Mod R.

Valuation framework

Our framework for modelling corporate CDS contracts classifies CDS credit events into two categories: hard and soft credit events.[6] Failure to pay and bankruptcy are hard credit events, while restructuring is the sole soft credit event.[7] In our model, following a hard credit event, all senior unsecured claims trade at the same recovery value; following restructuring, the value of senior unsecured debt is determined using default probabilities from a post-restructuring No R CDS spread curve.

Restructuring is modelled as a maturity extension of an obligation by a fixed term. Triggering after a restructuring allows the protection buyer to deliver the cheapest available obligation, but at the same time cancels the remaining hard credit event protection value of the contract. In this context, the payoff from the cheapest-to-deliver option is the difference between the proceeds from settlement and the remaining value of the CDS contract. This payoff is positive in cases where the protection buyer can deliver obligations that mature after the contract's maturity date. By assuming a fixed maturity extension period as well as a given post-restructuring No R CDS curve, we can compute the cheapest-to-deliver option value of Mod R, Mod Mod R, and Old R CDS contracts.

Panel 2 uses a simplified example to illustrate how a restructuring credit event generates value for the protection buyer. For simplicity, the example in Panel 2 assumes that the benefit from a restructuring credit event is constant over time. However, in the reminder of the chapter, we develop a more detailed model that allows the value of the restructuring credit event to depend on time.

Panel 2
THE CDS SPREAD DIFFERENCE BETWEEN CONTRACTS WITH AND WITHOUT THE RESTRUCTURING CREDIT EVENT.

Table A. Implied restructuring premium relative to a No R contract (% of initial CDS spread)

Cheapest-to-deliver bond price	Payoff from restructuring	Restructuring probability factor relative to a hard credit event			
		10%	25%	50%	100%
66	21	3.1	7.6	15.3	30.6
70	17	2.5	6.2	12.4	24.9
74	12	1.9	4.8	9.6	19.1
78	9	1.3	3.4	6.7	13.4
82	5	0.8	1.9	3.9	7.7
86	1	0.2	0.5	1.0	2.0

Source: Goldman Sachs

The CDS spread difference between a contract with the restructuring credit event (RCE) and one without it contains the market's expectations of:

❏ the probability of restructuring relative to a hard credit event; and
❏ par minus the value of the cheapest-to-deliver obligation following restructuring, relative to the remaining value of an equivalent No R contract.

We model the probability of restructuring as proportional to the probability of a hard credit event. A proportional restructuring probability factor of 50% means that for every two hard credit events, we observe one restructuring. The spread between a CDS contract with restructuring and one without can be decomposed into the combination of the market's expectation of the restructuring probability factor and the post-restructuring price of the cheapest-to-deliver obligation.

As an example, consider a five-year No R CDS contract with a market spread of 100 bps. Although in reality we expect a CDS spread curve to be wide and downward sloping just prior to restructuring, as the market worries about near-term liquidity, and tighter and upward-sloping following restructuring, for the purpose of this example we assume flat pre- and post-restructuring CDS curves. The spread duration of the contract is initially 4.6 years.

We assume a 30% recovery following a hard credit event. The

approximate five-year hard credit event market-implied probability is 6.6% = 4.6 / (1–30%). Also, we assume that following restructuring, the No R protection market level is 1,500 bps for the remainder of the term. For concreteness, we assume that restructuring will occur in year 4 and that the spread duration of the one-year No R spread will be 0.90 year.

An investor simultaneously buys Mod R CDS protection and sells No R protection on the same reference credit and with identical terms. Following restructuring, the investor triggers the Mod R contract and delivers the lowest-price bond. Simultaneously, the investor unwinds the remainder of the No R contract. Using our assumptions, the cost of unwinding the No R CDS after restructuring will be 12.6 points = –(100 – 1,500) × 0.90. The payoff from this strategy is: 100 – Price of Cheapest-to-Deliver Bond – 12.6. We convert the payoff into a running spread by multiplying by the restructuring probability and dividing by the initial spread duration of 4.6 years.

Table A shows the implied running-spread premium of a contract with restructuring relative to a No R contract as a function of the cheapest-to-deliver bond price and the RPF. The second column displays the payoff from restructuring. For cheapest-to-deliver obligation prices in the 70s and the RPF around 25%, the restructuring premium relative to a No R CDS contract is between 3% and 6% of the initial No R CDS curve.

The model

The model decomposes the valuation problem into two components:

1. a model for the probability of a restructuring credit event; and
2. a model for the payoff of the cheapest-to-deliver option in the case of a restructuring credit event.

The probability of the restructuring credit event is determined by assuming that at any point during the term of the CDS contract, the reference entity can be in one of three states:

❑ survival (no credit events);
❑ restructuring (soft credit event); or
❑ bankruptcy or failure to pay (hard credit event).

Starting in *survival*, the reference entity can suffer a soft or a hard credit event. Following a soft credit event, the reference entity can subsequently experience a hard credit event or remain in the restructured state. We do not permit the possibility of multiple restructurings for the sake of tractability. Once the entity enters the hard credit event state, it remains there for the term of the contract. We illustrate our model schematically in Figure 1.

In every period i, if the reference entity is in the *survival* state, a soft credit event can occur with a probability q_i^S, while a hard credit event can occur with probability q_i^H. Following a soft credit event, the reference entity can suffer a hard credit event with probability q_i^{SH} or remain in the soft credit event state with probability q_i^{SS}. The risk-neutral probability of a soft (restructuring) credit event is assumed to be k times more likely than a hard credit event, that is, $q_i^S = k \times q_i^H$. We label k the restructuring probability factor. The state transition probabilities – q_i^S, q_i^H, q_i^{SH}, and q_i^{SS} – are calibrated to the term structures of the No R CDS spread curve using the restructuring probability factor and the recovery rate assumption.

The base-case model parameter assumptions are listed in Figure 2. The initial No R CDS spread curve is assumed to be 100 bps per year for all maturities, while the post-restructuring No R CDS curve is taken to be 15%. Recovery following a hard credit event is 30%. The restructuring probability factor assumption of 25% corresponds roughly to that observed among all reference entities included in synthetic CDOs rated by Standard & Poor's.[8] A restructuring probability factor of 100% means that restructuring is equally likely as a hard credit event.

To compute the value of the cheapest-to-deliver option, we derive the expected discounted value of all bonds available for delivery into the CDS

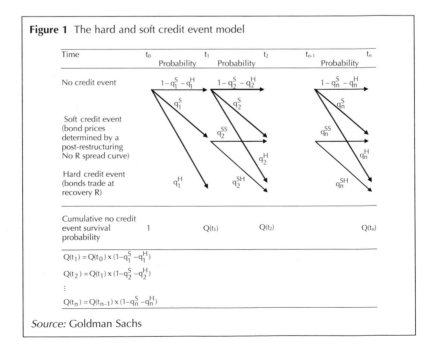

Figure 1 The hard and soft credit event model

Source: Goldman Sachs

Figure 2 Base-case assumptions

Parameter	Assumption
Bond maturity structure	Bonds maturing quarterly
Initial No R term structure of CDS spreads (bps)	100 (all maturities)
Post-restructuring No R CDS Spread (bps)	1,500
Restructuring probability factor (%)	25
Hard credit event recovery (%)	30
Restructuring maturity extension (years)	2

Source: Goldman Sachs

contract. These bond values are computed using default probabilities implied from the post-restructuring/no-restructuring CDS spread. We then assume that the lowest price obligation is delivered to settle the contract. For Mod R and Mod Mod R contracts, the cheapest-to-deliver bond is the one with maturity equal to the Mod R maturity limitation date. For Old R contracts, the 30-year bond (or the longest maturity bond outstanding) is delivered.

In Mod R and Mod Mod R CDS, triggering and delivering a bond with the same maturity as the contract to settle following a restructuring does not generate a substantial gain, if all outstanding bonds are then valued on the post-restructuring No R curve. The protection buyer receives par minus the value of the delivered bond times the contract notional, and loses the remaining value of the hard credit event protection of the CDS contract – this generates essentially a zero payoff.[9] The delivery option generates a positive payoff if the restructuring occurs when the contract allows the delivery of obligations with longer maturities than the CDS.

Results

Using the parameter values in Figure 2 and our assumption about state transitions, we compute the Mod R, Mod Mod R, and Old R CDS premiums relative to the No R CDS curve. Figure 3 shows the percentage increase over the 100 bps No R curve for Mod R, Mod Mod R, and Old R contracts at the five-year maturity point. With a restructuring probability factor of 25%, the Mod R contract commands a 1.9% theoretical premium and the Mod Mod R contract is 2.5% wider, while the Old R contract is 10.1% wider. For all three contracts, the premium over the No R CDS curve increases with the restructuring probability factor. Assuming that restructuring is as likely as a hard credit event – the restructuring probability

Figure 3 Percentage increase over the 100 bps five-year No R CDS spread. No R CDS Spread = 100 bps

| | Restructuring probability factor relative to a hard credit event | | | |
	10%	25%	50%	100%
Mod R	0.8	1.9	3.4	5.5
Mod Mod R	1.1	2.5	4.4	7.0
Old R	4.7	10.1	19.9	33.1

Source: Goldman Sachs

factor is 100% – produces 5.5%, 7.0%, and 33.1% premiums for Mod R, Mod Mod R, and Old R, respectively.

Figures 4, 5 and 6 graphically present the sensitivity of the cheapest-to-deliver option premium to the maturity of the CDS contract.[10] Figure 4 shows the Mod R, Figure 5 displays the Mod Mod R, while Figure 6 presents the Old R results. In all three cases, the value of restructuring, when expressed as a running basis point spread, is highly dependent on maturity. This result is explained by the fact that the cheapest-to-deliver option mostly has value during the last 30 months of a Mod R or a Mod Mod R CDS contract. The value of the option at the start of the contract declines with the term, since the probability of survival to the point when

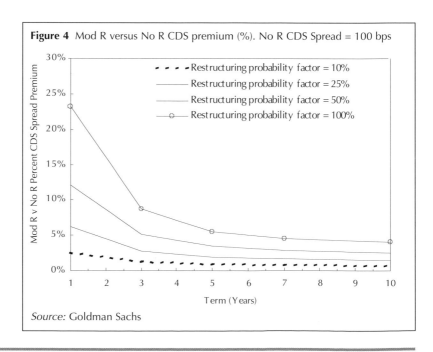

Figure 4 Mod R versus No R CDS premium (%). No R CDS Spread = 100 bps

Source: Goldman Sachs

the option has value falls over time. Additionally, converting the option value into a running spread produces lower values for longer-term contacts. This last effect also explains the drop in the Old R running premium for longer-term contracts, since in Old R contracts the option has value during the entire term. Panel 3 examines the sensitivity of the results to several other model parameter values.

The base-case analysis assumes a full-term structure of deliverable bonds; the reference entity has bonds maturing every quarter. At the other extreme is an issuer with only one bond that matures on the same date as the CDS contract. In this case, the model value of the cheapest-to-deliver option is essentially zero.[11] Of course, the model does not take into account the possibility that new bonds could be issued in the future, or that bonds may be cheap for other reasons (eg, foreign currency or convertible bonds). This simplifying assumption may cause the model to understate the value of the cheapest-to-deliver option.

While this report focuses on the effect of bond maturity on the post-credit event price, other bond characteristics may also affect value. For example, yen-denominated bonds issued by European and US incorporated entities may have lower prices relative to euro- or US dollar-denominated debt, even following a hard credit event. Similarly, a low coupon convertible bond will often be the cheapest-to-deliver bond. The existence of and the ability to deliver these potentially low-priced bonds can further increase the value of the cheapest-to-deliver option, even in No R

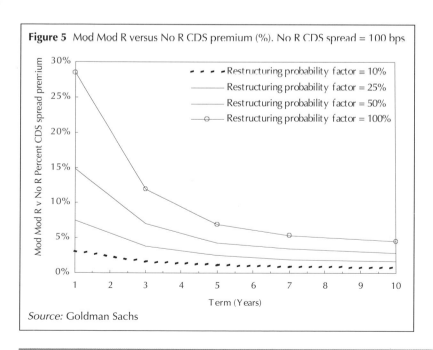

Figure 5 Mod Mod R versus No R CDS premium (%). No R CDS spread = 100 bps

Source: Goldman Sachs

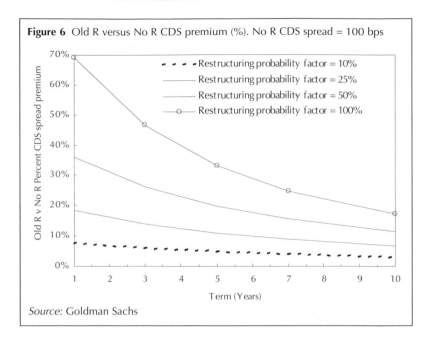

Figure 6 Old R versus No R CDS premium (%). No R CDS spread = 100 bps

Source: Goldman Sachs

contracts. For example, if we assume that post-restructuring the protection buyer will access a bond US$5 cheaper than the cheapest obligation priced on the post-restructuring No R curve, this approximately doubles the Mod R contract premium.

A second factor not explicitly considered in our framework is the impact of interest rates. The post-restructuring value of bonds will depend on

Panel 3
SENSITIVITY ANALYSIS FOR MODIFIED RESTRUCTURING MODEL

In this panel, we explore the sensitivity of the results described in this chapter to changes to the initial No R CDS curve and the post-hard credit event recovery. Figure A displays the results for the Mod R contract, while Figures B and C present the results for Mod Mod R and Old R, respectively.

The first graph of Figure A presents the sensitivity of the restructuring premium to the initial No R CDS curve. In terms of our model, the initial No R CDS curve incorporates both the probability of a direct hard credit event, as well as the probability of a soft credit event followed by a hard one. The results indicate that the short-maturity contract premiums are not very sensitive to the initial spread. At long maturities, the increase in the premiums for longer maturities is due to the compensation for the greater possibility of losing the running CDS spread in contracts with restructuring relative to No R.

The second graph of Figure A shows the sensitivity to the post-hard credit event recovery. The sensitivity of results to this parameter is generally small. A higher recovery rate implies a higher hard credit event probability for a given CDS curve. In the context of our model, a higher hard credit event probability implies a higher restructuring probability, which, in turn, implies a higher cheapest-to-deliver option

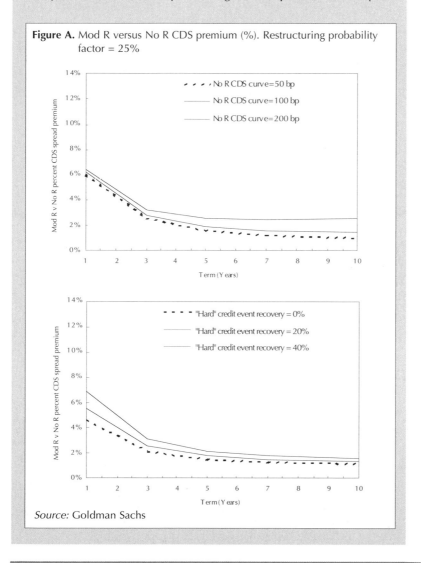

Figure A. Mod R versus No R CDS premium (%). Restructuring probability factor = 25%

Source: Goldman Sachs

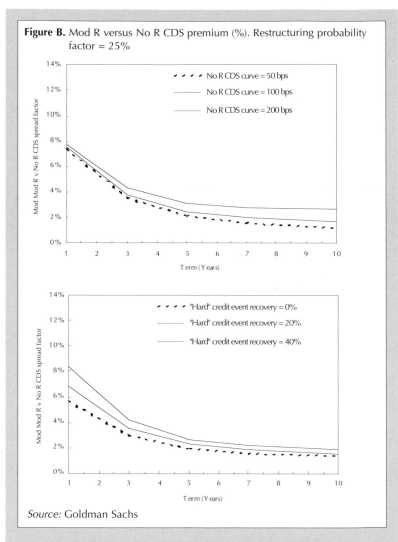

Figure B. Mod R versus No R CDS premium (%). Restructuring probability factor = 25%

Source: Goldman Sachs

value. The sensitivity is greater for short-maturity contracts, since the fixed increase in the value of the option is amortised over a shorter term.

Figures B and C show the sensitivities of the Mod Mod R and Old R contracts, which are broadly similar to Mod R. The exception is the sensitivity of the Old R premium to the post-hard credit event recovery. For Old R contracts, increasing hard credit event recovery generally decreases the running spread premium versus No R contracts. Since in Old R contracts the value of the option increases, albeit slowly, with the term of the contract, the increase in the hard credit event probability decreases the value of the option and the running premium.

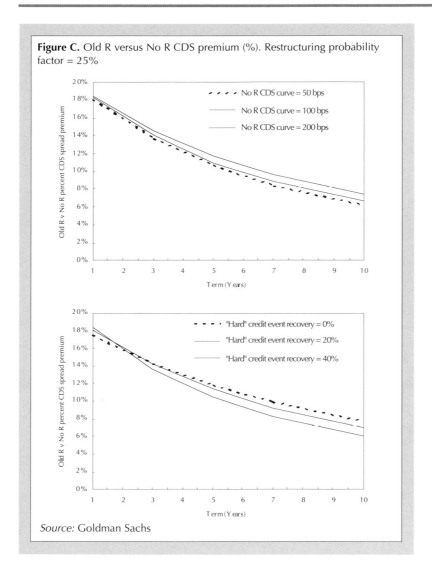

Figure C. Old R versus No R CDS premium (%). Restructuring probability factor = 25%

Source: Goldman Sachs

their coupons relative to prevailing interest rates. Following restructuring in an environment where rates are low, an issuer's bonds are likely to trade at relatively high US dollar prices – decreasing the value of the cheapest-to-deliver option. Conversely, if restructuring occurs in an environment where rates are generally higher than the coupons of outstanding fixed rate obligations, the value of the cheapest-to-deliver option may be greater.

Panel 4
THE CONSECO RESTRUCTURING EVENT

On September, 22, 2000, Conseco Inc. announced a US$2.8 billion loan restructuring agreement with its bank syndicate group.[1] At the time, the Conseco syndicated loan traded at a price of US$92, while the 9% bond of October 2006 traded at US$65. Conseco protection buyers could settle most CDS contracts by delivering the bonds. In this case, the net protection payment of US$35 (par minus recovery) was much larger than the US$8 loss on the restructured loan. Protection buyers who hedged a Conseco loan with CDS were able to realise US$27 (US$35 gain on the triggered contract – US$8 loss on the loan) following the restructuring.

Conseco protection sellers did not expect hedgers to trigger the contract and reap windfall gains. Following this episode, protection sellers noted that lenders who have hedged loans with CDS have an incentive to restructure the loan in order to collect the difference between the post-restructuring value of the loans and bonds. However, some protection buyers who use CDS to hedge loans argued that simply removing restructuring from the list of credit events would leave them with an incomplete hedge.

1 See Conseco, "Banks Agree to Restructure $2.8 Billion in Debt", Dow Jones News Service, September 22, 2000.

CONCLUSIONS

Our model allows investors to decompose the premium of CDS that include restructuring as a credit event relative to the No R CDS spread into two main components: the post-restructuring cheapest-to-deliver obligation price and the probability of restructuring, relative to a hard credit event. The analysis shows that for reasonable assumptions about the restructuring probability and the cheapest-to-deliver obligation price, the running premium of Mod R contracts relative to No R is in the 1–6% range, somewhat lower than what is currently observed in the market.

In practice, many of the model parameters are difficult to measure precisely for a given reference entity. Further complicating matters include the possibility that the entity alters the value of the cheapest-to-deliver option in the future by issuing long-maturity or foreign currency debt. For this reason, we do not expect the market to begin valuing the cheapest-to-deliver option using models. However, we believe that our framework will encourage investors to decompose the Mod R, Mod Mod R, and Old R premiums versus No R into the likelihood of restructuring relative to a hard credit event and the loss following a restructuring, enabling a comparison of the implied values with investors' intuition.

1   Under our base-case assumptions, for a five-year CDS contract, the value of Mod R is 1.9% of the No R spread, the value of Mod Mod R is 2.5%, and the value of Old R is 10.1%.

2   We estimate that at this time more than 90% of US investment grade corporate CDS contracts are executed with Mod R, while most contracts in Europe and Asia are executed with Old R.

3   See the Goldman Sachs Credit Derivatives Strategies November 2000 report, *Default Swaps: A Guide to Single-Name Credit Risk Transfer*, for an introduction to credit default swaps.

4   Obligation Acceleration was dropped as a credit event from standard US corporate CDS contracts in November 2001 on the grounds that it was unnecessary.

5   A second difference between Mod R and Mod Mod R is that under Mod R only fully trans-ferable obligations (no consent generally required to transfer) can be delivered, while Mod Mod R specifies that deliverable obligations may be conditionally transferable (ie, consent may be required so long as the loan documentation specifies that it may not be reasonably withheld). This distinction reflects the differences between the US and Europe in the typical underlying loan documentation as well as in perceptions regarding what transfer rights borrowers will permit.

6   The payoff from triggering a CDS contract following restructuring is the sum of the gain from the delivery of obligations in exchange for par and the loss of protection from possible future hard credit events.

7   At a restructuring probability factor of 25%, the Mod R contract commands a 1.9% theoret-ical premium over a 100 bps No R spread. The Mod Mod R contract is 2.5% wider, while the Old R contract is 10.1% wider.

8   See *Credit Event Data – What we observed on the front US & Europe*, presentation by Nik Khakee and Katrien Van Acoleyen at the Second Annual CDO Conference. Standard & Poor's reports that three out of 16 credit events reported in static synthetic CDOs rated by its Europe office were restructurings, while the corresponding figure for US transactions was four out of 30. Using these figures as indications of the likelihood of restructuring relative to bankruptcy and failure to pay results in empirical restructuring probability factors of 23% = 3/(16-3) and 15% = 4/(30-4), for Europe and the US, respectively.

9   The payoff is slightly positive, since the initial Mod R or Mod Mod R spread is wider than the No R spread. For this reason, the gain in value on the Mod R or Mod Mod R contract valued on the post-restructuring No R curve is slightly lower than the difference between par and the price of the delivered obligation.

10 The existence of potentially cheap bonds can further increase the value of the cheapest-to-deliver option.

11 The value is slightly positive because of the difference between the value of the bond following a restructuring credit event and an outstanding No R CDS contract. The difference is caused by a mismatch in cashflows: the bond pays semi-annually while the contract pays quarterly.

5

The debt and equity linkage and the valuation of credit derivatives

Sean C. Keenan, Jorge R. Sobehart, and Terry L. Benzschawel*

Citigroup Global Markets, New York[1]

INTRODUCTION

In their seminal article, Modigliani and Miller (1958) presented a theory that became a cornerstone of modern finance. Their paper explained the indeterminacy of corporate capital structure under certain idealised conditions. Several of these conditions are simplifying assumptions that could easily be relaxed. But crucial to their analysis is the assumption of complete contingent claims markets. Under these conditions, both investors and managers are indifferent as to whether firms finance projects using debt or equity, and projects expected to add value to future states of the world will be financed by one means or the other. All claims are contingent in a probabilistic sense, and corporate default risk is efficiently priced through consensus expectations about the relative likelihood of future states of the world.[2] Credit derivatives *per se* are unnecessary in this scenario, since each investor creates a portfolio of contingent claims diversified over all possible future world conditions. In simple terms, each investor holds a portfolio of assets, with each portfolio's return tied to the returns for all projects, in some specific future state of the world.

While consistent expectations about future project returns may never materialise, evolution toward the other key Modigliani–Miller precondition – complete contingent claims markets – has proceeded to exert a slow but transforming influence on global capital markets over recent decades. The increasing variety of contingent claims contracts, the evolution of markets on which to trade them and pricing techniques, and the growing dependence on derivatives by financial institutions and corporate obligors

* The authors would like to thank Jure Skarabot for helpful comments and suggestions.

continues to drive global markets in the direction of Modigliani–Miller. Credit derivatives are a recent addition to the contingent claims markets. This article considers the linkage between debt and equity markets, and the role that this connection plays in valuing credit derivatives.

THE EMERGENCE OF A DEBT-EQUITY LINKAGE

Presumably, if markets are to be (on average) fully informed and efficiently priced, multiple agents must perform the analytical legwork and trade sufficient volumes of securities to bring this about. The role of information-revealing investigative analysis is particularly important when firms face strong incentives to actively manage information flows. Clearly, if the debt and equity markets are to be tightly linked, there needs to be a common information set and a mechanism for maintaining the flow of information into and across markets.

Historically, however, equity analysts and bond analysts have tended to focus on different aspects of fundamental corporate finance data. Traditional fundamental credit analysis, performed by bond and loan analysts, focuses on those aspects of a company's financial statement that signal the ability of the firm to service its debt. The prime considerations of equity analysts are profitability, efficiency, and growth. Key measures include the price-to-earnings ratio, price as a multiple of cash flow, and price to book equity, none of which explicitly considers the capital structure of the firm. Equity analysts are also often associated with a heightened sensitivity to recent price movements, including the identification of "overbought" or "oversold" conditions, support and/or resistance levels, and especially the direction of "the market". Although such technical factors affect all securities markets, the lower liquidity, lower turnover, lesser importance of indexes, and lower retail participation in the fixed income markets all contribute to a greater emphasis on bottom-up, name-by-name analysis.

Throughout the 1960s, 1970s and early 1980s, corporate bond markets became increasingly oriented towards investment-grade issuers, with the agency ratings themselves playing a major role in providing liquidity and rationalising pricing. At year-end 1974, over 76% of rated bond issuers were rated investment-grade. With the exception of the Penn Central debacle of 1970, the all-corporate default rate averaged less than 1% over the 1971–1988 period, and large-scale corporate bankruptcies were rare. In this environment, not only were analytical techniques different, but the major players in bond and equity markets were different, and seemed to be separated by a wide cultural gulf – we were far from the idealised world of Modigliani–Miller.

However, the seeds of change were sown in 1973 with the publication of the Black–Scholes options pricing model and the resulting explosion of interest and trading in contingent claims contracts. While Black–Scholes alluded to a link between equity and corporate liabilities, it was Merton (1973, 1974) who detailed the relationship between a firm's equity price, the value of its assets and liabilities, and its likelihood of default.[3] The Merton–Black–Scholes insight was that equity could be viewed as a call option on the assets of the firm. Debt, under this characterisation, is equivalent to assets minus a call. Both debt and equity then, can be valued using the Black-Scholes options-pricing formula. The theory continues that if the value of the firm's assets evolve stochastically and we assume that options are deterministic functions of the underlying asset value, then there should be a functional relationship between debt and equity. The link to Modigliani–Miller was readily apparent: because of the embedded optionality of most corporate securities, contingent claims markets were far deeper than had been recognised, and to a large degree, equity and debt values should be functionally related to the time profile of expected payoffs.

The Black–Scholes model helped to fuel an explosion in options trading in stocks and commodities during the 1970s and 1980s. The success of this model in options pricing provided investors with tools for hedging and for increasing leverage in speculative trading. As liquidity in options markets increased, more sophisticated hedging and speculating strategies became feasible, allowing traders to bet on more specific patterns of price movement and volatility. The introduction of the OEX contract in 1983, an optionable futures contract on the S&P 100 index, ushered in the era of synthetic derivatives. Further developments included the so-called "exotic" options tied to more specific and complex future outcomes. Thus, from the mid-1970s to the late 1980s, contingent claims markets – for commodities and stock markets at least – were becoming more and more complete.

The debt markets were slower to embrace the Merton framework. Although contingent claims analysis was used to price corporate bonds with embedded options, the notion that valuation of corporate liabilities was itself an applied options-pricing problem, or that equities and debt were structurally linked derivatives of the firm's value, were not a part of the initial Black-Scholes revolution. In fact, early attempts to derive corporate bond spreads from the Merton model were unsuccessful.[4] It was not until the mid-1990s that a structural pricing model, which predicted probabilities of default rather than credit spreads, became commercially available.[5] The demand for bond pricing models grew in the late 1990s, along with the market for credit-based derivatives – eg, total return swaps, cash and synthetic collateralised debt obligations (CDOs), credit spread options, and credit default swaps (CDS). Credit derivatives have become important tools for institutions to hedge their bond and loan positions. They provide efficient ways to go long credit risk while remaining diversified, to short corporate credits, and to participate in the syndicated loan market. As these markets developed, the inadequacy of agency ratings for pricing and hedging credit derivatives stimulated industry and academic research on credit models. Furthermore, a rash of sudden blow-ups and high-profile defaults since 2000, for which the agency ratings appeared to lag bond spreads, has intensified the search for more forward-looking measures of corporate credit quality.

At present, there is little consensus on the correct methodology for pricing credit-related derivative instruments. Models described in the literature invariably take default probabilities and recovery rates (and sometimes downgrade probabilities) as input parameters.[6] Historical averages provided by rating agencies were used in the earliest days, but these were clearly insufficient for name-specific transactions. Current practice can be divided into two approaches:

❏ reduced-form models, which directly impute default probabilities and recovery rates from bond spreads; and
❏ structural models that use values obtained from equity markets in a Merton type model.

Each has its advantages and disadvantages. Both types of model can be formulated to predict default likelihood or credit spreads, either of which could be used to value credit derivatives.[7] In practice, the more empirical nature of the reduced form models often makes them preferable to current structural models for pricing purposes, while the forward-looking nature of the structural-type models are more suitable for prediction and analysis of fair value.

Modelling issues aside, a theoretical and practical problem has persisted: bond and equity markets often do not agree. For example, when bonds trade at a deep enough discount to imply impairment of principal, the corresponding equity should trade at zero, but this is often not the case. Inconsistencies have been observed not only for single names, but also for market aggregates. For example, from 1998–2002 the correlation between implied equity volatility as measured by the VIX index and investment-grade bond spreads was 0.52, while for speculative-grade spreads it was 0.51; however, the period was marked by several episodes in which sharply higher equity volatility occurred with minimal response in bond spreads.[8] These observations have resurrected interest in the theoretical debt-equity linkage implied by Merton, primarily from traders now seeking to identify arbitrage opportunities across all three markets. A few academic studies have sought to investigate this linkage empirically.[9] For example, Janosi, Jarrow, and Yildrim (2000, 2001) first estimate default intensities from bond prices using a reduced-form model, then estimate default intensities from equity prices, also using a reduced-form model, to see if the two markets are in agreement. Although model specifications used in these studies are too highly stylised to allow a precise measurement of cross-market agreement, they indicate the current level of interest in the debt-equity link, and the diversity of approaches now being used to try to understand it.

Importantly, for practitioners and academics alike, studying the debt-equity linkage is not merely a means to choosing between the Merton model and some reduced-form alternative. Rather, a clearer understanding of the debt and equity markets and their interrelationship is the first step towards a new and more reliable family of models for valuing corporate liabilities and their derivatives. In this chapter, we focus on the Merton framework and its implied linkage between the debt and equity markets. We suggest explanations for the observed inconsistencies between markets, and consider the implications for the credit derivatives markets.

A CLOSER LOOK AT THE MERTON-IMPLIED LINKAGE

In this section, we review the Merton model, focusing on the model's fundamental assumptions, their relation to actual debt and equity markets, and by extension, the implications for the debt-equity value relationship, which is critical to the credit-derivatives pricing issue.

Central to the Merton model is the idea that equity and debt can be viewed as options on the value of the firm's assets. In particular, ownership of common stock is seen as being equivalent to being long a call option on the firm's assets while ownership of debt is equal to ownership of the firm's assets minus the equity call. When evaluating Merton's assumption of an isomorphic price relationship between levered equity of the firm and a call option on its assets, it is not sufficient to simply evaluate the payoff profile of levered equity. We need to know which party owns the firm's assets at each point in time, and who has a conditional claim against those assets. A naïve interpretation of the exact call option analogy $E = C(A, t)$ would imply (counterfactually) that ownership of the assets is transferred temporarily to the debt holders once debt is issued. In this simplistic view, owners of the call options have the right to repurchase the assets at maturity if their value exceeds the exercise price D_0 – ie, the face value of the debt (see Figure 1a). From the call-put parity relationship, the complementary view is that equity is given by $E = A - D_0 e^{r(T-t)} + P(A, t)$, where $P(A, t)$ is the value of a put option with exercise price D_0 (see Figure 1b). In this alternative view, equity holders own the assets less the borrowed amount, and have the right to swap the assets' residual value for the borrowed amount if the assets' value falls below the payment promised to the bondholders – ie, the equity holders walk away from the assets. The timing of payment is, however, inconsistent with the put analogy, since the payment is made when the bonds are purchased. Thus, the assets continue to be owned by the equity investors, while bondholders hold only a conditional claim against a portion of those assets at the debt maturity. This becomes clear if we write $E = A - [A - C(A, t)]$ (see Figure 1c). Equity holders, through management, can dispose of the firm's assets as they see fit, even liquidating them if it serves their interests, while debt holders can do little to prevent this until after a default has occurred. Of course, debt holders may have covenant protections (contractual agreements) that limit management's freedom to dispose of the assets in certain ways. But management and equity holders still have limited liability and so can be forced to do no more than turn the assets – whatever their worth – over to debt holders. It is this limited liability feature that makes the equity payoff profile the same as that of a call option.

Looking at debt and equity in this way immediately suggests a conflict of interest between bondholders and stockholders. That is, if equity is truly an option on the firm's asset value, then its price can be raised by

Figure 1 Option payoff view of the firm's equity at time t_0: (a) right to repurchase the firm's assets at a fixed price; (b) residual value of the firm's assets plus right to sell the firm's assets at fixed price ; and (c) ownership of the firm's assets and obligation to repay due to limited liability

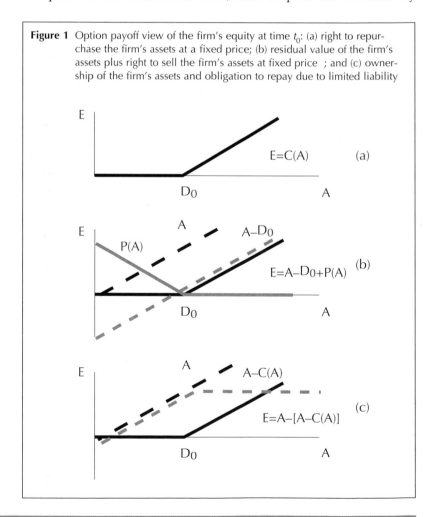

increasing the volatility of the firm's assets through risky investment and production decisions. Equity prices can also be raised by increasing dividend payouts, or by issuing debt to buy back stock. These increases in equity values come at the expense of the debt holders, because there is now a greater probability of default on the firm's debt. Both the increase in the firm's risk and the payment of dividends can be viewed as a transfer of wealth from debt holders to stockholders. Bond holders attempt to protect themselves from these tactics by including protective covenants that may limit the amount of dividends paid to stockholders and, to some extent, control the management's investment and production decisions by specifying the purpose of the debt proceeds.

Another problem is that observed equity prices reflect marginal values – ie, the amounts that investors are willing to pay for an incremental unit of the firm's assets. The difference between marginal and aggregate valuation can be seen during corporate take-overs, during which a firm's stock can move 30% or more from its pre-take-over price range. When such deals fall through, stock prices usually retreat quickly from the price that would have been required to purchase all of the firm's assets. Finally, there is the absence of a hedging motivation on the part of the equity holder's pre-leverage. In securities and commodities options markets, hedging activity is the initial source of market liquidity, with speculators playing a secondary role. If, as some argue, equity investors take on debt to hedge their initial ownership position against a catastrophic fall in the value of the firm's assets, they would want an instrument that paid off in cash under those circumstances. They do not receive any such benefit from an instrument (issuance of corporate debt) that pays off in advance, and whose proceeds are converted to additional assets to be claimed by bondholders in case of bankruptcy. Without a behavioural explanation for debt issuance consistent with the equity-as-option analogy, we are left only with the Modigliani–Miller consistent assumption that the firm's capital structure is determined purely by tax and cost-of-issuance considerations.

As previously stated, the acceptance of the Merton model as a tool for estimating default probabilities and pricing liabilities, and credit-related derivatives, was partly driven by its close connection with the highly successful Black–Scholes model for options pricing. As with the Black–Scholes model, the original Merton model has been extended, relaxing many of the simplifying assumptions including stochastic interest rates, various types of option structures, and more complex stochastic processes governing the evolution of the firm's assets. However, the derivation of the Merton and Black–Scholes models draw on similar key fundamental and technical assumptions:

a) the value of the firm's equity and debt is a deterministic function of the underlying value of the firm's assets and time to expiration;

b) an ideal self-financed hedge portfolio composed of risk-free bonds, the idealised equity described in (2), and the underlying firm's assets can be constructed; and

c) the ideal portfolio can be hedged at each point in time.

To obtain a tractable formalism that could lead to closed-form solutions, the following additional technical assumptions were also introduced by Merton (1974):

d) the risk free rate is constant;

e) the distribution for growth rates of the underlying assets is normal;

f) the volatility of the firm's assets is constant; and

g) there are no transaction costs, taxes, liquidity problems or problems with the indivisibility of assets, equity or debt.

Based on these assumptions, Merton derived a partial differential equation for pricing the firm's equity and its debt, which is equivalent to the Black–Scholes equation. In Merton's framework, the fundamental assumptions (a)–(c), together with the computational assumptions (d)–(g), lead to a riskless hedge strategy for an ideal portfolio that requires no initial investment and no additional funds to maintain the strategy – ie, the portfolio is self-financed. In Merton's ideal hedge strategy, the stochastic variations of the firm's equity (or debt) are balanced by the variations of the underlying firm's assets. As there could be no riskless strategy, at any point in time, that could yield a positive return with no initial investment and no additional funds, the return on the ideal hedge portfolio must be set equal to zero to avoid sustainable arbitrage opportunities.

Like the Black–Scholes model, one of the advantages of the Merton model is that it is not extremely demanding in terms of inputs. To estimate the value of equity E (an option on the firm's assets) the required variables are:

1. the current value of the underlying firm's assets A;
2. the volatility of the assets σ;
3. the riskless rate of return r; and
4. the *par* value of the debt D_0, and (5) the time to expiration $(T - t)$.

Also, as in the Black–Scholes model, the rate of return of the firm's assets does not appear in the debt-equity pricing formula. This is a consequence of both the continuous hedge argument and the instantaneous no arbitrage condition imposed on the hedge portfolio. As a result, the return on the underlying firm's assets is not required to price the firm's equity in the idealised no-arbitrage Merton framework. The main implementation problem for the Merton model is that the firm's assets are unobservable and need to be inferred from equity prices.

If the Merton model were a consistent representation of actual equity and debt price dynamics, then the substitution of the current equity market price – ie, the "implied" firm's assets price and volatility – into the formula derived by Merton (along with the specifics of the debt contract and the risk free rate) would result in credit spreads similar to those observed in bond markets. Unfortunately, the estimated spreads differ greatly to those observed in the market (Jones, Mason and Rosenfeld, 1984; and Gemmill, 2002). In fact, to obtain spreads of similar magnitude to the observed values, the volatility of the assets needs to be set to unrealistic values (Kim, Ramaswamy, and Sunderasan, 1993; and Cathcart and El-Jahel, 1998). Even worse, the values for the firm's assets and volatility implied from equity prices disagree with those obtained from bond prices. The observed implied volatility is usually interpreted as an estimate of the "future uncertainty" associated with investors' perceptions of the firm. The lack of predictability of the observed spreads is the main reason why adopters of market-based models typically restrict their use to estimating probabilities of default on payments, and rarely use them for pricing corporate bonds and loans, or for building trading strategies in credit markets (King, 2001).

Because assumptions (a) and (b) are thought to be fundamental to the Merton framework and its extensions, the discrepancy between the observed spreads and the model estimates is usually attributed to the simplifications introduced by the assumptions (c)–(g); extensions to the model have generally sought to relax them. This approach has been supported by the fact that these extensions of the Merton model – which include non-log-normal distribution of assets, stochastic interest rates and volatilities, and stochastic default points – show better fit at the expense of increased mathematical complexity (see Levin and van Deventer, 1997; Leland, 1999; and Bohn, 2002). However, these extensions to the original model remain unable to completely describe the observed term structure of corporate bond spreads without additional assumptions. Despite this, for many years models of this type have been used for hedging and capital structure arbitrage, with the trader exercising judgement in terms of the "limits" of the model. Panel 1 gives a more detailed overview of this and explains the use of the structural models to estimate both risk-neutral and real default probabilities.

We now turn to the implications of the assumptions (a)–(c), and focus on two technical problems in the debt valuation framework contained in Merton and its extensions. The technical problems are that:

❏ structural aspects of the corporate debt market that could prevent the no-arbitrage condition from holding; and
❏ equity market and debt market uncertainty is not accounted for within the Merton model.

Panel 1
PRACTICAL IMPLEMENTATIONS OF EQUITY TO CREDIT MODELS
Jean-Pierre Lardy, JP Morgan

Although the original articles of Black–Scholes (1973) and Merton (1974) are now 30 years old, the idea of assessing credit quality based on stock market information has increased in popularity over the past decade. Today it is widely adopted amongst credit portfolio managers and the large faction of traders and arbitragers involved in credit and equity derivatives, corporate debt and convertible bonds.

Commercial banks need to assess the quality of their large portfolio of borrowers and counterparts, many of which have no public rating or traded credit instrument. For them, equity-based models provide a real-time indicator of credit risk that complements internal rating systems. The metric for single-name credit quality is the expected default frequency (EDF) introduced by KMV. Moody's KMV and RiskCalc provide EDFs for 20,000 companies with public equity; Black–Scholes–Merton's original ideas are used to estimate a "distance-to-default" based on the underlying value of the assets compared to the debt of the firm, normalised by the asset volatility. The EDF relationship to the distance-to-default is calibrated on a historical default database. By construction, a firm's EDF is the historical default frequency of firms with similar distance-to-default.

On the trading desks, the idea of hedging the underlying credit risk of a non-investment-grade bond position with a short-stock position is certainly older than Black–Scholes–Merton's research. Today, with the development of credit derivatives, a rapidly growing number of desks are specialising in capital structure arbitrage. Here, Black–Scholes–Merton's ideas provide the basis for arbitrage strategies on the relative price relationships of traded equity and debt instruments or credit default swaps. The relevant metric is the risk-neutral probability of default, which, unlike the EDF, includes a risk premium required by the market to compensate for the variance of the default risk. RiskMetrics' CreditGrades provides 11,000 companies with direct calculation of such risk-neutral probabilities and the corresponding five-year credit default swap spread, utilising a simple equity-to-credit formula known as E2C (see Lardy, Finkelstein, Khuong-huu and Yang, 2000). The formula was inspired by the earlier refinements of Black–Scholes–Merton's ideas by Black and Cox (1976) and Leland (1994).

A common characteristic of these models is their ability to provide early warning signals and quite robust assessments of credit quality. However, one should not expect an unrealistic level of precision. Cox and Rubinstein (1985) describe how they invoke a powerful idea but ignore certain aspects of corporate finance and governance. Moreover, their implementation requires approximations and imprecise estimations of observable inputs. In practice, traders must learn to adapt their judgements and actions from an irreducible level of noise and event risk. Throughout 2001 and 2002, the correlation between equity and credit was particularly strong. The first half of 2003 has witnessed a

Table A Various estimations of default probabilities from commercial implementations

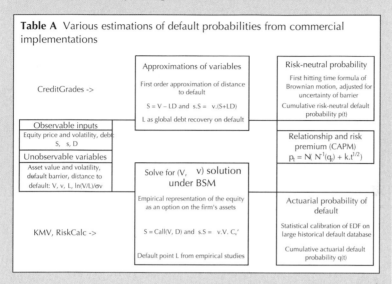

CreditGrades ->

Observable inputs
Equity price and volatility, debt:
S, s, D

Unobservable variables
Asset value and volatility,
default barrier, distance to
default: V, v, L, ln(V/L)/σv

KMV, RiskCalc ->

Approximations of variables
First order approximation of distance to default

$S = V - LD$ and $s.S = v.(S+LD)$

L as global debt recovery on default

Solve for (V, v) solution under BSM

Empirical representation of the equity as an option on the firm's assets

$S = Call(V, D)$ and $s.S = v.V. C_v'$

Default point L from empirical studies

Risk-neutral probability
First hitting time formula of Brownian motion, adjusted for uncertainty of barrier
Cumulative risk-neutral default probability p(t)

Relationship and risk premium (CAPM)
$p_t = N(N^{-1}(q_t) + k.t^{1/2})$

Actuarial probability of default
Statistical calibration of EDF on large historical default database
Cumulative actuarial default probability q(t)

Table B Various types of practical implementations and activities

Market participant	Goal	Strategy	Key resource	Risks
Bank credit portfolio managers	Complement internal risk ratings with real time information	Quantitative credit risk assesment from equity markets	Single name EDF and rating equivalents	Flawed credit assesment due to data quality or equity markets technicals
	Calculation of credit capital	Quantitative assesment of unexpected credit losses	Default correlation and distribution of portfolio losses	Poor calibration of unobservable parameters
Credit and equity derivatives dealers	Increase value-added client flow	Develop debt-equity axes and liquity	Transparent debt-equity pricing tools	Arbitrage risks
	Reduce P&L at risk and increase risk taking capacity	Hedge retained inventory (High Yield/Fallen Angels) with equity and equity derivatives	Simple equity to credit model consistent with credit and equity derivatives analytics	Adverse selection bias of a back book
Proprietary trading and hedge funds	Profit from market inefficiencies	Debt-equity opportunities on liquid names	Transparent debt-equity pricing tools	Arbitrage risks
	Profit from credit versus equity markets arbitrage	Diversify basis risk across large portfolio of debt-equity arbitrages	Simple equity to credit model consistent with credit and equity derivatives analytics	Concentrations in illiquid names, accumulation of basis risks
	Profit from volatility smile arbitrage	Credit as an exotic equity derivative	Advanced model and access to entire equity volatility curve	Model risk, poor calibration and corporate events

reversion to a more normal situation, where forward-looking assessments of volatility and anticipations of corporate activity are an integral part of the puzzle.

Table A summarises the various implementations of equity-based EDF and equity-based risk-neutral probabilities, illustrating how these concepts relate to each other.

Table B summarises various types of activities relying on these models. Dealers' credit or equity derivatives desks are offering debt-equity research, trade opportunities and arbitrage tools. Hedge funds and other arbitrage desks are placing bets accordingly. Some are managing portfolios of debt-equity arbitrages to diversify the basis and event risk of any particular name. More recently, sophisticated risk-reversal hedging strategies are being explored, along with advanced models based on jump-diffusion processes or non-parametric estimations of the stock-price evolution process.

The first problem concerns the appropriateness of the no-arbitrage condition being imposed on a portfolio composed of equity, debt and the firm's assets. The second relates to the model's failure to include the uncertainty of market participants on *how* to price equity and debt. Note that only the uncertainty of the firm's assets is represented in the Merton model and that the values of the firm's assets and their volatility have to be inferred from equity or debt prices. As we show below, due to the fact that the model does not include any uncertainty originating in – and remaining specific to – the equity and debt markets, implied asset values and volatilities could be seriously biased.

Concerns about the no-arbitrage condition are related to the fact that the Merton model draws an analogy between traded options on a liquid security, and the option-like features of equity for firms issuing debt. From this analogy, it is argued that the assumptions on which the Black–Scholes options-pricing equation is based can be transplanted, with little modification, into this new context – ie, the two valuation problems are isomorphic. However, the analogy is not as tight as it may initially appear, and each of these assumptions must be considered carefully in the context in which it is being used.

By assuming correlated uncertainty between equity and debt markets, Merton was able to build his model using the Black–Scholes structure. However, in the valuation of corporate liabilities there are at least two active derivative markets related to the value of the underlying: the equity market and the debt market. In contrast, in the Black–Scholes approach, there is only the equity derivative on the underlying security. Although Black–Scholes (1973) recognised that, due to the under- and overreaction of option traders, option prices could deviate temporarily from their fair value, they treated this as an empirical limitation rather than an additional source of noise. As we discuss below, this is a critical over-simplification, as it impacts the no-arbitrage condition and, along with issues regarding the debt-equity link, points to limitations of the Merton framework for pricing and hedging cash and derivative assets.

LOOSENING THE LINK: MARKET UNCERTAINTY AND INTER-MARKET ARBITRAGE

To recap, the Black–Scholes model is based on the assumption that the no-arbitrage condition would hold for a hedged portfolio composed of a stock and an offsetting short position in call options, requiring a liquid market for both the stock and its options. The authors point out that, "If this were not true, speculators would try to profit by borrowing large amounts of money to create such hedged positions, and would in the process force the returns down to the short term interest rate".[10]

This observation is made in recognition of the high liquidity in equity cash and derivatives markets, and the existence of arbitrageurs who work to exploit tiny temporary differences between stock and stock option prices. In the Merton context, the dynamic hedge portfolio is comprised of a firm's stock, its bonds, and a risk-free alternative. Critics of Merton's application of the options pricing framework to the valuation of risky corporate debt argue that the corporate debt market is too illiquid for the no-arbitrage assumption to hold.[11] However, the illiquidity in the market for corporate debt is an effect, rather than a cause, of the failure of the no-arbitrage assumption. That is, illiquidity is simply a reflection of the different purposes being served by market participants. As we argued above, the issuance of debt is not associated with any *bona fide* hedging activity that would result in a high volume of incremental reallocative trades. Instead, the difference between the large denomination bilateral transactions, thin trading in the bond market, and rapidly fluctuating equity prices traded on centralised exchanges is inconsistent with the characterisation of bondholders as writers of call options on the firm's assets. Thus, the relative illiquidity of the corporate bond market compared to the market for equities cannot be viewed merely as an institutional impediment to the satisfaction of the no-arbitrage condition. Rather, it must be seen as further evidence of the looseness of the analogy of equity-as-option in the sense proposed by Merton. Although this argument does not demonstrate that the no-arbitrage condition is never satisfied or cannot be satisfied, it does suggest that Black and Scholes' argument justifying the no-arbitrage condition between stocks and their associated options, is less compelling when applied to the debt/equity relationship.

Consider now the problem that separate uncertainty components, one for the equity market and one for the bond market, are not embedded in the Merton model. To see how the inclusion of only one source of uncertainty may bias the model, we reproduce the basic model structure in the equations below. Following Merton (1974), let us assume that the value of the firm's assets A follows a log-normal random walk given by the stochastic differential equation

$$dA = \mu\, A\, dt + \sigma\, A\, dX \tag{1}$$

Here the random variable X follows a Wiener process, μ is the rate of return of the security and σ is its volatility.

Following Merton, we construct a self-financing portfolio Φ composed of α shares in the firm's assets, β shares in the firm's equity, and a number of γ shares in a risk-free bond, whose price is $B(t)$.[12] In a self-financing portfolio, the investor reallocates wealth among different investments without adding or withdrawing capital. Merton's ideal portfolio requires no initial net investment at time t

$$\Phi(t) = \alpha A + \beta E + \gamma B = 0 \tag{2}$$

Also, the self-financing portfolio does not require any additional funds at the end of a small time increment $\Delta t \to 0$. That is, for the self-financing portfolio, the long positions are completely financed by short positions. This imposes a dynamic relation between the positions α, β and γ, whose values should be adjusted at the end of the time increment Δt to preserve the strategy.

$$d\Phi = \alpha\, dA + \beta\, dE + \gamma\, dB \tag{3}$$

A Taylor series expansion of the variation of the hedge portfolio $\Phi(A,\ t)$ in terms of the changes in the security's price in Equation (1) yields:

$$d\Phi = \sigma\, A\partial_A\Phi\, dX + (\partial_t\Phi + \mu\, A\partial_A\Phi + \tfrac{1}{2}\sigma^2 A^2 \partial_A^2\Phi)\, dt \tag{4}$$

Recognising that $dB = rB\, dt$ and that the tangent hedge strategy $\alpha = -\beta\partial E/\partial A$ partially removes the stochastic term in dX in Equation (3), the portfolio is claimed to become "riskless". To avoid arbitrage opportunities, the following no-arbitrage condition is imposed: $d\Phi = 0$. This immediately yields the options pricing equation

$$\partial_t E + r\, A\partial_A E + \tfrac{1}{2}\sigma^2 A^2\partial_A^2 E = rE \tag{5}$$

Notice that to derive Equation (5), we assumed that the value of the option is a deterministic function of the stochastic price of the underlying security and time. As a result of this assumption, the only source of uncertainty in the equity and debt values is the random variation of the value of the underlying firm's assets. This introduces perfect correlation between the stochastic price changes of the equity and debt, and those of the firm's assets (ie, changes in the random variable X). Again, because the purpose of the hedge is to remove the leading stochastic terms of the portfolio capital gains, this assumption is crucial to constructing the ideal hedge strategy proposed by Merton (a variant of the BS hedging strategy).

Because this relationship between changes in the firm's asset value, its equity and its debt requires perfect correlation, markets, in aggregate, would have to completely agree on how to value equity and debt at each point in time, even though the underlying assets of the firm are stochastic and unobservable. This would require equity traders and bond traders to:

1. have perfect information, in the sense of perceiving instantaneous changes in the firm's unobservable assets; and
2. to act simultaneously to changes in unobservable assets of the firm.

Thus, while the Merton model describes a relationship between the fair value of idealised equity and debt, and the dynamics of the firm's assets, it represents neither the instantaneous price nor the value of tradable equity and debt, because it does not include the uncertainty of the market participants. This is critical because pricing models based on hedging strategies and no arbitrage arguments can only be constructed with tradable instruments.

To reiterate, the assumption that the value of the option is a deterministic function of the stochastic price of the underlying security and time introduces information that is not contained in the original pricing problem. Merton's assumption is essentially a "no discrepancy" assumption that is not derived from the structure of the problem. To see this, note that in Merton's framework the relationship between equity, debt and the firm's assets is known with absolute certainty only at debt maturity, when assets are liquidated and the debt repaid. The debt payoff is given explicitly as a function of the firm's assets value. At any other time, the only information that investors actually have is that the equity price, the debt price and the underlying assets are changing randomly, and that pricing should not lead to sustainable arbitrage opportunities. This is significant for practical application, since equity prices are sometimes built on capitalised confidence about the firm's prospects and conceptual, rather than physical, assets. As has been seen recently, these assets can vanish overnight when investors lose confidence; this creates an additional layer of uncertainty in market prices.

Given the nature of actual markets and tradable instruments, it is more reasonable to assume that equity and debt are not *deterministic* functions of the underlying firm's assets price, but *stochastic* functions of the underlying assets. The additional random variations could be caused by the uncertainty of market participants on *how* to value equity (the equity market uncertainty) and debt (the bond–loan market uncertainty) given that all market participants will be only imperfectly informed or disagree on their valuation. Note that this approach does not increase the complexity of the original problem, but removes the additional require-ment of the Merton framework that all participants be perfectly informed. Technically, we can write its increment as the combination of the ideal Merton increment and random idiosyncratic variations:

$$dE = \left(\frac{\partial E}{\partial t} + \mu A \frac{\partial E}{\partial A} + \frac{\sigma^2}{2} A^2 \frac{\partial^2 E}{\partial A^2} \right) dt + \sigma \frac{\partial E}{\partial A} dX + E \frac{dY}{Z}(\varepsilon) \qquad (6)$$

$$dD = \left(\frac{\partial D}{\partial t} + \mu A \frac{\partial D}{\partial A} + \frac{\sigma^2}{2} A^2 \frac{\partial^2 D}{\partial A^2} \right) dt + \sigma \frac{\partial D}{\partial A} dX + E \frac{dZ}{Z}(\eta) \qquad (7)$$

Here, the symbolic terms $E\, dY/\, Y$ and $D\, dZ/\, Z$ represent idiosyncratic vari-ations of tradable equity $E = Y\, F(A,\, t)$ and debt $D = Z\, G(A,\, t)$ produced by the uncertainty of the market participants, and changes in supply and demand for the instruments. The parameters ε and η determine the magni-tude of the fluctuations of the random variables Y and Z respectively. The functions $F(A,\, t;\, \sigma)$ and $G(A,\, t;\, \sigma)$ represent the fair-value of the instru-ments in the absence of uncertainty, and reduce to the Merton solutions in the limit of perfectly informed markets. In this limit, we also obtain $Y \rightarrow 1$ and $Z \rightarrow 1$.

Also note that the introduction of two additional levels of uncertainty Y and Z destroys the similarity between the Black–Scholes and Merton model. As a result of the inclusion of these separate sources of uncertainty, it will be impossible to construct the riskless strategy proposed by Merton for realistic tradable instruments. The reason for this is that the stochastic variations associated with the valuation uncertainty cannot be removed by hedging against moves in the value of the firm's assets. This would explain why changes in the equity and bond prices of a firm could lead to incon-sistent estimates of the firm's unobservable assets. Importantly, while the existence of multiple sources does not imply any sustainable inter-market arbitrage opportunities, it is central to the question of how to construct models for estimating default probabilities, pricing credit derivatives, and hedging across asset classes.

Recently, Sobehart and Keenan (1999, 2003) discussed an alternative valuation framework using the generalised probabilistic representation of the valuation uncertainty shown in Equations (6) and (7). They discussed potential arbitrage opportunities and showed that the relationship between equity, debt and the firm's assets can exhibit random deviations consistent with the concept of market equilibrium. As mentioned above, the main motivation for the development of alternative debt valuation models is the empirical evidence that the Merton model exhibits pricing biases for equity and debt (see, for example, Wei and Guo, 1997; and Gemmill, 2002). This represents, perhaps, the greatest challenge to any acceptable alternative model that describes both equity and debt.

Consider the relevant differences of the distribution of equity and debt obtained from Equations (6) and (7). These equations indicate that there are random variations around the expected equity and debt prices. For simplicity, we focus our discussion on the firm's equity and assume that there is no uncertainty in the debt market. The discrepancy between the observed equity price $E = Y F(A, t; \sigma)$ and the Merton call-option formula $C(A, t; \sigma)$ is caused by the uncertainty of the equity market participants, including possible changes in their preferences and expectations. Note that if, at each point in time, the observed equity price E is fitted with the expression $C(A_1, t; \sigma_1)$, containing "implied" value of the firm's assets A_1 and volatility σ_1, the uncertainty generated by market participants will cause the implied parameters to exhibit continuous random changes. Because the Merton framework does not contain the uncertainty of the equity market, these changes will be erroneously attributed to changes in the value of the firm's assets and volatility and, hence, its creditworthiness. This would produce errors in the resultant estimates of the value of the debt, as well as errors in default probability estimates based on the model.

The uncertainty of market participants can not only affect instantaneous values, but also estimates of the implied assets and volatility based on the equilibrium (average) fair value of equity $E^Y(E|A, \sigma; t)$ observed in the market, where $E^Y(f|g)$ is the expectation of the variable $f(Y)$ conditional on g. The severity of the discrepancy between the "true" value of the firm's assets A and volatility σ, and the "implied" value of the firm's assets A_1 and volatility σ_1 is governed by the magnitude of the options market uncertainty and the non-linearity of the functions $F(A, t; \sigma)$ and $C(A_1, t; \sigma_1)$. To illustrate, consider $Y = e^w$, where w is the trading noise described by an ideal Ornstein–Uhlenbeck mean-reverting process. Also consider the case where the discrepancy between the implied assets and volatility and the firm's assets and volatility is small, and where the Black–Scholes–Merton formula is a good approximation to the fair value of equity – ie,

$$E^Y (E|A, t; \rho; \sigma) = E^w(e^w)F(A, t; \sigma) \approx C(A_1, t; r, \sigma_1) \qquad (8)$$

$$\sigma_E^2 \approx \Sigma^2(A_1, t; r, \sigma_1) \qquad (9)$$

where

$$\sigma_E^2 = \left(\frac{A}{F} \frac{\partial F}{\partial A} \right)^2 \sigma^2 + \gamma_w^2, \quad \Sigma^2(A_1, t; r, \sigma_1) = \left(\frac{A_1}{C} \frac{\partial C}{\partial A_1} \right)^2 \sigma_1^2 \qquad (10)$$

Here, σ_E is the observed volatility of the firm's equity, Σ is the volatility of the firm's equity obtained from the Merton model, and γ_w is the volatility of the trading noise w. Equations (8) and (9) have to be solved for the implied values assets A_1 and volatility Σ_1.

Notice that for the selected mean-reversion noise, Equation (6) yields a pricing equation similar to Equation (5), except that the risk-free rate is replaced by a risk-adjusted return ρ, which includes a risk premium required as a compensation for the additional uncertainty that cannot be hedged away. Thus, the functions $F(.)$ and $C(.)$ have the same formal dependence on their arguments:

$$F(A, t; \rho, \sigma) = C(A, t; \rho, \sigma) = A \, N(d_1{}^\rho) - e^{-\rho(T-t)} \, D_0 \, N(d_2{}^\rho) \qquad (11)$$

Here

$$d_0{}^\rho = \frac{1}{\sigma\sqrt{T-t}} \log\left(\frac{A e^{\rho(T-t)}}{D_T}\right)$$

$$d_1{}^\rho = d_0{}^\rho + \frac{\sigma}{2}\sqrt{T-t} \qquad (12)$$

$$d_2{}^\rho = d_0{}^\rho + \frac{\sigma}{2}\sqrt{T-t}$$

Expanding the solution $F(A, t; \rho, \sigma)$ in Taylor's series in terms of the firm's assets A, volatility σ and risk premium $\rho - r$, we obtain the first order approximations to the implied values of assets and volatility:

$$A_1 \approx A + \frac{1}{\Omega}\{\partial_\sigma \Sigma^2[(e^\delta - 1)C + e^\delta \partial_r C(\rho - r)] - \partial_\sigma C[\partial_r \sigma_E^2(\rho - r) + \gamma^2]\} \quad (13)$$

and

$$\sigma_1 \approx \sigma + \frac{1}{\Omega}\{\partial_\sigma \Sigma^2[(e^\delta - 1)C + e^\delta \partial_r C(\rho - r)] - \partial_\sigma C[\partial_r \sigma_E^2(\rho - r) + \gamma^2]\} \quad (14)$$

where

$$\Omega = \partial_A C \partial_\sigma \Sigma^2 - \partial_\sigma C \partial_A \Sigma^2 \text{ and } \delta = \log\left(\frac{E_t^w[e^w]}{E_T^w[e^w]}\right) \qquad (15)$$

In Equations (13) to (15), the functions and their derivatives are evaluated at $(A, t; r, \rho)$. Note that the implied assets' value A_1 and volatility σ_1 in Equations (13) to (15) are functions of both the time to maturity $T - t$, and the effective leverage term $d_0{}^\rho(A, \sigma)$. Because in the Merton model the creditworthiness of the firm is basically determined by the distance from default $d_0(A, \sigma)$, the use of implied assets and volatilities could seriously impair the ability of the model to generate an unbiased credit opinion.[13]

Figure 2 shows the probability of default estimated with the implied and true assets and volatility as a function of the distance from default for a one-year time horizon. The amount due is $D_0 = 1$, the riskless rate is $\rho = r = 5\%$, the volatility of the assets is $\sigma = 20\%$, the uncertainty of the market participants is $\delta = 0.2\sigma$ and the volatility of the trading noise is $\gamma_w = 0.25\sigma$. Note that for highly leveraged firms (low values of the distance from default) the probabilities of defaults are similar (see the solid triangle, Figure 2). However, for highly capitalised firms, the probability of default obtained using implied assets and volatility assigns a lower credit quality to the firm than it should (see the open circle and solid square, Figure 2).

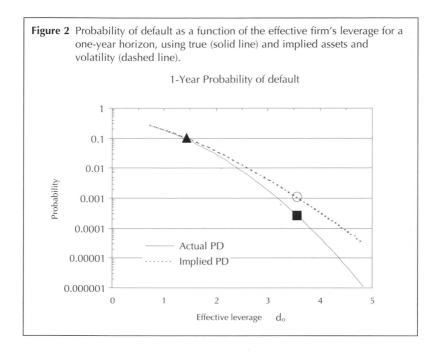

Figure 2 Probability of default as a function of the effective firm's leverage for a one-year horizon, using true (solid line) and implied assets and volatility (dashed line).

This is a consequence of the uncertainty introduced by the market participants; models based solely on market equity information erroneously interpret this as asset volatility. This also indicates that credit spreads for high-credit obligors will be higher than those obtained from the Merton model as observed in practice. The relevance of this effect as a function of the distance from default and time to debt maturity suggests that additional research is needed in the area of models of corporate liabilities based on market equity information.

Note that the uncertainty of the trading noise γ_w – which reflects the uncertainty of the equity market participants on *how* to price equity on the firm's assets – could be different for each individual firm or industry. Thus, the distance from default $d_0(A_1, \sigma_1)$ cannot be adjusted by introducing a single correction term for all firms. As a result, the comparison of the relative riskiness of firms using only the distance from default could be misleading.

Another problem with most extensions of the Merton model that impairs their usefulness for pricing credit derivatives is that short-term corporate-yield spreads converge to zero, which is not observed in practice, (see Huge, 2001). In contrast, a model that takes into account the market uncertainty can generate credit spreads that do not vanish for high quality obligors in the limit of high values of the effective leverage $d_0^r(A/D_T) \gg 1$ $(D_T/A \to 0)$, or close to maturity $(t \to T)$. To illustrate, if we

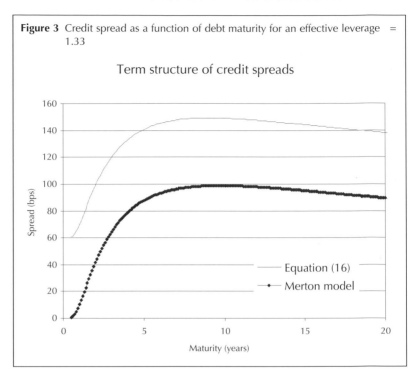

Figure 3 Credit spread as a function of debt maturity for an effective leverage =
1.33

Term structure of credit spreads

replace equity with debt in our example, the corresponding credit spread
ϕ with market uncertainty is (see Sobehart and Keenan, 2003).

$$
\phi = -\frac{1}{T-t} \log\left(\frac{E^w[D(A,\, t)]}{D_T}\right) - r
$$

$$
= -\frac{1}{T-t}\left[\log\left(\frac{Ae^{\rho(T-t)}}{D_T}(1-N(d_1{}^\rho)) + N(d_2{}^\rho)\right) + \delta\right] + (\rho - r)
$$

(16)

Here, δ is the term defined in Equation (15).

Note that investment grade firms with the highest credit quality can
have a finite spread above the risk-free rate. The reason is that the credit
spread reflects the uncertainty of the market participants as to how to
value the firm's equity and debt, which is assumed constant – the para-
meter $\gamma_w(\varepsilon)$, which affects the risk premium $\rho - r$. Figure 3 shows the spread
from Equation (16) and the spread obtained from the Merton model ($\delta = 0$,
$\rho = r$) as a function of the debt maturity. The parameters for our model are
$\sigma = 30\%$, $r = 4\%$, $\rho - r = 0.6\%$ and $\delta = 0$.

CONCLUSIONS

In theory, the connection between debt and equity values should only be
a function of seniority and the time structure of expected payoffs,

providing contingent claims markets are complete. However, complete contingent claims markets require participants to hold consistent sets of probabilities for future states of the world. In the Modigliani–Miller equilibrium, trades are stimulated only by differing preferences for risk and the time profile of payoffs. The development of active credit derivatives markets that dates from the early 1990s has the potential to drive the capital markets toward the Modigliani–Miller equilibrium by enabling a more fluid and granular transfer of current and future credit risk. However, efficient risk transfer is dependent on efficient pricing of these instruments. Unfortunately, the dominant approach for estimating default risk involves a theory (see Merton, 1973, 1974) that assumes a specific and tight linkage between debt and equity markets – ie, a link that is not completely supported by empirical evidence. Although the highly successful Black–Scholes model has revolutionised derivatives markets, it has been seen to yield options prices with a tendency towards bias (volatility smile and skew); these biases are exacerbated in the Merton model when it is used to calculate bond prices or probabilities of default. This is because the no-arbitrage condition, a crucial component of the model, is less likely to hold in the Merton context than it is in the Black–Scholes context. We advance two reasons to support this contention.

1. The Merton model is based on an analogy which requires debt trading as supporting the hedging activity in the equity markets. This analogy supports the existence of both a motivation and a mechanism through which arbitrage opportunities will be eliminated. However, the analogy is seen to be weak, and the idealised assumption of no arbitrage less compelling when applied to loans and bonds than when confined to equity markets.
2. The Black–Scholes model assumes only one source of uncertainty in both the market for a security and the market for its associated options. If this is true, the construction of a risk-free hedge portfolio is at least feasible, and the no-arbitrage assumption imposed on a hedge portfolio can be satisfied. On the other hand, in the Merton context, we would need to have a single source of uncertainty affecting a firm's asset value, as exhibited in the markets for its debt and equity – ie, two markets with different players, market mechanisms and dynamics. If bond traders disagree on how to price debt given the market price of the firm's equity, the no-arbitrage condition might not apply to Merton's hedge portfolio; both pricing and default predictions based on the Merton model will contain biases.

Actual inconsistencies across debt, equity, and CDS markets support two important conclusions, namely that:

❏ the Merton model's fundamental assumption about the relationship between debt and equity is often violated; and
❏ widespread use of mis-specified models for inputing default and recovery parameters may be creating, as opposed to eliminating, arbitrage opportunities in the credit derivatives market, and between equity and bond markets.

These observations suggest the need for more general types of contingent claims models for estimating default probabilities. A natural alternative to Merton-type models would involve the explicit inclusion of separate sources of uncertainty for the debt and equity markets. This would represent a generalisation rather than an extension of the basic Merton model – a generalisation with the potential to more consistently describe actual market dynamics. Such models do not introduce any additional complexity, but simply avoid the pitfall of assuming away a source of uncertainty – a source that does exist for tradable instruments, as described. In considering a more general class of models, we must also reconsider the value of non-market information in predicting default and estimating fair value prices for corporate liabilities. As has recently been shown in Sobehart and Keenan (2002a, 2002b), both the relaxation of the uncertainty restriction and the inclusion of accounting information can lead to models with lower bias, and therefore greater overall performance.

1   The analysis and conclusions set forth are those of the authors only. Citigroup is not responsible for any statement or conclusion herein, and no opinions, theories, or techniques presented herein necessarily reflect the position of the institution.
2   See Arrow (1964).
3   While Black–Scholes (1973) suggested that the options-pricing equation could be used to value corporate liabilities, their analysis focused on the valuation of options on traded securities.
4   See Jones, Mason, and Rosenfeld (1984).
5   See Crosbie (1999).
6   See, for example, Jarow, Lando, and Turnbull (1997), Duffie and Singleton (1999), Arvanitis (2000), and Hayt (2000).
7   CreditGrades, for example, is a commercial implementation of a structural model calibrated to spreads.
8   See Tierney (2003).
9   For example, Kwan (1996), Treptow (2002), Liu and Mamaysky (2002), and Campbell and Taksler (2003).
10 Black and Scholes (1973), p.643.
11 For example, see Kwan (1996).
12 Since Merton assumes that both equity and debt issues can be written as functions of the value of the assets and time only, the hedge portfolio can be constructed using either debt or equity.
13 With the appropriate correction for the actual growth of the firm's assets.

BIBLIOGRAPHY

Arrow, K., 1964, "The Role of Securities in the Optimal Allocation of Risk Bearing", *Review of Economic Studies*, 31, pp. 91–96.

Arvanitis, A, 2000, "Getting the Pricing Right", *Risk*, September, pp. 115–119.

Black, F., and M. Scholes, 1973, "The Pricing of Options and Corporate Liabilities," *Journal of Political Economy*, 81, pp. 637–659.

Bohn, J., 1999, "Empirical assessment of a simple contingent-claims model for the pricing of risky debt", Submitted as partial fulfillment of a PhD dissertation, University of California, Berkeley.

Campbell, J. and Taksler, G., 2003, "Equity Volatility and Corporate Bond Yields", *Journal of Finance*, December.

Cathcart I., and L. El-Jahel L., 1998 "Valuation of Defaultable Bonds", *The Journal of Fixed Income*, 8 (1), pp. 65–78.

Crosbie, P., (1999) "Modeling default risk", KMV Publication, KMV LLC, San Francisco, January 12, pp. 1-33.

Duffie, D. and Singleton, K., (1999) "Modeling term structures of defaultable bonds", *Review of Financial Studies*, 12 (4), pp. 687–720.

Gemmill G., 2002, *Testing Merton's Model for Credit Spreads on Zero-Coupon Bonds*, Faculty of Finance, City University Business School, Frobisher Crescent, UK.

Hayt, G., 2000, "How to Price a Credit Derivative", *Risk*, February, pp. 60–61.

Huge B., 2000, *On Default Claims and Credit Derivatives*, PhD Dissertation, Department of Statistics and Operations Research, University of Copenhagen, Denmark.

Janosi T., Jarrow R. A. and Y. Yildrim, 2001, *Estimating Default Probabilities Implicit in Equity Prices*, Johnson Graduate School of Management, Cornell University, working paper.

Janosi T., Jarrow R. A. and Y. Yildrim, 2000, *Estimating Expected Losses and Liquidity Discounts Implicit in Debt Prices*, Johnson Graduate School of Management, Cornell University, working paper.

Jarrow, R., Landow, D. and S. Turnbull, 1997, "A Markov Model for the Term Structure of Credit Risk Spreads", *Review of Financial Studies*, (10), pp. 481–523.

Keenan S.C., Hamilton D. and A. Berthault, Historical Default Rates for Corporate Bond Issuers: 1920–1999, Moody's Investors Service, Special Comment.

Kim J., Ramaswamy K., and S. Sunderasan, 1993, "Does Default Risk in Coupons Affect the Valuation of Corporate Bonds? A Contingent Claims Model," *Financial Management*, Autumn, 22 (3), pp. 117–131.

King M., 2001, *Using Equity to Price Credit*, JP Morgan Securities, London. Credit Strategy report, September.

Kwan, S., 1996, "Firm-Specific Information and the Correlation between Individual Stocks and Bonds", *Journal of Financial Economics*, (40), pp. 63–80.

Kwan, S., 1996, "On the Relation Between Stocks and Bonds", *Journal of Financial Economics*, 40, pp. 63–80.

Leland, H. E., 1999, "The Structural Approach to Credit Risk", *Frontiers in Credit-Risk Analysis* (AIMR Conference Proceedings), pp. 36–46.

Levin, J., van Deventer, W. and R. Donald, (ed. Cornyn, A.G. *et al.*), 1997, "The Simultaneous Analysis of Interest Rate and Credit Risk", *Controlling and Managing Interest Rate Risk*, New York Institute of Finance, NY, pp. 484–507.

Liu, J. and H. Mamaysky, 2002, *Correlations Between Bond and Stock Markets with Different Default Risks*, working paper, Yale University, November.

Merton, R. C., 1973, *Theory of Rational Option Pricing, Bell Journal of Economics and Management Science*, 4, pp. 141–183.

Merton, R. C., 1974, "On the Pricing of Corporate Debt: The Risk Structure of Interest Rates", *Journal of Finance*, 29, pp. 449–470.

Modigliani, F. and M.H. Miller, 1958, "The Cost of Capital, Corporate Finance and the Theory of Investment", *American Economic Review*, 48 (63), pp. 261–297.

Sobehart, J.R. and S.C. Keenan, 1999, *Equity Market Value and Its Importance for Credit Analysis; Facts and Fiction*, Moody's Risk Management Services, July, working paper.

Sobehart J.R. and S.C. Keenan, 2002a, "The Need for Hybrid Models", *Risk*, February 2002, pp. 73–77, and *Credit*, April, pp. 46–52.

Sobehart J.R. and S.C. Keenan, (Ong, M. ed.), 2002b, "Hybrid Contingent Claims Models: A Practical Approach to Modeling Default Risk", *Credit Ratings: Methodology, Rationale and Default Risk*, Risk Books, UK.

Sobehart J.R. and S.C. Keenan, 2003, "The Impact of Valuation Uncertainty in the Pricing of Risky Debt", *Journal of Risk Finance*, 4 (2), December, pp. 56–67.

Tierney, J., 2003, *Debt vs Equity: Where is the Trade?*, ICBI Global Derivatives Summit, conference presentation, www.icbi-derivatives.com.

Treptow, F., 2002, *Information Arbitrage Between Individual Stocks and Corporate Bonds*, working paper, March.

Vasicek, O.A., 1984, *Credit Valuation*, KMV Corporation.

Wei, D. G., and D. Guo, 1997, "Pricing Risky Debt: An Empirical Comparison of the Longstaff and Schwartz, and Merton Models", *The Journal of Fixed Income*, Autumn, pp. 8–28.

Section 2

Default Correlation and Credit Portfolio Risk

Introduction

Jon Gregory
BNP Paribas

Having discussed single-name credit risk in the last section, we now move on to portfolio credit risk in the context of portfolio management and capital allocation. We begin with a study of default correlation and basket default swaps (or nth to default swaps). A basket default swap is like a single-name CDS, except that it is referenced to a particular credit event (first, second and so on) on a basket of credits. These allow investors to take a leveraged exposure to a relatively small tailor-made pool of credits. A first-to-default basket could achieve a high return from exposure to high-quality assets while a second (or more) to default would be more suitable for a more risk-averse investor. **Douglas Lucas** and **Alberto Thomas** of UBS explain the structure and motivation of such basket structures and then move on to a detailed investigation of default correlation, which is important in determining their prices and risks. They present empirical behaviour and provide a thorough and intuitive description of the mathematical concepts, which is a useful precursor to the copula models presented later in Section 4. Default correlation tells us the degree to which default events will be clustered. It is of fundamental importance in determining the credit risk of a portfolio as well as pricing basket default swaps and CDO structures. As such, this is an extremely important theme for much of the rest of this book.

Based largely on the realisation that default correlation is so important, the past few years have seen a lot of work put into developing models for computing CreditVAR (value at risk due to credit). The motivation for this has been to use quantitative approaches for economic capital allocation and management. Gaussian approaches can lead to straightforward calculations and portfolio optimisation via the mean-variance approach of Markowitz (1952). The fat-tailed nature of credit loss distributions arising from correlated defaults and the fact that individual credit losses are low-probability but high-loss events means that Gaussian assumptions cannot be applied to portfolios of this type. As it became increasingly clear that credit portfolios had highly non-Gaussian behaviour, a number of risk management models, starting with CreditMetrics (see Gupton *et al*, 1997) have been developed to provide a more realistic treatment of portfolio credit risk and estimation of CreditVAR and economic capital. In the next chapter **Greg M. Gupton** of **Moody's KMV** discusses the different portfolio credit risk models available in the market, explaining the model that could be most relevant for particular situations. Each of these approaches represents a different quantitative methodology and each has different features and strengths. As well as producing a static view of a portfolio's credit risk, a credit portfolio model should be able to calculate quantities such as marginal contributions, which show how much each exposure contributes to the overall risk. This leads to suggestions of risk minimising or return maximising trades to achieve portfolio optimisation.

Credit derivatives offer the products to be able to actually implement dynamic portfolio management in practice. Portfolio optimisation ideas are attracting increasing interest for active management of credit portfolios by utilising dynamic measures of default probability and then combining these marginals to produce the portfolio loss distribution. This approach was first taken by KMV around a decade ago (see, for example, Crosbie and Bohn, 2002). **Alla Gil** of **Citigroup** concludes this section by extending the classical Markowitz approach to discuss credit portfolio optimisation by characterisation of the efficient frontier in a generalised approach with forward-looking dynamics. A model is described that is consistent with the ideas of Basel II and allows a credit portfolio to be optimised – that is, to move towards a point closer to the efficient frontier that represents a reduced risk or improved return or both. Various credit derivatives structures can aid transforming the current portfolio to an "optimal" one. The simplest example would be to use CDSs to buy protection on names for which the exposure needs to be reduced. This can be coupled with simultaneously selling protection on names on which it would be beneficial to have an increased exposure, even names not originally in the portfolio (which need obviously to be included as "dummy" names in the optimisation). CDOs provide potentially more efficient ways in which to optimise a credit portfolio but are harder to analyse than single-name positions (for example, it may be possible to sell risk on a certain pool of names but retain the equity tranche). The fact that the approach described uses Monte Carlo simulation should make such complex scenarios easy to analyse.

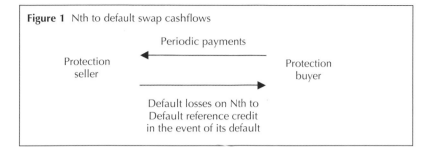

Figure 1 Nth to default swap cashflows

Periodic payments

Protection seller

Protection buyer

Default losses on Nth to
Default reference credit
in the event of its default

three to five underlying reference names rated A or AA. If rated, the nth to default note itself is usually rated A or BBB. The cash flows of an nth to default note are shown in Figure 2.

The interaction or intersection between the *credit swap* part the nth to default note and the *note* part of the nth to default note occurs when the protection seller/note purchaser owes default losses to the protection buyer/note issuer. The protection seller does not make a payment of default losses to the protection buyer. Rather, the protection buyer either delivers the deliverable obligation (physical settlement) or pays the protection seller the recovery value of the deliverable obligation. The note is thereby redeemed and the embedded swap terminated.

It is sometimes convenient for the protection seller that the nth to default swap be embedded in a note. An nth to default *note* isolates the protection buyer from the credit risk of the protection seller. By buying the note, the protection seller has effectively collateralised its potential obligation to the protection buyer. Almost the same result could be obtained, however, by having the protection seller of an nth to default swap collateralise the mark-to-market of the swap to the protection buyer. Within limits, this would give the protection seller the ability to choose what collateral it owns and posts to the protection buyer. The protection seller can also

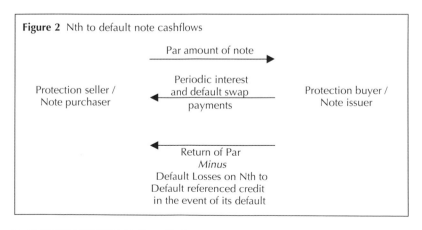

Figure 2 Nth to default note cashflows

Par amount of note

Protection seller /
Note purchaser

Periodic interest
and default swap
payments

Protection buyer /
Note issuer

Return of Par
Minus
Default Losses on Nth to
Default referenced credit
in the event of its default

replace one acceptable collateral instrument with another. But, in an nth to default note, the protection seller must buy the protection buyer's debt instrument.[3]

Also, in note form, the protection seller is now at risk to the protection buyer for what we have termed the protection seller's collateral, aka the principal amount of the note. An nth to default protection seller/note purchaser must consider not only the credit risks of the reference credits in the swap basket, but also the credit risk of the note issuer.

COMPARISON OF NTH WITH DEFAULT SWAPS TO OTHER CREDIT SWAPS

To help understand the risks of nth to default swaps, we will compare them with single-name default swaps and basket default swaps. We will look at the following six CDSs:

❑ a US$10 million *1st* to default swap on five underlying credits;
❑ a US$10 million *5th* to default swap on five underlying credits;
❑ a portfolio of *five separate US$2 million single-name CDS*;
❑ a portfolio of *five separate US$10 million single name CDS*;
❑ a US$10 *million subordinate basket CDS* responsible for the first US$10 million of default losses on a portfolio of five underlying credits of US$10 million each; and
❑ a US$10 *million senior basket CDS* responsible for default losses above US$40 million on a portfolio of five underlying credits of US$10 million each.

These credit swaps are shown in Figure 3, in order of their risk, which we define as the amount of potential default losses the protection seller might have to absorb. We assume that all credit swaps reference the same five names, and explain their relative risks.

The riskiest credit derivative in Figure 3 is the US$50 million swap portfolio comprising five separate US$10 million single-name CDS. This portfolio of separate swaps is more risky than the subordinated basket swap. Protection sellers in both situations are equally exposed to the first US$10 million of default losses from the five names. But the protection seller's aggregate exposure under the subordinate basket swap is capped at US$10 million. The protection seller of the five single-name swaps is exposed to an additional US$40 million of potential default losses.

The subordinate basket swap is riskier than the 1st to default swap. Protection sellers under both these swaps are equally exposed to default losses from the first of the credits to default. But the subordinate basket swap protection seller is also exposed to the 2nd, 3rd, 4th and 5th defaults in the portfolio up to US$10 million aggregate of default losses.

The 1st to default swap is more risky than the US$10 million swap port-

Figure 3 Comparison of dredit swaps		
Riskiness	**Credit default swap**	**Default loss exposure**
1	Portfolio of 5 separate US$10 million single name CDS	Default loss on each credit up to US$10 million; capped at US$50 million in aggregate
2	Subordinate basket swap. First US$10 million of default losses on portfolio of 5 names @ US$10 million each name	Default loss on each credit up to US$10 million; capped at US$10 million in aggregate
3	US$10 million 1st to default swap on 5 names	Default loss on first credit to default; capped at US$10 million
4	Portfolio of 5 separate US$2 million single name CDSs	Default loss on each credit up to US$2 million; capped at US$10 million in aggregate
5	US$10 million 5th to default swap on 5 names	Default loss on fifth credit to default; capped ay US$10 million
6	Senior basket swap. Last US$10 million of default losses on portfolio of 5 names @ US$10 million each name	Default loss after US$40 million of losses have already occurred; capped at US$10 million

folio comprising five separate US$2 million single-name CDS, but the situation is not as clear-cut. First, assume that default losses on any credit will be of equal percentage of par, say 50%. Upon the first default among the five names, the protection seller of the 1st to default swap pays US$5 million and the protection seller of the swap portfolio comprising five separate US$2 million single-name CDS pays US$1 million. The only way for the protection seller on the portfolio of swaps to pay US$5 million is if *all* five underlying credits default.

The only way that the protection seller on the portfolio of swaps would have to make larger total default loss payments is if there are specific patterns of defaults and percentage default losses among underlying credits. For example, suppose that default losses from the first defaulting credit were only 10% of par. The protection seller under the 1st to default swap would have to pay US$1 million while the protection seller on the portfolio of swaps would have to pay US$200,000. If one more credit defaulted with a default loss percentage above 40%, or if all four remaining credits defaulted with an average default loss percentage above 10%, then the protection seller of the portfolio of swaps would pay more than the protection seller of the 1st to default swap.

Note that if the loss percentage on the first credit to default was above 25%, it would take at least three defaults for the protection seller of the portfolio to possibly pay more than the protection seller of the 1st to default swap. While certain scenarios of this sort are possible, they are not as likely as situations where the 1st to default swap protection seller has to pay more default losses.

Similarly, the US$10 million swap portfolio comprising five separate US$2 million single-name CDS is more risky than the 5th to default swap. The only way that the protection seller of the 5th to default swap would have to make the larger default loss payment is if (1) all five credits default *and* (2) the average percentage loss on all five defaults was smaller than the default loss percentage of the fifth credit to default.

Finally, the 5th to default swap is more risky than the senior basket swap. Given that the protection seller under the senior basket swap has US$40 million of subordination below it, it is not exposed to the 5th credit to default unless previous default losses exceed US$30 million. Only if previous default losses have been US$40 million (ie, if all four credits have defaulted and their default losses were US$10 million each) would it be as exposed to the 5th credit to default in a way equal to the protection seller under the 5th to default swap.

PICTURING NTH TO DEFAULT RISK

In this section, we are going to explore nth to default risk another way, using Venn diagrams. These are intersecting circles that show the overlap or lack of overlap between two or more events or conditions. The area of circles labelled A, B and C in Figure 4 represent the probability that under-lying credits A, B or C are going to default over the term of an nth to default swap. In Figure 4, the circles have some overlap with each other. These overlaps represent the probability that more than one credit is going to default over the term of the nth to default swap. The "2s" in the Figure indicate the area where two of the circles overlap and therefore represent

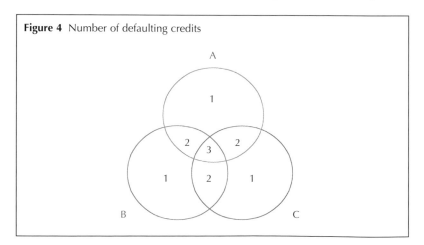

Figure 4 Number of defaulting credits

the probability that two of the three credits will default. There are three such overlaps, between circles (and credits) AB, BC and AC. There is also an area where all three circles overlap, representing the probability that all three credits will default over the term of the nth to default swap.

Figure 4 says something about the relative risks of 1st, 2nd, and 3rd to default swaps. The area within all three circles represents the probability that one or more credits will default. This is the probability that the protection seller of a 1st to default swap on these three underlying credits will have to pay default losses. The sections labelled "2" and "3" represent the probability that two or three credits will default. This is the probability that the protection seller of a 2nd to default swap on these three underlying credits will have to pay default losses. Finally, the section labelled "3" represents the probability that all three credits will default. This is the probability that the protection seller of a 3rd to default swap on these three underlying credits will have to pay default losses. (The undefined area outside the three circles represents the probability that *no* credits will default.)

From Figure 4, we can tell a lot about the probability of a default loss payout under an nth to default swap. However, this particular drawing is not the only way that credits A, B and C might behave with respect to defaulting. It might be, for example, that Figure 5 is a more accurate representation of how defaults occur among these credits.

What we see in Figure 5 is the situation where credits A, B and C *never* default at the same time. This is represented in the Figure by the lack of overlap among circles A, B and C. In this scenario, there is no risk to the protection seller of a 2nd or 3rd to default swap because 2nd and 3rd defaults among the portfolio will never occur. However, comparison of

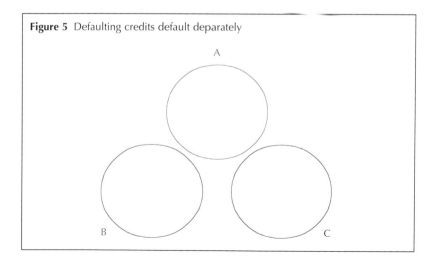

Figure 5 Defaulting credits default deparately

Figures 4 and 5 shows that there is *more* risk of one credit defaulting. The overlaps in Figure 4 are spread out in Figure 5 with the result that there is greater area covered by the circles, representing greater probability that *one* credit will default.

Figure 6 shows the opposite situation to Figure 5. Instead of defaults being spread out, and never occurring together, in Figure 6 defaults are bunched up and never occur separately. (Note that we draw the circles in Figure 6 a little offset so you can see that there are three of them. In theory, they rest exactly on top of each other.) Compared with both Figures 4 and 5, there is a lot of probability that two or three of the credits will default. In this scenario, there is relatively more risk to the protection seller of a 2nd or 3rd to default swap. However, there is less risk of one or more credits defaulting and therefore less risk to the protection seller of a 1st to default swap.

The difference between the default probability pictures in Figures 4, 5 and 6 is *default correlation*.

DEFAULT CORRELATION DEFINED

Default correlation is the phenomenon that the likelihood of one obligor defaulting on its debt is affected by whether or not *another* obligor has defaulted on *its* debts. A simple example of this is if one firm is the creditor of another: if Credit A defaults on its obligations to Credit B, we think it is more likely that Credit B will be unable to pay its own obligations. This is an example of *positive* default correlation. The default of one credit makes it *more* likely the other credit will default.

There could also be *negative* default correlation. Suppose that Credit A and Credit B are competitors. If Credit A defaults and goes out of business, it might be the case that Credit B will get Credit A's customers and be able to get price concessions from Credit A's suppliers. If this is true, the default of one credit makes it *less* likely that the other credit will default. This would be an example of *negative* correlation.

But default correlation is not normally discussed with respect to the

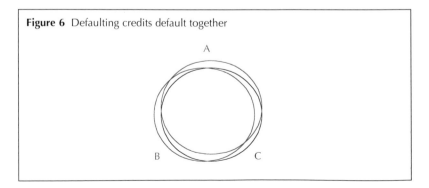

Figure 6 Defaulting credits default together

particular business relationship between one credit and another. And the existence of default correlation does not imply that one credit's default directly *causes* the change in another credit's default probability. It is a maxim of statistics that *correlation does not imply causation*. Nor do we think negative default correlation is very common. Primarily, we think *positive* default correlation generally exists among credits because the fortunes of individual companies are linked together via the health of the general economy or the health of broad subsets of the general economy.

DRIVERS OF DEFAULT CORRELATION

The pattern of yearly default rates for US corporations since 1920, shown in Figure 7, is notable for the high concentrations of defaults around 1933, 1970, 1991 and 2001. A good number of firms in almost all industries defaulted on their credit obligations in these depressions and recessions. The boom years of the 1950s and 1960s, however, produced very few defaults. To varying degrees, all businesses tend to be affected by the health of the general economy, regardless of their specific characteristics. The phenomena of companies tending to default together or not default together are indicative of positive default correlation.

But defaults can also be caused by industry-specific events that affect only firms in those particular industries. Despite a favourable overall economy, low oil prices caused 22 companies in the oil industry to default on rated debt between 1982 and 1986. Bad investments or perhaps bad regulation caused 19 thrifts to default in 1989 and 1990. Recently, we experienced the defaults of numerous dotcoms due to the correction of "irrational exuberance". Again, the phenomena of companies in a particular

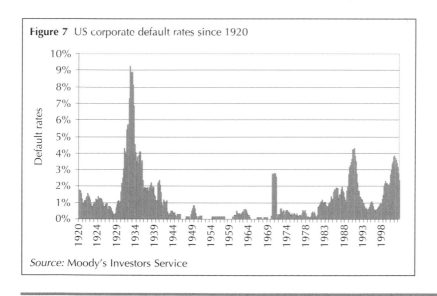

Figure 7 US corporate default rates since 1920

Source: Moody's Investors Service

industry tending to default together or not default together are indicative of positive default correlation.

There are other default-risk relationships among businesses that do not become obvious until they occur. The effect of low oil prices rippled through the Texas economy affecting just about every industry and credit in the state. A spike in the price of silver once negatively affected both film manufacturers and silverware makers. The failure of the South American anchovy harvest in 1972 drove up the price of grains and put both Peruvian fishermen and Midwest cattle farmers under pressure. These default-producing characteristics hide until, because of the defaults they cause, their presence becomes obvious.

Finally, there are truly company-specific default factors such as the health of a company's founder or the chance a warehouse will be destroyed by fire. These factors do not transfer default contagion to other credits.

Defaults are therefore the result of an unknown and unspecified multi-factor model of default that seems akin to a multifactor equity pricing model. Default correlation occurs when, for example, economy-wide or industry-wide default-causing variables assume particular values and cause widespread havoc. Uncorrelated defaults occur when company-specific default-causing variables cause trouble.

WHY WE CARE ABOUT DEFAULT CORRELATION

Default correlation is very important in understanding and predicting the behaviour of credit *portfolios,* including nth to default swaps. It directly affects the risk-return profile of investors in credit-risky assets and is there-fore important to the creditors and regulators of these investors. Default correlation even has implications for industrial companies that expose themselves to the credit risk of their suppliers and customers through the normal course of business. We will prove these assertions via an example.

Suppose we wish to understand the risk of a bond portfolio and we know that each of the 10 bonds in the portfolio has a 10% probability of default over the next five years. What does this tell us about the behaviour of the portfolio as a whole? Not much, it turns out, unless we also under-stand the default correlation among credits in the portfolio.

It could be, for example, that all the bonds in the portfolio always default together. Or, to put it another way, if one of the 10 bonds defaults, they all default. If so, this would be an example of "perfect" *positive* default correlation. Combined with the fact that each bond has a 10% probability of default, we can make a conclusion about how this portfolio will perform. There is a 10% probability that *all* the bonds in the portfolio will default. And there is a 90% probability that *none* of the bonds will default. Perfect positive default correlation, the fact that all the bonds will either default together or not default at all, combines with the 10% probability of default to produce this extreme distribution, as shown in Figure 8.

At the other extreme, it could be the case that bonds in the portfolio *always* default separately. Or, to put it another way, if one of the 10 bonds defaults, no other bonds default. This would be an example of "perfect" *negative* default correlation. Combined with the fact that each bond has a 10% probability of default, we can make a conclusion about how this portfolio will perform: there is a 100% probability that *one* and only one bond in the portfolio will default. Perfect negative default correlation, the fact that when one bond defaults no other bonds default, combines with the 10% probability of default to produce this extreme distribution, as shown in Figure 9.

The difference in the distributions depicted in Figures 8 and 9 has profound implications for investors in these portfolios. Remember that in

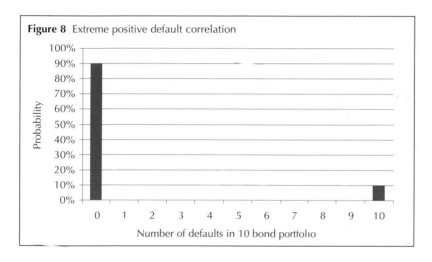

Figure 8 Extreme positive default correlation

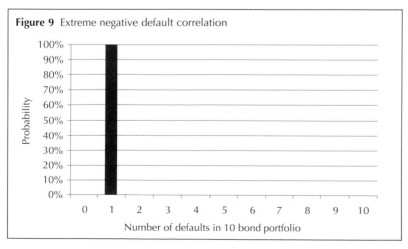

Figure 9 Extreme negative default correlation

both cases the default probability of bonds in the portfolio is 10% and the expected number of defaults is one. But one knows with *certainty* the result of the portfolio depicted in Figure 9: one and only one bond is going to default. This certainty would be of comfort to a lender to this investor. The lender knows with certainty that nine of the bonds are going to perform and that par and interest from those nine performing bonds will be available to repay the investor's indebtedness.

The investor in the portfolio depicted in Figure 8 has the greatest uncertainty. Ninety per cent of the time the portfolio will have no defaults and 10% of the time every bond in the portfolio will default. A lender to an investor with this portfolio has a 10% risk that *no* bonds in the portfolio will perform.

A complete analysis of the risk of these two example portfolios would depend on the distribution of default recoveries. But it is obvious that the portfolio depicted in Figure 8 is much more risky than the portfolio depicted in Figure 9, even though the default probabilities of bonds in the portfolios are the same. The difference in risk profiles, which is due only to default correlation, has profound implications to investors, lenders, rating agencies and regulators. Debt backed by the portfolio depicted in Figure 8 should bear a higher premium for credit risk and be rated lower. If this is a regulated entity, it should be required to have more capital.

DEFAULT PROBABILITY AND DEFAULT CORRELATION IN 1ST TO DEFAULT SWAPS

In Figure 10, we relate default correlation to 1st to default swaps. The Figure shows the probability that *at least one* of five credits will default. This is the risk to the protection seller of a 1st to default swap on five reference names. The Figure shows this probability assuming different levels of default correlation, from –0.05 to 1.00.[4] The line labelled "5% Default probability" also incorporates the assumption that each credit in the reference portfolio has a 5% probability of default.

Focusing on that line, note that over different default correlation assumptions it moves from 25% probability of at least one reference credit defaulting to 5% probability of at least one reference credit defaulting. At the most extreme negative default correlation, which is –0.05 for this default probability, none of the five underlying credits default at the same time. The probability of one underlying credit defaulting is therefore 5 * 5% or 25%. At 1.00 default correlation, when one of the credits defaults, they all default. The probability of one (or all five credits) defaulting is 5%.

Higher default correlation *always* reduces the risk to a 1st to default protection seller. Recall from Figure 6 that, when defaults happen together, there is more of a chance that *no* defaults will occur. (In the Figure, the probability of no defaults occurring is represented by the area outside circles A, B and C.) As default correlation increases, we are moving from a picture of defaults like the one shown in Figure 5 to a picture of defaults like the one shown in Figure 6. A probability distribution like the one pictured in Figure 6 is more likely to produce cases where there are *multiple* defaults and more likely to produce cases where there are *no* defaults. The increase in the probability of no underlying reference defaults reduces 1st to default risk.

Also in Figure 10, is a line labelled "7% Default probability", which incorporates the assumption that every reference credit has a 7% probability of default. Just like the 5% line, it moves, left to right, from only one credit defaulting at a time to all credits defaulting together. In this case, that means a 35% probability of a swap payout at –0.08 default correlation and a 7% probability of a payout at 1.00 correlation. From being 10% above the 5% default line in extreme negative correlations, the 7% default line declines at a faster rate than the 5% default line until it is 2% higher than the 5% line.

We can also compare, in Figure 10, the relative effects of underlying reference credit default probability and default correlation on the probability of a payout under a 1st to default swap. But first we need to decide where to look.

The historical evidence is that default correlation among *well-diversified* investment grade credits over five years is 0.00 or 0.01.[5] Researchers looking at intra-industry default correlation have estimated default correlation for investment-grade names in the same industry at as much as 0.10 or 0.20. So a very generous range of likely default correlations for a 1st to

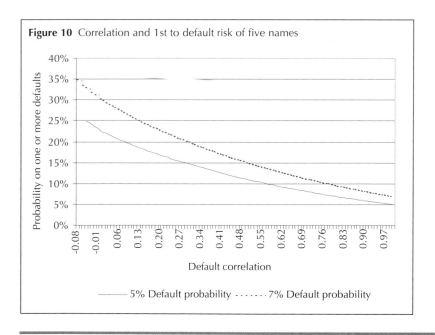

Figure 10 Correlation and 1st to default risk of five names

default swap is from 0.00 to 0.30. On the other hand, it seems pretty easy to us for someone to get default probability wrong by 2% over five years.

Looking at the line for 5% underlying reference credit default probability over the range of default correlation from 0.00 to 0.30, the risk that at least one reference credit will default ranges from 22.6% to 15.8%. This is a difference of 6.9%. Changing the underlying reference credit default probability from 5% to 7% increases the risk that at least one reference credit will default an average of 6.9%. It seems to us much more likely that a protection seller will be off 2% on the true probability of default for the underlying reference credits than off by 0.30 in their estimation of default correlation. Since both mistakes would have the same result, this shows that 1st to default swaps are much more sensitive to estimates of default probability than estimates of default correlation.

DEFAULT PROBABILITY AND DEFAULT CORRELATION IN 2ND TO DEFAULT SWAPS

In Figure 11, we address the risk of 2nd to default swaps, or the risk that at least *two* defaults will occur in our five-credit, five-year 2nd to default swap example. The situation with respect to default correlation is ambiguous. At first, default correlation increases the risk of a 2nd to default swap and then it decreases that risk. What happens is that as default correlation first increases the probability that credits default together, there is a greater chance that two, three, four and five credits will default together. The chance of *two or more* defaults increases. But, as default correlation increases still more, the chance of *exactly* two defaults peaks and then declines while the probability of three, four and five credits defaulting continues to increase. It happens that the decrease in the probability of exactly two defaults is greater than the increase in the probability of *three or more* defaults. Thus, 2nd to default risk decreases. We show this effect in Figure 12.

In the relevant range of default correlation, 0.00 to 0.30, the probability of a 2nd to default payoff, assuming 5% underlying reference credit default probability, ranges from 0.0% to 6.1%. Over this same range of default correlations, an increase in underlying reference default probability from 5% to 7% increases the probability of a 2nd to default payout an average of 2.4%. So we see that default correlation is much more important in the pricing of 2nd to default swaps than it is in the pricing of 1st to default swaps. This result generally holds for higher "nths" and different underlying reference credit default probabilities.

CONCLUSIONS

In this chapter, we explained the mechanics of nth to default swaps and notes and then compared them with portfolios of single-name default swaps and senior and subordinated credit swaps on a portfolio of names.

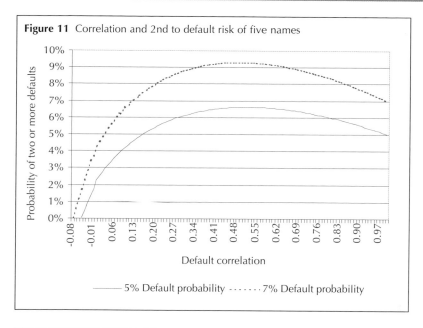

Figure 11 Correlation and 2nd to default risk of five names

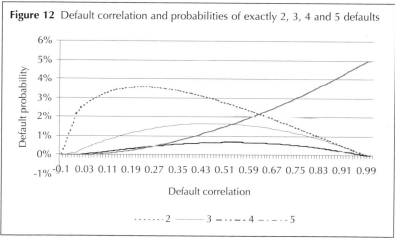

Figure 12 Default correlation and probabilities of exactly 2, 3, 4 and 5 defaults

We ranked different credit swaps in order of their risk to the protection seller. We next "pictured" nth to default risk via the use of Venn diagrams representing credits defaulting together or separately. This led right into a discussion of default correlation. We explained what negative and positive default correlation are, why default correlation is important in analysing credit-risky portfolios like nth to default swaps, and even the causes of default correlation.

Finally, we turned back to nth the default swaps and applied our understanding of default probability and default correlation. We addressed the probability of *at least one* credit defaulting out of a portfolio of five (1st to default risk) and the probability of at least *two* credits defaulting out of a portfolio of five (2nd to default risk). We saw that higher default correlation decreases 1st to default risk. But we said that reference credit default probability was relatively more important in estimating 1st to default risk than default correlation. We also saw that default correlation first increases and then decreases 2nd to default risk. And we pointed out that reference credit default correlation is relatively more important in estimating 2nd to default risk than default probability.

Nth to default swaps and notes allow investors to take on increased credit risk, but remain exposed only to investment-grade credits. The limited number of names in the portfolio allows protection sellers to thoroughly vet the names to which they are exposing themselves. And the static nature of the reference portfolio eliminates any surprise from an asset manager. It also allows the purchase of single-name default swaps later to hedge credit risks. Nth to default swaps are a particularly attractive product in low-spread environments. We expect to see greater use of nth to default swaps and notes to take on credit risk.

1   Much of the material on default correlation in this chapter is adapted from Douglas Lucas, 1989, *Rating Cash Flow Transactions Backed by Corporate Debt* (Moody's Investors Service), September, and Douglas Lucas, 1995, "Default Correlation and Credit Analysis," *Journal of Fixed Income*, March 1995.

2   The expert in credit default swap (CDS) documentation will note that we use a mix of official ISDA-defined terms and expressions whose meanings we feel are easier to understand. Thus "protection buyer" for "Fixed Rate Payer", "protection seller" for "Floating Rate Payer", "default" for the occurrence of a "Credit Event," and "default losses" for the difference between par and market value of the cheapest "Deliverable Obligation".

3   An alternative structure would have the protection seller buy a note for X amount of par, but be responsible for some Y amount of losses where Y > X. In this manner, the protection buyer is collateralised for the first X/Y% of default losses that might occur. The protection seller would still be responsible for uncollateralised default losses exceeding X/Y%. X would be set relative to Y to cover the most likely range of default losses.

4   We assume that default correlations between pairs of credits, the default correlation between a pair of credits and a third credit, the default correlation between three credits and a fourth credit, and the default correlation between four credits and a fifth credit are all equal. In Appendix 1 of Douglas Lucas, 2003, *CDO Insight* (UBS), 31 May, we discuss the insufficiency of pairwise correlations in describing the probability distributions of binomial events like default and the effect of "higher order" default correlations.

5   In Appendix 2 of Douglas Lucas, 2003, *CDO Insight* (UBS), 31 May, we show how measures of historical default correlation are biased to report results that are too high.

7

Portfolio credit risk models

Greg M. Gupton

Moody's KMV

There are several portfolio-level methodologies for estimating a portfolio's CreditVAR (value-at-risk due to credit quality changes). The natural question is, "which framework is best?" In a very significant way, this is driven by the data that are available. If the best data for evaluating credit quality are categorical credit ratings (either from credit rating agencies or a bank's own internal ratings), then the best models of credit risk will use these as input, likely apply Markov analysis, and end up looking like CreditMetrics or CreditPortfolioView. If the best (most timely and impartial) credit quality inferences can be extracted from equity prices, then the best models will use these, probably apply a Merton-type structural approach and end up looking like PortfolioManager. If better credit judgements are from default histories, then perhaps an actuarial model such as CreditRisk+ will dominate.

Similarly, the selection and application of available models is best made after first considering what data are available for user input. An analyst may deeply believe that, say, credit spreads contain the best credit-quality information. Nevertheless, if spreads for his particular set of obligors are very "noisy" due to illiquidity, then it is better to seek another alternative. There have been studies, such as Gordy (2000), that conclude that very different model frameworks can be made to produce very similar results. This chapter gives an overview of the four most broadly implemented and influential modelling frameworks:

1. CreditMetrics, as implemented in the RiskMetric's Group's CreditManager;
2. Expected default frequencies (EDFs), as are utilised in PortfolioManager by Moody's KMV;
3. CreditRisk+, developed by Credit Suisse Financial Products; and
4. CreditPortfolioView, developed by McKinsey & Company.

There is no single best modelling framework. There are only good matches between the best credit information available and a framework that can utilise it. To help guide this choice, this chapter discusses these frameworks with particular emphasis on what data are pivotal to them and what information is required from the user.

CREDITMANAGER, THE IMPLEMENTATION OF CREDITMETRICS

This model originated within JP Morgan for its internal risk management. It was repackaged for public release in early 1997 following JP Morgan's 1994 release of its strictly market risk methodology, RiskMetrics. In 1998, JP Morgan spun off the RiskMetrics Group, which is carrying the models forward. The analytical assumptions and methodology implemented in CreditManager is fully documented in the *CreditMetrics* Technical Document.[1] It is open to alternative user inputs addressing each aspect of its calculation of CreditVAR. This openness allows analysts to perform stress scenarios, assess model sensitivities, carry out what-if analysis and adapt the standard data sets to local market conditions.

Overall premise

This approach follows the idea that the value of an instrument changes with up-/downgrades (moving to a different credit spread curve) and default (realising only a recovery value). CreditMetrics defines credit risk as the uncertainty in instrument value across these credit quality "states" at the risk horizon. The credit rating migrations of each obligor are correlated with the migrations of every other obligor in the portfolio by "loading" each obligor onto a shared set of industry/country equity indices. Although this reference to equity prices is analogous to a Merton-type structural model of credit, CreditMetrics is *not*, strictly speaking, a structural model. CreditMetrics estimates default correlations as a structural model would, but it takes default likelihoods as *exogenous*. Default likelihoods are required inputs via transition matrices. The equity indices that are used here to drive credit events are better thought of as empirical indices of creditworthiness rather than a structural measure of firm unlevered asset value.

User inputs and data dependency

User inputs include each obligor's credit rating, industry and country, plus each instrument's recovery grade, term, amount and asset type. Different asset types may require some specific additional inputs such as the amount currently drawn down, amortisation, peak exposure, etc. Asset-type categories include loans, bonds, commitments and credit derivatives (credit default swaps or total return swaps). The rating system can be from an external agency such as Moody's Investors Service, S&P's and Fitch or perhaps an internal rating system developed within a user's financial institution.[2] All obligors who are assigned the same rating will have the same likelihood of upgrade, downgrade or default. The correlation of these credit events, however, is determined by the industry, country and rating grade of the obligor.

The most common credit derivative types can be directly entered into CreditManager with the programme's full reporting facilities available to show marginal effects, what-ifs and net benefits.

Outputs and available analysis

The reports generated by CreditManager are extensive. Across the portfolio aggregation, the distribution of portfolio value at the risk horizon (adjustable, but typically one year) is available with mean, variance and downside tail statistics. Risk statistics are also available within "grids", which divide the portfolio across the choice of dimensions, including industry, term, region, rating, size, obligor and asset type. For individual exposures, the marginal contribution of risk to the portfolio is calculable. Also available are what-if scenario analysis on individual or group-at-a-time analysis.

Implementation and calibration issues

One of the benefits of CreditManager is its extensive openness. Essentially, every aspect of the applied methodology can be parameterised to local client conditions. Of course, this freedom carries a burden for the user to validate and calibrate changes for not only individually parameters, but also to collectively assure that unanticipated adverse interactions do not occur.

Table 1 Relative strengths/weaknesses: CreditManager

Best strengths	Notable challenges
Flexibility: Essentially, every parameter of the methodology is adjustable by the user.	*Historical view*: All inputs are backward-looking unless the user projects his own (forecast) inputs.
Transparency: Essentially, every modelling assumption is disclosed and discussed in extensive detail.	*Default probabilities*: These must be provided by the user and are limited to categories rather than a continuous scale.
Reporting: Wide array of different reporting options.	*Correlations*: These are weighted sums of equity indices taken without any firm leverage adjustment.
Analysis: Wide variety of what-if, marginal and scenario analysis available.	*Corporate credit only*: The analytics are not well extendable across hundreds of thousands of exposures.

Panel 1
CASE STUDY: CREDITMANAGER

A bank has just completed an internal loss given default (LGD) study that shows its recoveries are much better than published averages. While pleased at this result, it carefully checks to confirm the validity of this before entering the higher recovery rates into CreditManager, which was otherwise running with parameters from the vendor. It found that it had a high proportion of defaulted loans that it was able to restructure with zero economic loss. This lowered its overall LGD estimate and led its risk management system to compute a lower overall CreditVAR result.

Problem: What was happening was that the bank used loan covenants that would classify borrowers as being in "technical default" long before actually missing a payment. This allowed loan officers entrée into distressed clients to actively find loan structures that would likely see the borrower through troubled times. While this benefited all parties economically, it meant that the bank was mixing two incompatible definitions of default into its credit risk management system; the recovery rate's breach of covenant definition with the transition matrix's missed payments definition.[1]

Resolution: The bank could fix this issue in two separate ways. First, it could retabulate its recovery rates over only the set of borrowers who actually missed an interest payment, including cases where the bank "forgave" a scheduled payment or where new lending was put forward to allow the borrower to thus "make" a payment. Alternatively, it could estimate its own institution's rate of technical default – as it practises it. While this second alternative is part of the applicability assurance required in Basel II, the author has seldom seen it done.

1 Published statistics typically follow rating-agency default definitions. Moody's Investors Service defines default as "any missed or delayed disbursement of interest and/or principal, bankruptcy, receivership, or distressed exchange where (i) the issuer offered bondholders a new security or package of securities that amount to a diminished financial obligation (such as preferred or common stock, or debt with a lower coupon or par amount) or (ii) the exchange had the apparent purpose of helping the borrower avoid default".

Best application/situation

CreditManager is targeted at portfolios of corporate obligors. While CreditManager is primarily oriented to loans and bonds, its openness lends itself towards a broader set of localised adaptation relative to other systems. Indeed, this openness across so many modelling inputs may be viewed as a comparative advantage and the best reason for a financial institution to choose CreditManager relative to alternative models. This openness also tends to allow each bank's credit experts to continue acting as experts and taking active responsibility for their decisions. However, the burden of model validation must be borne solely by the user.

PORTFOLIO MANAGER, BY MOODY'S KMV

The original focus of credit risk management systems from KMV (acquired by Moody's Corporation in 2002) was an extension of the structural model of credit first detailed by Merton (1974) to calculate "Expected default frequencies" (EDFs). This EDF model is based on a default data set whose size (which the author's group has recently examined) rivals Moody's own data sets.[3] Since the mid-1990s, PortfolioManager (a portfolio CreditVAR model) was added. Most recently, after Moody's and KMV joined, two new modules have been integrated into PortfolioManager: RiskCalc for private-firm EDFs and LossCalc for security-level LGD forecasting. These are both econometric rather than structural models. Unlike some of the other frameworks, there is no one definitive public document to lay out the details of PortfolioManager, but Crosbie and Bohn (2002) comes fairly close.[4]

Overall premise

KMV was the first to construct a commercially practical implementation of what has come to be known as the *structural* model of debt. The motivation for this model is that the best (most timely, most forward-looking, most accurate) measure of a firm's value is its stock price. Enormous market forces continually act to ensure that there is no better measure of firm value. The structural model treats the debt of a firm as if it were a short put option on the underlying assets of the firm. The likelihood that firm value falls below liabilities is the default probability, the EDF.

For portfolio CreditVAR, at least three more things are needed beyond EDFs:

1. an estimate of the change in debt value due to credit quality changes at the risk horizon;
2. an estimate of inter-firm dependencies of credit events; and
3. a forecast of LGD at the security level.

PortfolioManager models debt value changes on a continuous scale closely related to EDF changes. Inter-firm credit correlations are driven by a serially orthogonal factorisation of firm assets values. LGD is forecast with the LossCalc model that has predictive factors at the security level, firm, industry and over time.

User inputs and data dependency

PortfolioManager has a data set of many thousands of obligors worldwide. Indeed, this list covers essentially all the publicly traded companies in the world's major economies. Selecting an obligor from this list will provide to the model the firm's industry, country, debt structure, size and EDF. Private firms are addressed by inputting financial statement values into the econometric (non-structural) RiskCalc model for EDFs.

It is applicable to most credit-sensitive instruments, including bonds, amortising or bullet loans, revolvers and credit derivatives that can be assessed individually, combined with the exposure that it hedges, or broadly within a portfolio context.

Optionally, additional exposure-level information may be input for the forecasting of LGD for the security, such as asset type, seniority class and whether there is any debt in the capital structure with greater seniority than the one in question. This would free the user from having to assume some historical average recovery rate.

Outputs and available analysis

There is extensive and flexible reporting of standard CreditVAR-type analysis. Also, there is a selection of follow-on analysis programmed into PortfolioManager. These include:

❏ what-if analysis on candidate transactions;
❏ single-name risk contributions and sensitivities;
❏ identification of underperforming exposures within the portfolio; and
❏ portfolio optimisation to suggest risk minimisation or profit maximisation trades, etc.

There is analysis available for individual loan officers or traders, managers with portfolio responsibility and institution-wide risk departments.

Implementation and calibration issues

There is a fair amount of data assembly that is needed ahead of actually running PortfolioManager. Another way of saying this is that the system is tuned to make risk forecasts based on historical and market data, but it needs information about obligors and exposures in some detail. The counterpoint to this is that the system does not need much custom calibration by the particular financial institution that it is run in.

Best application/situation

PortfolioManager is best applied to large corporate names in, perhaps, the top 20 economies in the world. With the recent integration of RiskCalc, for private-firm EDFs, it is also well applied to private companies who are within any of the (currently) 18 economies that have RiskCalc coverage. These can be very large to fairly modest in size.

Panel 2
CASE STUDY: PORTFOLIOMANAGER AND EDFs

A New York bank prided itself on having market-leading risk management tools – most of which were designed and built in-house. They saw their competitive advantage as having top-rate in-house credit experts who were provided with the best tools available.

Problem: When evaluating PortfolioManager and EDFs, bank management reasoned that it could never serve as a competitive advantage since it was a vended tool available to anyone who bought it. In addition, EDFs were seen as displacing in-house credit expertise, with the fear that credit skills would atrophy over time. At the same time, larger-than-average defaults hit the loan book, which, in retrospect, EDFs would have flagged.

Resolution: PortfolioManager and EDFs were brought in, but no one was *required* to take their advice. Rather, each exposure was charged for its *model* credit risk. To the extent that a manager or loan officer's *realised* risk was less than the modelled risk, his compensation pool increased.

Table 2 Relative strengths/weaknesses: PortfolioManager and EDFs

Best strengths	Notable challenges
Forward-looking view: Equity prices implicitly contain the market's collective forecast of the future.	*View of credit as dynamic*: Traditionally, credit quality has been viewed as solely a gradual process.
Credit quality on a continuous scale: And through a validated system supported by large data sets.	*Set-up investment*: There is appreciable effort to first set up a portfolio and settings. It cannot be used casually.
Credit correlations: Defined and estimated to be consistent with the process of credit quality changes.	*Firm coverage*: Not every public firm worldwide is included in the EDF database.
Extensive vendor support: Models are maintained and extended. Staff are available to answer questions.	*Corporate credit only*: The analytics are not well extendable across hundreds of thousands of exposures.

CREDITRISK+, BY CREDIT SUISSE FINANCIAL PRODUCTS
In October 1997, Credit Suisse First Boston (CSFB) published the CreditRisk+ methodology, which brought the innovation of traditional actuarial statistics to the area of financial VAR analysis. Unlike other alter-

natives, it does not require a large simulation to produce the full distribution of credit value across the portfolio.[5] A potential issue for financial institutions considering its implementation is that it is no longer being developed and is not a supported system.

Overall premise

The two guiding principles of the CreditRisk+ methodology are that there are (1) very many discrete obligors in the portfolio – it is *fine-grained*; and (2) they all share the same default characteristics – it is *homogeneous* within each sector. An extreme example of this is a very large credit card portfolio composed of cardholders who were all sourced in a single focused campaign targeted at a narrow demographic and geography. A tangible example is LEASEUROPE (2003), which made a sensible application of CreditRisk+ on about 40,000 leases. Of course, every credit portfolio is different and the qualities of fine-grained homogeneity will inevitably vary on a continuous scale. Thus, validating model projections is a necessary step for course-grained and/or heterogeneous portfolios, but this is true for all of the modelling frameworks.

An important difference between CreditRisk+ and all the other frameworks in this chapter is that it was designed to focus only on the volatility of value (the risk) due to default and not to address the volatility of value due to price changes driven by credit quality migrations.

User input and data dependency

User input into CreditRisk+ is commonly seen as less onerous than it is for other models since little information is needed on the individual exposure level. The user simply has to enter the total exposure amount (net of anticipated recoveries) allocated to "sectors". For each "sector" within the portfolio, the user must provide the aggregate default rate and default volatility. Default rates can be either taken from history or asserted based on judgement. Default volatilities are a pivotal input to the model since they imply the correlation of default and the portfolio's diversifiable risk; higher default volatility directly implies higher default correlation. The framers of this system observe that default volatility is commonly half of the default rate, but to mechanically assume this value abdicates any realistic estimation of the loss distribution.

The default volatility is a primary driver in CreditRisk+, since it implicitly determines the effective correlation of defaults. Default correlations are a primary driver of the long downside "tail" of the credit loss distribution and its implied capital requirements. So, it is important to validate this assumption for the portfolio at hand. Sourcing the rate and volatility of defaults is straightforward if there is a sufficient history to look to that is consistent with the current portfolio composition.

The only way to enter credit derivatives into CreditRisk+ would be to net the exposure amount in the applicable sector. There would be no view of the credit derivative except as its marginal effect on the portfolio as a whole.

Outputs and available analysis

The only systems implementation of CreditRisk+ available from CSFB is an Excel spreadsheet. This spreadsheet has very limited reporting. It simply lists the portfolio aggregate mean, median and a number of downside tail percentiles. However, it also produces a full distribution of the aggregate portfolio: a list of hundreds of slices of the probability density function. From this detail, almost any descriptive statistic can be calculated. User modifications to do marginal analysis (ie, of what happens to the portfolio's distribution given some marginal change) are also possible. This would involve performing the calculation twice and each slice of the resulting density functions from its counterpart. Of course, maintenance and quality assurance of any extensions of the spreadsheet become the user's responsibility. As with any spreadsheet, it size and organisation may soon become unwieldy.

Implementation and calibration issues

Decisions need to be made about how to sensibly group exposures to be within "sectors" that are homogeneous. Not much can be done to change the granularity of the portfolios. So, if it is in question, then validation testing needs to be done. It is ironic that the model with the fewest required inputs is likely to be the one with the greatest calibration concerns. The model is quite dependent upon the ratio of the input default rate and the default volatility. If there are lengthy historical data, then these are straightforward to estimate. But there remains the need to verify that these historic estimates reflect the same context of the current portfolio.

Panel 3
CASE STUDY: CREDITRISK+

A financial institution has both a corporate lending division (CLD) and an equipment leasing division (ELD). These two groups had implemented different CreditVAR models with the ELD using CreditRisk+.

Problem: An appreciable number of obligors in the CLD portfolio also had leases outstanding. Loan covenants were always written such that the lease would be deemed in default if the loan defaulted. However, the current system did not capture this 100% default correlation.

Resolution: Leases to obligors who also have corporate loans are flagged. These are accounted for within the CLD when calculating obligor concentrations, while the ELD runs their CreditRisk+ in two ways:

1. including the flagged obligors, to manage the lease book; and
2. excluding the flagged obligors, which is handed up for overall corporate aggregation.

While this addressed the tactical issue of certain large obligors, the broader issue of aggregating these divisions' CreditVAR results at the institution level was unaddressed in this exercise.

Table 3 Relative strengths/weaknesses: CreditRisk+

Best strengths	Notable challenges
Speed: There is no simulation required. Application to even very large consumer portfolios is no slower.	*Burden of sourcing default rate volatility*: Although CreditRisk+ has few required inputs, this is both critical and often difficult to source.
Scalable: Readily handles arbitrarily large portfolios that are fine-grained and homogeneous.	*Lack of reporting/analysis*: The spreadsheet download is very sparse and virtually all reporting must be custom-made.
Data collection: No transaction or firm-level data are needed other than exposure amounts net of LGD.	*Lack of vendor support*: Credit Suisse Financial Products does not actively support this as a product.
Sharing and customisation: Its spreadsheet implementation is readily tailored and freely shared.	*System integrity*: Spreadsheets are notorious for potential bugs that can be introduced from prolonged uses by multiple people.

Best application/situation

CreditRisk+ could well be applied to a wide variety of credit portfolios. However, its comparative advantage in raw computation time, relative to other frameworks, is when it is applied to very large portfolios. With current desktop computers' power (3GHz at the time of writing) portfolios of 40,000 exposures are not a problem for any of the models discussed here. CreditRisk+ excels when applied to homogeneous exposures numbering in the hundreds of thousands and more.

CREDITPORTFOLIOVIEW, BY MCKINSEY & COMPANY

CreditPortfolioView was a consulting solution within McKinsey & Co published in November 1997. Although there are no longer any references to it across McKinsey.com, the approach continues to be implemented privately and remains an influential topic of discussion.

Overall premise

The methodology has a very similar orientation to CreditMetrics: credit quality is a user input by rating category, recovery rates are historical, transition matrices describe (prototypical) rating migration, and securities are revalued at the risk horizon by rediscounting at a new corporate spread curve. CreditPortfolioView diverges in the way it estimates how obligors potentially default at the same time. Rather than trying to estimate correlations, predictive macroeconomic models (typically by country) are employed to forecast the health of the credit environments. Specifically, these macroeconomic models forecast the speculative grade default rate. The resulting credit forecast is used to adjust (or "twist") the probabilities in the transition matrix.

So, for example, during economic declines the probabilities of default rise, which then also implies increases in the chance of downgrades and decreases in the chance of upgrades. This effect is applied to all exposures across the scope of each macro-model. In this way, default correlation is addressed implicitly. All obligors experience a higher chance of default during the same times and, thus, default correlation occurs.

User inputs and data dependency

Inputs are very much like CreditManager with additions such as country rating, a parent-versus-domestic-country distinction and a "business unit name" (to aid in organising the outputs). The macroeconomic models are specified ahead of time and it is not recommended that they be continuously updated. The main driver of CreditVAR is the macroeconomic model, one per country covered, as well as a country-by-country correlation matrix. These can be changed, but are not part of the typical user input. Adjusting position inputs manually can represent basic credit derivative positions.

Outputs and available analysis

There are an extensive number of output reports available. Many of these are similar to the instrument and portfolio group type of reporting of CreditManager. There is, in addition, further reporting to reflect the macro economy and credits extended into the future.

Implementation and calibration issues

One issue to be addressed is more on the policy side of how the model will be used to guide decisions. As CreditPortfolioView generates portfolio CreditVAR measurements each month, the numbers will vary. Those changes will be attributable to two separate things: changes in portfolio composition and changes in indications from the macroeconomic models.

Panel 4

CASE STUDY: CREDITPORTFOLIOVIEW

A European bank chose CreditPortfolioView because of its ability to attribute different default behaviour to credits within each of the three countries in its lending territory. Management felt good about the system and wanted to update the macro models, since it had been a few years since the system was installed.

Problem: This work highlighted two issues. The first issue was a choice between statistically fitting the default data and consistency. GNP could be consistently applied in each country and it predicted at least moderately well everywhere. Industrial production predicted very well in two countries but poorly in the third country, the largest. The second issue was that applying these two alternative model formulations to the past data would have calculated CreditVAR that was both different from each other and different from the old system.

Resolution: Management chose to sacrifice consistency by picking the most predictive model reformulations for each of their three countries. This choice led to an appreciable one-time shift in their calculated CreditVAR compared with their current system. To isolate and better understand the impact of macroeconomic change in the model, they now run the model three ways each month:

1. apply this month's new macro variable values to last month's portfolio;
2. apply last month's macro variables to this month's portfolio; and
3. apply this month's new macro variable values to this month's portfolio.

In this way, bank management feel they can distinguish between changes in CreditVAR that are attributable to the economic environment versus changes in portfolio size and composition.

Best application/situation

CreditPortfolioView is targeted at portfolios of corporate obligors, but it is likely best applied to smaller corporate names that are engaged in fairly standard asset types and are located in multiple countries. This allows the macroeconomic models to provide an additional layer of insight into potential drivers of the credit environment. This different view of the credit process can help stimulate debate among local credit experts.

SUMMARY

These portfolio credit value-at-risk models grew out of a basic industry need to understand and to manage risk. Three of these were published in

Table 4 Relative strengths/weaknesses: CreditPortfolioView

Best strengths	Notable challenges
Forward-looking: macroeconomic model component projects shifts in upgrade/downgrade tendencies.	*Maintaining macro models*: over time the macroeconomic models lose relevance and need to be respecified.
Thought-provoking view of credit: the exercise of thinking about the credit environment in a structured way is useful.	*Default probabilities*: these must be provided by the user and are limited to categories rather than a continuous scale.
Reporting: wide array of different reporting options.	*Lack of vendor support*: McKinsey is no longer supporting this product.
Not only "How much", but also "Why": helps to start answering why credit risks change.	*Corporate credit only*: the analytics are not well extendable across hundreds of thousands of exposures.

1997 – well ahead of the current regulatory push towards quantitative and historically supported models. These models are capable of estimating aggregate (and marginal) credit risk with greater obligor and instrument-specific information than is required in any proposed regulation. This allows portfolio managers, traders, bankers and deal originators to speak a common language. Importantly, it allows an insight into the drivers of credit risk and so facilitates greater proactive management of these risks through credit derivatives and other means.

PORTFOLIO CREDITVAR MODEL COMPARISON

Table 5 Feature comparison across the major value-at-risk models for credit portfolios

Vendor	RiskMetrics	Moody's KMV	CSFB	McKinsey & Co
Model	CreditManager: CreditMetrics	PortfolioManager: EDFs, RiskCalc, LossCalc	CreditRisk+	CreditPortfolioView
Risks included	Change in market value due to defaults and change in credit rating category	Change in market value due to defaults and change in EDFs	Defaults only	Change in market value due to defaults and change in credit rating category
Measure of obligor credit quality	User input: credit-rating categories (must be accompanied by a transition matrix)	Model output: continuous scale, expected default frequency (EDF)	User input: default rate (constant across a "sector", but can have multiple sectors)	User input: credit rating categories (must be accompanied by a transition matrix)
Risk drivers	Credit ratings and equity indices	Firm equity, leverage and defaulted debt prices	Input default rates and default volatilities	Credit ratings and macro factors
Rating transition and process	Constant historical averages	Dynamic at firm level; driven by equity and leverage	N/A	Dynamic at sector-level; driven by macro factors
Credit correlations	Multivariate normal equity index returns	Serially orthogonal factoring of unlevered asset returns	Sector level implied from default volatilities	Macroeconomic "twisting" of transition matrix. Correlations implicit in co-twists

Table 5 Continued

Vendor	RiskMetrics	Moody's KMV	CSFB	McKinsey & Co
Loss given default (expectation)	User input: flexible but typically by security category	Forecast based on security, firm, industry and macro factors	User input: credit exposure entered net of recoveries	User input: flexible but typically by security category
Loss given default (uncertainty)	Beta distributed historical volatility	Forecast as above: beta distributed	Not captured in this framework	"Random": details are undocumented
Processing	Simulation/analytic	Simulation/analytic	Analytic (spreadsheet)	Econometric simulation
Pivotal	Transition matrix, equity indices by industry and country, LGD by category	Equity prices, balance-sheet items, defaulted debt prices	Default rates and volatilities by sector	Transition matrix, macroeconomic models, LGD by category
Model data				
Secondary model data	Credit spreads	Credit spreads	-	Credit spreads
User inputs	Obligors: industry, country, size	Exposures: company ID, amount	Sector definitions, default rates and volatilities by sector	Obligors: industry, country
	Exposures: asset type, rating, seniority, term, amount			Exposures: asset type, rating, seniority, term, amount

1   Gupton, Finger and Bhatia (1997), http://www.defaultrisk.com/ pp_model_20.htm.
2   If a custom rating system is used, then the user must supply a transition matrix to embody how that rating system will behave.
3   After the Moody's acquisition of KMV, we were able to compare the two institutions' databases of defaulted companies. Though comparable in size, they each excelled in different market segments. Thus, their joining lead to a better inference of the total market's default rate (see Dwyer and Stein, 2003).
4   Crosbie and Bohn (2002), downloadable at http://www.moodyskmv.com/research/ whitepapers.html.
5   The CreditRisk+ methodology and a spreadsheet that implements it are available at http://www.csfb.com/creditrisk/.

BIBLIOGRAPHY

Bluhm, C., L. Overbeck and C. Wagner, 2002, *An Introduction to Credit Risk Modeling* (Chapman & Hall).

Crosbie, P. J., and J. R. Bohn, 2002, "Modeling Default Risk", Moody's KMV.

Crouhy, M., D. Galai and R. Mark, 2000, "A Comparative Analysis of Current Credit Risk Models", *Journal of Banking & Finance*, 24, pp 59–117.

Derviz, A. and N. Kadlčáková, 2001, "Methodological Problems of Quantitative Credit Risk Modeling in the Czech Economy", working paper, Czech National Bank.

Dwyer, D., and R. Stein, 2003, "Inferring the Default Rate in a Population by Comparing Two Incomplete Default Databases", working paper, Moody's KMV.

Gordy, M. B., 1998, "From CreditMetrics to CreditRisk+ and Back Again", working paper, Board of Governors of the Federal Reserve System.

Gordy, M. B., 2000, "A Comparative Anatomy of Credit Risk Models", *Journal of Banking & Finance* 24, pp. 119–49.

Gupton, G. M., C. C. Finger and M. Bhatia, 1997, "CreditMetrics – Technical Document", Morgan Guaranty Trust Company.

Gupton, G. M. and R. Stein, 2002, "LossCalc Moody's Model for Predicting Loss Given Default (LGD)", working paper, Moody's KMV.

Kern, M. and B. Rudolph, 2001, "Comparative Analysis of Alternative Credit Risk Models: an Application on German Middle Market Loan Portfolios", working paper, Ludwig-Maximilians University. LEASEUROPE: European Federation of Leasing Company Associations: URL: http://www.leaseurope.org/Pages/Agenda_and_ Minutes/ (16 January 2003).

Martin, R., K. Thompson and C. Brown, 2003, "Taking to the Saddle", in M. B. Gordy (ed), *Credit Risk Modeling*, pp 137–43 (Risk Books).

Merton, R. C., 1974, "On the Pricing of Corporate Debt: The Risk Structure of Interest Rates", *Journal of Finance* 29, pp. 449–70.

Wilde, T., 1997, "CreditRisk+ A Credit Risk Management Framework", Credit Suisse First Boston.

8

Credit derivatives as an efficient way of transitioning to optimal portfolios

Alla Gil

CitiGroup

The key challenge in optimising credit-risky portfolios is measuring risk/return trade-off consistently with the pricing of overlaying instruments used for transition to an optimal portfolio. This chapter describes an original hybrid methodology that measures portfolio credit risk consistently with the pricing and hedging techniques. We construct an efficient frontier for the given portfolio, explicitly taking into consideration possible default events. Then we identify the optimal portfolio on the frontier that is the most appropriate for the nature of existing portfolio. Finally, we demonstrate how to overlay various credit derivatives structures in order to transform the current portfolio into the optimal one.

INTRODUCTION

As discussed in the last chapter, the last decade has seen a number of methodologies for evaluating credit risk on a portfolio basis has greatly increased and now includes such well-known packages as KMV (see Kealhoffer, 1995), CreditPortfolioView (see Wilson, 1997), CreditRisk+ (see Credit Suisse Financial Products, 1997) and CreditMetrics (see CreditMetrics). This increase is the direct result of the development of credit derivatives markets. While credit risk has always existed in the financial markets, quantifying it without being able to mitigate would be a nerve-racking experience, and useless to boot.

Credit derivatives, the market for which has grown up significantly in the past few years, allow portfolio managers (including managers of investment portfolios of insurance companies and pension funds, asset managers and managers of bank loan portfolios) to eliminate only the unwanted portion of credit risk. The first step here is to separate fundamentals, ie, risk imbedded in portfolio positions that reflects the managers' views of expected exposures, and excess risk inherent in portfolio positions. In other words, expected exposures represent the portion of risk for which a portfolio manager is compensated with portfolio returns, while the unexpected losses are auxiliary to his investment objectives and thus have to be hedged away. By definition, economic capital is supposed to cover for the losses above and beyond the expected loss (that risk takers are compensated for) up to some reasonable level (established by the risk policies).

The concept of risk/return trade-off is different for credit portfolios and for individual credit-risky investments. Thus investing in an AA-rated name is less profitable (from credit spread point of view) and safer (judging from the default probabilities) than in an A-rated name. At the same time, a well-diversified portfolio with a weighted average credit rating of single A can be less risky than a very concentrated AA-rated (on average) portfolio. This means that average credit rating does not adequately measure tail risk on a portfolio basis.

Economic capital provides a comprehensive measure of such portfolio risk. It enables us to construct efficient frontiers for credit-risky portfolios (Figure 1).

Economic capital here represents the major characteristic of the unexpected loss. It allows for quantifying different portfolio strategies and choosing a robust direction for portfolio optimisation.

The efficient frontier in Figure 1 is different from the classic concept because it includes the possibility of default events and takes into consideration not just historical information, but the forward-looking dynamics of underlying market factors, as well. The following sections describe our methodology for measuring risks on a portfolio level. This methodology uses the concept of economic capital extended from the standard Basel II notion to generalised value at risk (VAR) approach appropriate for both

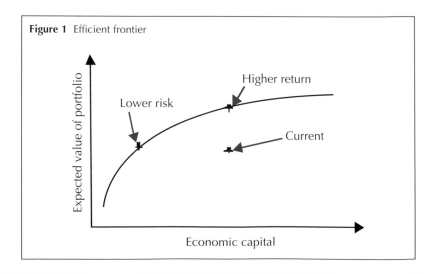

Figure 1 Efficient frontier

market and credit risk and consistent with the pricing and hedging techniques. Then we discuss how to identify the right position on the efficient frontier for the given portfolio and what is the best way to achieve it.

Economic capital as an efficient measure of risk

In traditional portfolio management and asset allocation, an investor would choose the instruments based on his views of market dynamics and use mean-variance optimisation to construct efficient frontier. However, this approach is plagued with serious inadequacies when it comes to credit-risky portfolios. The main one is an assumption of normal distribution of portfolio returns that works quite well when underlying instruments are not prone to extreme risks. For the portfolios where assets can default, or are exposed to political or Emerging Market risk, the distribution of returns has strongly non-Gaussian behaviour. Thus economic capital replaces the traditional measure of risk – variance – for such portfolios (as shown on Figure 1).

There is another aspect of risk assessment: should it be measured on an absolute or relative (with respect to a given performance benchmark portfolio) basis?

Asset managers usually apply tracking error (relative risk) methodology to make sure that their portfolio performance does not deviate from the investment benchmark too much. Even if their portfolio has incurred absolute losses, they are happy as long as they are outperforming the benchmark. But tracking error methodologies don't give portfolio managers an idea of how much can be lost with what probability.

Bank loan portfolio managers measure market risk by looking at the absolute losses using the standard VAR methodology. But credit risk is usually analysed on a name-by-name basis and the decisions to extend credit or not are based on industry or name specific credit lines.

When measuring credit risk on a portfolio level, it is natural to expand existing methodologies to apply to the new forms of risk. But these methodologies do not always accurately account for the extreme forms of risk (defaults).

The question of how to measure market and credit risk consistently has been especially popular in light of Basel II.

After the first Basel Accord was introduced in 1988, banks developed risk-based policies to effectively address the regulatory capital requirements. The first stage of development of credit derivatives markets focused on regulatory arbitrage and exploited the inefficiencies of the rigid regulatory rules.

Basel II is intended to correct some of these inefficiencies and give banks greater incentives to measure and manage risk using economic principles. It introduces economic capital as a measure of capital adequacy that accurately reflects on risks inherent in banks assets. Economic capital can be calculated using a more or less sophisticated (advanced or standard) approach (see Basel Committee). Banks which will obtain permission (according to Basel II rules) to switch to economic measure of capital adequacy, can be much more efficient in their business practices.

As financial institutions realise that economic capital can serve in a much wider role as a strategic measure of asset allocation efficiency, they start developing return on economic capital requirements for different asset classes.

Economic capital became a standard term for effectively measuring market, credit and operational risk. The methodology proposed here is fully consistent with the Basel II Advanced Approach to economic capital.

In the context of credit-risky portfolios, economic capital can be utilised as a unified measure for market and credit risk (see Figure 2). Portfolio value is exposed to two different types of uncertainty: two-sided or reversible exposures (or market risk based on interest rate, currency and credit spread fluctuations), and one-sided exposures associated with irreversible losses due to defaults or necessity to sell some assets in order to cut losses. The latter can happen when an issuer falls below the lowest credit rating category allowed by investment guidelines. These types of risk are not independent: when credit spread widens enough, the probability of default might increase substantially, not necessarily proportionally to the spread growth.

The proposed approach looks at both types of risk consistently while assessing their relation to each other in dynamics.

Market risk has been traditionally measured with the VAR approach. This has meant measuring a 95% confidence interval based on historical statistics of market changes and applying it forward for a 10–30-day horizon. This methodology works quite well for market risks but is not

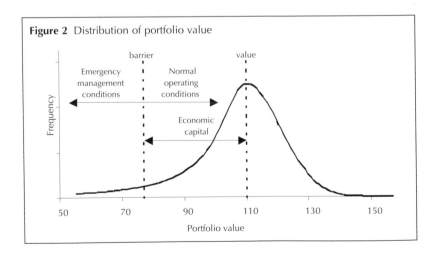

Figure 2 Distribution of portfolio value

appropriate for credit risks for the following reasons:

❏ historical statistics cannot predict the events that never happened in the past, and by definition all (or almost all) holdings in the current portfolio have never defaulted before;
❏ credit risks represent fat-tailed distributions where the normalised return assumptions and 95% confidence intervals do not cover a reasonable and foreseeable amount of losses; and
❏ short-term horizon analysis is deceptive: for a portfolio of reasonably high-quality holdings, the probability of default over a 10-day horizon is negligibly small, while over a longer-term horizon it can grow, accumulate and become quite substantial.

Still, VAR is a very attractive methodology, because it describes the probability of feasible losses, P(x > X), or probability of loss crossing the given threshold. It summarises the worst-case loss faced by a portfolio manager over a target horizon with a given confidence interval in a single measure.

If this measure cannot be expanded directly onto other components of economic capital (credit and operational risk), what should replace it? We suggest a generalised VAR approach, ie, a methodology that allows us to answer the same question the traditional VAR addresses but that overcomes its shortcomings when applied to credit and operational risks. The generalised VAR approach is based on forward-looking analysis of future uncertainties. In order to calculate how much can be lost with a given probability, according to VAR, one needs to construct a loss distribution function (see Figure 3).

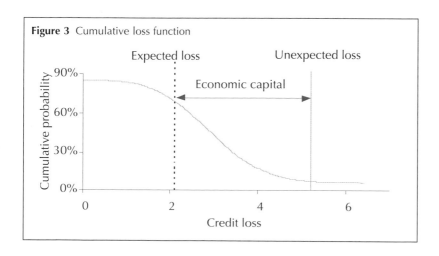

Figure 3 Cumulative loss function

This in turn can be used to calculate probabilities of different loss ranges.

MODELLING RISK IN THE PRESENCE OF DEFAULT EVENTS

We are going to develop a methodology that allows us to apply a generalised VAR measure to fat-tailed behaviour of loss distributions.

It is known from empirical data that most financial distributions are fat-tailed (see Mandelbrot, 1963). In the situations where rare events are involved, fat tails cannot be ignored or approximated with normal or lognormal distributions. Predicting rare or unique events is essential for risk management process. As a rule, most instruments in fixed-income portfolios are issued by companies that haven't defaulted yet – but counting on their continued survival would not be prudent. Thus possible future defaults (and other rare events) create loss distributions where substantial amounts can be lost with non-negligible probability.

The common definition of the fat-tailed distribution is that tails of its density function decay at power rate (versus exponential or faster decay for thin-tailed distribution):

$$P(x > x) > k(x)x^{-\alpha}$$

Panel 1

EXTREME VALUE THEORY

One of the popular methodologies that study the behaviour of fat tails is extreme value theory (EVT). EVT is often used by insurance companies to estimate probabilities of rare events. It addresses the fat-tailed distribution issue by modelling the tails separately from the centre. It helps to estimate the probability of events that might not have happened before. But it has a number of drawbacks, too. Since it is dealing with rare events, it requires long historical time series, which are often unavailable.

But the major disadvantage in using this theory for assessing losses in credit-risky portfolios is that the risk evaluation is inconsistent with the pricing of hedging instruments (ie, credit derivatives) that are to be used to curb this risk.

EVT provides static assessment of tail distribution. But the credit spreads are dynamic and probabilities of default embedded in them are changing with the changes in credit quality.

While EVT is a powerful tool for studying the tail behaviour of a distribution, one must be aware of its limitations when applied to financial risk management. It is best as a complementary analysis for generalised VAR in cases when there are no readily available hedging instruments on the market (as in the case with operational risk).

Analysis of risk in portfolios with credit exposures should combine reliable historical information (eg, rating transition matrices, historical recovery distributions and corporate bond prices) with current market dynamics of credit spreads and yield curves (observed in asset and credit default swap (CDS) and callable bond markets). It should also use available information reflecting the current credit quality and its transition, as well as estimates of loss amount in the event of default. Market (interest rate, spread, foreign exchange and equity) and credit risk should be evaluated using a consistent modelling platform. Assessing these types of risk should be compatible with pricing and hedging models and methodologies. It should also take into consideration the existing portfolio benchmark and investment guidelines of a given portfolio manager.

DESCRIPTION OF PROPOSED APPROACH
There are two major approaches to assessing credit risk:

❏ the *structural approach* is based on the information extracted from the traded equity and the fundamental analysis of the balance sheet of a firm (see Merton, 1974);
❏ reduced-form approach uses information from the market credit spreads (see Madan, Unal, 1998; and Duffie, Singleton, 1999).

We propose to use the hybrid approach that combines the best features of the existing ones.[1] It utilises all available information and allows for consistent integration of market and credit risk.

Credit spreads of the instruments available on the market (corporate bonds, CDS, asset swaps, etc) are observable indicators of the credit risk. They are composed of several components reflecting both market-wide or systematic risk, and company-specific, idiosyncratic risk.

Liquidity is one of the components of credit risk. We define liquidity as the portion of the credit spread that is market-wide, ie, not associated with any credit fears, and doesn't include premium charged for unpopular (illiquid) industries or names. It can be estimated by considering the spread of illiquid but credit risk-free instruments to the Treasury yield curve. For example, Libor, government agency or AAA-industrial curves can serve this purpose under different circumstances. The part of the credit spread that is charged for possible changes in credit quality, or is industry- or name-specific, reflects credit fears and is not included in definition of liquidity.

Another clearly distinguished component of credit spread is expected recovery in the event of default. Recovery represents investors' expectation of what they can obtain in bankruptcy proceedings. After the default event has been announced, prices of distressed bonds reflect these expectations and are used for defining recovery in credit derivatives contracts.

The major factors impacting expected recovery are collateralisation conditions, seniority of the obligation, industry affiliation and the value of the assets. For example, US non-financial assets, on average, recover 41.7%, while US banks only 22% (see Amner, Packer). Expected recoveries are also correlated with default frequency.[2] Thus expected recoveries are best estimated through the fundamental analysis and can be calibrated using the structural approach. Since this approach models the value of the firm, it is possible to record the total asset value at the time of default. Using historical ratios of senior secured recovery rates to unsecured to subordinate, etc, it is possible to determine on each defaulted path how much is recovered by issues of each seniority level. As a result, we construct the entire distribution of recoveries that can be used later in modelling portfolio value, see Gil, Polyakov, (2003).

The remaining components of credit spread reflect the dynamics of credit quality and consist of migration and default risk. Understanding the dynamic nature of these components is quite important for modelling credit risk.

Historical migration risk is reflected in rating transition probability matrices published by rating agencies. But the credit ratings do not change often and they usually lag behind the continuously changing credit quality. Market prices change in credit quality continuously and anticipate changes in credit ratings. Even downgrades do not – in most cases – cause abrupt changes in affected bond prices, because they have already been adjusted to the respective level. Thus, in developed markets, the changes in credit quality can be described by a smooth diffusion process.

When it comes to default, though, bond prices usually drop abruptly causing the fat-tailed nature of loss distribution functions for credit-risky portfolios. However, the process can be different, depending on pre-default credit quality. Thus investment-grade companies are most likely to

Figure 4 Rating transition matrix

Credit spread ranges	Transition probabilities	AAA	AA	A	BBB	BB ...	Default
L_{AAA}–U_{AAA}	AAA	$P_{AAA, AAA}$	$P_{AAA, AA}$	$P_{AAA, A}$	$P_{AAA, BBB}$	$P_{AAA, BBB}$	$P_{AAA, D}$
L_{AA}–U_{AA}	AA	$P_{AA, AAA}$	$P_{AA, AA}$	$P_{AA, A}$	$P_{AA, BBB}$	$P_{AA, BB}$	$P_{AA, D}$
L_A–U_A	A	$P_{A, AAA}$	$P_{A, AA}$	$P_{A, A}$	$P_{A, BBB}$	$P_{A, BBB}$	$P_{A, D}$

default by a catastrophic event while a lower-grade company could be driven into bankruptcy even by a regular market move.

The ratio between these two components – the smooth diffusive one reflecting migration risk and the other representing jump to default – changes over time. This split can be calibrated using rating transition matrices on each random path at each point in time. As the credit spread widens and narrows due to spread volatility but remains within the range associated with the current credit rating, the ratio between jump and diffusion remains the same, as it is defined by the same row of transition probabilities (see Figure 4).

Here L_K and U_K are lower and upper spread bounds for the credit rating K; $P_{I,J}$ is the transition probability from rating I to rating J.

The process of applying rating transition matrices to modelling migration and default risk is suggested in Jarrow, Lando, Turnbull (1997). We use these historical matrices for identifying which portion of the spread is charged for migration risk and which for the probability of default. When the spread widens (or narrows) enough to cross into a different range, the split changes as it is determined by the ratio of cumulative downgrade migrations to the probability of default.

To summarise, we propose to measure fat-tails of loss distribution functions and estimate generalised VAR with a given confidence interval using jump-diffusion processes based on dynamics of credit spreads. The amount of loss in the event of default is estimated using a structural approach.

ASSESSING CREDIT RISK ON PORTFOLIO LEVEL

To construct loss distribution function for a credit-risky portfolio, we need to simulate jointly distributed spreads of the underlying obligors, see Gil, Polyakov, (2003).

Correlation between the issuers' credit spreads is the major driver of the fatness of the tails, see Gil, Klymchuk, (2002). Correlation within the industry (on average 70% on a lognormal basis) is usually a much higher one than average correlation between the industries (10–20%).

The observable spread correlations can be estimated using the historical time series. Most often market crises are characterised by a significant increase in correlations, both systematic (when all spreads widen) and idiosyncratic (when more defaults happens together). Our approach allows for stress-testing correlation assumptions by calibrating them to a specific stressful period of market history. At the same time, the implied default correlation is dynamic. When the spreads widen together the implied probabilities of default increase simultaneously for highly correlated names. This way more default events can happen over a given time interval, which raises the implied correlation of defaults.

Equation 1 is used to simulate credit spreads (we use the spread over Libor to eliminate the market-wide liquidity component):

$$s_i (p, t) = \hat{s}_i(t) \exp\left(-\frac{\sigma^2}{2} t + \sigma \sqrt{t} z_i \right) \tag{1}$$

where s_i is a credit spread for the ith obligor in the portfolio on the path p and $\hat{s}_i(t)$ is its mean at time t; σ_i is credit spread volatility; z_i is a standard normal random variable. When credit spread curves are jointly simulated, we use correlated z_i with historically estimated correlations.

Then, according to the methodology described above, the credit spread is split into diffusive $\psi_i(t)$ (used for marking positions to market) and jumpy $\psi_i(t)$ (used as rate of arrival of default events and for simulating whether default has happened on a given path) components.

$$s_i (t) = \varphi_i(t) + \psi_i(t) \tag{2}$$

The smooth changes in credit quality and the mark-to-market impact of credit spread volatility represent market risk. Portfolio managers associate credit risk with the events that cause abrupt and significant losses in the portfolio (such as defaults). The reason why credit spread dynamics has to be separated into two components is the necessity to analyse market and credit risk on an integrated basis and observe their mutual interdependence. The split into the two components, according to Equation 2, on each path is time-dependent. This provides us with the flexibility to impose stress-testing not only on spread levels, volatilities and correlations, but on the rate of deterioration in credit quality. It is important to do this, because the annual probability of downgrade in some rating categories was almost 10 times higher in the past two years than an average taken over 15 years of history.

The principal difference between market and credit risk cannot just be described by default versus gradual credit deterioration. It really boils down to distinction between the two-sided risk, when you can wait and hope that your positions will recover, and one-sided risk, when you have to realise your losses at once (which often happens when the obligor defaults). But there are other examples. If a portfolio manager is not allowed by investment policies to keep the names below a certain credit rating in the portfolio, then the investment would have to be sold soon after it falls out of the respective category, even if the manager believes that there is a good upside potential.

The described portfolio methodology can be used to help senior management design efficient investment, risk management and hedging policies consisting of the following steps:

❏ diagnostics: what are the current risks in the portfolio?, which risks one is compensated for?, what are the current capital provisions and requirements?;

❑ positioning: how to identify the right risk tolerance, what is an appropriate level of risk for this portfolio?, what is the right place on the efficient frontier that has been constructed for integrated market and credit risk considerations?; and

❑ transition: how to reach the right position on the frontier, whether it should be done through increased returns, reduced unexpected losses or both in the cash markets by selling and buying assets and changing portfolio composition or synthetically by using hedge overlays, what is the best way to conduct risk mitigation, ie, to transform the current portfolio to the portfolio with maximum return for an appropriate level of risk.

Table 5 Allocation by rating

Credit rating	Current portfolio	
	Number of obligors	Size (%)
Aaa	20	73.9
Aa1	3	2.2
Aa2	1	0.5
Aa3	5	2.6
A1	2	1.6
A2	5	3.8
A3	5	6.5
Baa1	4	2.7
Baa2	4	5.1
Baa3	1	0.7
Ba2	1	0.5
Ba3	–	–
B1	–	–
B2	–	–
B3	–	–
Caa-C	–	–
Total	**51**	**100**

Let us consider the following example. The portfolio has 51 instruments with average credit spread over Libor of 32 basis points (bps) and an average weighted credit rating of Aa1. This portfolio is mostly concentrated in names belonging in the Sovereign, Banking, and asset-backed securities (ABS) sectors (they represent almost 88% of total portfolio value). The portfolio has the following distribution of weights by credit rating according to Table 5.

Applying the methodology described above to this portfolio, ie

❑ simulating correlated credit spreads according to Equation 1 for the next five years using 5,000 paths per credit curve at each time point (we used six-month intervals for simulation frequency). The number of paths in this example is fairly robust. Suggested stress testing of underlying parameters for simulation impacts the efficient frontier much more than doubling the number of paths or changing the seed. The critical point is that credit derivatives instruments used for hedging are evaluated on the same paths as the underlying portfolio – only this allows us to construct robust optimal hedging strategy;

❑ for a given path p and time t, we find an interval [L(K), U(K)] containing spread s(p,t) for that point. Based on the implied rating K, we find the respective row of the matrix (Figure 4), the ratio of downgrade to default probability in that row, and apply Equation 2 to find the diffusive component $\varphi(t)$ and rate of arrival of default $\varphi(t)$ at each time point and on every path;

❑ simulating the default event itself with this probability of default and assuming that in case default occurs the value of the investment falls down to the level of recovery rate, which in turn is picked out of historical or implied distribution;

❑ a diffusive component is used for discounting non-defaulted cashflows on the path in addition to credit risk free discounting;

we have found that the expected value of the portfolio is US$386 million. Because of all of the market uncertainties including yield curve and credit spread volatilities, possible downgrades and default, 1% of simulated outcomes falls below US$380 million. The difference (US$6 million) represents the integrated market (reinvestment, rating migration) and credit

Table 6 Suggested allocation by rating

Credit rating	Current portfolio		Optimal portfolio	
	Number of obligors	Size (%)	Number of obligors	Size (%)
Aaa	20	73.92	10	25.55
Aa1	3	2.15	18	23.88
Aa2	1	0.48	13	18.26
Aa3	5	2.62	17	20.40
A1	2	1.58	2	1.58
A2	5	3.79	5	3.79
A3	5	6.54	5	6.54
Baa1	4	2.69	–	–
Baa2	5	5.05	–	–
Baa3	1	0.66	–	–
Ba1	–	–	–	–
Ba2	1	0.53	–	–
Ba3	–	–	–	–
B1	–	–	–	–
B2	–	–	–	–
B3	–	–	–	–
Caa-C	–	–	–	–
Total	51	100	70	100

(possible defaults) risk. This is the economic capital requirement for the portfolio measured over a five-year horizon. Out of this US$6 million, US$3.7 million represents losses that occur due to defaults only, a number obtained from the default subset of all paths that resulted in defaults.

The average loss in the portfolio accumulated over the five-year horizon is US$0.5 million and the worst-case outcome (with 99% confidence interval) is US$4.2 million. So we can see that average portfolio rating does not reflect the tail risk.

An efficient frontier for this portfolio can be constructed either in the form specified in Figure 1 or using the 99% worst-case outcome as a risk measure (horizontal axis).

In order to build the frontier we need to find a modification of the current portfolio that will have the highest expected value for every level of required economic capital. Thus for each set of weights $\{w_1, w_2, ..., w_n\}$ (n is the number of all instruments that could be used for portfolio composition), we come up with a loss distribution that supplies both the algorithmically defined objective function (expected value) and constraint (required economic capital). The optimisation algorithm is described in detail in Gil, Polyakov (2003). It consists of jointly simulating the credit curves for the current obligors in the portfolio and the ones that can be possibly added to it. The initial weights for the latter ones are zeros. If some obligors do not have representative credit curves, they can be aggregated by industry and credit rating. Once possible losses of the underlying names are pre-computed, the loss distribution function can be constructed for each set of weights produced by the optimiser.

The tracking error representing the deviation from a given benchmark can be used as an additional constraint. In fact, this approach to analysing the absolute risk of the portfolio can be used to identify the right benchmark in the first place.

Implementation of the optimal solution should also consider investment guidelines and market and accounting constraints.

When we apply the optimisation algorithm to the above example in order to bring the portfolio to the highest return for the same level of risk, it proposes the following changes:

This recommendation significantly decreases both ends of the allocation distribution by credit ratings (Aaa and Baa and below) and suggests a reallocation of this portion of the portfolio into Aa category while increasing the portfolio granularity (from 51 to 70 names). That leads to an increase of the expected portfolio value to US$389 million and the 99% worst-case outcome to US$383 million, leaving economic capital requirements at the same level of US$6 million. The weighted average credit rating of the new portfolio falls down to Aa2 but average annualised spread increases to 50 bps, which proves again that the average credit rating of a portfolio doesn't adequately measure the entire distribution of risk. Figure 7

rioration and default events in the underlying asset pool. The securities issued by CDOs are tranched into classes that can be rated by the agencies. Detailed descriptions of CDO structures can be seen in Bluhm, Overbeck, Wagner (2003).

Buying a tranche of CDO is practically equivalent to selling protection to obtain synthetic exposure on a portion of the underlying pool. In recent years CDOs have received some bad publicity because of tranche deteriorations and downgrades. Some asset managers prefer to stay away from them despite tremendous diversification benefit and return enhancement that these products are offering. CDOs as an investment opportunity must be considered with extreme caution, though, because of their complexity and, additionally, because it is very difficult to identify the marginal impact of a CDO tranche on the overall portfolio.

In order to use CDOs to their full advantage, it is important to understand conceptually whether they are appropriate for one's investment profile. This means having the ability to analyse the risk of the tranche one plans to buy, not just on a standalone basis, but in the context of the overall portfolio. In most cases (at least up until the time of writing) CDOs are not liquid securities, being more appropriate for a buy-and-hold investor. When purchasing a CDO tranche, one has to significantly stress-test one's expectations of the future market environment and credit dynamics. It is important to be able to digest possible losses in one's portfolio and still be better off with this investment than without it (instead of hoping that one could sell one's investment if it started to deteriorate).

The methodology described in this chapter allows us to analyse credit risk and performance measures of CDO tranches (as well as other complex structured finance products) and their impact on the overall performance of the existing portfolio.

In order to do this in the most consistent manner, the entire collateral pool (or multiple pools) should be simulated simultaneously with the existing portfolio. This way all credit dynamics, implied increase in default correlations and overall possible concentrations of risk are taken into account. Then, on each path, at every point in time, the algorithm has to identify which losses belong to which tranche of each collateral pool and accumulate only the ones that the current portfolio is exposed to (or considers to acquire). At the same time all of the losses that come from the existing portfolio should be counted in full.

This will capture possible single-name exposure across all CDOs and the existing portfolio, take into account the degree of correlation among assets belonging to different industries and rating categories across all collateral pools and provide a comprehensive picture of the overall portfolio performance and of marginal impact of different CDO tranches on this performance. The resulting distribution can be used for detailed quantitative and qualitative comparison among different portfolio allocations.

In the considered example, a collection of mid-A-rated CDOs tranches of uncorrelated collateral pools can provide the transition to the described optimal portfolio if a portfolio manager obtains around US$30 million worth of such exposure.

To summarise, in order to effectively use credit derivatives for transitioning to an optimal portfolio, it is necessary to decide what risk tolerance is appropriate, to choose the respective position on the efficient frontier and then structure a credit derivatives instrument that allows a portfolio manager to arrive at that optimal position in the most efficient way; satisfying the constraints associated with investment guidelines, benchmark considerations and accounting and regulatory rules.

CONCLUSIONS

The proposed methodology demonstrates how to consistently evaluate market and credit risk and capital requirements for an existing portfolio and how to optimise them using credit derivatives. It allows us to analyse extreme (ie, tail) events consistently with the rest of the distribution. Such an approach for analysing portfolio risk is consistent with pricing of derivatives securities and allows us to quantify risk/return trade-off of different investment, hedging or return enhancement strategies. The loss distribution function enables investors to establish the benchmark criteria for the strategic portfolio rebalancing.

In the dynamic market environment, realised future trends could be far away from the projected ones. It is important to measure the entire distribution of portfolio values, as significant shifts of market trends (change in paradigm) can affect the tail distribution also. This approach allows for stress-testing of the underlying parameters while creating a transparent strategic methodology for weathering perfect storms.

1   See Gil, Polyakov (2003).
2   See Altman, Resti, Sironi, (2001).

BIBLIOGRAPHY

Altman, E., A. Resti and A. Sironi, 2001, "Analyzing and Explaining Default Recovery Rates", working paper (report submitted to ISDA).

Amner, Packer, working paper.

Basel Committee on Banking Supervision, 1988, "Internal Convergence of Capital Measurements and Capital Standards" (Basel: Bank for International Settlements).

Basel Committee on Banking Supervision, 1999a, "A New Capital Adequacy Framework" (Basel: Bank for International Settlements).

Basel Committee on Banking Supervision, 1999b, "Credit Risk Modelling: Current Practices and Applications" (Basel: Bank for International Settlements).

Bluhm, C., L. Overbeck and C. Wagner, 2003, *An Introduction to Credit Risk Modeling* (Chapman & Hall).

Brace, A., D. Gatarek and M. Musiela, 1997, "The market model of interest rate dynamics", *Mathematical Finance* 7(2), pp 127–55.

Black, F., and M. Scholes, 1973, "The pricing of options and corporate liabilities", *Journal of Political Economy* 81, pp 637–54.

Bohn, J.R., 1999, "A survey of contingent-claims approaches to risky debt valuation", working paper, June.

Credit Suisse Financial Products, 1997, "CreditRisk+, A Credit Risk Management Framework".

CreditMetrics, technical document, URL: http://www.riskmetrics.com/cmtdovv.html.

Das, S.R., 1995, "Credit risk derivatives", *Journal of Derivatives* 2(3), pp 7–23, Spring.

Das, S.R., and Peter Tufano, 1994, "Pricing credit-sensitive debt when interest rates, credit ratings and credit spreads are stochastic", working paper (Harvard Business School), December.

Das, S.R. (ed), 1998, "Credit Derivatives: Trading and Management of Credit and Default Risk" (New York, Chichester, Singapore: John Wiley & Sons).

Duffie, D., and K.J. Singleton, 1997, "An econometric model of the term structure of interest-rate swap yields", *Journal of Finance* 52(4), pp 1287–322.

Duffie, D., and K.J. Singleton, 1999, "Modeling term structures of defaultable bonds", *Review of Financial Studies* 12(4), pp 687–720.

O'Shea, S. Bonelli and R. Grossman, 2001, "Bank Loan and Bond Recovery Study: 1997-2001", Fitch, March.

Flesaker, B., L. Hughston, L. Schreiber and L. Sprung, 1994, "Taking all the credit". *Risk,* 7, pp 105–8.

Francis, J.C., J.A. Frost and J.G. Whittaker, 1999, *The Handbook of Credit Derivatives* (New York: McGraw-Hill).

Gil, A., and T. Klymchuk, 2002, "Derivatives Use", *Trading & Regulation* 7(4), pp 324–36.

Gil, A., and Y. Polyakov, 2003, "Integrating Market and Credit Risk In Fixed Income Portfolios", in S. Satchell and A. Scowcroft, *Advances in Portfolio Construction and Implementation* (Butterworth-Heinemann Finance).

Heath, D., R .Jarrow, and A. Morton, 1992, "Bond pricing and the term structure of interest rates: A new methodology for contingent claims valuation", *Econometrica* 60, pp 77–105.

Hull, J., and A. White, 2000, "Valuing Credit Default Swaps II: Modeling default correlations", working paper, April.

Jamshidian, F., 1997, "LIBOR and swap market models and measures", *Finance and Stochastics* 1(4), pp 293–330

Jarrow, R., and D. Madan, 1995, "Option pricing using the term structure of interest rates to hedge systematic discontinuities in asset returns", *Mathematical Finance* 5(4), pp 311–336.

Jarrow, R.A., and S.M. Turnbull, "Pricing derivatives on financial securities subject to credit risk", *Journal of Finance* 50, pp 53–85.

Jarrow, R.A., D. Lando and S.M. Turnbull, 1997, "A Markov model for the term structure of credit risk spreads", *Review of Financial Studies* 10(2), pp 481–523.

Hayne E.L., 1994, "Risky debt, bond covenants and optimal capital structure", *Journal of Finance* 49, pp 1213–52.

Kealhoffer, S., 1995, "Managing Default Risk in Derivative Portfolios", in D. Shimko (ed.), *Derivative Credit Risk: Advances in Measurement and Management* (London: Risk Books).

Kolyuoglu, II.U., and A. Hickman, 1998, "Reconcilable differences", *Risk*, October.

Longstaff, F., and E. Schwartz, 1995, "The pricing of credit risk derivatives", *Journal of Fixed Income* 5(1), pp 6–14, June.

Madan, D., and H. Unal, 1998, "Pricing the risks of default", *Review of Derivatives Research* 2(2/3), pp 121–60.

Mandelbrot, B., 1963, *Journal of Business*, 36, pp 394–419.

Merton, Robert C., 1974, "On the pricing of corporate debt: The risk structure of interest rates", *Journal of Finance* 29, pp 449–70.

Hamilton, D., G. Gupta and A. Berhault, 2001, "Default and Recovery Rates of Corporate Bond Issuers: 2000" (Moody's) February.

Wilson T., 1997, "Portfolio credit risk," *Risk* pp 111-17, September, pp 56–61, October.

Schönbucher, P.J., 1998, "Term structure modeling of defaultable bonds", Review of Derivatives Studies, special issue, *Credit Risk* 2(2/3), pp 161–92.

Schönbucher, P.J., 2000 (revised), "A LIBOR market model with default risk", working paper, original December 1999.

Vasicek, O., 1977, "An equilibrium characterisations of the term structure", *Journal of Financial Economics*, 5, pp 177–88.

Zhou, C., 1997, "A jump-diffusion approach to modeling credit risk and valuing defaultable securities", Finance and Economics Discussion Paper Series[MFE70], 1997/15 (Board of Governors of the Federal Reserve System), March.

Zhou, C., 1997, "Default Correlation: an analytical result", Finance and Economics Discussion Paper Series, 1997/15 (Board of Governors of the Federal Reserve System), May.

Section 3

Structured Credit Derivatives

Introduction

Jon Gregory

BNP Paribas

In the last section, we discussed portfolio credit risk and the impact of default correlation. Now we move on to tackle the products that have formed a very large part of the credit derivatives market, namely collateralised debt obligations or CDOs. As with basket default swaps, the risks of these products are very sensitive to default correlation. CDO structures allow investors to gain leveraged exposure to a diversified pool of assets (and perhaps sectors they would otherwise not have access to) as well as potentially benefiting from the skills of an asset manager. Some transactions are motivated by arbitrage while others are driven by balance-sheet management. The basic idea of a CDO is that a pool of cash or synthetic credit exposures is divided into tranches (usually at least three), to give a set of exposures with new risk/return characteristics, which are sold to parties either in cash or synthetic form. **Eileen Murphy** of **Barclay's Capital** begins this section by giving an overview of the CDO market, charting its development and evolution, describing the major participants in the market and looking at the various types of structures. These structures will then be analysed in greater detail in subsequent chapters.

The CDO market has developed thanks to the application of securitisation techniques, allowing banks to sell portfolios of various types of debt. The traditional method of securitisation, involving the actual transfer of assets to an SPV, is more complex. Synthetic securitisation, allowing the transfer of risk on debt instruments via credit derivatives, offers many advantages. Under Basel I, corporate credit risk (bonds, loans and other credit facilities) carries an 8% capital charge irrespective of its credit quality and maturity. Banks have therefore obtained regulatory capital relief by transferring lower-yielding assets that require the same capital but generate lower returns off their balance sheet. The first CDO structures involved the actual transfer of the underlying assets to an SPV, which then issued notes backed by the cashflows on this portfolio. Increasingly, however, CDSs have been used to transfer the credit risk to the SPV synthetically. The first such transaction of this type was JP Morgan's BISTRO in 1997. Aside from balance-sheet CDOs, the other main class of transactions is the so-called arbitrage deals. Since the rating of a particular tranche determines largely the spread that must be paid in the market for this risk, there is a potential for the originator to exploit the difference between this and the spread that can be earned on the underlying port-folio. This spread difference between assets and liabilities is maximised by choosing the widest spreads available for each given rating (although this is of course almost certainly not in the interests of the investor) while maintaining a reasonably well-diversified pool of credits overall.

Paul Hawkins of **Merrill Lynch** compares synthetic and cash CDO structures, discussing the advantages of synthetic deals such as speed, funding considerations, improved yields and lower fees. The variety of asset classes used for both types of these securitisations is discussed, from loans or CDSs to mortgage and asset-backed securities. CDO tranches are commonly rated by one or more rating agencies to give investors the confi-dence in their future performance based on a statistical analysis of the component cashflows. It is important to understand how rating agencies arrive at ratings for tranches of portfolio transactions. All agencies will review the unique characteristics of each pool starting with the rating of underlying assets (if available) and working through other major issues, such as recovery assumptions and any structural factors, such as subordi-nation, that help protect a rating. Defaults and recoveries are stressed as a reflection of the uncertainty of the historical data. Rating agency approaches are discussed in several of the chapters in this section and also later on in Chapter 20. The rating agencies have an important role in giving investors an impartial assessment regarding the relative safety or risk of what is a rather complex product. This chapter also compares and contrasts the different rating agency methodologies. This is important, as there are substantial differences between the rating agencies: for example, Moody's considers the expected loss to be the main indicator while Standard & Poor's and Fitch consider only the default probability without taking into account the expected recovery rate, which can potentially be quite high.

Next, **Moorad Choudhry** of **KBC Financial Products** takes a closer look at synthetic CDO structures, from an investor and issuer perspective, giving examples of the various types, for instance, funded versus unfunded, balance sheet and arbitrage and single tranche. The author includes case studies of some innovative transactions that illustrate the rapid progression of the CDO market over the past few years. A detailed analysis of such structures should allow the reader to become well acquainted with the most important features of such transactions. This chapter also proposes a new structure as a clue to the next generation of products. This product aims to be flexible in terms of the asset and liability structure (cash and synthetic) and thus affords the maximum flexibility in term of structuring and could appeal to a wider range of investors

In the earlier days of the CDO market, static deals predominated. Static portfolios would be selected at the start of the transaction (or during some ramp-up period) and then would not change over time. Lately, managed deals have become more popular (at least for arbitrage structures, as balance-sheet transactions are not investor-driven) as explained by **Alexander Batchvarov, Jenna Collins** and **William Davies** of **Merrill Lynch**, who also give more perspectives on the cash-versus-synthetic topic in this context. Such transactions are managed to a greater or lesser degree by a third-party asset manager who has the aims of maximising returns and/or minimising losses. The management may be extremely active or involve only a few substitutions, and the asset manager may be limited to a certain percentage of the portfolio (the trading bucket) or certain types of trading such as credit improvement trades. Managed CDOs have become popular more recently, perhaps due to the relatively large number of credit events that have impacted static pools. The collateral manager will normally retain a share of the first loss or equity piece, which may help to avoid adverse selection issues. Unlike a static deal, a managed transaction affords the opportunity to substitute a name before it has a bad effect on the pool or to participate in relative value type trading. However, if the portfolio is already well diversified, it is perhaps questionable to what value an asset manager can add to the structure, given the additional costs this will introduce.

Ideal assets for securitising via a CDO are those that are of investment grade, provide a high-spread income, are relatively illiquid and add a reasonable level of diversification. This makes CDO tranches themselves potential candidates for inclusion in new CDO structures as described by **Darren Smith** of **Dresdner Kleinwort Wasserstein**. This chapter outlines the potential value of so-called "CDOs of CDOs" and describes applications of CDO-of-CDO technology. Not only do investors have the benefit of improved diversification, but they also gain from two levels of subordination, as there is first-loss protection embedded in the constituent structures. The CDO-of-CDO product presents a significant challenge for modelling, as the underlying loss distribution is a rather complex function of the individual losses. Some of the potential approaches to modelling are explained, including rating-agency approaches, which, the author argues, are conservative in terms of their treatment of the diversification. However, it is not easy to understand or capture the dependencies and complex dynamics inherent to this type of product. A Monte Carlo type of approach, where underlying default times are modelling and then the overall payoff is determined by losses flowing from constituent CDOs to the CDO-of-CDO tranche, would seem to be the best one.

A tranche of a CDO will normally promise a higher yield than that of an equivalently rated corporate. This is some recognition that these portfolio structures may be inherently more risky. Indeed, the joint effects of (correlated) credit-rating changes are implicitly not taken account of. This could mean that a CDO tranche with a small expected loss could nevertheless have an unusually high chance of being downgraded. It is not clear whether the large number of downgrades of CDO tranches recently is due simply to the relatively high number of corporate defaults or whether the structures themselves are inherently more risky. The tightening spreads in the first half of 2003 together with the relatively large number of downgrades (and no upgrades) have created difficult conditions for the development of the CDO market.

The risk on a CDO tranche depends on the loss distribution of the underlying portfolio, which defines the probability of all possible future losses up to a given point in time. This distribution depends on individual default probabilities and recoveries, but also (as discussed in Chapter 6 in the last section) rather critically on the default correlation, which is a measure of the diversification (or lack of it) in the portfolio. This latter point is extremely important, as a senior tranche on a well-diversified portfolio should be far less risky than if the portfolio were highly correlated. The rating agencies employ models to combine the individual statistics of each name in the pool, via some correlation assumptions to estimate the portfolio loss distribution and also the rating on a tranche. As we saw above, there are significant differences between the major rating agencies' models (Moody's, S&P's and Fitch) in terms of default statistics and correlation assumptions. The rating agencies are making a concerted effort to improve their models for computation of portfolio loss distribution. For example, Moody's have applied Fourier transform to facilitate fast computations similar to the ideas that have been applied in some proprietary valuation models as described in the first chapter of the next section. A potential worry with CDOs is that numerous deals have been packaged and sold to relatively small institutions. It is not clear whether investors clearly understand the structures and their associated risks and more analysis of actual losses and better tools for assessing portfolio credit risk should aid transparency on these points. Furthermore, rather than reply solely on the rating agencies' assessment of credit worthiness, investors should be encouraged to form their own quantitative and qualitative assessments of the real value of the product. Such confidence and understanding from the buy side of the market can only help in the development of an increasingly sophisticated product range of portfolio credit risk transactions.

BIBLIOGRAPHY

Bund, S., M. Neugebauer and K. Gill, 2003, "Global Rating Criteria for Collateralised Debt Obligations", Fitch Ratings Structured Finance, Criteria Report, July.

Bund, S., M. van der Weijden and M. Lench, 2001, "European SME CDOs: an Investor's Guide to Analysis and Performance", Fitch, Ibca, Duff and Phelps European Structured Finance Special Report, October.

Cifuentes, A. and G. O'Connor, 1996, "The Binomial Expansion Method Applied to CBO/CLO Analysis", Moody's Investors Service Global Credit Research, December.

Debuysscher, A. and M. Szegö, 2003, "The Fourier Transform Method – Technical Document", Moody's Investors Service International Structured Finance Working Paper, January. "Global Cash Flow and Synthetic CDO Criteria", 2002, Standard & Poor's Structured Finance, March.

Turnbull, S., A, Jackson and K. Gill, 2002, "Global Rating Criteria for Synthetic CDOs", Fitch Ratings Structured Finance Credit Products/Europe Special Report, September. "Using Standard & Poor's CDO Evaluator 2.0", 2003, Standard & Poor's Structured Finance, January.

Yoshizawa Y., 2003, "Moody's Approach to Rating Synthetic Collateralised Debt Obligations", Moody's Special Report.

9

Overview of the CDO market

Eileen Murphy

Barclays Capital

INTRODUCTION

Collateralised debt obligations (CDOs) represent one of the fastest-growing segments of the structured finance world and are sometimes lumped together with asset backed securities (ABSs). However, there are several fundamental differences between CDOs and ABSs. CDOs allow for the pooling and retranching of credit risk with pools that are almost always much lumpier than their ABS cousins and with structures that can be tailored to a particular asset class, pool or manager. The flexibility of the CDO product has important repercussions in terms of understanding the product and in determining which analytical methods are best used to evaluate them. Accordingly, analytical approaches must move away from an actuarial method to one that recognises the heterogeneous nature of the pools.

Any evaluation of CDOs must also take into account that CDOs represent the far end of the continuum that begins with single-name default trades, continues with baskets of possible defaults and finally goes to the extreme of those rare CDOs that have thousands of underlying credits. Finally, CDOs, unlike ABS transactions, usually have an asset manager actively buying and selling assets in the pool due to credit and diversification concerns.

NOMENCLATURE

The generic term *collateralised debt obligation* refers to a variety of structured transactions that resemble a closed-end mutual fund and have an underlying exposure to a variety of debt capital market instruments, including some underlying assets that are not at all debt in nature. *Collateralised bond obligation* (CBO) or *collateralised loan obligation* (CLO) refers to such pools containing bonds or loans, respectively, which bankers tranche to distribute credit risk in order to provide optimal funding for an issuer or to tailor exposures to investor demand. As assets have evolved, new acronyms have appeared to describe them including, for example, CDOs that contain exposures to private equity. This chapter will cover most of these variants with the assurance that new structures and exposures will continue to appear. The one constant of the CDO market we can all be sure to observe is its inexorable tendency to evolve continuously.

Background

The illustration in Figure 1 shows a special purpose vehicle (SPV) that has issued multiple classes of rated debt to finance the purchase of a pool of assets. The premise underlying CDOs is that the interest and principal generated by a pool of assets will be more than adequate to pay liabilities issued by the issuer sequentially starting with the senior-most class of debt and ending with an unrated equity or first-loss tranche.

EVOLUTION OF THE PRODUCT ON THE ASSET SIDE

CDO transactions have a provenance that belies their usefulness and flexibility in allocating resources and providing risk capital to many different markets. The earliest CDO transactions arose during the final days of the house of Drexel. In fact, high-yield bonds sold by Drexel to a financial institution comprised the assets in the Long Run Bond transaction executed in 1988, which was the first CBO ever rated by Moody's Investors Service. Milken discovered the theoretical underpinnings for the CBO product while still in undergraduate school. There he began his fascination with below-investment-grade bonds. He read a study written by W Braddock Hickman of below-investment-grade bonds from 1919 to 1945,

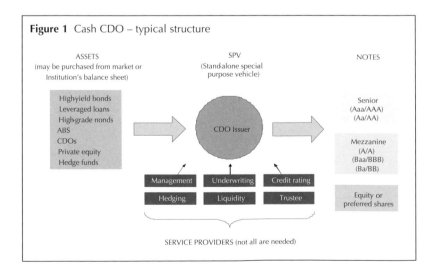

Figure 1 Cash CDO – typical structure

ASSETS
(may be purchased from market or
Institution's balance sheet)

SPV
(Stand-alone special
purpose vehicle)

NOTES

Highyield bonds
Leveraged loans
Highgrade nonds
ABS
CDOs
Private equity
Hedge funds

CDO Issuer

Senior
(Aaa/AAA)
(Aa/AA)

Mezzanine
(A/A)
(Baa/BBB)
(Ba/BB)

Management　Underwriting　Credit rating

Hedging　Liquidity　Trustee

Equity or
preferred shares

SERVICE PROVIDERS (not all are needed)

which demonstrated that diversified pools of high-yield bonds would outperform similar pools of investment-grade debt without any greater risk. This thesis was confirmed by a later study in the 1960s as well.

Other early transactions were composed entirely of leveraged loans. In 1990, Chancellor Senior Secured Management began the first of a line of early CLOs named ROSA. These structures were relatively simple in terms of tranching and not all sought Aaa ratings for the most senior class of debt. Not long after the ROSA structures developed, hybrid transactions containing both bond bonds and loan appeared in the market.

The first CDO of emerging market assets took place in 1995 with the issuance of the IFC's Latin American and Asian Loan Trust. The CDO market developed slowly as a relatively unknown part of the private placement market until 1996 and 1997 when large bank balance sheet transactions began to appear in the UK and the US and added significantly to volume. In the years following, every conceivable loan type found its way into CLOs, whether such loans were term, revolver, secured, unsecured, syndicated, bilateral or middle market in nature. Issuance volume increased significantly as the chart in Figure 2 shows.

There was a significant increase in CDO issuance in 1996 as investors welcomed a wave of transactions, including the first pool of emerging market assets managed by a private sector asset manager. Market value transactions also made their entrance. Then, in 1997, some investment banks introduced synthetic baskets into structures as well as including provisions for inclusion of structured finance securities in limited amounts. The appearance of transactions that would be entirely composed of structured finance securities or fully synthetic would not be far behind.

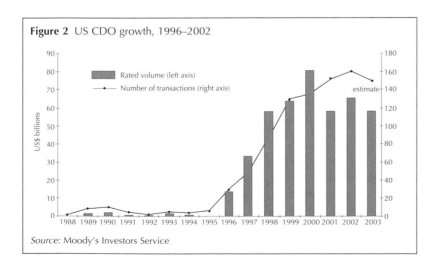

Figure 2 US CDO growth, 1996–2002

Source: Moody's Investors Service

The Glacier transaction structured by SBC Warburg in 1997 featured credit linked notes (CLNs) to transfer the risk of a pool of borrowers to an SPV. JP Morgan's BISTRO product appeared soon thereafter. A detailed discussion of synthetic CDOs can be found in Chapter 10.

The search for assets with appropriate spread that would also provide diversifying exposures led to project finance loans being placed on the structurer's desk and into transactions in 1998. The first CDO of CDO assets took place in 1999 with the ZAIS Investment Grade Limited transaction. Chapter 11 contains further information regarding CDOs built from CDO assets. CDOs of ABS, or "resecuritisation" transactions, quickly followed this development. In resecuritisations, a wide variety of structured finance assets, including ABSs, MBSs and commercial mortgage backed securities (CMBSs), would be pooled together, perhaps with a portion of REIT paper. Other noteworthy assets found in CDO pools include distressed assets, trust preferred stock and forfeit paper. Each different type of asset requires a careful examination of rating criteria and assumptions to be sure that the methodology and risk manager keeps up with market developments.

In Europe, asset transfer issues and the desire for confidentiality led to an emphasis on synthetic transactions rather than cash. Cash transactions involving European high-yield and investment-grade debt flourished during the peak of the internet IPO bubble. The high-yield transactions have largely ceased issuance. European SME transactions containing loans to small and medium-sized enterprises have remained popular with investors and issuers alike. The option to transfer credit risk through default swaps has great value and tremendous room for growth. However, investors and issuers need to be cognisant of the additional risks to which one can be exposed with these structures. Chapter 1 provides a valuable overview of the topic which should be read heeding the notes of

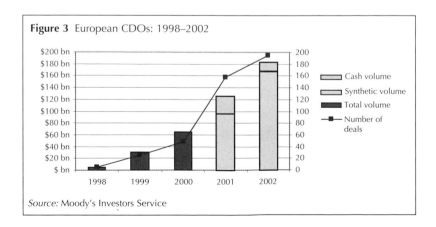

Figure 3 European CDOs: 1998–2002

Cash volume
Synthetic volume
Total volume
Number of deals

Source: Moody's Investors Service

caution expressed by Jesper Andreasen in his chapter "Dynamite dynamics". In Asia, local currency CDOs have become widely accepted by investors who can avoid the cost or risk of investing in foreign currency transactions, while they also avoid assets from economies that they may not understand or trust to the same extent as those found within their own country or region.

The CDO structurer's art and powers of negotiation with the rating agencies have been most recently put to the test in securitisations of private equity and hedge fund exposures, which have been slowly gaining acceptance among some CDO investors. The key consideration for these transactions is the availability and suitability of data covering private equity or funds of funds. The next wave of transactions would appear to be CDOs of insurance exposures following along the same lines as the trust preferred market for banks.

One final development that bears close scrutiny would be the advent of single-tranche collateralised synthetic obligations (CSOs), wherein an investor chooses a pool of reference assets by themselves or pursuant to negotiation with a banker, who then tailors a specific liability exposure for the investor. The arranger then retains the remainder of the risk and either distributes other "tranches", if possible, to other investors or retains the residual risk and dynamically hedges the structure in the dealer's trading book. Time will tell whether investors and bankers have adequately intensified and controlled the credit and market risks embedded in these structures.

Evolution of the product on the liability side

The liability side of CDOs was considerably simpler in early transactions. Typically, there would be only one or two rated tranches in addition to an equity class, which often had a cap on payments. The ratings sought for the earlier structures would often not include an Aaa tranche and rarely a below-investment-grade tranche. By 1995, many transactions had multiple layers of debt (including Aaa) above an equity tranche. In 1996, structures with ratings for a minimum coupon appeared, allowing for higher ratings with reduced promises that were utilised for some liabilities in the structures. With the integration of ABS investors and structurers into the CDO market in the years following 1997, an ever-increasing number of tranches, mirroring the multi-tranched nature of some ABS structures, appeared in some underwriters' transactions.

More recent developments include that underwriters have at times adjusted liabilities to match the revolving nature of assets. Others have designed variable funding notes and money market tranches for some of their transactions.

TAXONOMY: CLASSIFICATION BY SOURCE OF REPAYMENT, ISSUER MOTIVATION OR EXECUTION

Source of repayment: cashflow versus market value transactions

Most CDOs are cashflow transactions where the focus is on the sufficiency of cashflows generated by underlying assets, notwithstanding assumed defaults in the pools. As so well demonstrated by the variety of assets discussed above, the same creativity used in sourcing assets needs to be used when including assets in structures. As a general matter, as long as an asset produces some predictable cashflow, it can be included in a pool.

Market value transactions focus on the market value of the underlying assets in comparison to the liabilities for the issuer. These transactions rely on haircuts for illiquidity and market volatility to ensure payment of liabilities when matured. Market value structures rely at the same time on the assumption that you can trade assets that become impaired or at least become worrisome for a manager. While these transactions appear to have much greater enhancement relative to other CDOs, this may be counterbalanced in the minds of some by their exposure to the vagaries of the market coupled with the need for the manager not only correctly to assess the credit calls but also to stay on top of other market movements across multiple asset classes. This is a balancing act requiring a skill set that few managers or organisations can consistently deliver.

Market value structures are most appropriate for assets that do not generate predictable cashflows or where managers want very broad trading flexibility not just in terms of discretionary trading but also in order to move opportunistically entirely out of one asset class to another, which is not possible in cashflow transactions. Another contrast to cashflow transactions is that market value transactions normally have bullet maturities rather than amortising structures.

Issuer motivations: balance sheet versus arbitrage transactions

The preponderance of CDOs are arbitrage transactions, which means the transaction is driven by the existence of a difference between the return earned on assets compared with that paid on the issuance of primarily investment-grade liabilities. Spread earned on assets that do not carry ratings as high as most of the liabilities and presumably pay higher coupons, can more than compensate for the costs of issuance and payment of manager fees while also providing a return that is sufficient enough to attract investment. Obviously, the greater the spread between asset and liabilities, the higher the potential profit for the equity.

CDO issuers can be motivated by many different factors. The most common include transactions driven by collateral managers seeking to increase assets under management (and therefore fees) as well as balance sheet trades driven by the desire to achieve diversification/reduce over-concentrations or address regulatory arbitrage or economic capital concerns.

Balance sheet transactions have almost always been the focus of financial institutions. These trades may be executed by selling assets from the balance sheet in cash form or through synthetic transfer where assets remain on the balance sheet but credit risk is transferred through CLNs or CDSs. The reason for such sales may be due to anything from prudential concerns regarding over concentration of risk to a single name to more onerous reasons, such as concern over credit deterioration or even exiting a relationship with a borrower altogether. Synthetic transactions also allow one to disaggregate funding from credit since it is often possible to fund more economically at one entity while the credit risk is actually held elsewhere. Some of the issues arising from balance sheet transactions have been the thin amounts of equity layers, adverse selection in collateral pools and large quantities of unrated assets requiring "mapping" of internal systems to external methodologies, particularly outside the US.

Execution: cash versus synthetic

The major difference between cash and synthetic CDOs is the use of credit derivatives in the synthetic structures. The reason for the use of credit derivatives may be that the desired credit cannot be obtained in the cash market or for confidentiality or legal reasons, a cash sale is not feasible. The transfer could be achieved in funded form using CLNs, or unfounded form using CDSs. Figure 4 depicts a typical synthetic CDO structure.

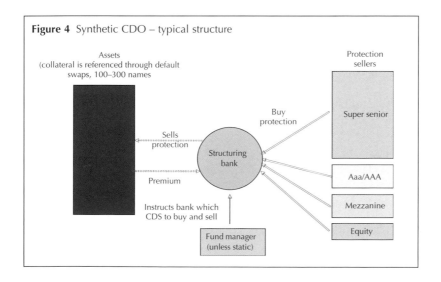

Figure 4 Synthetic CDO – typical structure

Manager involvement: managed versus static

While most cashflow CDOs are actively managed pursuant to a predetermined set of rules, there is a subset of transactions that either has limited management activity or is static. The advantage of static transactions over managed would be that there is no fee paid to a manager. However, many investors found this to have been painful when assets showed clear signs of deterioration and there was no mechanism to sell or replace them. A middle ground has been found in transactions like the Orix CDO, which uses a qualifying special purpose entity (QSPE) structure providing for application of a pre-determined set of rules as if a manager were there to sell credit once pre-determined triggers or deterioration takes place.

Rating methodologies and assumptions

All of the rating agencies active in the CDO market seek to assist investors in the product by expressing their assessment regarding the relative safety or risk of a CDO tranche. Whether they express that opinion in terms of expected loss or as the point of first US dollar of loss, this judgement is the end result of quantitative stresses, including simulation in some cases, as well as more qualitative factors such as review of documentation and operational and credit reviews of the collateral manager.

All agencies will review the unique characteristics of each pool starting with the rating of underlying assets (if available) and working through other major issues such as recovery assumptions and any structural mitigants that may help protect a rating. Defaults and recoveries as well as timing are stressed as a reflection of the uncertainty as to whether each agency's unique historical data may or may not be observed during the life of the pool. An in-depth review of the approaches adopted by each of the agencies should be obtained directly from each of them, as such details are beyond the scope of an overview chapter. However, rating agency approaches have been included for several of the CDO subcategories discussed in the chapters immediately following this introduction.

It should be noted that, in the indenture for each transaction, issuers agree to maintain certain coverage tests for par and interest as well as minimum assumptions used in evaluating individual credits in the pools, as well as satisfying portfolio tests.

Market participants

No overview of the market would be complete without a discussion of the major participants in the CDO market. Primary among these would be investors and managers.

Investors range from senior note investors, such as banks and structured investment vehicles (SIVs), who are looking for spread with a high certainty of repayment, to mezzanine investors, who may be hedge funds or other CDOs looking for higher spread with some risk to return of principal, all the way to equity or first-loss investors, who seek leveraged returns in exchange for much higher risk to principal. In addition to receiving all excess spread in structures, equity investors also have an option to call transactions after a specified period of time, which may become quite valuable over time. CDO investors often invest in transactions as a way to outsource management of exposures needed for the investor without having to make the commitment for staff and resources that might be beyond its reach. CDOs permit investors also to gain exposure to assets that would not otherwise be accessible, or might even be impermissible in a different form.

CDO asset managers can range from the largest banks globally (as issuers) or well-established asset managers to boutique firms that only manage structured finance assets, or only utilise CDO structures for the assets they manage. The motivation for most asset managers is to lock up assets under management and also capture the fees such assets would generate. As a practical matter, CDO managers may be removed pursuant to the terms of the collateral management agreement negotiated among the investors manager and the investment bank. Such removal typically would be related to performance problems but could also be for no reason at all if the necessary note is obtained from the deal investors.

Monolines

Monoline insurance companies provide financial guarantees to bonds issued in the CDO market. Their presence, which provides external credit enhancement, can mean the difference between a transaction being issued or not. As such, monoline insurers can command a fair amount of attention in the structuring and documentation of a CDO. Monolines will assess the strength of a manager and can often negotiate broad power to manage alongside or replace a manager who has underperformed. Even where a monoline does not exert control rights in a structure, they will review and comment extensively on the structure and documentation.

Rating agencies

Even more critical than the monolines are the rating agencies that are responsible for setting the criteria for a transaction and to a large extent enforcing the rules of the indenture and other documents agreed to by the parties. The agencies will conduct a thorough review of the manager's qualifications, experience and systems before approving a transaction. If a rating agency is not satisfied with the terms of a transaction, an issuer may have to restructure a transaction or give it up completely. Once a transaction is issued, a rating agency will actively monitor its progress and will take rating activity consistent with the terms of the indenture and other documents, as well as the agency's unique view concerning a structure of CDO market developments generally.

Trustees

Every CDO transaction has a trustee, which represents the rights of the note holders in a transaction. The trustee must be a third party with the systems and technical expertise to assist the rating agencies, asset manager and investors in ensuring that the terms of all agreements have been adhered to. CDO trustees receive compensation well in excess of amounts paid to ABS trustees and there is a correspondingly higher expectation of proactive, professional oversight.

Vendors

The incredible growth of the CDO market has produced opportunities for data and professional service providers to specialise in the CDO product. From bond trustees to data service providers, the quest for greater transparency and the development of a secondary market in CDO paper has resulted in greater availability of CDO transaction information in a form accessible to any person considering investing in such deals. Obtaining all the details regarding a transaction can be very difficult without offering materials and updated trustee reports. It is no longer necessary to own CDO paper in order to get some of this information about individual transactions. There is a growing subset of CDOs for which information is available publically including cashflow information on third party databases. While much room for improvement exists, vendors will continue to refine the effectiveness and thereby broaden the reach of their products, which should help to expand the CDO investor universe.

CDO secondary activity

In the early days of the CDO market, very little trading of CDO liabilities took place and it most often involved senior note sales. The market dislocation of late 1998, culminating in LTCM's demise, seriously dampened a nascent CDO trading market. This market has slowly rebuilt itself around the efforts of several firms including Lehman Brothers, Bear Stearns, Merrill Lynch and Morgan Stanley. Industry sources estimate US$5 billion in CDO paper traded in 2002, with another US$10 billion having changed hands by the middle of 2003. Since visibility is limited in this market due to its private placement nature, it is hard to accurately gauge the depth of the market. There is no exchange or clearing house for this product, due to the unique characteristics of each CDO and the lack of uniformity in strucure and documentation. It should be noted that since 2002 there have been times when an overhang of secondary product seriously impacted the primary market by taking investing capacity and attention away from the new issue. This is understandable since secondary product in the CDO market often has an attractive pricing profile especially when a seller is forced or impatient.

As the CDO market has increased in size, increasing numbers of vendors have worked to develop systems to facilitate the review and trading of CDOs. The proliferation and affordability of technology with which to perform the simulations and cash flow modelling necessary to adequately evaluate the quantitative aspects of these structures has greatly enhanced investor comfort in purchasing and selling CDOs in the secondary market. Increased transparency of rating methodologies and asset information has also been a catalyst for growth. The secondary market will continue to grow as investors prune, upgrade or diversify their book of CDO exposures. Finally, as new classes of investors such as hedge funds become more firmly involved with the product, it is only natural that the trading of CDOs will become more frequent, since the funds will have the capital and an existing comfort with trading and the risk aspects of trading, what has been, quite illiquid paper.

10

Synthetic securitisation and structured portfolio credit derivatives

Paul Hawkins

Merrill Lynch

INTRODUCTION

The single name, credit default swap (CDS) market trades expected loss (EL), is well-established and is increasingly liquid and standardised. The market for small basket transactions, referencing multiple entities, is growing and diverse. With first, second and nth to default structures, products exist to trade and transfer correlation risk.

Pricing and trading portfolio credit risk is a more complex undertaking. Transactions are individually tailored with a large choice of structural, portfolio and tranching alternatives. Portfolio transactions trade complex correlation and loss combinations.

While single name CDSs pay in the event of credit losses from a single reference entity, small baskets and large portfolios reference multiple entities. The payoff, often called the cash settlement amount, is determined by a formula. The cash settlement amount may include all losses from any reference entity, or it may be defined as losses from the first or second entity to default. In large portfolios it is more common to calculate cash settlement amounts on a tranche, that is, losses between some subordination threshold and some upper band (sometimes called attachment and detachment points).

A securitisation is a repackaging of future cashflows in order to raise cash or transfer risk. For the purpose of this chapter, we use the slightly narrower definition of a securitisation as a repackaging of debt instruments into a tranched structure. Classical cash securitisation involves the sale of the instruments, often to a special purpose vehicle (SPV). In a synthetic securitisation, the risk transfer is instead achieved by means of a credit derivative, usually a portfolio CDS. The reference obligations under the portfolio CDS are the debt instruments in the reference portfolio, so cash settlement amounts are payable on the CDS if losses occur on the reference portfolio, above a certain threshold.

The use of credit derivative instruments for synthetic securitisations is becoming increasingly popular as an investment – or capital and risk management – technique for a number of asset classes. There is no sale or purchase of the underlying debt instruments. Instead, the assets' owner retains them on its balance sheet and continues to be the legal owner of the portfolio; alternatively, the underlying portfolio is not owned by any party but is constructed purely synthetically. The arranger or originator buys portfolio-CDS protection against the credit losses in the asset portfolio, effectively transferring the risk without selling the assets. Rating agencies tranche the portfolio using their established methodologies.

A synthetic securitisation transaction can be a partially funded public deal involving the issuance of listed notes, bringing publicity for the originator or arranger. Alternatively, the transaction can be a private deal involving risk transfer exclusively through portfolio CDS or privately placed notes.

This chapter will focus on portfolio risk transfer, investigating motivations for trading and hedging portfolio credit risk. It will also describe the trading, modelling and pricing of portfolio risk transfer using synthetic securitisation, with a particular focus on rating agency methodologies. It will also look at example transactions.

SYNTHETIC AND CASH SECURITISATION
Development of synthetic securitisation
The technology to execute synthetic transactions has been developed relatively recently. The credit derivatives market began to develop in the mid- to late-1990s, with CDSs and total return swaps referencing single credits or reference obligations. The first trades to reference multiple credits followed, and then in the late 1990s, the first large portfolio transactions were executed. The early credit derivatives market consisted largely of private over-the-counter transactions; many of the early portfolio trades followed this pattern.

Meanwhile, the cash securitisation market was already well-developed. Credit card and mortgage securitisations, especially in the US, had been executed for many years; in many areas, they were highly standardised by the mid-1990s. The collateralised debt obligation (CDO) market was at that time growing strongly. A CDO is a securitisation of loans or bonds, and by that time increasing numbers of portfolios of bonds and loans had been securitised in cash format. These were typically public transactions for arbitrage purposes, with portfolios managed by some third party. The junior portion was placed to investors driven by minimum return requirements, while the senior tranches were placed to capital-markets bond investors.

By the late 1990s, the credit derivative market was developing with increasingly complex transactions. Trades were executed for baskets of reference obligations, sometimes with payments linked to the first or second name to default in the basket.

In 1998 and 1999, the two separate product groups of securitisation and credit derivatives met with fully tranched portfolio structures that were similar in profile to securitisations, but with credit derivative risk transfer mechanisms. A groundbreaking European balance sheet synthetic was CStar, which referenced a €4 billion portfolio of loans on Citibank's balance sheet in 1999. These transactions were often motivated by banks wishing to manage their balance sheet – eg, in terms of capital requirements.

At the same time as the first transactions were being executed for balance sheet purposes, a growing number of synthetic CDOs were being executed by investors seeking high returns. These transactions continued to be mainly private, often executed under programs such as Bistro or Taurus.

Since that time, the market has developed with increasing numbers of more standard transactions – eg, under the Promise and Provide programs. Promise and Provide are sponsored by the German agency KfW for balance sheet securitisation of loans to small- and medium-sized enterprises. New structural features have developed for both arbitrage and balance sheet securitisations, and recent times have seen the advent of single tranche arbitrage synthetics and new asset classes for balance sheet deals.

Figure 1 shows the development of public cash and synthetic securitisa-

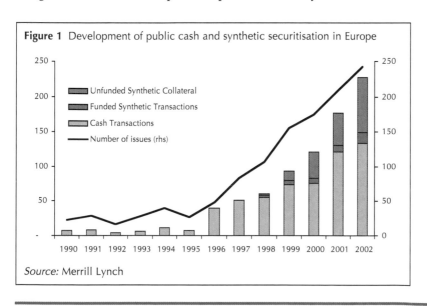

Figure 1 Development of public cash and synthetic securitisation in Europe

Source: Merrill Lynch

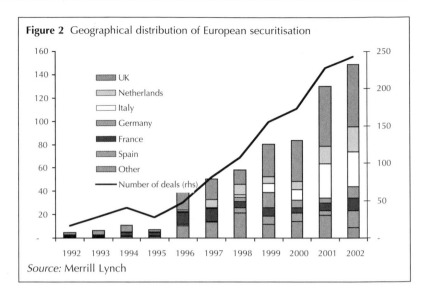

Figure 2 Geographical distribution of European securitisation

Source: Merrill Lynch

tion in Europe over the past 12 years and illustrates the huge growth of synthetic securitisations. This continued in 2002 with growth of above 68% in synthetic transactions. This consisted of 70% growth in unfunded synthetic and 61% growth of funded synthetic. Synthetic transactions grew to represent 41% of transactions in 2002.

Synthetic securitisations have been executed over a wide variety of asset classes and geographies. By way of illustration, we show the overall development of securitisation business by country, together with the latest breakdown by underlying asset class.

While there are some differences between the distribution of cash and synthetic transactions, the UK remains the most important market overall, with 36% of European issuance volume in 2002 (see Figure 2). However, the Spanish market is now the fastest growing – in 2002, a growth rate of over 200% reached 9% of overall European issuance volume. In the same year, German issuance doubled its annual volume, growing to represent 6% of overall European issuance volume.

The sector breakdown for European securitisations is shown in Figure 3. Year-to-year growth in 2002 was highest in MBS, which is rather more dominated by cash issuance, and which increased more than 45% from US$47 billion in 2001 to US$68 billion in 2002.

Characteristics of cash and synthetic securitisation
It is useful to contrast some features of synthetic securitisations and cash securitisations. Cash transactions are relatively complicated, due to factors such as the complexity of transferring the assets into an SPV. The legal work involved in completing a transfer can be relatively easy for publicly

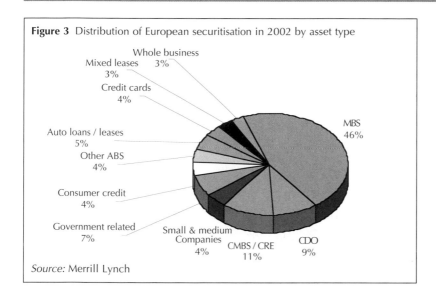

Figure 3 Distribution of European securitisation in 2002 by asset type

Whole business 3%
Mixed leases 3%
Credit cards 4%
Auto loans / leases 5%
Other ABS 4%
Consumer credit 4%
Government related 7%
Small & medium Companies 4%
CMBS / CRE 11%
CDO 9%
MBS 46%

Source: Merrill Lynch

traded bonds, but can be far more complex for loans requiring significant due diligence or consent from the borrowers. On the other hand, the assets need to be transferred to the SPV by means of a true sale, in order to ring-fence them from the seller. This means that all the cashflows are transferred, a process made lengthier by the analysis and modelling of the more complex cashflows. The issues become even more pronounced if the portfolio is multi-jurisdictional or has assets with different maturity profiles, interest types or currencies.

Synthetic securitisation addresses these issues with greater flexibility. This is due to the risk transfer being accomplished through a credit derivative instead of a true sale. The underlying assets remain on the balance sheet of the buyer of protection, or are not required to be held at all. There is no need for borrower consent, and the legal due diligence can be avoided by representations from the protection buyer. Because the exact cashflows are not transferred, there is greater flexibility which enables the cashflows to be defined to the investors in a simpler way, unaffected by the exact cashflows on the underlying.

KEY CONSIDERATIONS AND MOTIVATION FOR PORTFOLIO CREDIT DERIVATIVES

To execute a portfolio credit derivative transaction, a number of building blocks need to be in place. Although each transaction is unique and tailored, some aspects are more typical of many synthetic securitisation structures. The structure has to address not only the economic risk transfer, but also the exact form and legal structure required by the involved parties.

Key considerations
The following aspects all need to be considered when structuring a synthetic securitisation:

1. choice of exact portfolio – ie, size, concentrations, diversification, credit quality, etc;
2. management of transaction – ie, static management, replenishment, defensive management, active management, etc;
3. substitution criteria to be used;
4. whether it is funded or unfunded;
5. choice of tranching – ie, first loss size, mezzanine tranche sizes, senior tranche size, etc;
6. whether it is public or private;
7. tenor of transaction – ie, call options, substitution period, early amortisation triggers, etc;
8. risk transfer – ie, credit events, loss valuation mechanism, etc; and
9. other structural enhancements.

Motivation for executing synthetic securitisation
The structure of a synthetic securitisation depends highly on the motivation for entering into the transaction. Two quite distinct forms of synthetic securitisation have developed: arbitrage and balance sheet.

Arbitrage synthetic
An arbitrage synthetic transaction is often labelled a *synthetic CDO* or *portfolio CDS* (although these terms can also apply to balance sheet synthetics), or it is termed as *collateralised synthetic obligation* (CSO). The transaction is often driven by investors. An investor may be looking for a return linked to a diversified portfolio of credit assets, in order to take advantage of relatively high returns or credit spreads. To do this in an efficient way, the investor may wish to invest in an arbitrage synthetic transaction. These transactions typically offer investors a wide choice of possible risk profiles depending on the preference. This is because of the tranched nature of CDO transactions, which means that investors can choose tranches with different subordinations and, therefore, different risk profiles. Should an investor wish to assume leveraged exposure, then they would invest in a junior, or subordinated, tranche. The same would be true should they wish to obtain the highest potential returns for a set notional amount of investment. Alternatively, should the investor require a steady return, and wish to have significant cushion against losses, they would prefer to invest in a more senior tranche.

Balance sheet synthetic

A balance sheet synthetic securitisation is often labelled a *synthetic CLO* or *synthetic ABS* transaction. The transaction is often driven by an originator who may have built up portfolios of debt assets that give rise to significant risk exposure or capital requirements. In the interest of managing their operations and balance sheets efficiently, originators seek a low cost of capital, or a high return on capital, and aim to have the best risk-return profile for the institution and its equity investors. Often the originators are bank lenders who are constrained by regulatory capital requirements, internal capital limits, and – increasingly – economic capital. A balance sheet synthetic securitisation transfers risk and may lead to significant relief based on these or other constraints – eg, credit lines used, risk capacity in a sector, and impact on credit ratings.

The transaction is not primarily driven by the yields or spreads on the portfolio of assets, for the assets were typically entered during the normal course of the originator's business over time and usually the originator retains the most junior tranche. Instead, the cost is determined by the total cost of transferring the risk on the mezzanine and senior tranches.

ASSET CLASSES FOR SYNTHETIC SECURITISATIONS

Synthetic securitisation is the transfer of risk, by means of credit derivatives, on portfolios of debt instruments. So just as the universe of debt instruments is very large, the variety of asset classes available for synthetic securitisation is wide. This section describes some of the asset classes that have been traded using synthetic securitisation. We start by looking at synthetic CDOs with underlying CDSs.

Credit default swaps

When synthetic CDOs backed by portfolios of CDSs are referred to, the transaction has been executed using a portfolio default swap that mirrors the terms in the single name CDS for each reference entity in the portfolio. So when one reference entity defaults, the impact on the portfolio is the size of the loss on the single name CDS. Because the terms are similar, the arranger or broker can hedge its exposure to the reference entities cleanly and efficiently in the single name CDS markets.

The true underlying obligations in the synthetic CDO are the same as those referenced in the single name CDS, typically comprising money borrowed by the reference entities. The cash settlement payments in the synthetic CDO are determined by the prices of the same deliverable obligations as the single name CDSs, which is typically a range of bonds and loans of the reference entity. One key difference is that while single name CDSs are mostly physically settled by delivery of the obligation, synthetic CDOs are cash-settled by determination of the price of the deliverable obligation. The synthetic CDO will usually be tranched, so the investor is only exposed to risk between a certain threshold and an upper band. More recently, single-tranche synthetics have been issued, where the arranger or broker issues one tranche tailored to the investor, and hedges its exposure to that tranche dynamically by selling partial protection on the reference entities.

Because single name CDSs have standard maturities – eg, five years – it is simpler to construct a transaction with a fixed maturity profile.

More detail on arbitrage synthetics based on CDS portfolios can be found in Batchvarov, Collins and Hani (2002) and Yan, Zhu and Castro (2003) and in the following two chapters.

Unsecured corporate bonds or loans

If the securitisation is backed by individual corporate bonds or loans, then the reference obligations are limited to single obligations, instead of any borrowed money of the reference entity. Consequently, the effect on the portfolio is limited to events related to that obligation, together with the value of that specific obligation in a default scenario.

Balance sheet securitisations frequently reference portfolios of bank loans. The originating bank will have a portfolio of loans it has built up over time, and the bank will buy credit protection on the loans in a portfolio default swap.

For balance sheet securitisation, the credit events are often limited to bankruptcy of the reference entity and failure to pay of the reference obligation.

Commercial mortgages

Instead of referencing unsecured bonds or loans, the reference obligations in a portfolio default swap can be restricted to corporate loans which are secured on mortgages. Because the reference obligations are limited to these specific mortgage loans, the transaction benefits from the real estate collateral against the loans, as the loans have security over the property. This collateral implies higher recovery rates than for unsecured loans and can lead to significantly improved tranching compared with unsecured transactions.

If the commercial mortgages are located in many jurisdictions, synthetic securitisation becomes significantly more efficient than cash securitisation. The legal due diligence and costs associated with transferring complex loans under many different legal systems can be prohibitive, but by defining the loans as reference obligations in a synthetic securitisation, these issues can be substantially mitigated.

Residential mortgages

There is no limit to the number of assets that can be referenced in a portfolio default swap. Consequently, consumer assets can be synthetically securitised in the same way as corporate assets. A number of synthetic residential-mortgage securitisations have been executed, especially in jurisdictions such as Germany, where cash securitisation raises additional complications. As these portfolios are often extremely granular and highly secured, they can obtain very good tranching levels.

Asset-backed corporate loans

Apart from real estate, many other types of security exist for loans – eg, cars, fixed assets in project finance, and other types of equipment. One notable asset class is transportation, namely aircraft and shipping. Synthetic CLOs referencing both classes of transportation assets have been executed, including the Leonardo and Latitude transactions. These more esoteric asset classes rely on CDSs that are highly tailored in order to address the specific natures of the loans.

Asset-backed securities (ABS)

As the structured finance and cash securitisation markets have grown, asset-backed securities have represented an increasing proportion of debt issuance. As with any other type of debt, the potential exists for asset-backed securities to be referenced in synthetic securitisations, and an increasing number of CDOs of ABS are being executed, both in cash and synthetic format.

STRUCTURAL ISSUES FOR SYNTHETIC SECURITISATION

One of the key structural aspects in a synthetic securitisation is the degree of flexibility for the portfolio to change after execution. Transactions range from completely static, with no ability to remove or insert assets, to completely flexible, where assets can be inserted and removed at any time, often by a portfolio manager. Some of the options are characterised below.

Static

A static transaction is one in which the reference portfolio cannot change from the original portfolio. The portfolio can be completely known for the whole life of the transaction, meaning that the potential losses are limited to credit events on a specific list of reference entities.

Replenishable

A replenishable transaction is one where the reference obligations are amortising over time or have the potential to repay or prepay. If these events occur, new reference obligations can be inserted into the portfolio, provided that they meet certain replenishment conditions. These conditions typically state that the portfolio quality, as defined by specified characteristics, is not significantly deteriorated by the replenishment. Criteria often used include limits on single obligor exposure, industry concentrations, average rating and maximum maturity.

Substitution

It may be the case that, in addition to adding reference obligations for amortisations, an originator or manager has the right to substitute names from the portfolio with new names. Again, this will be subject to certain conditions, which may be stricter than the replenishment conditions. A substitution right can be useful if an originator has bought protection on a portfolio, but then later sells some of its exposures in the market. In that case, the protection would be obsolete, so it is useful to be able to substitute new reference obligations. Typically, the gain or loss that the originator has made in the sale is not passed on to the synthetic securitisation transaction, because the control of the originator could lead to a potential for moral hazard.

Managed

Investors may wish to use the expertise of a third party to make decisions about the portfolio and the selection of names to invest in. In this case, a manager may be appointed to decide when to make changes to the portfolio; they may select the initial portfolio. Again, the changes must be subject to certain criteria. If there are gains or losses due to buying or selling names for the portfolio, these will be passed on to the portfolio. An investor may wish to either manage their own portfolio, have some control over the manager, or be completely independent. The management guidelines may indicate more defensive management, aimed primarily at preventing large losses, or may be geared towards a more proactive style.

TYPICAL SYNTHETIC SECURITISATION STRUCTURE

Figure 4 shows a typical structure for synthetic securitisation. The risk in the portfolio is divided into tranches, with any losses that occur on the portfolio allocated first to the junior tranche, or first loss position. Only if total losses exceed the first loss threshold, and the first loss position is written down to zero, is there any loss to the mezzanine tranches. Only when total losses exceed the first loss and the mezzanine positions are any losses allocated to the senior tranche.

We now look at the main parts of the typical structure in turn.

Portfolio

The portfolio is a collection of debt assets, which may be loans, bonds or CDSs. The portfolio originates either from a balance sheet – eg, a bank's loan book – or is purchased from or hedged in the market by a broker, arranger or manager (see Figure 5).

Credit default swaps

The owner of the portfolio, or the CDS counterparty, buys credit protection on the portfolio by means of a CDS. The swap pays a fixed premium, in exchange for payments when the cumulative losses exceed the relevant thresholds.

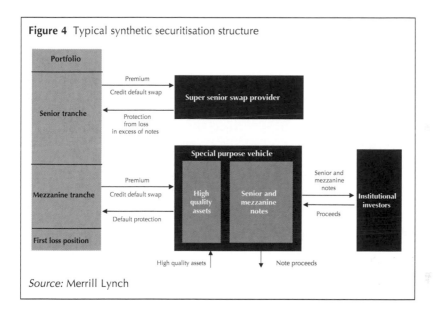

Figure 4 Typical synthetic securitisation structure

Source: Merrill Lynch

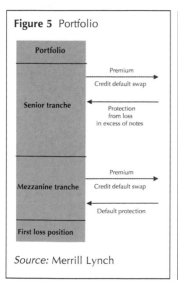

Figure 5 Portfolio

Source: Merrill Lynch

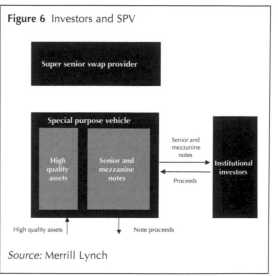

Figure 6 Investors and SPV

Source: Merrill Lynch

Investors

The super-senior tranche of a synthetic securitisation is typically the largest tranche, rated AAA. It can often be most efficiently executed in unfunded form, with the investor selling protection in a default swap without the issue of notes or up-front cash payments. The mezzanine tranche is often placed in the form of credit linked notes (CLNs). Investors pay cash up front and receive their principal at maturity less any losses in the portfolio. The notes are often rated and/or listed (see Figure 6).

Special purpose vehicle

In order to issue funded CLNs, the proceeds from the issuance must be invested, often through a ring-fenced issuance by an SPV. The SPV may invest the proceeds in highly rated or low risk-weighted collateral. In turn, the SPV enters a default swap with the portfolio owner and uses the proceeds to both make payments under the default swap and redeem the notes.

TRANCHING AND MODELLING A SYNTHETIC SECURITISATION

We now discuss the different tranching and modelling approaches and methods.

Definition of risk tranches

The key attribute of portfolio risk transfer or securitisation is the division of the portfolio into risk tranches. In constructing the tranching, the risk of losses on the portfolio is assigned to a number of tranches in a sequential way – ie, the first credit losses to occur on the portfolio are apportioned to the junior or first loss tranche. Only when this tranche is written down to zero are losses then applied to the mezzanine tranches – ie, the mezzanine tranches are only exposed to losses above some threshold. The senior tranche only suffers losses when all of the junior and mezzanine tranches have been wiped out.

In a cash securitisation, the risk is split into tranches by means of so-called cash waterfalls. That is, proceeds from interest and principal on the portfolio are paid first to the senior tranches. Provided sufficient cash proceeds remain, proceeds are then paid to the more junior tranches. In a synthetic securitisation, the risk is split in a different way: legal documents define that cash settlement amounts are applied first to the junior tranche, writing down the size of the tranche, and subsequently to the more senior tranches.

We now describe a tranching mathematically, and then investigate the optimal choice of tranching.

Figure 7 shows a single tranche in a portfolio, together with the portfolio's loss distribution at the termination date. Zero losses are an unlikely outcome, as are large-sized losses. The most probable outcome is some

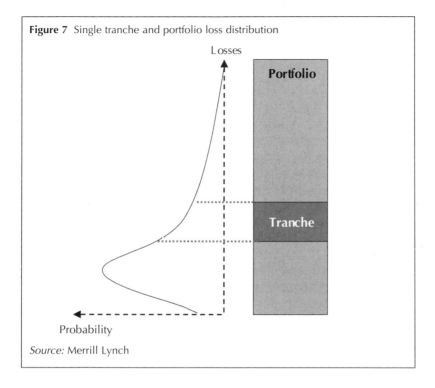

Figure 7 Single tranche and portfolio loss distribution

Source: Merrill Lynch

small amount of losses. The tranche's loss distribution is determined by the part of the loss distribution next to, and senior to the tranche.

A securitised portfolio is simply a collection of tranches with different sizes and subordination levels which together comprise the entire portfolio, as illustrated in Figure 8. The total cost of the securitisation is the sum of the costs of the various tranches; these costs are determined by the loss distribution of the underlying tranches.

Mathematically, a tranching is a set of k subordination levels $t_1, ..., t_k$ with $t_1 = 0$, $t_i \le t_j$ for $i < j$ and $t_i \le 100\%$ for all i.

If $F(x) = p(L_p \le x)$ is the cumulative distribution of losses on the portfolio L_p, with marginal distribution $f(x)$, then q_i, the default probability for tranche i is given by:

$$q_i = 1 - p(L_p \le t_i) = 1 - F(t_i) = 1 - \int_0^{t_i} f(x)dx$$

The loss experienced on the tranche is a function of the losses in the portfolio. If losses are below the threshold, no loss is experienced on the tranche; if losses exceed the upper band, the entire tranche is lost. The EL l_i for tranche i is the aggregate of the loss in each scenario multiplied by the

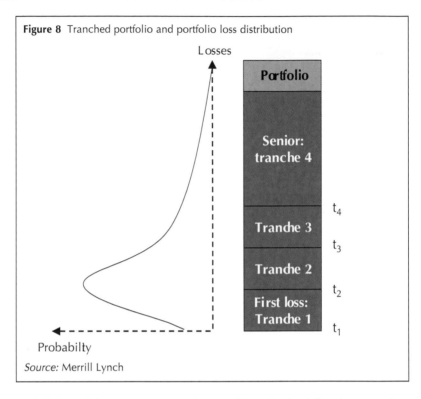

Figure 8 Tranched portfolio and portfolio loss distribution

Losses

Portfolio

Senior:
tranche 4

t_4

Tranche 3

t_3

Tranche 2

t_2

First loss:
Tranche 1

t_1

Probabilty

Source: Merrill Lynch

probability of the scenario occurring, as shown in the following equation. The first term relates to partial losses on the tranche, when portfolio losses are between the threshold and upper band, and the second term relates to loss of the entire tranche.

$$l_i = \int_{t_i}^{t_{i+1}} \left(\frac{x - t_i}{t_{i+1} - t_i} \right) \cdot f(x)dx + \int_{t_{i+1}}^{1} f(x)dx$$

Choice of tranching

When structuring a synthetic securitisation, one of the key questions is the exact choice of tranching – ie, the number of tranches, and their size and subordination, how large should the first loss junior tranche be, and how large can the senior tranche be? The parties to the transaction are seeking the most efficient tranching, ie, the tranching that gives the least cost overall, or the highest return on investment. So, in general, lower risk tranches with lower spreads should be as large as possible. Investors are seeking good returns with the minimum of risk, so they will want tranches with a reasonable subordination and sufficient return.

Mathematically, say that each obligation *i* in the portfolio of n obligations has the following characteristics:

❑ X_i exposure to obligation;
❑ G_i geographical location of obligation;
❑ R_i rating of obligation;
❑ S_i sector or industry of obligation;
❑ B_i borrower or obligor;
❑ D_i loss of obligation given default; and
❑ M_i maturity of obligation.

Factors such as these define other characteristics of the obligations and portfolio, such as the default probability of the obligations p_i. The portfolio is the set of all obligations $P = \{$all $i: i = 1, ..., n\}$, and has characteristics such as

$$\text{Portfolio size } X_P = \sum_{i=1}^{n} X_i$$

The aim of modelling the portfolio is to determine or approximate the loss distribution $F(x) = p(L_P \leq x)$ in order to determine the loss profile of a tranche and assign a rating or a price to that tranche.

The amount lost for each obligation is a random variable L_i dependent on X_i, p_i, D_i, and M_i. The distribution of the total losses is a function of these factors and additional factors such as G_i and S_i which determine the relationship between the obligors. The distribution may therefore be stated as the following:

$F(x) = p(L_P \leq x) = p(sum\ L_i \leq x) = p(function(X, G, p, S, B, D, M) \leq x)$

As the general solution to this problem is impossible to state or calculate, some assumptions must be made.

RATING AGENCY MODELLING OF SYNTHETIC SECURITISATIONS

One of the drivers of investor demand and pricing is the rating of a tranche. The credit rating agencies are third parties whose credit ratings are designed to be arrived at in an objective and impartial way, and issued as a result of a thorough analysis of a transaction. A tranche with a rating of AAA will, with everything else being equal, require a lower return than a tranche with a rating of BBB. Therefore, a key consideration when deciding on a tranching is to maximise the size of higher-rated tranches and minimise the size of lower-rated tranches.

Due to the concentration of risk in lower tranches, the junior first-loss portion will often not be given a rating, but by contrast there may be a very large AAA-rated tranche at the top of the capital structure. Depending on the portfolio and structure, the size of the AAA-tranche may make up the majority of the size of the portfolio.

Because pricing is linked to credit ratings, it is important to understand how the rating agencies assign ratings to portfolio transactions. The major, international credit rating agencies all have specific quantitative methodologies and models for assessing the risk of securitisation tranches.

The main conceptual difference between the views of Moody's, Standard and Poor's (S&P) and Fitch on credit ratings is the measure that the rating is evaluating. A Moody's rating is an assessment of the EL of a debt instrument, whereas an S&P or Fitch rating is an assessment of the instrument's default probability. This means that a Moody's rating takes the expected recovery of an instrument into account; Moody's therefore gives a higher rating for an instrument with higher recovery but similar default probability. S&P and Fitch, however, measure only the default probability, and so, for S&P and Fitch, the rating of two instruments with the same default probability should be the same, regardless of expected recovery.

For tranched portfolios, these measures are important factors in how the rating agencies view the size and subordination of tranches. An instrument that is linked to the performance of a tranche will default when losses in the portfolio exceed the subordination threshold of the tranche. So the probability of default (PD) of the instrument is simply the probability that losses exceed the threshold. That is, the subordination of the tranche is enough to determine the default probability of the instrument, and therefore is sufficient to establish the Fitch and S&P ratings.

However, the subordination level is not sufficient to determine the ELs in a tranche. If a tranche is very small, and if the first dollar is lost on the tranche, it is very likely that the remainder of the tranche is quickly lost, so the loss given default is likely to be high. However, if the tranche is large, there may be a high probability of losses exceeding the threshold, but a low chance of losses exceeding the upper band, leading to a lower EL. So the Moody's rating, which is driven by the EL, is determined not only by the subordination, but also by the size of the tranche.

Apart from their differing philosophies in assigning ratings, the rating agencies have somewhat more tangible differences to their modelling approaches. Moody's is well known for its diversity score model, whereas S&P uses its CDO Evaluator. Below, we give an overview of the main models.

Moody's: diversity score model and binomial expansion methodology

The Moody's diversity score methodology has been established for a number of years and forms the basis for Moody's evaluation and rating of many cash and synthetic CDOs.

The concept underlying the Moody's model is as follows. Any diverse portfolio with many obligations of differing size, default probability and tenor, has equivalent loss characteristics to a new portfolio in which all obligations have equal size, default probability and tenor.

Under this assumption, the EL of any tranche can be found explicitly. The process by which Moody's implement this model has two steps. In the first, the existing diverse portfolio is transformed into the equivalent portfolio using the diversity score model. In the second step, the loss distribution of the equivalent portfolio is found using the Binomial Expansion Method.

So when using this methodology, Moody's key assumption is that the non-homogeneous portfolio P is equivalent, for the purpose of rating the tranches, to a homogeneous portfolio $\bar{P}$, so $L_P \sim L_{\bar{P}}$. The rationale is that if there are many large peak exposures, the EL of mezzanine and senior tranches increases. If there is a smaller number of obligors, or more obligors in one industry sector, the default probability of mezzanine and senior tranches increases. Starting with a portfolio with different exposure sizes and correlations, the diversity score model transforms the portfolio into an equivalent portfolio that is uncorrelated and has equal exposure sizes by reducing the number of obligors.

In the first step of this model's implementation, we must first assume that each obligation is issued by a separate obligor. (If not, then group the exposures of each obligor into one obligation with combined size and weighted average default probability, loss given default and maturity.) The first step is to transform the portfolio into an equivalent portfolio that is still correlated, but which has equal exposure sizes. The number of obligors in each industry in this equivalent portfolio is defined as:

$$score_{ind} = \sum_{\substack{all\ i \\ in\ sector\ s}} \min(1, \frac{X_i}{\bar{X}}) \text{ where } \bar{X} = \frac{1}{n}\sum_i X_i \text{ is the average exposure.}$$

The next step is to find the equivalent number of uncorrelated assets by mapping each industry score (found in the first step) to an industry diversity score. The higher the industry score, the higher the impact of the mapping – eg, an industry score of 3 maps to a diversity of 2, but an industry score of 10 maps to a diversity of just 4. The mapped scores are summed to give the diversity score:

$$d = \sum_{all\ sectors} div(score_s)$$

As a result, the homogeneous portfolio $\bar{P}$ is defined under the diversity score model as $\bar{P} = \{j : j = 1, ..., d\}$ where the number of obligations d in the transformed portfolio $\bar{P}$ is the diversity score as determined using the following steps.

1. Exposure $\forall j\ X_j = \bar{X}$

2. Default Probability $\forall j\ p_j = p = \frac{1}{n}\sum_i p_i$

3. Loss of obligation given default $\forall j$ $L_j = \dfrac{1}{n} \sum_i L_i$

4. Maturity of obligation $\forall j$ $M_j = \dfrac{1}{n} \sum_i M_i$

with each obligation j deemed to be independent of each other obligation.

Given that this transformed portfolio $\bar{P}$ is a portfolio of equal-sized, equal-default probability, uncorrelated obligations, the EL of any tranche can be found explicitly, based on the probability of r obligors defaulting, P_r, being given by the binomial formula.[1]

$$P_r = \frac{d!}{r!(d-r)!} \, p^r \, (1-p)^{d-r}$$

Moody's apply stresses to account for factors not otherwise taken into consideration, and applies recovery rates dependent on the portfolio. For European portfolios, a distribution of recovery rates is used.

Other Moody's methodologies
Moody's do not rely solely on the diversity score mapping methodology. This is particularly so in the case of portfolios that are highly non-homogeneous – eg, where the portfolio consists of a higher-rated portion and a lower-rated portion, Moody's uses a double-binomial or multi-binomial model. When using this methodology, the portfolio is split into subportfolios that are more homogeneous, each of which is assigned a diversity score and modelled using the binomial expansion technique. The loss distributions are then combined so the probability of losses on the entire portfolio exceeding specified levels can be found.

For portfolios of asset backed securities and single industry CDOs, Moody's use alternative methods to evaluate the diversity score.[2] When evaluating and rating larger, more diverse portfolios, Moody's have recently introduced a model based on Fourier Transforms, which provides a faster way of calculating losses than Monte Carlo simulation, under certain assumptions about the pool.[3]

For esoteric portfolios, such as aircraft and shipping portfolios, Moody's uses a methodology based on Monte Carlo simulation of underlying defaults based on a correlation structure, and then applies stresses to the collateral based on given factors. For large homogeneous portfolios, such as residential mortgages or credit card loans, Moody's uses a method based on analysis of historical losses.

It is worth noting that the rating agency models are generally applied regardless of whether a transaction is a cash or synthetic securitisation. For cash securitisations, additional modelling of cashflows based on waterfalls is required, whereas for synthetic securitisation, the exact mechanism of risk transfer is examined, eg, the credit event and cash settlement mechanism. For both cash and synthetic, the rating agencies usually conduct a full due diligence and review of the structure, together with legal documentation, in accordance with their criteria

Standard and Poor's CDO evaluator

S&P do not use a diversity score approach to account for correlations in portfolio transactions. Historically, they have captured correlations by applying stresses to the default probabilities. This stress is higher for industries which have a higher correlation.

In 2001, S&P released their CDO Evaluator model. Rather than introducing correlation through increased default rates, this model applies pair-wise correlations directly to the random trials of the Monte Carlo simulation by applying a Cholesky decomposition to the correlation matrix. To construct the correlation matrix, obligors in the same industry are assumed to have a higher correlation, whereas the correlation between industries is assumed to be much lower.

Based on portfolio correlation and ratings as determined by the portfolio, along with recovery rate assumptions, the CDO Evaluator calculates the percentiles of the portfolio loss distribution. For a given subordination level, the probability of losses exceeding that level is found. If this probability is less than the default rate associated with a desired rating (which is stressed by S&P) then the tranche is able to obtain that rating. So for example, if the probability of losses exceeding 30% is calculated to be 0.001%, and the AAA default probability is 0.002%, then a tranche with 30% subordination can gain a AAA rating.

S&P's and Fitch's rating methods are only dependent on default probabilities, rather than ELs, therefore, given required ratings for each class, calculating the optimal tranching is straightforward. This is because the problem reduces to finding the lowest subordination for each tranche. So if rating r_i implies tranche i requires PD less than or equal to $p(r_i)$ then the solution is

$$\forall_i \quad \min t_i \text{ s.t. } q_i \leq p(r_i)$$
$$\Rightarrow \forall_i \quad \min t_i \text{ s.t. } 1 - F(t_i) \leq p(r_i)$$
$$\Rightarrow \forall_i \quad \min F(t_i) \geq 1 - p(r_i)$$
$$\Rightarrow \forall_i \quad \min t_i \text{ s.t. } t_i \geq F^{-1}(1 - p(r_i)) \text{ because } F \text{ is a cumulative density function}$$
$$\Rightarrow \forall_i \quad t_i = F^{-1}(1 - p(r_i))$$

Again, S&P have different approaches for other types of assets. For esoteric assets, such as aircraft and shipping, they use a Monte-Carlo methodology similar to the CDO Evaluator, but with the added complexity of a stochastic process for the value of the collateral backing the loans.

For large granular portfolios, S&P also rely on a historical loss methodology, measuring losses over a period of time and stressing them for the desired rating level.

is the loss to the originator in the worst case defined by a particular confidence level. So, if in 99.9% of cases, the bank loses US$30 million or less, then the economic capital required using a 99.9% confidence level is US$30 million.

Many different methods exist to calculate economic capital requirements, including different implementations of correlation and copula models, often using Monte Carlo simulation, many of which are discussed elsewhere in this book. The economic capital amount depends on many factors including diversity, probability of loss and severity of loss.

To illustrate the concept of economic capital, Figure 10 shows a portfolio loss distribution, demonstrating the economic capital amount. Figure 10 also shows the following factors:

1. on the basis of experience, knowledge of the portfolio assets, etc, the originator has its own view as to the level of likely losses on the portfolio (equal to 1 in the example);
2. such ELs are generally covered by reserving or provisioning policies;
3. unexpected losses are covered by capital (regulatory and economic); and
4. the confidence level is chosen in relation to the insolvency probability of the bank

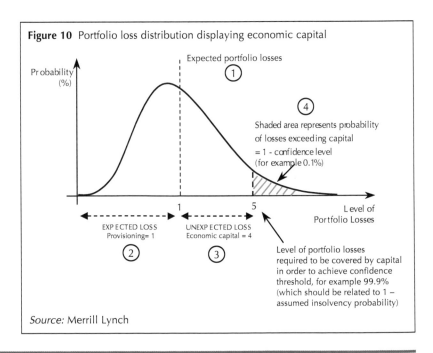

Figure 10 Portfolio loss distribution displaying economic capital

Source: Merrill Lynch

In a securitisation where the originator retains the first loss and places the remainder of the risk in a portfolio, the originator's losses after the transaction are capped at the size of the first loss. This places a cap on the economic capital after the securitisation. If this first loss is less than the size of the reserves plus the initial economic capital, the transaction reduces the economic capital amount. The optimal transaction and portfolio can be selected, based on the size of the economic capital reduction and the cost of the transaction.

SUMMARY

Synthetic securitisations and portfolio credit derivatives come in many different forms. Some transactions are motivated by arbitrage while others are driven by balance sheet management. While arbitrage transactions typically mirror the single name CDS terms, balance sheet securitisations reference specific bonds or loans, sometimes secured on real estate or other assets. The portfolios can be static or have some degree of active management.

Synthetic securitisations are tranched structures with losses being applied first to some junior position. Many methods exist to model the tranches, including established rating agency methodologies, such as Moody's diversity score methodology and S&P's CDO evaluator.

1 See Cifuentes and O'Conner (1999)
2 See Gluck and Remeza (2000).
3 See Debuysscher and Szegö (2003).
4 For full details on Fitch's previous approach, see Turnbull, Jackson and Gill (2002) and Bund, van der Weijden and Lench (2001).
5 See Bund, Neugebauer and Gill (2003).

BIBLIOGRAPHY

Batchvarov, A., J. Collins and C. Hani, 12 September, 2002, "Synthetic Static and Dynamic Arbitrage CDOs", Merrill Lynch Global Securities Research & Economics Group.

Bund, S., M. Neugebauer and K. Gill, 14 July 2003, "Global Rating Criteria for Collateralised Debt Obligations", Fitch Ratings Structured Finance, Criteria Report.

Bund, S., M. van der Weijden and M. Lench, 2 October, 2001, "European SME CDOs: an Investor's Guide to Analysis and Performance", Fitch, Ibca, Duff and Phelps European Structured Finance Special Report.

Cifuentes, A., and G. O'Connor, 19 December, 1996, "The Binomial Expansion Method Applied to CBO/CLO Analysis", Moody's Investors Service Global Credit Research.

"CStar – C*Strategic Asset Redeployment Program 1999–1 Limited", 30 June, 1999, Information Memorandum.

Debuysscher, A., and M. Szegö, 30 January, 2003, "The Fourier Transform Method – Technical Document", Moody's Investors Service International Structured Finance Working Paper.

"Global Cash Flow and Synthetic CDO Criteria", 21 March, 2002, Standard & Poor's Structured Finance

Gluck, J., and H. Remeza, 15 September, 2000, "Moody's Approach to Rating Multisector CDOs", Moody's Investors Service Structured Finance Special Report.

Turnbull, S., A. Jackson and K. Gill, 5 September, 2002, "Global Rating Criteria for Synthetic CDOs", Fitch Ratings Structured Finance Credit Products / Europe Special Report.

"Using Standard & Poor's CDO Evaluator 2.0", 22 January, 2003, Standard & Poor's Structured Finance.

Yan, D., W. Zhu and D. Castro, 19 March, 2003, "Synthetic CDO Valuation", Merrill Lynch Global Securities Research & Economics Group.

11

Integrating credit derivatives and securitisation technology: the collateralised synthetic obligation

Moorad Choudhry*

KBC Financial Products (UK) Limited

This chapter is an analysis of the synthetic collateralised debt obligation (CDO), or collateralised synthetic obligation (CSO). We focus on the key drivers of this type of instrument, from an issuer and investor point of view, before assessing the mechanics of the structures themselves. The latter takes the form of a case study-type review of selected innovative transactions. Finally, we propose a new structure that combines the advantages of existing deal types to date, which presents features of interest for a wide group of investors and issuers alike. We begin with a brief introduction to the concept of the CDO, a progressive development of well-established securitisation techniques.

SECURITISATION AND THE CDO

A *cashflow* CDO is a structure represented by an issue of the notes with interest and principal payments linked to the performance of the underlying assets of the vehicle. These underlying assets act as the *collateral* for the issued notes, hence the name. There are many similarities between CDOs and the asset-backed securities (ABS) that pre-dated them. The key difference between CDOs and other ABS and multi-asset repackaged

* The views, thoughts, and opinions expressed in this chapter are those of Moorad Choudhry in his individual private capacity, and should not be taken to be representative of KBC Financial Products (UK) Ltd or KBC Bank N.V., or of Moorad Choudhry as an employee, director or representative of KBC Financial Products (UK) Ltd or KBC Bank N.V.

securities is that the collateral pool is usually (although not always) actively managed by a collateral portfolio manager. Generally, CDOs feature a multi-tranche overlying note structure, with most or all of the notes being rated by one or more of the public credit ratings agencies. The priority of payment of the issued securities reflects the credit rating for each note, with the most senior note being the highest rated. The term *waterfall* is used to refer to the order of cashflow payments. Sufficient underlying cashflows must be generated by the issuing vehicle in order to meet the fees of third-party agency servicers and all the note issue liabilities. In Europe, issued securities may pay a fixed or floating coupon, usually on a semi-annual, quarterly or monthly basis, with senior note issues rated from AAA to A, and junior and mezzanine notes rated BBB to B.[1] Unrated, subordinated and equity pieces may also be issued. The equity note is actually a bond, and represents the shareholding interest in the vehicle; its return is variable and linked to the performance of the collateral pool. Investors in the subordinated notes receive coupons after payment of servicing fees and the coupon on senior notes. The equity and subordinated note are the first loss pieces and, as they carry the highest risk, have a higher expected return compared to that of the underlying collateral.

In a CDO, the cashflows of the underlying assets are used to fund the liabilities of the overlying notes. As the notes carry different ratings, a *priority of payment* must be followed – this is the cashflow waterfall illustrtated in Figure 1. The most senior payment must be paid in full before the next payment can be met, and so on until the most junior liability is discharged. If insufficient funds are available, the most senior notes must be paid off before the junior liabilities can be addressed. Before paying the next priority of the waterfall, the vehicle must pass a number of compliance tests on the level of its underlying cashflows. These include interest coverage and principal (par) coverage tests.

Banks and financial institutions use CDOs to diversify their sources of funding, manage portfolio risk and obtain regulatory capital relief. Investors are attracted to the senior notes in a transaction because these allow them to earn relatively high yields compared to other asset-backed bonds of a similar credit rating. Other advantages for investors include:

❏ exposure to a diversified range of credits;
❏ access to the fund management and credit analysis skills of the portfolio manager; and
❏ a typically lower level of uncertainty and risk exposure compared to a single bond of similar rating.

A recommended reading on CDOs is Fabozzi and Goodman (2001).

Panel 1
THE FULLY UNFUNDED SYNTHETIC CDO

A fully unfunded deal can be on balance sheet or source reference assets externally. Because it is fully unfunded, the liabilities of the deal structure are comprised purely of credit default swaps (CDSs), meaning it can also be structured with or without an SPV. This example shows a hypothetical deal structure with the following terms.

Originator:	Banking institution
Reference Portfolio:	€900m notional
	80–100 corporate names sourced in the market
CDS tranching:	Super-senior CDS €815 million notional
	"Class A" CDS €35 million notional
	"Class B" CDS €15 million notional
	"Class C" CDS €20 million notional
	"Class D" or Equity CDS €15 million notional

The structure diagram is shown in Figure 9.

The key difference with this structure is that it can be arranged by the originating institution direct: there is no need to set up an SPV. In fact, this is also an on-balance sheet deal. The rating of the tranches is based on the loss allocation, with credit events among reference assets being set up so that the junior note suffers losses first. This follows traditional structured finance technology. However, unlike traditional structures, the interest payments on the liability side are not subject to a waterfall, but are guaranteed to investors. This increases the attraction of the deal for investors. Thus, on occurrence of a credit event, interest payments are still received by investors. It is the notional amount, on which interest is calculated, that is reduced, thereby reducing the interest received. Losses of notional value above the Class D threshold eat into the Class C swap notional amount.

This is a version of an arbitrage deal, with the originating bank taking the role of a fund manager. It displays the following features.

❑ The bank selects the initial portfolio, using its credit skills to select credits in the market, which are referenced via CDSs. The bank sells protection on these assets; the premium received exceeds the premium paid out on the liability side, creating the arbitrage gain for the bank. The reduced premium payable on the liability side reflects the tranches arrangement of the liabilities.
❑ The reference assets are sourced by the bank on its own balance sheet, before the CDO itself is closed in the market.
❑ The bank has the freedom to dynamically manage the portfolio during the life of the deal, taking a view in credits in line with its fundamental analysis of the market.

❏ Trading profits are trapped in a "reserve account", which is also available to cover trading losses and losses suffered due to credit events.

As part of the rating requirements for the deal, the originating bank will follow certain eligibility constraints on which exposures it can take on. Restrictions may include:

❏ reference entities being rated at investment grade by the ratings agencies;
❏ no single reference credit may exceed a total exposure of more than €10 million;
❏ the reference entity being incorporated in a specified list of countries;
❏ specified geographical and industrial concentration;
❏ a trading turnover limit of 20% of notional value per annum; and
❏ a Moody's diversity score of at least 45 on closing and no lower than 42 during life of deal.

In addition to the "guaranteed" nature of interest payments for investors (subject to leave of credit events), the principal advantage of this structure is that it may be brought to market very quickly. There is no requirement for the originator to set up an SPV, and no need to issue and settle notes. The originator can therefore take advantage of market conditions and respond to investor demands for return enhancement and diversification fairly quickly.

THE SYNTHETIC CDO

Synthetic CDOs were introduced to meet differing needs of originators in instances when credit risk transfer is of greater importance than funding considerations. Compared with conventional cashflow deals, which feature an actual transfer of ownership or *true sale* of the underlying assets to a separately incorporated legal entity, a synthetic securitisation structure is engineered. This enables the assets' credit risk to be transferred by the transaction's sponsor or originator from the asset itself to the investors, by means of credit derivative instruments. The originator is therefore the credit protection buyer and investors are the credit protection sellers. This credit risk transfer may be undertaken either directly or via an SPV. Using this approach, underlying or *reference* assets are not necessarily moved off the originator's balance sheet. Consequently the approach is adopted whenever the primary objective is to achieve risk transfer rather than balance sheet funding. The synthetic structure enables removal of credit exposure without asset transfer, and so may be preferred for risk management and regulatory capital relief purposes. From banking institutions' point of view, it also enables loan risk to be transferred without sale of the

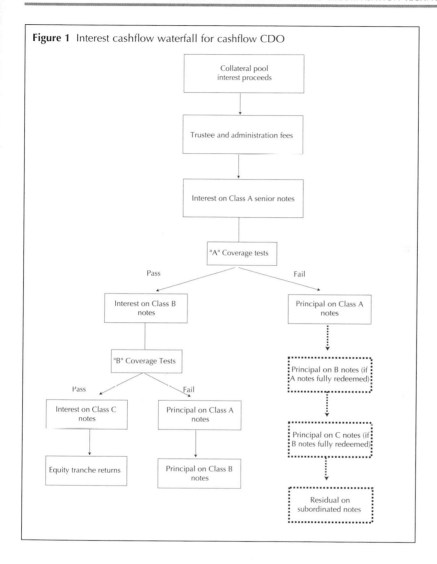

Figure 1 Interest cashflow waterfall for cashflow CDO

loans themselves, thereby allowing customer relationships to remain unaffected. The first synthetic deals were observed in the US market, while the first deals in Europe were observed in 1998. Figure 2 illustrates market growth in Europe.

Assessing the genesis of the synthetic CDO
The original cashflow-style CDO was a tool for intermediation. In this respect, it can be viewed as a (mini-) bank, although it presents a more efficient intermediation tool than a bank. Where it differs is the composition of its asset pool: unlike a bank, this is not diverse, but will have been

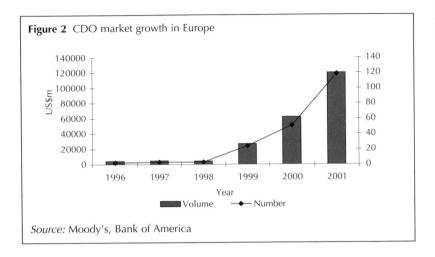

Figure 2 CDO market growth in Europe

Source: Moody's, Bank of America

tailored to meet the specific requirements of both the originator and the customer (investor). It is this tailoring that generates the economic efficiencies of the CDO. In an institutional scenario, as exists within a bank, assets are effectively priced at their lowest common denominator. Hence, a bank that has 10% of its assets held in the form of emerging market debt would be priced at a lower value than an equivalent institution that does not hold such risky assets. The CDO-structure's liabilities will also be more tailored to specific needs, with a precise mix of equity holders, AAA-liabilities and so on.

Thus far, we may view the CDO-type entity as being a tool for the intermediation of risk, and similar to a banking institution. A synthetic CDO may be viewed in similar terms, although it is more similar to an insurance company than a bank. This is due to the separation of funding from credit risk that is facilitated by the synthetic approach; the resulting ability to price pure credit is a risk management mechanism analogous to the operations of an insurance company. The investors in a synthetic CDO do not purchase the assets that are referenced in a vehicle, but merely wish an economic exposure to it. This is made possible through the use of credit derivatives in the CDO structure.

The process of combining securitisation technology with credit derivatives within synthetic structures was particularly suited to the European market, with its myriad of legal and securitisation jurisdictions. The European market viewed the traditional method of securitisation, used for balance sheet and risk management purposes and involving the sale of assets into a special purpose vehicle, as being less efficient than it had actually had proved in the North American market. This can be attributed to the following differences in the markets:

Panel 2

THE AAA-RATED REFERENCE PORTFOLIO CDO

This illustration is of a hypothetical managed synthetic CSO that generates value from low-risk reference assets. During a period of economic downturn and widening spreads, higher yields on AAA-rated securities enable synthetic CDOs to be structured with the backing of a pool of AAA-rated collateral. Thus, a very low-risk CDO vehicle can be created, providing investors with favourable risk/reward profiles. In this structure, investors are exposed to ratings downgrade risk rather than default risk, since it is extremely unlikely that an AAA-rated entity will experience default during the life of the deal.

This transaction features:

❏ a reference portfolio comprised solely of AAA credits – this can be a mixture of conventional bullet bonds, ABS and MBS securities and CDSs;
❏ a liability notes structure tranched so that the junior note is BBB-rated, but whose effective risk is actually lower than this rating suggests – thus a favourable risk/reward profile is created for investors;
❏ a return on a note that is BBB-rated (and hence paying BBB-note interest spread over Libor) but which is, in effect, AAA-rated given the nature of the collateral backing; and
❏ all notes paying a fixed spread over Libor.

The structure is illustrated in Figure 11. The proceeds of the note issues are held in a reserve account that is authorised to invest in "eligible investments". These are typically a cash account (or "GIC" account), Treasury bills and Treasury securities or other AAA-rated sovereign bonds. This reserve account is used to pay for any losses incurred by the reference portfolio; surplus reserves are for the benefit of the originating bank.

The risk/reward profile of the issued notes is made possible because the reference assets are all AAA-rated. Investors in this deal are being exposed to spread risk rather than default risk (because an AAA-rated asset can be downgraded). Nevertheless, BBB noteholders are able to earn an attractive return at what is, for practical purposes, a risk exposure considerably lower than BBB-rated risk.

❏ In the US market, commercial banks were traditionally lower-rated than their European counterparts. Hence the funding element of a cashflow securitisation was a key motivating factor behind a deal, as the originator could secure lower funding costs by means of the securitisation.

❑ European banks, being higher-rated than US banks, had less need of the funding side in a securitisation deal – compared to US banks, they obtained a greater share of their funding from their retail customer base. A significant portion of their funding was obtained at Libor-minus, compared to the Libor-flat funding of US banks.

So while European banks had an interest in wanting to transfer risk from their balance sheet, they had less need of the funding associated with a traditional securitisation. This rendered a cashflow CDO less economic and therefore less relevant. However, banks still needed to reduce regulatory capital requirements and transfer credit risk, and this led to the first static balance-sheet synthetic CDO. Known as BISTRO, it was originated by JP Morgan in 1997.

The first synthetic CDOs were balance-sheet driven: banks structured deals for regulatory capital management purposes. These deals reflected a desire by banks to shift their credit risk and, in so doing, manage capital more efficiently. Later deals followed an arbitrage model: they were originated by fund managers, who were recognised by investors as being more professional at managing risk. Hence the "second generation" of CDO structures, which reflected the comparative advantage generated as insurance companies were able to divide an overall "pool" of risk into separate pieces, which were tailored to specific investor preferences. As with cashflow structures, synthetic structures were able to separate the risk transfer element from the funding element. This mirrors what occurred in the early 1980s with interest-rate swaps, which also split the interest-rate risk from the funding risk, being off-balance sheet instruments with no exchange of principal. This is the case with credit derivatives, and mirrors exactly what has happened in the credit derivatives market.

Deal motivations
Differences between synthetic and cash CDOs are perhaps best reflected in the different cost-benefit economics involved in issuing each type, which in turn reflect the different motivations behind these issues. A synthetic CDO can be seen as being constructed out of the following:

❑ a short position in a credit default swap (CDS) – bought protection – by which the sponsor transfers its portfolio credit risk to the issuer; or
❑ a long position in a portfolio of bonds or loans, which produces a cashflow which enables the sponsor to pay liabilities of overlying notes.

The originators of the first synthetic deals were banks who sought to manage the credit risk exposure of their loan books, without having to resort to the administrative burden of true sale cash securitisation. They are also central to the development of credit derivative structures, with single name CDSs being replaced by portfolio default swaps. Synthetic CDOs can be "de-linked" from the sponsoring institution, so that investors do not have any credit exposure to the sponsor itself. The first deals were introduced in 1998, at a time when widening credit spreads and worsening credit quality among originating firms meant that investors were sellers of cash CDOs that retained a credit linkage to the sponsor. A synthetic arrangement also means that the credit risk of assets that are otherwise unsuitable for conventional securitisation may be transferred, while assets are retained on the balance sheet. Such assets include bank guarantees, letters of credit, or cash loans that have some legal or other restriction regards securitisation. For this reason, synthetic deals are more appropriate for assets that are described under multiple legal jurisdictions.

The economic advantage of issuing a synthetic versus a cash CDO can be significant. Put simply, the net benefit to the originator is the gain in regulatory capital cost, minus the cost of paying for credit protection on the CDS side. In a partially funded structure, a sponsoring bank will obtain full capital relief when note proceeds are invested in 0% risk weighted collateral such as Treasuries or gilts. The super senior swap portion will carry a 20% risk weighting.[2] It is unsurprising that a synthetic

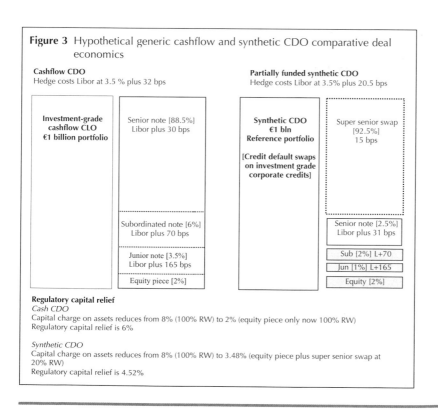

Figure 3 Hypothetical generic cashflow and synthetic CDO comparative deal economics

Cashflow CDO
Hedge costs Libor at 3.5 % plus 32 bps

Partially funded synthetic CDO
Hedge costs Libor at 3.5% plus 20.5 bps

Investment-grade cashflow CLO €1 billion portfolio	Senior note [88.5%] Libor plus 30 bps
	Subordinated note [6%] Libor plus 70 bps
	Junior note [3.5%] Libor plus 165 bps
	Equity piece [2%]

Synthetic CDO €1 bln Reference portfolio [Credit default swaps on investment grade corporate credits]	Super senior swap [92.5%] 15 bps
	Senior note [2.5%] Libor plus 31 bps
	Sub [2%] L+70
	Jun [1%] L+165
	Equity [2%]

Regulatory capital relief
Cash CDO
Capital charge on assets reduces from 8% (100% RW) to 2% (equity piece only now 100% RW)
Regulatory capital relief is 6%

Synthetic CDO
Capital charge on assets reduces from 8% (100% RW) to 3.48% (equity piece plus super senior swap at 20% RW)
Regulatory capital relief is 4.52%

deal should be cheaper: if CDSs are used, the sponsor pays a basis point fee, which for AAA security might be in the range 10-30 bps, depending on the stage of the credit cycle. In a cash structure where bonds are issued, the cost to the sponsor would be the benchmark yield plus the credit spread, which would be considerably higher compared to the CDS premium. This is illustrated in Figure 3, where we assume certain spreads and premiums in comparing a partially funded synthetic deal with a cash deal. The assumptions are that:

❏ the super senior credit swap cost is 15 bps, and carries a 20% risk weight;
❏ the equity piece retains a 100% risk-weighting;
❏ the synthetic CDO invests note proceeds in sovereign collateral that pays sub-Libor.

Synthetic deals can be unfunded, partially funded or fully funded. An unfunded CDO would be comprised wholly of CDSs, while fully funded structures would be arranged so that the entire credit risk of the reference portfolio was transferred through the issue of credit-linked notes (CLNs). We discuss these shortly.

Within the European market, static synthetic balance sheet CDOs are the most common structure. The reasons that banks originate them are two-fold:

1. *Capital relief*: Banks can obtain regulatory capital relief by transferring lower-yield corporate credit risk such as corporate bank loans off their balance sheet. Under Basel I rules, all corporate debt carries an identical 100% risk-weighting; therefore with banks having to assign 8% of capital for such loans, higher-rated (and hence lower-yielding) corporate assets will require the same amount of capital but will generate a lower return on that capital. A bank may wish to transfer such higher-rated, lower-yield assets from its balance sheet; this can be achieved via a CDO transaction. The capital requirements for a synthetic CDO are lower than for corporate assets – for instance, the funded segment of the deal will be supported by high quality collateral such as government bonds, and via a repo arrangement with an OECD bank, which would carry a 20% risk weighting, as does the super senior element.

2. *Transfer of credit risk*: The cost of servicing a fully funded CDO, and the premium payable on the associated CDS, can be prohibitive. With a partially funded structure, the issue amount is typically a relatively small share of the asset portfolio. This substantially lowers the default swap premium. Also, as the CDO investors suffer the first loss element of the portfolio, the super senior default swap can be entered into at a considerably lower cost than that on a fully funded CDO.

Deal mechanics

A synthetic CDO is so-called because the transfer of credit risk is achieved "synthetically" via a credit derivative, rather than by a "true sale" to an SPV. Thus, in a synthetic CDO, the credit risk of the underlying loans or bonds is transferred to the SPV using CDSs and/or total return swaps (TRS). However the assets themselves are not legally transferred to the SPV, and they remain on the originator's balance sheet. Using a synthetic CDO, the originator can obtain regulatory capital relief and manage the credit risk on its balance sheet, but will not be receiving any funding.[3] In other words, a synthetic CDO structure enables originators to separate credit risk exposure and asset funding requirements. The credit risk of the asset portfolio, now known as the reference portfolio, is transferred, directly or to an SPV, through credit derivatives. The most common credit contracts used are CDSs. A portion of the credit risk may be sold on as CLNs. Typically, a large majority of the credit risk is transferred via a "super-senior" CDS, which is dealt with a swap counterparty, but is usually sold to monoline insurance companies at a significantly lower spread over Libor compared with the senior AAA-rated tranche of cashflow CDOs.[4] This is a key attraction of synthetic deals for originators. Most deals are structured with mezzanine notes sold to a wider set of investors, the proceeds of which are invested in risk-free collateral such as Treasury bonds or *Pfandbriefe* securities. The most junior note, known as the "first-loss" piece, may be retained by the originator. On occurrence of a credit event among the reference assets, the originating bank receives funds remaining from the collateral after they have been used to pay the principal on the issued notes, less the value of the junior note.

In the generic synthetic CDO structure, as shown in Figure 4, the credit risk of the reference assets is transferred to the issuer SPV, and ultimately to the investors, by means of the CDS and an issue of CLNs. In the default swap arrangement, the risk transfer is undertaken in return for the swap premium, which is then paid to investors by the issuer. The note issue is invested in risk-free collateral rather than passed on to the originator, in order to de-link the credit ratings of the notes from the originator's rating. If the collateral pool were not established, a downgrade of the sponsor could result in a downgrade of the issued notes. Investors in the notes expose themselves to the credit risk of the reference assets, and if there are no credit events, they will earn returns at least equal to the collateral assets and the default swap premium. If the notes are credit-linked, they will also earn excess returns based on the performance of the reference portfolio. If there are credit events, the issuer will deliver the assets to the swap counterparty and will pay the nominal value of the assets to the originator out of the collateral pool. CDSs are unfunded credit derivatives, while CLNs are funded credit derivatives where the protection seller (the investors) fund the value of the reference assets up-front, and will receive a reduced return on occurrence of a credit event.

Funding mechanics
As the super-senior piece in a synthetic CDO does not need to be funded, it provides the key advantage of the synthetic mechanism compared to a cashflow arbitrage CDO. During the first half of 2002, the yield spread for the AAA note piece averaged 45–50 basis points (bps) over Libor, while the cost of the super-senior swap was around 10–12 bps.[5] This means that the CDO manager can reinvest in the collateral pool risk-free assets at Libor minus 5 bps, and is able to gain from a saving of 28–35 bps on each nominal US$100 of the structure that is not funded. This is a considerable gain. If we assume that a synthetic CDO is 95% unfunded and 5% funded, this is equivalent to the reference assets trading at approximately 26–33 bps cheaper in the market. There is also an improvement to the return on capital measure for the CDO manager. Since, typically, the manager retains the equity piece, if this is 2% of the structure and the gain is 33 bp, the return on equity will be improved by [0.36/0.02] or 16.5%.

Another benefit of structuring CDOs as synthetic deals is their potentially greater attraction for investors (protection sellers). Often, selling CDS protection on a particular reference credit generates a higher return than going long of the underlying cash bond. This is usually because, due to a number of reasons, the CDS price is greater than the asset swap price for the same name, for a number of reasons (as explained in detail in Chapter 3). For instance, during 2001 the average spread of the synthetic price over the cash price was 15 bps in the five-year maturity area for BBB-rated credits.[6] The main reasons why default swap spreads tend to be above cash spreads are as follows (as discussed also in Chapter 3).

❏ Bond identity, in that the bondholder is aware of the exact issue that they are holding in the event of default, however, default swap sellers may receive any bond from a basket of deliverable instruments that rank *pari passu* with the cash asset; this is the delivery option afforded the long swap holder.
❏ The borrowing rate for a cash bond in the repo market may differ from Libor if the bond is to any extent special; this does not impact the default swap price which is fixed at inception.
❏ Certain bonds rated AAA (such as US agency securities) sometimes trade below Libor in the asset swap market. However, a bank writing protection on such a bond will expect a premium (positive spread over Libor) for selling protection on the bond.
❏ Depending on the precise reference credit, the default swap may be more liquid than the cash bond, resulting in a lower default swap price, or less liquid, resulting in a higher price.

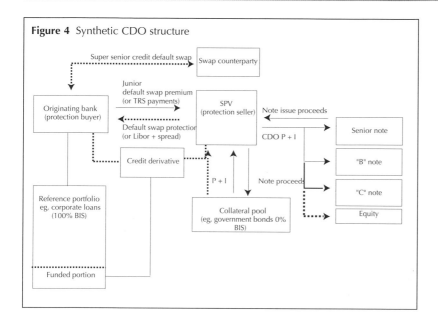

Figure 4 Synthetic CDO structure

❏ Default swaps may be required to pay out on credit events that are technical defaults, and not the full default that impacts a cash bond-holder. Protection sellers may demand a premium for this additional risk.

❏ For assets trading below par, the protection seller is covering a greater loss than is the cash bondholder. This is because CDSs are "par products" and pay out the par value of the reference asset, minus the market value at time of termination. This means that for an asset trading below par, the protection seller is protecting a greater value than the actual loss suffered by someone who is holding the cash bond.

Summary: advantages of synthetic structures

Synthetic securitisation vehicles were introduced in response to the specific demands of sponsoring institutions, so present certain advantages over traditional cashflow structures.

❏ Implementation is fast: a synthetic transaction can, in theory, be placed in the market sooner than a cash deal, with the time from inception to closure being as low as four weeks. Average execution time can be six to eight weeks compared to three to four months for the equivalent cash deal. This reflects the shorter ramp-up period noted above.

❏ There is no requirement to fund the super-senior element.

❏ For many reference names, the CDS is frequently cheaper than the same name underlying cash bond.

❏ Transaction costs such as legal fees can be lower, as there is no necessity to set up an SPV.

❏ Banking relationships can be maintained with clients whose loans need not be actually sold off the sponsoring entity's balance sheet.

❏ The range of reference assets that can be covered is wider, and includes undrawn lines of credit, bank guarantees and derivative instruments that would give rise to legal and true sale issues in a cash transaction.

❏ The use of credit derivatives introduces greater flexibility to provide tailor-made solutions for credit risk requirements.

❏ The cost of buying protection is usually lower, for there is little or no funding element and the credit protection price is below the equivalent-rate note liability.

This does not mean that the cash transaction is now an endangered species, for it retains certain advantages of its own over synthetic deals.

❏ There is no requirement for an OECD bank (the 20% BIS risk-weighted entity) to act as the swap counterparty to meet capital relief requirements.

❏ Lower capital relief is available, compared to the 20% risk weighting on the OECD bank counterparty.

❏ The potential investor base is larger, and the number of counterparties potentially greater (certain financial and investing institutions have limitations on the degree of usage of credit derivatives).

❏ There is a lower degree of counterparty exposure for originating entity. In a synthetic deal, the default of a swap counterparty would mean cessation of premium payments or more critically a credit event protection payment, and termination of the CDS.

Investment banking advisors will structure the arrangement that best meets their sponsoring client's requirements. Depending on the nature of these, it may be either a synthetic or cash deal.

SYNTHETIC CDO DEAL STRUCTURES
We now look in further detail at the various types of synthetic CDO structures.

Generic concept
Synthetic CDOs have been issued in a variety of forms, labelled in generic form as arbitrage CDOs or balance-sheet CDOs. Structures can differ to a considerable degree from one another, having only basic features in common. The latest development is the *managed synthetic* CDO.

A synthetic arbitrage CDO is originated generally by collateral managers who wish to exploit the difference in yield between that obtained on the underlying assets and that payable on the CDO, both in note interest and servicing fees. The generic structure is as follows.

❏ A specially created SPV enters into a total-return swap with the originating bank or financial institution, referencing the bank's underlying portfolio (the reference portfolio).
❏ The portfolio is actively managed and is funded on the balance sheet by the originating bank.
❏ The SPV receives the "total return" from the reference portfolio, and in return it pays Libor plus a spread to the originating bank.
❏ The SPV also issues notes that are sold into the market to CDO investors – these can be as high as AAA, being backed by high-quality collateral, which is purchased using the note proceeds. A typical structure is shown in Figure 5.

A balance-sheet synthetic CDO is employed by banks that wish to manage regulatory capital. As before, the underlying assets are bonds, loans and credit facilities originated by the issuing bank. In a balance-sheet CDO, the SPV enters a CDS agreement with the originator, with the specific collateral pool designated as the reference portfolio. The SPV receives the premium payable on the default swap, and thereby provides credit protection on the reference portfolio. There are three types of CDO within this structure. A fully synthetic CDO is a completely *unfunded* structure which uses CDSs to transfer the entire credit risk of the reference assets to investors who are protection sellers. In a *partially funded* CDO, only the highest credit risk segment of the portfolio is transferred. The cashflow that would be needed to service the synthetic CDO overlying liability is received from the AAA-rated collateral that is purchased by the SPV with the proceeds of an overlying note issue. An originating bank obtains maximum regulatory capital relief by means of a partially funded

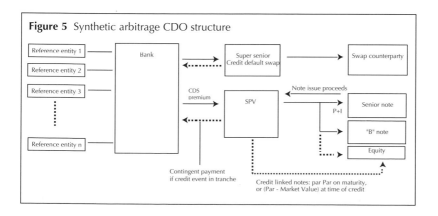

Figure 5 Synthetic arbitrage CDO structure

structure, through a combination of the synthetic CDO and what is known as a *super senior swap* arrangement with an OECD banking counterparty. A super senior swap provides additional protection to that part of the portfolio – ie, the senior segment – that is already protected by the funded portion of the transaction. The sponsor may retain the super senior element or may sell it to a monoline insurance firm or CDS provider.

Some commentators have categorised synthetic deals using slightly different terms. For instance, Boggiano, Waterson and Stein (2002) define the following types:

❑ balance-sheet static synthetic CDO;
❑ managed static synthetic CDO;
❑ balance-sheet variable synthetic CDO; and
❑ managed variable synthetic CDO.

As described by Boggiano *et al*, the basic structure is that already described for a partially funded synthetic CDO. In fact, there is essentially little difference between the first two types of deal; in the latter, an investment manager rather than the credit-swap counterparty selects the portfolio. However, the reference assets remain static for the life of the deal in both cases. For the last two deal types, the main difference would appear to be that an investment manager, rather than the originator bank, trades the portfolio of credit swaps under specified guidelines. It is this author's belief that this is not a structural difference; for this chapter, we will consider both to be managed CDOs, which are described later in this chapter.

Synthetic deals may be either static or managed. Static deals hold the following advantages:

❑ there are no ongoing management fees to be borne by the vehicle; and
❑ the investor can review and grant approval to credits that are to make up the reference portfolio.

Funded and unfunded deals

Synthetic deal structures are arranged in a variety of ways, with funded and unfunded elements available to meet investor and market demand. In a generic, partially funded synthetic transaction, as shown in Figure 6, an arrangement exists whereby the issuer enters into two CDSs: the first with an SPV that provides protection for losses up to a specified amount of the reference pool, and the second with the OECD bank or – occasionally – an insurance company.[7,8]

A *fully funded* CDO is a structure whereby the credit risk of the entire portfolio is transferred to the SPV via a CDS. In a fully funded – or just "funded") synthetic CDO, the issuer enters into the CDS with the SPV, which itself issues CLNs to the entire value of the assets on which the risk has been transferred. The proceeds from the notes are invested in risk-free government or agency debt such as gilts, bonds or *Pfandbriefe*, or in senior unsecured bank debt. Should there be a default on one or more of the underlying assets, the required amount of the collateral is sold and the proceeds from the sale paid to the issuer to recompense for the losses. The premium paid on the CDS must be sufficiently high to ensure that it covers the difference in yield between that on the collateral and that on the notes issued by the SPV. The generic structure is illustrated in Figure 7.

Fully funded CDOs are relatively uncommon. One of the advantages of the partially funded arrangement is that the issuer will pay a lower premium compared to a fully funded synthetic CDO, because it is not required to pay the difference between the yield on the collateral and

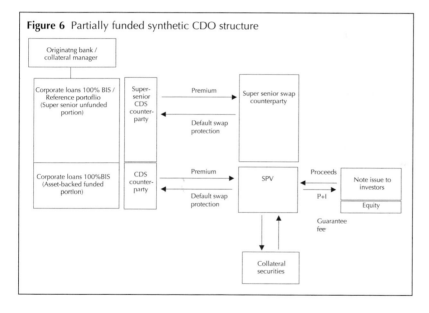

Figure 6 Partially funded synthetic CDO structure

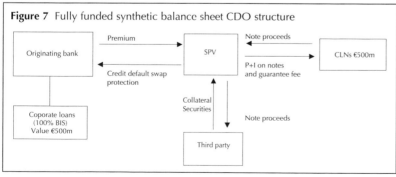

Figure 7 Fully funded synthetic balance sheet CDO structure

the coupon on the note issue (the unfunded part of the transaction). The downside is that the issuer's risk weighting for capital purposes will be reduced to 20% for the risk transferred via the super senior default swap.

The fully *unfunded* CDO uses only credit derivatives in its structure. The swaps are rated in a similar fashion to notes, and there is usually an "equity" piece that is retained by the originator. The reference portfolio will again be commercial loans, usually 100% risk-weighted, or other assets. The credit rating of the swap tranches is based on the rating of the reference assets, as well as other factors such as the diversity of the assets and ratings performance correlation. In the typical structure, as shown in Figure 8, there will be the equity tranche, plus one or more junior tranches, one or more senior tranches and a super-senior tranche. The senior tranches are sold on to AAA-rated banks as a portfolio CDS, while the junior tranche is usually sold to a an OECD bank. The ratings of the tranches will typically be:

- ❏ super-senior: AAA;
- ❏ senior: AA to AAA;
- ❏ junior: BB to A; and
- ❏ equity: unrated.

The CDSs are not single-name swaps, but are written on a class of debt. The advantage for the originator is that it can name the reference asset class to investors without having to disclose the name of specific loans. Default swaps are usually cash-settled and not physically settled, so that reference assets can be replaced with other assets if the sponsor wishes.

The managed synthetic CDO

Managed synthetic CDOs are the latest variant of the synthetic CDO structure.[9] They are similar to the partially funded deals we described earlier, except that the reference asset pool of credit derivatives is actively traded by the sponsoring investment manager. It is the maturing market in CDSs, resulting in good liquidity in a large number of synthetic corporate credits, that has facilitated the introduction of the managed synthetic CDO. With this structure, originators can use credit derivatives to arbitrage cash and synthetic liabilities, as well as leverage off their expertise in credit trading to generate profit. The advantages for investors are the same as with earlier generations of CDOs, except that with active trading they are gaining a still-larger exposure to the abilities of the investment manager. The underlying asset pool is, again, a portfolio of CDSs. However, these are now dynamically managed and actively traded under specified guidelines. This affords greater flexibility to the sponsor; the vehicle will record trading gains or losses as a result of credit derivative trading. In most

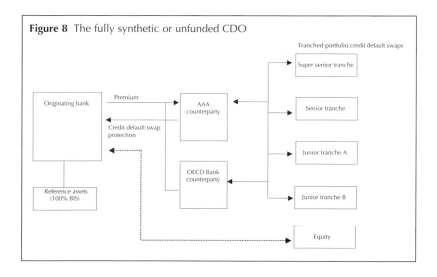

Figure 8 The fully synthetic or unfunded CDO

structures, the investment manager can only buy protection (short credit) in order to offset an existing sold protection default swap. For some deals, this restriction is removed and the investment manager can buy or sell credit derivatives to reflect its view.

Structure

The structure of the managed synthetic CDO is similar to the partially funded synthetic CDO, with a separate legally incorporated special purpose vehicle (SPV).[10] On the liability side there is an issue of notes, the proceeds of which are invested in collateral or *eligible investments*. This is one or a combination of the following:

❑ a bank deposit account or guaranteed investment contract (GIC) which pays a pre-specified rate of interest;[11]
❑ risk-free bonds such as US Treasury securities, German *Pfandbriefe* or AAA-rated bonds such as credit-card ABS securities;
❑ a repo agreement with risk-free collateral;
❑ a liquidity facility with a AA-rated bank; or
❑ a market-sensitive debt instrument, often enhanced with the repo or liquidity arrangement described above.

On the asset side, the SPV enters into CDSs and/or TRSs, selling protection to the sponsor. The investment manager (or "collateral manager") can trade in and out of CDSs after the transaction has closed in the market.[12] The SPV enters into credit derivatives via a single basket CDS to one swap counterparty, written on a portfolio of reference assets, or via multiple single-name credit swaps with a number of swap counterparties. The latter

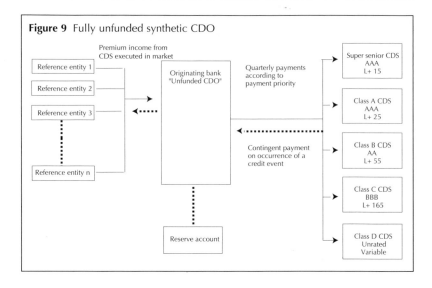

Figure 9 Fully unfunded synthetic CDO

arrangement is more common and is referred to as a multiple dealer CDO. A percentage of the reference portfolio will be identified at the start of work on the transaction, with the remaining entities being selected during the ramp-up period ahead of closing. The SPV enters into the other side of the CDSs by selling protection to one of the swap counterparties on specific reference entities. Thereafter, the investment manager can trade out of this exposure in any of the following ways.

❏ By buying credit protection from another swap counterparty on the same reference entity. This offsets the existing exposure. However, there may be residual risk exposure unless premium dates are matched exactly, or if there is a default in both the reference entity and the swap counterparty.

❏ By unwinding or terminating the swap with the counterparty.

❏ By buying credit protection on a reference asset that is outside the portfolio. This is uncommon, as it will leave residual exposures and may affect premium spread gains.

The SPV actively manages the portfolio within specified guidelines, the decisions being made by the investment manager. Initially, the manager's opportunity to trade may be extensive, but this will be curtailed if there are losses. The trading guidelines will extend to both individual CDSs and at the portfolio level. They may include:

❏ parameters under which the investment manager (in the guise of the SPV) may actively close out, hedge or substitute reference assets using credit derivatives; or

❏ guidelines under which the investment manager can trade credit derivatives to maximise gains or minimise losses on reference assets that have improved or worsened in credit quality or outlook.

CDSs may be cash settled or physically settled, with physical settlement being more common in a managed synthetic deal. In a multiple dealer CDO, the legal documentation must be in place with all names on the counterparty dealer list, which may add to legal costs as standardisation may be difficult.

Compared to vanilla synthetic deals, investors who are interested in this structure are seeking the following advantages:

❏ active management of the reference portfolio and the trading expertise of the investment manager in the corporate credit market;
❏ a multiple dealer arrangement, so that the investment manager can obtain the most competitive prices for default swaps; and
❏ the fact that under physical settlement, the investment manager (via the SPV) has the ability to obtain the highest recovery value for the reference asset.

A generic managed synthetic CDO is illustrated in Figure 10.

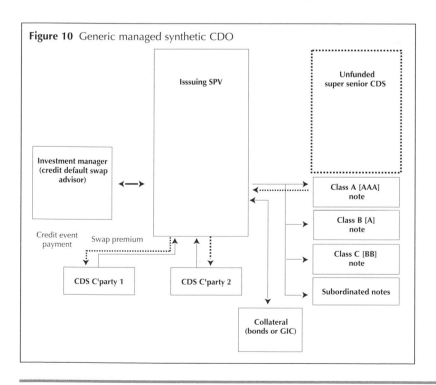

Figure 10 Generic managed synthetic CDO

The single-tranche synthetic CDO

One of the advantages offered to investors in the synthetic market is the ability to invest at maturities required by the investor, rather than at maturities selected by bind issuers. Figure 12 illustrates how synthetic products allow investors to access the full credit curve, while the bond market provides assets only at selected points on the curve.

The flexibility of the CSO, enabling deal types to be structured to meet the needs of a wide range of investors and issuers, is well-illustrated with the tailor-made or "single-tranche CDO" structure.[13] This structure has been developed in response to investor demand for exposure to a specific part of a pool of reference credits. With this structure, an arranging bank creates a tailored portfolio that meets specific investor requirements with regard to:

❑ portfolio size and asset class;
❑ portfolio concentration, geographical and industry variation;
❑ portfolio diversity and rating; and
❑ investment term-to-maturity.

The structure is shown in Figure 13.

Under this arrangement, there is only one note tranche. The reference portfolio, made up of CDSs, is dynamically hedged by the originating bank itself. The deal has been arranged to create a risk/reward profile for one investor only, who buys the single tranche note. This also creates an added advantage that the deal can be brought to market very quickly. The key difference with traditional CSOs is that the arranging bank does not transfer the remainder of the credit risk of the reference pool. Instead, this risk is dynamically managed, and hedged in the market using CDSs.

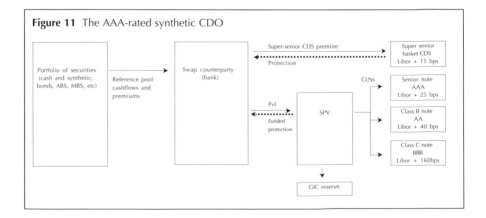

Figure 11 The AAA-rated synthetic CDO

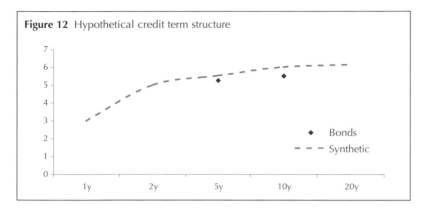

Figure 12 Hypothetical credit term structure

Deal structure

The investor in a single-tranche CDO will decide on the criteria of assets in the portfolio, and the subordination of the issued tranche. Typically this will be at the mezzanine level – eg, covering the 4–9% loss level in the portfolio. This enables a very favourable risk return profile to be set up: a CDO tranche that is exposed to 4–9% losses has a very low historical risk of default (approximately equivalent to a Moody's A2 rating), and a high relative return given its tranching of around Libor plus 200 bps as at May 2003. The risk represented by a mezzanine tranche is illustrated in Figure 4 of Chapter 13. A hypothetical portfolio is shown in Figure 14.

Unlike a traditional CDO, a single-tranche CDO has a very simple cashflow "waterfall". Unlike the waterfall for a cash CDO, a single-tranche waterfall will consist of only agency service and hedge costs, and the coupon of the single tranche itself.

Some of the issues the investor will consider when working with the arranging bank to structure the deal include:

❑ the number of names in the credit portfolio, usually ranging from 50 to 100 names;

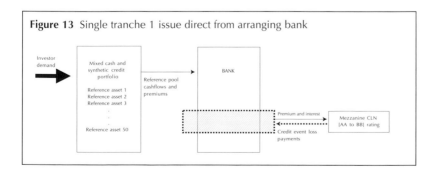

Figure 13 Single tranche 1 issue direct from arranging bank

❏ the geographical split of the reference names;
❏ the required average credit rating and average interest spread of the portfolio; and
❏ the minimum credit rating required in the portfolio.

As with any CDO type, if the deal is being rated, the mix of assets will need to meet ratings agency criteria for diversity and average rating. The diversity score of a portfolio is a measure of the diversity of a portfolio based on qualities such as industrial and geographical concentration. It can be defined as the number of equivalent uncorrelated assets in the pool.

The position and rating of the issued single tranche is as required by the investor. The subordination of the note follows from the required rating of

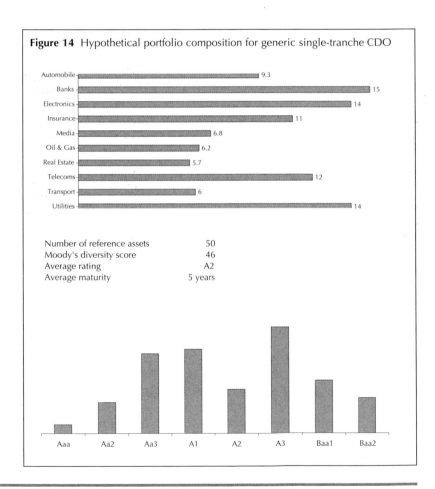

Figure 14 Hypothetical portfolio composition for generic single-tranche CDO

Number of reference assets	50
Moody's diversity score	46
Average rating	A2
Average maturity	5 years

the investor. For instance, the investor may require an A2 rating for the note. The process for doing this involves:

❏ targeting the required rating on the issued tranche;
❏ setting the required return on the note, and hence determining where the tranche will lie;
❏ defining the percentage of first loss that must occur before the issued tranche is impacted by further losses;
❏ setting the size of the note issue, in line with investor requirements – ie, if the investor wishes to place US$20 million in the note, and the reference pool is US$800 million nominal value, this will imply a 2.5% tranche.

As with the previous synthetic CDOs, a single-tranche CDO can be either a static or a managed deal. In a managed deal, the investor can manage the portfolio and effect substitutions if this is part of its requirement. To facilitate this, the deal may be set up with one or more fund managers in place to deal with the investor who requests substitutions. Alternatively, an investor may leave trading decisions to a fund manager.

Advantages of the single-tranche structure
For certain investors, the single-tranche CDO presents a number of advantages over the traditional structure.

❏ It is flexible, in that investment features can be tailor-made to suit the investors needs precisely. The investor can select the composition of the portfolio, the size of the tranche and its subordination level.
❏ The note terms are exactly as required: the coupon and maturity of the note are tailor-made for the investor.
❏ The timeframe is shorter: the deal can be brought to market relatively quickly, (in as little as four weeks), compared to anything from two months to one year for a conventional CSO.
❏ The cost of issue is lower, and includes lower legal costs due to the short time to issue and lack of protracted marketing effort by the arranger.

The flexibility of the single-tranche structure means that the market can expect to see more variations in their arrangement, as more investors evaluate it as an asset class.

INVESTOR RISKS AND RETURN
Fund managers consider investing in CDO-type products because they represent a diversification in the European bond markets, with yields that are comparable to credit-card or auto-loan ABS assets. A CDO also gives investors exposure to sectors in the market that may not otherwise be

accessible to most investors, eg, credits such as small- or medium-sized corporate entities that rely on bank finance alone. Also, the extent of credit enhancement and note tranching in a CDO means that they may show better risk/reward profiles that straight conventional debt, with a higher yield but incorporating both asset backing and insurance backing. In cash and synthetic CDOs, the issues notes are often bullet bonds, with fixed term to maturity, whereas other ABS and MBS product are amortising securities with only average (expected life) maturities. This may suit certain longer-dated investors.

An incidental perceived advantage of cash CDOs is that they are typically issued by financial institutions such as higher-rated banks. This usually provides comfort not only on the credit side, but also on the underlying administration and servicing side with regard to underlying assets. In this respect, they compare favourably to consumer receivables securitisations. A comparison of yields across asset classes is show in Figure 15.

Investor risk considerations

The key structural differences between a synthetic and conventional securitisation are the absence of a true sale of assets and the use of credit derivatives. Investors must therefore focus on different aspects of risk that the former instrument represents. Although it might be said that each securitisation – irrespective of whether it is cash or synthetic – is a unique transaction with its own characteristics, synthetic deals are very transaction-specific because they can be tailor-made to meet very specific requirements; requirements may concern reference asset type, currency, underlying cashflows, credit derivative instrument, etc.

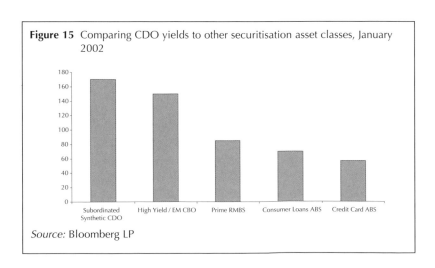

Figure 15 Comparing CDO yields to other securitisation asset classes, January 2002

Source: Bloomberg LP

Investor risk in a synthetic deal centres on the credit risk inherent in reference assets and the legal issues associated with definition of credit events. The first risk is closely associated with securitisation, but particularly with synthetic securitisation. Remember that the essence of the transaction is credit risk transfer, and investors (protection sellers) desire exposure to the credit performance of reference assets. So investors are taking on the credit risk of these assets, be they conventional bonds, ABS securities, loans or other assets. The primary measure of this risk is the credit rating of the assets, taken together with any credit enhancements, as well as their historical ratings performance.

The second risk is more problematic and open to translation issues. In a number of deals, the sponsor of the transaction is also tasked with determining when a credit event has taken place – as the sponsor is also buying protection, there is scope for conflict of interest here. The more critical concern, and one which has given rise to litigation in past cases, is that of what exactly constitutes a credit event. A lack of clear legal definition can lead to conflict when the protection buyer believes that a particular occurrence is a credit event and therefore the trigger for a protection pay-off, but this is disputed by the protection seller. For more information on this subject see Chapter 4. Generally, the less specific the definition of a credit event, the greater is the risk of a dispute. Trigger events should therefore be defined as closely as possible in the governing legal documentation.

This is crucial: most descriptions of events defined as trigger events, include those listed in the 1999 ISDA *Credit Derivatives Definitions* (see Chapter 19), include circumstances that fall short of a general default, meaning that pay-offs can be enforced when the reference asset obligor is not in default. This means that the risk taken on by investors in synthetic deals is higher than that taken on in a conventional cash deal (see Choudhry, 2002). It is important for investors to be aware of this: credit ratings for a bond issue will not reflect all the credit events that are defined by ISDA. This means that the probability of loss for a synthetic note of a specific rating may be higher than for a conventional note of the same reference name.

CASE STUDIES
The latest manifestation of synthetic securitisation technology is the managed synthetic CDO or CSO. In Europe these have been originated by fund managers, with the first example being issued in 2001. Although they are effectively investment vehicles, the disciplines required to manage what is termed a "structured credit product" is not necessarily identical to those required for a corporate bond fund. Investment bank arrangers are apt to suggest that a track record in credit derivatives trading is an essential pre-requisite to being a successful CSO manager. There is an element of reputational risk at stake if a CDO suffers a downgrade; eg, during 2001,

Moody's downgraded elements of 83 separate CDO deals, across 174 tranches, as underlying pools of investment-grade and high-yield corporate bonds experienced default.[14] Thus, managing a CDO presents a high-profile record of a fund manager's performance.

In Europe, fund managers that have originated managed synthetic deals include Robeco, Cheyne Capital Management, BAREP Asset Management, and Axa Investment Managers. In the second part of this article, we look at three specific deals as case studies, issued in the European market during 2001 and 2002.

We now consider a number of specific deals that illustrate the progressive development of the synthetic CDO market since inception. These are:

❏ BISTRO – the first static synthetic balance-sheet CDO;
❏ ALCO1 – a balance-sheet deal arranged for credit risk management and regulatory capital purposes;
❏ Blue Chip Funding – a managed synthetic CDO; and
❏ Jazz I CDO – a managed synthetic "hybrid" CDO.

These deals exemplify innovative structures and a creative combination of securitisation technology and credit derivatives. They show how a portfolio manager can utilise vehicles of this kind to exploit its expertise in credit trading as well as provide attractive returns for investors. Managed synthetic CDOs also present fund managers with a vehicle to build on their credit derivatives experience. As the market in synthetic credit – in Europe at least – is frequently more liquid than the cash market for the same reference names; it is reasonable to expect more transactions of this type in the near future.

BISTRO: the first synthetic securitisation

Generally viewed as the first synthetic securitisation, BISTRO is a JP Morgan vehicle brought to market in December 1997. The transaction was designed to remove the credit risk on a portfolio of corporate credits held on JP Morgan's books, with no funding or balance sheet impact. The overall portfolio was US$9.7 billion, with US$700 million of notes being issued in two tranches by the BISTRO SPV. The proceeds of the note issue were invested in US Treasury securities, which in turn were used as collateral for the CDS entered into between JP Morgan and the vehicle. This is a five-year swap written on the whole portfolio, with JP Morgan as the protection buyer. BISTRO, the protection seller, pays for the coupons on the issued notes from funds received from the collateral pool and the premiums on the CDS. Payments on occurrence of credit events are paid out from the collateral pool.

Under this structure, JP Morgan has transferred the credit risk on US$700 million of its portfolio to investors, and retained the risk on a first-loss piece and the residual piece. The first loss piece is not a note issue, but a US$32 million reserve cash account held for the five-year life of the deal. First losses are funded out of this cash reserve which is held by JP Morgan. This is shown in Figure 16.

The asset pool is static for the life of the deal. The attraction of the deal for investors included a higher return on the notes compared to bonds of the same credit rating and a bullet-maturity structure, compared to the amortising arrangement of other ABS asset classes.

The BISTRO deal featured:

❏ the credit risk exposure of a pool of assets being transferred without moving the assets themselves from the balance sheet;
❏ a resultant reduction of the credit exposure for the originator;
❏ no funding element for the originator – ie, a securitisation deal that separated the liquidity feature from the risk transfer;
❏ the application of structured finance rating technology; and
❏ unfunded liabilities which were nevertheless tranched, as in a traditional cashflow securitisation, so that these liabilities could be rated.

Investors in the deal, who are in fact taking on the credit risk of the assets on the originator's balance sheet, were attracted to the deal because:

1. the deal provided exposure to particular credits and credit risk/return profile, but without a requirement for this exposure to be funded;

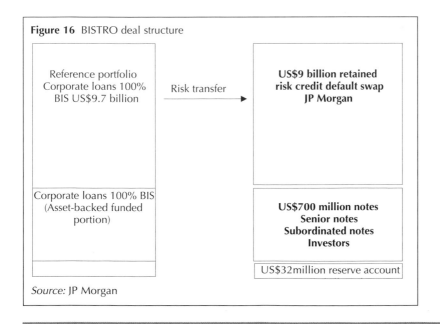

Figure 16 BISTRO deal structure

| Reference portfolio Corporate loans 100% BIS US$9.7 billion | Risk transfer → | **US$9 billion retained risk credit default swap JP Morgan** |

| Corporate loans 100% BIS (Asset-backed funded portion) | | **US$700 million notes Senior notes Subordinated notes Investors** |
| | | US$32million reserve account |

Source: JP Morgan

2. the deal economics are aimed at a precise transfer of specifically-packaged segments of risk, with the investor realising greater value; and

3. the equity holder gains from a leveraged exposure, which means the cost of this exposure is lowered.

The originating bank retained a comparative advantage on the funding, while the investor gained the required exposure to the credit risk. The investor effectively provides the comparative advantage because it is not subject to regulatory capital requirements. In short, the deal is a win-win transaction for both the bank and the investor. The investor – in this instance, typically a fund manager or insurance company – is an expert in the market, so can price the risk very efficiently. It also benefits from the cheap(er) funding that the bank is able to source.

ALCO 1 Limited

The ALCO 1 CDO is described as the first rated synthetic balance-sheet CDO from a non-Japanese bank.[15] It is a US$2.8 billion structure sponsored and managed by the Development Bank of Singapore (DBS). The structure diagram is shown in Figure 17.

The structure allows DBS to shift the credit risk on a US$2.8 billion reference portfolio of mainly Singapore corporate loans to a special purpose vehicle, ALCO 1, using CDSs. As a result, DBS can reduce the risk capital it has to hold on the reference loans, without physically moving the assets from its balance sheet. The structure is US$2.45 billion super-senior tranche – unfunded CDS – with US$224m notes issue and US$126m first-loss piece retained by DBS. The notes are issued in six classes, collateralised by Singapore government T-bills and a reserve bank account known as a "GIC" account. There is also a currency and interest-rate swap structure in place for risk hedging, and a put option that covers purchase of assets by arranger if the deal terminates before expected maturity date. The issuer enters into CDSs with a specified list of counterparties. The default swap pool is mainly static, but there is a substitution facility for up to 10% of the portfolio. This means that under certain specified conditions, up to 10% of the reference loan portfolio may be replaced by loans from outside the vehicle.

The first rated synthetic balance sheet deal in Asia, ALCO 1-type structures, have subsequently been adopted by other commercial banks in the region. The principal innovation of the vehicle is the method by which the reference credits are selected. The choice of reference credits on which swaps are written must, as expected with a CDO, follow a number of criteria set by the ratings agency, including diversity score, rating factor, weighted average spread, geographical and industry concentration, among others.

Structure and mechanics

The issuer enters into a portfolio CDS with DBS as the CDS counterparty to provide credit protection against losses in reference portfolio. The CDSs are cash settled. In return for protection premium payments, after aggregate losses exceeding the US$126 million "threshold" amount, the issuer is obliged to make protection payments to DBS. The maximum obligation is the US$224m note proceeds value. In standard fashion associated with securitised notes, further losses above the threshold amount will be allocated to overlying notes in their reverse order of seniority. The note proceeds are invested in collateral pool comprised initially of Singapore Treasury bills.

ALCO 1 note tranching is shown in Figure 18.

During the term of the transaction, DBS as the CDS counterparty is permitted to remove any eliminated reference obligations that are fully paid, terminated early or otherwise no longer eligible. Additionally, DBS has the option to remove up to 10% of the initial aggregate amount of the reference portfolio, and substitute new or existing reference names.

For this structure, credit events are defined specifically as failure to pay and bankruptcy. Note how this differs from European market CDOs, where the list of defined credit events is invariably longer, frequently including restructuring and credit rating downgrade.

The reference portfolio is an Asian corporate portfolio, but with a small percentage of loans originated in Australia. The portfolio is concentrated in Singapore (80%). The weighted average credit quality is Baa3/Ba1, with

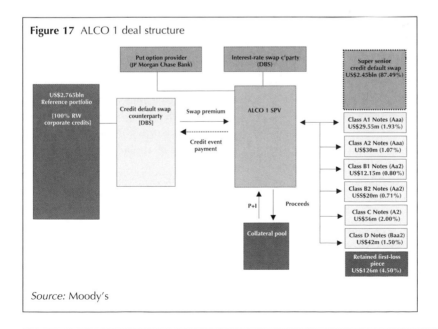

Figure 17 ALCO 1 deal structure

Source: Moody's

Figure 18 ALCO 1 note tranching

Class	Amount (US$m)	%	Rating	Interest rate
Super senior swap	2.450	87.49	NR	N/A
Class A1	29.55	1.93	Aaa	3m USD Libor + 50 bps
Class A2	30	1.07	Aaa	3m SOR + 45 bps
Class B1	12.15	0.80	Aa2	3m USD Libor + 85 bps
Class B2	20	0.71	Aa2	3m SOR + 80 bps
Class C	56	2.00	A2	5.20%
Class D	42	1.50	Baa2	6.70%

Source: Moody's

an average life of three years. The Moodys' diversity score is low (20), reflecting the concentration of loans in Singapore. There is a high industrial concentration. The total portfolio at inception was 199 reference obligations amongst 136 reference entities (obligors). By structuring the deal in this way, DBS obtains capital relief on the funded portion of the assets, but at lower cost and less administrative burden than a traditional cashflow securitisation, and without having to have a true sale of the assets.

Blue Chip Funding 2001-1 plc

Blue Chip Funding is a managed synthetic CDO originated by Dolmen Securities, which closed in December 2001. The deal has a €1 billion reference portfolio.

The structure is partially funded, with €80 million of notes issued, or 8% of the nominal value. The share of the unfunded piece is comparatively high. The proceeds from the notes issued are invested in AAA securities, which are held in custody by the third-party agency service provider, which must be rated at AA- or higher. The diversity of the structure is reflected in there being 80 different credits, with a weighted average rating of A-, with no individual asset having a rating below BBB-. The structure is shown in Figure 19.

With this deal, the managers have the ability to trade the CDSs with a pre-specified panel of dealers. The default swap counterparties must have a short-term rating of A-1+ or better. Trading will result in trading gains or losses. This contrasts with a static synthetic deal, where investors have not been affected by trading gains or losses that arise from pool substitutions. The deal was rated by Standard & Poor's, which in its rating report described the management strategy as "defensive trading" to avoid acute credit deteriorations. There are a number of guidelines that the manager must adhere to, including the following:

❏ The manager may both sell credit protection and purchase credit protection; however the manager may only short credit (purchase credit protection) in order to close out or offset an existing previous sale of protection.

❏ There is a discretionary trading limit of 10% of portfolio value.

❏ A minimum weighted average premium of 60 bps for swaps must be maintained.

❏ A minimum reinvestment test must be passed at all times: this states that if the value of the collateral account falls below €80 million, interest generated by the collateral securities must be diverted from the equity (Class C and D notes) to the senior notes until the interest cover is restored.

The issuer has sold protection on the reference assets. On occurrence of a credit event, the issuer will make credit protection payments to the swap counterparty. If the vehicle experiences losses as a result of credit events or CDS trading, these are made up from the collateral account.

Jazz CDO I BV

Jazz CDO I BV is an innovative CDO structure and one of the first *hybrid* CDOs introduced in the European market. A hybrid CDO combines elements of a cashflow arbitrage CDO and a managed synthetic CDO – consequently, the underlying assets are investment grade bonds and loans, and synthetic assets such as CDSs and TRSs. The Jazz vehicle

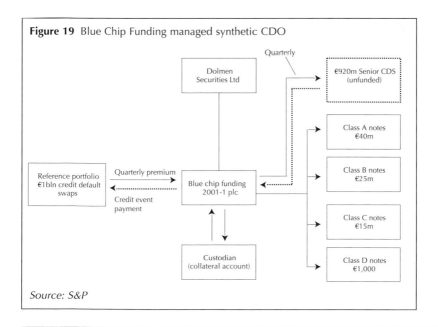

Figure 19 Blue Chip Funding managed synthetic CDO

Source: S&P

comprises a total of €1.5 billion of referenced assets, of which €210 million is made up of a note issue. Its hybrid arrangement enables the portfolio manager to take a view on corporate and bank credits in both cash and synthetic markets. Thus, a structure like Jazz bestows the greatest flexibility for credit trading on CDO originators. The vehicle is illustrated in Figure 20.

The main innovation of the structure is a design that incorporates both funded and unfunded assets, as well as funded and unfunded liabilities. This arrangement means that the portfolio manager is free to trade both cash and derivative instruments, thereby exploiting its experience and knowledge across the markets. During 2001–02, a time of increasing defaults in CDOs, static pool deals began to be viewed unfavourably by certain investors, because of the inability to offload deteriorating or defaulted assets. Jazz CDO I is an actively managed deal, and its attraction reflects, to a great extent, the perception with which the portfolio manager is viewed by investors. For this reason, the role of the portfolio manager was critical to the ratings analysis of the deal. This covered:

❏ experience in managing cash and synthetic assets;
❏ its perceived strength in credit research;
❏ previous experience in managing CDO vehicles; and
❏ infrastructure arrangements, such as settlement and processing capability.

These factors, together with the traditional analysis used for static pool cash CDOs, were used by the ratings agencies when assessing the transaction.

The assets in Jazz CDO I may be comprised of CDSs, TRSs, bonds and loans, at the manager's discretion. The asset mix is set up by:

❏ purchase of cash assets, funded by the proceeds of the note issue and the liquidity facility;
❏ selling protection via CDSs;
❏ buying protection via CDSs; and
❏ entering into TRSs, whereby the total return of the reference assets is received by the vehicle in return for a payment of Libor plus spread (on the notional amount) – this is funded via the liquidity facility.

The liability side of the structure is a combination of the super-senior CDS, and issued notes and equity piece. However, the asset and liability mix can be varied by the portfolio manager at its discretion, and can be expected to change over time. In theory, the asset pool can comprise 100% cash bonds or 100% CDSs; in practice we should expect to see a mixture.

Figure 20 Jazz CDO I B.V. structure diagram

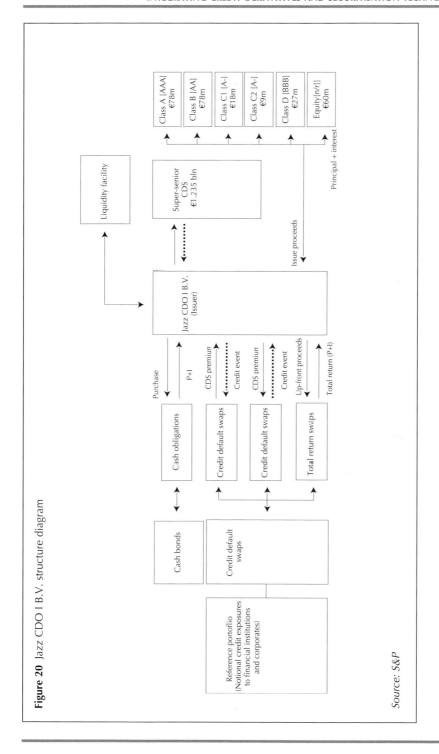

Source: S&P

The TRS and the Jazz I CDO

A variation on the generic TRS has been used in structured credit products such as synthetic CDO.[16] In the Jazz I CDO structure, which is a vehicle that can trade in cash bonds as well as CDSs and TRSs, the TRS is a funded credit derivative because the market price of the reference asset is paid in advance by the Jazz vehicle to the swap counterparty. In return, the swap counterparty pays the principal and interest on the reference asset to Jazz CDO. The Jazz CDO has therefore purchased the reference asset synthetically. On occurrence of a credit event, the swap counterparty delivers the asset to the CDO and the TRS is terminated. Because these are funded credit derivatives, a liquidity facility is needed by the vehicle, which it will draw on whenever it purchases a TRS. This facility is provided by the arranging bank to the structure. The TRS arrangement in the Jazz structure is shown in Figure 21.

Liquidity facility

A liquidity facility of €1.7 billion is an integral part of the structure. It is used as a reserve to cover losses arising from CDS trading, occurrence of credit events, and to fund any purchases when the mix of cash versus synthetic assets is altered by the manager. This can include the purchase of bonds and the funding of TRSs. The facility is similar to a revolving credit facility and is provided by the arrangers of the transaction.

If the manager draws on the liquidity facility, this is viewed as a funded liability, similar to an issue of notes, and is in fact senior in the priority of payments to the overlying notes and the super-senior CDS.

Trading arrangements

Hybrid CDOs are the latest development in the arena of managed synthetic CDOs. The Jazz CDO structure enables the portfolio manager to administer credit risk across cash and synthetic markets. The cash market instruments that may be traded include investment grade corporate bonds, structured

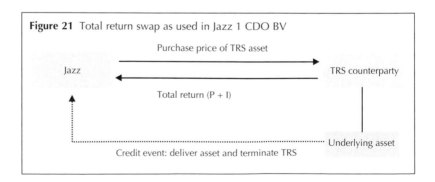

Figure 21 Total return swap as used in Jazz 1 CDO BV

Purchase price of TRS asset

Jazz — TRS counterparty

Total return (P + I)

Underlying asset

Credit event: deliver asset and terminate TRS

finance securities such as ABS or MBS, and corporate loans. The portfolio manager may buy and sell both types of assets, ie, it may short credit in accordance with its view. In other words, the restriction that exists with the Blue Chip and Robeco III deals is removed in Jazz CDO. Therefore, the portfolio manager can buy protection in the credit derivative market as it wishes, and not only to offset an existing long credit position (sold protection). The only rules that must be followed when buying protection are that the counterparty risk is of an acceptable level, and there are sufficient funds in the vehicle to pay the credit derivative premiums.

The manager may trade where existing assets go into default, or where assets have either improved or worsened in credit outlook (to take or cut a trading profit/loss). Another significant innovation is the ability of the vehicle to enter into basis trades in the credit market. An example of such a trade would be to buy a cash bond and simultaneously purchase protection on that bond in the CDS market. Similar to trades undertaken in the exchange-traded government bond futures market, this is an arbitrage-type strategy where the trader seeks to exploit price mismatches between the cash and synthetic markets.

The various combinations of trades that may be entered into are treated in different ways for counterparty risk and regulatory capital. For an off-setting position in a single name, the options are:

1. using only CDSs to cancel out an exposure, with both CDSs traded with the same counterparty – this is netted out for risk purposes;
2. using CDSs only, but with different counterparties – there will be a set-aside for counterparty risk requirement exposure;
3. using CDS and cash bond – regarded as a AAA-rated asset for capital purposes.

The Offering Circular for the deal lists a number of trading guidelines that must be followed by the manager. These include a limit of 20% by volume annual turnover level.

INTEGRATING CASH AND SYNTHETIC MARKETS: THE MULTI-SPV CREDIT HYBRID CDO STRUCTURE

The synthetic CDO is well-established as a vehicle for facilitating balance-sheet capital management, credit risk transfer and credit trading. It merges traditional securitisation technology with credit derivative instruments. In this section, we propose an innovative new structure that combines a multi-Special Purpose Vehicle (SPV) arrangement, together with a hybrid cash and synthetic element that splits the vehicle into stand-alone pieces to suit specific investor requirements. The structure uses existing technology, packaged together in a way that integrates cash and synthetic markets. This results in a product offering greater flexibility than has been issued in the market before now, and enables financial institutions that already originate cash or synthetic CDOs to benefit from this flexibility.

The new structure may be used to achieve one or a combination of the following:

❏ credit risk transfer and/or regulatory capital management of assets already on the balance sheet;
❏ exploiting arbitrage opportunities between cash and synthetic credits;
❏ obtaining funding for acquiring assets subsequently used in an arbitrage synthetic transaction;
❏ a significant increase in potential deal size, due to the benefits arising from the multi-SPV structure;
❏ any combination of conventional bonds, structured financial products (ABS, MBS and CDO), loans and synthetic assets such as CDSs in the reference portfolio;
❏ leveraging the credit expertise of a fund manager to deliver gains for the equity participants in the vehicle; and
❏ meeting the requirements of a varied class of investors by means of the multi-SPV structure, including multi-currency requirements and specific fund management styles.

A description of the proposed structure follows, commencing with an assessment of the origins and efficacy of the synthetic CDO structure and its use of credit derivatives. This is followed by a description of the proposed new structure, and an illustration of how originators would benefit from adopting this approach when bringing new transactions to the market.

Since the inception of the first synthetic deals, the market has evolved, with continuing development of newer structures to meet differing originator and investor requirements. The proposed multi-SPV may be considered the "fourth-generation" of such products, following the structures introduced earlier (see Choudhry, 2004). This is shown in Figure 22.

As we have seen elsewhere in this chapter, the first European synthetic deals were balance-sheet CLOs, with underlying reference assets being commercial loans on the originator's balance sheet. Originators were typically banking institutions. Arbitrage synthetic CDOs have also been introduced, typically by fund management institutions, and involve sourcing credit derivative contracts in the market and then selling these on to investors in the form of rated notes, at the arbitrage profit. Within the synthetic market, arbitrage deals were the most frequently issued during 2001, reflecting certain advantages they possess over cash CDOs (see McPherson *et al*, 2002).

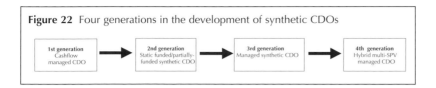

Figure 22 Four generations in the development of synthetic CDOs

| 1st generation
Cashflow
managed CDO | ➡ | 2nd generation
Static funded/partially-
funded synthetic CDO | ➡ | 3rd generation
Managed synthetic CDO | ➡ | 4th generation
Hybrid multi-SPV
managed CDO |

The multi-SPV credit hybrid vehicle

By integrating the cash and synthetic credit markets in one vehicle, originators will be able to attract wider investor interest. Such a vehicle combines both a cash-funded element and a synthetic element – hence the term "hybrid". The active management of the vehicle will be similar to that already described in the section on managed synthetic CDOs.

Deal structure
The structure is comprised of:

❏ a reference portfolio sourced in the market or on originator's balance sheet;
❏ a TRS set up for funding purposes;
❏ a back-to-back TRS;
❏ a second-loss credit protection CDS;
❏ a funded element of CLNs issued by SPV 2; and
❏ if required, a managed arbitrage-element of CDS trading undertaken out of SPV 1.

The structure diagram is shown in Figure 23, with illustrative terms in Figure 24.

Deal arrangement

The reference portfolio may be comprised of conventional bonds, asset-backed securities (ABS), loans, or synthetic assets such as CDSs. The type of assets that can be placed in the portfolio are dictated by the deal terms and conditions. The portfolio is actively managed by the fund manager, which retains an equity participation in the deal. Assets can be substituted by the fund manager acting under portfolio guidelines.

The funding stage of the transaction is executed first. This enables the deal to acquire assets. This SPV enters a back-to-back TRS with the originator that transfers the total return of assets to the originator and eventually on to a swap counterparty via SPV 1. The fund manager can execute credit derivatives in the market via SPV 1, and a multi-dealer arrangement that would be conducted in a managed arbitrage synthetic deal (see Choudhry, 2002).

The cash CDO element of the structure is executed by SPV 2, which

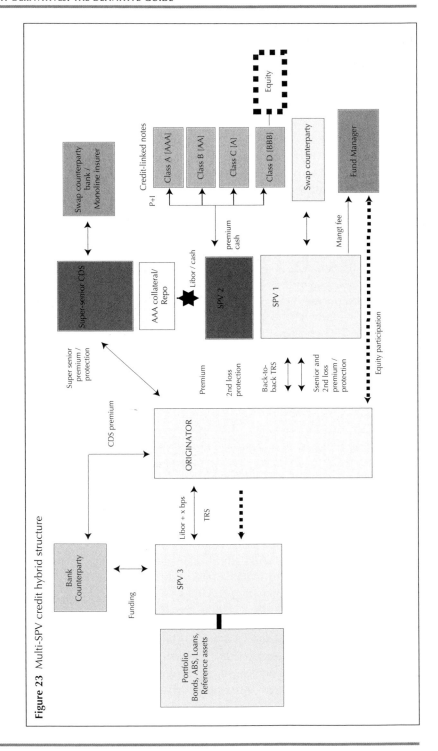

Figure 23 Multi-SPV credit hybrid structure

Figure 24 Hypothetical (proposed) deal terms

Multi-SPV credit hybrid structure	
Portfolio size	€1bln -€7bln
Trade date	Month 1 Year 1
Ramp-up end date	Month 1 Year 2
Call date	Month 1 Year 7
Final maturity	Month 1 Year 20

issued credit-linked notes. This SPV provides the "second-loss" protection for the originator. Proceeds of the note issue are invested in risk-free assets such as T-bills, or placed in a reserve cash account or structured deposit. If proceeds are invested in eligible investments, these are placed in a repo with a counterparty bank. The return on the issued notes is linked to the return from the collateral pool and the premium payments received by the SPV from the originator for taking on the second-loss risk protection.

The originator retains equity participation in the structure to benefit from gains made by the fund manager in running the portfolio and in entering into CDS trading.

Deal highlights
For a balance-sheet-type transaction, the originator is able to transfer credit risk of assets held on its balance sheet. It can also benefit from the arbitrage gain from sourcing credit protection on these assets in the CDS market compared to the return received on these assets in the cash market. As we have seen earlier, there is significant saving in regulatory capital charge from the partially-funded structure. In addition, the managed element of the deal, which is undertaken via SPV 1 and a multi-dealer counterparty arrangement, will allow the originator to undertake credit trading in the market.

Under the multi-SPV structure, the originator benefits from the following.

❏ Structure and close large volume deals, achieved by placing risk across a wide range of investors, including cash bond investors and credit derivative counterparties.
❏ A vehicle that enables each investor an opportunity to tailor the SPV to meet their specific investment requirements and criteria – ie, specific requirements in terms of currency requirements, market sector and particular fund management style.
❏ A vehicle that allows the portfolio manager to leverage experience from different areas of its firm to blend skills into the management of the overall deal.

❏ Scope to use existing market familiarity with credit derivatives, cash and synthetic CDOs and managed arbitrage synthetic CDOs to introduce a more complex product across a wider range of investors and markets.
❏ A flexible deal structure that enables risk exposure of any asset class to be transferred, while any asset class can be targeted in the market for credit trading.
❏ The ability to securitise both cash and synthetic assets as required.

Due to existing familiarity with the CDO product across US and European legal jurisdictions, it will be possible to bring the new structure to the market under existing legislation.

Summary
The synthetic CDO structure is well-established in the debt capital markets. In its different variants, financial institutions have employed the product for balance sheet management, credit risk transfer and credit trading. The above shows how the deal mechanics can be advantageous for commercial banks wishing to effectively control regulatory capital. The greater liquidity of the synthetic credit market, compared to the cash market, has made synthetic CDO accessible for investors.

The next generation of this product will be designed to integrate cash and synthetic markets. By engineering one transaction that can generate interest across a wider range of investors, the originator will benefit from a greater deal flexibility. This has significant implications for efficient balance sheet management.

CONCLUSIONS
The case studies considered in this chapter are innovative structures that present a creative combination of securitisation technology and credit derivative instruments. Later structures have been introduced into the market that make use of TRSs as well as CDSs, while removing the restriction on shorting credit. Analysis of these vehicles shows how a portfolio manager can utilise the arrangement to exploit its credit trading expertise and its experience of the credit derivatives market to provide attractive returns for investors. The most flexible vehicles, such as Jazz CDO I, theoretically allow more efficient portfolio risk management when compared to static or more restrictive deals. As the market in synthetic credit, in Europe at least, is frequently more liquid than the cash market for the same reference names, it is reasonable to expect more transactions of this type in the near future.

ACKNOWLEDGEMENTS

The author would like to thank Ketul Tanna and Chee Hau at JP Morgan Chase, Richard Pereira at Dresdner Kleinwort Wasserstein, Rod Pienaar and Suleman Baig at Deustche Bank AG, Aaron Nematnejad and Abukar Ali at Bloomberg LP, Didier Joannas at Sungard and Mohamoud Dualeh for their constructive review comments on an earlier draft. Any errors are the responsibility of the author.

1 This shows that Eurobonds, defined as international securities issued by a syndicate of banks and clearing in Euroclear and Clearstream, may pay coupon on frequencies other than an annual basis.

2 Providing the counterparty is an OECD bank, which is invariably the case.

3 This is because reference assets that are protected by credit derivative contracts, and which remain on the balance sheet, will – under Basel rules – attract a lower regulatory capital charge.

4 So called because the swap is ahead of the most senior of any funded (note) portion, the latter being "senior", which means that the swap must be "super-senior".

5 Averaged from the yield spread on 7 synthetic deals closed during January– December 2002, yield spread at issue, rates data from Bloomberg.

6 UBS Warburg, *CDO Insight*, 29 March 2002.

7 In practice, to date this portion has been between 5% and 15% of the reference pool.

8 An "OECD" bank, thus guaranteeing a 20% risk weighting for capital ratio purposes, under Basel I rules.

9 These are also commonly known as collateralised synthetic obligations (CSOs) within the market. *Risk* magazine has called them collateralised swap obligations, which handily also shortens to CSOs. Boggiano *et al*, (2002) refer to these structures as managed variable synthetic CDOs, although the author has not come across this term in other literature.

10 This is also referred to as a special purpose entity (SPE) or special purpose company (SPC).

11 A GIC has been defined either as an account that pays a fixed rate of interest for its term, or more usually an account that pays a fixed spread below Libor or euribor, usually three-month floating rolled over each interest period.

12 This term is shared with other securitisation structures: when notes have been priced and placed in the market, and all legal documentation signed by all named participants, the transaction has closed. In effect this is the start of the transaction, and, all being well, the noteholders will receive interest payments during the life of the deal and principal repayment on maturity.

13 These deals have been arranged by a number of investment banks, including JP Morgan Chase, Bank of America and Credit Agricole Indosuez. They are known variously as *tailor-made CDOs, tranche-only CDOs, on-demand CDOs, iCDOs and investor-driven CDOs*, as well as *single-tranche CDOs*. The author prefers the last one.

14 Source: CreditFlux, April 2002

15 Source: Moody's

16 See Choudhry, M., *et al*, 2002, An Introduction to Credit Derivatives (www.YieldCurve.com).

BIBLIOGRAPHY

Anson, M., 1999, *Credit Derivatives* (New Hope, PA: FJF Associates).

Boggiano, K., Waterson, and Stein, C., 2002, "Four forms of synthetic CDOs", *Derivatives Week*, Euromoney Publications, 11(23), pp. 12–14.

Bomfim, A., 2002, "Credit Derivatives and Their Potential to Synthesize Riskless Assets", *Journal of Fixed Income*, September 2002, pp. 6–16.

Choudhry, M., 2001, "Some issues in the asset-swap pricing of CDSs", *Derivatives Week*, Euromoney Publications, 2 December 2001, pp. 4–5.

Choudhry, M., 2002, "Trading credit spreads: the case for a specialised exchange-traded credit futures contract", *Journal of Derivatives Use, Trading and Regulation*, 8(1), pp.46–61.

Choudhry, M., 2002, "Combining securitisation and trading in credit derivatives: an analysis of the managed synthetic collateralised debt obligation", *Euromoney Debt Capital Markets Yearbook* (London: Euromoney Publications).

Choudhry, M., 2004 (forthcoming), *Structured Credit Products: Credit Instruments and Synthetic Securitisation* (Singapore: John Wiley & Son).

Das, S., 2001, *Structured Products and Hybrid Securities* (Singapore: John Wiley & Son).

Fabozzi, F., and L. Goodman (ed), 2001, *Investing in Collateralised Debt Obligations* (New Hope, PA: FJF Associates).

Kasapi, A., 1999, *Mastering Credit Derivatives* (London: FT Prentice Hall).

McPherson, N., H. Remeza, and D. Kung, 2002, *Synthetic CDOs and CDSs* (London: CSFB).

12

Considerations for dynamic and static, cash and synthetic collateralised debt obligations

Alexander Batchvarov, Jenna Collins and William Davies

Merrill Lynch

European collateralised debt obligations (CDOs) have evolved from early, static, balance-sheet cash transactions to utilise synthetic execution, synthetic assets and various dynamic forms of credit portfolio management. As the market continues to evolve, diversification takes on new dimensions, potential volatility and complexity of excess cash flow may increase, currency risk is more dynamic, liquidity needs often become more significant, losses may crystallise due to trading behaviour rather than simply credit risk, obligation settlement and valuation requires careful definition, and management flexibility and/or investor input often increases. Although the market often refers to CDOs as existing in one form versus another – static or managed, cash or synthetic – clear distinctions in nomenclature have diminished in practice, and the increasing degree of variety within the market necessitates new questions from CDO investors.

CDO MARKET ROADMAP

CDOs have established themselves in the market as a distinct sector, and one can argue that the sector has matured, given that it went through severe stresses in recent years. The moniker "CDO" covers a broad range of products and is more of a description of a certain type of structure. As such, the CDO product can be structured on the basis of different fixed-income instruments (for example, bonds, private equity, loans or asset-backed securities) as well as credit default swaps. The pool of exposures (cash or synthetic) is tranched to create a new set of exposures with a different risk profile, which are then distributed to parties willing to assume such new exposures either in cash or synthetic format.

All CDOs have this technique in common and can be categorised by collateral or reference entity type, the way the underlying pool exposure is created, motivations of the different parties to the CDO transaction, ways in which exposures to the CDO are assumed, the degree of management of the underlying pool of exposures and so on. Such categorisation is helpful in creating a clearer picture of the market, but can be imprecise, given the overlap of different categories and sectors within an increasingly hetero-geneous CDO world.

CDOs are usually divided into three broad sub-sectors, collateralised bond obligations (CBO), collateralised loan obligations (CLO) and collat-eralised synthetic obligations (CSO):

❏ CDOs consisting of loan collateral (mezzanine, leveraged, senior-secured or unsecured, loan commitments) are called collateralised loan obligations (CLOs).
❏ CDOs consisting of bond collateral are called collateralised bond oblig-ations (CBOs). CBOs may therefore contain asset-backed bonds, as well as corporate (investment-grade and high-yield), and emerging market bonds.
❏ If the underlying the CDO pool of exposures are created through CDS, one may refer to it as CSO (collateralised synthetic obligation).
❏ A mixture of bond and CDS leads to a hybrid structure, and a mixture of bonds and loans in a pool is classified depending on which instru-ment dominates or simply referred to as CDO.

CDOs are also, separately, differentiated as to whether the deal is "arbi-trage-driven" or "balance-sheet-driven":

❏ Managers of arbitrage-driven deals exploit spread differences between the assets and liabilities of the CDO structure.
❏ By contrast, balance-sheet transactions are done primarily to improve the economics of a bank's balance sheet by transferring credit risk from their loan book and gaining commensurate regulatory capital relief and/or by accessing alternative off-balance-sheet funding sources.

CDOs are further categorised as cash-flow, market-value or synthetic structures:

❏ Cash-flow CDOs rely on the amortisation of the underlying assets for both interest and principal debt service. In this respect they are similar to other traditional financial receivable-backed, asset-backed securities. In Europe, cash-flow CDOs historically relied on static portfolio of credits, but the market has developed to allow for some substitution and management of deteriorated credits, or to embrace full manage-ment of the portfolio.

❏ While debt interest service in cash "market value"-driven structures is also drawn from underlying bond and loan payments, debt principal repayment is met by selling securities (ultimately liquidating the portfolio) in the open market – hence the term "market-value structures". The asset manager in market-value structures takes a hands-on role in maximising the arbitrage yield, as well as the value of the portfolio, and may engage in active trading.

❏ Synthetic CDOs use credit-default swaps (CDS) in some aspect of the structure. The term "synthetic" may refer to the asset side of the CDO balance sheet, to the liability side of the balance sheet or both. If it is referring to the asset side of the balance sheet, the portfolio of assets would comprise CDS (either in whole or in part). When it refers to the liability side of the balance sheet, the risk of the portfolio is transferred to third parties by means of one or more portfolio CDS.

Synthetic techniques are applied to bank balance-sheet reference portfolios – collateralised loan obligations – (CLOs) as well as arbitrage portfolios:

❏ For a synthetic CLO, the CDS mechanism allows an originating bank to hedge the credit exposure on a portfolio of reference assets, without having to sell the portfolio outright. Yet, despite there being no transfer of underlying reference assets, the transaction is typically structured to de-link the ratings of the risk tranches (swaps and notes) from the originating bank.

❏ Alternatively, synthetic arbitrage CDOs aim at creating an investor-portfolio product and finding the best investment opportunities in CDS markets. Synthetic arbitrage transactions increasingly consist of hybrid portfolios, allowing the portfolio manager to take positions in both the cash bond and CDS markets.

Synthetic transactions may issue "funded" credit-linked notes (CLN) in addition to, or instead of, directly placing CDS with (ie, buying protection from) third-party investors:

❏ If a synthetic CDO is "funded", it means that some or all of the CDS were linked to cash notes that are then issued to investors (who may not be able to sell protection in a pure form). In this context, the term "funded" does not mean that the notes provide any funds to the issuer. The cash raised from the note issuance is used instead to buy high-quality "collateral", ie, highly rated government securities or quasi-government securities. This collateral is used to repay the notes at maturity, and to help service the interest payments on the notes. If losses are incurred by the reference pool during its life, the collateral is used to cover those losses, hence reducing the amount of collateral available to repay CDO investors upon maturity.

Synthetic structures are again split as to whether they reference static portfolios or dynamic portfolios:

❏ Static credit portfolios, at the extreme, are portfolios that are selected at the start of a transaction (or during some ramp-up period), and for which the composition of the portfolio does not change over time, other than as assets within the portfolio mature, are called, or default. The spread generated by such portfolios is a function of the credit spreads on the assets – there are no trading gains or losses, little or no substitution of assets, and no manager oversight after issuance.

❏ Managed and/or "dynamic" credit portfolios are portfolios that are managed, to a greater or lesser degree, by a third-party manager that is given a level of discretion to buy and sell bonds or protection in market, in order to maximise returns and minimise losses in the CDO. In more recent transactions, some of the functions can be performed by an investor(s).

Furthermore, synthetic structures can be executed as:

❏ Full liability structures – with tranches spanning from most senior to "equity"; and

❏ Single tranche structures, where a single tranche is created for a given investor, and the portions below and above that particular tranche are hedged.

We emphasise again that despite these distinctions, it is increasingly common that CDO issuer motivations, asset types, investor involvement and the degree of management overlap among the categories above.

SYNTHETIC CDO MECHANICS

As a subsector within the broader CDO market, the synthetic CDO market has experienced nothing short of phenomenal growth in recent years, particularly in Europe. From 1 January 2002 to 30 May 2003, roughly US$77 billion in risk transfer was executed via CDOs in Europe (see Table 1, excluding small and medium-sized enterprise CLOs). Of this amount, nearly 90% was executed synthetically.

The synthetic CDO market started with mostly private transactions in the latter part

Table 1. European *Arbitrage and Balance Sheet* CDO total risk transfer: 1 January 2002 to 30 May 2003 US$ billions

	Cash	Synthetic
Dynamic	8.4	36.2
Static	1.7	31.1

of the 1990s. It further developed in both the private and public domains in 2000 and 2001. Due to a spate of downgrades that plagued a number of static investment-grade CDOs, the market has again become more bespoke and increasingly private in nature, giving individual investors and managers a more custom-tailored product than was offered in the recent past. The initial black-box structures have also given way to more transparent structures, and exclusively static portfolios have increasingly given way to, more recently, dynamic portfolios (those allowing a degree of credit substitution or active management).

The mechanics of a typical synthetic CDO are as follows (see Figure 1):

❑ A special-purpose vehicle ("SPV") issues bonds (for most of the risk tranches) and uses the proceeds to purchase the aforementioned "collateral" for the notes.

❑ The sponsor bank or counterparty enters into a CDS with the SPV. This is the component of the structure that transfers credit risk on the pool of reference assets to the investors. The losses are allocated to investors by reducing the amount of collateral held by the SPV, which is then applied sequentially to the capital structure, taking into account the tranche seniority.

❑ Interest debt service is met by the collateral yield, CDS premiums (or guarantee fees) due from the sponsor bank and repo payments (if any). The structure provides for the premium payments, coupled with any repo interest, to cover the residual negative carry (or interest deficiency) that would inevitably exist given lower coupons accruing to the collateral versus interest due under the capital structure. Unlike cash CDOs, debt service is not met by interest payments or amortisation of the asset portfolio itself.

❑ Principal repayment is met from the liquidation or redemption of the separate collateral pool. Other forms of structural credit support ensure that the likelihood of cash flows due to investors is consistent with the assigned ratings.

One of the attractions of synthetic CDO execution is that it involves much less transaction documentation compared with cash executed transactions. For example, an asset sale and transfer agreement are not required for the referenced obligation in a synthetic transaction. In addition, synthetic CLOs allow banks to avoid the onerous process of combing through each underlying loan document and unravelling assignment clauses or other restrictions in order to sell the asset. As a result, transaction execution is much simpler. However, investors should not be lulled into a false sense of security, given the complexity and potential pitfalls of another aspect of synthetic CDO documentation – that of the credit default swap itself.

Executing a transaction using synthetic liabilities also typically involves

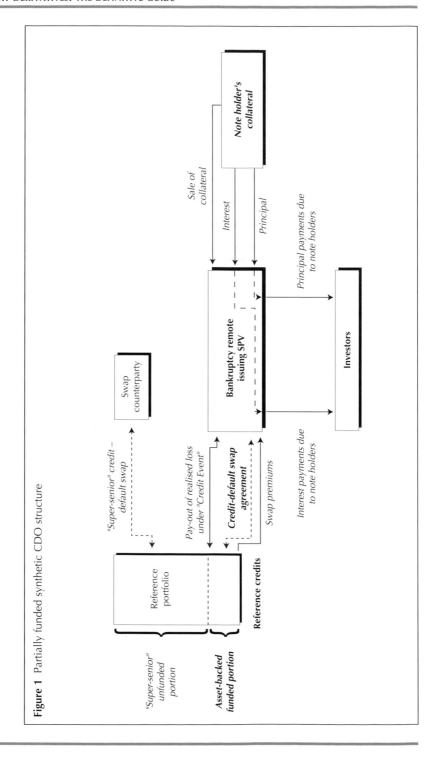

Figure 1 Partially funded synthetic CDO structure

lower all-in costs than a conventional structure, and is thus popular with both banks and investment managers. The lower all-in costs are largely a result of an "incomplete" cash market that does not reward tranching of risk beyond the triple-A level, due to the opportunity cost of cash (a floor exists at the yields of triple-A government debt). In the synthetic market, however, risk can be tranched at any level and remunerated. Hence, the transactions have historically created a risk tranche that is senior to the triple-A tranche, the "super-senior tranche", paying premiums of 10 to 15 basis points (bps). Increasingly, the super-senior tranche is tranched even further, per investor requirements and in order to optimise execution.

COUNTERPARTY RISK

Given that the CDS implicit in the reference portfolio and the risk transfer in a synthetic CDO are agreements between a protection seller and a protection buyer and the related payment flows going in both directions, the buyer and the seller have credit exposure to each other, ie, counterparty risk. Counterparty risk is an additional risk in synthetic CDOs that is usually present only to a limited degree in cash CDOs, ie, in any currency or interest-rate swaps. If a CDS counterparty defaults, it would have implications for:

❏ Regular payments of protection premiums by the protection buyer. The protection seller may, in some cases, mitigate this counterparty risk by requiring the buyer to make protection payments in advance, ie, at the beginning of the protection period.
❏ Event-related, one-time protection payments due from the protection seller. The risk of absence of this payment when needed is usually addressed by requiring a minimum-rating trigger on the protection seller. A trigger breach requires a replacement of the protection seller by one of an acceptable rating, a guarantee of the protection seller's obligation by an appropriately rated third party, or posting of collateral by the protection seller (the level of collateral depends on the level of deviation from the minimum required rating).
❏ CDS mark-to-market (MTM) valuation in case of termination, and a requirement for funding of such termination payment (repayment at par) through a liquidity line or through a senior position in the transaction's cash-flow allocation. This MTM should not erode the subordination levels in the transaction.

Early synthetic CDOs usually involved the transfer of the risk of the entire portfolio through a single-basket CDS from one counterparty to another single counterparty, often the SPV. In partially funded synthetic CDOs, there are usually two separate risk transfers: one portfolio CDS directly with the super-senior protection provider and one with the SPV that issues the remaining tranches of risk.

These transfers are applicable to both static and dynamic arbitrage synthetic CDOs, the use of one or more counterparties depends on the level of management anticipated in a given transaction. For a static transaction, protection is purchased for a portfolio held by a single CDS counterparty (eg, a bank for a synthetic CLO). Any modifications to the initial portfolio are traded by the SPV through a single counterparty. As the level of management and manager discretion increases, the number of counterparties of the SPV can increase into multiple counterparties with which the manager trades (in the way of a traditional credit portfolio manager).

The simplicity and ease of execution of the static balance sheet structures are replaced with higher documentation complexity of actively managed CDS structures to allow for active and more efficient portfolio management. While the need for competitive pricing for trading and settlement of CDS requires several CDS counterparties, using an excessive number of counterparties may inadvertently create the additional problems of documentation complexity and, more importantly, management of counterparty risk. For example, hedging and offsetting trades for a single credit position with two different counterparties creates additional complexities in determining the credit risk of the net position.

So the questions in synthetic CDOs are not only the traditional "how many credits (or CDS) are present in a transaction?" but also:

❑ How many swap counterparties are used?
❑ How is counterparty risk managed?
❑ Is it necessary to have multiple counterparties, ie, is the portfolio expected to be actively managed?

CASH OR SYNTHETIC EXPOSURES

Synthetic securitisation initially referred specifically to the form of transfer of the credit risk of the securitisation pool. More recently, the question as to whether a CDO transaction is "cash or synthetic" is equally applicable to the way the exposures in the CDO portfolio are created, whether via:

❑ *CDS*: selling protection on given credits or buying protection (which is the equivalent of cash bond shorting);
❑ *Cash*: buying exposure to given credits in the form of bond purchases (short-selling of bonds is generally not allowed); or
❑ *Hybrid*: a combination of the two above; to these two broad categories of assets, one can also add total rate-of-return swaps, and bivariate risk positions, which are generally used infrequently.

Because of the increasing ability to mix CDS and cash exposures within transactions, the key questions are not so much how the reference pool is created, or what format credit exposure takes (CDS or cash bonds), but rather:

❑ What is the credit quality of the portfolio, and what is the distribution of credit quality?
❑ What level of diversification can be achieved and maintained?
❑ Does the presence of CDS modify the loss distribution of the pool?

Given that CDS exist primarily on investment grade corporates (a limited pool of names), in order to improve the diversification of a CDS pool, cash bonds are often a welcome addition. Cash exposures can take the form of corporate and sovereign bonds, asset-backed and other structured-finance securities ("ABS"), as well as stripped convertible bonds.

ABS, in its broadest meaning (that is, all structured finance asset classes), is increasingly added to the portfolio to provide diversification into credit sectors not easily available through CDS or other cash alternatives. Such sectors include consumer loan portfolios (as in the traditional asset-backed and residential mortgage-backed securities), and corporate CDO portfolios on names for which CDS are scarce (high-yield) or nonexistent (eg, mezzanine loans, small and medium sized enterprise bank loans, commercial real estate loans). Such hybrid portfolios will generally benefit from broader defensive diversification and higher rating stability, as indicated by recent studies of rating transitions of different fixed-income instruments over similar time frames. These studies also emphasise the difference in transition ratios and spread volatility for ABS and corporate bonds under the similar economic conditions of duress, ie, that experienced in the period 1998 to 2002. This further evidences lower correlation between the two sectors, and is of particular benefit for investors in senior tranches of synthetic CDOs.

A hybrid managed CDO also allows CDO managers to explore possible relative value opportunities that may emerge between CDS and cash assets for the benefit of investors in the respective CDO. It also allows the manager the opportunity to achieve better returns through more efficient leverage. Overall, a hybrid structure should allow for the optimisation of asset allocation given a CDO manager's skills and sector knowledge.

One should not forget that, regardless of how a transaction is structured, it is, after all, mainly about credit. All portfolios of credits – cash bonds or reference entities – require similar analysis in terms of credit quality, diversification, single credit exposure, risk and return, default and recovery expectations. The default and recovery expectations for the same exposure may be different depending on whether such exposure is assumed in cash form (long a bond) or synthetic form (selling protection). Despite constant refinement of structural features within CDOs, investors must continue to have a view as to the credits within the portfolio in which they invest.

EXCESS MARGIN VERSUS EXCESS SPREAD

In both cash and synthetic securitisations, excess cash flow arises from the difference between the cash flows generated by the assets and the cash flows needed to service the liabilities of the structure. In both cases key questions of the investor analysis, particularly by investors at the lower steps of the capital structure, are:

❑ At what level are the excess cash flows likely to be during the life of the transaction?
❑ Which are the key variables that can affect excess spread negatively?
❑ How is excess cash flow used in the structure?

Unlike cash CDOs, in synthetic CDOs, the excess cash flows are not only related to credit quality and margin of the asset portfolio, but also a function of, among other things, trading strategies, counterparty risk and short trading of CDS, as well as MTM variations. Some of these aspects differ from the traditional cash CDOs and should be carefully examined in conjunction with the other elements of the synthetic CDO structure discussed previously.

In general, the use of excess cash flow in the structure can fall into one of three categories:

❑ *Never used*, that is, released to equity holders and the manager.
❑ *Always used*, or retained in a reserve account for future use or used to purchase additional collateral, thus creating additional credit protection in the form of over-collateralisation, or ability to pay down liabilities, thus allowing for the deleveraging of the structure.
❑ *Used under certain circumstances*, such as the increase of portfolio losses beyond a certain level or breach of over-collateralisation or other tests.

In a synthetic managed CDO, the level of excess margin may be used as a trigger allowing (or disallowing) short CDS trades. As shorting CDS involves payment, rather than receipt, of premiums, it may lead to spread erosion in the pool and to additional counterparty risk, both of which could translate into liquidity shortfalls.

CURRENCY RISK

Most securitisations usually have assets and liabilities in the same currency, or if there is a mismatch between the two it is easy to address on an SPV level. In cash CDOs, the mismatch usually occurs on the asset side of the CDO balance sheet: for instance, if a CDO is funding in euros and the CDO asset pool is a combination of euro- and US dollar-denominated bonds, whose relative share of the pool can change over time. The currencies are usually known from the outset and the respective hedging mechanisms can be established. In contrast, in a CDS pool, the potential currency mismatches and the currencies involved may not be known in advance, and can spontaneously arise in the event of a delivery of a foreign-currency-denominated bond, should a credit event occur and is settled. Currency risk therefore arises due to the risk of cash shortfall as a result of conversion risk. So the question changes from the cash CDO question of "how is currency risk hedged?" into the synthetic CDO questions of:

❑ What currency mismatches can potentially arise?
❑ How are investors protected against them?

As mentioned above, currency risk can arise from the delivery, in case of a credit event, of a bond for which the currency is not pre-determined and could be different from the currency of the CDO's assets and liabilities. This currency risk does, however, apply only to recoveries, so it may play a relatively small role, given the lower prices associated with obligations for which a credit event has occurred. To avoid the currency concerns, the simplest solution, usually employed in CDO structures, is to opt for a cash settlement and/or to fix exchange rates at transaction onset. Alternatively, the use of a liquidity facility and/or rolling spot-forward hedging after a credit event can mitigate this currency risk.

LIQUIDITY NEEDS

In a typical cash CDO structure, given the pass-through nature of the cash flows emanating from the asset pool and directed to servicing the CDO liabilities, liquidity may be needed to cover temporary cash-flow shortfalls usually due to timing mismatches between asset and liability payments. These concerns are not present in a synthetic CDO structure and, in managed synthetic CDOs, particular needs for liquidity may or may not arise. Therefore, instead of an assumption that there is a liquidity facility in the deal, the questions instead should be:

❑ Is there a need for a liquidity facility in a given synthetic CDO structure?
❑ How is the liquidity facility sized and procured?

Particular need for liquidity in a synthetic CDO are created by:

❑ shorting CDS (payment, rather than receipt of premiums);
❑ trading losses crystallised by termination; and
❑ credit events requiring cash settlement or bond delivery (where a bond must be purchased).

Liquidity may also play an active part in the execution of portfolio management strategy and facilitate changes in asset allocation.

For certain trading strategies, eg, uncovered short CDS, the liquidity needs may be substantial and can be satisfied only through a dedicated liquidity facility. Short CDS also often precipitate collateralised swaps, to minimise the counterparty risk of the trade. The size and cost of such a facility are of key importance, as high liquidity costs may reduce the benefit of savings achieved on the liability side of the synthetic CDO through the low-cost super-senior tranche hedging.

Liquidity facilities may also be used to meet shortfalls of subordinated class interest payments. However, CDOs often remove this need for extra liquidity by introducing payment-in-kind interest ("PIKable interest") for these classes. PIKable tranches typically capitalise any missed interest if interest payments are missed for two consecutive periods for single-A-rated tranches or indefinitely for the triple-B-rated tranches.

LOSS CRYSTALLISATION

In traditional cash-flow CDO structures, losses crystallise to tranched notes and equity in relation to frequency and severity of credit losses on the underlying credit or reference portfolio. By way of contrast, in dynamically managed synthetic CDOs (not unlike market-value cash CDOs) profit or loss instead arise due to credit losses and trading losses. In dynamic synthetic CDOs, these trading losses may result from the unwinding of a CDS or offsetting trades.

The questions are, therefore, not only "what is the expected and sustainable frequency and severity of losses within the CDO?" but also:

❏ How does loss arise?
❏ How is the loss determined and what is the nature of the bidding process in the case of a credit event?
❏ How is the loss covered?

In a synthetic CDO, if a loss arises from offsetting trades, it will be covered by the premium flows and hence absorbed by the excess margin. In contrast, a loss due to termination must be funded in cash, although it can be amortised over time through the interest flows or be funded by a liquidity facility.

Furthermore, in CDOs (and portfolio CDS) as opposed to single-name CDS, losses are often settled in cash, to avoid currency risk and provide for a reduced administrative burden for the manager. However, this must be balanced with the reduced pressure to sell a delivered obligation if physically settled, giving a portfolio manager the ability to maximise proceeds at the opportune time.

DIFFERENT RISKS FROM THOSE IN CASH CDOS

Although synthetic CDOs can be a more effective method of risk transfer and portfolio management and CDS can often offer more attractive arbitrage opportunities than cash bonds, there are different risks in the synthetic CDOs from those in its cash counterpart, as explored above.

Synthetic CDOs have credit risk, counterparty risk and collateral risk (if funded notes are used), but less servicing risk than cash transactions.

❑ Synthetic CDOs incorporate not only credit risk of the reference portfolio, but also the counterparty risk of the entities required to pay premiums or protection payments.

❑ Investors in funded notes of synthetic CDOs also have exposure to the credit risk of the collateral purchased to defease the notes at maturity. This collateral may be highly rated, but also has transition and default probabilities on top of that of the underlying portfolio. To minimise the impact on investors in the event that such collateral experiences ratings downgrades, the credit risk of collateral is increasingly structured with over-collateralisation or replacement triggers.

❑ Servicing risk present in traditional receivables-backed ABS as well as cash CLOs, related to the timeliness of receipt of interest and principal payments from the underlying loans, is not much of a concern when the transaction is executed synthetically, as these payments do not service the debt issued to investors in funded notes.

Synthetic CDOs have more complex settlement and valuation issues related to transaction credit events in comparison with the cash-based structures, where loss crystallisation and its impact on the transaction's liabilities are relatively straightforward:

❑ Credit events and payout amounts in synthetic CLOs, for example, are predefined, whereas in cash- or "true sale"-based structures any form of underlying non-payment or default adversely affects investors. This feature of synthetic CLOs is clearly investor-positive. However, credit events that are too broadly defined may trigger prematurely and result in more severe losses for note holders. In transactions where the credit events are not clearly described, investors would have to rely on a third party for the interpretation and validation of an event covered under the swap. It suffices to mention restructuring, as a credit event that continues to raise controversy in contrast to the generally accepted credit events of bankruptcy and failure to pay.

❑ Credit events in CDS within the portfolio of a static or dynamic synthetic CDO can also be varied, and, *inter alia*, such events, reference entities, deliverable obligations and maturities must be the same for any offsetting CDS in order to properly hedge an exposure.

Third parties, such as trustees, have different responsibilities:

❑ There is a greater reliance on trustees in being able to protect the interests of note holders, particularly in synthetic CLOs prior to insolvency of the originator. Among other duties, the trustee in synthetic CLOs will be required to be vigilant *vis-à-vis* monitoring and selling the collateral as required and verifying the determination and allocation of losses.
❑ Unlike cash CDOs, in the event of the insolvency of the originating bank or counterparty, the trustee does not have the responsibilities to wind down a portfolio to pay down the notes. Such insolvency is simply a default under the swap agreement, necessitating a termination payment.

Utilising the super-senior swap in a partially funded synthetic CDO places senior note holders in a more leveraged position than senior note holders in a similar fully funded or cash flow CLO:

❑ Senior note holders could face greater relative losses (as a proportion of principal) compared with senior investors in fully funded or conventional structures, should defaults reach a level where all subordination is removed. Nevertheless, the likelihood of such high defaults is extremely remote and is consistent with triple-A ratings.
❑ In the subordinated tranches, however, note holders in partially funded structures are no more aggressively long the underlying credit exposure from either a "first dollar of loss" or "expected loss" position compared with their counterparts in a conventional cash or fully funded structure.

GROWTH IN DYNAMICALLY MANAGED SYNTHETIC CDOS
Although static CDOs laid the groundwork for the synthetic CDO market, dynamically managed CDOs have taken over since 2002 and will likely remain the governing force in the synthetic CDO market going forward. The static format remains preferred for synthetic balance sheet transactions, as such transactions are not driven by an investor, arranger or investment manager, but rather a bank seeking capital relief and/or risk management. However, the arbitrage-driven synthetic CDO is increasingly dominant, representing three-quarters of total European CDO risk transfer for the period 1 January 2002 to 30 May 2003 (see Figure 2). Moreover, the arbitrage synthetic CDO is becoming more managed but with significantly different degrees of freedom. Over the same period, 77% of European synthetic arbitrage CDOs utilised some degree of active management, ranging from limited ability to substitute credits and leeway to minimise losses for deteriorating credits, to more active management,

including the ability to undertake naked short CDS positions.

The reasons behind the dramatic growth in the synthetic CDO sector, and particularly in managed synthetic CDOs, can be summarised as follows:

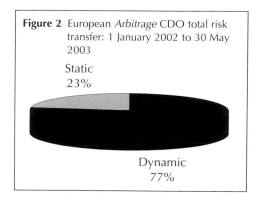

Figure 2 European *Arbitrage* CDO total risk transfer: 1 January 2002 to 30 May 2003

Static 23%

Dynamic 77%

❏ In 2002, there was a window of opportunity to capture the arbitrage between the wide corporate CDS spreads and relatively stable CDO spreads, ie, between the asset and liability side of the CDO balance sheet. This arbitrage will continue to reappear periodically as the technical dynamics between the two markets continue to differ fundamentally.

❏ Opportunities arise to capture the arbitrage between CDS and cash bonds (trading this difference is referred to as "basis trading").

❏ Opportunities arise to benefit from greater leverage as the credit quality of the synthetic CDO assets and reference entities is generally higher than cash CDOs and CLOs, requiring less equity support to achieve top ratings.

❏ CDO arbitrage has been further improved by the price and size of the super-senior tranche, resulting in reduced requirement to sell cash rated notes on the market.

MANAGER VERSUS INVESTOR CONTROL

Investors debate the strengths and weaknesses of static versus dynamic CDO transactions, including both those with mere substitution rights and those that are more actively managed. Static transactions allow investors to familiarise themselves with a pool of credits from the outset, and require less ongoing monitoring of the portfolio manager's trading decisions. Furthermore, given the diversified portfolio of credits within a transaction, it may be argued that the remaining risk of the portfolio at senior tranches level is largely systemic risk. Most studies have shown that investment managers (generally in the equity and total-return fixed-income markets), cannot perform better than the market after transaction costs, cannot remove systemic risk, and therefore add little value to management of a well diversified portfolio. Nevertheless, a number of static transactions have experienced downgrades as credits deteriorated and there was no party that could trade out of securities or CDS in order to minimise or prevent losses.

So, investors have turned (for a fee) to actively managed portfolios, relying on the expertise of a portfolio manager to maximise returns and minimise risks by making timely and shrewd investment decisions. It may be argued that the limited size of the CDS market in particular and/or the composition of a "diversified" CDO is not a true approximation of the market portfolio, and therefore has "unsystemic" risk that may be managed more appropriately by an expert portfolio manager. On the other side, CDOs that incorporate a greater or lesser degree of management may perform better than a comparable static portfolio, but they also may perform worse depending on the portfolio manager's actions. The direction the market seems to be taking is to find ways to mitigate the downside of each of the two structures by balancing between the familiarity of a static pool of credits, defensive management of such a portfolio, and delegating more active management to managers who may be able to outperform the market.

Because of these developments, the market is increasingly difficult to categorise solely as static or dynamic and is evolving into a more nuanced market reflecting management ability and investor preferences, differing transaction to transaction. Increasingly, in order to assess the risks and rewards that a transaction may offer, the key questions an investor must ask are not whether the pool of referenced obligations is, therefore, static or dynamic, but rather:

❑ Who selects the referenced obligations?
❑ Who has the right to change one or more of them, when and how?

Many variations are possible. The ability to make changes in the portfolio can vary from broad to increasingly restricted, the latter being more widely used recently. On one end, portfolios may change via replenishment only upon prepayment or amortisation of credits during a period specified at the beginning of the transaction. On the other end, a manager may have full discretion to manage the portfolio for the life of a transaction. Most synthetic CDOs lie increasingly in between these two extremes, where managers have the right to trade for a limited proportion of the portfolio.

In addition, the CDO equity investor, CDO arranger, the CDO manager or a CDO debt investor may select the referenced pool. In the first three cases, there is greater ground for moral hazard, due to the possible diverging interests of these parties when compared with those of the senior and mezzanine debt investors. In some cases, the role of the manager may be assumed by the CDO arranger or CDS counterparty (thus saving on management fees). However, this may often result in the selection of the cheapest to include credits, ie, those with market-implied higher default probability than peer credits of the same rating.

The case where a CDO equity investor or CDO manager selects referenced obligations is the classic case of moral hazard demonstrated in many cash CDO deals and motivated by reward. With their position at the bottom of the capital and payment structure, these parties may take above-average risks, particularly in the short run, to recover their investment and achieve a level of equity returns at the expense of the more senior tranches of risk. There are a number of ways to mitigate this risk or, in other words, to realign the interest of the equity and debt holders.

MINIMISING CONFLICTS BETWEEN DEBT INVESTORS, CDO MANAGERS AND EQUITY INVESTORS

The potential (or realised) conflicts between the interests of debt investors and of CDO managers or equity investors (as well as the mechanism of manager compensation) have been used partially to explain the underperformance of arbitrage cash-flow CBOs over the period 1998 to 2002. In general, the equity investor is more concerned with defaults than rating migration, while the latter, especially in its more acute form, is the primary preoccupation of the mezzanine and other, more senior, investors. Static and managed synthetic CDOs are not immune to similar shortcomings; in fact, they can be magnified given the higher leverage often achieved in a managed synthetic CDO due to a predominantly investment-grade credit portfolio.

In static synthetic CDOs, these conflicts have been addressed by writing the equity tranche down by the difference between the notional amount and settlement amount as a credit event is crystallised. The write-down depends on the level of recoveries. As the tranches further down the capital structure of a CDO pay higher coupons, the reduction in CDO liabilities also reduces the CDO debt costs by a potentially larger degree than the CDO income, thereby boosting excess spread flowing out of (or captured by) the structure.

In a managed synthetic structure, a CDO manager may have the incentive through the remuneration structure (being an equity investor and receiving a performance fee) to buy CDS paying higher premium for the same-rated risk in order to boost excess margin. This, arguably, exposes the transaction to riskier names for a given rating, as the market perception of risk is greater than that contemplated by the rating alone. This is an investment strategy similar to deep-discount buying in managed, high-yield CBOs and may make such a portfolio more susceptible to downward credit migration, and may particularly impact ratings on the mezzanine tranches of synthetic CDOs.

To mitigate this tendency and minimise aggressive trading, either the CDO investor or manager may be allowed to replace referenced names only under certain conditions, and within strict predetermined eligibility criteria, including limits on asset classes, geographic concentrations, reference entity exposures, credit and counterparty concentrations. The ability of a party to change the portfolio and to what degree also depends on the investment strategy permitted by the CDO. Because of this, the range of ability to change the portfolio can be wide not only in terms of market sectors and eligibility criteria as mentioned above, but also in terms of investment strategies used to achieve such portfolio repositionings.

The CDO manager's trading discretion, if allowed, may be limited to a certain percentage of the pool (the "trading bucket") or may be restricted by certain conditions for trading. The manager's ability to trade may be limited to "credit improvement trades" (linked to spread tightening beyond a certain pre-determined level, premium ratios and other tests) or "credit deterioration trades" (risk of a credit event occurring as assessed by the manager). Managers may also be allowed to undertake long and short positions, with short positions being used for hedging purposes or, alternatively, naked short positions, used for speculation or arbitrage. Managers may also be allowed to take a view as to basis positioning, and be given the ability to add and unwind basis trades.

Furthermore, trading itself may be accomplished either by terminating or offsetting exposures. The level of prescribed use of termination and/or offsetting trades often differentiates transactions. A transaction structure may direct the manager to:

❏ Pursue a termination in case of an improved credit, thus generating cash into the structure; or

❏ Pursue an offsetting trade in case of a deteriorated credit, not requiring any cash outflow from the structure, in contrast to the termination of a similarly deteriorated credit.

Investors should consider the degree of defensive versus discretionary trading to be inversely proportional to their confidence in the manager, and related to the quality of the referenced pool and their investment objectives. A wider discretion in trading is probably more appropriate for high-yield portfolios (not yet in the CDS domain) and more experienced managers. In any individual case, it is a balance between flexibility granted to the manager and complexity of the deal associated with that given level of flexibility. It is critical for investors to estimate objectively whether the results of a manager's use of the flexibility given will materialise in rewards sufficient to compensate for the additional complexity fees and lack of investor control.

Other mechanisms embedded in CDO structures' attempts to realign investors' and managers' interests include:

❏ Definition of "credit-impaired" assets – definition can be changed to incorporate a rating downgrade or spread-movement concept in the event that losses erode a portion of the subordinated tranches or an overcollateralisation test is breached.

❏ Retained tranches – managers may buy both at the equity and debt level of the capital structure of the respective synthetic CDO. In some cases managers have purchased a piece of every single tranche of the capital structure, while in others they have purchased pieces of the equity and mezzanine tranches.

❏ Equity IRR – if the CDO management promise a moderate (rather than aggressive) IRR on the equity tranche this generally indicates a more conservative management.

❏ Controlling position – in a typical CDO only the controlling class, ie, the senior and super-senior tranches, have the right to remove a CDO manager and approve a replacement. In some cases, such rights are granted to the mezzanine tranche investors, giving them additional rights of control and protection and putting them on a par with the senior investors, to some degree. Granting of such rights may be linked to a threshold of losses due to credit events or to a notional amount of reference entities that have experienced credit events.

❏ Utilisation of excess margin – as addressed above.

❏ Management fee – just as in the cash CDO market, it has become the norm to split the fee into two components: one flat fee higher up in the waterfall and a second one based on performance at the bottom of the waterfall. Variations of the latter are possible, and the key issue is how the manager's motivation or course of action may be altered by the fee structure.

INVESTOR STRATEGIES

Investors should look at the CDO product from the perspective of their entire portfolio and assess how adding a respective CDO exposure complements and diversifies their existing holdings. A starting point is an investor's self-evaluation of the level of credit skills with regard to corporate and ABS bond pools.

Credit-savvy investors, who for a number of reasons may not want to manage their own CDS or corporate portfolios, who may not have access to certain kinds of credits or assets, or who want to take a defined risk exposure to a diversified credit portfolio, should consider the CDO product in two forms: static pool and pools with substitution. The logic behind this is that an investor who can formulate his or her own opinion about specific credits, can also assess the composition of a credit pool and forecast the future performance of such a pool within a reasonable range. Hence, the investor can assume some of the selection and substitution decisions, without the need for an outside manager and, importantly, the related expenses. A well-chosen portfolio should perform within initial expectations.

On the other hand, investors who do not have the necessary credit skills should consider managed CDOs, as they can rely on a specialised manager for the respective credit decisions. Nevertheless, such investors must still be able to assess the quality of portfolio managers and have a good general understanding of credit market trends and developments.

After determining the degree of management most suitable for an investor's portfolio and credit expertise, the next question becomes, what is the most appropriate position within the capital structure of the CDO to invest?

Credit-intensive investors comfortable with a particular credit pool may choose to leverage their exposure, and may select lower-rated or unrated tranches of such CDOs. In contrast, more passive credit investors may focus on the senior tranches CDOs, as their senior position should cushion them to large degree against potential negative developments in the portfolio.

In addition to the basic level of credit expertise of an investor, just as in other portfolio management decisions, investors in CDOs must consider their view on the correlation of assets within the credit portfolio. Low-asset correlation benefits the senior tranches of a CDO as the loss distribution for such a portfolio approximates a normal (or lognormal) distribution and, hence, the probability of any large losses eroding subordination is very small. As correlation of a portfolio increases, senior tranches become more risky, but subordinate tranches actually become less risky. This is because, as correlation increases, the loss distribution becomes closer and closer to a binomial distribution. In such a situation, the probability of loss for these subordinate tranches (equity in particular) is equal to the probability of loss for the weakest credit in the pool (ie, less than the sum of the probabilities of defaults of all credits in the pool).

Given this, if an investor estimates that the correlation of a synthetic CDO asset (or reference) pool is actually lower than that which the rating agencies assume and/or is priced by the market, senior tranches will offer higher risk-adjusted returns. If, on the other hand, the correlation within the pool is higher than that which the rating agencies assume and/or is priced by the market, junior tranches will instead offer higher risk-adjusted returns.

13

CDOs of CDOs: art eating itself?

Darren Smith

Dresdner Kleinwort Wasserstein*

DEVELOPMENT OF THE MARKET

The collateralised debt obligation (CDO) market has grown from virtually nothing in the early 1990s to a market growing at an annual rate of over US$150 billion rated notes per annum. The CDO or collateralised bond obligation (CBO) market, as it was initially, grew out of the junk-bond market meltdown of the early 1990s. After that market recovered, there was no new issuance for a period of five years or so, from which there was an explosion of issuance. So, although the market has been technically in existence since the late 1980s, the real growth occurred from the middle 1990s (see Figure 1).

The CDO-of-CDO market, or CDO-squared market, was a natural extension of the market much the same way CMOs extended the mortgage market. The technology can be used for a number of different purposes, including arbitrage, repackaging risk and capital arbitrage. The CDO-of-CDO market did not develop until the late 1990s and was pioneered originally by the ZING transactions by the ZAIS Group.

CDOs, particularly the mezzanine tranches, proved to be ideally suited to being repackaged, as they were of investment grade or just below investment grade, provided a high-spread income and, as there is no ready after-market, liquidity is relatively low – all hallmarks of assets ideally suited to securitisation.

While the idea of retranching and repackaging CDOs within CDOs is a bit strange to many investors and may seem at first – a bit like "the art

* The views, thoughts and opinions expressed in this chapter represent those of the author in his individual capacity and should not in any way be attributed to, or to the author as a representative, officer or employee of, Dresdner Kleinwort Wasserstein or its affiliated entities. The author would like to thank Richard Pereira, Christopher Cloke-Brown and Anthony Brown for their assistance in reviewing this chapter and Arturo Cifuentes, Patrick Galloway, Mari Kawawa and Eddie Lee for their insights and contributions on the subject over the years.

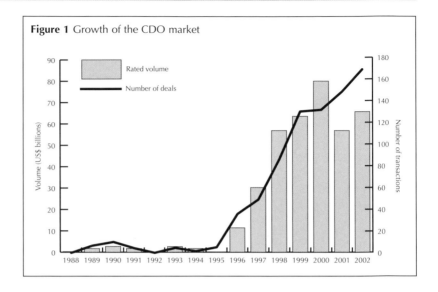

Figure 1 Growth of the CDO market

eating itself" – in fact one of the largest purchases of CDO mezzanine debt has been, for some time, other CDOs. Most CDOs have a "structured finance basket" for the purchase of asset-backed securities (ABS), credit-linked notes (CLNs) and CDOs. It has been a useful addition to corporate credit trades, as, again, they often yield more than similarly rated corporate debt. The original idea behind a CDO of CDOs was most likely an extension of the structured finance-basket concept.

Recent performance issues in CDOs, particularly in the US high-yield sector, have given rise to a requirement for liquidity for senior tranche sellers. 2002 was a record year for downgrades in CDOs with more than 150 transactions downgraded and 246 downgraded more than once (see Table 1 for details of downgrades). Many senior tranche investors have rating restrictions on which tranches they hold. Downgrades tend to force these holders to sell often at a more distressed level than that implied by the perceived risk. The inception of more CDO of CDOs and the creation of CDO investment funds has been the market response to the potential value in those assets.

USES OF THE TECHNOLOGY
CDO-of-CDO technology has several applications:

❑ rating arbitrage
❑ capital relief/arbitrage
❑ repackaging

Table 1. CDO downgrades by vintage and type (1995–2002)

Deal	Type/Vintage	1995	1996	1997	1998	1999	2000	2001	2002	Total
Arbitrage Cash flow (ACF) CBO										
Deals			4.3%	6.2%	10.5%	19.1%	8.1%	1.0%		49.3%
Tranches			4.0%	6.8%	10.8%	23.6%	8.5%	0.8%		54.6%
Arbitrage synthetic non-US$										
Deals						0.50%	2.90%	12.9%		16.3%
Tranches						0.20%	3.60%	8.9%		12.7%
Arbitrage synthetic US$										
Deals						0.5%	1.0%	4.8%	0.5%	6.7%
Tranches						0.4%	0.8%	5.5%	0.4%	7.2%
Balance sheet synthetic US$										
Deals				0.5%	1.4%	0.5%	1.4%	1.0%		4.8%
Tranches				0.8%	2.1%	0.4%	2.1%	1.3%		6.8%
Arbitrage cash flow (ACF) CLO										
Deals			1.4%	2.4%	3.3%		0.5%			7.7%
Tranches			1.1%	1.5%	2.8%		0.4%			5.7%
Arbitrage cash flow (ACF) investment grade (IG) CBO US$										
Deals					0.5%	0.5%	1.0%	3.3%		5.3%
Tranches					0.2%	0.2%	0.6%	3.6%		4.7%
Balance sheet synthetic non-US$										
Deals						0.5%	1.9%	1.4%		3.8%
Tranches						0.2%	2.5%	1.7%		4.5%

Source: Mody's Investor Services

Table 1. Continued

Deal	Type/Vintage	1995	1996	1997	1998	1999	2000	2001	2002	Total
Resecuritisations										
Deals						0.5%	0.5%	1.4%		2.4%
Tranches						0.2%	0.4%	0.6%		1.3%
Market value										
Deals						1.0%				1.0%
Tranches						1.1%				1.1%
Emerging markets										
Deals		0.5%	0.5%		0.5%					1.4%
Tranches		0.4%	0.2%		0.2%					0.8%
Balance sheet cash flow US$										
Deals						1.0%				1.0%
Tranches						0.4%				0.4%
Arbitrage cash flow (ACF) investment grade (IG) non-US$	IG									
Deals								0.5%		0.5%
Tranches								0.2%		0.2%
Totals:										
Deals		0.5%	6.2%	9.1%	16.3%	23.9%	17.2%	26.3%	0.5%	209
Tranches		0.4%	5.3%	9.1%	16.1%	26.8%	19.1%	22.7%	0.4%	471

Source: Mody's Investor Services

Rating arbitrage

Rating arbitrage involves creating a leveraged fund under the supervision of a third-party manager who has the experience, expertise and resources to evaluate primary and secondary CDO offerings and combine them in a portfolio. The typical approach is to buy primary mezzanine pieces and discounted secondary, more senior assets. Acquiring the assets usually requires a "ramp-up" period of several months, which is highly dependent on the new-issue pipeline, and often requires bridging finance or a warehouse line from a bank.

Capital relief/arbitrage

Banks have traditionally been investors in CDOs as a compliment or replacement to traditional lending business. However, the capital available to support investment in CDO tranches may be limited. In order to support continued investment, banks have often used CDO-of-CDO technology to transfer some of the more senior risk to obtain some capital relief.

For example, investment-grade tranches of CDOs are 100% risk-weighted in the banking-book regime under Basel. The Cooke ratio is a bank's capital as a percentage of assets. The original Basel agreement proscribed this at a minimum of 8%, of which at least half was to be equity. Therefore, if a bank wished to preserve a Cooke ratio of 8% then a €100 million portfolio of CDOs would require 8% or €8 million of capital. If the bank could transfer, say, 96% of the credit risk through a portfolio credit derivative, then, even if the residual risk is deducted directly from capital

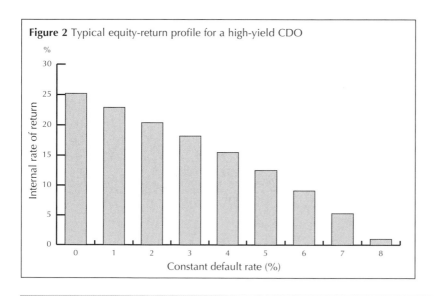

Figure 2 Typical equity-return profile for a high-yield CDO

(ie, the capital can be reduced to €4 million). The bank could then use this freed capital to support an additional €50 million of new assets.

Basel II, which is currently in consultation, aims to shift banks' attention to economic capital rather than regulatory capital and does this by varying capital requirements relative to perceived rating risk. A likely impact of this regime will be to incentivise banks to transfer risk on portfolios of lower-rated tranches.

Repackaging

Lead managers and arrangers of CDOs often have small residual positions on their books from prior transactions, which, under trading-book treatment, may attract aged inventory charges. These small residual positions may not be of sufficient size to attract investors. However, by repackaging these small residual positions as part of a CDO-of-CDO trade, it enables the lead manager to move the positions and offers the investor a larger, more liquid investment.

VALUE PROPOSITION

All CDOs are rated on the expected loss and variance in the expected loss (the "unexpected loss") of the portfolio, with each tranche taking less risk and consequently less reward as the risk is transferred up the capital structure. Figure 3 shows how the risk of a portfolio of high-yield credit may be typically tranched.

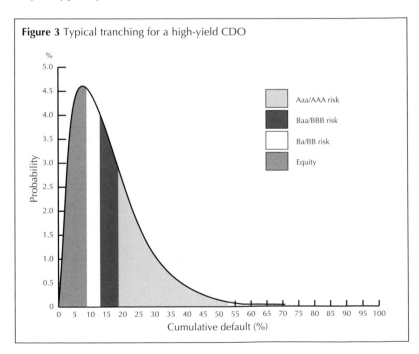

Figure 3 Typical tranching for a high-yield CDO

The equity investors typically take the first-loss position in return for leveraged investment in the underlying risk. For example, high-yield-bond CBO equity investors historically targeted potential returns in the 20–30% range at a base case. A typical return profile for the equity investors is shown in Figure 2. The key points to note are that returns are reduced immediately in line with defaults, and the return profile is highly dependent on recovery rates and timing. From a risk/return point of view, the equity acts more as an interest-only, or IO, security than a bond, and has often been described as a race between defaults and return.

Whereas a CDO-of-CDO transaction typically holds investments in at least second-loss positions (see Figure 4) and is consequently more resilient to the defaults in the underlying obligors; initial defaults in the underlying portfolios are borne by the investor in the original deals and are absorbed outside of the deal. CDO-of-CDO equity investors have the benefit of first-loss protection provided by the original transaction investors. Mezzanine and senior note investors therefore have effectively double subordination. This is the attraction for equity investors in CDO-of-CDO transactions. Equity returns are very stable compared with those that are experienced with most corporate credit-backed CDOs, with near depression level of ongoing underlying defaults required before a loss occurs (see Figure 5).

Diversity measures, as discussed below, will tend to underestimate the diversity in the portfolio.

RATING AGENCY APPROACH

A CDO-of-CDO transaction, like most other CDOs, is a rating arbitrage transaction. Assets are purchased by the issuance of rated debt secured on those assets. The spreads paid on the debt are linked to ratings obtained on the debt. While earlier in the CDO market, investors discriminated

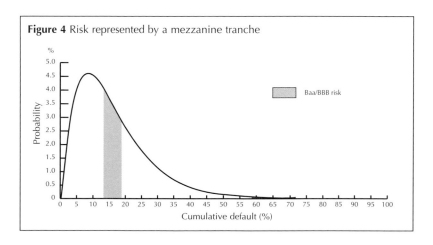

Figure 4 Risk represented by a mezzanine tranche

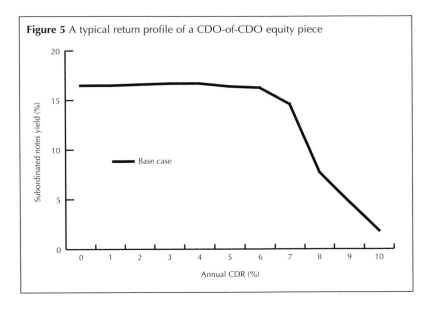

Figure 5 A typical return profile of a CDO-of-CDO equity piece

largely on the ratings for price, ie, Aaa was Aaa, they are currently more discerning and the spreads for the rated debt also depend on the perceived underlying risk as well as the rating. The arbitrage works if the difference between the spread paid on the rated debt and received on the assets is sufficient to compensate the investor in the first-loss or equity piece.

RATING ISSUES
The main issues with rating a CDO-of-CDO transaction are:

❏ correlation
❏ recoveries
❏ default data; and
❏ cash-flow management

Correlation
All three agencies avoid the complications of looking through the structures into the underlying risk and treat CDOs as part of a general multi-sector asset-backed-security (ABS). They divide the structured finance universe into "sectors" as an extension of industry sectors for corporate risk. The sectors broadly breakdown into ABS (consumer, commercial, esoteric), commercial mortgage-backed-securities (CMBS), (large loan, credit tenant lease, conduit); residential mortgage-backed-securities (RMBS), (first lien, home equity, manufactured housing); real estate investment trusts (REITs), (hotels, retail, industrial, office, diversified); and CDOs. However, they all retain the option of addressing the concentration

issues by adjusting correlations and placing additional restrictions such as servicer concentrations, and vintage restrictions, ie, limiting the number of deals originated within a given calendar period.

Fitch's approach

Fitch extends the concept of diversity from the corporate credit side and divides the structured finance universe into "sectors" to mirror their approach to industry sectors for corporate credit. Fitch in July 2003 announced a major revision to its CDO rating methodology, called VECTOR. VECTOR is a multi-period Monte Carlo simulation model, which simulates the potential changes to the value of a firm's assets and compares that to a threshold to measure the likelihood of default, a so-called structural model. The model in effect is simulating insolvency, ie, the point where a firm's liabilities exceed its assets. Like the S&P approach to multi-sector ABS assets, correlations are implied at the transaction level from educated "guestimates".

Moody's

Moody's approach is similar to the original Fitch approach but slightly more sophisticated in that a diversity score is calculated on a per-asset correlation and cross-correlation basis.

Two estimates of diversification are generated and the lower of the two is used.

In order to facilitate the calculation of diversity, Moody's have prepared a diversity calculation kit, an interesting side benefit being that it can also be used to calculate diversity for credit portfolios where the assumption of zero correlation between industries is relaxed.

Standard & Poor's

Standard & Poor's have adapted their CDO evaluator technology to incorporate multi-sector structured-finance assets. S&P's CDO evaluator is based on a Monte Carlo simulation and is used to generate loss rates to different levels of confidence corresponding to different rating levels. The CDO evaluator has replaced S&P's risk tabulator and CDO structuring models, allowing concentration risk to be addressed via correlation rather than the previous approach of notching ratings. Like Moody's and Fitch, S&P's divide the structured-finance universe into sectors and have estimated the correlations between the sectors.

Implications of diversity assumptions

These approaches tend to significantly underestimate diversity. For example, a typical CDO of CDOs may have 25 different tranches in it. Let us assume that they are all high-yield bond tranches (which in itself would be unusual). A high-yield bond CDO portfolio typically contains 50 to 70 obligors with corresponding diversity score of at least 40. Hence, with 50 names and 25 tranches, we have 1,250 potential exposures, typically at a second or higher loss position. Even allowing for some overlap among the exposures, the risk will represent that of a broad market index and hence be very insulated from idiosyncratic risks. A diligent manager would aim to reduce this correlation risk significantly. An alternative view of the port-folio is that of an index of names in a secondary loss position. However, the likely diversity scores from Moody's and Fitch will be single digits to low teens.

Recoveries

Low diversity numbers are often compensated for in the rating process by assuming higher recoveries than for equivalently rated corporate debt. This is probably justifiable for most ABS-type securities, as the debt holder is secured against a portfolio of assets, which may be readily liquidated, transferred or refinanced as required. However, CDOs reference "lumpy" credit and it is difficult to imagine high recoveries over the short to medium term for mezzanine CDO debt in the event of anything other than a technical default on the indenture. Recoveries for senior tranches will be driven by covenant-related pay-downs as well as underlying asset values. Many distressed seniors that have suffered downgrades in the past have been upgraded or are since eligible for upgrade, as prepayment of the senior notes to cure covenant breaches ultimately improves asset coverage and reduces leverage. However, mezzanine recoveries will be delayed in the event of distress to the underlying portfolio and may be fully realised only over the long term. The only interim remedy would be to sell the tranche early into a very illiquid market. Realised recoveries on the distressed positions will be low. The availability of such distressed CDO paper is of interest to distressed CDO funds and it helps drive the arbi-trage for CDO-of-CDO transactions.

Default data

Default data on CDOs has historically been very sparse. Currently the probability of default (PD) of rated CDO tranches is derived from similarly rated corporate debt.

However, recognising a default is also problematic, as most mezzanine tranches of CDOs are capital instruments designed to absorb losses in the CDO by deferring and capitalising interest. So a failure to pay on a coupon date is not necessarily a default event for a CDO tranche. In the worst case it may not be clear that a default will occur until the final maturity is reached and the principal on the tranche finally comes due.

Many of the agencies recognise this problem and address it via a down-ward adjustment to the tranche ratings. So the rating of the tranche that is not currently paying will become more speculative over time. For the purposes of obtaining a rating for a CDO-of-CDO transaction, Moody's assume a tranche default after more than two missed or deferred payments.

Cash-flow management

Most cash-flow CDO-of-CDO transactions have a significant proportion of deferrable-interest mezzanine or PIKs (payment-in-kind) securities. As the payments on the senior liabilities of the CDO are to be met solely from the income on the portfolio, this can be of some concern to the rating agencies. Consequently, most CDO-of-CDO transactions will require some degree of liquidity facility to ensure timely payment on the most senior tranches. A third party often provides the liquidity facility in the form of a limited-advance facility, ie, advances are made to meet shortfalls in return for a senior claim on interest and principal on the underlying assets.

PREREQUISITES

Structuring and managing a CDO-of-CDO is a very data-intensive process. To begin assessing the underlying risk and value of a potential investment, information on the portfolio and the structure of the transaction is required and needs to be of sufficient detail to reverse-engineer the deal. Portfolio information required includes prices, obligor ratings, industry classifications and hedge information. Structural information is derived from the Offering Memoranda and Trustee reports. In order to be efficient in evaluating opportunities, it is important to have an infrastructure capable of reverse-engineering a potential investment within a couple of

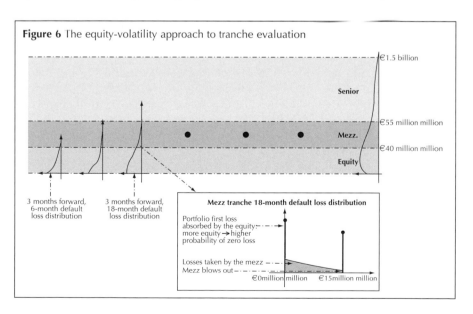

Figure 6 The equity-volatility approach to tranche evaluation

days. Much longer and the investment opportunity may no longer be available.

There is also a need to assess valuation and risk for each tranche individually, and with respect to the overall portfolio.

VALUATION

The lack of readily available and market-acceptable models on a common platform means that it is currently very difficult for market participants to agree on the value of CDO tranches. Historically, projected cash flows and portfolio information have been privately maintained by the originating investment bank and largely been made available only to investors. Information systems for CDOs are in a similar position to those of the mortgage market and ABS markets prior to the development of analytics on Bloomberg and systems such as INTEX. The lack of deal transparency is one of the major determining factors affecting liquidity in the CDO market and one of the drivers behind arbitrage CDO-of-CDO transactions. The lack of standard valuation approaches and models has encouraged investment boutiques such as ZAIS, Triton Partners and Coast to develop their own approaches to determine tranche value and has consequently made arbitrage CDO-of-CDO transactions an attractive value proposition. However, for other investors there is some relief on the horizon, as several investment banks are now making the deal information available through systems such as INTEX. Also, trustees such as JP Morgan Chase and rating agencies (Moody's) are providing deal information and valuation models. Ultimately, if one of these systems becomes the market standard, the opportunities for CDO-of-CDO arbitrage transactions may be greatly diminished in the future.

VALUATION APPROACHES

In determining relative value of a tranche, both a quantitative assessment and a subjective assessment of the tranche are required. Quantitative measures include estimating the expected loss, variance in the expected loss and variance of returns. The subjective measures relate to the evaluating manager experience and expertise, structural features and legal issues.

Manager evaluation is the most subjective and looks into the manager's style, experience in the asset class particularly with problem assets, and resources in terms of initial analysis and ongoing maintenance. Expertise references both the underlying assets and the expertise required to manage the assets within the structure. Similarly, manager experience with both the underlying assets and the extent of experience in managing the assets within a CDO are important considerations. Also to be considered are the manager infrastructure, investment process and reporting frequency and contact. Due-diligence visits with the manager have often

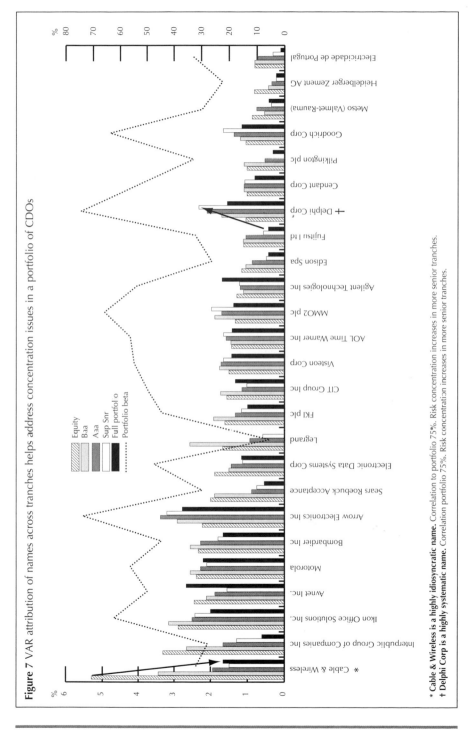

Figure 7 VAR attribution of names across tranches helps address concentration issues in a portfolio of CDOs

* **Cable & Wireless is a highly idiosyncratic name.** Correlation to portfolio 75%. Risk concentration increases in more senior tranches.
† **Delphi Corp is a highly systematic name.** Correlation portfolio 75%. Risk concentration increases in more senior tranches.

been required in the past to ascertain the above information. This may be less necessary in the future with many top-tier asset managers having assessments and "being rated" by the rating agencies. Agency reports will be an important source of information for investors and underwriters with all agencies working with asset managers to demystify and to quantify performance. Style and experience in the underlying assets, management style with regard to trading, and loss/gain experience with defaults and trading distressed assets, are important considerations. Reviewing past experience in CDO management concentrates on asset selection and the review process, trading record, trends in overcollateralisation triggers and compliance with credit quality tests. Dependence on key personnel and how they are retained is a particular consideration for the smaller investment boutiques.

Structural considerations will address issues such as

❏ eligible assets;
❏ trading quotas and restrictions; and
❏ basket limitations for items such as structured finance and CCC/Caa-rated assets.

A major focus will also be on alignment of interests between the various classes. This typically manifests itself in examining retained manager interest, management fees (and how they are split), the waterfall and how windfall gains are dealt with.

Other issues include the manager's resources in terms of administering the transaction, ie, settlement, cash management, reporting etc.

Legal issues to be addressed are:

❏ controlling class;
❏ who decides to control assets in the event of default;
❏ voting rights;
❏ to do with calling the deal and selection of the asset manager;
❏ taxation issues (jurisdiction, calls for tax changes, any for withholding make-wholes); and
❏ true sale/fair transfer opinions.

There are several different approaches used by managers of CDO portfolios to assess the relative value of a tranche. I have detailed the most common approach, that of re-rating, and aim to give a flavour of newer techniques used by the market. These involve:

❏ re-rating
❏ Monte Carlo simulation

❑ analytical approaches
❑ equity volatility models

Rerating

A common approach used to evaluate a secondary position is to re-rate the deal using the current portfolio, interest rates and capital structure to assess the implied rating.

It requires a lot of data, including trustee reports, hedge details, legal documents and prices. A flexible model or library of models is required to reverse-engineer the deal and, using credible assumptions, estimate the rating as obtained by the agencies.

A re-rating approach, like the original rating process, does not typically use the actual underlying obligors but is rated to the original indenture constraints. Moody's and Fitch (prior to VECTOR) reduce the actual portfolio to one or more homogeneous equivalent portfolios of independent obligors. Even approaches such as the CDO evaluator and VECTOR are often rated to the indenture constraints, which are more general than the initial target portfolio.

If the deal is sufficiently impaired, then some licence with the terms of the indenture is required: that is, if the CCC+/Caa-rated bucket was above an acceptable threshold (usually 5%) of the portfolio size, then it would be unlikely to be issued like that.

The difficulty with rerating for transactions suffering some impairment is what to do about the distressed assets. A conservative approach is to write them down as defaulted immediately. Another approach advocates looking at the asset price: if the price is sufficiently distressed, then assume default within a one-year period, or else assume normal default profiles.

One variation on re-rating includes enhancements to the rating process. One such approach is used by Triton Partners (Triton), a CDO-of-CDO manager. Triton extended the binomial expansion technique in several directions to improve the information it provided. The first was to recalculate the diversity score but after relaxing the assumption of zero correlation between industries, a more generic diversity calculation was made. Moody's use a similar approach in their diversity calculator for multi-sector deals.

A variation on re-rating would be to retranche the deal as well and use current asset prices to determine appropriate yield measures for each of the tranches. By then comparing the new attachment points to the old attachments, value estimates could be obtained for each tranche. For example, say the initial transaction was a three-tranche deal, equity, BBB and Aaa, of, say, 12.5%, 20%, 68% with, say, a B1/B+ average rating, and that the excess spread on the transaction was initially 2% and Libor was 3%. Then return on equity would be 19%, ie, 8 x 2% plus 3%. Now if the pool declines in price to, say, 90%, the yield will increase on the pool by, say, 1.5%, assuming portfolio duration of 6.67 years. Assuming the pool quality has also declined to an average B3/B- the new tranches would require, say, a 15% equity piece, a 20% BBB and a 65.5% Aaa. Now, assuming the collateral price improvement on the deal is compressed into the equity, which means that equity on a market value is now worth 33%, the equity cash flow would largely be the same, but slightly lower because of the lower leverage. However, the yield would have increased greatly and would have more than doubled. Using the implied yields and attachment points enables us to estimate values and prices. Hence the original 12.5% equity should be discounted at the new yield.

However, the old BBB tranche now effectively consists of 2.5% equity and 17.5% BBB. Discounting at the blended yield is one effective approach to valuation. So, assuming original spread on BBB was Libor + 3% (for a combined coupon of 6%), the blended yield would be 10.25%, assuming a 40% equity yield. If the duration of BBB was seven years, then a 4.25% increase in yield would imply a price decline of around 30%. Similarly, the old Aaa tranche consists of 2.5% Baa/BBB and 65.5% Aaa. Say the blended yield is (assuming Aaa at Libor+60) 4.7%, a 90- basis point (bps) increase. With a similar duration the price would have declined to 93.70.

MONTE CARLO SIMULATION

A common approach in valuing CDO tranches, particularly for synthetic CDOs, is to use a Monte Carlo simulation in a structural model (see Chapters 5 or 18 for more detail). Simulation techniques based upon structural models build upon the work of Merton and infer the likelihood of default as the point of insolvency, ie, when the value of a firm's liabilities exceeds that of its assets. That is, the Merton approach views the value of a company's equity as the call option on the excess of its assets less its liabilities. Conversely, investors in a company's debt are seen as being short a put option on the assets. Actual systems using the Merton approach, such as KMV, adjust the strike to take into account the time horizon of the liabilities, as it may be possible for companies to continue to service their longer-dated liabilities, even if they may appear technically insolvent. Recent examples of this have been insurance companies and pension funds.

In order to ascertain the likelihood of default, a distribution of asset values, an assumed asset volatility and a threshold (in terms of multiples of standard deviations), below which a default is implied a normal distribution of the value of the firm over the period of interest is normally assumed. The asset volatility is inferred from the common stock volatility via an option-pricing model, and a threshold level of default is implied either via market prices for the debt or using historical default rates.

There are two broad approaches to simulation of portfolios:

❑ discrete period-by-period approach, and
❑ correlated times to default.

Discrete period-by-period approach

The drawbacks of the discrete approach were addressed by Li (2000) in the approach described in Chapter 14. In this approach structural-form models were initially single-period models in which the tenor of the investment was the period over which defaults were to be considered.

This single-period model was extended to multiple periods by various entities such as RiskMetrics and the rating agencies. It forms the basis of many of the simulation techniques used at rating agencies for evaluating both CDOs (S&P CDO evaluator, FITCH VECTOR) and ith to default baskets (Moody's).

The main extensions to the single-period model are to add period-by-period default thresholds and to generate marginal conditional probabilities by calibrating the variance and correlation to the market.

A correlation structure is imposed via a covariance matrix. Correlation structures can be a flat spearman rho-type correlation, which is time-invariant, or more typically a time dependence is introduced via copulas. Simply put, copulas allow for the co-dependence between two random variables to vary, as some other variable (typically time), such that the probability of one variable influencing another is higher in the immediate vicinity of the event. They do so by linking marginal univariate distributions to the joint multivariate distribution. There are many choices for copula functions but the most common choice seems to be a normal or Gaussian copula.

The multi-period discrete approach requires the simulation and tabulation of the survivors for every period and does not give any information with regard to time to default. Which is fine for evaluating write-down synthetic CDO structures directly, but it is only useful to generate loss thresholds on the portfolio for more complicated waterfall structures with cash-flow diversion. Cash-flow diversion structures require a default-time distribution to assess the benefit that diversion provides. The requirement to track survivors and simulate draws for each period means that multi-period discrete models are also computationally intensive and relatively slow.

Correlated times to default

The drawbacks of the discrete approach were addressed by David Li at RiskMetrics through his model based on time-to-default copulas, which was adopted by RiskMetrics for their CDO manager product. In this approach, correlated default times are generated over the life of the transaction and not period by period. It typically involves generating draws from a multivariate normal distribution. The draws are then mapped back to another distribution, such as an exponential distribution, to generate a default time.

Simulation approaches, to be successful, typically have to cope with the following problems:

❏ speed;
❏ realistic codependence structure; and
❏ need to generate "positive definite" covariance matrix.

Speed is usually the largest problem, as it depends on the number of obligors within the portfolio, and the tenor of the transaction. Calculating the "fair value" for a particular tranche may not be too difficult but evaluating sensitivities of a portfolio or of tranches can be vary time consuming.

The codependence structure is the most subjective topic to address, copula approaches are the typical approach and the selection of the copula is often a trade-off between tractability and realism. One of the biggest criticisms of time-to-default approaches is that the correlation factors dominate the result and are unobservable in the market. How do you know that you are using the appropriate factors? Some practitioners are quite critical of using such a complicated approach that allows for so much subtlety when the result is dominated by the unobservable. Simulation models are used to measure "fair value" and are the basis of many banks' "fair-value" models – ie, models to attribute risk and reward across the different tranches of a CDO by taking the credit spread of the portfolio and attributing it across each tranche in an "arbitrage-free" way.

However, the level of correlation dominates the result in that it is probably more useful to evaluate tranches on a comparative basis rather than an absolute measure, ie, by holding correlation assumptions constant and examining the expected value and variance in returns.

The need to invert the covariance matrix to generate the draws means that there are limits to the degree of correlation between pairs of obligors. Also, if you are measuring sensitivities to correlation, note that there are limits to the ranges of correlation.

Another difficulty in using simulation techniques to address losses in CDOs is for non-credit-related assets. Most CDOs have a basket for structured finance and there is currently a preponderance in the market towards multi-sector-type deals with ABS. The loss distributions for ABS may depend on the underlying assets. The main problem is the correlation with credit assets. There is no observable method of measuring the correlation with other assets so at best we have educated guesses. This is certainly the problem that Standard & Poor's seemed to have with their early releases of the CDO evaluator technology and multi-sector deals.

ANALYTICAL APPROACHES

In a series of recent papers Moody's have advocated the use of Fourier transforms to aggregate loss distributions via convolution in the frequency domain.[1] This particularly has advantages for multi-sector transactions, as well as transactions with low diversification or a large dispersion in credit quality, as, rather than using a predetermined loss distribution for the portfolio, the portfolio loss distribution is created by convolving individual asset-loss distributions.

The main advantage of analytical approaches over Monte Carlo techniques is that of speed. However, the Fourier transform technique, like binomial expansion technique, is a single-period model, with the typical period being the tenor of the transaction, and does not typically address default timing. As previously discussed, this is more of an issue in more complicated cash-flow waterfalls in which subordination is dependent on cash-flow diversion and hence varies with default timing.

A new variation on the analytical approach is the application of the saddle-point technique to calculate credit VAR, see Martin *et al.* The method is based on the use of moment-generating functions (MGFs) of probability distributions and uses a saddle-point approximation to calculate the Fourier transform of the probability density function (PDF) in the tails of the distribution, as an alternative to the fast Fourier transforms (FFT), by finding the saddle points of the PDF, and using Gaussian quadrature to approximate the integral. Like the FFT, the saddle-point method can be adapted to any distribution, at least those for which the first and second derivatives are available, and is therefore not confined to a normal distribution. The credit VAR can be calculated analytically without recourse to simulation by using root-finding techniques to find the threshold at a given probability or percentile in the cumulative distribution.

A recent extension of this modelling approach used at Dresdner, Kleinwort Wasserstein, in CreditHorizons, extends the credit VAR approach for the portfolio by attributing their products across each tranche for a CDO by obligor.

For each payment point over the CDO lifetime the forward equity distribution is generated, from which, via a Merton-style model, the credit spread is derived. At each point the credit VAR is calculated and the fair spread for each tranche calculated by comparing premiums paid for protection versus projected losses. The portfolio VAR per underlying risk is calculated, as is the fair-spread contribution per asset. The credit VAR is allocated as to the sensitivity of the fair spread to a change in asset allocation (see Figures 6 and 7).

MEASURING VALUE AND RISK IN A PORTFOLIO OF CDOs

As well as assessing the risk/reward of an individual tranche in isolation, it is equally if not more important to examine the impact of exposures from the portfolio perspective. The portfolio is likely to contain investments that have exposures to the same credits but that may have differing degrees of credit enhancement and subordination. For example, a default of a credit that appears in more than one transaction is likely to have a larger impact on a mezzanine position than, say, a position in another more senior tranche. As discussed earlier, the CDO portfolio investor is less concerned about the underlying defaults, because they are typically absorbed by more junior investors, and more concerned about the combinations of defaults impacting the portfolio.

One simple approach to examining the defaults is to stratify the exposures in each transaction by size, rating, industry and region, then, for each investment, to prepare a loss look-up table based upon, say, a binomial expansion that is based upon ideal independent obligors. Say, for example, the tranche contemplated for investment had an equally weighted portfolio of 50 obligors totalling €500 million and a corresponding diversity score of 40. Then the individual "real" obligor exposure would be €10 million but the incremental exposure for the binomial expansion would be €12.5 million. Probabilities of default by real exposures can then be interpolated. A conservative approach would be to take the worst paths of exposures by size and stratification across the whole portfolio and aggregate the incremental effect of exposures.

In effect, by ordering the defaults and assigning some probability – whether it be a simple uniform distribution or related to the probability of default (depending on the stratification strategy) – an estimate of worst-case exposure can be obtained. More sophisticated approaches would involve using the approaches indicated above for single tranches:

❏ Monte Carlo simulation;
❏ equity-option models; and
❏ applying them across the whole portfolio.

That is, the main advantage of analytical approaches is that they quickly enable credit VAR to be calculated per name in a portfolio of CDOs both on a tranche level and composite level, which in turn allows portfolio managers the opportunity to optimise their portfolios by buying tranches at different seniorities in order to "flatten" their risk profile. (See Figure 7 for actual risk attribution for a CDO using an equity-option model.) This optimisation approach is one of the drivers behind bespoke single-tranche CDOs.

NEW TRENDS
Synthetic multi-sector deals.
A prevalent transaction, originated primarily by European banks, has been the synthetic multi-sector CDO. Typically the bank originates or purchases structured-finance assets and funds them. In order to obtain capital relief and create an arbitrage, the bank will transfer the majority of the risk via credit-derivative portfolio swap.

The credit events required for structured finance transactions are very different from those for corporate credits. The main credit events for corporate credit are:

❏ bankruptcy;
❏ failure to pay; and
❏ restructuring.

Bankruptcy
As most ABS are created as bankruptcy remote vehicles, then the bankruptcy as an event is both unlikely and largely irrelevant.

Failure to pay
Failure to pay in a corporate sense is the failure to pay scheduled principal or interest. ABS, particularly mezzanine securities, can PIK or capitalise interest, a failure to pay scheduled interest may not be an event required to be protected from. However, with other types of multi-sector deals, particularly consumer leasing or loan deals, which have a known amortisation schedule, protection against lack of payment on scheduled amortisation date may be required. Synthetic multi-sector deals break failure to pay down into:

❏ failure to pay ABS principal; and
❏ failure to pay ABS interest.

Restructuring
As any restructuring of an ABS transaction, including CDOs, is to be controlled by a committee of creditors, then protection against restructuring is not required and is largely irrelevant.

Other events for which banks have sought protection for synthetic multi-sector deals – including synthetic CDOs of CDOs – include:

❏ CDO tranche write-down; and
❏ ABS tranche downgrade triggers.

CDO tranche write-down events are largely used for synthetic write-down structures that have no recourse to excess spread to absorb losses, but rely solely on the amount of subordination. Once a write-down has occurred, then a loss is realised.

ABS tranche downgrade triggers are becoming less common but, as some ABS tranches will not realise an actual default to the final payment date, then banks have often sought protection against ultimate losses by triggering credit events based on the credit rating of the tranche. If a CDO tranche has not paid interest for some time or has experienced a write-down, or if the underlying assets no longer cover the debt issued, then it is likely that the tranche will be downgraded below investment grade long before a default is realised.

A major development in the CDO market in recent years has been that of the synthetic single-tranche transaction. The transactions are based on a portfolio of CDS on corporate credits, but, unlike a traditional transaction, which involves the investment bank selling the whole capital structure (or conversely buying protection on the whole portfolio), modelling and hedging techniques allow the investment bank to buy protection via a single tranche. The advantages of this approach are that transactions:

❏ can be executed more quickly; and
❏ can be tailored to a specific client rather than be a compromise among several clients and thus closely complement an existing portfolio.

These single-tranche transactions are already finding their way into multi-sector deals, "structured finance baskets" of corporate CDOs, and CDOs-of-CDOs. Portfolio managers by buying and selling single tranches in conjunction with portfolio risk models will look to "flatten" risk profiles in their portfolios in the future.

CONCLUSION

Current rating-agency approaches for CDOs are by their very nature on the whole conservative, as the complexity and detail required to evaluate the underlying risk is quite daunting. However, for investors there is some relief on the horizon with increasing availability of deal information provided by system providers such as RiskMetrics/JP Morgan Chase, Intex and the rating agencies. Then the underlying CDO performance will become more transparent and the risks associated with holding a portfolio of CDOs will be more readily assessed. The increased transparency of the market should increase the secondary market for CDO pieces and may actually ultimately reduce the opportunities for arbitrage CDOs of CDOs.

The advent of single-tranche technology, coupled with more sophisti-cated risk models, will mean that CDO-of-CDO technology and CDO port-folio techniques will become increasingly more widely used.

1 See Debuysscher *et al.*

BIBLIOGRAPHY

Cifuentes, A., and G. O'Connor, 1996, "The Binomial Expansion Method Applied to CBO/CLO Analysis", Moody's Special Report.

Cifuentes, A., 2001 "Evaluating CDO Structures and Performance", a presentation.

Debuysscher, A., and M. Szegö, 2003, "The Fourier Transform Method – Overview", Moody's Special Report.

Debuysscher, A., and M. Szegö, 2003, "The Fourier Transform Method – Technical Document", Moody's Working Paper.

Finger, C., 2000, "A comparison of stochastic default rate models", Working Paper.

Gluck, J., and H. Remeza, 2000, "Moody's Approach to Rating Multi-sector CDOs", Moody's Special Report.

Hrvatin, R., H. Katz and J. Schiavetta, 2000, "Rating Criteria for Cash Flow ABS/MBS CDOs", Fitch Managed Funds Special Report.

Li, D., 2000, "On default correlation: a copula approach", Journal of Fixed Income 9, March.

Merton, R.C., "On the Pricing of Corporate Debt: The Risk Structure of Interest Rates", *Journal of Finance*, 29, pp. 449–70.

Martin, R., K. Thompson and C. Browne, 2003, "Taking to the saddle", in M. B. Gordy (ed.) *Credit Risk Modelling*, pp 137–43 (Risk Books).

Nazarian, D., K. Feinzig, M. Miagkova and C. Kim, 2003, "Credit Migration of CDO Notes, 1996–2002 , for U.S. and European Transactions", Moody's Special Report.

Section 4

Models and Valuation

Introduction

Jon Gregory

BNP Paribas

Credit derivative pricing models can be broadly divided into two categories, with so-called structural models applied mainly to modelling contracts sensitive to default correlation and more traditional reduced-form approaches applied to other products. The first two chapters of this section are concerned with the structural models that have been applied to the correlation products, namely basket default swaps and the synthetic CDO structures described in detail in the last section. For such portfolios to be effectively priced and risk-managed on a name-by-name basis, we must understand not only the credit risk of each individual name but also the correlation between credit events. The paper by Li (2000) introduced the use of copula functions as a means to model multi-underlying credit products in a "Default Time Model". In this context, a copula function combines the information from all the individual credits assuming some underlying correlation structure between them. In our first chapter, **David X Li** and **Jure Skarabot** of **Citigroup** present this approach for pricing synthetic CDO tranches (this model being also applicable to basket default swaps). The authors describe the ease of implementation of such a model and how factor models can be used to further simplify the calculations and the calibration of the correlation structure. They also illustrate pricing examples and discuss sensitivity analysis and hedging issues. It should be noted that these approaches can also be extended to cash CDO structures as well as the somewhat easier-to-model synthetic ones. To do this requires additional features such as the "waterfall" prioritisation of cash-flows and excess spread as well as overcollateralisation and interest coverage tests.

The Default Time Model using a Gaussian copula has been quite widely adopted by market practitioners for credit portfolio pricing in general. The dependence structure of asset returns is central to this model and in the Gaussian structure this is fully characterised by a correlation matrix.

Commonly, equity returns are used as proxies for asset return correlation, which (even for high-yield corporates) is strongly supported by the analysis of **Roy Mashal, Marco Naldi** and **Assaf Zeevi** of **Lehman Brothers**. The main point of this chapter is to investigate the validity of the (multivariate) Gaussian assumption for modelling (joint) asset returns. The authors show how to extend the approach of the previous chapter to incorporate extreme events into the model. An empirical analysis of equity returns leads to an outright rejection of Gaussian behaviour in favour of a "fat-tailed" approach. This obviously leads to some significant pricing deviations, most notably for low-correlation and senior tranches of synthetic CDOs. The latter point is not surprising since the payoff depends on multiple credit events and so the "tails" of the distribution will be important in pricing such a contract appropriately. A model such as this will also lead to default correlation even when the asset return correlation (linear dependence) is zero. These observations are also important for calculating credit VAR (which, like senior risk, is very sensitive to the tail of the distribution) and economic capital and should be incorporated into models for this purpose.

Our focus then moves on to reduced-form models (also known as *hazard rate* or *intensity* models). These approaches are more in line with those used for other asset classes, such as interest-rate or equity derivatives. Reduced-form models offer several advantages in terms of implementation and calibration, since they consider the actual underlying credit spreads rather than the unobservable asset value. **Leif Andersen** of **Banc of America** explains the basics of reduced-form models and discusses credit curve stripping and pricing of "flow" products such as CDSs, bonds and asset swaps. The author then shows how such an approach can be extended to price quanto products, volatility products, interest-rate hybrids and convertible bonds. This chapter keeps the underlying modelling simple, not considering, for example, smile, stochastic volatility or jumps. We could argue that the liquidity of the credit default swap market is not nearly high enough to warrant application of a more complicated model, a sort of Occam's razor applied to credit derivatives telling us to use simpler models, more likely to be correct than complex ones.[1] On the other hand, we should beware of potentially extreme distributional behaviour in credit spreads and be open to more complex approaches, even if they will lead to further parameters and uncertainties that the market cannot calibrate for us. This is particularly important for some credit products where the possibility of default should have a significant impact on the tail of the credit-spread distribution. Two examples of contracts where this could be important could be out of the money credit spread put option or a credit-contingent cross-currency, where a default could trigger a swing in the currency (or vice versa).

These observations bring us to the chapter by **Jesper Andreasen** of

Nordea Markets, who describes a reduced-form model with richer dynamics. This approach captures all the dynamic properties we may expect from credit spreads (smile, sudden and gradual defaults, and a potentially flexible correlation structure). In this model, default will usually occur following a significant increase in the credit spread as opposed to the sudden or anticipated default, which are respectively characteristics of standard reduced-form and structural models. The Andreasen approach makes use of explosive processes and herein lies the downside, as the cost of the richer dynamics is that implementation will certainly not be easy, in terms of both calibration and pricing. However, the author shows how to price basic products (CDSs, bonds, asset swaps) in closed form and gives relatively standard numerical integration schemes for pricing options. Portfolio products would need to be handled by Monte Carlo simulation. Clearly, the explosive model is going to offer a number of challenges in terms of implementation and calibration, but, on the other hand, it is not particularly restricted to certain situations or products. It potentially offers a "generic" framework for handling volatility, correlation and hybrid products within a single framework, albeit with some rather complex implementation issues. One question that remains is: does the development of models of this type *depend* on or are they a *prerequisite* for a more mature and liquid credit derivatives market? The answer is probably somewhere between the two.

Finally, this section concludes with the chapter by **Monique Jeanblanc** of **Universite d'Evry Val d'Essonne** and **Marek Rutkowski** of **Warsaw University of Technology**, giving us all the mathematical tools for pricing and hedging default risk. Although this may seem rather theoretical in nature, such rigour will become increasingly vital as the credit derivative market matures and issues that are sometimes glossed over – such as arbitrage-free dynamics and complete replication – are tackled formally. This chapter describes in detail structural models, showing how the work of Merton was extended by Black and Cox (1976) and Leland (1994), giving more theoretical depth into the material in Chapter 5. But the chapter is not biased towards the structural approach and covers also reduced-from models, for both approaches discussing hedging considerations by replication with the relevant risky and non-risky underlying securities.

It is now half a century since Markowitz laid down the foundations of modern portfolio theory and three decades after the brilliant Black–Scholes–Merton work on the pricing of options and corporate liabilities. Major advances have been made in financial engineering in terms of the use of stochastic volatility, jump diffusion and market models for pricing the ever more complex array of derivatives instruments. To support the growth and continuing complexity of the credit derivatives market will require increasingly complex approaches to credit modelling. To some extent, quantitative innovations in other product areas can be utilised but care must be exercised when applying these models naïvely to the credit market. Issues such as default correlation, the distributional behaviour of credit spread and difficulties in parametrising credit models are leading to the creation of a whole new field of quantitative finance for credit derivatives.

1 William of Occam (Ockham), 12th-century: "Pluralitas non est ponenda sine neccesitate" or "plurality should not be posited without necessity."

BIBLIOGRAPHY

Arvanitis, A, and J. Gregory, 2001, *Credit: The Complete Guide To Pricing, Hedging and Risk Management* (Risk books, London).

Black, F., and J. C. Cox, 1976, "Valuing Corporate Securities: Some Effects of Bond Indenture Provisions", *Journal of Finance* 31(2) pp 351–67.

Black, F., and M. Scholes, 1973, "The Pricing of Options and Corporate Liabilities", *Journal of Political Economy* 81, pp. 637–659.

Leland, H. E., 1994, "Corporate Debt Value, Bond Covenants, and Optimal Capital Structure", Journal of Finance, 49(4), University of California, Berkeley, pp. 1213–52.

Li, D. X., 2000, "On Default Correlation: A Copula Function Approach", *Journal of Fixed Income,* pp. 43-53, March.

Merton, R. C., 1974, "On the Pricing of Corporate Debt: The Risk Structure of Interest Rates", *Journal of Finance,* 29, pp. 449–70.

Markowitz, H., 1952, "Portfolio Selection," *Journal of Finance* 17(1) March.

Schonbucher, P. J., 2003, "Credit Derivatives Pricing Models: Models, Pricing & Implementation" (John Wiley & Sons).

14

Valuation and risk analysis of synthetic collateralised debt obligations: a copula function approach

David X. Li, Jure Skarabot

Global Credit Derivatives Research, Citigroup Global Markets Inc.[1]

INTRODUCTION

Development of credit derivatives markets

The need to efficiently manage credit risk generated a strong foundation for the expansion of suitable market instruments. Serving this purpose, credit derivatives products are one of the most effective solutions, providing various methods for transfer of credit risk between the market participants. Credit derivatives markets have been through a rapid growth over the last several years. New findings and improvements in credit risk modelling have fuelled the widespread use of credit derivative products. These not only provide the method for credit risk management, but they also allow for alternative investment opportunities and deliver a range of new investment products tailored to their specific requirements to investors.

The main goal of credit derivatives is to transfer reference credit risk between the buyers and sellers of credit protection. Originally, investors were focused on the credit risk associated with the individual names, but today the portfolio risk transfers are increasingly prevalent. It became evident that the credit risk of portfolios could not be managed properly on an individual, name-by-name level, without taking the correlation between credit events into account. The portfolio approach to credit risk allowed for efficient allocation of capital and optimisation of returns for a given level of credit risk. Investors could then identify the concentration risk due to specific credit events and set the proper limits. The portfolio credit model provided the sensitivity analysis, which led to the development of hedging tools and overall credit risk management. All of these factors influenced the expansion of portfolio credit derivatives solutions, and we expect to see further growth and innovations in this market segment.

Credit derivatives are structured in different forms and types. From a general perspective, they can be classified into single-name credit derivatives and portfolio credit products. Single-name credit derivatives products, such as the credit default swap (CDS) and total return swap, are the most basic and common instruments. Single-name CDSs were designed with the initial intention of providing insurance protection against credit events related to a single reference name. Today they are still used primarily for this original purpose, but in addition to providing the default protection, CDSs are building blocks for most of the structured credit products.

As the single-name credit products became established, portfolio credit derivatives products gained in their popularity and acceptance among the investors. In a similar way to single-name credit derivatives, portfolio products provide loss protection on a given part of a portfolio of risky credits. Portfolio products vary from relatively simple instruments, such as first-to-default baskets, to more complex instruments, such as portfolio default swaps and synthetic collateralised debt obligations (CDOs). In case of first-to-default baskets, the protection payment is contingent on the time and identity of the first-to-default issuer in a given credit risk portfolio. Therefore, these instruments can be viewed as an extension of single-name CDSs. In case of portfolio default swaps and synthetic CDOs, the protection payment is contingent on the cumulative loss of a given portfolio before a given time in the future.

The basic portfolio credit derivative instruments are portfolio default swaps, which provide the protection against the loss on a whole portfolio of underlying issuers. Portfolio swaps can be applied as stand-alone derivative instruments between two parties, but in most cases they act as a building element for more complex structured credit products. In instances when the credit risk of a portfolio is distributed to different classes of investors according to their risk/return preferences, the majority of portfolio credit derivatives are usually structured as tranched products. Tranches of synthetic CDOs are a good example of this type of credit derivatives product. Investors in a tranche of a synthetic CDOs make payment only when the cumulative portfolio loss exceeds a certain level, and the total loss exposure for that tranche is limited by the tranche size.

Portfolio credit derivatives are contingent on the credit risk of a portfolio of credits, and not just the risk associated with one single-name credit. Valuation of portfolio products does not depend only on the understanding of the credit risk associated with each individual name, but represents a much more sophisticated problem. Consequently, the correct analysis of correlation between the credit risk of individual names is critical.

Regardless of the more complicated modelling and structuring issues, the market for portfolio credit derivatives has increased dramatically in recent years. For example, the issue of synthetic CDOs more than doubled during 2001 and 2002. According to the estimates provided by CreditFlux, the notional size of synthetic CDOs issued in 2002 reached almost US$300 billion, with a higher rate of growth in arbitrage structures than in the balance sheet synthetic CDOs.[2] The same growth trend can be observed in other portfolio credit derivatives products, where managed portfolio products are becoming increasingly sophisticated and more widespread among market participants.

Portfolio credit products are destined to expand further as the institutions address the need to manage their credit risk exposure on a portfolio level, and investors become more comfortable with the risk/return profile of structured portfolio credit derivatives. In this process, valuation and risk analysis models for portfolio credit products play an important role. Modelling of credit risk on a portfolio level – although a considerable challenge – is one of the key inputs in establishing a liquid market for portfolio credit derivatives.

Key issues in credit portfolio modelling

There are several steps associated with the modelling of credit portfolio transactions. The valuation process depends on two main inputs: derivation of individual default probabilities associated with each credit name in a portfolio, and estimation of the joint distribution of correlated default probabilities.

In order to build a valuation model for the portfolio products, we first need to model the credit risk associated with each name in the portfolio. There are multiple ways to determine the default probabilities for the individual obligations. Some of the approaches result in the risk-neutral probabilities of default, while others deliver probabilities of default under the statistical (historical) probability measure.

Estimation of individual default probabilities can be achieved in different ways. We can use the historical default experience studies from rating agencies; we can reduce the information from other risky credit instruments traded in the market; or we can rely on a structural-type model of credit risk, which determines the default probabilities of risky obligation from the process for the value of the firm (as described in more detail in Chapter 4).

A second key valuation input for modelling credit products is the derivation and implementation of the joint probability of default timing for all the credits in a given portfolio. Because these products, unlike other credit-sensitive instruments such as credit card or consumer loan portfolios, do not involve a large sample of credits, we cannot approach this problem statistically using actuarial methods. On the other hand, a typical reference portfolio associated with the portfolio credit products also includes too many credits to allow for an exhaustive scenario analysis that covers all the possible outcomes associated with default events. The issue of how to model the default correlation for the credits in the reference portfolio is extremely challenging. In addition to this, when modelling structured portfolio credit products, such as synthetic CDOs, time-to-default is an important factor. This means that instead of relying on the static/discrete models of correlated default events, we need to use a model that captures the distribution of time-to-default for each single-name credit, before combining them in a joint distribution of correlated defaults.

Although rare, an event wherein default of one credit directly triggers default of another is not purely random – in fact, defaults tend to cluster together as shown empirically in Chapter 6. Default correlation is generally small, but it has a huge impact on the modelling of portfolio credit products. The correlation between the defaults affects the liabilities in tranched portfolio credit products in an uneven fashion. For example, we observe that the correlation has a significant role in analysis of senior and first-loss tranches, where some mezzanine tranches might be less sensitive to the correlation changes. Clearly, the correlation between rare events is hard to model but it is too important to ignore. Chapter 6 illustrates some inherent problems in the estimation and modelling of default correlation directly. We will see that the use of copula functions is one way to attempt to circumvent such problems.

Copula modelling approach

The complexity involved in portfolio credit derivatives modelling can be addressed from various angles, but one of the most elegant approaches is the copula function method. Li (2000) introduced the copula function approach to credit portfolio modelling and this method quickly became a standard modelling technique used in valuation of portfolio credit derivatives.[3] In this approach, the modelling is based on a random variable called survival time, characterised by its hazard rate function. That approach specified the default timing over any time horizon. Li resolved the problem of determining the joint distribution of default timing for a credit portfolio by the application of the copula function. Copula function combines the information from the individual credits using the assumptions about the correlation structure between them. This concept allows for the construction of a joint distribution of survival times with given marginal distributions specified by the individual credit curves. Finally, in order to perform valuation and pricing in a risk-neutral world, Li used a scheme for the construction of individual credit curves using the pricing information for other risky credit products issued by the same issuer, such as CDSs, assets swaps, or risky bonds.

In the following sections, we review the modelling of individual risky credits and summarise the copula function approach. We analyse the loss distribution of a synthetic credit portfolio and examine the effect of tranching on the valuation of synthetic CDOs. We conclude the chapter with the sensitivity analysis of synthetic CDOs and a review of hedging approaches. Our analysis should thereby provide a consistent valuation and modelling scheme for synthetic CDO structures.

PRICING OF SINGLE-NAME CREDIT OBLIGATIONS

If we want to generate the joint distribution of survival times for a given credit portfolio, we need to determine the marginal survival time distributions for each individual credit in the portfolio. These marginal survival times can be reduced from the observed prices on the credit instruments issued by each obligor. We determine the survival time distribution through the construction of the credit curve. Using a model for pricing risky securities, the observed prices will allow us the reduce hazard rate functions , which define the distribution of the survival times for each credit. Using these curves and the structure of the correlation between default, we can link the individual credits in a portfolio and provide a model for the joint distribution of defaults.

Characterisation of default times

A credit curve gives an instantaneous default probability of the reference obligation at any time in the future. Construction of the credit curve is based on market observed information such as bond prices, asset swap spreads, or default swap spreads. These probabilities are risk-neutral default probabilities. In general, they are much higher than the historical default probabilities for the rating class to which the credit belongs. Here, we briefly describe how a credit curve is constructed (for more details, see Li, 1998).[4]

In order to construct the credit curve for a party issuing a security A, which is subject to default, we introduce a random variable T called *time-until-default* to denote the length of the time between the current date and the occurrence of the default. We characterise *time-until-default* with the distribution function of T, giving us $F(t) = \Pr(T \leq t)$. We define a survival function $S(t)$ as $S(t) = 1 - F(t)$, which provides the probability that a security, A, will attain age t. The random variable *time-until-default* or survival time can be characterised by a probability density $f(t)$, giving us $f(t) = F'(t) = -S'(t)$. We define additional notation:

$$_t q_x = \Pr(T - x \leq t \mid T > x)$$

$$_t p_x = 1 - {_t q_x} = \Pr(T - x > t \mid T > x)$$

The symbol $_t q_x$ can be interpreted as the conditional probability that the security, A, will default within the next t years, conditional on the survival in the first x years. The symbol $_tp_x$ can be interpreted as the conditional probability that the security will survive over the next t years conditional on the survival in x years. In the case that $t = 1$ we omit the prefix t and use the notation

$$q_x = \Pr(T - x \le 1 \mid T > x)$$

$$p_x = 1 - q_x = \Pr(T - x > 1 \mid T > x)$$

Probabilities q_x are called marginal *conditional default probabilities*, which represent the probability of default in period of $[x, x + 1]$ conditional on the survival to the beginning of the period.

Default times are characterised by a *credit curve* for security A, which is defined as the sequence $\{q_0, q_1, ..., q_n\}$

Hazard rate

We can also characterise distribution functions $F(t)$ and $S(t)$ using the hazard rate. The hazard rate function gives the instantaneous default probability for credit that attained given age. This probability is defined

$$\Pr[x < T \le x + \Delta x \mid T > x] = \frac{F(x + \Delta x) - F(x)}{1 - F(x)} \cong \frac{f(x) + \Delta x}{1 - F(x)}$$

and we define the hazard rate function as

$$h(x) = \frac{f(x)}{1 - F(x)} = -\frac{S'(x)}{S(x)}$$

From the last expression we can see that the survival function $S(t)$ can be expressed in terms of the hazard rate $S(t) = e^{-\int_0^t h(s)ds}$ and the density function $f(t)$ can be expressed as

$$f(t) = h(t)e^{-\int_0^t h(s)ds}$$

The marginal conditional survival probability can be expressed in terms of the hazard rate function as

$$_tp_x = e^{-\int_x^{x+t} h(s)ds}$$

and marginal conditional default probability can be written as

$$_tq_x = e^{-\int_x^{x+t} h(s)ds}$$

For the implementation purposes, a typical modelling assumption is that the hazard rate is either constant or piece-wise constant. In this way, we can fit the hazard rate function to the observed market prices for which we usually have only a discrete set of observations. Specifically, in the case of a constant hazard rate, the density function is given as $f(t) = he^{-ht}$ defining the exponential distribution. This specific distribution implies useful scaling properties, which can be used to determine the default probabilities over shorter time intervals.

Valuation of risky bonds

In order to price risky claims subject to default in a risk-neutral setting, we need to derive risk-neutral default probabilities. We can choose different approaches, depending upon which prices we can observe in the market. Traditionally, default probabilities have been modelled using the yields on corporate bonds with different maturities. As the CDS instruments have developed, the default market has become a more liquid sector, thereby providing an alternative source for the estimation of the default probabilities and derivation of the credit curve. In most of the current implementations, CDS spreads are used to extract the risk-neutral default probabilities for pricing of credit sensitive instruments.

We usually assume that the hazard rate is a piece-wise constant function, in which the number of steps matches the number of observed prices. Accordingly, we can use a simple "bootstrap" procedure to construct the discrete credit curve from the observed prices. Extracting default probabilities from the credit curve depends on the assumed recovery treatment of default, so we need to provide the model for the recovery process following default. A few different approaches are utilised in the credit derivative modelling literature.[5] However, none of these models fully reflects the legal treatment of the corporate defaults. We usually adopt the Duffie–Singleton [1999] approach to model the recovery process, since their framework allows risky cash flows to be valued by discounting at the risk-free rate plus the mean loss, where the mean loss is defined as the product of probability of default and the loss given default.

Using this valuation approach, we can extract marginal default probabilities and build a credit curve from the market prices for bonds with maturities t_1, t_2, ..., t_n. If we assume that the hazard rate is piece-wise constant, $h(t) = h_i$, $t_{i-1} \leq t < t_i$ and that the recovery is exogenous and constant, we can determine the complete hazard rate function by simply iterating the valuation equation for the risky bond. Starting with the first period, we price the bond with maturity t_1 and extract the corresponding hazard rate h_1. We continue the same process step-by-step, using the bonds with longer maturities, and then bootstrap the remaining default probabilities recursively.

Valuation of CDSs

A CDS is a bilateral contract where one party (the protection buyer) buys default protection from another party (the protection seller) with respect to a reference entity. The protection buyer pays a premium in the form of periodic payments to the protection buyer. In exchange, the protection seller pays a contingent payment to the protection buyer in case the credit event occurs with respect to the reference entity. The contracts have stated maturity, and they terminate if the credit event occurs. The credit event is a legally defined occurrence that includes bankruptcy, failure-to-pay, and some forms of debt restructuring. If no credit event occurs, the only cash-flow is the premium (ie, the credit default spread) paid by the buyer to the seller. If a credit event occurs, the premium payments stop and the trans-action is settled either physically or as cash settlement.

A CDS consists of two sides: the premium leg and the default payment leg. The present value of the default swap is equal to the sum of the present value of the premium leg and the present value of the default payment leg. CDS spread is the premium, which sets the present value of the default swap equal to zero. Using the constructed credit curve for an individual credit, we can apply a simple valuation model and derive the required annualised CDS premium π, which equates the premium side and the loss payment side of a CDS.[6]

In the first stylised model presented below, we ignore the premium accrued.[7] We also make an assumption that the premium is paid at the end of each period.

Under these assumptions, the present value of premium leg can be expressed as

$$PV^{premium} = \pi \sum_{i=1}^{n} \Delta_{i-1,i} P(0,t_i)_{ti} P_0 = \pi \sum_{i=1}^{n} \Delta_{i-1,i} P(0,t_i) e^{-\int_0^{t_i} h(s)ds}$$

where $\Delta_{i-1,i}$ denotes the tenor between the successive payment dates and $P(0,t_i)$ is the risk-free discount factor. If we assume that the hazard rate $h(t)$ is constant over the interval $[t_{i-1}, t_i]$, then we can express the present value of premium payments as follows

$$PV^{premium} = \pi \sum_{i=1}^{n} \Delta_{i-1,i} P(0,t_i) e^{-\sum_{j=1}^{t} h_j(t_j - t_{j-1})}$$

The present value of loss payment leg can be written as

$$PV^{loss} = (1-R) \int_0^{t_n} P(0, t) f(t)dt = (1-R) \int_0^{t_n} P(0, t)h(t)e^{-\int_0^{t} h(s)ds} dt$$

If we assume that the hazard rate $h(t)$ and the interest rate $r(t)$ are constant over the small intervals $[t_{i-1}, t_i]$, then the present value of loss payments can be calculated as follows

$$PV^{loss} = (1-R) \sum_{i=1}^{n} \frac{h_i}{r_i + h_i} (1 - e^{-(r_i + h_i)(t_i - t_{i-1})}) P(0, t_{i-1}) e^{-\sum_{j=1}^{i-1} h_j(t_j - t_{j-1})}$$

Therefore, the CDS spread π is determined as the premium for which

$$PV^{premium} = PV^{loss}$$

That condition implies that the CDS spread π is given as

$$\pi = \frac{\displaystyle\sum_{i=1}^{n} \Delta_{i-1,i}\, P(0,t_i) e^{-\int_0^{t_i} h(s)\,ds}}{(1-R) \displaystyle\int_0^{t_n} P(0,\,t) h(t) e^{-\int_0^{t} h(s)\,ds}\, dt}$$

Under the assumption of piece-wise constant hazard and interest rate, premium is defined as

$$\pi = \frac{\displaystyle\sum_{i=1}^{n} \Delta_{i-1,i}\, P(0,t_i) e^{-\sum_{j=1}^{i} h_j(t_j - t_{j-1})}}{(1-R) \displaystyle\sum_{i=1}^{n} \frac{h_i}{r_i + h_i} \left(1 - e^{-(r_i+h_i)(t_i - t_{i-1})}\right) P(0,\, t_{i-1}) e^{-\sum_{j=1}^{i-1} h_j(t_j - t_{j-1})}}$$

This formula can be easily modified to take the accrued premium payments into account. Assuming that the premiums are paid at the end of the period, then if the default occurs at time τ between two payment periods $[t_{i-1},\, t_i]$, the buyer of protection must pay the credit swap premium that has accrued since the last payment date. The accrued premium will be approximately equal to

$$\left(\frac{\tau - t_{i-1}}{t_i - t_{i-1}}\right) \Delta_{i-1,i}\, \pi$$

For reasonably small default probabilities and coupon periods, the expected difference between the default event and the coupon date is approximately half of the length of the payment period. Therefore, as a first approximation, we could estimate the accrued premium by adding one half of coupon period to each premium payment when valuing the premium leg.

To be more exact, we need to calculate the present value of the accrued premium. Again, if we assume that the hazard rate $h(t)$ and the interest rate $r(t)$ are constant over the interval $[t_{i-1},\, t_i]$, then the present value of accrued at time t_{i-1} can be calculated following integration by parts as

$$PV^{accrued}_{t_{i-1}} = \frac{\Delta_{i-1,i}\, \pi}{t_i - t_{i-1}} \left[\frac{h_i}{r_i + h_i} \left[\frac{1}{r_i + h_i} - \left(\frac{1}{r_i + h_i} + (t_i - t_{i-1})\right) e^{-(r_i+h_i)(t_i - t_{i-1})} \right] \right]$$

Therefore, the present value of all expected accrual payments is given as

$$PV^{accrued} = \sum_{i=1}^{n} \frac{\Delta_{i-1,i}\,\pi}{t_i - t_{i-1}} \left[\frac{h_i}{r_i + h_i} \left[\frac{1}{r_i + h_i} - \left(\frac{1}{r_i + h_i} + (t_i - t_{i-1}) \right) \right. \right.$$

$$\left. \left. e^{-(r_i+h_i)(t_i-t_{i-1})} \right] P(0,t_{i-1}) e^{-\sum_{j=1}^{i-1} h_j(t_j - t_{j-1})} \right]$$

Now we can estimate the modified CDS premium π as the rate, which equates the following equation

$$PV^{premium} + PV^{accrued} = PV^{default}$$

As a further extension of the presented valuation model for CDSs, we could consider the dependence between the hazard default probabilities, risk-free rate, and the recovery process. In addition, both parties involved in the CDS contract are exposed to their (counterparts) default risk, which might be correlated with the default risk of the reference obligation. The CDS-valuation model presented here can be modified to properly take the above considerations into the account

GENERAL FRAMEWORK OF COPULA FUNCTIONS

It is well understood that in the modelling of portfolio credit products, correlation between the credit events plays a primary role. The default correlation is not only a crucial input for the valuation of synthetic CDOs and credit derivatives baskets, but it is an important factor in estimating various risk exposures, from the counter-party settlement risk to the general risk exposure in the fixed income portfolios. For that reason, it is important to define the correlation between the credit events in a proper way, linking it correctly with the default probabilities for each individual credit.

When introducing the default correlation into the modelling, we can select from different approaches. Appropriate quantities can range from correlation between default indicator variables to the correlation between continuous default variables. For example, we could define default correlation based on the discrete events of survival, or default over some specific time interval. That means that if E_A and E_B are default events of credits A and B over a given time horizon, and $q_A = \Pr(E_A)$, $q_B = \Pr(E_B)$, and $q_{AB} = \Pr(E_A E_B)$ are the probabilities of individual and joint defaults, then the correlation between two discrete default events is defined as

$$\rho_{AB} = \frac{q_{AB} - q_A q_B}{\sqrt{q_A(1 - q_A)\, q_B(1 - q_B)}}$$

This approach to modelling correlation between credit events has several shortcomings. Default is a time-dependent event; therefore, default correlations are also time-dependent. Using this approach, potentially useful information about the term structure of the default rates will not be taken into the account. In addition, choice of the time interval used in the definition of the default is arbitrary. As the discrete default correlation could be applicable to the shorter time horizon, in the case of portfolio credit derivatives products, we need to analyse the correlations over longer time horizons. For this reason, we believe that the discrete default correlation measure is not the best measure for the modelling of portfolio credit products.

As an alternative approach, we define default correlation between credits A and B as the correlation between their survival times T_A and T_B

$$\rho_{T_A T_B} = \frac{E(T_A T_B) - F(T_A)E(T_B)}{\sqrt{Var(T_A)Var(T_B)}}$$

We can observe that the survival time correlation $\rho_{T_A T_B}$ is a far more general concept than the discrete default correlation ρ_{AB}. For example, knowing the distribution of survival time variables allows us to calculate the discrete default correlation. However, we cannot determine the correlation between survival times using the distribution for the discrete default events.

Note that from the estimation perspective, correlation between the fundamentals of the firms in addition to the correlation in macro and industry factors should be an input for extracting default correlations. We will discuss the estimation procedure more in detail later.

In a previous section, we illustrated how to generate marginal distributions of survival time for each specific credit, using the market data. Now we need to construct a joint distribution that will be consistent with the marginal distributions and the correlation structure. Obviously, this problem does not have a unique solution. A copula function approach is a simple and convenient method that combines marginal probability distributions into a joint distribution with a specified correlation structure. It also allows us to use a variety of different specifications and choose different copula functions to combine marginal default probabilities. A copula function approach allows us to independently estimate marginal distributions of default, separately from their dependence structure.

Among those choices, use of normal copulas has several advantages. It is relatively straightforward to simulate correlated normal distribution using Cholesky decomposition. In addition, correlation parameters in normal copulas can be interpreted as the asset correlations. That step simplifies the modelling task even further, because we can empirically determine the correlations between the assets returns and feed it back into the copula model.

Defining a copula function

A copula function method approach is a specification on how to use univariate marginal distributions to form a multivariate distribution. If we have n correlated and uniformly distributed random variables, then the joint distribution function C, defined as

$$C(u_1, u_2, ..., u_n) = \Pr[U_1 \leq u_1, U_2 \leq u_2, ..., U_n \leq u_n]$$

is called *copula*.[8]

If we have n marginal distributions $F_i(T_i)$ and a copula function C, then using the fact that $F_i(T_i)$ are uniformly distributed on the unit interval, we can show that the function

$$C(F_1(T_1), F_2(T_2), ..., F_n(T_n)) = F(T_1, T_2, ..., T_n)$$

presents a joint distribution function for random variables $F_i(T_i)$ and its marginal distributions are

$$F_1(T_1), F_2(T_2), ..., F_n(T_n)$$

Following the theorem by Sklar, the reverse statement is also true. Any multivariate distribution can be written in a form of a copula function. For a given joint distribution $F(T_1, T_2, ..., T_n)$ and marginal distributions $F_1(T_1)$, $F_2(T_2), ..., F_n(T_n)$, a copula associated with $F(T_1, T_2, ..., T_n)$ is a function C such that

$$F(T_1, T_2, ..., T_n) = C(F_1(T_1), F_2(T_2), ..., F_n(T_n))$$

If $F(T_1, T_2, ..., T_n)$ is continuous, then the copula C is unique.

Copula approach simplifies the simulation of correlated survival times. If we can simulate uniform random variables $U_1, U_2 ..., U_n$ with the proper joint probability distribution of $(F_1(T_1), F_2(T_2), ..., F_n(T_n))$, then we can simulate survival times $T_1, T_2, ..., T_n$ by simply inverting $F_i(T_i) = U_i$. More detail and a graphical illustration of this simulation algorithm is given in the following chapter.

Copula choice and calibration

The copula function approach represents an intuitive and clear way to combine individual distribution function into a joint distribution. Which copula function is the most suitable for the estimation of joint survival time distributions remains an open question. In addition, after we decide on a choice of copula, we need to find a way to estimate the parameters efficiently.

As we discussed above, the marginal credit curves can be constructed from the observed market information, such as credit default spreads, asset swap spreads, or bond prices. In order to define the default event, we assume that there exists a standardised asset return $\bar{r}_i$ and a threshold level

r_i such that the default is triggered if the return falls below the threshold level r_j.

One of the most standard classes among copulas are the elliptical copulas, and a generic example is the normal copula[9]

$$C(u_1, ..., u_n) = \Phi_n \left(\Phi^{-1}(u_1), ..., \Phi^{-1}(u_n), \Sigma \right)$$

where $\Phi_n(x_1, ..., x_n, \Sigma)$ is the standard multivariate normal distribution with the correlation matrix Σ and denotes the inverse of the univariate normal distribution.

Normal copulas have the advantage of establishing a framework to esti-mate the correlation parameters Σ from the assets returns. In case of two credits, if we assume that asset returns follow bivariate normal distribu-tion $\Phi_2(x, y, \rho)$ with correlation coefficient ρ, the joint probability is given by

$$\Pr\left(\tilde{r}_1 \leq r_1, \tilde{r}_2 \leq r_2 \right) = \Phi_2 \left(\Phi^{-1}(q_1), \Phi^{-1}(q_2), \rho \right)$$

where

$$\Pr(\tilde{r}_1 \leq r_1) = \Phi(r_1) = q_1$$
$$\Pr(\tilde{r}_2 \leq r_2) = \Phi(r_2) = q_2$$

This illustration shows that if we use normal copula function, we can apply asset return correlations as the correlation parameter in copula func-tion. Using the estimation of pair-wise asset correlation, then the simula-tion of correlated default times should be a straightforward process. In order to simulate a distribution of correlated normal variables Y_i with a given correlation matrix Σ, we use Cholesky algorithm to triangulate the correlation matrix Σ and apply it to the sample of independent normal variables to derive the joint distribution of correlated normal variables. After that step, we translate the normal random variables Y_i into uniforms $U_i = \Phi(Y_i)$. From these uniforms we derive the survival times for each credit by inverting individual distribution functions $F_i(T_i) = U_i$.

SPECIFICATION OF THE CORRELATION MATRIX

As shown earlier, the correlation parameters in the normal copula function can be roughly interpreted as the standardised asset return correlations. We have the following few ways to specify the asset return correlation matrix.

We could use an economic asset correlation model based on equity returns. To assure a stable asset correlation, we tend to apply factor analysis to broad equity indices, and then regress the asset return to the chosen set of factors. Some other approaches start by mapping each credit into country, sector and industry, based on its revenue sources. Two credits are therefore correlated because they share these common factors.

The idiosyncratic risk of each credit has been shown to be linked to the company asset size. Intuitively, if a company is big in terms of asset size, it would move in tandem along with the market it forms a part of, and therefore presents a less idiosyncratic risk. On the other hand, if a company is small in terms of asset size, it moves more independently, and hence presents a larger idiosyncratic risk. An example of this approach is the one used by CreditMetrics.

In a trading environment, we tend to calibrate the correlation parameters to traded portfolio products, like default baskets or tranches of CDOs written on the same collateral assets.[10] For most practical purposes, we use a parsimonious representation of the correlation matrix by using only one parameter, which implies that all credits are driven by one common factor. If we use one correlation parameter ρ in the copula function, then that parameter can be associated with the one-factor asset return model where we assume the distribution of the return r_i is driven by the common factor r_m and the idiosyncratic risk factor ε_i

$$r_i = \sqrt{\rho}\, r_m + \sqrt{1-\rho}\, \varepsilon_i$$

More often than not, we use two correlation parameters: the inter- and intra-industry correlations. It is assumed that the two credits from the same industry are more correlated than the two from different industries. This two parameters assumption in the correlation matrix can also be expressed in terms of factor models. If we use two correlation parameters, inter-industry correlation and intra-industry correlation then each asset return can be expressed as follows

$$r_i = \sqrt{\rho_1 - \rho_0}\, r_k + \sqrt{\rho_0}\, r_m + \sqrt{1-\rho_1}\, \varepsilon_i$$

where r_k is the return for each industry sector, r_m is the common factor for all credits, and ε_i is the independent noise factor. Using this two-parameter correlation specification, we can reduce the number of independent factors to $n + 1$, where n is the total number of industry groups for a given industry classification. This reduction of dimensionality can substantially improve the speed of calculation of any credit portfolio, since the number of fundamental driving factors is fixed, irrespective of the number of credits in the portfolio. Conditional on these factors, all credits are independent from each other. We can then explore various techniques to calculate the total loss distribution for a portfolio of independent credits. The factors can then be averaged out using numerical integration.

LOSS DISTRIBUTION OF A SYNTHETIC CREDIT PORTFOLIO

In the valuation of synthetic credit portfolio structures, estimating the total loss distribution over a given period is the most important step. To this end, we need to calculate the present value of the expected loss or the discounted expected loss (EDL) that is the required premium, if the premium is a lump-sum payment made at the origination. However, in reality, the premium is usually paid in instalments and is contingent on the evolution of the loss distribution across time, up to the maturity of the portfolio transaction. In the case of tranched portfolio credit products, estimating the EDL for an individual tranche presents an additional step in valuation.

The estimation of the loss distribution is based on the following key inputs:

❏ marginal default probabilities from individual credit curves, which could be based from historical information, implied from market default swap spread or Merton type structural model;
❏ the correlation matrix , which is the key input for modelling joint distribution of correlated defaults; and
❏ assumptions about the recovery rate for the individual names in the portfolio.[11]

Once we have all these inputs in place, we can begin to calculate the loss distribution. We can do this in one of several ways.

The simplest approach is the one introduced by Li (2000). In this approach, we first simulate correlated normal distribution Y_i's and then use the following formula $T_i = F_i^{-1}(\Phi(Y_i))$ to translate Y_i's into survival time.[12] This approach has several advantages. First, it is easy to implement; second, under each simulation it gives the time of each default. The disadvantage is that the convergence is slow, especially when we deal with credit with lower default probabilities. If we use historical simulation for an AAA credit, the 5-year default probability is 0.0029%, so it takes about 34,483 runs to have one case of default. Using this approach would require a large number of simulations to achieve stable results, especially when we use historical information or value super senior CDO tranches.

There are a variety of enhancements we can implement to improve the simulation framework. The most commonly used improvement techniques are the following: importance sampling, quasi-Monte Carlo simulation, reduction of dimensionality, and Fast Fourier Transform (FFT). For further discussion on different approaches to the estimation of loss distribution and valuation of synthetic credit portfolio structures, see recent publications by Schmidt and Ward (2002) or Gregory and Laurent (2003).[13]

Knowing the distribution of losses not only allows us to determine the EL and derive the premium, but also leads to various loss measures, such as the unexpected loss (defined as volatility of losses), VAR/Credit VAR losses, and expected shortfall or tail VAR.

When we analyse the loss on a portfolio, we prefer to use the distribution of excess loss, which is defined as the probability of loss larger than a given loss amount $S(l) = \Pr(L > l)$. The reason that we use the excess loss distribution instead of the loss distribution defined as $F(l) = 1 - S(l)$ is that many properties of loss can be visible better if the loss measure is expressed as the excess loss. For example, the EL for the whole portfolio can be expressed in two ways

$$EL = \int_0^\infty lf(l)dl = \int_0^\infty S(l)dl$$

which is the area below the excess loss distribution curve. Some other quantities, such as the EDL of tranched synthetic-credit portfolios can be expressed more simply if we use the excess loss function. We will return to this point in the next section, when we discuss valuation of synthetic CDOs.

To illustrate the concept of excess loss, we present an example of a model portfolio and generate the distribution of excess loss. This portfolio has 100 names, the credit spread for each name is 200 bps, maturity is five years and the recovery rate is 30%. Figure 1 shows the distribution of excess loss, where the x-axis is the loss amount and the y-axis is the probability of loss larger than given amount. If we include zero loss in the calculation of excess loss probability, then the probability of having a non-negative loss is always 1. We purposely exclude the zero loss in the calculation, so that we can explicitly see the probability of suffering no losses.

Figure 1 shows the impact of correlation on the distribution of excess loss. We can see that the probability of no losses rises from almost 0% to

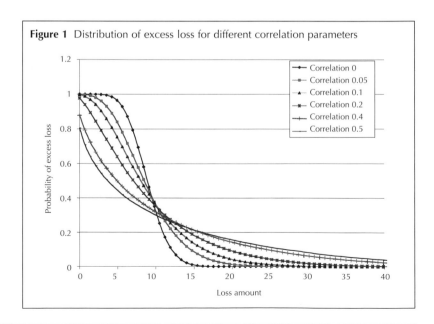

Figure 1 Distribution of excess loss for different correlation parameters

20% as the correlation changes from 0% to 50%. It is clear that in the case of independent names, the probability of no default in a portfolio is extremely small.[14] When the correlation is high, the defaults are more likely to occur in a group, and this increases the probability of no loss to 20%. In the case of high correlation, losses are concentrated more in the tail of the distribution. Therefore, in a portfolio with high correlation between the credits, the probability of severe losses increases.

Figure 2 Credit VAR for different correlation parameters

Correlation	1% credit VaR
0%	14.7
10%	25.2
20%	32.9
50%	53.9
75%	67.2

From the perspective of a whole portfolio, the EDL doesn't depend on correlation, however, measures of loss variation, such as unexpected loss or expected shortfall, are dependent on correlation. We can observe that the correlation has an important impact on the loss distribution. This can be shown using a measure like Credit VAR, which is defined as the excess loss that the probability of a loss larger than that value is less than a given percentage. The 1% Credit VAR for our model portfolio is given in Figure 2.

TRANCHING AND VALUATION OF SYNTHETIC CDO
Pricing of the portfolio default swaps
The portfolio default swap is a contract that transfers the credit risk of a portfolio from the originator (the protection buyer) to the investors (the protection sellers). The protection buyer usually retains first-loss tranche and transfers the second-loss part. The redistribution of the risk is specified in terms of the percentage of the portfolio loss. The reference portfolio typically consists of 100–200 credit names. Portfolio default swaps can be implemented as stand-alone instruments, although they usually play a role of the building blocks for synthetic CDOs.

Valuation of the portfolio default swaps follows a similar procedure to the valuation of single-name default swaps. A portfolio default swap consist of two parts, the loss payment leg and the premium leg. Breakeven spread is the premium, which the protection buyer pays to the protection seller for the compensation of potential aggregated losses on a portfolio of credits.

In order to determine the breakeven spread, we need to derive the distribution of cumulative losses from the origination date to the maturity of the portfolio swap. If the probabilities of default are set in the risk-neutral world, then the discounted value of loss payments at the risk-free rate represents the present value of the loss payment leg. On the other side, we can determine the distribution of the outstanding principal from the distribution of cumulative losses. The portfolio default-swap premium is a flat rate applied to the current outstanding principal. That defines the distribution of payments on the premium side and the present value of the premium payments – again, discounted at the risk-free rate in the risk-neutral world – needs to be equated to the present value of the protection loss payments. In that way, the breakeven spread is uniquely defined.

Pricing of the tranched synthetic CDOs

As we mentioned earlier, the majority of the portfolio credit products are offered in a tranched form, and our main goal is to provide the valuation and risk analysis for the synthetic CDOs.

Synthetic CDOs combine traditional CDO technology with the synthetic transfer of credit risk. Compared to cash CDOs, these structures decouple the funding from the credit risk transfer. The originator transfers the credit risk of a pool of reference assets using portfolio default swaps and issues liabilities in an unfunded or partially funded form. Synthetic CDOs can be static or managed structures and they are divided into two classes:

❏ balance sheet synthetic CDOs, structured to improve originators' return on regulatory capital and manage the credit exposure; and
❏ arbitrage synthetic CDOs, designed to exploit the yield mismatch between spreads on synthetic credit products and synthetic CDO liabilities.

In the case of synthetic CDOs, investors provide the protection only for certain level of aggregated losses, limited by the floor β_{i-1} and cap β_i. For example, investors in the first loss tranche are exposed to the losses up to β_1, investors in the next tranche are exposed to losses between β_1 and β_2, and so on.

Pricing of the tranched synthetic CDOs closely follows the valuation of the portfolio default swaps. Instead, for a whole portfolio, we need to calculate the present value of the expected payments for the premium leg and expected payments for the loss protection leg for each tranche separately. Present values of both payment sides determine the breakeven spread for a given tranche. Following the allocation of the losses from the first-loss tranche to the more senior tranches, we can derive the distribution of cumulative tranche losses from the aggregate distribution of losses on a portfolio.

Again, the investors who sell the protection on a tranche i, provide the protection against the total loss L of a whole portfolio with notional amount N over a certain range $[B_{i-1}, B_i]$. We call the first-loss tranche $[0, B]$ the *equity tranche*, and the most senior tranche $[B_{m-1}, B_m]$ the *senior* or *super-senior tranche*. We can observe that the tranche loss has a different structure depending on the seniority order. This variation in the loss allocation has an important effect on the valuation of risk analysis of tranched synthetic CDOs.

If $L(t)$ is the cumulative loss on a whole portfolio up to time t, then the cumulative loss on the tranche is defined as

$$L_i(t) = \begin{cases} 0 & L(t) \leq B_{i-1} \\ (L(t) - B_{i-1}) & B_{i-1} < L(t) \leq B_i \\ B_i - B_{i-1} & B_i < L(t) \end{cases}$$

or it can be expressed as

$$L_i(t) = \min[\max[(L(t) - B_{i-1}), 0], (B_i - B_{i-1})]$$

In Figure 3, we show the loss function for a five-tranche CDO against the total distribution.

We can observe that buying a super senior tranche is equivalent to selling a call option on the total loss of the portfolio with a strike of the lower subordination level of super senior tranche. Buying an equity tranche is equivalent to selling a put option with the strike price equal to the equity size. An investment in mezzanine tranche is equivalent to putting on a spread option strategy in which the investor is long a call option with strike B_i and short a call with a strike price of B_{i-1}.

We define the total cumulative expected loss EL_i for a given tranche is given as

$$EL_i = \int_0^\infty lf_i(l)dl$$

where $f_i(e)$ is the density function of the loss distribution for tranche i, but for the valuation purposes we need to determine the expected values of all discounted loss payments at the risk-free rate.

If $P(0, t)$ is the risk-free discount factor, and T is the maturity of the portfolio default swap, then we can write the present value of the loss payment leg as

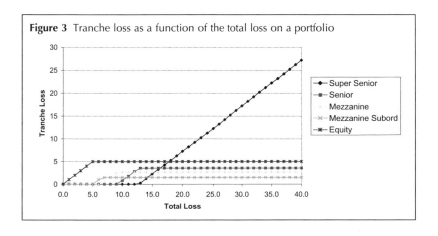

Figure 3 Tranche loss as a function of the total loss on a portfolio

305

$$PV^{loss_i} = E^P\left[\int_0^T P(0, t)dL_i(t)\right]$$

with the expectation calculated under the risk-neutral measure. We can use integration by parts and change the order of integration in the second integral by Fubini's theorem, before rewriting the present value of the loss payment side as

$$PV^{loss_i} = P(0, T)E^P(L_i(T)) - \int_0^T f(0, t)P(0, t)E^P(L_i(t))dt$$

where $f(0, t)$ denotes the instantaneous forward rate

$$f(0, t)dt = \frac{dP(0, t)}{P(0, t)}$$

As with single-name default swaps, we determine the break-even spread paid by the default protection buyers to the default protection seller as the premium, which equates the present value of the premium leg with the present value of the loss payment leg. The value of the premium leg depends on the evolution of the outstanding principal $P_i(t)$ of the tranche. In the same way that we determined the loss, it can be shown that the outstanding principal on a tranche can be expressed as

$$P_i(t) = \min[\max[(B_i - L_i(t)), 0], (B_i - B_{i-1})]$$

Therefore, the value of the premium leg can be written as

$$PV^{premium_i} = \pi_i E^P\left[\sum_{j=1}^n \Delta_{j-1,j}\, P(0, t_j)P_i(t_j)\right]$$

$$= \pi_i E^P\left[\sum_{j=1}^n \Delta_{j-1,j}\, P(0, t_j)\min\left[\max\left[(B_i - L_i(t_j)), 0\right], (B_i - B_{i-1})\right]\right]$$

with the expectation calculated under the risk-neutral measure.

The fair spread on the tranche is the premium π_i such that $PV^{loss_i} = PV^{premium}$

Figure 4 Pricing of a sample synthetic CDO

Name	National %	Expected loss	Breakeven spread (bp)
Super senior	88	281,325	1
Senior	4	1,425,417	77
Senior mezzanine	3	4,306,068	323
Junior mezzanine	2	6,987,661	877
First loss	3	22,344,375	3104

In Figure 4, we give a numerical example of a synthetic CDO pricing model for different correlation levels. We choose a model portfolio with 100 credits with average spread of 80 bps. Maturity is five years and the pairwise correlation is 12.5%.

Note that the derived fair spreads presented in Figure 4 can differ from the observed spreads on the actual tranched portfolios. Different factors can affect the discrepancy. We assumed that the total spread for each individual name is attributed to the default risk. In reality, this is not the case, as other non-default factors (eg, liquidity) represent a portion of the credit spreads. Our choice of copula function is only one of the approaches in incorporating single-name default distributions into a joint distribution of defaults. Different copula functions could be applied to generate the joint distribution. Also, we don't incorporate the stochastic nature of the default intensities into the model, which could have an effect on the valuation.

RISK ANALYSIS AND HEDGING

We can analyse the risk associated with the portfolio credit derivatives in different ways. To extract the sensitivity of the losses on a portfolio as a whole, and the sensitivity of individual tranche losses, we define various measures that estimate the variation in the present value of expected losses as the key individual factors change. Essentially, such measures provide the sensitivity analysis to various key input factors.

Risk sensitivity measures

Several risk sensitivity measures are common in analysis of tranched credit portfolios:

❏ *Credit01*: This quantity measures the sensitivity of the tranche *I* with the respect to a single-name *j*. In this definition of Credit01, we evaluate the change in the present value of a tranche, given a parallel shift in spreads for an individual single-name credit. We can apply a modified definition of Credit01, whereby we measure the effect on the value of the tranche given a parallel shift in spreads for all names.
❏ *Correlation01*: This quantity measures the sensitivity of tranche *I* to the change in the correlation parameters. If we use a factor model for the correlation input, Correlation01 can be evaluated to each individual.
❏ *Default01*: This quantity measures the sensitivity of tranche *I* to the default of an individual credit in the portfolio.
❏ *MCF*: This quantity measures the sensitivity of the tranche *I* when one of the individual names in the portfolio changes from a risky credit to a risk-free asset.

We can observe several properties of risk measures for a tranched synthetic CDO portfolio. The EDL on a portfolio on each individual

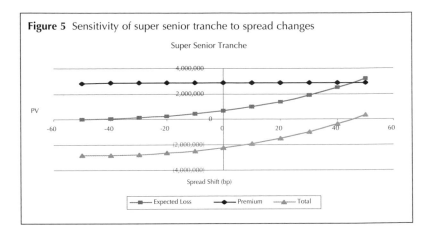

Figure 5 Sensitivity of super senior tranche to spread changes

tranche increases as the spreads increase. Clearly, the EDL on each tranche is capped by the notional amount of that tranche and the total loss on a portfolio is capped with the notional amount. As the spreads on individual credits widen, a greater proportion of Credit01 migrates from junior tranches to senior tranches. EDL on senior tranches is positively convex, and we therefore observe negative price convexity (see Figure 5). We can also observe that it is more sensitive to the spread increases when the spreads are wider.

For the mezzanine tranches, the effect of spread widening can act in either direction. As the spreads increase, EDL on mezzanine tranches shifts from being positively convex to negatively convex (see Figure 6). This is mainly due to the EDL already being high at the high levels of spreads in the reference portfolio. Being close to the total size of the tranche, any further spread increases would not affect the mezzanine in a more significant way. This phenomena is even more apparent in the equity tranche, where the EDL is negative convex (see Figure 7).

Although the EDL of a whole portfolio doesn't depend on the correlation, the change in correlation has a strong impact on the expected losses of the individual tranches. In general, increase in the correlation increases Correlation01 of most senior tranches as the chance of extreme events increase. On the other hand, a decrease in correlation increases the losses in the most junior tranche, as the distribution of losses is shifted more towards the first loss position. There is a certain level of uncertainty in the impact of correlation changes for the mezzanine tranches. As we noted, the loss distribution on a mezzanine tranche is non-linear and is similar to the payoff of a spread option. Certain mezzanine tranches can be an inflection point, in the sense that the expected losses would initially increase as the correlation increases. After reaching some threshold level, the expected losses on that tranche would start decreasing with an increase in the

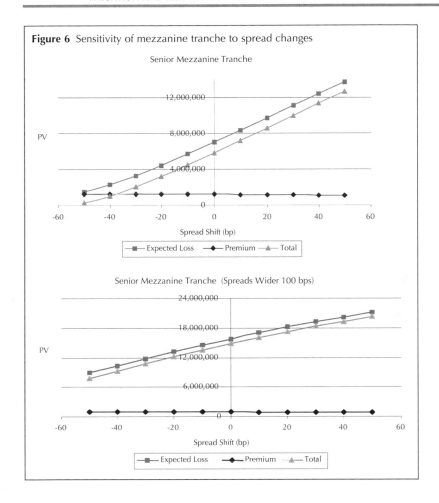

Figure 6 Sensitivity of mezzanine tranche to spread changes

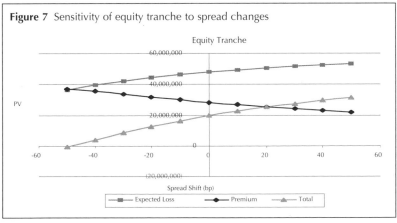

Figure 7 Sensitivity of equity tranche to spread changes

correlation. For that specific tranche, the sensitivity to an increase in correlation starts following the equity pattern, after acting as a senior tranche. With a high average spread of a reference portfolio, the "inflection" tranche is higher on the capital structure of the synthetic CDO; with low average spreads in a reference portfolio, the inflection tranche is lower on the capital structure of the synthetic CDO. Again, this phenomena is driven by the fact that an increase in correlation shifts the distribution of total losses towards more senior tranches.

As an additional input to the sensitivity analysis, we can aggregate certain measures defining the quantities associated with the variation of losses, loss percentiles and expected tail loss. These measures can be designed in such a way that they target each individual tranche or a portfolio as a whole.

Hedging

After we have defined the risk measure Credit01, we can estimate the proper hedge ratios for a tranche, which neutralise the effect of the potential changes in spreads.

The spread hedge ratio of a tranche I with the respect to a given credit j is defined as

$$HedgeRatio_I^j = -\frac{Tranche\ Credit01}{Name\ Credit01}$$

This ratio defines the percentage of the notional of the individual default swap, which needs to be sold to hedge the corresponding tranche Credit01.

Note that due to the differences between the premium received in the default swap and the premium paid for the protection on the tranche, in addition to the effect of the correlation, the hedge ratio on a portfolio (summed over all tranches) is less then 100%.

It is clear that we cannot optimally hedge both spreads and defaults with the set on individual single-name CDSs.[15] Individual defaults can be hedged by buying 100% notional protection for each single name. Such hedging strategy over-hedges to the changes in spreads.

It can be empirically estimated that for the mezzanine tranches, the spread hedge ratios and default hedge ratios are approximately the same. Therefore, it is possible to approximately hedge changes in spreads and defaults simultaneously, with the same set of underlying CDSs. For the remaining tranches, it would be feasible to design a portfolio of hedges, which would minimise the combination of spread and default sensitivity for each credit at some given risk level.

CONCLUSIONS

We have presented a flexible framework for the valuation and risk analysis of portfolio credit derivative products using the copula approach. We focused our analysis on the synthetic CDOs, although the valuation scheme is general enough to cover various portfolio credit products.

The valuation structure consists of two building parts: characterisation of the default times for single-name credits in the reference portfolio, and the construction of a joint distribution of correlated default times for the whole portfolio. Distribution of the default times for the single-name credit obligations is specified using the hazard-rate function; we have illustrated the method to reduce the default probabilities from the observed market prices for traded obligations such as risky bonds. We characterised joint distribution of defaults using the copula function. In particular, we focused on the use of normal copula and discussed the input of the correlation structure.

For the purpose of valuation of portfolio credit derivatives, we introduced the notion of excess loss, which allows us to examine the portfolios in an intuitive way. For synthetic CDOs, we derived the valuation of premium and loss payment parts, and we determined the breakeven spread for a given tranche. We provided numerical illustration for pricing of a sample portfolio and we discussed risk analysis for different CDO tranches.

There are several issues in the modelling of synthetic CDOs and general portfolio credit derivatives that can be developed as an extension of the valuation framework presented here. The speed of the copula portfolio modelling approach can be enhanced using certain statistical properties and faster numerical procedures (eg, Fast Fourier Transform). Stochastic credit spread models for reference credits and the implementation of alternative copula functions should improve the accuracy of the valuation models. Finally, the issue of optimal hedging for the tranches of synthetic CDOs can be explored further, taking default and spread movements into account simultaneously. We believe that these enhancements will lead to improved accuracy and efficiency of the valuation models for synthetic CDOs.

1   The authors would like to thank Graham Murphy for his comments in the preparation of the paper.

2   *CreditFlux*, February 2003.

3   "On Default Correlation: A Copula Function Approach", David Li, *Journal of Fixed Income*, March 2000, pp. 43–53.

4   "Constructing a Credit Curve", David Li, *Credit Risk, RISK Special Report*, November 1998, pp. 40–44.

5   The three most common approximations for the recovery process are the "Recovery of Market Value" approach (see Duffie, D. and K. Singleton, 1999, "Modeling Term Structure of Defaultable Bonds", *Review of Financial Studies*, pp. 687–720), the "Recovery of Treasury"

approach (see Longstaff, F. and E. Schwartz, 1995, "Simple Approach to Valuing Risky Fixed and Floating Rate Debt", *Journal of Finance*, pp. 789–819), and the "Recovery of Face Value" approach (see Jarrow, R., Lando, D. and S. Turnbull, 1997, "A Markov Model for Term Structure of Credit Risk Spreads", *Review of Financial Studies*, pp. 482–523).

6   That premium ("credit default spread") is expressed in basis points per annum on the notional amount and the typical day count convention for corporate credits is Actual/360 with quarterly payments.

7   In case the credit event occurs between the payment dates, the protection buyer will typically have to pay the premium accrued between the credit event date and the last payment date.

8   We can also provide an equivalent axiomatic definition of copula, where a copula is any increasing function $C: [0, 1]^n \to [0, 1]$ with the properties that it has uniform marginals $C(1, ..., 1, x_i, 1, ..., 1) = x_i$ and that the volume of any hypercube in $[0, 1]^n$ is non-negative.

9   Elliptical copulas are distributions that have ellipsoid density contours. Important examples in this family are normal copulas and student t-copulas.

10 Ideally, if we could observe the prices of all possible credit default baskets, we could infer the implied correlation parameters between all the possible pairs of credit. These implied correlation parameters should have the same role as the implied volatility parameters in the equity derivatives markets, and should provide the complete correlation input for the valuation of the portfolio credit products.

11 Note that the recovery rate assumption for the individual credit in the portfolio can be different form the recovery rate used in the extraction of individual default probabilities.

12 Implementation of the normal copula function can be extended to other copulas. For example, valuation based on the Student t-copula function follows similar steps as the valuation based on the normal copula function.

13 Schmidt and Ward, 2002, "Pricing Default Baskets", Risk, January; Gregory and Laurent, 2003, "I will Survive", Risk, June.

14 The default probability over five years for each name is $1 - e^{-5.0.200/(1-0.3)} = 0.133$. In case of independent names, probability of no default in a portfolio is $(1 - 0.133)^{100}$, which is practically 0.

15 Theoretically, such hedging should be possible if we have 2n independent obligations for a portfolio with n credits. For example, we could apply the simultaneous spread/default strategy using CDSs with different maturity or a combination of CDSs and CDS options.

15

Extreme events and multi-name credit derivatives[1]

Roy Mashal, Marco Naldi and Assaf Zeevi

Lehman Brothers; Columbia University

The dependence structure of asset returns lies at the heart of a class of models widely employed for the valuation of multi-name credit derivatives, as we saw in the last chapter. In this chapter, we study the dependence structure of asset returns using copula functions. Employing a statistical methodology that relies on a minimal amount of distributional assumptions, we first investigate whether the popular tenet of Normal dependence between asset returns is supported on the basis of empirical observations. We also compare the dependence structures of asset and equity returns to provide some insight into the common practice of estimating the former using equity data. Our results show that the presence of joint extreme events in the data is incompatible with the assumption of Normal dependence, and support the use of equity returns as proxies for asset returns. Furthermore, we present evidence that the likelihood of joint extreme events does not diminish as we decrease the sampling frequency of our observations. Building on our empirical findings, we then describe how to capture the effects of joint extreme events by means of a simple and computationally efficient time-to-default simulation. Using a t-copula model, we analyse the impact of extreme events on the fair values and risk measures of popular multi-name credit derivatives such as nth-to-default baskets and synthetic loss tranches.

INTRODUCTION

The valuation of default-contingent instruments calls for the modelling of default mechanisms. A well-known dichotomy in credit models distinguishes between a "structural approach", where default is triggered by the market value of the borrower's assets falling below its liabilities, and a "reduced-form approach", where the default event is directly modelled as an unexpected arrival.

Currently, a major challenge facing credit models is represented by the rapid growth of multi-name instruments, whose valuation entails modelling the joint default behaviour of a set of reference names. Although both the structural and the reduced-form approaches can, in principle, be extended to the multivariate case, the calibration of the parameters governing the likelihood of joint defaults poses a number of problems.

If we think of defaults as being generated by asset values falling below a given boundary, then the probabilities of joint defaults over a specified horizon must follow from the joint dynamics of asset values. Consistent with their descriptive approach of the default mechanism, multivariate structural models rely on the dependence of asset returns in order to generate dependent default events. In the first part of this chapter, we focus on the empirical properties of the dependence structure – also known as the *copula function* – of asset returns. Roughly speaking, the copula function summarises the dependence structure of a multivariate distribution by "factoring out" the marginals (see the section on *Dependence Structure Modelling*).

The last chapter described a multivariate Normal model for generating the joint default distributions. Indeed, several well-known multivariate models assume a joint normal distribution for asset returns. For example, Hull and White (2001) generate default dependence by simulating correlated Brownian motions that are supposed to mimic the asset values dynamics. Similarly, two of the most commercially successful multi-name models, developed by KMV and CreditMetrics, rely on the joint normality of the default-triggering variables.[2] The widespread use of the multivariate Normal distribution is certainly related to the simplicity of its dependence structure, which is fully characterised by the correlation matrix.

A number of recent studies have shown that the joint behaviour of *equity* returns is not consistent with the correlation-based Gaussian modelling paradigm. In particular, extreme co-movements between equities tend to be more adequately described by a fat-tailed dependence structure – eg, the one derived from the Student-t multivariate distribution (the so called *t*-copula). To that end, empirical evidence suggests that correlation, and therefore the Gaussian dependence structure (aka Normal-copula), are not sufficient to appropriately characterise the dependencies between equity returns.[3]

This observation is particularly relevant to the world of default-contingent instruments. The evidence in favour of a fat-tailed dependence structure implies that the likelihood that equity values exhibit large co-movements is higher than correlation-based models would predict. Since the payoffs of credit instruments are triggered by defaults, and defaults are typically modelled as tail realisations, the increased likelihood of such *extremal events* has substantial implications on the analysis and valuation of these instruments.

Of course, to substantiate the discussion above, one needs to first verify whether the joint behaviour of asset returns is similar to that found in equity returns, as – according to the "structural approach" – it is the former that governs the risk profile of default-contingent instruments. Given that asset returns are not directly observable, it has become customary to proxy asset dependence with equity dependence, and to estimate the parameters governing the joint behaviour of asset returns from equity return series. Fitch Ratings (2003), for example, have recently published a special report describing their methodology for constructing portfolio loss distributions: it is based on a Gaussian copula parameterised by equity correlations.

The use of equity returns to infer the joint behaviour of asset returns is often criticised on the grounds of the different leverage of assets and equity. Even those who accept it as a valid approximation for high-grade issuers are often critical of this approach when applied to low-grade borrowers. This is because a high-quality issuer has a relatively low probability of default, and every variation in the market value of its assets translates almost dollar-by-dollar into a variation of its market capitalisation. On the other hand, high-yield borrowers are closer to the default threshold, and a variation in their asset value can also produce a significant variation in the market value of their debt. This "leverage effect" may generate significant differences in the joint dynamics of equity and asset values.

This chapter has three main objectives.

1. We test whether evidence of extreme events in asset return data is statistically significant, as it was found to be in equity return data. Building on dependence concepts, we find that this question can be answered affirmatively; our statistical study also sheds some light on the magnitude of the error induced by using equity data as a proxy for actual asset returns.
2. Based on these findings, we then illustrate how one can construct simple models that support extremal dependencies in defaults times. We require that such models be easily calibrated to empirical data and be computationally tractable. This culminates in a simple simulation algorithm based on a t-copula model of correlated defaults.
3. Finally, based on these models for correlated default times, we illustrate the impact of extreme event modelling on the practical issue of measuring and pricing the risk of two popular multi-name credit products, namely nth-to-default baskets and synthetic loss tranches. We close with comments on our results and offer some concluding remarks.

DEPENDENCE STRUCTURE MODELLING

At this point we will briefly describe some dependence modelling concepts to be used in the chapter. The key ingredient in modelling and testing dependencies is the observation that any d-dimensional multivariate distribution can be specified via a set of d marginal distributions that are "knitted" together using a *copula function*. Alternatively, a copula function can be viewed as "distilling" the dependencies that a multivariate distribution attempts to capture by factoring out the effect of the marginals. More formally, a copula function is a multivariate distribution defined over $[0,1]^d$, with uniform marginals. It is possible to confirm that copula functions capture the dependence structure of a multivariate distribution from the following fundamental result; this is known as Sklar's theorem and is adapted from Theorem 1.2 of Embrechts *et al* (2001).

Sklar's Theorem
Given a d-dimensional distribution function H with continuous marginal cumulative distributions $F_1, ..., F_d$, there exists a unique d-dimensional copula $C: [0,1]^d \rightarrow [0,1]$ such that

$$H(x_1, ..., x_d) = C(F_1(x_1), ..., F_d(x_d)) \tag{1}$$

In particular, the copula is given by

$$C(u_1, ..., u_d) = H(F_1^{-1}(u_1), ..., F_d^{-1}(u_d)) \tag{2}$$

where $u_i \in [0,1]$ and $F_i^{-1}(\cdot)$ denotes the inverse of the cumulative distribution function F, for $i = 1, ..., d$.

By plugging in various multivariate distributions – eg, the Gaussian distribution – for H, one produces the various copulas that underlie these distributions and are derived from them. This study focuses on a natural generalisation of the Gaussian dependence structure, namely the Student-t copula. To this end, let t_v denote the (standard) univariate Student-t cumulative distribution function with v degrees-of-freedom, namely,

$$t_v(x) = \int_{-\infty}^{x} \frac{\Gamma((v+1)/2)}{\Gamma((v/2)(v\pi)^{1/2}} (1 + y_2 / v)^{-(v+1)/2} dy \tag{3}$$

Then, for $u = (u_1, ..., u_d) \in [0,1]^d$

$$C(u_1, ..., u_d; v, \Sigma) = \int_{-\infty}^{t_v^{-1}(u)} \frac{\Gamma((v+d)/2)}{|\Sigma|^{1/2}\Gamma((v/2)(v\pi)^{1/2}} (1 + y^T\Sigma^{-1} y / v)^{-(v+d)/2} dy \tag{4}$$

is the Student-t copula parameterised by (v, Σ), where Σ is the correlation matrix, and

$$y = t_v^{-1}(u) := (t_v^{-1}(u_1), ..., t_v^{-1}(u_d))$$

The density of the t-copula, $c(\cdot; v, \Sigma)$, is obtained by differentiating the t-copula w.r.t. $u_1, ..., u_d$ (see, for example, Embrechts *et al*, 2001).

While the Gaussian copula lies at the heart of most financial models and builds on the concept of correlation, a number of alternative dependence models have been proposed in the literature: the Clayton, Frank, Gumbel and Student-*t* are probably the most notable examples. In this chapter, we focus on the dependence structure underlying the multivariate Student-*t* distribution for a number of reasons.

First, Mashal and Zeevi (2003) compare the different copulas mentioned above in the context of modelling the joint behaviour of financial returns. Applying a formal test, they find that the *t*-copula provides a better fit than the others (see also the study by Bremann *et al* (2003), which also finds empirical support for the *t*-copula using a different statistical test).

Second, the *t*-copula retains the notion of correlation while adding an extra parameter into the mix: the degrees-of-freedom (DoF). The latter plays a crucial role in modelling and explaining extreme co-movements of financial variables, and is of paramount importance for the valuation and risk management of default-sensitive instruments. Moreover, it is well known that the Student-*t* distribution is very "close" to the Gaussian when the DoF is sufficiently large (say, greater than 30); thus, the Gaussian model is nested within the *t* family. The same statement holds for the underlying dependence structures, and the DoF parameter effectively serves to distinguish the two models. This suggests how empirical studies might test whether the ubiquitous Gaussian hypothesis is valid or not. In particular, these studies target the dependence structure rather than the distributions themselves, thereby eliminating the effect of marginal returns that would "contaminate" the estimation problem in the latter case.

To summarise, the *t*-dependence structure constitutes an important and quite plausible generalisation of the Gaussian modelling paradigm, which is our main motivation for focusing on it in this chapter. For a further discussion of copulas, and the many important characteristics that make them a central concept in the study of joint dependencies, see, eg, the recent survey paper by Embrechts *et al* (2001).

THE DEPENDENCE STRUCTURE OF ASSET RETURNS: EMPIRICAL EVIDENCE AND MODELLING IMPLICATIONS

We continue with a discussion of how asset return data are "backed out" from observable equity return values via the Merton model. We will go on to describe a semi-parametric methodology that allows for the estimation of the dependence structure of a set of returns without imposing any parametric restriction on their marginal distributions. After introducing a test statistic that can be used to evaluate the significance of our point estimates, we apply this methodology to study the dependence structure of asset returns, comparing it with that of equity returns. Next, we present a fully-parametric model with a *t*-copula and *t*-marginals; the empirical results show that, since the univariate t-distribution accurately fits the time-series of equity returns, a fully-parametric t-model produces estimates of the dependence parameters that are extremely close to the one produced by the semi-parametric methodology. We then provide some concluding remarks and a summary of our empirical results.

The Merton model and implied asset values

Obviously, the main obstacle when attempting to estimate the dependence structure from historical data is that asset returns are not directly observable. In fact, the use of unobservable underlying processes is one of several criticisms directed at the structural approach over the years. To provide a plausible answer to these questions, we first need to "back out" asset values from observable data. One way to estimate the market value of a company's assets is to implement a univariate structural model. Using Merton's (1974) approach – ie, recognising the identity between a long-equity position and the payoff of a call option written on the asset value process – one can apply standard option pricing arguments to derive two conditions that can be simultaneously solved for the asset value of the company and its volatility. This procedure is at the heart of KMV's CreditEdge, a popular credit tool that first computes a measure of distance-to-default and then maps it into a default probability (EDF) by means of a historical analysis of default frequencies. The empirical analysis that follows employs the asset value series generated by KMV's model to study the dependence properties of asset returns.

A semi-parametric estimation procedure and a test for fat-tailed dependence

We now describe an estimation procedure that is used to calibrate a certain class of dependence structures to the equity and asset returns data. Bearing our earlier discussion in mind (see the section on *Dependence Structure Modelling*), the key question that we now face is how to estimate the parameters of the dependence structure. In particular, consider a basket of d names, each following an arbitrary marginal F_i, $i = 1, ..., d$, and having a joint distribution H with underlying t-dependence structure, which is denoted by $C(\cdot; v, \Sigma)$, see Equation (4) for the precise parametric form. Here, Σ denotes the correlation matrix and v the DoF parameter. Suppose we have n observations $\{x_i\}_{i=1}^n$ on these d names, where the returns $x_i = (x_{i1}, ..., x_{id})$ are assumed to be mutually independent and distributed according to H.

If the marginal distributions were known, then we could use Sklar's Theorem to conclude that $U := F(X_i) \sim C(\cdot; v, \Sigma)$, where $F(X_i) := (F_1(X_{i1}), ..., F_d(X_{id}))$ is the vector of marginal distributions, the symbol ":=" reads "defined as", and the symbol "~" reads "distributed according to".

Since the structure of the marginals is arbitrary and unknown to us, we propose to use the empirical distribution function as a surrogate, that is,

$$\hat{F}_j(\cdot) := \frac{1}{n} \sum_{i=1}^{n} I\{X_{ij} \le \cdot\}, j = 1, ..., d \tag{5}$$

where $I\{\cdot\}$ is the indicator function, ie,

$$I(A) := \begin{cases} 1, & \text{if } A \text{ occurs,} \\ 0, & \text{otherwise} \end{cases}$$

We then work with the *pseudo-sample* observations:[4]

$$\hat{U}_i = \left(\hat{F}_1(X_{i1}), ..., \hat{F}_d(X_{id})\right), i = 1, ..., n$$

Focusing on the t-dependence structure $C(\cdot; \nu, \Sigma)$ – formally given by the t-copula in Equation (4) – let us denote by

$$\Theta = \left[(\nu, \Sigma): \nu \in (2, \infty)\right], \Sigma \in R^{d \times d} \text{ is symmetric and positive definite}\}$$

the feasible parameter space, and set $\theta := (\nu, \Sigma)$.

Then, for a given pseudo-sample $\{U_i\}_{i=1}^{n}$ we set the *pseudo log-likelihood* function to be

$$L_n(\theta) = \sum_{i=1}^{n} \log c\,(\hat{U}_i; \theta)$$

where $c(\cdot; \theta)$ is the t-copula density function associated with C. Now, let $\theta := (\hat{\nu}, \hat{\Sigma})$ denote the *maximum likelihood* (ML) estimator of the DoF and correlations, ie, the value of $\theta \in \Theta$ maximising $L_n(\theta)$. This maximisation is generally very involved, and a naive numerical search is likely to fail because of the high dimensionality, $(1 + d(d-1)/2)$, of the parameter space. A simpler way to search for a maximum in this large parameter space is to estimate the correlation matrix using Kendall's Tau (see Lindskog, 2000) and then maximise the likelihood over the DoF parameter. The results reported in this study refer to estimates obtained in this manner. We note in passing that the estimator based on Kendall's Tau is efficient, in the sense that it achieves the minimal asymptotic variance in this context of the t-family – see, for example, Embrechts *et al*, (2001).

As we mentioned earlier, the DoF parameter ν controls the tendency to exhibit extreme co-movements, and also measures the extent of departure from the Gaussian dependence structure. Given its pivotal role, we subsequently focus on the accuracy of the DoF estimates in a more detailed manner.

Specifically, we use a *likelihood-ratio* formulation to test whether empirical evidence supports or rejects a given value of ν. To begin with, we fix a value of the DoF parameter ν_0 and consider the hypotheses $H_0: \theta \in \Theta_0$ vs. $H_1: \theta \in \Theta$ where $\Theta_0 = \{\theta \in \Theta: \nu = \nu_0\} \subset \Theta$.

Then, we set the *likelihood-ratio test statistic* to be

$$\Lambda_n \left(\hat{\nu} \mid \nu_0 \right) = -2 \log \frac{\sup_{\theta \in \Theta_0} \prod_{i=1}^{n} c\left(\hat{U}_i; \theta \right)}{\prod_{i=1}^{n} c\left(\hat{U}_i; \hat{\theta} \right)} \tag{6}$$

To determine the adequacy of each value of ν_0, we need to characterise the distribution of the statistic $\Lambda_n \left(\hat{\nu} \mid \nu_0 \right)$. Since this distribution is not tractable, the standard approach is to derive the asymptotic distribution and use that as an approximation. Specifically, Mashal and Zeevi (2002) arrive at the approximation

$$\Lambda_n \left(\hat{\nu} \mid \nu_0 \right) \approx (1 + \gamma) \chi_1^2 \tag{7}$$

where $\gamma > 0$ is a constant that depends on the null hypothesis, χ_1^2 denotes a random variable distributed according to a Chi-squared law with one degree-of-freedom, and "$\approx$" reads "approximately distributed as" (for large values of n).[5] Thus, we can calculate approximate p-values as a function of ν_0 as follows

$$p - \text{value}(\nu_0) \approx P\left(\chi_1^2 \geq \frac{\Lambda_n \left(\hat{\nu} \mid \nu_0 \right)}{(1 + \gamma)} \right)$$

By letting the *null hypothesis* ν_0 vary over the parameter space, we can compute the corresponding p-values and detect the range of Dof that are supported (or rejected) by the observed return data. Notice that *large* values of the test statistic correspond to *small* p-values, thus indicating that the hypothesised ν_0 is not plausible on the basis of the empirical observations. This hypothesis testing formulation illustrates the "sharpness" of the estimation results in a much stronger manner than if we had just focused on the associated confidence intervals for the parameter estimates.

Empirical evidence

We now apply the methodology outlined above to study the dependence structure of asset returns and compare it with that of equity returns. For consistency, asset and equity values are both obtained from KMV's database. The reader should keep in mind, however, that equity values are observable, while asset values have been "backed out" by means of KMV's CreditEdge implementation of a univariate Merton model. We use daily data covering the period from December 31, 2000 to November 8, 2002, and focus our attention on two portfolios, the 30-name Dow Jones Industrial Average and a 20-name high-yield portfolio.

DJIA Portfolio

Following the semi-parametric methodology described in the previous section, we estimate the number of DoF of a t-copula without imposing any structure on the marginal distributions. Using the test statistic we introduced, Figure 1 presents a sensitivity analysis for various null hypotheses of "joint-tail fatness", as captured by the DoF parameter. The two horizontal lines represent significance levels of 99% and 99.99%; a value of the test statistic falling below these lines corresponds to a value of DoF that is not rejected at the respective significance levels.

The minimal value of the test statistic is achieved at 12 DoF (v =12) for asset returns and at 13 DoF (v =13) for equity returns. In both cases, we can reject any value of the DoF parameter outside the range [10,16] with 99% confidence; in particular, the null assumption of a Gaussian copula ($v = \infty$) can be rejected with an infinitesimal probability of error.

Finally, notice that the point estimate of the asset returns' DoF lies within the non-rejected interval for the equity returns' DoF, and vice versa, indicating that the two are essentially indistinguishable from a statistical significance viewpoint. Moreover, the difference between the joint tail behaviour of a 12- and a 13-DoF t-copula is negligible in terms of any practical application.

Figure 2 reports the point estimates of the DoF for asset and equity returns in the DJIA basket, as well as for three subsets consisting of the first, middle, and last 10 names (in alphabetical order). The similarities

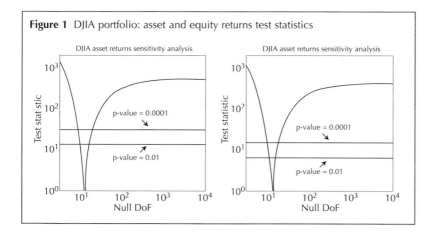

Figure 1 DJIA portfolio: asset and equity returns test statistics

Figure 2 Maximum likelihood estimates of DoF for DJIA portfolios

Portfolio	Asset Returns DoF	Equity Returns DoF
30-Name DJIA	12	13
First 10 names	8	9
Middle 10 names	10	10
Last 10 names	9	9

between the joint-tail behaviour (as measured by the DoF) of asset and equity returns are quite striking.[6]

Next, we compare the remaining parameters that define a t-copula, ie, the correlation coefficients. Using robust estimates based on Kendall's rank statistic, we compute the two 30×30 correlation matrices from asset and equity returns. The maximum absolute difference (element-by-element) is 4.6%, and the mean absolute difference is 1.1%, providing further evidence of the similarity of the two dependence structures.

To summarise, the empirical evidence strongly supports the widespread practice of using equity return series to estimate underlying dependencies between asset returns.

High-yield portfolio

We now investigate whether the similarities between the dependence structures of asset and equity returns persist when we restrict our attention to lower-quality, higher-leverage issuers. Figure 3 shows the constituents of a 20-name portfolio that we have randomly selected from the universe of publicly traded, high-yield companies covered by KMV.

Figure 3 The constituents of the high-yield portfolios

Names 1–5	Names 6–10	Names 11–15	Names 16–20
AES	Atlas Air Worldwide Holding Inc.	MGM Mirage	Safeway Inc.
Adaptec Inc.	Echostar Communication Corp.	Navistar International	Saks Inc.
Airgas Inc.	Gap Inc.	Nextel Communications	Service Corporation International
AK Steel Holding Inc.	Georgia-Pacific Corp.	Northwest Airlines Corp.	Solectron Corp.
Alaska Air Group Inc.	L-3 Communications Holdings Inc.	Royal Caribbean Cruises Ltd.	Sovereign Bancorp Inc.

Figure 4 Maximum likelihood estimates of DoF for high-yield portfolios

Portfolio	Asset Returns DoF	Equity Returns DoF
20-Name portfolio	15	16
Names 1–5	15	13
Names 6–10	14	12
Names 11–15	10	10
Names 16–20	13	15

Figure 4 reports the ML estimates for the DoF of asset and equity returns for this 20-name high-yield portfolio, as well as for the four 5-name sub-portfolios. Once again, the estimated DoF for asset and equity returns are very close. When analysing correlations, a similar behaviour is also observed: specifically, the maximum absolute difference in the correlation coefficients is 6.7% and the mean absolute difference is 1.6%.

A fully-parametric *t*-model

In order to estimate the dependence structure of equity returns, one needs to estimate the whole multivariate distribution. Namely, even though the marginal distributions of returns can be estimated without any assumption on the dependence structure, the inference of the dependence structure cannot be done without estimating the marginal distributions.

Earlier, we used the empirical marginals to estimate a *t*-dependence for returns and test the null hypothesis of Gaussian dependence. In this section, we show how to estimate the copula of equity returns while modelling the marginals as shifted, scaled *t*-distributions.[7] The numerical examples we now utilise show that, since the univariate *t*-distribution generally represents a good probability model for unconditional equity returns, the estimates of the parameters of the *t*-copula are not very sensitive to the choice between the two methods.

There is plethora of evidence that the *t*-distribution accurately fits univariate equity returns (see Praetz, 1972; Blattberg and Gonedes, 1974; Glasserman *et al*, 2002). As an example, in Figure 5 we use a quantile-to-quantile (Q-Q) plot to show that a *t*-distribution with four degrees of freedom offers a much better fit for the daily equity return series of Boeing than the Normal distribution.

Figure 5 Q-Q plots of BA return vs. normal and t_4 distributions

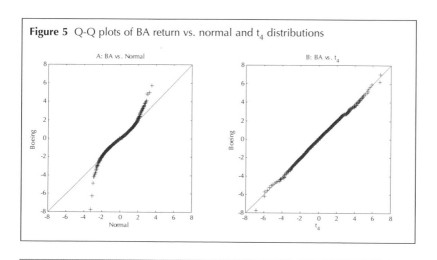

As before, we take advantage of Sklar's Theorem to split the estimation of the multivariate distribution into the following two steps:

1. estimating each marginal by itself, as the marginals are independent from each other and from the dependence structure, and
2. estimating the dependence structure based on the estimated marginals and the copula representation.

This procedure, which separates the estimation of the marginals from the joint dependence parameters, is sometimes referred to as IFM (see the monograph by Joe, 1997). To accomplish the first step, we now fit univariate t-distributions to the individual time-series of returns rather than using the empirical distributions as we did earlier. As for the second step, we follow exactly the same procedure described earlier.

The density of the standard t-distribution is given by the derivative of Equation (3):

$$f_v(x) = \frac{\Gamma((v + 1)/2)}{\Gamma((v/2)\sqrt{\pi v}} (1 + x^2 / v)^{-(v+1)/2}, \ x \in R \tag{8}$$

where v represents the degrees of freedom (DoF) parameter. The variance of the t-distribution is equal to $v/(v - 2)$, $v > 2$. We model each equity return series by means of a shifted and scaled t-distribution (see Raiffa and Schlaifer, 1961, Section 7.9). Given a univariate return sample $\{X_i\}_{i=1, \ldots, n}$, where n is the number of observations, we assume that $\tilde{X}_i := (X_i - m) / \sqrt{H}$ is distributed according to a standard t-distribution, where m denotes the shift parameter and H denotes the scale parameter. Next we define $\theta^u = (m, H, v)$,

$$\Theta^U = \{\theta^U \colon m \in R, H > 0, v > 2\}$$

and the maximum likelihood estimator

$$\theta^U = (\hat{m}, \hat{H}, \hat{v}) = \arg \max_{\theta^U \in \Theta^U} \prod_{i=1}^n f_v(\tilde{X}_i)$$

which can be found by means of a simple numerical search.

The purpose of the univariate estimation is to enable the transformation of equity returns into the domain of the copula. This is achieved by computing

$$\hat{U}_i := t_{\hat{v}}^{-1} \left[(X_i - \hat{m}) / \sqrt{\hat{H}} \right]$$

Performing the above procedure for every return series we get

$$\{\hat{U}_{ij}\}, \ i = 1 \ldots n, \ j = 1 \ldots d$$

and we can now estimate the copula following the steps described earlier.

Numerical examples and the effect of the sampling frequency

We will now use our two t-models to estimate the multivariate distribution of several 5- and 10-name baskets belonging to the Dow Jones Industrial Average. We use both daily and monthly equity return data, ranging from January 1991 to December 2001, for a total of 2,526 daily and 119 monthly observations.

Estimating the t-marginals

To implement the fully parametric methodology, we first need to estimate the t-marginals. Figure 6 presents the estimates of the shift, scale and DoF parameters for the 30 DJIA stocks (membership as of February 2002).

Figure 6 MLE for shift, scale and DoF parameters for DJIA stocks

Ticker	Daily			Monthly		
	$\hat{m}$	$\hat{H}$	$\hat{v}$	$\hat{m}$	$\hat{H}$	$\hat{v}$
AA	$-1.4 \cdot 10^{-4}$	4119	4.8	$1.1 \cdot 10^{-2}$	231	4.9
AXP	$6.2 \cdot 10^{-4}$	3455	5.6	$2.6 \cdot 10^{-2}$	285	4.6
T	$-1.2 \cdot 10^{-4}$	6304	3.4	$4.6 \cdot 10^{-3}$	242	4.6
BA	$1.2 \cdot 10^{-4}$	5432	4.0	$1.1 \cdot 10^{-2}$	245	8.1
CAT	$1.4 \cdot 10^{-4}$	4027	4.8	$1.2 \cdot 10^{-2}$	180	10.2
C	$1.0 \cdot 10^{-3}$	3021	6.2	$2.9 \cdot 10^{-2}$	162	7.9
KO	$4.2 \cdot 10^{-4}$	5702	5.2	$1.9 \cdot 10^{-2}$	339	4.2
DD	$1.4 \cdot 10^{-4}$	4910	5.1	$8.2 \cdot 10^{-3}$	206	>100
EK	$-1.1 \cdot 10^{-5}$	6338	4.0	$4.5 \cdot 10^{-3}$	301	5.3
XOM	$3.5 \cdot 10^{-4}$	7768	5.8	$1.0 \cdot 10^{2}$	612	27.4
GE	$8.1 \cdot 10^{-4}$	6427	6.1	$1.8 \cdot 10^{-2}$	281	144.2
GM	$-1.3 \cdot 10^{-5}$	3409	7.5	$5.3 \cdot 10^{-3}$	149	11.1
HD	$1.1 \cdot 10^{-3}$	3658	5.2	$2.3 \cdot 10^{-2}$	182	18.3
HON	$5.1 \cdot 10^{-4}$	5118	3.9	$1.8 \cdot 10^{-2}$	312	3.2
HWP	$8.6 \cdot 10^{-4}$	2667	4.7	$2.0 \cdot 10^{-2}$	106	10.1
IBM	$1.8 \cdot 10^{-4}$	4536	4.0	$8.9 \cdot 10^{-3}$	134	31.1
INTC	$1.5 \cdot 10^{-3}$	2214	5.3	$3.2 \cdot 10^{-2}$	97	7.7
IP	$-2.1 \cdot 10^{-4}$	4534	4.7	$3.1 \cdot 10^{-3}$	229	4.7
JPM	$1.5 \cdot 10^{-4}$	5410	4.0	$1.2 \cdot 10^{-2}$	273	4.7
JNJ	$5.5 \cdot 10^{-4}$	5137	7.1	$1.4 \cdot 10^{-2}$	206	>100
MCD	$3.1 \cdot 10^{-4}$	5431	5.5	$1.3 \cdot 10^{-2}$	236	>100
MRK	$5.6 \cdot 10^{-4}$	4649	6.5	$1.6 \cdot 10^{-2}$	188	22.2
MSFT	$1.1 \cdot 10^{-3}$	2870	5.9	$2.7 \cdot 10^{-2}$	129	6.0
MMM	$1.8 \cdot 10^{-4}$	8776	3.7	$8.3 \cdot 10^{-3}$	541	4.5
MO	$5.2 \cdot 10^{-4}$	5845	3.4	$1.2 \cdot 10^{-2}$	193	6.1
PG	$4.9 \cdot 10^{-4}$	6144	4.8	$1.6 \cdot 10^{-2}$	388	4.1
SBC	$4.5 \cdot 10^{-4}$	5911	4.4	$1.0 \cdot 10^{-2}$	295	10.9
UTX	$4.7 \cdot 10^{-4}$	5974	4.4	$2.0 \cdot 10^{-2}$	336	4.6
WMT	$5.1 \cdot 10^{-4}$	3942	4.9	$1.6 \cdot 10^{-2}$	185	14.8
DIS	$2.5 \cdot 10^{-4}$	5039	4.5	$9.7 \cdot 10^{-3}$	214	9.3

The DoF estimates are quite low, confirming the well-documented non-normality of equity returns. It is interesting to note that the DoF of most names increases as we decrease the sampling frequency from daily to monthly. This might be due to aggregation (similar to the type of behaviour observed in the Central Limit Theorem, which states that sums of random variables converge to a Gaussian distribution). However, this effect varies considerably across tickers: some names show a far more "stable" additivity than others.

It is also clear that the estimated DoF differ significantly across names, independently of the frequency. This confirms that in order to estimate the copula correctly, one should allow for different DoF in the marginals rather than fitting a multivariate t-distribution to the data.

Estimating the t-copula

To provide numerical examples for the estimation of the t-dependence structure, we choose nine baskets consisting of members of the DJIA. The semi-parametric model employs the empirical marginals to map each equity return series into the unit interval, while the fully parametric method utilises the estimates described in the previous section. In both cases, the t-copula is then estimated using Kendall's Tau transform for the correlation matrix and maximising the likelihood function over the DoF parameter.

Figure 7 shows the estimated DoF of the t-copula for the nine baskets (the term "Emp-marginals" refers to the non-parametric assumption on the distribution of the marginals). First, notice that the two methodologies produce very similar results, confirming that the univariate t-distribution generally represents a good probability model for the univariate equity return series. Second, note that while the estimates of the marginal DoF appear to decrease systematically as we increase the frequency of the observations, the estimates of the copulas' DoF do not change significantly. In other words, while the marginal fat tails get thinner due to potential aggregation effects, there is no evidence that a similar phenomenon is driving the behaviour of the joint tails.

Our results echo the recent work of Breymann, Dias and Embrechts (2003) on the joint behaviour of FX financial series. Breymann *et al* employ a t-copula to model the dependence structure of a set of exchange rates, and show that the DoF parameter is almost independent of the sampling window. Moreover, this parameter is small (of order 4–6), indicating that the t-copula provides a more accurate description of the data than the Gaussian counterpart. Their study also compares the t-copula to various competing models and finds further empirical support for the former.

Summary

Our empirical investigation of the dependence structure of asset returns sheds some light on two main issues that were raised in the introduction.

Figure 7 Estimates of DoF of the *t*-copula for different DJIA baskets

Basket	Tickers	*t*-marginals		Emp-marginals	
		Daily	Monthly	Daily	Monthly
1	AA, AXP, T, BA, CAT	8	7	8	6
2	C, KO, DD, EK, XOM	10	12	9	10
3	GE, GM, HD, HON, HWP	9	7	8	6
4	IBM, INTC, IP, JPM, JNJ	8	8	7	5
5	MCD, MRK, MSFT, MMM, MO	9	6	8	5
6	PG, SBC, UTX, WMT, DIS	8	7	7	5
7	Baskets 1+2	10	10	10	8
8	Baskets 3+4	10	11	10	8
9	Baskets 5+6	9	8	9	6

DoF estimates for the *t*-copula of different DJIA baskets under a fully parametric and a semi-parametric model. The semi-parametric specification uses the empirical distributions to estimate the marginals. The estimates are provided for two different sampling frequencies (daily and monthly)

First, the assumption of Gaussian dependence between asset returns can be rejected with extremely high confidence in favour of an alternative fat-tailed dependence. Second, the dependence structures of asset and equity returns appear to be strikingly similar. The KMV algorithm that produces the asset values used in our analysis is nothing more than a sophisticated way of de-leveraging the equity to get to the value of a company's assets. Therefore, the popular conjecture that the different leverage of assets and equity will necessarily create significant differences in their joint dependence seems to be empirically unfounded, even when we analyse the value processes of low-grade issuers. Instead, our results suggest that the differences in leverage are mostly reflected in the marginal distributions of returns. From a practical point of view, these results represent good news for practitioners who only have access to equity data for the estimation of the dependence parameters of their credit models.

Our analysis also shows that imposing *t*-marginals on the equity return series, rather than using their empirical distributions, does not have significant consequences for the estimation of the dependence parameters. Thus, the *t*-copula with *t*-marginals provides a simple and parsimonious model that can be used in various financial applications in a much more straightforward manner than the semi-parametric model based on the *t*-copula. Finally, the presence of fat-tailed dependence does not seem to diminish as we decrease the sampling frequency of our data. In other words, there is no evidence that the dependence structure of equity returns approaches the Gaussian dependence structure as we increase the measurement intervals and allow for aggregation.

EXTREME EVENTS AND CORRELATED DEFAULTS

A number of different frameworks have been proposed in the literature for modelling correlated defaults and pricing multi-name credit derivatives. Hull and White (2001) generate dependent default times by diffusing correlated latent variables and calibrating default thresholds to replicate a set of given marginal default probabilities. Multi-period extensions of the one-period CreditMetrics paradigm are also commonly used, even though they produce the undesirable serial independence of the realised default rate. A computationally more expensive approach is that based on the implementation of stochastic intensity models, as proposed by Duffie and Singleton (1998) and Duffie and Garleanu (1998). Finger (2000) offers an excellent comparison of several multivariate models in terms of the default distributions they generate over time when calibrated to the same marginals and first-period joint default probabilities. While most multi-name models require simulation, the need for accurate and fast computation of greeks has pushed researchers to look for modelling alternatives. Finger (1999) and, more recently, Gregory and Laurent (2003) show how to exploit a low-dimensional factor structure and conditional independence to obtain semi-analytical solutions.

In an influential paper, Li (2000) presents a simple and computationally inexpensive algorithm for simulating correlated defaults. His methodology builds on the implicit assumption that the multivariate distribution of default times and the multivariate distribution of asset returns share the same copula, which he assumes to be Gaussian. The approach described in the previous chapter is based on this model. The results of our earlier statistical analysis suggest that the dependence structure of asset returns is very similar to the dependence structure of equity returns, and that the dependence structure of equity returns is better described by a t-dependence than by a Gaussian copula.

Therefore, it seems natural to modify Li's methodology to account for the likelihood of extreme joint realisations, and simulate correlated default times under the assumption that their dependence structure is the same as that of the associated equity returns.

Simulating default times with fat-tailed dependence

To construct the multivariate distribution of default times under the objective probability measure, we first need to estimate the marginal distributions, which we will denote with $F_1, F_2, ..., F_d$. These can be derived from univariate structural models (such as KMV's EDF) or simply estimated using observed default frequencies within relatively homogeneous peer groups (such as Moody's default frequencies by rating). We then join these marginals with a t-copula, and estimate the dependence parameters (correlation matrix Σ and DoF v) from equity returns using either one of the two procedures described earlier.

For valuation purposes, we need to construct the multivariate distribution of default times under the risk-neutral probability measure. In this case, it is common practice to back out the marginals F_1, F_2, ..., F_d from single-name defaultable instruments (such as credit default swaps). Given the low liquidity of multi-name instruments, it is not yet possible to use their market prices to obtain implied values for the dependence parameters. Instead, practitioners generally estimate the copula using historical data, implicitly relying on the extra assumption that the dependence structure of default times remains unchanged when we move from the objective to the pricing probability measure.

Simulating default times from this multivariate distribution is straight-forward:

1. Commence by simulating a multivariate-t random vector $X \in R^d$ with correlation Σ and v DoF.
2. Next, transform the vector into the unit hyper-cube using $U = (t_v(x_1), t_v(x_2), ..., t_v(x_d))$
3. Translate U into the corresponding default times vector τ using the inverse of the marginal distributions: $\tau = (\tau_1, \tau_2, ..., \tau_d) = (F_1^{-1}(u_1), F_2^{-1}(u_2), ..., F_d^{-1}(u_d))$.

The simulation algorithm is illustrated in Figure 8.

It is easy to verify that τ has the given marginals and that its dependence structure is given by a t-copula with correlation Σ and v DoF. The logic of the proof can be established via the following.

❑ X has a $t_{\Sigma,v}$ copula by definition.
❑ Since copulas are preserved by strictly monotonic transformations of the variables and the univariate t-distribution is strictly increasing, U also possesses a $t_{\Sigma,v}$ copula.

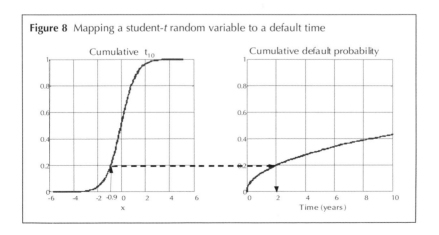

Figure 8 Mapping a student-t random variable to a default time

❑ Since copulas are preserved by strictly monotonic transformations of the variables, while the marginal distributions of default times are strictly monotonic, τ also has a $t_{\Sigma,v}$ copula.
❑ Since $t_{\Sigma,v}$ has marginals, U has uniform marginals.
❑ Since U has uniform marginals, τ has F_1, F_2, ..., F_d marginals.

Asset correlation, default time correlation and default event correlation
The simulation algorithm discussed above is based on the assumption that asset returns and default times share the same copula, and consequently share the same correlation matrix. To understand better the impact of different dependence assumptions on the valuation and risk measures of default-contingent instruments, it is useful to introduce the concept of "default event correlation".

Default event correlation measures the tendency of two credits to default jointly within a specified horizon. Formally, it is defined as the correlation between two binary random variables that indicate defaults, ie,

$$\rho_D = \frac{p_{AB} - p_A p_B}{\sqrt{p_A(1 - p_A)}\sqrt{p_B(1 - p_B)}} \tag{9}$$

where p_A and p_B are the marginal default probabilities for credits A and B, and p_{AB} is the joint default probability. Of course, p_A, p_B and p_{AB} all refer to a specific horizon. Notice that default event correlation increases linearly with the joint probability of default, and is equal to zero if – and only if – the two default events are independent.

Default event correlations are the fundamental drivers in the valuation of multi-name credit derivatives. Unfortunately, the scarcity of default data makes joint default probabilities, and therefore default event correlations, very hard to estimate directly. As a result, researchers rely on alternative methods to calibrate the frequency of joint defaults within their models: the method we described above solves this problem by assuming that rarely observable default times and frequently observable equity returns share the same copula.

It is interesting to see how the DoF parameter – which regulates tail dependence and the likelihood of joint extreme events – influences default event correlations. Using a 5-year horizon and two credits whose default times are exponentially distributed with hazard rates of 1%, Figure 9 compares a normal copula and a t-copula with three and 10 degrees of freedom. Tail dependence increases default event correlation for any value of asset correlation. In particular, notice that even when asset returns are uncorrelated (ie, they are linearly independent), tail dependence can produce a significant amount of default event correlation.

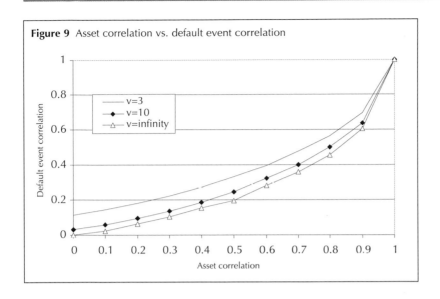

Figure 9 Asset correlation vs. default event correlation

MULTI-NAME CREDIT DERIVATIVES

In the previous section, we proposed an algorithm to simulate tail-dependent defaults under either the objective or the pricing measures. Fair values and risk metrics for any multi-name credit derivative can now be easily computed. In this section, we analyse the consequences of making different assumptions with respect to the dependence structure of default times. Specifically, we focus on two popular multi-name credit instruments, namely nth-to-default baskets and portfolio loss tranches.

nth-to-default baskets

In an nth-to-default basket swap, two counterparties agree on a maturity and a set of reference assets, and enter into a contract whereby the protection seller periodically receives a premium (also called "basket spread") from the protection buyer. In exchange, the protection seller stands ready to pay the protection buyer par minus recovery of the nth referenced defaulter in the event that the nth default occurs before the agreed-upon maturity. First- and second-to-default swaps are the most popular orders of protection.

Taking extreme events into account has significant consequences on the estimate of the Expected Discounted Loss (EDL) of a basket swap (see the previous chapter for the definition of the EDL). This is because, other things equal, simulating defaults by means of a fat-tailed copula increases the probability of joint defaults, and thus default event correlation (see Equation 9). We focus on EDL because this measure relates both to agency rating methodologies (when computed under real-world probabilities)

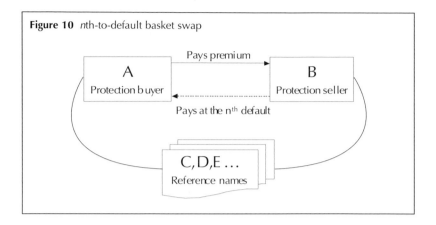

Figure 10 *n*th-to-default basket swap

and to the fair compensation for the default risk exposure (when computed under risk-neutral probabilities).

The sign of the relation between EDL and default event correlations, however, depends on the order of the basket. The EDL of a first-to-default exposure is always monotonically decreasing in default event correlations. In terms of valuation, this means that allowing for joint extreme events makes first-to-default protection unambiguously cheaper.

The EDL of a second-to-default exposure is not necessarily monotonic in default event correlations. Rather, it generally increases up to a maximum, then it starts decreasing. The location of the turning point depends on all other parameters and, in particular, on the number of names in the basket. With a low number of names, the EDL of a second-to-default exposure is generally increasing in default event correlations over most of the domain. Intuitively, with only a handful of names in the portfolio, the event that at least two of them default becomes more likely as we increase their tendency to default together.

These qualitative relations are consistent with the results reported in Figure 11, where we compare the EDL of five-year first-, second-, and third-to-default exposure on a 5-name basket using both a Normal copula and a *t*-copula with 12 DoF. In both cases, the marginal distributions of default times are assumed to be defined by a constant yearly hazard rate equal to 1%, recovery rates are known and equal to 40%, and the risk-free discounting curve is flat at 2%. We compute EDL for three different levels of asset correlations, namely 0%, 20%, and 50%. The standard errors of the Monte Carlo estimators are reported in brackets and represent the simulation standard error for the EDL as a percentage of the EDL. As one would expect, the percentage difference between the Gaussian copula and the *t*-dependence is higher when the triggering event is less likely.

Figure 11 Expected discounted loss of nth-to-default baskets

Asset Correlation	Copula	1st-TD	2nd-TD	3rd-TD
0%	Normal	0.1265 (0.059%)	0.0121 (0.206%)	0.0006 (0.898%)
	t12	0.1207 (0.059%)	0.0167 (0.169%)	0.0017 (0.566%)
	% Difference	−5%	38%	185%
20%	Normal	0.1151 (0.066%)	0.0205 (0.155%)	0.0033 (0.380%)
	t12	0.1094 (0.063%)	0.0239 (0.137%)	0.0051 (0.155%)
	% Difference	−5%	17%	55%
50%	Normal	0.0934 (0.072%)	0.0305 (0.131%)	0.011 (0.231%)
	t12	0.0888 (0.071%)	0.0318 (0.129%)	0.0127 (0.197%)
	% Difference	−5%	4%	15%

Normal vs. Student t-copula with DoF=12, 10M- path Monte Carlo simulation, standard errors in parenthesis

Portfolio loss tranches

According to a recent survey published in Risk Magazine (February 2003), portfolio loss tranches have become one of the most common types of multi-name credit exposures traded in the market.[8] In a typical portfolio loss tranche, a protection buyer pays a periodic premium to a protection seller, who, in exchange, stands ready to compensate the buyer for a pre-specified slice (tranche) of the losses affecting a set of reference obligations. The reference portfolio is generally composed of dozens (and sometimes hundreds) of credits, and each name is represented in the portfolio according to a given notional amount.

Here we consider a portfolio of 100 names, each with US$1 million notional. A tranche exposure is defined by a lower and an upper percentile of the total notional. For example, the seller of protection on the 5%–10% tranche of our 100-name portfolio will be responsible for covering losses exceeding US$5 million and up to US$10 million (US$5 million exposure). Losses are defined as the notional amount of defaulted credits times the associated loss given default (LGD). In our example, we assume uniform recovery rates of 35%, ie, 65% LGD for every credit in the reference port-folio.

We first consider a valuation exercise using the following parameters:

❑ 1% risk-neutral hazard rate for each reference name;
❑ 20% asset correlation between every pair of credits;
❑ flat risk-free curve at 2%; and
❑ a 5-year maturity deal.

Figure 12 compares the risk-neutral EDL for several tranches under the two alternative assumptions of Gaussian dependence and t-dependence with 12 DoF. The results show the significant impact that the (empirically motivated) consideration of tail dependence has on the distribution of losses across the capital structure: expected losses are clearly redistributed from the junior to the senior tranches, as a consequence of the increased default event correlations. This implies that the Gaussian assumption underestimates the fair compensation for senior exposures and overestimates the fair compensation for junior risk.

Even larger differences can be observed if one compares higher moments or tail measures of the tranches' loss distributions. Let us now assume that each of the 100 reference names has an objective default

Figure 12 Expected discounted loss of portfolio tranches

Tranche	Normal Copula EDL (Std Err)	t-Copula DoF=12 EDL (Std Err)	% Difference
0% – 5%	2,256,300 (0.14%)	2,012,200 (0.23%)	–11%
5% – 10%	533,020 (0.63%)	601,630 (0.66%)	13%
10% – 15%	146,160 (1.37%)	221,120 (1.06%)	51%
15% – 20%	41,645 (1.70%)	90,231 (1.62%)	117%
20% – 100%	16,188 (4.94%)	59,042 (2.79%)	265%

Normal vs. Student t-copula with DoF=12, 100K-path Monte Carlo simulation, standard errors in parenthesis

Figure 13 Value-at-risk and expected shortfall at the 95th percentile

Tranche	Copula	VAR$_{95\%}$	ES$_{95\%}$
0% – 5%	Normal	5,000,000	5,000,000
	t12	5,000,000	5,000,000
	% Difference	0%	0%
5% – 10%	Normal	850,000	3,119,812
	t12	2,150,000	4,278,209
	% Difference	153%	37%
10% – 15%	Normal	0	600,480
	t12	0	1,583,187
	% Difference	0%	164%
15% – 20%	Normal	0	124,750
	t12	0	584,986
	% Difference	0%	369%
20% – 100%	Normal	0	32,747
	t12	0	339,124
	% Difference	0%	936%

Normal vs. Student t-copula with DoF=12, 100K-path Monte Carlo simulation intensity equal to 0.5%. The remaining parameters are unchanged. Figure 13 compares the two dependence assumptions in terms of the 95% VAR and expected shortfall that they produce for a number of loss tranches.

CONCLUSIONS

The empirical study presented in the first part of this chapter has two main findings. First, empirical evidence suggests that large joint movements of equity values occur with higher likelihood than what is predicted by correlation-based models. In particular, empirical evidence seems to favour a fat-tailed dependence structure instead of the widely-used Gaussian one. The second observation is that the dependence structures of asset and *equity* returns appear to be strikingly similar.

One interesting corollary to these empirical findings is the lack of support for the popular conjecture regarding the ways in which the different leverage of assets and equity create significant differences in their joint dependence. To this end, the KMV algorithm that we use to "back-out" asset values from observed equity data can be viewed simply as a means for de-leveraging the equity to arrive at the value of a company's assets. Our results suggest that the differences in leverage are mostly reflected in the marginal distributions of returns. A practical consequence is that (observed) equity data seem to provide a valid and consistent proxy for (unobserved) asset returns, at least for the purpose of calibrating the dependence structure.

We conclude our empirical study with a recommendation for a simple and parsimonious framework that can be used to model asset dependencies. (Such a model will also drive the analysis of multi-name credit derivatives.) Specifically, this is a fat-tailed multivariate distribution, having marginals that each follow a univariate t-distribution (with possibly different parameters), and with a dependence structure given by a t-copula. It is important to note that while the estimates of the parameters of the marginals (in particular, the degrees-of-freedom which dictates the fatness of the marginal tail) may depend on the sampling frequency of the data, the tail behaviour in the dependence structure seems to be quite insensitive in this regard. In particular, there is no empirical evidence that the dependence structure of equity returns approaches the Gaussian dependence structure as we increase the measurement intervals and allow for aggregation.

These empirical findings have significant bearing on multi-name credit derivatives models. In particular, the results described above indicate that asset returns exhibit non-negligible tail dependence; therefore, if one follows the "structural approach", default times seem to be more accurately modelled using a t-dependence structure rather than the widely used Gaussian one. The examples on the valuation of first- and second-to-default baskets illustrate the importance of the modelling choice for pricing purposes. In addition, the example that considers synthetic loss tranches suggests that multivariate Gaussian models will generally underestimate default correlations and thus overestimate the expected loss of junior positions and underestimate the expected loss of mezzanine and senior tranches.

1 We would like to thank Mark Broadie, Paul Glasserman, Mark Howard, Prafulla Nabar, Dominic O'Kane, Lutz Schloegl and Stuart Turnbull for comments and suggestions on earlier versions of this document. The usual disclaimer applies.

2 A description of these models can be found in Kealhofer and Bohn (2001) and Gupton, Finger and Bhatia (1997).

3 See, for example, Mashal and Naldi (2002), Mashal and Zeevi (2002) and Breymann et al (2003).

4 This approach follows the semi-parametric estimation framework developed in a more abstract context by Genest et al (1995).

5 A rigorous derivation and an explicit characterisation of γ is given in Appendix A of Mashal and Zeevi (2002) who also validate this asymptotic numerically.

6 The range of accepted DoF is very narrow in each case, exhibiting similar behaviour to that displayed in Figure 1.

7 This should not be confused with a multivariate-t model, since we are not restricting the copula and all of the marginals in order to achieve the same DoF parameter.

8 See "Credit derivatives survey, flow business booms", by Navroz Patel, Risk Magazine, February 2003, pp. S20-S23.

BIBLIOGRAPHY

Blattberg, R. C. and N. J. Gonedes, 1974, "A Comparison of the Stable and Student Distributions as Statistical Models for Stock Prices", *Journal of Business*, 47, pp. 244–80.

Breymann, W., A. Dias and P. Embrechts, 2003, "Dependence Structures for Multivariate High-Frequency Data in Finance", Working Paper, Department of Mathematics, ETH Zurich.

Duffie, D. and N. Garleanu, 2001, "Risk and Valuation of Collateralized Debt Obligations", *Financial Analyst Journal*, 57, pp. 41–59.

Duffie, D. and K. Singleton, 1998, "Simulating Correlated Defaults", Working Paper, Stanford University, Stanford.

Embrechts, P., F. Lindskog and A. J. McNeal, 2001, "Modelling Dependence with Copulas and Applications to Risk Management", Working Paper, Risklab, ETH, Zurich.

Finger, C., 1999, "Conditional Approaches for CreditMetrics Portfolio Distributions", RiskMetrics Group, New York.

Finger, C., 2000, "A Comparison of Stochastic Default Rate Models", RiskMetrics Group, New York.

Fitch Ratings, 2003, "Default Correlation and its Effect on Portfolios of Credit Risk", Structured Finance, Credit Products Special Report, February.

Genest, C., K. Ghoudi and L-P. Rivest, 1995, "A Semiparametric Estimation Procedure of Dependence Parameters in Multivariate Families of Distributions", Biometrika, 82, pp. 543–52.

Glasserman P., P. Heidelberger and P. Shahabuddin, 2002, "Portfolio Value-at-Risk with Heavy-Tailed Risk Factors", *Mathematical Finance*, 12, pp.239–70.

Gregory, J. and J-P. Laurent, 2003, "I Will Survive", *Risk*, June, pp. 103–107.

Gupton, G.M., C.C. Finger and M. Bhatia, 1997, "CreditMetrics – Technical Document", J.P. Morgan, New York.

Hull, J. and A. White, 2001, "Valuing Credit Default Swaps II: Modelling Default Correlations", *Journal of Derivatives*, 8, pp. 12–22.

Joe, H., 1997, *Multivariate Models and Dependence Concepts*, "Monographs on Statistics and Applied Probability", 37, Chapman and Hall, London.

Kealhofer, S. and J.R. Bohn, 2001, "Portfolio Management of Default Risk", KMV, San Francisco.

Li, D., 2000, "On Default Correlation: a Copula Function Approach", *Journal of Fixed Income*, 9, pp. 43–54.

Lindskog, F., 2000, "Linear Correlation Estimation", Working Paper, RiskLab, ETH Zurich.

Mashal, R. and M. Naldi, 2002, "Extreme Events and Default Baskets" *Risk*, June, pp. 119–122.

Mashal, R. and A. Zeevi, 2002, "Beyond Correlation: Extreme Co-Movements between Financial Assets", Working Paper, Columbia University, New York.

Mashal, R. and A. Zeevi, 2003, "Inferring the Dependence Structure of Financial Assets: Empirical Evidence and Implications", Working Paper, Columbia University, New York.

Merton, R.C., 1974, "On the Pricing of Corporate Debt: The Risk Structure of Interest Rates", *Journal of Finance*, 2, pp. 449–70.

Praetz, P.D., 1972, "The Distribution of Share Price Changes", *Journal of Business*, 45, 49–55.

Raiffa, H. and R. Schlaifer, 1961, *Applied Statistics Decision Theory*, Harvard University Press, Boston.

16

Reduced-form models: curve construction and the pricing of credit swaps, options and hybrids

Leif Andersen

Banc of America Securities

INTRODUCTION

In the analysis of credit risk, it is often assumed that a default event is triggered when firm assets fall to a sufficiently low level relative to the notional of outstanding debt. In this line of thinking, models of credit risk naturally involve joint assumptions of the stochastic evolution of the individual components of the firm capital structure – ie, assets, debt, and equity. Such an approach is clearly "deep" in the sense that the analysis aims not only to quantify the credit risk itself, but also to understand the causal factors behind it.

The description of credit risk through an analysis of balance sheet information and other fundamental factors is the domain of the so-called *structural models*. While such models have their uses (see Chapters 5, 7, 14 and 15), it is often more practical to work at a higher level of abstraction and simply treat credit events as point processes with parameters that can be inferred from observations. This approach is known as *reduced-form* modelling. While reduced-form models are, in a sense, less fundamental than structural models, they offer the financial engineer large advantages in terms of implementation, analytic manipulations, and the all-important calibration to market-observed prices.

In this chapter, we shall give a detailed description of reduced-form models and their applications to the pricing and hedging of single-name credit-sensitive instruments. Initially, our focus is on basic survival-curve construction and the pricing of flow-products such as bonds, asset swaps, and credit default swaps (CDSs). Later, we move on to more complicated products, ranging from "quanto-ed" CDSs to option products, interest rate hybrids, and convertible bonds.

Much of the material in this chapter is fairly technical in nature. While we shall develop a fair part of the theory and notation from scratch, we assume that the reader has a basic knowledge of derivatives pricing theory (eg, on the level of Hull, 2000).

SOME BASIC TECHNICAL PREREQUISITES
Poisson and Cox processes

As Poisson processes are at the heart of the reduced-form approach, we shall start with a brief survey of results for this class of processes. Recall that a Poisson process N is a counting process taking values in the set of natural numbers. Sample paths of the Poisson process are flat across time, except for a number of random arrival times x_i, $i = 1, 2, ...$, where the process exhibits upward jumps of unit magnitude: $N(x_i) - N(x_i-) = 1$, $i = 1$, $2, ...$ In the classical (time-homogenous) Poisson process, for any time t, the likelihood of a jump over an infinitesimal time-step $[t, t + dt]$ is λdt, where λ is a positive constant known as the *Poisson intensity* or *hazard rate*. Notice that jumps in the Poisson process are completely unpredictable, in the (loose) sense that if λ is known, then observation of the past path of the process does not reveal any information about the time of occurrence of future jumps. With the convention that $N(0) = 0$, a classical result is that

$$\Pr(N(t) = i) = e^{-\lambda t} \frac{(\lambda t)^i}{i!}, \; i = 0, 1, ... \tag{1}$$

where $\Pr(\cdot)$ is a probability measure. We recognise that the right-hand side of this equation is the probability function of the Poisson distribution with mean λt. The waiting times between jumps are independent and identically exponentially distributed:

$$\Pr(x_{i+1} - x_i > t) = \Pr(x_1 > t) = \Pr(N(t) = 0) = e^{-\lambda t}, \; t \geq 0, \; i = 0, 1, ... \tag{2}$$

where we have relied on Equation (1) in the last equality.

We will now extend the basic Poisson process in two steps. First, consider allowing the Poisson hazard rate to be a deterministic non-negative function of time, $\lambda = \lambda(t)$. The resulting process is known as a *non-homogenous Poisson process*. As one would expect, we essentially have to replace λt in (1) with a time integral

$$\Pr(N(s) - N(t) = i) = e^{-\int_t^s \lambda(u)du} \frac{\left(\int_t^s \lambda(u)du\right)^i}{i!}, \; s \geq t, \; i = 0, 1, ... \tag{3}$$

Due to the time-dependence of the hazard rate, Equation (2) does not hold and has to be replaced by

$$\Pr(x_{i+1} - x_i > s \mid x_i = t) = e^{-\int_t^s \lambda(u)du}, \; s \geq t$$

In a second step, we extend the definition further by allowing $\lambda(t)$ to be random, giving rise to the so-called *Cox process*. In the prescription for the creation of a Cox process, we proceed by first drawing the full path of $\lambda(t)$

and then treat this hazard rate process as given. In other words, *conditionally* given $\lambda(t)$, $t \geq 0$, the Cox process is simply defined as a non-homogenous Poisson process with hazard rate $\lambda(t)$. The unconditional distribution of the Cox process then requires integration against the distribution of the hazard rate path:

$$\Pr(N(s) - N(t) = i) = E\left(e^{-\int_t^s \lambda(u)\,du} \frac{\left[\int_t^s \lambda(u)\,du\right]^i}{i!} \right), \quad s \geq t,\ i = 0,\ 1,\ \ldots \quad (4)$$

where $E(\cdot)$ is the (time 0) expectations operator. The result in Equation (4) gives probability as of time 0, but by making the expectation conditional on information available at later times, we can easily generalise. For instance, consider the important special case

$$\Pr(N(s) = 0 \mid \mathfrak{I}_t) = 1_{N(t)=0}\, E\left(e^{-\int_t^s \lambda(u)\,du} \mid \mathfrak{I}_t \right) \equiv 1_{N(t)=0}\, E_t\left(e^{-\int_t^s \lambda(u)\,du} \right), \quad s \geq t \quad (5)$$

where 1_A is the indicator function for the set A, and $\mathfrak{I}_t$ represents the information available at time t. The result shown in Equation (5) was first used in a default setting in Lando (1998) and is key to reduced-form modelling of credit derivatives.

Default modelling and basic building blocks

We now move into a financial setting where we assume the existence of a risk-neutral probability measure Q, consistent with the absence of arbitrage. Given a process for the short-term interest rate r, we first introduce regular (default-free) zero-coupon bond prices, given as

$$P(t,\ T) = E_t^Q\left(e^{-\int_t^T r(u)\,du} \right)$$

where $E_t^Q(\cdot)$ is the time t risk-neutral expectations operator. In other words, $P(t,\ T)$ represents the price at time t of US\$1 delivered for sure at time T.

Consider now the price of a default-risky zero-coupon bond Z, paying US\$1 at time T, if and only if some underlying reference firm does not default before T. To model the embedded credit risk of this security, we assume that the time of default τ can be modelled reduced-form style as the first jump in a Cox process with hazard rate process $\lambda(t)$: $\tau \equiv x_1$. Accordingly, by standard arbitrage results,

$$Z(t,\ T) = E_t^Q\left(e^{-\int_t^T r(u)\,du}\, 1_{\tau > T} \right) = 1_{\tau > t}\, E_t^Q\left(e^{-\int_t^T [r(u) + \lambda(u)]\,du} \right)$$

where the second equality follows from Equation (5). Notice how the hazard rate process affects risky zero-coupon bonds by effectively acting as a spread on the regular interest rate. As both hazard rates and interest rates can be interpreted as "killing rates", this result is quite intuitive.

The above expression for Z is generally easier to work with if written to separate the interest rate and default contributions. For this, we can write

$$E_t^Q\left(e^{-\int_t^T [r(u)+\lambda(u)]du}\right) = P(t,\ T)E_t^T\left(e^{-\int_t^T \lambda(u)du}\right) = P(t,\ T)X(t,\ T) \qquad (6)$$

where $E_t^T(\cdot)$ denotes expectation with respect to the so-called *forward T-measure* Q^T.[1] Note that the quantity $X(t,\ T)$ defined above has the interpretation of being the time t *survival probability* to time T, given that no default took place before time t.

Risky zero-coupon bonds are important building blocks for credit-derivative pricing, just as regular zero-coupon bonds are important for interest-rate derivative pricing. Another important building block deals with

---

Panel 1

MEASURE SHIFTS FOR CREDIT DERIVATIVES

Here we give some technical results about certain types of measure changes that frequently can be used to simplify computations involving survival probabilities.

Consider the problem of establishing

$$E_t^P(X(T)Y(T)) = E^P(X(T)Y(T) \mid \Im_t)$$

where P is a probability measure, and where $\Im_t$ represents information available at time t. Define the process

$$\xi(t) = E_t^P(X(T))\ /\ E^P(X(T)) \qquad (1)$$

which, by the law of iterated expectations, defines a martingale with $\xi(0) = 1$. Assuming that ξ is strictly positive, it can be used to define a shift of probability measure from P to, say, M, governed by the Radon-Nikodym derivative (see, for example, Duffie, 1996)

$$\frac{dM}{dP} \mid \Im_t = \xi(t)$$

By the Radon-Nikodym Theorem, we can write

$$E_t^P(X(T)Y(T)) = E_t^M(\xi(t)\xi(T)^{-1}X(T)Y(T)) = E_t^P(X(T))\ E_t^M(Y(T)) \qquad (2)$$

Here, the second equality follows from the fact that $\xi(t)\ /\ \xi(T) = X(T)^{-1}$ $E_t^P(X(T))$. To give an example of the use of Equation (2), consider evaluation of

$$E_t^Q\left(e^{-\int_t^T [r(u)+\lambda(u)]du}\right)$$

where Q is the usual risk-neutral probability measure. Setting $X(T) = \exp(-\int_0^T r(u)du)$ and $Y(T) = \exp(-\int_0^T \lambda(u)du)$ in Equation (2), we achieve

---

$$E_t^Q\left(e^{-\int_t^T [r(u)+\lambda(u)]du}\right) = E_t^Q\left(e^{-\int_t^T r(u)du}\right) E_t^T\left(e^{-\int_t^T \lambda(u)du}\right)$$

$$= P(t, T)E_t^T\left(e^{-\int_t^T \lambda(u)du}\right) \qquad (3)$$

where $P(t, T)$ is simply the time t discount bond to time T, and E_t^T denotes expectation under a measure Q^T given by the Radon-Nikodym derivative (see Equation (1))[1]

$$\xi(t) = E_t^Q(X(T)) / E^Q(X(T)) = \frac{P(t, T)}{e^{\int_0^t r(u)du} P(0, T)}$$

The measure Q^T is often known as the forward-T measure and corresponds to using $P(t,T)$ as a pricing numeraire, rather than the rolling money market account $\exp(\int_0^t r(u)du)$ used in the risk-neutral measure.

To add some more structure to the measure shift governed by Equation (1), assume now that the martingale process $\xi(t)$ is driven by a Brownian motion W_ξ under P

$$d\xi(t) / \xi(t) = \sigma_\xi(t)dW_\xi(t) \qquad (4)$$

for some stochastic volatility process $\sigma_\xi(t)$ satisfying certain regularity conditions (eg, the Novikov condition). By Ito's Lemma $\xi(t)$ is an exponential martingale

$$\xi(t) = e^{-\frac{1}{2}\int_0^t \sigma_\xi(u)^2 du + \int_0^t \sigma_\xi(u)dW_\xi(u)}$$

Now, assume that the process Y above is driven by another Brownian motion, under P

$$(P) \quad dY(t) = \mu_Y(t)dt + \sigma_Y(t)dW_Y(t) \qquad (5)$$

To compute the expectation $E_t^M(Y(T))$ in Equation (2), we need to establish the dynamics of Y under M. A straightforward application of the Girsanov Theorem (Duffie, 1996) yields, under M,

$$(M) \quad dY(t) = \left(\mu_Y(t) + \rho(t)\sigma_Y(t)\sigma_\xi(t)\right)dt + \sigma_Y(t)d\tilde{W}_Y(t) \qquad (6)$$

where $d\tilde{W}_Y(t)$ is a Brownian motion under M, and where the correlation coefficient ρ is defined through $dW_Y(t)dW_\xi(t) = \rho(t)dt$.

1 Not to be confused with the probability measure P used earlier in Panel 1.

instruments that contain a provision that calls for the payment of a possibly random recovery amount $\alpha(\tau)$ at the time of default, provided that $\tau < T$. Let us denote the time t price of this security $Y(t, T; \alpha)$. To compute it, first notice that when conditioned upon a particular path of λ, the time t risk-neutral probability of the default event taking place over $[s, s + ds]$, $s \geq t$, is simply

$$\Pr(\tau \in [s, s + ds] \mid \mathfrak{I}_t) = \lambda(s)ds \cdot 1_{\tau > t} e^{-\int_t^s \lambda(u)du}$$

which we recognise as the likelihood of having a Poisson jump on $[s, s + ds]$, multiplied by the likelihood of having had no jumps before time s. Incorporating discounting, taking expectations over all paths of λ, and summing over all ds-buckets, we get

$$Y(t, T; \alpha) = 1_{\tau > t} E_t^Q \left(\int_t^T \alpha(s)\lambda(s)e^{-\int_t^s \lambda(u)+r(u)du} ds \right) \tag{7}$$

Under the assumption that the default payout $\alpha(t)$ is independent of interest rates and credit spreads, we can simplify this expression as follows:

$$Y(t, T; \alpha) = 1_{\tau > t} \int_t^T E_t^Q \left(\alpha(s)\lambda(s)e^{-\int_t^s [\lambda(u)+r(u)]du} \right) ds$$

$$= 1_{\tau > t} \int_t^T E_t^Q \left(\alpha(s) \middle| P(t, s) E_t^s \left(\lambda(s)e^{-\int_t^s \lambda(u)du} \right) \right) ds \tag{8}$$

$$= -1_{\tau > t} \int_t^T E_t^Q \left(\alpha(s) \middle| P(t, s) \frac{\partial X(t, s)}{\partial s} ds \right.$$

In deriving this equation, we have first relied on an inter-change of integration and expectation, and then on a measure change, similar to the one that leads to Equation (6). Finally, we have also used the fact that

$$\frac{\partial X(t, s)}{\partial s} = E_t^s \left(\frac{\partial}{\partial s} e^{-\int_t^s \lambda(u)du} \right) = -E_t^s \left(\lambda(s)e^{-\int_t^s \lambda(u)du} \right)$$

Quanto effects

Consider now the pricing of a US$-denominated, risky zero-coupon Z written on a *foreign* company A.[2] The time t survival curve associated with A, as seen from the perspective of an investor based in the same country as A, is assumed given and denoted $X_f(t, T)$. Similarly, we use the notation $P_f(t, T)$ to denote foreign-currency denominated discount bonds. Letting $E(t)$ be the time t US$ per foreign currency exchange rate, we can then write

$$Z(t, T) = 1_{\tau > T} P(t, T) E_t^T \left(e^{-\int_t^T \lambda(u)du} \right) = 1_{\tau > t} E(t) P_f(t, T) E_t^{T,f} \left(e^{-\int_t^T \lambda(u)du} E^{-1}(T) \right)$$

where $E_t^{T,f}(\cdot)$ denotes expectation with respect to the probability measure Q_f^T induced by using $P_f(t, T)$ as a *numeraire*. In the second part of this expression, we effectively price the risky bond in the foreign currency, and then convert it to US$ through the factor $E(t)$. Notice in particular that the factor $E(T)^{-1}$ converts the US$1 terminal payment to foreign currency.

To proceed, define $M(t, T) = E(t)^{-1}P(t, T) / P_f(t, T)$ which defines the foreign/domestic forward exchange rate to time T. It is easy to see that $E(t)^{-1}P(t, T)$ defines a foreign-currency denominated asset, whereby $M(t, T)$ by standard arguments, must be a martingale in the Q_f^T measure.[3] We then write

$$Z(t, T) = 1_{\tau > T} P(t, T) E_t^{T,f}\left(e^{-\int_t^T \lambda(u)du} M(T, T) / M(t, T) \right)$$

whereby the survival curve as seen in the US$ forward-T measure becomes

$$X(t, T) = E_t^{T,f}\left(e^{-\int_t^T \lambda(u)du} M(T, T) / M(t, T) \right) = X_f(t, T) E_t^H(M(T, T) / M(t, T)) \quad (9)$$

where H is a probability measure given by the Radon-Nikodym Theorem (see Panel 1):

$$\frac{dH}{dQ_f^T} \Big| \mathfrak{I}_t = \frac{X_f(t, T)}{e^{\int_0^t \lambda(u)du} X_f(0, T)} \equiv \xi(t)$$

While Equation (9) is completely general, it has too little structure for practical computations. To proceed, we can, for instance, assume that $X_f(t, T)$ and $M(t, T)$ follow geometric Brownian motion processes with deterministic volatility functions $\sigma_X(t, T)$ and $\sigma_M(t, T)$, respectively. In other words

$$d\xi(t) / \xi(t) = \sigma_X(t, T) dW_X(t)$$
$$dM(t, T) / M(t, T) = \sigma_M(t, T) dW_M(t)$$

where W_X and W_M are Brownian motions under Q_f^T. Defining the deterministic correlation $\rho(t)dt = dW_X(t)dW_M(t)$, we get from Equation (6) in Panel 1 that the process for M under measure H is

$$dM(t, T) / M(t, T) = \rho(t)\sigma_M(t, T)\sigma_X(t, T)dt + \sigma_M(t, T)d\widetilde{W}_M(t)$$

where $\widetilde{W}_M$ is a Brownian motion under H. Hence,

$$E_t^H(M(T, T) / M(t, T)) = e^{\int_t^T \rho(u)\sigma_M(u, T)\sigma_X(u, T)du} \quad (10)$$

Equations (9) and (10) together describe how to "quanto-adjust" a foreign survival curve $X_f(t, T)$ to turn it into a US$ (domestic) survival curve $X(t, T)$. Later, we will take a closer look at typical magnitudes of the quanto-adjustment.

CREDIT DEFAULT SWAPS, BONDS, AND ASSET SWAPS

We have now established the basic framework for single-firm, reduced-form default modelling. We continue by applying the basic results to price a number of simple "static" instruments, namely bonds, asset swaps, and credit default swaps (CDSs). More complicated instruments – hybrids and options – are discussed in later chapters.

Credit default swaps (CDSs)

Consider a CDS indexed to some underlying company A with random default time τ. Under the terms of the CDS, the default protection buyer makes a periodic fee payment (the "premium leg") in return for the right to exchange at time τ a reference bond of company A for par (the "default leg"). Let us consider the value of the two legs to the swap in separation.

Starting with the premium leg, let the remaining payments be made on a schedule $\{t_i\}_{i=1}^n$, with t_n being the maturity of the CDS. We let t denote current time, and assume that $t_1 > t$ (as we only need to consider future payments). Let the annualised premium fee be c, whereby the cash payment made at t_i for the period $[t_{i-1}, t_i]$ is $c\Delta_i$, with Δ_i being a day-count fraction (typically close to $t_i - t_{i-1}$). Assuming for simplicity that no accrued interest is paid for the period in which default takes place, the present value of the premium leg is simply

$$PV_{fix}(t) = \sum_{i=1}^n c\Delta_i Z(t, t_i) = 1_{\tau>t} \sum_{i=1}^n c\Delta_i P(t, t_i)X(t, t_i) \tag{11}$$

This equation simply expresses the fact that a cash payment of $c\Delta_i$ will be made at time t_i if and only if the company has not defaulted before time t_i. As such, the premium leg is just a weighted sum of risky zero-coupon bonds.

Turning to the default leg, let us first make the common assumption that the underlying reference bond will recover a fixed fraction R of its notional in default. Typically, $R \approx 40\%$, but obviously depends on the specifics of company A. Assuming that the CDS notional is US\$1, the default payment α on the default leg is then simply $\alpha(\tau) = 1 - R$, provided that $\tau \leq t_n$. Using the result given in Equation (8), we thereby have

$$PV_{float}(t) = Y(t, t_n; 1 - R) = -1_{\tau>t}(1 - R) \int_t^{t_n} P(t, s) \frac{\partial X(t, s)}{\partial s} ds$$

In practice, we would discretise this integral on some timeline $\{T_i\}_{i=0}^N$, with $T_0 = t$ and $T_N = t_n$. For instance, we could use the simple approximation

$$PV_{float}(t) = 1_{\tau>t}(1 - R) \sum_{i=1}^N P\left(t, \frac{1}{2}(T_i + T_{i-1})\right)(X(t, T_{i-1}) - X(t, T_i)) \tag{12}$$

Note that the $\{T_i\}$ integration timeline generally does not need to coincide with the premium leg schedule $\{t_i\}$.

To the buyer of default protection – ie, the premium leg payer – the present value of the CDS is simply

$$PV_{CDS}(t) = PV_{float}(t) - PV_{fix}(t) \tag{13}$$

The value to the default leg payer is then obviously $-PV_{CDS}(t)$. We note that a CDS newly issued at time t always satisfies $PV_{CDS}(t) = 0$ by means of setting the premium leg fee coupon to its *break-even* or *par value*.

$$c_{par}(t, t_n) = -(1 - R) \int_t^{t_n} P(t, s) \frac{\partial X(t, s)}{\partial s} ds \Big/ \sum_{i=1}^n \Delta_i P(t, t_i) X(t, t_i) \quad (14)$$

While it is convenient to omit accrued interest in premium-leg CDS computations in case of default, many actual CDS contracts require that the premium-leg payer is responsible for paying any interest that has accrued up to the day of default. Let us briefly describe how to handle this. For convenience, let $n(\tau)$ denote the (random) index of the premium-leg schedule bucket surrounding the default time: $\tau \in (t_{n(\tau)-1}, t_{n(\tau)})$. In this case, provided that $\tau < T$, the accrued interest is to close approximation $a(\tau) = c\Delta_{n(\tau)}(\tau - t_{n(\tau)-1}) / (t_{n(\tau)} - t_{n(\tau)-1})$.[4] The present value of accrued interest can then easily be computed from Equation (8) with $\alpha(t) = a(t)$. This value would then be added to the premium leg value PV_{fix} as computed in Equation (11).

Bond and asset swap pricing

Let us now turn to the pricing of a coupon bond paying a coupon of c on a schedule $\{t_i\}_{i=1}^n$, with $t_1 > t$ and with t_n being the final maturity of the bond. Assuming that the issuing company does not default over the life of the bond, at time t_n the bond will repay the notional, here assumed to be US\$1. Assuming for a moment that the investor will not recover anything on the bond in case of default, the bond price can obviously be written as a sum of risky zero-coupon bonds:

$$B_{NR}(t) = c \sum_{i=1}^n Z(t, t_i)\Delta_i + Z(t, t_n) = 1_{\tau > t} \left(c \sum_{i=1}^n P(t, t_i)X(t, t_i)\Delta_i + P(t, t_n)X(t, t_n) \right)$$

The two terms in this equation correspond to the value of the coupons and the terminal redemption of notional, respectively. To the expression above, we then must add the value of receiving the recovery value of the bond in case of default. It is common and reasonable to assume that the recovery of the bond is some constant fraction R of the bond notional, irrespective of the coupon. Seen in isolation, the value of this recovery amount is then simply $Y(t, t_n; R)$ – see Equation (8) – resulting in the following total value B of the bond:

$$B(t) = B_{NR}(t) + Y(t, t_n; R)$$

$$= 1_{\tau > t} \left(c \sum_{i=1}^n P(t, t_i)X(t, t_i)\Delta_i + P(t, t_n)X(t, t_n) - R \int_t^{t_n} P(t, s) \frac{\partial X(t, s)}{\partial s} ds \right) (15)$$

Notice that this expression gives the so-called *dirty price* of the bond. The clean price can be found by subtraction of the interest accrued to time t from the most recent past coupon date, if any.

In practice, bond prices are often quoted through an asset swap convention. Specifically, consider adding a fixed-for-floating interest rate swap to the bond, where the coupons of the bond are swapped against Libor plus a spread; the combined position of the bond and the swap is known as an *asset swap package*. Under standard market conventions, the spread on the floating side that makes the value of the asset swap package equal to par is known as the (clean) *asset swap spread* ε_B. The fixed side of the asset swap always matches exactly the coupon payments of the bond. For dates between schedule dates of the bond, the standard convention for the floating leg is to use a short first stub and an interpolated Libor rate, making the value of the pure floater (excluding the asset swap spread) worth par. Typically, the floating leg pays using a different day-count basis than the bond; let us use d_i to denote the floating leg day-count fraction for the period $[t_{i-1}, t_i]$. We can then write for the value of an asset swap package issued at time t

$$PV_{pkg}(t) = B(t) - \left\{ c \sum_{i=1}^{n} P(t, t_i)\Delta_i + P(t, t_n) \right\}$$

$$+ \left\{ 1 + \varepsilon_B d_1 \frac{t_1 - t}{t_1 - t_0} P(t, t_1) + \varepsilon_B \sum_{i=2}^{n} P(t, t_i)d_i \right\} \equiv 1 \qquad (16)$$

Here, the terms in the two curly brackets are the values of the fixed and floating side of the swap, respectively. Notice that the floating side of the swap is explicitly defined to have a short first stub, with t_0 being defined as the most recent past payment date of the bond. Also note that a known bond price allows us to derive the current market asset swap spread ε_B from Equation (16).

Finally, we briefly comment on basis risk and liquidity premia. Suppose that the functions $X(t, T)$ have been constructed, as is common, from liquid quotes of CDS spreads.[5] A direct application of Equation (15) is unlikely to recover exactly the dirty price of a bond, as quoted in the market. There are multiple reasons for this.

1. The liquidity of CDS and bond markets are typically quite different.
2. The price of an individual bond is often affected by a number of issue-specific effects – eg, tax, position in capital structure, investor coupon preferences, issue size, etc – that go beyond mere default risk.
3. It is not quite clear which proxy for risk-free interest rate should be used in Equation (15). For US investors, the US Treasury curve appears the most logical choice for a risk-free benchmark rate, yet issues of liquidity and the limited number of on-the-run instrument maturities

have made many market participants increasingly question the robustness and reliability of the Treasury curve. Indeed, as discussed in Golub and Tilman (2000), an argument could be made that Libor or agency curves are currently more reasonable benchmarks. Indeed, the market-standard interest-rate benchmark for CDS pricing is the Libor curve.[6]

Regardless of which rate is used, for a given bond price $B(t)$ and given term curves for P and X, we can always be pragmatic and introduce "plug" spreads on either or both of the survival curve or the risk-free discount curve to ensure that the right-hand side of Equation (15) match a quoted price. For instance, if we add a discount spread l_p, we write

$$B(t) = 1_{\tau > t} c \sum_{i=1}^{n} e^{-l_p(t_i - t)} P(t, t_i) X(t, t_i) \Delta_i + 1_{\tau > t} e^{-l_p(t_N - t)} P(t, t_n) X(t, t_n)$$

$$-1_{\tau > t} R \int_t^{t_n} e^{-l_p(s - t)} P(t, s) \frac{\partial X(t, s)}{\partial s} ds$$

and can search for a value of l_p that will make the computed bond price equal the market quote. If a spread l_x is instead added to the survival curve, we instead write

$$B(t) = 1_{\tau > t} c \sum_{i=1}^{n} e^{-l_x(t_i - t)} P(t, t_i) X(t, t_i) \Delta_i + 1_{\tau > t} e^{-l_x(t_n - t)} P(t, t_n) X(t, t_n)$$

$$-1_{\tau > t} R \int_t^{t_n} P(t, s) e^{-l_x(s - t)} \left(-l_x X(t, s) + \frac{\partial X(t, s)}{\partial s} \right) ds$$

which works even if we do not have any estimate whatsoever for the survival curve – we then simply set $X(t, T) = 1$ for all values of t and T.

CURVE CONSTRUCTION AND QUANTO-EFFECTS
Survival curve construction from CDS quotes
We now turn to the question of how to estimate time 0 survival curves $X(0, T)$ from observed credit-derivative prices. In principle, one can construct these curves from an arbitrary mix of, for instance, bonds, CDSs, and asset swaps, but we shall here focus on the important practical question of constructing the survival curves from CDS quotes only. The algorithm discussed here, however, easily extends to a more general setting.

Assume that time 0 CDS par spreads $c(0, T_i)$ – see Equation (14) – are given for some set of maturities $\{T_j\}_{j=1}^{K}$. A typical set of maturities might be 1, 2, 3 and 5 years. With only K instruments given, we clearly cannot hope to construct a continuous survival curve unless we add to the problem some kind of interpolation rule. For this, consider introducing two new functions $\hat{\lambda}(T)$ and $s(T)$, given by

$$X(0, T) = e^{-\int_0^T \hat{\lambda}(u)du} = e^{-s(T)T} \qquad (17)$$

In other words, $\hat{\lambda}(T)$ represents the forward hazard rate over $[T, T + dT]$, as seen from time 0; and $s(T)$ represents the term hazard rate over $[0, T]$. One commonly used interpolation rule treats $\hat{\lambda}(T)$ as piecewise constant, with discontinuities at the maturity dates $\{T_i\}_{i=1}^K$. An alternative rule treats $s(T)$ as piecewise linear, with the linear segments connected at $\{T_i\}_{i=1}^K$. There are other interpolation rules in use, including various types of smoothing or tension splines, but the two interpolation rules described here are the most common and suffice for most practical applications.

Let us state the two interpolation rules above a bit more precisely:

1. For K constants $\hat{\lambda}_i$, $i = 1, 2, \ldots, K$, let $\hat{\lambda}(t) = \hat{\lambda}_i$, for $T_{i-1} \le t < T_i$

2. For $K + 1$ constants s_i, $i = 0, 1, 2, \ldots, K$, let $s(t) = s_{i-1}\dfrac{T_i - t}{T_i - T_{i-1}} + s_i\dfrac{t - T_{i-1}}{T_i - T_{i-1}}$,

   for $T_{i-1} \le t < T_i$

In both cases, we use the convention that $T_0 = 0$. With the application of (17), the two interpolation rules transform the problem of constructing the survival function $X(0, T)$, $T \in [0, T_K]$ into a simple search for a finite set of constants. These can be found in classical "bootstrap" fashion, where a one-dimensional root-search algorithm is applied one time-step at a time. For instance, for interpolation rule 1, the bootstrap algorithm becomes:

a) assume that $\hat{\lambda}_i$ is known for all $i \le j$;
b) to solve for λ_{j+1}, make a guess for this quantity and compute the par spread $c(0, T_{j+1})$ using Equation (14), with the necessary survival function values computed from Equation (17); and
c) if the computed par spread equals the spread quoted in the market, stop; otherwise, return to step (b).

The updating of guesses when looping over steps (b) and (c) can be handled by any standard root-search algorithm – eg, the Newton–Raphson or secant methods. The algorithm can easily be extended to interpolation rule 2. However, we notice that since rule 2 involves $K + 1$ constants and we only have K quoted spreads, an additional constraint on the s_i constants must be added to obtain a unique solution. For instance, we could assume that the first piece of the $s(t)$-function is flat – ie, we would set $s_0 = s_1$.

In Figure 1, we have demonstrated the results of applying the algorithm above on a set of quoted CDS spreads for maturities of one, two, three and five years. The figure shows term hazard rates as defined in Equation (17) as well as forward hazard rates given by

$$\hat{\lambda}(T) = -\partial \ln X(0, T) / \partial T$$

For both rules, term hazard rates are continuous functions of T. For interpolation rule 1, the forward hazard curve is piecewise flat by construction, whereas interpolation rule 2 gives rise to a saw-tooth shaped curve. Smooth forward curves can be obtained using spline methodologies, at a significant increase in algorithmic complexity.

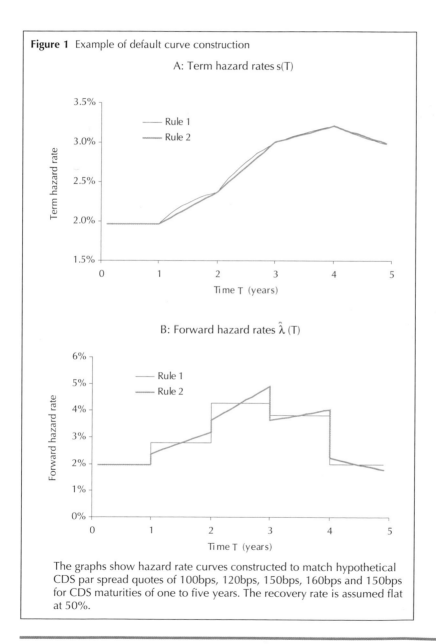

Figure 1 Example of default curve construction

A: Term hazard rates s(T)

B: Forward hazard rates $\hat{\lambda}$ (T)

The graphs show hazard rate curves constructed to match hypothetical CDS par spread quotes of 100bps, 120bps, 150bps, 160bps and 150bps for CDS maturities of one to five years. The recovery rate is assumed flat at 50%.

Quanto effects

Assume now that the algorithm outlined earlier (see *Survival curve construction from CDS quotes*) has been applied to construct a survival curve for a company based outside the US. We now wish to take the constructed survival curve $X_f(0, T)$, $T > 0$, and quanto-adjust it for applications by a US investor. From Equations (9) and (10), we have

$$X(0, T) = X_f(0, T)e^{\int_0^T \rho(u)\sigma_M(u, T)\sigma_X(u, T)du}$$

where σ_M and σ_X are the volatilities of the forward FX rate and the survival probability, respectively. Equivalently, we can relate the quanto-adjusted US\$ forward hazard rate $\hat{\lambda}$ to the foreign forward hazard rate $\hat{\lambda}_f$ as

$$\hat{\lambda}(T) = \hat{\lambda}_f(T) + \rho(T)\sigma_S(0, T)\sigma_M(0, T)$$

More generally, let $\hat{\lambda}(t, T) = -\partial \ln X(t, T)/\partial T$ (and similar for $\hat{\lambda}_f$), whereby

$$\hat{\lambda}(t, T) = \hat{\lambda}_f(t, T) + \rho(T)\sigma_S(t, T)\sigma_M(t, T)$$

We notice that the quanto "spread" to a given fixed maturity T, $\rho(T)\sigma_S(t, T)$ $\sigma_M(t, T)$, depends on current time t.

To make matters more concrete, we now assume that the volatility of the forward FX rate is constant at the level σ_M and that $\lambda(t)$ follows a mean-reverting Gaussian model with instantaneous (normal) volatility of v_λ and mean-reversion κ. Then

$$\sigma_X(t, T) = \kappa^{-1}v_\lambda[1 - e^{-\kappa(T-t)}]$$

As it is often more convenient to work with a log-normal specification, we introduce an approximate log-normal equivalent hazard rate volatility as $\sigma_\lambda\lambda \approx v_\lambda$, whereby we can write

$$\hat{\lambda}(t) \approx \hat{\lambda}_f(t)[1 + \kappa^{-1}\rho\sigma_\lambda\sigma_M(1 - e^{-\kappa(T-t)})]$$

turning the quanto spread into a quanto multiplier $[1 + \kappa^{-1}\rho\sigma_\lambda\sigma_M(1 - e^{-\kappa(T-t)})]$.

Often, it is more informative to look at the quanto-adjustment on term hazard rates $s(t, T)$, defined by the following (see also Equation (17))

$$s(t, T) = -\ln X(t, T)/(T - t) = (T - t)^{-1}\int_t^T \hat{\lambda}(u)du$$

For our model setup, we get after a few manipulations

$$s(t, T) \approx s_f(t, T)\left(1 + \kappa^{-1}\rho\sigma_M\sigma_\lambda(1 - \kappa^{-1}(1 - e^{-\kappa(T-t)})/(T - t))\right) \equiv s_f(t, T)\Omega(t, T)$$

Setting $\sigma_M = 0.15$ and $\sigma_\lambda = 0.7$, the tables in Figure 2 summarise the adjustment multiplier Ω for various values of ρ, κ, and $T - t$.

We notice that generally speaking, the adjustments are fairly modest for short- to medium-term horizons. For instance, for a five-year CDS (which depends on risky bonds from one to five years), we would expect multiplicative quanto-adjustments to the par spread to stay in the range of

Figure 2 The adjustment multiplier Ω for various values of ρ, κ, and $T - t$

Term hazard curve multiplier Ω, $\kappa = 0$ ($\sigma_M = 0.15$, $\sigma_\lambda = 0.7$)

$T - t$	$\rho = -0.2$	$\rho = 0.2$	$\rho = 0.4$	$\rho = 0.6$
1	0.990	1.010	1.021	1.031
2	0.979	1.021	1.042	1.063
3	0.969	1.031	1.063	1.094
4	0.958	1.042	1.084	1.126
5	0.948	1.052	1.105	1.157
7	0.927	1.073	1.147	1.220
10	0.895	1.105	1.209	1.314
15	0.843	1.157	1.313	1.470
20	0.791	1.209	1.417	1.626

Term hazard curve multiplier Ω, $\kappa = 0.1$ ($\sigma_M = 0.15$, $\sigma_\lambda = 0.7$)

$T - t$	$\rho = -0.2$	$\rho = 0.2$	$\rho = 0.4$	$\rho = 0.6$
1	0.990	1.010	1.020	1.030
2	0.980	1.020	1.039	1.059
3	0.971	1.029	1.057	1.086
4	0.963	1.037	1.074	1.111
5	0.955	1.045	1.089	1.134
7	0.941	1.059	1.118	1.177
10	0.923	1.077	1.155	1.232
15	0.899	1.101	1.202	1.304
20	0.881	1.119	1.238	1.358

0.95–1.15 for correlation and mean reversion parameters similar to those used in the tables (see Figure 2).

EUROPEAN OPTIONS ON CDS, BONDS, AND ASSET SWAPS
Next, we will demonstrate how careful choice of pricing numeraires will allow us to price European options on CDSs and bonds in closed form. We will cover callable (Bermudan) style securities later, along with a number of other more complex credit derivatives.

European CDS options
Consider an option C that grants its holder the right, but not the obligation, to enter into a CDS at some future point in time, $t_0 > t$. The premium to be paid on the CDS is fixed in advance, at some strike level c. Let the CDS contract be defined as above (see *Credit default swaps, bonds, and asset swaps*), with payments taking place on a schedule $\{t_i\}_{i=1}^n$, with $t_1 > t_0$.[7] Assuming that the option contract does not grant any type of protection

for defaults taking place before time t_0, the time t_0 value of the option is defined as[8]

$$C(t_0) = 1_{\tau > t_0}(\phi PV_{CDS}(t_0))^+$$

where PV_{CDS} is defined in Equation (13), and the sign-flag ϕ takes the value +1 (−1) for an option on a CDS where the option holder pays (receives) the fixed premium. From Equation (13), we can rewrite the payout as

$$C(t_0) = 1_{\tau > t_0}\left(\phi c \sum_{i=1}^{n} P(t_0, t_i)X(t_0, t_i)\Delta_i + \phi(1-R)\int_{t_0}^{t_n} P(t_0, u)\frac{\partial X(t_0, u)}{\partial u} du\right)^+ \quad (18)$$

$$= 1_{\tau > t_0} A(t_0)\left(\phi\left(c - c_{par}(t_0, t_n)\right)\right)^+, \quad A(t) \equiv \sum_{i=1}^{n} P(t, t_i)X(t, t_i)\Delta_i$$

where we have introduced a risky annuity $A(t)$. To price the option at some $t < t_0$, we first define a *forward par CDS spread* θ_0 through

$$\theta_0(t, t_n) \equiv -(1-R)\int_{t_0}^{t_n} P(t, u)\frac{\partial X(t, u)}{\partial u} du \cdot A(t)^{-1} \quad (19)$$

whereby obviously

$$c_{par}(t_0, t_n) = \theta_0(t_0, t_n)$$

By standard theory we then have

$$C(t) = E_t^Q\left(e^{-\int_t^{t_0} r(u)du} 1_{\tau > t_0} A(t_0)\left(\phi\left(c - \theta_0(t_0, t_n)\right)\right)^+\right)$$

$$= 1_{\tau > t} E_t^Q\left(e^{-\int_t^{t_0}[r(u)+\lambda(u)]du} A(t_0)\left(\phi\left(c - \theta_0(t_0, t_n)\right)\right)^+\right)$$

Notice that

$$E_t^Q\left(e^{-\int_t^{t_0}[r(u)+\lambda(u)]du} A(t_0)\right) = E_t^Q\left(e^{-\int_t^{t_0}[r(u)+\lambda(u)]du}\sum_{i=1}^{n} e^{-\int_{t_0}^{t_i}[r(u)+\lambda(u)]du}\Delta_i\right)$$

$$= E_t^Q\left(\sum_{i=1}^{n} e^{-\int_t^{t_i}[r(u)+\lambda(u)]du}\Delta_i\right) = A(t)$$

where we have relied on iterated conditional expectations in the first equality. As $A(t)$ is strictly positive, we can use the result earlier (see Equation (2), Panel 1) to write

$$C(t) = 1_{\tau > t} A(t)E_t^A\left(\left(\phi\left(c - \theta_0(t_0, t_n)\right)\right)^+\right) \quad (20)$$

where E_t^A denotes expectation with respect to the probability measure Q^A generated by using A as a numeraire. The Radon-Nikodym derivative for the measure shift is (see Equation (1), Panel 1),[9]

$$\frac{dQ^A}{dQ} \Big| \mathfrak{I}_t \equiv \xi(t) = e^{-\int_0^t [r(u)+\lambda(u)]du}\, A(t)\, /\, A(0),\ t \in [0,\ t_0]$$

Then,

$$E_t^A(\theta_0(t_0,\ t_n)) = E_t^A\left(-(1-R)\int_{t_0}^{t_n} P(t_0,\ s)\,\frac{\partial X(t_0,\ s)}{\partial s}\, ds \cdot A(t_0)^{-1}\right)$$

$$= E_t^A\left((1-R)\int_{t_0}^{t_n} e^{-\int_{t_0}^s [r(u)+\lambda(u)]du}\lambda(s)ds \cdot A(t_0)^{-1}\right)$$

$$= E_t^Q\left((1-R)\int_{t_0}^{t_n} e^{-\int_{t_0}^s [r(u)+\lambda(u)]du}\lambda(s)ds \cdot A(t_0)^{-1}\xi(t_0)\, /\, \xi(t)\right)$$

$$= E_t^Q\left((1-R)\int_{t_0}^{t_n} e^{-\int_t^s [r(u)+\lambda(u)]du}\lambda(s)ds \cdot A(t)^{-1}\right)$$

$$= -(1-R)\int_{t_0}^{t_n} P(t,\ s)\,\frac{\partial X(t,\ s)}{\partial s}\, ds \cdot A(t)^{-1} = \theta(t)$$

which demonstrates, not surprisingly, that $\theta_0(t,\ t_n)$ is a martingale under Q^A.

Having established the martingale property of $\theta_0(t,\ t_n)$, the form of the valuation Equation (20) allows us to write closed-form formulas for CDS option prices if the process for $\theta_0(t,\ t_n)$ is chosen to be sufficiently simple. For instance, we can assume that $\theta_0(t,\ t_n)$ is a log-normal diffusion process with deterministic volatility

$$d\theta_0(t,\ t_n)\, /\, \theta_0(t,\ t_n) = \sigma_\theta(t)dW(t) \tag{21}$$

where W is a Brownian motion under Q^A. We then get the explicit Black–Scholes type result

$$C(t) = 1_{\tau > t}A(t)\phi(c\Phi(-\phi d_-) - \theta_0(t,\ t_n)\Phi(-\phi d_+)) \tag{22}$$

$$d_\pm = \frac{\ln(\theta_0(t,\ t_n)\, /\, c) \pm \dfrac{1}{2}\displaystyle\int_t^{t_0} \sigma_\theta(u)^2 du}{\sqrt{\displaystyle\int_t^{t_0} \sigma_\theta(u)^2 du}}$$

where Φ is the standard cumulative Gaussian distribution function. Other tractable processes, such as the constant elasticity of variation (CEV) process, can obviously be used instead of Equation (21) and may offer advantages if one wishes to explicitly model a volatility smile in CDS options. At present, liquidity in CDS options is probably not high enough to warrant applications of models much more complicated than Equations (21) and (22).

European bond options

For short-dated bond options, the market convention is to use a simple, price-based Black–Scholes model. For medium- to long-dated options, however, such an approach is inadequate. We will now briefly outline a closed-form pricing technique consistent with a reduced-form framework.

As before (see *Credit default swaps, bonds, and asset swaps*), we work with a bond paying a coupon rate of c on a schedule $\{t_i\}_{i=1}^n$. Assume that we are given a bond option C maturing at some date t_s in the schedule of the bond, $1 \leq s \leq n$.[10] On default, the bond holders recover a fraction of R of the bond notional. Using K to denote the strike on the bond, the option payout is defined as

$$C(t_s) = 1_{\tau > t_s}\left(\phi(B(t_s) - K)\right)^+ \tag{23}$$

where ϕ is +1 for a call and –1 for a put. Notice that we here have assumed that the option holder recovers nothing if the bond defaults before the option maturity. This may not be reasonable for put options, but the present value of any option recovery can easily be computed as $Y(t, t_s; R_C)$, where R_C is the option recovery rate and the function Y is defined in Equation (8).[11] In light of this, we focus our attention on the no-recovery payout shown in Equation (23).

To proceed, let us now define a risky forward break-even yield ("yield-to-strike") as

$$y_K(t) = A(t)^{-1}\left(KP(t,t_s)X(t,t_s) - P(t,t_n)X(t,t_n) + R\int_{t_s}^{t_n} P(t,u)\frac{\partial X(t, u)}{\partial u}\, du\right), \; t \leq t_s$$

$$A(t) = \sum_{i=s+1}^{n} P(t, t_i)X(t, t_i)\Delta_i$$

whereby the option payout can be re-written as

$$C(t_s) = 1_{\tau > t_s}A(t_s)\left(\phi(c - y_K(t_s))\right)^+ \tag{24}$$

Notice the similarity between Equation (24) and the CDS option payout in Equation (18). Proceeding along the same lines as before (see *European CDS options*), we write

$$C(t) = 1_{\tau > t}E_t^Q\left(e^{-\int_t^{t_s}[r(u)+\lambda(u)]du}A(t_s)\left(\phi(c - y_K(t_s))\right)^+\right) = 1_{\tau > t}A(t)E_t^A\left(\left(\phi(c - y_K(t_s))\right)^+\right)$$

where we have performed a measure shift similar to the one that leads to Equation (20). Using the same technique as before, it is straightforward to establish that y_K must be a martingale under the Q^A-measure. Assuming that y_K is log-normal with deterministic volatility $\sigma_y(t)$, we can then write down an explicit option pricing formula:

$$C(t) = 1_{\tau > t}A(t)\phi(c\Phi(-\phi d_-) - y_K(t)\Phi(-\phi d_+)) \tag{25}$$

$$d_{\pm} = \frac{\ln(y_K(t) / c)) \pm \frac{1}{2} \int_t^{t_s} \sigma_y(u)^2 du}{\sqrt{\int_t^{t_s} \sigma_y(u)^2 du}}$$

Again, more complicated martingale processes for y_K can be used if generation of a volatility smile/skew is required.

Finally, a few words about the practical application of Equation (25). First, in the definition of y_K we require knowledge of the survival curves X. In general, these are hard to bootstrap out of bonds and it is often reasonable to use the survival curves generated from CDS quotes. As discussed earlier (see *Bond and asset swap pricing*), adjustments of the CDS survival curve (or, alternatively, the discount curve) will then likely be required to ensure that Equation (15) recovers the quoted price of the bond underlying the option. In the case that no CDS curve exists, a pragmatic approach is to assume that forward hazard rates are flat, and then search for the level that values the underlying bond correctly. Second, in the estimate of the yield volatility σ_y, it is often useful to break the yield into a default-free yield r_K plus a credit spread l_K, along the lines of, for instance,

$$y_K(t) = r_K(t) + l(t), \quad r_K(t) \equiv \frac{KP(t, t_s) - P(t, t_n)}{\sum_{i=1}^n P(t,t_i)\Delta_i}$$

The volatility of r_K can often be estimated with high precision from the swaption market. If the volatility of the credit spread l_K can be estimated, σ_y can then be computed (eg, by moment-matching) for any given correlation between r_K and l_K.

Options on asset swap packages

To round off our discussion of European options, consider the pricing of an option to either buy or sell at par an asset swap package with a predetermined asset swap spread ε_K. Let the asset swap package be written on a bond $B(t)$ with the same schedule and characteristics as before (see *European bond options*). With the option maturity being t_s, from Equation (16) the payout of the option can be written

$$C(t_s) = 1_{\tau > t_s} \left(\phi \left(B(t_s) - c \sum_{i=s+1}^n P(t_s, t_i)\Delta_i - P(t_s, t_n) + \varepsilon_K \sum_{i=s+1}^n P(t_s, t_i)d_i \right) \right)^+ \quad (26)$$

where again we are focusing only on the non-recovery part of the option payout (see *European bond options* for the adjustment needed to incorporate non-zero option recovery). In Equation (26), the sign flag ϕ is +1 if the option-holder has the right to buy the asset swap package (bond call) and −1 if they own the right to sell (bond put).

To write the option payout in a more manageable form, define first a new numeraire

$$D(t) = E^Q_t\left(e^{-\int_t^{t_s}\lambda(u)du}\sum_{i=s+1}^{n}P(t,\,t_i)d_i\right),\ t\le t_s \tag{27}$$

and a forward asset swap level (compare to Equation 16)

$$\varepsilon_F(t) \equiv \frac{c\sum_{i=s+1}^{n}P(t,t_i)[1-X(t,t_i)]\Delta_i + P(t,t_n)[1-X(t,t_n)] + R\int_{t_s}^{t_n}P(t,s)\dfrac{\partial X(t,s)}{\partial s}ds}{D(t)} \tag{28}$$

From the bond pricing Equation (15), a little thought shows that the payout in Equation (26) can now be written as

$$C(t_s) = 1_{\tau > t_s}\sum_{i=s+1}^{n}P(t_s,\,t_i)d_i\big(\phi\big(\varepsilon_K-\varepsilon_F(t_s)\big)\big)^+$$

Hence, the time t price of the option becomes

$$C(t) = 1_{\tau > t}E^Q_t\left(e^{-\int_t^{t_s}[r(u)+\lambda(u)]du}\sum_{i=s+1}^{n}P(t_s,t_i)d_i\cdot\big(\phi\big(\varepsilon_K-\varepsilon_F(t_s)\big)\big)^+\right)$$

$$= 1_{\tau > t}D(t)E^D_t\left(\big(\phi\big(\varepsilon_K-\varepsilon_F(t_s)\big)\big)^+\right)$$

where E^D_t is the expectations operator in the measure Q^D induced by using D as a numeraire. The second equality follows directly from Equation (2) in Panel 1.

From its definition in Equation (28) and the results already mentioned from earlier sections, we see that the forward asset-swap spread is a martingale under Q^D. For variety and to incorporate the fact that asset swaps spreads occasionally go negative, we could here assume dynamics of the *displaced* log-normal type

$$d\varepsilon_F(t) = \sigma_\varepsilon(t)(v+\varepsilon_F(t))dW(t),\ v\ge 0$$

which allows $\varepsilon_F(t)$ to take values on $[-v,\infty)$. It is then easily derived that

$$C(t) = 1_{\tau > t}D(t)\phi((v+\varepsilon_K)\Phi(-\phi d_-) - (v+\varepsilon_F(t))\Phi(-\phi d_+)) \tag{29}$$

$$d_\pm = \frac{\ln\left(\dfrac{\varepsilon_F(t)+v}{\varepsilon_K+v}\right) \pm \dfrac{1}{2}\int_t^{t_s}\sigma_\varepsilon(u)^2 du}{\sqrt{\int_t^{t_s}\sigma_\varepsilon(u)^2 du}}$$

The somewhat unusual form of the numeraire D is a consequence of the fact that the option payout involves cashflows beyond t_s, yet default risk only matters on the interval $[0,t_s]$. In practice, the computation of the numeraire D from Equation (27) is often non-trivial and may require either an approximation or the outright assumption that credit spreads are independent of interest rates. In the latter case, we simply get

$$D(t) = \sum_{i=s+1}^{n} X(t, t_s)P(t, t_i)d_i$$

GENERAL VALUATION PDE, BERMUDAN OPTIONS, AND HYBRIDS

We have now dealt with a number of European options for which closed-form solutions can be found for sufficiently simple assumptions about certain break-even spreads and yields. For more complicated securities, we will typically have to go back to basics and build models directly around specified dynamics for more fundamental quantities, such as credit intensities and the short interest rate. For most process specifications, closed-form solutions for derivatives prices will then not be possible, and we must rely on numerical methods. While we so far have relied on expressing securities prices as expectations under certain probability measures, for numerical implementation it is often more convenient to reformulate the pricing problem in a partial differential equation (PDE) framework. We will now introduce the PDE method and give some brief examples of its usage on Bermuda-style cancellable CDS options as well as "hybrid" credit/fixed income securities.

Basic pricing PDE

Assume for simplicity that interest rates are deterministic and let us assume that the risk-neutral hazard-rate process is a Markov diffusion process of the form

$$d\lambda(t) = \mu_\lambda(t, \lambda(t))dt + \sigma_\lambda(t, \lambda(t))dW(t) \tag{30}$$

for given well-behaved functions μ_λ, σ_λ. Consider a security V that pays $V(T) = h(\lambda(t))$ at terminal maturity T if and only if no default takes place on $[0, T]$. In case of pre-maturity default, the recovery of V is assumed to be a given function R of time and λ: $V(\tau) = R(\tau, \lambda(\tau))$, $\tau \leq T$. Writing $V(t) = V(t, \lambda(t))$ and assuming that no default has taken place before time t, we get from Ito's lemma:

$$dV(t) = \left\{ \frac{\partial V}{\partial t} + \mu_\lambda \frac{\partial V}{\partial \lambda} + \frac{1}{2} \sigma_\lambda^2 \frac{\partial^2 V}{\partial \lambda^2} \right\} dt + \sigma_\lambda \frac{\partial V}{\partial \lambda} dW(t) + (R - V(t-))dN(t)$$

where $t- = \lim_{\varepsilon \downarrow 0} t - \varepsilon$ and where we have suppressed most function arguments for brevity. Notice the presence of the Poisson (Cox) term, which merely states that V jumps to its recovery term R in case of default. Taking expectations and expressing the fundamental arbitrage restriction that

$$E_t^Q(dV(t)) = r(t)V(t)dt$$

we arrive at the backward pricing PDE for $V(t, \lambda)$

$$\frac{\partial V}{\partial t} + \mu_\lambda(t, \lambda)\frac{\partial V}{\partial \lambda} + \frac{1}{2} \sigma_\lambda(t, \lambda)^2 \frac{\partial^2 V}{\partial \lambda^2} - (r(t) + \lambda)V(t, \lambda) + \lambda R(t, \lambda) = 0 \tag{31}$$

This equation is subject to the terminal boundary condition $V(T, \lambda) = h(\lambda)$; further boundary conditions can be added to capture – for instance – early exercise rights or the existence of knock-in/out barriers (we will see some examples of this later).

Generally speaking, Equation (31) cannot be solved analytically and a numerical solution is required. An obvious and general choice of a numerical scheme is the *finite difference method* where the equation is discretised on a (t, λ)-grid using difference approximations for the derivatives in Equation (31) – see Tavella and Randall (2000) for more details of this.

Example: Bermuda-style CDS option in an affine framework

To make the above treatment a bit more concrete, let us consider pricing Bermuda-style options in the popular *affine hazard rate model*:

$$d\lambda(t) = \kappa(t)(\theta(t) - \lambda(t)) + \sigma(t)\sqrt{\alpha(t) + \beta(t)\lambda(t)}\,dW(t) \tag{32}$$

where $\kappa(t) \geq 0$ and $\theta(t)$ denote time-dependent mean-reversion speed and level, respectively, and α, β, σ are deterministic functions of time defining the local volatility of the hazard rate. Certain regularity requirements are needed for the process above to make sense. For instance, if $\beta \neq 0$, for the square root in Equation (32) to be well-defined, we need to ensure that the drift term in that equation has the same sign as β when $\alpha(t) + \beta(t)\lambda(t) = 0$. That is, for $\beta(t) \neq 0$ we must have

$$\kappa(t)\beta(t)(\theta(t) + \alpha(t) / \beta(t)) \geq 0$$

Stronger conditions are needed to ensure strict positivity – see Duffie and Kan (1996) for more details about this. Note that if β is allowed to be zero at some points in time, λ can become negative. This is generally not desirable, so we typically would insist that $\beta(t) > 0$ for all t.

The advantage of the affine process in Equation (32) is the fact that the PDE in Equation (31) can be solved for certain simple, but important, instruments. In particular, consider setting $R(t, \lambda) = 0$ and $h(\lambda) = V(T, \lambda) = 1$, in which case Equation (31) describes a T-maturity risky zero-coupon bond: $V(t) = P(t, T)X(t, T)$. Guessing at the solution

$$V(t, \lambda) = P(t, T)e^{A(t, T) + B(t, T)\lambda} = e^{-\int_t^T r(u)du}\, e^{A(t, T) + B(t, T)\lambda} \tag{33}$$

we find by insertion into Equation (31) that the coefficients A and B must satisfy Ricatti differential equations

$$\frac{\partial A}{\partial t} - \kappa(t)\theta(t)B + \frac{1}{2}\sigma(t)^2\alpha(t)B^2 = 0$$

$$-\frac{\partial B}{\partial t} + \kappa(t)B + \frac{1}{2}\sigma(t)^2\beta(t)B^2 = 1$$

subject to the boundary conditions $B(T,T) = A(T,T) = 0$. These equations can easily be solved for all t and T using, for instance, a Runge-Kutta ODE solver – see Press *et al*, (1992) for more details.

The existence of the explicit expression in Equation (33) for $P(t,T)X(t,T)$ – and thereby for $X(t,T)$ – has a number of practical advantages. First, for given volatility function and mean reversion $\kappa(t)$, we can use the result derived from Equation (33) to quickly calibrate the function θ to the observed time 0 initial term curves of risky zero-coupon bonds $P(0, t)$ $X(0,t)$, $t > 0$.[12] Second, Equation (33) allows us to express directly the prices of traded instruments such as CDSs and bonds as functions of the PDE state variable λ, making it easy to apply boundary conditions.[13] For instance, for a European option to buy protection through a CDS with a fixed spread c, we simply get the boundary condition (for the right to sell protection, just reverse the sign)

$$V(T, \lambda) = V_{CDS}(T, \lambda)$$

$$= (1 - R) \sum_{i=s+1}^{n} P\left(T, \frac{1}{2}(t_i + t_{i-1})\right)\left(e^{A(T,t_{i-1})+\lambda B(T, t_{i-1})} - e^{A(T,t_i)+\lambda B(T, t_i)}\right) \quad (34)$$

$$-c\sum_{i=s+1}^{n} \Delta_i P(T, t_i)e^{A(T,t_i)+\lambda B(T, t_i)}$$

where we have used the same notation and approximation as in Equations (11) to (13). Also, we have used an integration timeline on the default leg coinciding with the premium leg schedule. Notice that the option is assumed to mature at a date in the premium leg schedule t_s, $s \geq 1$.

Going beyond the purely European specification, we notice that many practical contracts grant the option holder a right to exercise the option prematurely, on a given set of dates. Assuming that these dates are finite in number – ie, that the option is Bermuda-style – and falling on the coupon dates t_b, t_{b+1}, ..., $t_s = T$, $b \geq 1$, we need to supply to the PDE the additional free boundary conditions:

$$V(t_j, \lambda) \geq V_{CDS}(t_j, \lambda), j = b, ..., s \quad (35)$$

Here, we understand that in the determination of the right-hand side of this expression, the sums in Equation (34) are supposed to run from j to n. Implementation of Equation (35) in a finite difference solver is straightforward: whenever the finite difference solver rolls back over an exercise date t_j, we use the relationship

$$V(t_j -, \lambda) = MAX(V(t_j +, \lambda), V_{CDS}(t_j, \lambda))$$

While the details are outside the scope of this chapter, let us make a few comments on the calibration of the affine model shown in Equation (32). In practice, the parameter κ would be set based on observation of the auto-correlation structure of the hazard rates, as well as the decay of term volatilities of European option as a function of option maturities. The parameters α, β determine the volatility skew and would be set to match any observations or beliefs about the skew.[14] The parameters θ and σ would then finally be jointly calibrated such that risky zero coupon bonds (as reflected in quoted bonds and/or CDS prices) and European credit option prices would be matched. Good closed-form approximations exist for European options in the affine model (see, for example, Colin-Dufresne and Goldstein, 2001), which can be combined with Equation (33) to make such a joint calibration computationally efficient.

Two-factor PDE and hybrids

The PDE in Equation (31) holds under the assumption of deterministic interest rates. This assumption is often sufficient for instruments such as CDS options that have fairly limited interest rate volatility exposure. A number of "hybrid" credit structures, however, have sufficiently strong interest-rate dependence to make it necessary to work with models where both interest rates and credit spreads are stochastic. The classical example of a hybrid contract is a credit derivative that protects against credit losses on a specific portfolio of fixed income derivatives. Often the underlying fixed-income derivatives are swaps – in which case the hybrid is known as a "risky swap" contract – but structures on more complicated fixed income derivatives also exist. Notice that a regular bond option (see *European bond options*) could be considered a hybrid, as it has significant exposure to both interest rates and credit spreads.

As above, assume now that the hazard rate process is of the form shown in Equation (30). Moreover, let the short-term interest rate follow the risk-neutral process

$$dr(t) = \mu_r(t, r(t))dt + \sigma_r(t, r(t))dW_r(t)$$

for given well-behaved functions μ_r, σ_r calibrated to the market for fixed-income options and swaps/bonds. The instantaneous correlation between interest rates and the hazard rate is $\rho(t)$, such that $dW(t)dW_r(t) = \rho(t)dt$. A security V that depends on both r and λ then must satisfy the two-factor PDE

$$\frac{\partial V}{\partial t} + \mu_\lambda(t,\lambda)\frac{\partial V}{\partial \lambda} + \mu_r(t,r)\frac{\partial V}{\partial r} + \frac{1}{2}\sigma_\lambda(t,\lambda)^2\frac{\partial^2 V}{\partial \lambda^2} + \frac{1}{2}\sigma_r(t,r)^2\frac{\partial^2 V}{\partial r^2}$$

$$+ \rho(t)\sigma_\lambda(t,\lambda)\sigma_r(t,r)\frac{\partial^2 V}{\partial r \partial \lambda} - (r+\lambda)V(t,r,\lambda) + \lambda R(t,r,\lambda) = 0 \qquad (36)$$

subject to appropriate boundary conditions. The PDE above can be handled by two-dimensional finite difference solver (such as an alternating directions implicit method), at a significant increase in computation time relative to the one-dimensional Equation (31). Notice that the recovery value R in Equation (36) can depend on both interest rates and hazard rates. Indeed, interest rate dependent recovery is obviously key to the modelling of credit derivatives that insure against credit losses on specific fixed income instruments.

In many instances of practical importance, making the additional assumption that interest rates are independent of credit spreads will make Equation (36) quite tractable. For instance, consider the case where a derivative V pays out an interest rate dependent quantity $R(\tau, r(\tau))$ at the time of default τ, provided that $\tau < T$. From the basic Equation (7) we then have

$$
\begin{aligned}
V(t) &= 1_{\tau > t} E_t^Q \left(\int_t^T R(s,\, r(s)) \lambda(s) e^{-\int_t^s [\lambda(u) + r(u)] \, du} \, ds \right) \\
&= 1_{\tau > t} E_t^Q \left(\int_t^T R(s,\, r(s)) e^{-\int_t^s r(u) \, du} \, ds \right) E_t^Q \left(\int_t^T \lambda(s) e^{-\int_t^s \lambda(u) \, du} \, ds \right) \qquad (37) \\
&= -1_{\tau > t} \int_t^T E_t^T \big(R(s,\, r(s)) \big) P(t,\, s) \frac{\partial X(t,\, s)}{\partial s} \, ds
\end{aligned}
$$

where the second and third equality both rely on the assumed independence of rates and credit spreads. In the equation above, $E_t^T\big(R(s, r(s))\big)$ is simply the time t forward value of $R(s, r(s))$, a quantity that is normally straightforward to compute. Indeed, Equation (37) simply expresses the value of V as a weighted sum of forward values, with each weight being a default probability.

REDUCED-FORM MODELS AND EQUITY HYBRIDS
Motivation
As we discussed at the start of this chapter, many structural models are built around fundamental relationships between a company's equity and its creditworthiness. Having such a causal link is a general strength of structural models, particularly when it comes to the modelling of securities that involve both equity and credit components. The classical example of such a security is a convertible bond, a coupon-paying security with a built-in American option to convert the security into a fixed number of equity shares. Other important applications for joint credit/equity models include the increasingly popular usage of equity price process to predict default and/or to determine credit spreads – for instance, see the KMV or CreditGrades commercial applications – and the usage of equity positions to hedge credit exposure in cases where CDS markets have insufficient liquidity.

To further illustrate the link between equity and credit spreads, consider taking a position in a T-maturity European put option on an equity price S. If the strike on the put option is sufficiently low, the option will practically only pay out if the company defaults and the stock price drops to zero (or very close to zero). As an approximation for small strikes, we can then write for the time t value of the put option

$$PV_{put}(t) = P(t,T)E_t^T\left((K - S(T))^+\right) \approx P(t,T)KE_t^T(1_{\tau \leq T})$$
$$= P(t,T)K\left(1 - 1_{\tau > t}X(t,T)\right) = K(P(t,T) - Z(t,T))$$

which demonstrates a close link between low-strike equity options and credit spreads. Notice that the above result can be made more succinct by taking the limit:

$$P(t,\ T) - Z(t,\ T) = \frac{\partial PV_{put}(t)}{\partial K}\ \big|_{K \downarrow 0} \tag{38}$$

For situations where joint modelling of equity and credit spreads is important, it is natural to ask whether the basic reduced-form framework can be adapted to this task. In fact, this can be done in a number of ways; we shall present one particularly appealing approach in the next section.

A reduced-form defaultable equity model

Consider a stock S with a bounded state-dependent volatility $\sigma(t,\ S)$. We wish to introduce a default mechanism in the process for S, under the following assumptions:

a) default is triggered by the first jump in a Cox process $N(t)$;
b) at the time of default, the stock is driven into 0 where it will stay forever; and
c) the hazard rate λ of the Cox process is a deterministic function of the stock price, $\lambda = \lambda(t,\ S)$.

The first of these assumptions simply states that we wish to stay inside the reduced-form framework, whereas the second assumption makes the reasonable assertion that equity-holders are left with no residual value after a default. The third assumption, suggested originally by Davis and Lishka (1999), adds further structure to the model and serves to provide the desired link between credit spreads and the equity price.

With the risk-free interest rate r and the instantaneous dividend yield q both assumed deterministic, the assumptions (a) to (c) give rise to risk-neutral stock dynamics of the form

$$dS(t)/S(t-) = (r(t) - q(t) + \lambda(t,S(t-)))dt + \sigma(t,S(t-))dW(t) - dN(t) \tag{39}$$

Let us make a few comments on this SDE. First, notice the drift term $\lambda(t, S(t-))$, which compensates for the expected downward drift of the Cox process term: $E_t^Q(dN(t)) = \lambda(t,\ S(t-))dt$. The drift compensation is required for the process to satisfy the arbitrage restriction that $S(t)\exp(-\int_0^t[r(u) - q(u)]du)$ be a martingale in the risk-neutral probability measure. Second, notice that when N jumps from 0 to 1, $dS(t) = -S(t-)$, the stock is driven into 0, as desired.

Given Equation (39), consider now the pricing of a contingent claim V with maturity T. Writing $V = V(t, S)$, we can use techniques similar to those already discussed (see *Basic pricing PDE*) to derive that V must satisfy the following backward PDE, subject to a boundary payoff condition at T

$$\frac{\partial V}{\partial t} + (r(t) - q(t) + \lambda(t, S))S\frac{\partial V}{\partial S} + \frac{1}{2}\sigma(t, S)^2 S^2 \frac{\partial^2 V}{\partial S^2} = (r(t) + \lambda(t, S))V - \lambda(t, S)R(t, S) \quad (40)$$

Here, $R(t, S)$ is the recovery value of V in case of default at time t; the recovery value can be allowed to depend on both time and the pre-default value of the stock price. The PDE above is similar to Equation (31) and can be solved numerically using finite difference methods.[15]

Calibration issues

Consider first the parameterisation of the function $\lambda(t, S)$, the main driver of the dependence between credit spreads and stock prices in the model shown in Equation (39). As stock price and credit-worthiness can be empirically observed to be inversely related to each other, we would normally want to use specification for $\lambda(t, S)$ that is decreasing in S. For instance, an often-used parameterisation is

$$\lambda(t, S) = a(t)S^{-p} \quad (41)$$

for some deterministic function a and a constant $p \geq 0$. The value of p can be estimated by, say, time-series regression of stock prices against credit spreads or by noting that, from Ito's lemma,

$$d\lambda(t) / \lambda(t) = \ldots dt - p\sigma(t, S)dW(t)$$

which identifies p as the ratio of credit spread volatility to equity volatility, two quantities that can often be observed with a reasonable degree of precision. Typical values for p range from 1 to 3.

Leaving aside momentarily the question of how to determine the function $a(t)$ in Equation (41), consider now the question of calibrating the volatility function $\sigma(t, S)$. As a first observation, we note that this function *cannot* be imported directly from a regular pure-diffusion equity option system. In particular, we notice that the effective implied volatility of the process Equation (39) will contain a contribution from the jump-term $dN(t)$, causing us to over-price European stock options unless the diffusion volatility in this equation is lowered relative to the volatility used in a default-free stock model. As documented in detail in Andersen and Buffum (2002), failure to adequately account for this effect can lead to very substantial pricing errors.

As it transpires, it is in principle possible to compute $\sigma(t, S)$ non-parametrically from observations of the volatility smile of European equity options. To state this result, let us use $C(T, K)$ to denote the time 0 price of a European equity call option with strike K and maturity T. Then, as demonstrated in Andersen and Buffum (2002), for known λ we have the explicit relationship

$$\sigma(T,K)^2 = \frac{\dfrac{\partial C}{\partial T}+(q-K\lambda'(T,k))C+(r-q+\lambda(T,K))K\dfrac{\partial C}{\partial K}-K\int_K^\infty C(T,k)\lambda''(T,k)dk}{\dfrac{1}{2}K^2\dfrac{\partial^2 C}{\partial K^2}} \tag{42}$$

where we have suppressed dependence on T for r and q, and where hyphens denote derivatives with respect to T.[16] This expression is similar in spirit to the result of Dupire (1992) for standard diffusion processes.

The result derived in Equation (42) depends on the existence of call options traded at a continuum of strikes and a continuum of maturities. This is obviously never the case in practice, whereby implementation of Equation (42) must rely on various interpolation/extrapolation techniques. This exercise can be quite challenging and normally requires regularisation techniques to avoid unstable values of $\sigma(t, S)$. Rather than try to fit to an entire surface of call options, we could instead rely on a more pragmatic approach, where we fit only to at-the-money options (the "centre" of the smile) and to risky zero-coupon bonds (the extreme "left wing" of the smile – see Equation 38). This approach is typically sufficient for most applications and ensures that our model is in line with straight debt (eg, CDS or bond) prices as well as the most liquid equity options. With only two instruments per maturity to fit, it suffices to write $\lambda(t, S) = \lambda(S; a(t))$ and $\sigma(t, S) = \sigma(S; b(t))$ for two unknown functions of time, a and b. The calibration then simplifies to a joint search for a and b such that at-the-money options and risky zero coupon bonds at all maturities are replicated by the model. The lack of closed-form results for equity options and risky zero-coupon bonds in the model shown in Equation (39) requires application of numerical methods for the calibration – see Andersen and Buffum (2002) for discussion of an efficient forward induction technique.

Example: convertible bonds

Assume now that $\sigma(t, S)$ and $\lambda(t, S)$ have been estimated such that we are ready to apply the pricing PDE of Equation (40). To illustrate this process, consider a classical example of an equity/credit hybrid, namely a *convertible bond*. In a nutshell, a convertible bond is a regular coupon bond (the so-called *bond floor*) combined with an American-style option to convert the bond into a number of equity shares. Specifically, let $V(t)$ be the time t price of a T-maturity convertible bond paying an annualised coupon rate of c on some schedule $\{t_i\}_{i=0,...,K}$, $t_0 = 0$, $t_K = T$. The stream of cash-flows introduce the following jump-type boundary conditions for V

$$V(t_i-) = V(t_i+) + c(t_i - t_{i-1}), \ i = 1, 2, \ldots, K-1, \ V(T) = 1 + c(T - t_{K-1}) \quad (43)$$

where we have assumed a (normalised) notional of US\$1 and ignored the finer details of bond accrual conventions. On dates t where the bond can be exercised into shares, we impose the free boundary condition

$$V(t) \geq L(t)S(t) \quad (44)$$

where L is the possibly time-dependent conversion ratio (normalised to apply to a notional of US\$1). A simple technique to deal with free boundary conditions in a finite difference grid was discussed in our earlier example. For our purposes, Equations (43) and (44) serve to define a plain-vanilla convertible bond, but we point out that realistic convertibles often come with a number of additional features, including issuer-owned call rights and investor-owned put rights. Grimwood and Hodges (2002) provide terminology and a discussion of advanced features of convertible bonds; Andersen and Buffum (2002) and Ayache et al (2002) discuss how to implement some of these features in a PDE solver.

Equations (43) and (44) specify the boundary conditions that characterise our simple convertible bond. To complete the specification, we still need to make an assumption for the recovery rate $R(t, S)$ of the bond in default. While a number of such assumptions can be found in the literature, the most reasonable one is to use the same recovery as we would use

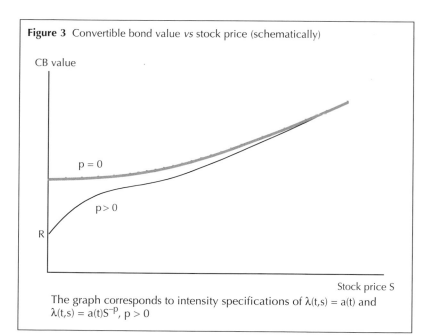

Figure 3 Convertible bond value *vs* stock price (schematically)

The graph corresponds to intensity specifications of $\lambda(t,s) = a(t)$ and $\lambda(t,s) = a(t)S^{-p}$, $p > 0$

for a regular coupon bond (see *Bond and asset swap pricing*): $R(t, S) = R$, where R is a constant fraction of the bond notional (here US$1).

Using the hazard rate specification of Equation (14), Figure (3) shows stylistically how convertible bond prices $V(0, S)$ emerging from a numerical solution of Equation (40), depend on the stock price S. Consider the limits $S \to \infty$ and $S \to 0$. For large enough S, the convertible bond holder will convert the bond, whereby the asymptote for $S \to \infty$ is simply $L \cdot S$. As for the lower limit, notice that when $p > 0$, we have $\lambda(t, S) \to \infty$ for $S \to 0$, whereby $V(t, 0) = R$; in other words, the convertible bond approaches its recovery value as the stock approaches 0. This is obviously quite reasonable behaviour and induces a characteristic "negative convexity" of the convertible bond price for low values of the stock price. Such negative convexity is indeed empirically observable for distressed convertible bonds. Notice that when $p = 0$ in Equation (41), the hazard rate does not depend on the stock price and the negative convexity effect will disappear, as indicated in Figure (3). More detailed numerical examples can be found in Andersen and Buffum (2002) and Ayache *et al* (2002).

1   See Panel 1, Equation (3) for details about the measure shift leading to this expression.
2   This section contains fairly advanced technical material and can be skipped at a first reading. The results used in applications are listed in Equations (9) and (10).
3   Recall that, roughly speaking, a martingale is a process with no drift.
4   If necessary, more exact day-counting could be applied here.
5   See *Curve construction* and *Quanto-effects* in this chapter for details.
6   Being swaps – and thereby involving a fairly balanced set of both negative and positive cashflows – the choice of discount basis is less important for CDSs than for bonds.
7   That is, the CDS contract is forward starting.
8   We use the usual notation $x^+ = \max(x, 0)$.
9   The following somewhat technical derivation serves to demonstrate that θ_0 is a martingale process under Q^A. For those not interested in this derivation, the final option pricing result is in Equations (21) and (22).
10 The discussion can easily be extended to options maturing between schedule dates.
11 Assuming that the option accelerates its payout in case of an early default, the recovery rate would be $R_c = (\phi(\alpha - K))^+$ where α is the recovery fraction on the bond. For normal values of the strike K, only put options would have a non-zero recovery.
12 Notice that θ might be a very noisy function as it contains the derivative of the forward hazard rate curve, which may not be smooth. While outside the scope of this article, we note that this problem can be overcome by changing variables in the PDE, so instead work with $z(t) = \lambda(t) + \partial \ln X(0,t)/\partial t$.
13 In models where this is not the case, a time-consuming "roll-back" procedure is required to compute risky zero-coupon bond prices numerically.
14 For a richer and more realistic modelling of volatility skews, it may be beneficial to allow the intensity process to jump, ie to turn Equation (32) into a jump-diffusion. As it turns out, the affine framework allows such extensions without losing much analytical tractability (see, for example, Duffie and Kan, 1996). When jumps are added, the PDE in Equation (31) would be turned into a partial integro-differential equation (PIDE) which can be solved using the techniques discussed in Andersen and Andreasen (2000).
15 See Andersen and Buffum (2002) or Ayache *et al* (2002) for details.

16 A result also exists for λ's that are not differentiable with respect to time. See Andersen and Buffum (2002) for details.

BIBLIOGRAPHY

Andersen, L., and J. Andreasen, 2000, "Jump-diffusion processes: Volatility smile fitting and numerical methods for option pricing", *Review of Derivatives Research*, 4, pp. 231–62.

Andersen, L., and D. Buffum, 2002, "Calibration and Implementation of Convertible Bond Models", Working Paper, Banc of America Securities.

Ayache, E, P. Forsyth, and K. Vetzal, 2002, "The Valuation of Convertible Bonds with Credit Risk", Working Paper, University of Waterloo.

Colin-Dufresne, P., and R. Goldstein, 2001, "Pricing swaptions within the affine framework", Working paper, Carnegie-Mellon University.

Davis, M., and F. Lischka, 1999, "Convertible Bonds with Market Risk and Credit Risk", Working Paper, Tokyo-Mitsubishi International.

Duffie, D., 1996, *Dynamic Asset Pricing Theory*, (Princeton University Press).

Duffie, D., and R. Kan, 1996, "A yield-factor model of interest rates", *Mathematical Finance*, 6, pp. 379–406.

Dupire, B., 1994, "Pricing with a Smile", *Risk*, January, pp. 18-20.

Grimwood, R., and S. Hodges, 2002, "The Valuation of Convertible Bonds: A Study of Alternative Pricing Models", Working Paper, University of Warwick.

Hull, J., 2000, *Options, Futures, and Other Derivatives*, 4th Edition, (London: Prentice Hall).

Lando, D., 1998, "On Cox Processes and Credit Risky Securities", *Review of Derivatives Research*, 2, pp. 99–120.

Press, W., B. Flannery, S. Teukolsky, and W. Vetterling, 1992, *Numerical Recipes in C*, (Cambridge University Press).

Tavella, D., and C. Randall, 2000, *Pricing Financial Instruments: The Finite Difference Method*, (John Wiley & Sons).

17

Dynamite dynamics

Jesper Andreasen

Nordea Markets

INTRODUCTION

In the context of stochastic models, *explosion* means that the variable that is modelled can go to infinity with positive probability. An example of this is the following model:

$$x(t) = \frac{1}{a - W(t)}$$

where a is a positive constant and W is a Brownian motion with $W(0) = 0$. Here x will go to infinity as W approaches a, and the process x is thus only well defined up to the *first passage time* of W to the level a.

In most finance models the stochastic dynamics of the modelled variables are restricted to prevent explosions, as we are rarely interested in prices or rates that are infinite. But in this chapter we actually make use of explosive processes to give us more realistic dynamics of credit default swap (CDS) spreads.

The case for this is based on the observation that defaults can be anticipated as well as unanticipated. If a default is anticipated it is well known in the market that the company has financial problems and the actual default will tend to happen after a period of steep increases in credit spreads and corresponding declines in bond and equity prices. Default can also be a complete surprise to the financial markets, in which case the spreads and prices do not react before the actual default event occurs. An example of this is when a company is bankrupted following accidents or natural disasters.

A second observation is that credit spreads tend to jump up and fall back a lot more than, for example, interest rates. This essentially means that the standard processes used for interest rates are not necessarily applicable for accurately describing the dynamics of credit spreads, and models with more probability mass in high-rates scenarios are required.

This chapter follows the base concept of the reduced-form models by assuming that the probability of default occurring over a small time interval is proportional to the length of the time interval, ie,

$$\Pr(\tau \in dt \mid \tau > t) = \lambda(t)dt$$

where τ is the default time, and λ is a stochastic process. But, contrary to most other reduced-form models, *the default intensity λ is not modelled as a standard well-behaved process*, but rather as a mean-reverting but explosive process with domain on the full positive real axis – infinity included.

This means that we obtain a model with the two types of default: *anticipated* when default occurs when the default intensity is high and on its way to infinity; and *unanticipated* when default occurs when the default intensity is low. Further, due to the trade-off between mean reversion and explosion, we get high likelihood of scenarios where the default intensity, and thereby the CDS spread, gaps out and falls back without default actually occurring. Figure 1 shows the path of an explosive default intensity process.

It is well known that correlating standard processes of the default intensity has very little effect on the correlation of actual default events of different names and this has led to the development of models with explicit modelling of the correlated default events, such as, for example, the Gaussian copula model.

However, in an explosive credit model of multiple names, positively correlated default intensities mean that one name going into an explosion

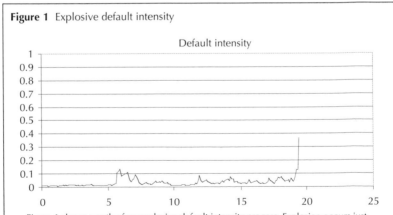

Figure 1 Explosive default intensity

Default intensity

Figure 1 shows a path of an explosive default intensity process. Explosion occurs just before year 20. Default can be unanticipated and occur when the default intensity is low or be anticipated and occur when the default intensity is exploding and on its way to infinity.

scenario will tend to drag other names with it. This in turn means that in this type of model correlating default intensities has much larger and more direct and realistic effects on the correlation of actual default events. This implies that the explosive model can be used as an alternative to the copula model for the pricing of credit-correlation products such as first-to-default baskets and CDO tranches. The advantage of the explosive model over the copula models is that it explicitly incorporates the dynamics of the credit spreads.

For an explosive model to be practically applicable it needs to be analytically tractable. The model that we present here allows for calculation of survival probabilities and Green's function in closed form. This means that standard CDSs can be priced in closed form and that all single-name European options, as, for example, options on bonds and CDSs, can be priced by one-dimensional numerical integration. Further, we show how a single parameter of the model can be made time-dependent so that is it possible to fit the model to the CDS market.

The rest of this chapter is organised as follows: the second section of the chapter presents the mathematical formulation of the model; the third and fourth sections consider the pricing of linear credit instruments such as for CDSs and bonds and European options on those; the fifth and sixth sections consider numerical pricing by Monte-Carlo simulations and finite difference methods; the seventh section considers the calibration of the model; and a final section considers the pricing of credit correlation products in the explosive model. We round off the chapter with a short conclusion.

THE EXPLOSIVE CREDIT MODEL

We are going to work directly under a risk-neutral measure under which all discounted asset prices are martingales. All probabilities and expectations in the following will be under this measure.

We assume that

$$Pr(\tau \in dt \mid \tau > t, x(t)) = \lambda(t)dt \tag{1}$$

where $\lambda(t) = 1/x(t)$ is the default intensity and

$$dx(t) = (\theta - \kappa(t)x(t))dt + \sigma \sqrt{x(t)}dW(t) \tag{2}$$

where W is a Brownian motion, $\kappa(\cdot)$ is a deterministic function and θ, σ are constants. Note here that we do not put any conditions on θ, σ, $\kappa(\cdot)$ being positive or negative.

Using the technique of speed and scale measures – see for example Borodin and Salminen (1996) – it is straightforward to show that $x = 0$ is an unattainable boundary for the process x if $2\theta \geq \sigma^2$. If this is not the case the additional boundary conditions for the behaviour at $x = 0$ are sometimes needed. So, if the boundary $x = 0$ is attainable, we will assume that

x is absorbed in 0. For these cases the default intensity will be an explosive process.

Using the terminology of Borodin and Salminen (1996), one can view the process specification (1–2) as a square-root process with absorption in $x = 0$ and *exponential killing* at the rate $1/x$.

Ito's lemma can be used to derive that

$$d\lambda(t) = (\kappa(t) - (\theta - \sigma^2)\lambda(t))\lambda(t)dt - \sigma\lambda(t)^{3/2}dW(t) \tag{3}$$

on $\{\lambda < \infty\}$. So the default intensity is a process with non-linear drift and diffusion, specifically, the power on the diffusion is $3/2$. Hence, we would expect that the options written on CDS spreads would exhibit an implied volatility skew opposite to that we typically see in interest rate markets – but in line with equity volatility skews in the sense that there would be excessive probability mass in the high-spreads/low-equity price state relative to the Gaussian case.

The parameter κ is left time-dependent to be able to calibrate to quoted CDS prices, σ controls the volatility of the CDS spread, whereas the parameter θ controls the probability of explosion relative to the total probability of default (PD). We will return to how one can set the parameters from market data in more detail in a subsequent section.

The model (2) for the default intensity is the same as Ahn and Gao (1999) used for the short-term interest rate. However, contrary to Ahn and Gao (1999), we do not put explicit constraints on the parameters to avoid explosion.

The specific choice of model made in this section allows for a range of closed-form results that we are going to present in the following sections. For brevity and minimal mathematical complexity, we have omitted the derivation of these results and refer to Andreasen (2000) for the technical details.

PRICING CREDIT DEFAULT SWAPS AND BONDS

If we make the assumption that the default intensity, interest rates and recovery are mutually independent, we have that a CDS paying a time-dependent continuous coupon of q up to maturity T has the time t value

$$C(t, x(t)) = \int_t^T P(t, u)[-L_T(t, x(t); u)(1 - R(t, u)) - L(t, x(t); u)q(u)]du$$

where $R(t, u)$ is the time t expected recovery rate of the underlying bonds if default happens at time u, $P(t, u)$ is the time t value of a zero-coupon bond maturing at time u, and where

$$L(t, x(x); T) = \Pr[\tau > T \mid \tau > t, x(t)] = E[e^{-\int_t^T \lambda(u)du} \mid x(t) \tag{3}$$

is the *survival probability*. We note that per arbitrage $L_T \leq 0$.

Likewise the value of a bullet bond with maturity T paying a continuous coupon of p is

$$B(t, x(t)) = \int_t^T P(t, u)[L(t, x(t); u)p(u) - L_T(t, x(t); u)R(t, u)]du + P(t, T)L(t, x(t); T)$$

So, in order to value these instruments, it is necessary to compute the survival probability. We see from (3) that computing the survival probability is similar to solving for a zero-coupon bond price in a short-rate interest rate model, and that the survival probability can be computed as the solution to the partial differential equation (PDE)

$$0 = L_t - \frac{1}{x}L + (\theta - \kappa x)L_x + \frac{1}{2}\sigma^2 x L_{xx} \tag{4}$$

on $\{t < T, x > 0\}$ subject to the boundary conditions

$$L(t, 0; T) = 0, \, t \le T$$
$$L(T, x, T) = 1, \, x > 0$$
$$L(t, \infty, T) = 1, \, t \le T$$

Luckily, our model permits calculation of the survival probability in closed form. It is given by

$$L(t, x; T) = \frac{\Gamma(\beta - \gamma)}{\Gamma(\beta)}M\left(\gamma, \beta, -\frac{x}{2K(t, T)}\right)\left(\frac{x}{2K(t, T)}\right)^\gamma, \, t < T, x > 0 \tag{4}$$

where

$$\gamma = \frac{-(\theta - \sigma^2/2) + \sqrt{(\theta - \sigma^2/2)^2 + 2\sigma^2}}{\sigma^2}$$

$$\beta = 2(\gamma + \theta/\sigma^2)$$

and

$$k(t, T) = e^{\int_t^T \kappa(u)du}, \, K(t, T) = \frac{\sigma^2}{4}\int_t^T k(t, u)du$$

and where $M(\cdot)$ and $\Gamma(\cdot)$ are respectively the *Kummer* and the *Gamma* functions defined by

$$M(a, b, z) = \sum_{n=0}^{\infty} \frac{(a)_n}{(b)_n} \frac{z^n}{n!}, \, (c)_n = \prod_{j=0}^{n-1} (c + j), \, (c)_0 = 1$$

$$\Gamma(z) = \int_0^\infty u^{z-1}e^{-u}du$$

Press *et al* (1992) gives a simple and very accurate algorithm for evaluating the Gamma function. As for evaluation of the Kummer function, we note that straightforward implementation of the above power series representation will give excellent results for $|z| < 10$. However, for large $|z|$ one can run into trouble with numerical overflow on standard computers, in which case the asymptotic expansion of Abramowitz and Stegun (1972), 13.5.1, is very useful. This can be combined to give routine for the survival probability with excellent accuracy that is only a little bit more costly to evaluate numerically than an exponential. Hence, evaluating CDSs and bonds is only marginally more costly in our model than evaluating them straight off a curve of pre-computed survival probabilities.

PRICING CREDIT OPTIONS

If we additionally make the assumption that interest rates are deterministic, the option to enter a CDS of maturity T at the fixed spread q at time s, contingent on no default up to time s, has the time t value[1]

$$V(t) = P(t, s)E[e^{-\int_t^s \lambda(u)du} C(s, x(s))^+ \mid x(t)] \tag{5}$$

$$= P(t, s) \int_0^\infty G(t, x(t); s, \bar{x})C(s, \bar{x})^+ d\bar{x}$$

where $G(\cdot)$ is the Green's function, formally given by

$$G(t, x(t); s, \bar{x}) \equiv E[e^{-\int_t^s \lambda(u)du} \delta(x(s)) - \bar{x}) \mid x(t)] \tag{5}$$

and $\delta(\cdot)$ is Dirac's delta function.[2]

The Green's function is essentially the state price of the joint event $\{x(s) = \bar{x}, \tau > s\}$. Hence,

$$G(t, x(t); s, \bar{x}) / L(t, x(t); s) \tag{6}$$

is the risk-neutral density of $\{x(s) = \bar{x}\}$ given that we have survived up to time s. In the context of interest-rate models where we could think of λ as a short-term interest rate (6) would be the maturity forward risk-adjusted density of $\{x(s) = \bar{x}\}$.

So, given that we can find the Green's function, it is possible to compute prices of all types of European options on linear credit instruments by numerical integration of (5).

The Green's function is given by

$$G(t, x; T, \bar{x}) = \frac{k(t, T)}{2K(t, T)} e^{\frac{x + \bar{x}k(t,T)}{2K(t,T)}} \left(\frac{x}{\bar{x}k(t, T)}\right)^{\gamma - \vartheta'/2} I_{|\vartheta'|}\left(\frac{\sqrt{x\bar{x}k(t, T)}}{K(t, T)}\right)$$

$$\equiv \left(\frac{x}{\bar{x}k(t, T)}\right)^{\gamma} h_{\vartheta'}(t, x; T, \bar{x})$$

where $\vartheta' = 2(\gamma + \theta/\sigma^2) - 1$ and $I_a(\cdot)$ is the *modified Bessel* function of index a defined by

$$I_a(z) = \sum_{j=0}^\infty \frac{(z/2)^{a+2j}}{j!\Gamma(a + j + 1)}.$$

Press *et al* (1992) contains algorithms for computing the modified Bessel function. Alternatively, one can use that

$$\int_0^{\bar{x}} h_{\vartheta'}(t,\, x;\, T,\, y)dy = \chi^2\left(\frac{\bar{x}k(t,T)}{K(t,T)},\, 2+2\vartheta',\, \frac{x}{K(t,T)}\right) \tag{7}$$

where $\chi^2(\cdot,\, f,\, \theta)$ is cumulative distribution function for a non-central χ^2-distributed random variable with non-centrality parameter θ and f degrees of freedom.

When using (7) one would take the numerical derivative of expression (7) to get $g_{\vartheta'}(t,\, x;\, T,\, \cdot)$ and then multiply with $(x/k\bar{x})^\gamma$ to obtain $G(t,\, x;\, T,\, \cdot)$. The advantage of this approach is that $\chi^2(\cdot)$ can be computed very accurately and efficiently with a combination of the normal distribution approximation of Johnson and Kotz (1981) for large x and $\bar{x}$, and the expansion and algorithm of Ding (1992) for small x and $\bar{x}$. In both cases, more than 20 terms are rarely needed for 10^{-8} accuracy. In practice this means that computing prices of European options on CDSs or bonds by numerical integration under our model assumptions is only about 5–10 times as computationally demanding as it would be under Gaussian assumptions.

SIMULATING THE EXPLOSIVE MODEL

For Monte-Carlo simulation of the explosive model we need to derive the conditional distribution. Let

$$g(t,\, x;\, T,\, \bar{x}) = E[\delta(x(T) - \bar{x})|x(t) = x]$$

be the conditional density of $\{x(T) = \bar{x}\}$ given $x(t) = x$, we have that

$$g(t,\, x;\, T,\, \bar{x}) = h_\vartheta(t,\, x;\, T,\, \bar{x}),\ \vartheta = 2\theta/\sigma^2 - 1 \tag{8}$$

Here, it can again be beneficial to compute (8) using the non-central χ^2 distribution function. We have

$$Y(\bar{x}|x) = \Pr(x(T) < \bar{x}\,|x(t) = x) = \begin{cases} 1 - \chi^2\left(\dfrac{x}{K(t,T)},\, -2\vartheta,\, \dfrac{\bar{x}k(t,T)}{K(t,T)}\right),\ \vartheta < 0 \\[3mm] \chi^2\left(\dfrac{\bar{x}k(t,T)}{K(t,T)},\, 2+2\vartheta,\, \dfrac{x}{K(t,T)}\right),\ \vartheta \geq 0 \end{cases} \tag{9}$$

From this we see that for $\vartheta < 0$, ie, when explosions occur, the probability of *no explosion* over a specific time interval is given by

$$H(t,\, x(t);\, T) = \Pr[\lambda(T) < \infty \mid x(t)] = \chi^2\left(\frac{x(t)}{K(t,\, T)},\, -2\upsilon,\, 0\right) \tag{10}$$

Additionally, we note that the probability of survival conditional on $x(t)$ and $x(T)$ is given by

$$P(x,\, \bar{x}) = \Pr[\tau > T|x(t) = x,\, x(T) = \bar{x},\, \tau > t]$$

$$= \frac{\Pr[x(T) \in d\bar{x}, \ \tau > T \,|\, x(t) = x, \ \tau > t]}{\Pr[x(T) \in d\bar{x} \,|\, x(t) = x, \ \tau > t]} \tag{11}$$

$$= \frac{G(t, x; T, \bar{x})}{g(t, x; T, \bar{x})}$$

This means that the system (1–2) can be simulated at the discrete dates t_0, t_1, K, t_m using the scheme:

i. Generate two sequences of mutually independent uniform random variables on (0, 1):

$$\{u(t_0), \ \dots, \ u(t_{m-1})\} \text{ and } \{v(t_0), \ \dots, \ v(t_{m-1})\}$$

ii. For each time step t_i to t_{i+1} use (9) and the random draw $u(t_i)$ to generate $x(t_{i+1})$ from $x(t_i)$ by setting

$$x(t_{i+1}) = \Upsilon^{-1}(u(t_i) \,|\, x(t_i)), \ i = 0, \ \dots, \ m-1$$

iii. For each time step t_i to t_{i+1} use (11) and the random draw v_i to determine whether there is a default or not by setting

$$\{\tau > t_{i+1}\} = \{v(t_i) < \Psi(x(t_i), x(t_{i+1}))\}, \ i = 0, \ \dots, \ m-1$$

Consider now the multiname model

$$dx_j(t) = (\theta_j - \kappa_j(t)x_j(t))dt + \sigma_j \sqrt{x_j(t)}dW_j(t), \ \lambda_j(t) = \frac{1}{x_j(t)}, \ j = 1, \ \dots, \ n$$

$$dW_j(t) \cdot dW_k(t) = \rho_{jk}dt$$

with (ρ_{jk}) being a constant $n \times n$ correlation matrix.

A scheme for simulating this type of model is the following. Let

$$z(t_i) = Rw(t_i)$$

where R is the Cholesky decomposition of the correlation matrix (ρ_{jk}), and $w(t_i) = (w_1(t_i), \ \dots, \ w_n(t_i))'$ are independent standard normal random variables. The uniform random variables in (6) are then generated by

$$u_j(t_i) = \Phi(z_j(t_i)), \ j = 1, \ \dots, \ n$$

where $\Phi(\cdot)$ is the standard normal cumulative distribution function. As we are not drawing the distribution directly from the joint distribution function for $(x_1, \ \dots, \ x_n)$, this simulation mechanism is not unbiased. However, as the time-step size goes to zero the bias disappears and practical experiments suggest that the bias is negligible compared with the typical simulation error when the time-step size is less than one year. Alternatively, if the time-step bias turns out to be a problem, one may consider using a finer time stepping when one x_j is close to zero.

FINITE-DIFFERENCE SOLUTION OF THE EXPLOSIVE MODEL

Bermudan options on CDSs and bonds are obvious candidates for finite-difference solution of the model. Under the assumption of deterministic interest rates these types of instruments satisfy the PDE

$$0 = \left[\frac{\partial}{\partial t} + D \right] F$$

$$D = -\left(r + \frac{1}{x} \right) + (\theta - \kappa x) \frac{\partial}{\partial x} + \frac{1}{2} \sigma^2 x \frac{\partial^2}{\partial x^2} \tag{12}$$

on $\{x > 0\}$, where r is the instantaneous continuously compounded interest rate. The PDE (12) is of course subject to appropriate boundary conditions defining the particular claim under consideration.

The most efficient way of solving this type of PDE is to use the Crank-Nicolson split:

$$\left[\frac{1}{\Delta t} - \frac{1}{2} D \right] F(t, \cdot) = \left[\frac{1}{\Delta t} + \frac{1}{2} D \right] F(t + \Delta t, \cdot) \tag{13}$$

Various types of artificial boundary conditions can be used in the numerical solution of (13). As there generally will be a high probability of x values close to 0, we favour using a value condition as for example

$$F(t, x = 0) = 0$$

rather than a derivative condition. For the other end of the grid a simple derivative condition like

$$F_{xx}(t, x = \infty) = 0$$

will work fine.

The standard way of finite difference solution of a system like (13) is to use a uniform spacing of the points in the x direction. However, in this model a lot of the "action" will take place close to $x = 0$ and we may therefore wish to include more grid points close to the $x = 0$ than uniform spacing would suggest. One way of doing this is to use a discretisation in the x direction with

$$x_k = O(k^2)$$

The alternative to numerical solution in the transformed variable $y = \sqrt{x}$ will introduce an infinite drift term in the PDE, so this route cannot be recommended.

The non-uniform spacing means that the finite-difference representation of (13) involves non-central difference operators and that we theoretically get a slower convergence of the numerical solution than the standard

$0(\Delta x^2)$. However, the latter has not shown to be a practical problem in our implementation.

CALIBRATION OF THE MODEL

Given a choice of the parameters θ and σ, it is possible to calibrate the model to a term structure of observed CDS spreads by appropriately choosing the curve $\{\kappa(t)\}_{t \geq 0}$, or equivalently choosing an increasing curve $\{K(0, T)\}_{T \geq 0}$. In fact, we note from (4) that

$$\frac{\partial L(0, x(0); T)}{\partial T} = \frac{\partial L(t, x(0); T)}{\partial K(0, T)} \frac{\partial K(0, T)}{\partial T} < 0, \ T \geq 0$$

and therefore that if a curve of observed survival probabilities $\{L_{obs}(0, T)\}_{T \geq 0}$ satisfy the arbitrage condition

$$\frac{\partial L_{obs}(0, T)}{\partial T} < 0, \ T \geq 0$$

then it is possible to calibrate the model for any choice of θ, σ. This is not *generally* the case for short-rate yield-curve models – for example, not for the Cox, Ingersoll and Ross (1985) model with time-dependent mean reversion level.

This suggests that we first compute the curve of survival probabilities from observations of market prices of CDS and/or bonds. Then we use the survival probability formula (4) to back out the curve $\{\kappa(t)\}_{t \geq 0}$. We may here use simple bootstrapping to obtain the κ curve, but we actually prefer to use a smooth spline method similar to those often used in the context of yield-curve estimation, since the bootstrapping methodology in some cases can be unstable and produce oscillating κ curves.

The parameter σ is of course linked to the instantaneous volatility of the credit spreads or, equivalently, the volatility of the *term hazard rates*

$$l(t, T) \equiv -\frac{1}{T - t} \ln L(t, T)$$

Specifically, we have that

$$dl(t, t + T) = -\frac{1}{T} \frac{L_x(t, x(t); t + T)}{L(t, x(t); t + T)} \sigma \sqrt{x(t)} dW(t)$$

This means that in the (likely) case of absence of implied credit volatility data, the parameter σ will have to be estimated from time-series observations of $l(t, t + T)$. In such an estimation we find it safe to ignore the drift term. If European option prices on, for example, CDS or bonds can be observed we can of course use the pricing relation (5) to deduce an implied volatility parameter σ.

The last parameter θ controls the probability of explosion relative to the total probability of default. The lower θ is, the more likely it is that the model will explode. We define the *term explosion rate* as

$$h(t,\,T) = -\frac{1}{T-t}\ln H(t,\,T) = -\frac{1}{T-t}\ln \Pr[x(T) > 0 \,|\, x(t)]$$

Figure 2 shows the curves of term explosion rates for seven different models, all with the same σ but different values of θ, and all calibrated to give the same total term hazard rates by having different κ curves.

The associated κ curves are shown for each of the models in Figure 3.

CREDIT CORRELATION PRODUCTS IN THE EXPLOSIVE MODEL

The higher the likelihood of explosion is in the model, the higher the impact of default intensity correlation (ρ_{jk}) is on the correlation of actual default events. In this section we illustrate this by considering the pricing of digital first-to-default swaps.

A digital first-to-default swap pays a continuous coupon of q against receiving a payment of US$1 at the first default among n companies, if such an event occurs before the final maturity T. Under the assumption of deterministic interest rates, the value of such a claim is

$$V(0) = E[P(0,\,\tau)1_{\tau \le T} - q \int_0^{\min(\tau,T)} P(0,\,u)du],\ \tau = \min(\tau_1,\,K,\,\tau_n)$$

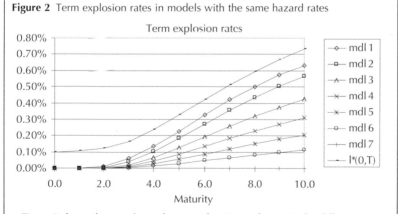

Figure 2 Term explosion rates in models with the same hazard rates

Term explosion rates

Figure 2 shows the term hazard rates as functions of maturity for different models that are calibrated to the same term hazard rate curve, the top blue curve l*(0,T) which in turn is generated from the parameters $\theta = 60$, $\kappa = 0.06$, $\sigma = 12$, $x(0) = 1000$. For all the models we have $\sigma = 12$, $x(0) = 1000$, whereas we let $\theta = 0, 45, 60, 65, 68, 70, 72$ for the models 1, 2, ..., 7 in respective order. In all cases the function $\kappa(\cdot)$ is calibrated so that all models hit the term hazard rate curve l*(0,T).

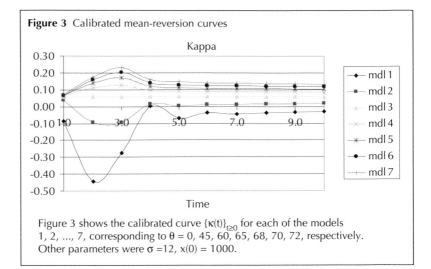

Figure 3 Calibrated mean-reversion curves

Figure 3 shows the calibrated curve $\{\kappa(t)\}_{t\geq0}$ for each of the models 1, 2, ..., 7, corresponding to $\theta = 0, 45, 60, 65, 68, 70, 72$, respectively. Other parameters were $\sigma = 12$, $x(0) = 1000$.

Table 1 Basket default swap par coupons under different model parameters

ρ	$\theta = 72$	$\theta = 70$	$\theta = 68$	$\theta = 65$	$\theta = 60$	$\theta = 45$	$\theta = 0$
0.00	3.50%	3.50%	3.50%	3.50%	3.50%	3.50%	3.50%
0.25	3.25%	3.18%	3.16%	3.14%	3.13%	3.11%	3.08%
0.50	3.02%	2.94%	2.85%	2.84%	2.73%	2.62%	2.55%
0.75	2.76%	2.68%	2.61%	2.49%	2.34%	2.15%	2.03%
0.95	2.43%	2.31%	2.18%	2.07%	1.88%	1.65%	1.45%
1.00	2.37%	2.25%	2.11%	1.97%	1.72%	1.35%	1.10%

Table 1 reports the par coupon for a 10-year first-to-default swap on five homogenous names as function of the default intensity correlation and the parameter θ. The basket default swap is assumed to pay annual coupons and the interest rate is supposed to be zero. Other parameters are $x_j(0) = 1000$, $\sigma_j = 12$ for $j = 1, ..., 5$. In all cases the curves $\{\kappa_j(t)\}_{t\geq0}$ are calibrated to produce the same survival probabilities, that corresponding to $\theta = 60$. The par coupon on a single name default swap is in all cases 0.73%. All reported numbers are based on 10,000 Monte-Carlo simulations.

where τ_j is the default time of company j. So the par coupon is

$$q = \frac{E[P(0,\tau)1_{\tau<T}]}{E[\int_0^{min(\tau,T)} P(0,u)du]}$$

Table 1 reports the par coupon as function of the "explosion tendency" parameter θ and default intensity correlation ρ.

Table 1 shows that the impact of correlation increases dramatically as the tendency to explode is increased, ie, θ is decreased. The reason for this is that if one name explodes and defaults then it will tend to drag other names with it.

CONCLUSION

We have presented a model that is attractive from a number of perspectives. First, it explicitly models the dynamics of credit spreads in such a way that defaults can be both anticipated and unanticipated. Second, the number of parameters is limited to one controlling the volatility of credit spreads, one that controls the explosion tendency of the model, and a time-dependent parameter that allows the model to be calibrated to observed CDS prices. Third, closed-form expressions can be derived for all linear credit instruments such as CDSs and bonds, and all European credit options on a single name can be handled by simple one-dimensional numerical integration. Bermudan credit options on a single name can be handled in a relatively standard one-dimensional finite-difference grid, whereas multiname products must be handled by Monte-Carlo simulations. The latter is also generally, but not always, the case for the more standard reduced-form models such as the Gaussian copula model.[3] However, the explosive model allows for pricing a range of products that the Copula models cannot handle – for example, Bermudan callable CDO tranches and other products explicitly involving the dynamics of the multiple credit spreads.

1 Here we use the notation $y^+ = \max(0,y)$
2 Dirac's delta function has the formal properties
3 What we are referring to here is that recently a number of banks have developed analytical methods for pricing standard CDOs and nth-to-default baskets in Copula models that eliminate the need for Monte-Carlo solution. However, these analytical methods do not apply to all credit correlation products. One exception is, for example, baskets of baskets and CDOs with a so-called collection account.

BIBLIOGRAPHY

Abramowitz, M. and I. Stegun, 1972, *Handbook of Mathematical Functions* (New York: Dover Publications Inc).

Ahn, D.-H., and B. Gao, 1999, "A Parametric Nonlinear Model of Term Structure Dynamics", *The Review of Financial Studies* 12(4), 721–62.

Andersen, L. and J. Andreasen, 2000, "Volatility Skews and Extensions of the Libor Market Model", *Applied Mathematical Finance* 7, 1–32.

Andersen, L. and J. Andreasen, 2001, "Factor Dependence of Bermudan Swaptions: Fact or Fiction?", *Journal of Financial Economics* 62, 3–37.

Andreasen, J., 2000, "Credit Explosives", working paper, General Re Financial Products.

Borodin, A. and P. Salminen, 1996, *Handbook of Brownian Motion – Facts and Formulae* (Basel: Birkhauser Verlag).

Cox, J., J. Ingersoll, and S. Ross, 1985, "A Theory of the Term Structure of Interest Rates", *Econometrica* 53, 385–408.

Craig, I. and A. Sneyd, 1988, "An Alternating Implicit Scheme for Parabolic Equations with Mixed Derivatives", *Compu. Math. Applic* 16(4), 341–50.

Ding, C., 1992, "Algorithm AS275: Computing the Non-Central – Distribution Function", *Applied Statistics* 41, 478–82.

Johnson, N., and S. Kotz, 1981, *Continuous Univariate Distributions*, Vol. 2 (John Wiley & Sons).

Mitchell, A. and D. Griffiths, 1981, *The Finite Difference Method in Partial Differential Equations* (John Wiley & Sons).

Press, W., S. Teukolsky, W. Vetterling, and B. Flannery, 1992, *Numerical Recipes in C* (Cambridge University Press).

Schroder, M., 1989, "Computing the Constant Elasticity of Variance Option Pricing Formula", *Journal of Finance* 44(1), 211–18.

18

Modelling and hedging of default risk

Monique Jeanblanc and Marek Rutkowski

Université d'Evry Val d'Essonne
and Warsaw University of Technology

INTRODUCTION

Our aim in this chapter is to present the fundamental methods and results relating to the valuation and hedging of credit derivatives (defaultable claims) within the structural and reduced-form approaches. In contrast to some other works that address this issue by invoking a suitable version of the martingale representation theorem, we directly analyse the possibility of replication of a given contingent claim by means of a trading strategy based on default-free and defaultable securities. It should be stressed that not only is the exact replication of the value process of a defaultable claim valid prior to the default time, but it also includes the jump of this value at time of default, if it occurs prior to or at the maturity date of this claim. We believe that such an approach, motivated by Vaillant (2001), is far more intuitive and leads directly to explicit forms for replicating strategies. Moreover, the issue of a judicious choice of tradeable securities appears in a natural way.

Although the approach may be applied to the general set-up of random interest rates and stochastic intensity, we deliberately focus on the case of deterministic interest rates and default intensity. In this case, one deals with a single volatility parameter of the underlying asset, rather than with the volatilities of the underlying asset, the default-free zero-coupon bond, and the intensity process. The case of random interest rates can be easily dealt with by working with the forward prices and using the concept of the forward measure. In addition, we consider here the basic case of a zero recovery scheme in case of default.

MODEL BUILDING

Financial modelling aimed at the valuation and hedging of derivative assets is the topic of several textbooks. Therefore, we here restricted ourselves to listing the most important aspects of constructing a model. These are:

❏ the specification of risk-sensitive contracts under considerations;
❏ identification of all essential risk factors;
❏ choice of a family of tradeable (liquid) instruments;
❏ choice of the most convenient and adequate models;
❏ construction of self-financing replicating strategies;
❏ valuation of standard derivative products;
❏ calibration of the model to market prices of standard derivatives;
❏ valuation of exotic products; and
❏ calculation of sensitivities.

Hedging credit derivatives

The most straightforward approach to the hedging of credit derivatives is based on the exact replication of a given defaultable claim. The possibility of replication depends heavily on the choice of model and the set of tradeable securities. In the case of the so-called structural approach, this is done in a similar way to the classic case of market models without the possibility of default. Dynamic replication of defaultable claims within the reduced-form approach has been previously analysed in many publications.

Of course, the dynamic (or static) replication is only possible for the so-called attainable contingent claim within a given framework. In the case of non-attainable defaultable claims, one may apply one of the following mathematical methods, which were developed to value and hedge non-attainable contingent claims.

❏ superhedging (see Collin-Dufresne and Hugonnier, 1999);
❏ quantile hedging (see Lotz, 1998);
❏ utility-based hedging (see Collin-Dufresne and Hugonnier, 1999); or
❏ risk-return approach (see Bielecki and Jeanblanc, 2002).

Formally, all existing credit risk models are covered by the general theory of arbitrage pricing of financial derivatives. This occurs due to the introduction of specific discontinuous martingales and the associated martingale (predictable) representation theorems. Credit-risk specific issues include:

❏ correct specification of the credit/default risk;
❏ judicious choice of tradeable instruments;
❏ risk-neutral valuation of non-tradeable claims; and
❏ explicit determination of particular replicating strategies based on default-free and defaultable securities.

STRUCTURAL APPROACH TO DEFAULT EVENT

In this section, we provide a brief overview of the classic structural models. Our goal is limited: we would like to stress the main difference between the strucural approach, in which the default time is usually a predictable stopping time with respect to the reference filtration, and the reduced-form approach (examined in some length in the next section), in which the default time is a totally inaccessible stopping time with respect to the reference filtration. This important feature makes the hedging of credit derivatives within the reduced-form approach qualitatively different from the hedging within the structural approach.

Merton's Model

Following Merton (1974), we assume that the short-term interest rate is constant and equals r. Therefore, the price at time t of the unit default-free zero-coupon bond with maturity T is easily seen to be $B(t, T) = exp(-r(T-t))$.

This formula can be easily extended to the case of a deterministic continuously compounded interest rate $r: \mathbf{R}_+ \to \mathbf{R}$. We denote by $E(V(t))$ $(D(V(t)),$ resp.) the value of the firm's equity (debt, resp.) at time t. Hence, the total value of the firm's assets satisfies $V(t) = E(V(t)) + D(V(t))$. We postulate that the firm's value process V follows a geometric Brownian motion under the spot martingale measure P^*, specifically,

$$dV_t = V_t\big((r - \kappa)dt + \sigma\, dW_t^*\big) \tag{1}$$

where σ is the constant volatility coefficient of the value process V and the constant κ represents the payout ratio, provided that it is non-negative. Otherwise, κ reflects an inflow of capital to the firm. The process W^* is the one-dimensional standard Brownian motion under P^* with respect to some reference filtration $\mathbf{F} = (F_t)$ (it is common to take $\mathbf{F} = \mathbf{F}^{W^*}$). Notice that the dynamics in Equation (1) can only be justified under the assumption that the total value of the firm's assets represents a traded security.

We postulate that the default event may only occur at the debt's maturity date T. Specifically, if at the maturity T the total value $V(T)$ of the firm's assets is less than the notional value L of the firm's debt, the firm defaults and the bondholders receive the amount $V(T)$. Otherwise, the firm does not default, and its liability is repaid in full. We are thus dealing here with a rather elementary example of a defaultable claim with recovery at maturity. We have

$$D(T, T) = L\, \mathbf{1}(\tau > T) + V(T)\, \mathbf{1}(\tau \le T) = L\, \mathbf{1}(V(T) \ge L) + V(T)\, \mathbf{1}(V(T){<}L)$$

or, equivalently,

$$D(T,T) = min\, (V(T),L)\, \mathbf{1}(V(T) \ge L) + min(V(T),L)\, \mathbf{1}(V(T){<}L) = min\, (V(T),L)$$

The fixed amount L may be interpreted as the face value (or par value) of a corporate zero-coupon bond maturing at time T. Since $D(T,T) = min$

$(V(T),L) = L - (L - V(T))^+$ where $x^+ = max\ (x,0)$ for any real number x, the price process $D(t,T)$ of a defaultable zero-coupon bond is manifestly equal to the difference in the value of a default-free zero-coupon bond with the face value L and the value of a European put option written on the firm's assets, with the strike price L and the exercise date T. This put option, with the terminal payoff $(L - V(T))^+$, is commonly referred to in the present context as the *put-to-default*. Formally, the value of the firm's debt at time t thus equals

$$D(V(t)) = D(t,T) = L\ B(t,T) - P(t) \qquad (2)$$

where $P(t)$ is the price of the put-to-default, and where $D(t,T)$ is the price of a defaultable bond:

$$D(t,T) = B(t)\ E_{P*}(B^{-1}(T)\ D(T,T)/\ F_t)$$

It is apparent from Equation (2) that the value at time t of the firm's equity satisfies

$$E(V(t)) = V(t) - D(V(t)) = V(t) - L\ B(t,T) + P(t) = C(t) \qquad (3)$$

where $C(t)$ denotes the price at time t of a call option written on the firm's assets, with the strike price L and the exercise date T. To justify the last equality in Equation (3), we may observe that at time T we have

$$E(V(T)) = V(T) - D(V(T)) = V(T) - min\ (V(T),L) = (V(T) - L)^+$$

and thus the firm's equity can be seen as a call option on the firm's assets.

Combining Equation (2) with the Black–Scholes formula for the arbitrage price of a European put option, Merton (1974) derives a closed-form expression for the arbitrage price of a corporate bond. In what follows, N denotes the standard Gaussian cumulative distribution function:

$$N(x) = (2\pi)^{-1} \int_{-\infty}^{x} exp\ (-u^2/2)\ du$$

Let us state without proof Merton's result.

Proposition 1
For every $0 \le t < T$ we have

$$D(t,T) = V(t)\ e^{-\kappa(T-t)}\ N(-d_1(V(t),T-t)) + L\ B(t,T)\ N(d_2(V(t),T-t)) \qquad (4)$$

where

$$d_1(V(t),T-t) = \frac{ln(V(t)/L) + (r - \kappa + \frac{1}{2}\sigma^2)(T-t)}{\sigma\sqrt{T-t}} \qquad (5)$$

and

$$d_2(V(t),T-t) = d_1(V(t),T-t) - \sigma\sqrt{T-t}$$

Observe that the bond price can be re-expressed as follows:

$$D(t,T) = L\, B(t,T) - DP \times EDL$$

where $DP = N(-d_2) = P^*(V(T)<L)$ is the (risk-neutral) default probability and EDL is the expected default loss $EDL = B(t,T)$.

Hedging a corporate bond

Merton's formula can be seen as a variant of the Black–Scholes valuation result. Therefore, the form of the replicating (ie, self-financing) trading strategy for a defaultable bond can be easily deduced from the well-known expressions for the Black–Scholes hedging strategy for a European put option. For the sake of convenience, we state the following corollary to Proposition 1, in which we write $D(t,T) = u(V(t),t)$.

Corollary 1
The unique replicating strategy for a defaultable bond involves at any time $0 \le t < T$ holding $\phi^1(t)V(t)$ units of cash invested in the firm's value and $\phi^1(t)$ $B(t,T)$ units of cash invested in default-free bonds, where:[4]

$$\phi^1(t) = u_V(V(t),t) = e^{-\kappa(T-t)}\, N(-d_1(V(t),T-t))$$

and

$$\phi^2(t) = (D(t,T) - \phi^1(t)V(t))/B(t,T) = L\, N(d_2(V(t),T-t))$$

Credit spreads

An important characteristic of a defaultable bond is the difference between its yield and the yield of an equivalent default-free bond – ie, the credit spread. Recall that the credit spread $S(t,T)$ is defined through the formula $S(t,T) = Y^d(t,T) - Y(t,T)$, where the yields $Y^d(t,T)$ and $Y(t,T)$ are given by:

$$Y(t,T) = -\frac{\ln B(t,T)}{T-t}, \quad Y^d(t,T) = -\frac{\ln D(t,T)}{T-t}$$

In Merton's model, the yield on a default-free bond is equal to the short-term interest rate – ie, $Y(t,T) = r$. Using the formula for $D(t,T)$ with $L = 1$, we arrive at the following representation for the credit spread in Merton's model:

$$S(t,T) = -\frac{\ln(V(t)\, e^{-\kappa(T-t)} N(-d_1)\,/\,LB(t,T) + N(d_2))}{T-t}$$

Let us now analyse the asymptotic behaviour of the credit spread when time converges to the debt's maturity. It is easy to check that $\lim_{t \to T} N(-d_1(V(t), T-t)) = 1$ on the set $(V(T) < L)$, and $\lim_{t \to T} N(-d_1(V(t), T-t)) = 0$ on the set $\{V(T) > L\}$. Similarly, we have $\lim_{t \to T} N(-d_2(V(t), T-t)) = 0$ on the set $\{V(T) < L\}$, and $\lim_{t \to T} N(-d_2(V(t), T-t)) = 1$ on the set $\{V(T) >$

L}. Using these relationships, the reader can readily verify that the credit spread tends to infinity when the default is imminent, specifically,

$$lim_{t \to T} S(t, T) = \infty \qquad (6)$$

on the set {$V(T) < L$}. On the other hand, we have $lim_{t \to T} S(t, T) = 0$ on the set {$V(T) > L$}.

An essential feature of Merton's model is that the default time τ appears to be a predictable stopping time with respect to the filtration generated by the value process V, as it is announced, for instance, by the following sequence of stopping times:

$$\tau_n = inf \, (t \geq T - (1/n): V(t) < L \,) \qquad (7)$$

with the usual convention that inf $\emptyset = \infty$.

The Black and Cox model

Black and Cox (1976) have made an attempt to relax the most unrealistic features of Merton's model (1974). Their approach accounts for such specific features of debt contracts as safety covenants and debt subordination. Since they assume that the firm's stockholders (or bondholders) receive a continuous dividend payment proportional to the current value of the firm, the risk-neutral dynamics of the firm's value are exactly the same as in Merton's model:

$$dV(t)=V(t) \, ((r - \kappa) \, dt + \sigma \, dW^*(t)) \qquad (8)$$

where the constants $\kappa \geq 0$ and $\sigma > 0$ represent the payout ratio and the volatility coefficient, respectively. As in Merton's model, the short-term interest rate r is assumed to be constant, so that the interest-rate risk is neglected is this approach as well.

Safety covenants

Let us first focus on the safety covenants in the firm's indenture provisions. Generally speaking, safety covenants provide the firm's bondholders with the right to force the firm to bankruptcy or reorganisation if the firm is doing poorly according to a set standard. The standard for a poor performance is set in Black and Cox (1976) in terms of a time-dependent deterministic barrier $v(t) = Ke^{-\gamma(T-t)}$ for some constants γ and $K > 0$. They postulate that as soon as at some date $t < T$ the value of firm's assets crosses this lower threshold, the bondholders take over the firm. Otherwise, default takes place at debt's maturity or not, depending on whether $V(T) < L$ or not. In other words, the default event occurs at the first time $t < T$ at which the firm's value $V(t)$ falls below the level $v(t)$, where $v(t) = Ke^{-\gamma(T-t)}$ for $t < T$ and $v(T) = L$. Thus the default time τ is given by the formula

$$\tau = inf \, \{ \, t \in \, [0, T]: V(t) < v(t) \, \} \qquad (9)$$

If default happens at maturity date T, the recovery payoff is proportional to the value process at this date; specifically, it equals $\beta_1 V(T)$ for some constant $0 \leq \beta_1 \leq 1$. The recovery payoff in case of premature default equals $\beta_2 V(\tau)$, where $0 \leq \beta_2 \leq 1$ is a constant.

It is natural to postulate that $v(t) \leq L\ B(t, T)$ or, more explicitly, that

$$Ke^{-\gamma(T-t)} \leq Le^{-r(T-t)} \qquad (10)$$

so that, in particular, $K \leq L$. Equation (10) ensures that the payoff to the bondholder at the default time τ never exceeds the face value of debt, discounted at the risk-free rate.

The valuation of the corporate bond relies on the following probabilistic representation of the price $D(t,T)$ prior to default:

$$
\begin{aligned}
D(t, T) &= E_{P*}(Le^{-r(T-t)}\ \mathbf{1}(\tau \geq T, V(T) \geq L) \mid F_t) \\
&+ E_{P*}(\beta_1 V(T)e^{-r(T-t)}\ \mathbf{1}(\tau \geq T, V(T) < L) \mid F_t) \\
&+ E_{P*}(K\beta_2\ e^{-\gamma(T-\tau)}\ e^{-r(\tau-t)}\ \mathbf{1}(t < \tau < T) \mid F_t)
\end{aligned}
$$

Using the well known results concerning the law of the first hitting time, Black and Cox (1976) were able to derive an explicit formula for the bond's price. Let us denote:

$$v = r - \kappa - \frac{1}{2}\sigma^2$$

and $\alpha = (v - \gamma)\sigma^{-2}$. The following result was established by Black and Cox (1976).

Proposition 2
Assume that $(v - \gamma)^2 + 2\sigma^2(r - \gamma) > 0$. Then the price $D(t, T)$ of a defaultable bond equals prior to default

$$
\begin{aligned}
D(t, T) &= LB(t, T)\ [\ N(h_1(V(t), T - t)) - R_t^{2\alpha} N(h_2(V(t), T - t))\ ] \\
&+ \beta_1\ V(t)\ e^{-\kappa(T-t)}\ [\ N(h_3(V(t), T - t)) - N(h_4(V(t), T - t))\ ] \\
&+ \beta_1\ V(t)\ e^{-\kappa(T-t)}\ R_t^{2\alpha+2}\ [\ N(h_5(V(t), T - t)) - N(h_6(V(t), T - t))\ ] \\
&+ \beta_2\ V(t)\ [\ R_t^{2\theta+\varsigma} N(h_7(V(t), T-t)) + R_t^{\theta-\varsigma} N(h_8(V(t), T - t))\ ]
\end{aligned}
$$

where $R_t = v(t)/V(t)$, $\theta = \alpha + 1$ and $\varsigma = \sigma^{-2}\sqrt{(\gamma)^2 + 2\sigma^2\gamma)}$. Furthermore

$$h_1(V(t), T - t) = \frac{\ln(V(t)/L) + v(T-t)}{\sigma\sqrt{T-t}},$$

$$h_2(V(t), T - t) = \frac{\ln v^2(t) - \ln(LV(t)) + v(T-t)}{\sigma\sqrt{T-t}},$$

$$h_3(V(t), T - t) = \frac{\ln(L/V(t)) - (v + \sigma^2)(T-t)}{\sigma\sqrt{T-t}},$$

$$h_4(V(t), T - t) = \frac{\ln(K/V(t)) - (v + \sigma^2)(T - t)}{\sigma \sqrt{T - t}},$$

$$h_5(V(t), T - t) = \frac{\ln v^2(t) - \ln(LV(t)) + (v + \sigma^2)(T - t)}{\sigma \sqrt{T - t}},$$

$$h_6(V(t), T - t) = \frac{\ln v^2(t) - \ln(KV(t)) + (v + \sigma^2)(T - t)}{\sigma \sqrt{T - t}},$$

$$h_7(V(t), T - t) = \frac{\ln(v(t)/V(t)) - \varsigma\sigma^2(T - t)}{\sigma \sqrt{T - t}},$$

$$h_8(V(t), T - t) = \frac{\ln(v(t)/V(t)) - \varsigma\sigma^2(T - t)}{\sigma \sqrt{T - t}},$$

Let us now analyse some special cases involving the Black–Cox valuation formula. We shall assume that $\beta_1 = \beta_2 = 1$ and the barrier function is chosen in such a way that $K = L$. Then necessarily $\gamma \geq r$ (since if not, Equation 10 would be violated). Obviously, if $K = L$. then we have $D(t, T) = D_1(t, T) + D_2(t, T)$, where in turn

$$D_1(t, T) = LB(t, T) \left[N(h_1(V(t), T - t)) - R_t^{2\alpha} N(h_2(V(t), T-t)) \right] \quad (11)$$

and

$$D_2(t, T) = V(t) \left[R_t^{\theta+\varsigma} N(h_7(V(t), T - t)) + R_t^{\theta-\varsigma} N(h_8(V(t), T - t)) \right] \quad (12)$$

Case 1: $\gamma = r$
In this case, we assume that $\gamma = r$, meaning that simple calculations yield

$$V(t)R_t^{\theta+\varsigma} = LB(t, T) \text{ and } V(t)R_t^{\theta-\varsigma} = LB(t, T)R_t^{2\alpha}$$

In addition, it is easy to see that

$$h_1(V(t), T - t) = -h_7(V(t), T - t) \text{ and } h_2(V(t), T - t) = h_8(V(t), T - t)$$

We conclude that if $v(t) = L\, e^{-r(T-t)} = LB(t, T)$, then $D(t, T) = LB(t, T)$. This result is quite intuitive; a defaultable bond with a safety covenant represented by the barrier function, which equals the discounted value of the bond's face value, is obviously equivalent to a default-free bond with the same face value and maturity. Notice also that when $\gamma = r$ but $K < L$, then we have

$$D_2(t, T) = K B(t, T) P^* (\tau < T| F_t)$$

Case 2: $\gamma > r$
If $K = L$ but $\gamma > r$, one would expect that $D(t, T)$ would be smaller than $LB(t, T)$. We shall show that when γ tends to infinity (all other parameters being fixed), the Black and Cox price converges to Merton's price – following on from Equation (4),

$$lim_{\gamma \to \infty} D(t, T) = V(t)\, e^{-\kappa(T-t)}\, N(-d_1(V(t), T - t)) + L\, B(t, T)\, N(d_2(V(t), T - t))$$

First, it is clear that $h_1(V(t),\ T - t) = d_2(V(t),\ T - t)$. Furthermore, straightforward calculations show that

$$lim_{\gamma \to \infty} R_t^{2\alpha}\, N(h_2(V(t),\ T - t)) = lim_{\gamma \to \infty} R_t^{\theta - \varsigma}\, N(h_8(V(t),\ T - t)) = 0$$

and thus the second term on the right-hand side of Equation (11), as well as the second term on the right-hand side of Equation (12), vanishes. Finally,

$$lim_{\gamma \to \infty} R_t^{\theta + \varsigma}\, N(h_7(V(t), T - t)) = e^{-\kappa(T-t)}\, N(-d_1(V(t), T - t))$$

$$\text{since } lim_{\gamma \to \infty} R_t^{\theta + \varsigma} = e^{-\kappa(T-t)} \text{ and } h_7(V(t), T - t) = -d_1(V(t), T - t)$$

Market completeness

In most models developed within the structural approach, the presence of default does not induce a new kind of incompleteness. If the default-free market is complete, as in both Merton's and Black and Cox's models, the defaultable market is also complete, since the default time is a stopping time in the asset's filtration. Note that the definition of completeness depends strongly on the choice of the filtration (as well as the choice of tradeable assets).

In the two previous models, the default time was also a predictable stopping time. This property is no longer valid in the case of Zhou's model (1996), where the dynamics of the firm's value are driven by a jump-diffusion process. In that case, both the defaultable and default-free markets are incomplete.

Valuation and hedging of credit derivatives

As soon as the default-free market is complete, one can hedge any contingent claim in the terminal filtration of the prices, and consequently any defaultable contingent claim. In a non-defaultable set-up, the hedging of credit derivatives is quite similar to that of standard or exotic options. Since this area is fairly well-known, we do not go into details here.

Partial observations

Until now, we have implicitly assumed that all agents possess perfect knowledge of the firm's current value. Following Duffie and Lando (2001), we now examine the case of a market model in which the agents have only partial information about the firm's assets. Specifically, the agents fully observe the prices only at discrete (ie, fixed) times $t_1, t_2, ..., t_n$. In addition, at any date the agents know whether the default has already happened or not. As before, we postulate that $dV(t) = V(t)\,((r - \kappa)\, dt + \sigma\, dW^*(t))$. Let $\mathbf{K} \subset \mathbf{F}$ be the filtration generated by the information flow available to an agent. Under the present assumptions we have $K_t = \sigma(V(t_1), V(t_2), ..., V(t_i), \{\tau > t_i\})$

for every t belonging to $[t_i, t_{i+1}]$. The default time is modelled as $\tau = inf \{ t \leq T: V(t) \leq \alpha \}$ for some constant $\alpha > 0$. In the case of deterministic interest rates, the value of a defaultable zero-coupon bond with zero recovery is $D^0(t, T) = B(t, T) P^* (\tau > T \mid K_t)$.

We write $V(t) = V(0)exp(\sigma X(t))$ where $X(t) = vt + W^*(t)$ and $v = (r/\sigma) - \sigma/2$. Finally, we denote $a = \sigma^{-1} \ln (V(0)/\alpha)$. For $t_i < t < t_{i+1}$ we have

$$D^0(t,T) = B(t,T) P^*(\tau > T \mid K_t) = B(t,T) P^*(\tau > T \mid \sigma(V(t_1), V(t_2), ..., (V(t_i), \{\tau > t_i\})))$$

Using standard computations based on the Markov property, we obtain that for $t_i < t < t_{i+1}$

$$D^0(t,T) = B(t,T) P^*(\tau > T \mid \sigma(V(t_i), \{\tau > t_i\})) = B(t,T) P^*(inf_{s<T} X(s) > a \mid \sigma(V(t_i), \{\tau > t_i\}))$$

$$= \mathbf{1}(\tau > t_i) B(t,T) P^*(inf_{t_i \leq s < T} X(s) > a \mid \sigma(V(t_i))) = \mathbf{1}(\tau > t_i) B(t,T) \Phi(T - t_i, a - X(t_i))$$

where the function Φ is given by, for $z < 0$ and $t \geq 0$,

$$\Phi(t,z) = P^*(inf_{u<t}(vu + W^*(u)) > z) = N\left(\frac{vt - z}{\sqrt{t}}\right) - e^{2vz} N\left(\frac{vt + z}{\sqrt{t}}\right)$$

For $z \geq 0$ and $t \geq 0$ we have $\Phi(t,z) = 0$, and for $z < 0$ we set $\Phi(t,z) = 1$. Notice that the process $D^0(t, T)/B(t, T)$ is increasing on the interval $[t_i, t_{i+1})$, its jump at time t_i on the set $\{\tau \leq t_i\}$ is

$$\Delta(D^0(t_i, T)/B(t_i, T)) = \mathbf{1}(\tau > t_{i-1}) \Phi(t_i - t_{i-1}, a - X(t_{i-1}))$$

and on the set $\{\tau > t_i\}$ the jump equals

$$\Delta(D^0(t_i, T)/B(t_i, T)) = \Phi(t_i - t_{i-1}, a - X(t_{i-1})) - 1$$

REDUCED-FORM APPROACH TO DEFAULT EVENT

One of the major drawbacks of the structural approach is that the default time is a predictable stopping time (at least, it is so in Merton's and Black and Cox's models). To capture the idea of a default that occurs by a total surprise, one can use a *totally inaccessible* stopping time – ie, a stopping time that cannot coincide with a predictable one on a set of a strictly positive probability. The most typical example of these times is the jump time of a Poisson process.

Let N be a Poisson process with the intensity $\lambda > 0$, defined on a probability space (Ω, A, Q). We denote by τ the random time of the first jump of N, that is, $\tau = inf \{t \geq 0: N(t) \geq 0\}$.

This time cannot be announced; however, its law is well known – this is an exponential law with parameter λ. The *intensity coefficient* λ is uniquely characterised by the fact that the *compensated process* $N(t) - \lambda t$ is a martingale (hence the stopped process $M(t) = N(t \wedge \tau) - \lambda(t \wedge \tau)$ is a martingale as well).

This can be generalised to the case of an inhomogeneous Poisson process – ie, a process N such that $N(t) - \int_0^t \lambda(s)ds$ is a martingale with respect to the filtration generated by N.

If λ is a given non-negative function (or even a non-negative stochastic process), it is easy to construct such a process. Indeed, let $\tilde{N}$ be a Poisson process with the constant intensity equal to 1, and let us set $\tilde{N}(t) = N(\Lambda(t))$ where $\Lambda(t) = \int_0^t \lambda(u)du$. Then, the probability law of the first jump time of $\tilde{N}$ is given by $Q^*(\tau \le t) = 1 - \exp(-\int_0^t \lambda(s)\,ds)$. In this case, the stopped process

$$N(t \wedge \tau) - \int_0^{t \wedge \tau} \lambda(s)ds = H(t) - \int_0^t \mathbf{1}(s < \tau)\lambda(s)ds$$

is a martingale with respect to the filtration $\mathbf{H}$ generated by the jump process $H(t) = \mathbf{1}(\tau \le t)$. However, we do not need the whole structure of the Poisson process, since only the first jump is usually taken into account. In the case of a stochastic intensity process λ, one starts with a given process λ, adapted to a given filtration $\mathbf{F}$, and one enlarges the filtration in order to construct the Poisson process with a stochastic intensity λ.

Default time

We shall now formally introduce the notion of a stochastic intensity of the default time. Let τ be a non-negative random variable on a probability space (Ω, A, Q^*), referred to as the *default time*. Recall that we have introduced the jump process $H(t) = \mathbf{1}(\tau \le t)$, and we denoted by $\mathbf{H}$ the filtration generated by this process.

Hazard process

We now assume that some reference filtration $\mathbf{F}$ is given. We set $\mathbf{G} = \mathbf{F} \vee \mathbf{H}$ so that $G_t = F_t \vee H_t$ for every t. The filtration $\mathbf{G}$ is referred to as the *full filtration*. It is clear that $\mathbf{G}$ includes, in particular, the observations of default event. Of course, τ is an $\mathbf{H}$-stopping time, as well as a $\mathbf{G}$-stopping time (but not necessarily an $\mathbf{F}$-stopping time). The concept of the *hazard process* of a random time t is closely related to the conditional distribution function $F(t)$ of τ. We define $F(t) = Q^*(\tau \le t \mid F_t)$ and $G(t) = 1 - F(t) = Q^*(t < \tau \mid F_t)$. We postulate that $G(t) > 0$, hence, we exclude the case where τ is an $\mathbf{F}$-stopping time. The process $\Gamma : \mathbf{R}_+ \to \mathbf{R}_+$ given by the formula $\Gamma(t) = -\ln(1 - F(t)) = -\ln G(t)$ is called the *hazard process* of a random time τ with respect to the reference filtration $\mathbf{F}$.

Deterministic default intensity

The study of a simple case when the reference filtration $\mathbf{F}$ is trivial, and thus the hazard process is deterministic, may be instructive. Assume that τ is a given random time. Assume that $Q^*(\tau > t) > 0$ for every $t \in \mathbf{R}_+$, and that the cumulative distribution function $F(t) = Q^*(\tau \le t)$ is an absolutely continuous function: $F(t) = \int_0^t f(u)du$ for some function $f: \mathbf{R}_+ \to \mathbf{R}_+$. Then we have $\Gamma(t) = \int_0^t \gamma(u)du$ where $\gamma(t) = f(t)/(1 - F(t))$. It is clear that the function $\gamma: \mathbf{R}_+ \to \mathbf{R}_+$ is non-negative and satisfies $\int_0^\infty \gamma(u)du = \infty$. The function γ is called the *intensity function* or the *hazard rate* of τ. It can be checked by direct calculations that the process $H(t) - \int_0^{t \wedge \tau} \gamma(u) du$ is an **H**-martingale.

Note that when the agent has no information on the prices – ie, only partial information is available – we can consider the case as when **F** is the trivial filtration.

Stochastic default intensity
In terms of the stochastic intensity, the conditional probability of the default event $\{t < \tau \le T\}$, given the full information G_t available at time t, equals

$$Q^*(t < \tau \le T/ G_t) = \mathbf{1}(t < \tau)\, E_{Q^*}(1 - exp(-\int_0^t \gamma(u)du) \,/\, F_t)$$

Thus

$$Q^*(T < \tau/ G_t) = \mathbf{1}(t < \tau)\, E_{Q^*}(exp(-\int_0^t \gamma(u)du) \,/\, F_t)$$

and consequently

$$Q^*(t < \tau \le t + dt \,/\, G_t) \approx \mathbf{1}(t < \tau)\gamma(t)dt$$

The latter formula shows that $\gamma(t)dt$ gives the conditional probability of the default occurrence in a short time after t, given that it has not yet occurred, and that we observe all events from the reference σ-field F_t. In addition, it can be shown that the process

$$H(t) - \int_0^{t \wedge \tau} \gamma(u)du = H(t) - \Gamma(t \wedge \tau) = H(t) - \int_0^t (1 - H(u))\,\gamma(u)du$$

is a (purely discontinuous) **G**-martingale.

Explicit construction of a default time
We now briefly describe the most commonly used construction of a default time associated with a given hazard process Γ. It should be stressed that the random time obtained through this particular method – which we will call the *canonical construction* – has certain specific features that are not necessarily shared by all random times with a given **F**-hazard process Γ. We start by assuming that we are given an **F**-adapted, right-continuous, increasing process Γ defined on a filtered probability space (Ω_1, A_1, P^*). As usual, we assume that $\Gamma(0) = 0$ and . In many instances, Γ is given by the equality $\Gamma(t) = \int_0^t \gamma(u)du$ for some non-negative, **F**-progressively measurable, default intensity process γ.

To construct a random time τ such that Γ is the **F**-hazard process of τ, we need to enlarge the underlying probability space. This also means that Γ is not the **F**-hazard process of τ under P^* but rather the **F**-hazard process of τ under a suitable extension Q^* of the probability measure P^*. Let ξ be a random variable defined on some probability (Ω_2, A_2, Q_2), uniformly distributed on the interval $[0,1]$ under Q_2. We consider the product space $\Omega = \Omega_1 \times \Omega_2$, endowed with the product σ-field $A_1 \otimes A_2$ and the product probability measure $Q^* = P^* \otimes Q_2$. The latter equality means that for arbitrary events $A \in A_1$ and $B \in A_2$ we have $Q^*(A \times B) = P^*(A) Q_2(B)$.

We define the random time $\tau: \Omega \to \mathbf{R}_+$ by setting

$$\tau = \inf\{t \in \mathbf{R}_+ : \exp(-\Gamma(t)) \leq \xi\} = \inf\{t \in \mathbf{R}_+ : \Gamma(t) \geq \eta\}$$

where the random variable $\eta = -\ln \xi$ has a unit exponential law under Q^*. It is not difficult to find the process $F(t) = Q^*(\tau \leq t/F_t)$. Indeed, since clearly $\{\tau > t\} = \{\xi < \exp(-\Gamma(t))\}$ and the random variable $\Gamma(t)$ is F_∞-measurable, we obtain

$$Q^*(\tau > t/F_\infty) = Q^*(\xi < \exp(-\Gamma(t))/F_\infty) = Q_2(\xi < \exp(-x)_{x=\Gamma(t)}) = \exp(-\Gamma(t)) \quad (14)$$

Consequently, we have

$$1 - F(t) = Q^*(\tau > t/F_t) = E_{Q^*}(Q^*(\tau > t/F_\infty)/F_t) = \exp(-\Gamma(t)) \quad (15)$$

and so F is an $\mathbf{F}$-adapted, right-continuous, increasing process. It is also clear that the process Γ represents the $\mathbf{F}$-hazard process of τ under Q^*.

Note that an alternative way of achieving much the same goal relies on postulating that the underlying probability space (Ω, A, P^*) is sufficiently rich to support a random variable ξ uniformly distributed on the interval $[0,1]$, and independent of the σ-algebra F_∞ under P^*, where $F_\infty \subset A$. In this version of the construction, Γ represents the $\mathbf{F}$-hazard process of τ under P^*.

Technical comment

As an immediate consequence of Equations (14) and (15), we obtain the following interesting property of the canonical construction of the default time:

$$Q^*(\tau \leq t/F_\infty) = Q^*(\tau \leq t/F_t) \quad (16)$$

Let us now analyse some important consequences of Equation (16). First, we obtain

$$Q^*(\tau \leq t/F_\infty) = Q^*(\tau \leq t/F_u) = Q^*(\tau \leq t/F_t) = \exp(-\Gamma(t)) \quad (17)$$

for arbitrary two dates $0 \leq t \leq u$. Notice that only the last equality in Equation (17) is necessarily satisfied by the $\mathbf{F}$-hazard process Γ of τ; the first two equalities are additional features of the canonical construction of τ, which means that they do not necessarily hold in a general set-up. Equation (17) entails the conditional independence under Q^* of the σ-fields H_t and F_t, given the σ-field F_∞. Such a property of the two filtrations $\mathbf{H}$ and $\mathbf{F}$ is usually termed *hypothesis* (H). It can be shown that *hypothesis* (H) is equivalent to the following condition: an arbitrary $\mathbf{F}$-martingale also follows a $\mathbf{G}$-martingale under Q^*.[5]

PRICING AND HEDGING OF CREDIT DERIVATIVES

We now analyse the valuation and replication of defaultable claims within the reduced-form set-up. As we mentioned in the introduction, we only present the basic results under several simplifying assumptions. For more general results, see Jeanblanc and Rutkowski (2003).

Default-free and defaultable assets

We now examine the possibility of an exact replication of defaultable claims within various models of defaultable markets. We argue that the choice of a particular setting (in particular, of default-free and defaultable tradeable assets) is an essential step in model-building. From the practical perspective, the valuation and hedging of credit derivatives should always be done with respect to liquid credit-risk sensitive instruments of a similar nature; ie, of a similar exposure with respect to the relevant risk factors. The latter point is illustrated by means of a credit default swap (CDS).

Default-free market

Consider an economy in continuous time, with time parameter $t \in \mathbf{R}_+$. We are given a filtered probability space (Ω, A, P^*) endowed with a one-dimensional standard Brownian motion W^*. It is convenient to assume that $\mathbf{F}$ is the P^*-augmented and right-continuous version of the natural filtration generated by W^*. As we shall now see, the filtration $\mathbf{F}$ will also play the role of the *reference filtration* for the default intensity. It is important to notice that all martingales with respect to a Brownian filtration $\mathbf{F}$ are necessarily continuous processes; this well-known property is used frequently below.

First, we introduce an arbitrage-free market model for default-free securities. Notice that all price processes introduced in this subsection are $\mathbf{F}$-adapted and continuous. In the default-free market, we have the following primary tradeable assets:

❏ a money market account B satisfying

$$dB(t) = r(t)B(t)dt, \ B(0) = 1$$

or, equivalently,

$$B(t) = exp\left(\int_0^t r(u)du\right) \qquad (18)$$

where $r(t)$ is an $\mathbf{F}$-adapted stochastic process;
❏ a default-free zero-coupon bond with the price process

$$B(t,T) = B(t) \ E_{Q^*}(B^{-1}(T)/F_t), \ t \leq T \qquad (19)$$

where T is the bond's maturity date; and
❏ a risky asset whose price dynamics under P^* are

$$dS(t) = S(t)(r(t) \ dt + \sigma(t) \ dW^*(t)), \ S(0) > 0, \qquad (20)$$

for some $\mathbf{F}$-progressively measurable volatility process σ.

For the sake of expositional simplicity, we assume that our model of default-free market is complete. The probability P^* is thus the unique martingale measure for the default-free market model. Let us finally notice that we may equally well assume that the Wiener process W^* is d-dimensional and $S = (S^1, ..., S^d)$ is the vector of prices of d risky assets. Recall that the completeness of such a market model is essentially equivalent to the non-degeneracy of the volatility matrix $\sigma(t)$.

Defaultable market
Most approaches have the following common features:

❑ completeness of a default-free market model is assumed;
❑ a default even is introduced through a suitable enlargement of the reference filtration;
❑ the default time is specified by postulating the form of the default intensity under an objective or a martingale probability;
❑ the enlarged model, with possibility of default, is consequently incomplete, unless tradeable defaultable securities are introduced; and
❑ default-free and defaultable contingent claims are priced through the risk-neutral valuation formula.

From the practical viewpoint, we are mainly interested in:

1. hedging default (jump) risk with the use of defaultable securities with similar features (jump and recovery rate) as the considered defaultable claim; and
2. hedging residual risk (credit spread risk) using either defaultable or default-free securities.

We might, for example, consider the hedging of a non-standard CDS using liquid (standard) CDSs of different maturities.

Simplified approach
In the financial industry, a simplified practical approach to the hedging of credit risk is commonly used. This is based on the following presumptions.

❑ A pure credit risk instrument (eg, a basic CDS) is considered.
❑ One considers a one-sided counterparty risk with a fixed recovery rate (the recovery rate is the same for a derivative product and for a corporate bond).
❑ Non-negativity of the marked-to-market value of the contract to a non-defaultable counterparty is postulated (defaultable loans and vulnerable options are thus covered, but defaultable swaps are beyond the scope).
❑ Independence of market and credit risks is assumed.

399

❑ Existence of a non-defaultable version of the contract and of a liquid market in corporate bonds is taken for granted.

Basic valuation formulae

We now present the basic valuation formule for defaultable claims within the reduced-form approach.

Default time

Let us assume that we are given the **F**-adapted, right-continuous, increasing process Γ on (Ω, A, P*). The default time t and the probability measure Q* are assumed to be constructed (see *Explicit Construction of a Default Time*, above). The probability Q* will play the role of the *martingale probability* for the defaultable market. It is essential to observe that:

❑ the Wiener process W* is also a Wiener process with respect to Γ under the probability measure Q*; and
❑ the restriction of Q* to F_t coincides with P* for every $t \in [0, T^*]$.

Defaultable term structure

For a defaultable discount bond with zero recovery it is natural to adopt the following definition of the price[6]

$$D^0(t, T) = B(t)E_{Q^*}(B^{-1}(T)\mathbf{1}(\tau > T)/G_t) = \mathbf{1}(t < \tau)\, D^{0,*}(t, T)$$

where $D^{0,*}(t, T)$ stands for the *pre-default value* of the bond. It can be shown to be given by the following equality

$$D^{0,*}(t, T) = \hat{B}(t)\, E_{Q^*}(\hat{B}^{-1}(T) \mid F_t)$$

where the *risk-adjusted savings account* $\hat{B}(t)$ equals

$$\hat{B}(t) = exp\left(\int_0^t (r(u) + \gamma(u))\, du\right)$$

Since **F** is assumed to be the Brownian filtration, the process $D^{0,*}(t, T)/\hat{B}(t)$ is a continuous, strictly positive, **F**-martingale. Therefore, the pre-default bond price $D^{0,*}(t, T)$ is a continuous, strictly positive F-semi-martingale. In the very special case when r and γ are constants, we obtain a simple representation

$$D^{0,*}(t, T) = exp(-(r + \gamma)(T - t)) = exp(-\gamma(T - t))\, B(t, T)$$

Note that the probability measure Q*, introduced above, is an essential input to the specification of defaultable term structure. Let us stress that we are here dealing with the modelling of bond prices $D^0(t, T)$, rather than with the arbitrage valuation of contingent claims. In this sense, the probability Q* is implied by the market through the calibration procedure, rather than derived through some formal mathematical arguments.

Valuation of a defaultable claim

Let Y be an F_T-measurable random variable representing the *promised payoff* at maturity date T. We consider a defaultable claim of the form $X = 1(T < \tau)Y$ – ie, a defaultable claim with zero recovery in case of default. A common approach to the valuation of defaultable claims is based on the following *risk-neutral valuation formula*

$$B(t)\, E_{Q^*}(B^{-1}(T)X/G_t) = B(t)\, E_{Q^*}(B^{-1}(T)Y\, 1(T < \tau)/G_t) = 1(t < \tau)V_t(X) \quad (21)$$

where

$$V_t(X) = \hat{B}(t)\, E_{Q^*}(\hat{B}^{-1}(T)Y\, /F_t) \quad (22)$$

The process $V_t(X)$ represents the *pre-default value* of X at time t. Notice that the process $V_t(X)/\hat{B}(t)$ is a continuous **F**-martingale (therefore $V_t(X)$ is a continuous **F**-semimartingale). The valuation formula presented in Equation (21), as well as the concept of pre-default value, should be supported by replication arguments. To this end, we must first construct a suitable model of a defaultable market. In fact, if we wish to use Equation (21), we need to know the joint law of all random variables involved – this is a non-trivial issue.

Trading strategies: default-free case

Next, we aim to present basic results relating to the concept of a self-financing trading strategy for a market model involving default-free and defaultable securities. For convenience's sake, we shall first briefly discuss the classic concepts of self-financing cash and futures strategies in the context of a default-free market model. It appears that in case of defaultable securities, only minor adjustments in definitions and results are needed.[7]

Cash strategies

Let $Z^0(t)$ and $Z^1(t)$ be the cash prices at time t of two tradeable assets, where Z^0 and Z^1 are continuous semi-martingales. Additionally, assume that the process Z^0 is strictly positive. We denote by $V(t)$ the wealth of the cash strategy (ϕ^0, ϕ^1) at time t, so that

$$V(t) = \phi^0(t)\, Z^0(t) + \phi^1(t)\, Z^1(t)$$

We say that the cash strategy (ϕ^0, ϕ^1) is self-financing if

$$dV(t) = \phi^0(t)dZ^0(t) + \phi^1(t)dZ^1(t)$$

This yields

$$dV(t) = (V(t) - \phi^1(t)Z^1(t))(Z^0(t))^{-1}\, dZ^0(t) + \phi^1(t)\, dZ^1(t)$$

Let us introduce discounted (relative) values $V^0(t) = V(t)/Z^0(t)$ and $Z^{1,0}(t) = Z^1(t)/Z^0(t)$. Using Itô's lemma, we get

$$V^0(t) = V^0(0) + \int_0^t \phi^1(u)dZ^{1,0}(u)$$

A similar result holds for any finite number of cash assets. Let $(Z^0(t),Z^1(t),...,Z^k(t))$ be cash values at time t of $k + 1$ primary assets. As before, $(Z^0,Z^1,...,Z^k)$ are assumed to be continuous semimartingales. Then the wealth process equals

$$V(t) = \phi^0(t) Z^0(t) + \phi^1(t) Z^1(t) + ... + \phi^k(t) Z^k(t)$$

and the strategy $(\phi^0, \phi^1, ..., \phi^k)$ is said to be self-financing if

$$dV(t) = \phi^0(t) dZ^0(t) + \phi^1(t) dZ^1(t) + ... + \phi^k(t) dZ^k(t)$$

By combining the last two formulae, we obtain

$$dV(t) = (V(t) - \sum_{i=1}^{k} \phi^i(t)Z^i(t)) (Z^0(t))^{-1} dZ^0(t) + \sum_{i=1}^{k} \phi^i(t) dZ^i(t)$$

Choosing Z^0 as a numeraire and denoting $V^0(t) = V(t)/Z^0(t)$, $Z^{i,0}(t) = Z^i(t)/Z^0(t)$, we get the standard result

$$V^0(t) = V^0(0) + \sum_{i=1}^{k} \int_0^t \phi^i(u) \, dZ^{i,0}(u)$$

Futures strategies
Now let $Z^0(t)$ and $Z^1(t)$ represent the cash and futures prices of some assets at time t, respectively. As before, we assume that Z^0 and Z^1 are continuous semi-martingales and Z^0 is a strictly positive process. In view of specific features of futures contracts, it is natural to postulate that the wealth V satisfies

$$V(t) = \phi^0(t) Z^0(t) + \phi^1(t) 0 = \phi^0(t) Z^0(t)$$

The futures strategy (ϕ^0, ϕ^1) is self-financing if

$$dV(t) = \phi^0(t) dZ^0(t) + \phi^1(t) dZ^1(t) \tag{23}$$

Thus, we have

$$dV(t) = V(t)(Z^0(t))^{-1} dZ^0(t) + \phi^1(t) dZ^1(t)$$

Proposition 3
The process $V^0(t) = V(t)/Z^0(t)$ satisfies $V^0(t) = V^0(0) + \int_0^t \phi^{1,0,\alpha}(u) \, dZ^{1,\alpha}(u)$ where

$$\phi^{1,0,\alpha}(t) = \phi^1(t)e^{\alpha(t)}/Z^0(t), \quad Z^{1,\alpha}(t) = Z^1(t) \, e^{-\alpha(t)}$$

and $\alpha(t) = \langle \ln Z^0, \ln Z^1 \rangle_t$.
This is proven because the above combined with Equation (23) yields

$$dV^0(t) = (Z^0(t))^{-1}dV(t) + V(t) \, d(Z^0(t))^{-1} + d<(Z^0)^{-1}, V>_t$$

$$= \phi^0(t)(Z^0(t))^{-1} \, dZ^0(t) + \phi^1(t)(Z^0(t))^{-1} \, dZ^1(t) + \phi^0(t)Z^0(t)d(Z^0(t))^{-1}$$

$$\phi^0(t)(Z^0(t))^{-2}d<Z^0, Z^0>_t - \phi^1(t)(Z^0(t))^{-2} \, d<Z^0, Z^1>_t$$

$$= \phi^1(t)(Z^0(t))^{-1} \, dZ^1(t) - \phi^1(t)(Z^0(t))^{-2} \, d<Z^0, Z^1>_t$$

$$= \phi^1(t) \, e^{\alpha(t)}(Z^0(t))^{-1} \, (e^{-\alpha(t)}dZ^1(t) - Z^1(t) \, e^{-\alpha(t)}d\alpha(t))$$

and the result follows.

Special cash strategies
Assume now that three assets are traded on the market and let (ϕ^0, ϕ^1, ϕ^2) be a self-financing strategy such that at any time there is zero net investment in Z^1 and Z^2 so that $\phi^1(t)Z^1(t) + \phi^2(t)Z^2(t) = 0$ or, equivalently, $\phi^2(t) = -\phi^1(t)Z^1(t)/Z^2(t)$.

Then, from

$$V(t) = \phi^0(t)Z^0(t)$$

and

$$dV(t) = \phi^0(t)dZ^0(t) + \phi^1(t)dZ^1(t) + \phi^2(t)dZ^2(t)$$

we get

$$dV(t) = V(t)(Z^0(t))^{-1} \, dZ^0(t) + \phi^1(t)(dZ^1(t) - Z^1(t)(Z^2(t))^{-1} \, dZ^2(t)) \qquad (24)$$

Let us denote

$$Z^{0,2}(t) = Z^0(t)/Z^2(t), \; Z^{1,2}(t) = Z^1(t)/Z^2(t)$$

The following result extends Proposition 3.

Proposition 4
The process $V^0(t) = V(t)/Z^0(t)$ satisfies

$$V^0(t) = V^0(0) + \int_0^t \phi^{1,0,\alpha}(u) \, dZ^{1,2,a}(u)$$

where

$$\phi^{1,0,a}(t) = \phi^1(t)e^{\alpha(t)}/Z^0(t), \; Z^{1,2,a}(t) = Z^{1,2}(t)e^{-a(t)}$$

and

$$a(t) = < \ln Z^{0,2}, \ln Z^{1,2} >_t$$

This is proven because when the discounted values of all considered processes are considered, with the price Z^2 being chosen as a numeraire, Equation (24) becomes

$$dV^2(t) = V^2(t)(Z^{0,2}(t))^{-1} \, dZ^{0,2}(t) + \phi^1(t) \, dZ^{1,2}(t)$$

where $V^2(t) = V(t)/Z^2(t)$. To conclude, it suffices to apply Proposition 3, and to note that $V^0(t) = V^2(t)/Z^{0,2}(t)$.

Note: suppose that $\sigma^{0,2}$ and $\sigma^{1,2}$ are the volatilities of $Z^{0,2}$ and $Z^{1,2}$ respectively, so that

$$dZ^{i,2}(t) = Z^{i,2}(t) \, (\mu^{i,2}(t) \, dt + \sigma^{i,2}(t) \, dW^*(t))$$

for $i = 0,1$. Then clearly

$$a(t) = \int_0^t \sigma^{0,}u \bullet \sigma^{1,2}(u) \, du$$

where $\bullet$ denotes the inner product. In a typical case, $\sigma^{0,2}(t)$ and $\sigma^{1,2}(t)$ (and thus also $a(t)$) will be deterministic functions.

Self-financing strategies with defaultable assets
First, we examine basic properties of general financial models involving default-free and defaultable securities. At this stage, our goal is to derive fundamental relationships. Subsequently, we will be more specific about the nature of these securities, and will furnish closed-form solutions for specific defaultable claims.

Case A: single defaultable tradeable asset and two default-free assets
For simplicity's sake, we assume zero recovery for the defaultable contingent claim X, as well as for the defaultable tradeable asset with the price process Z^0. Thus, at time τ, the wealth process of any strategy that replicates X should necessarily jump to zero. The process Z^0 vanishes at time of default (and thus also after this date). Nevertheless, it can be used as a numeraire prior to τ. Indeed, we have

$$Z^0(t) = \mathbf{1}(\tau > t)Z^{0,*}(t)$$

for some **F**-adapted process $Z^{0,*}(t)$. We assume that $Z^{0,*}$ is a strictly positive continuous **F**-semi-martingale (clearly $Z^{0,*} = V(X)$ for some defaultable claim X that settles at T, cf. (21)–(22)). On the other hand, it is obvious that the price process Z^0 jumps from $Z^{0,*}(t-)$ to 0 at default time τ.

Continuous **F**-semi-martingales Z^1 and Z^2 are assumed to model cash prices of tradeable default-free securities. We postulate that Z^2 is a strictly positive process. It is convenient to assume that the processes Z^1 and Z^2 are stopped at τ. Since we are going to deal with defaultable claims that are subject to the zero recovery scheme, it will be sufficient to examine replicating strategies on the random interval $[0, \tau \wedge T]$. For this reason, we shall postulate throughout that processes (ϕ^0, ϕ^1) and ϕ^2 are **F**-predictable, rather than **G**-predictable. In fact, it can be formally shown that for any **G**-predictable process ϕ there exists a unique **F**-predictable process Y such that $\mathbf{1}(\tau > t)\phi(t) = \mathbf{1}(\tau > t)Y(t)$ for every $t \in R_+$.

We consider a self-financing cash strategy (ϕ^0, ϕ^1, ϕ^2) such that at any time there is zero net investment in Z^1 and Z^2

$$\phi^1(t)Z^1(t) + \phi^2(t)Z^2(t) = 0, \tag{25}$$

that is,

$$\phi^2(t) = -\phi^1(t)Z^1(t)/Z^2(t)$$

We thus have $V(t) = \phi^0(t)Z^0(t)$ and

$$dV(t) = V(t-)(Z^{0,*}(t))^- \, dZ^0(t) + \phi^1(t)(dZ^1(t) - Z^1(t)(Z^2(t))^{-1} \, dZ^2(t))$$

Let us denote $Z^{0,*,2} = Z^{0,*}/Z^2$, $Z^{1,2} = Z^1/Z^2$. As the next result is a direct counterpart of Proposition 4, we do not present the proof here.

Proposition 5
The process V satisfies for $t \in [0,T]$

$$V(t) = Z^0(t) \left(V^0(0) + \int_0^t \phi^{1,b,*}(u) \, dZ^{1,2,b}(u)\right)$$

where

$$V^0(0) = V(0)/Z^{0,*}(0) = V(0)/Z^0(0)$$

and

$$\phi^{1,b,*}(t) = \phi^1(t)e^{b(t)}/Z^{0,*,2}(t) \quad Z^{1,2,b} = Z^{1,2} \, e^{-b(t)}, \quad b(t) = < \ln Z^{0,*,2} \,,\, \ln Z^{1,2} >_t$$

Case B: two defaultable tradeable assets
Assume that Z^0 and Z^1 are defaultable tradeable assets with zero recovery, and a common default time t. Then

$$Z^0(t) = \mathbf{1}(\tau > t) \, Z^{0,*}(t), \, Z^1(t) = \mathbf{1}(\tau > t) \, Z^{1,*}(t)$$

for some processes $(Z^{0,*}, Z^{1,*})$ that are assumed to be strictly positive, continuous, F-semimartingales. In this case, for any trading strategy (ϕ^0, ϕ^1) we have

$$V(t) = \phi^0(t) \, Z^0(t) + \phi^1(t) \, Z^1(t) = 0$$

on the set $\{\tau \le t\}$, ie, after default. In principle, we may thus directly apply such a strategy to the replication of a defaultable claim with zero recovery. We say that (ϕ^0, ϕ^1) is self-financing provided that

$$dV(t) = \phi^0(t-) \, dZ^0(t) + \phi^1(t-) \, dZ^1(t).$$

Simple considerations show that the wealth process V satisfies

$$dV(t) = (V(t-) - \phi^1(t-) \, Z^1(t-)) \, (Z^0(t-))^{-1} \, dZ^0(t) + \phi^1(t-)dZ^1(t)$$

or, equivalently,

$$dV(t) = (V(t-) - \phi^1(t-) \, Z^{1,*}(t-)) \, (Z^{0,*}(t))^{-1} \, dZ^0(t) + \phi^1(t-) \, dZ^1(t)$$

Proposition 6
The wealth process V satisfies for $t \in [0,T]$

$$V(t) = Z^0(t) \left(V^{0^*}(0) + \int_0^t \phi^1(u) \, dZ^{1^*,0^*}(u) \right)$$

where

$$V^{0^*}(0) = V(0)/Z^{0,*}(0) = V(0)/Z^0(0) \text{ and } Z^{1^*,0^*}(t) = Z^{1,*}/Z^{0,*}$$

To prove this, it is sufficient to note that, setting

$$V^*(t) = \phi^0(t) \, Z^{0,*}(t) + \phi^1(t) \, Z^{1,*}(t)$$

we have

$$dV^*(t) = \phi^0(t) \, dZ^{0,*}(t) + \phi^1(t) dZ^{1,*}(t)$$

Case C: single defaultable tradeable asset and a single default-free asset
Let us finally consider the case of two tradeable assets, with prices $Z^0(t) = \mathbf{1}(\tau > t) \, Z^{0,*}(t)$ and $Z^1(t)$, where $Z^{0,*}$, Z^1 are strictly positive, continuous, F-semi-martingales. We now have

$$V(t) = \phi^0(t)Z^0(t) + \phi^1(t)Z^1(t) = \phi^0(t)\mathbf{1}(\tau > t) \, Z^{0,*}(t) + \phi^1(t) \, Z^1(t)$$

and

$$dV(t) = (V(t-) - \phi^1(t)Z^1(t))(Z^{0,*}(t))^{-1} \, dZ^0(t) + \phi^1(t) \, dZ^1(t)$$

It is clear that the condition $V(t) = 0$ on $\{\tau \leq t\}$ implies $\phi^1(t) = 0$ for every $t \in \mathbf{R}_+$. Therefore,

$$dV(t) = V(t-)(Z^{0,*}(t))^{-1} \, dZ^0(t)$$

and the possibility of replication of a defaultable claim with zero recovery is unlikely within this setup (except for some trivial cases).

Replication and valuation of defaultable claims

First, we examine the possibility of an exact replication of a generic defaultable contingent claim with zero recovery. Formally, we consider a claim of the form $X = \mathbf{1}(\tau > T)Y$, where Y is some F_T-measurable random variable, representing the *promised payoff*.

Case A: single defaultable tradeable asset and two default-free assets
In view of Proposition 5, it is clear that a trading strategy (ϕ^0, ϕ^1, ϕ^2) replicates X whenever the following equality holds:

$$Z^{0,*}(T)\left(V^0(0) + \int_0^t \phi^{1,b,*}(t) \, dZ^{1,2,b}(T) \right) = Y$$

As usual, we say that a defaultable claim is *attainable* if it admits at least one replicating strategy. We thus have the following result.

Corollary 2

Suppose that a defaultable claim X is attainable. Let $Q^\#$ be a probability measure such that $Z^{1,2,b}$ is an F-martingale under $Q^\#$. Then the value at time 0 of X equals

$$V_0(X) = Z^0(0)E^\#(\,Y/Z^{0,*}(T))$$

Here $E^\#$ stands for the expectation under the probability $Q^\#$.

It is useful to notice that within the present setup the defaultable market is complete, provided that the underlying default-free market is complete (see *Default-free market*, above, for this assumption). Generally speaking, the attainability of a defaultable claim X is equivalent to attainability of the promised payoff Y in the default-free market.

Case B: two defaultable tradeable assets

We shall now make use of Proposition 6. Let us consider two defaultable tradeable assets Z^0 and Z^1, and an associated trading strategy (ϕ^0, ϕ^1). Clearly, it replicates a defaultable claim X whenever

$$Z^{0,*}(T)\,(V^0(0) + \int_0^T \phi^1(t)dZ^{1*,0*}(t)) = Y$$

Corollary 3

Suppose that a defaultable claim X is attainable. Let $Q^\wedge$ be a probability measure such that $Z^{1*,0*}$ is an **F**-martingale under $Q^\wedge$. Then the value at time 0 of X equals

$$V_0(X) = Z^0(0)\,E^\wedge(Y/Z^{0,*}(T))$$

Here $E^\wedge$ is the expectation under the probability $Q^\wedge$.

From the viewpoint of market completeness, the situation is different to the previous case. Indeed, a defaultable claim X is attainable if – and only if – the associated promised payoff X can be replicated with the use of pre-default value processes $Z^{0,*}$ and $Z^{1,*}$. In addition, even if a default-free asset is introduced, a replicating strategy for an arbitrary defaultable claim will always involve a null position in this asset. Therefore, the introduction of a tradeable default-free asset is not relevant if we restrict our attention to defaultable claims.

Equity derivatives

The dynamics of the stock price S are given by Equation (20). As a main example, we now show how to value and hedge a vulnerable European call option with the terminal payoff

$$\hat{C}(\,T) = \mathbf{1}(\tau > T)(S(T) - K)^+$$

Formally, we have

$$\hat{C}(\ T) = \mathbf{1}(_\tau > T)(S(T)\mathbf{1}(\tau > T) - K)^+ = (S(T)\mathbf{1}(\tau > T) - K)^+$$

and thus the contract can also be seen as either a vulnerable or non-vulnerable option on a defaultable stock. We argue that the financial interpretation of a particular real-life derivative contract is of great importance here. To show this, we consider several possible models, with different choices of tradeable assets that are used for hedging purposes. We show that both the claim's price and its hedging strategy depends on the model's choice.

Case A: single defaultable tradeable asset and two default-free assets
We first consider the case of a vulnerable option written on a non-defaultable stock. Specifically, the stock price process is assumed to be tradeable and default-free. In addition, we postulate that the default-free and defaultable zero-coupon bonds, maturing at time T, are also tradeable.

To value a vulnerable call option, we apply Corollary 2. Let us denote $F^S(t) = S(t)/B(t, T)$ and $\Gamma(t, T) = D^{0,*}(t, T)/B(t, T)$. It is important to observe that the process $\Gamma(t, T)$ is a continuous $\mathbf{F}$-sub-martingale, and it is an increasing process (in fact, an increasing function) if the intensity γ is deterministic (deterministic or random characters of interest rates are not relevant here).

Corollary 2 yields

$$\hat{C}(\ 0) = D(0,\ T)\ E^{\wedge}(Y) = \Gamma(0,\ T)\ B(0,\ T)\ E^{\wedge}(Y)$$

where $Q^{\wedge}$ is the martingale measure for the process $S^{\wedge}(t) = F^S(t)e^{-b(t)}$, and where in turn $b(t) = <\ln \Gamma(t, T), \ln F^S >_t$. If $\Gamma(t, T)$ is an increasing process, we have that $S^{\wedge}(t) = F^S(t)$ is the forward price of the stock. If interest rate r is deterministic then (see Equation 20)

$$dS^{\wedge}(t) = S^{\wedge}(t)\ \sigma\ dW^*(t),\ S^{\wedge}(0) = S(0)/B(0, T) \qquad (26)$$

The price $\hat{C}(\ 0)$ thus equals $\Gamma(0,T)C(0)$, where $C(0)$ denotes the Black–Scholes price of a (non-vulnerable) European call. This result can be easily generalised to the case of random interest rates (eg, within the Gaussian HJM framework).

Let us now examine hedging of a vulnerable option. In general, the replicating strategy for X satisfies, on the set $\{\tau > t\}$,

$$\phi^0(t)D^{0,*}(t, T) + \phi^1(t)S(t) + \phi^2(t)B(t, T) = V_t(X)$$

and

$$\phi^0(t)dD^{0,*}(t, T) + \phi^1(t)dS(t) + \phi^2(t)dB(t, T) = dV_t(X)$$

To hedge the jump risk perfectly, we need to take $\phi^0(t) = V_t(X)/D^{0,*}(t, T)$. Therefore necessarily $\phi^1(t)S(t) + \phi^2(t)B(t,T) = 0$. The *spread risk* (or the *volatility risk*) is hedged by matching the diffusion terms (recall that the completeness of the underlying default-free market was postulated). Note that the above trading strategy replicates the claim after the default time as well. The component ϕ^0 hedges the *jump risk* and the components (ϕ^1, ϕ^2) hedges the *spread risk*.

Now we formally consider a self-financing cash strategy (ϕ^0, ϕ^1, ϕ^2) such that at any time t there is zero net investment in stock and default-free bond, so that

$$\phi^1(t)S(t) + \phi^2(t)B(t, T) = 0$$

The following result is a straightforward consequence of Proposition 5.

Corollary 4
Assume that the default intensity γ is deterministic. Then the process V satisfies for $t \in [0,T]$

$$V(t) = D^0(t, T) \left[V(0)/D^0(0, T) + \int_0^t \phi^{1,\wedge}(u) \, dS^\wedge(u) \right]$$

where $\phi^{1,\wedge}(t) = \phi^1(t)\Gamma(t, T)$ and $S^\wedge(t) = F^S(t)$
This is proven, since because $\Gamma(t, T)$ is of finite variation, we have

$$b(t)=0, \ \phi^{1,\wedge}(t) = \phi^1(t)\Gamma(t,T) \text{ and } S^\wedge(t) = F^S(t)$$

Now consider the defaultable claim $\hat{C}(T) = \mathbf{1}(\tau > T)(S(T) - K)^+$. In view of Corollary 4, we need to find a constant c and a process $\phi^{1,\wedge}$ such that

$$c + \phi^{1,\wedge}(u) \, dS^\wedge(u) = c + \phi^{1,\wedge}(u) \, dF^S(u) = (S(T) - K)^+$$

It is clear that $\phi^{1,\wedge}$ coincides with the Black–Scholes replicating strategy and $V(0)/D^0(0, T) = C(0)/B(0, T)$, where $C(0)$ is the Black–Scholes price of a European call option. Thus the price at time 0 of $\hat{C}(T)$ equals $\Gamma(0, T)C(0)$.

Corollary 5
We have $\phi^{1,\wedge} = \psi$ where ψ is the Black–Scholes hedge ratio for the call option. The pre-default price at time t of $\hat{C}(T)$ equals $V_t(X) = \Gamma(t, T)C(t)$.

The component ϕ^0 of the replicating strategy for the vulnerable call option satisfies, on the set $\{\tau > t\}$,

$$\phi^0(t) = V_t(X)/D^{0,*}(0, T) = C(t)/B(t, T)$$

Moreover $\phi^1(t) = \psi(t)\Gamma(t, T)$ and $\phi^2(t) = \psi(t)\Gamma(t, T) \, F^S(t)$.
In a special case, assume that r and γ are constant. Then

$$\phi^0(t) = C(t)e^{r(T-t)}, \ \phi^1(t) = \psi(t) \, e^{-\gamma(T-t)}, \ \phi^2(t) = -\psi(t) \, e^{-(r-\gamma)(T-t)} \, S(t)$$

where $\psi(t) = N(d_1(S(t), T - t))$ is the classic Black–Scholes delta of a European call option.

Case B: two defaultable tradeable assets
We shall now consider the payoff

$$C^d(T) = \mathbf{1}(\tau > T)(S^*(T)\mathbf{1}(\tau > T) - K)^+ = (S^*(T)\mathbf{1}(\tau > T) - K)^+$$

representing a (vulnerable or non-vulnerable) option written on a default-able stock. To replicate this claim, we postulate that the stock price process is a tradeable, but defaultable, asset. Therefore, the price of the stock admits the following generic representation $S(t) = \mathbf{1}(\tau > t)\, S^*(t)$ where, by assumption, the pre-default price is governed by

$$dS^*(t) = S^*(t)\,(\mu(t)\,dt + \sigma\,dW^*(t))$$

In addition, we postulate that that the defaultable zero-coupon bond with maturity T is tradeable, with the price $D^0(t,T)$ and the pre-default price $D^{0,*}(t,\,T)$.

The valuation procedure is based on Corollary 3. The martingale property of the process $S^{*,0}(t) = S^*(t)/D^{0,*}(t,\,T)$ under $Q^\wedge$, is equivalent to

$$dS^*(t) = S^*(t)\,((\gamma(t) + r(t))dt + \sigma\,dW^*(t)).$$

The price at time 0 of the contract equals

$$C^d(0) = D^0(0,\,T)\,E^-(Y) = \Gamma(0,\,T)\,B(0,\,T)\,E^-(Y)$$

where Q^- is the martingale measure for the process $s^{*,0}(t)$ or, more explicitly,

$$C^d(0) = \Gamma(0,\,T)\,B(0,\,T)\,E^-(S^*(t) - K)^+.$$

In a special case, wherein r and γ are constant, the result is exactly the same as the Black–Scholes price of a European call, under the assumption that the interest rate equals $r^\wedge = r + \gamma$

Regards hedging: using Proposition 6, we arrive at the following equality for the wealth process V of a self-financing strategy:

$$V(t) = D^0(0,\,T)\,(V^0(0) + \int_0^t \phi^1(u)\,dS^{*,0}(u))$$

where $V^0(0) = V(0)/S(0)$. Replication of the claim $C^d(T)$ is thus equivalent to the following equality

$$c + \int_0^t \phi^1(u)\,dS^{*,0}(u) = (S^*(T) - K)^+$$

Again, it is rather clear that in the case of constant r and γ, the hedging strategy will be exactly the same as in the Black–Scholes model, but with the default-free interest rate substituted with the risk-adjusted interest $r^\wedge = r + \gamma$.

Credit derivatives

The most popular credit derivatives are CDS, total rate of return swap and credit linked notes (CLN). Furthermore, typical credit derivatives are linked to the default (credit) risk of several reference entities. We shall consider two examples: a CDS and and a specific first-to-default contract.

Credit default swap (CDS)
A generic CDS is a derivative contract that allows us to directly transfer the credit risk of the reference entity from one party (the risk seller) to another (the risk buyer). The contingent payment is triggered by the default event, provided that it occurs before the maturity of the contract. In one version of a CDS, the contract is settled at time t and the recovery payoff equals

$$Z(\tau) = (1 - \delta\, B(\tau,\, T))$$

The following two market conventions are common:

1) the buyer pays a lump sum at inception (*default option*), and
2) the buyer pays annuities k at the dates $0 < t_1, \ldots, t_{n-1} < t_n = T$ prior to τ (*default swap*)

In the first convention, the value $V(0)$ of the default option equals

$$V(0) = E_{Q^*}\, (B(\tau)^{-1}\, (1 - \delta\, B(\tau,\, T))\, \mathbf{1}(\tau \leq T))$$

In the second convention, the value of the contract at time 0 should be equal to zero. The right level of the annuity k can be found from the equality

$$V(0) = \kappa\, E_{Q^*}\!\left(\sum_{i=1}^{n} B^{-1}(t_i)\, \mathbf{1}(t_i < \tau) \right)$$

Digital CDSs
The fixed leg of a CDS can be represented as the sequence of payoffs $C_i = \kappa \mathbf{1}(t_i < \tau)$ at the dates t_i for $i = 1, \ldots, n$. The fixed leg of a CDS is, therefore, simply a portfolio of defaultable zero-coupon bonds. We consider a digital CDS and postulate that the floating leg is represeneted by the following sequence of payoffs

$$d_i = \delta\, \mathbf{1}(t_i < \tau \leq t_{i+1}) = \delta\, \mathbf{1}(\tau \leq t_{i+1}) - \delta\, \mathbf{1}(\tau \leq t_i)$$

at the dates t_{i+1} for $i = 1, \ldots, n - 1$. Clearly

$$d_i = \delta(1 - \mathbf{1}(t_{i+1} < \tau)) - \delta(1 - \mathbf{1}(t_i < \tau))$$

It is sufficient to value and replicate the payoff of the form $\mathbf{1}(t < \tau)$ which occurs at time t_{i+1}.

Delayed defaultable bond
Now we consider the payoff of the form $\mathbf{1}(T < \tau)$ which occurs at time $U > T$. To replicate this claim, it suffices to assume that default-free bonds with maturities T and U, as well as the defaultable bond with maturity T are tradeable.

The payoff $1(T < t)$ at time U is equivalent to $B(T, U)1(T < \tau)$ at time T. We are in position to apply Proposition 5 and Corollary 2. Thus, we have $\phi^1(t)$ $B(t, U) + \phi^2(t) B(t, T) = 0$ and the total pre-default value is invested in defaultable bonds. Moreover

$$b(t) = \int_0^t d_1(u,T) \bullet d_2(u,T) \, du$$

where $d_1(t,T)$ and $d_2(t,T)$ are the volatilities of $D^{0,*}(t,T)/B(t,T)$ and $B(t,U)/B(t,T)$, respectively. These volatilities depend on the model of default-free term structure and on the default intensity.

Basket credit derivatives
We shall now examine very briefly the valuation and hedging of *basket credit derivatives*. The main issue arising in this context is the modelling of dependent (correlated) defaults. We shall focus on the intensity-based approach to this problem.[9]

We make the basic assumption that the reference filtration is trivial, so that no volatility risk is present. Our goal is to show that the jump risk can be hedged using the underlying defaultable zero-coupon bonds with default times $\tau_1, \ldots, \tau_n$.

Recovery schemes and the values of (deterministic) recovery rates should, of course, be specified as well. This does not make the problem more complicated if the recovery schemes for the derivative contract and the hedging instruments are the same, albeit with possibly different values of recovery rates.

Let us describe very briefly Kusuoka's (1999) construction of default times for $n = 2$.[10] Under the original probability Q, the random times $\tau_i =$ $1, 2)$ are independent random variables with exponential laws with parameters λ_1 and λ_2, respectively. For a fixed $T > 0$, we define

$$dQ^* = \eta(T) \, dQ, \quad Q - a.s$$

where the process $\eta(t)$, $t \in [0, T]$, satisfies

$$\eta(t) = 1 + \sum_{i=1}^{2} \int_0^t \eta(u-)\kappa^i(u) \, dM^i(u)$$

where in turn

$$M^i(t) = 1(\tau_i \leq t) - \int_0^t 1(\tau_i > u)\lambda_i \, du$$

and

$$\kappa^1(t) = 1(\tau_2 < t)(\alpha_1 - \lambda_1)/\lambda_1, \quad \kappa^2(t) = 1(\tau_1 < t)(\alpha_2 - \lambda_2)/\lambda_2$$

It appears that the 'martingale intensities' under Q^* are

$$\lambda^1(t) = \lambda_1 \, 1(\tau_2 > t) + \alpha_1 \, 1(\tau_2 \leq t), \quad \lambda^2(t) = \lambda_2 \, 1(\tau_1 > t) + \alpha_2 \, 1(\tau_1 \leq t)$$

The following result shows that the intensities λ^1 and λ^2 can be interpreted as the *local intensities* of default with respect to the information available at time t. Therefore, the model can be reformulated as a two-dimensional Markov chain, see Lando (1998).

Proposition 7
For $i = 1, 2$ and every $t \in [0, T]$, we have

$$\lambda_i = lim_{h \downarrow 0} \, (1/h) \, Q^*(t < \tau_i \le t + h \mid \tau_1 > t, \tau_2 > t)$$

Moreover,

$$\alpha_1 = lim_{h \downarrow 0} \, (1/h) \, Q^*(t < \tau_1 \le t + h \mid \tau_1 > t, \tau_2 \le t)$$

and

$$\alpha_2 = lim_{h \downarrow 0} \, (1/h) \, Q^*(t < \tau_2 \le t + h \mid \tau_2 > t, \tau_1 \le t)$$

The next step is the valuation of defaultable bonds. As before, we assume that the defaultable bond is subject to zero recovery rule. Consequently, the price of the bond issued by the ith-firm is given by

$$D^0_1 (t, T) = Q^* (\tau_1 > T \mid H^1_t \vee H^2_t)$$

provided that the interest rate $r = 0$. The case of non-zero (or even random) interest rates can be dealt with in an analogous way.

Proposition 8
Assume that $\lambda_1 + \lambda_2 - \alpha_1 \ne 0$. Then on the set $\{t_1 > t\}$ the pre-default bond price $D^{0,*}_1(t, T)$ equals

$$D^{0,*}_1(t, T) = \mathbf{1}(\tau_2 > t)(\lambda - \alpha_1)^{-1} (\lambda_2 \, e^{-\alpha_1(T-t)} + (\lambda_1 - \alpha_1) \, e^{-\lambda(T-t)}) + \mathbf{1}(\tau_2 \le t) \, e^{-\alpha_1(T-t)}$$

where $\lambda = \lambda_1 + \lambda_2$.

Of course, an analogous formula holds for the price $D^0_2 (t, T)$ of the bond issued by the second firm. As an example of a basket credit derivative, we consider the first-to-default zero-coupon bond under the zero recovery rule. Thus we deal with the claim $X = \mathbf{1}(\tau > T)$ where $\tau = min(\tau_1, \tau_2)$. As hedging instruments, we take defaultable zero-coupons with default times τ_1 and τ_2.

Let us now describe the replicating strategy. At time t we hold $\phi_i(t)$ units of the bond defaulting at τ_j where $j \ne i$ and

$$\phi_i(t) = (\lambda_1 \lambda_2 \alpha_j) \, [(\alpha_1 - \lambda_1)(\alpha_2 - \lambda_2) - \lambda_1 \lambda_2]^{-1}$$

On the set $\{\tau > t\}$ we have

$$V_t(X) = \phi_1(t) \, D^{0,*}_1(t, T) + \phi_2(t) \, D^{0,*}_2(t, T)$$

where $D^{0,*}{}_i(t, T)$ are (explicitly known) pre-default values of defaultable bonds. On the set $\{\tau \leq t\}$ the wealth of the replicating strategy, as well as the value process $V_t(X)$, vanish.

CONCLUSIONS

As manifested by general results and illustrated by means of specific examples, the exact replication of credit derivatives is feasible within both the structural and the reduced-form frameworks, when suitable assumptions are made as to the availability of tradeable non-defaultable and/or defaultable securities that can be used for hedging.

Complete case: replication

Let us summarise once again the main steps of the replication procedure for a particular credit derivative:

1. specification of essential contractual features of a credit-risk-sensitive contract under study;
2. identification of risks – in most cases both the market and the credit risks are involved;
3. choice of the most convenient and adequate model – ie, structural, reduced-form or hybrid;
4. arbitrage-free valuation with respect to a martingale measure;
5. identification of tradeable (liquid) instruments – eg, corporate bonds – that can be used for hedging;
6. construction of a self-financing strategy, which replicates the value of a contract up to default time; and
7. calibration of the model to market prices of liquid instruments.

As in the case of non-defaultable claims, the practical hedging would be based on sensitivities of the price of a given contract with respect to risk factors, rather than on the dynamic replication. The study of the replicating strategy is therefore only the first step towards a real-life hedging.

Incomplete case: mean-variance hedging

Generally speaking, if the set of tradeable assets does not include a defaultable asset, the defaultable market is incomplete and thus exact replication of defaultable claims is not feasible. In this context, the issue of imperfect hedging of contingent claims therefore arises in a natural way. For more details on a specific way of mean-variance hedging of credit derivatives, we suggest the recent work by Bielecki and Jeanblanc (2003).

BIBLIOGRAPHY

Bélanger, A., S. Shreve, and D. Wong, 2001, "A Unified Model for Credit Derivatives", to appear in *Mathematical Finance*.

Bielecki, T., and M. Jeanblanc, 2003, "Mean-Variance Hedging of Credit Risk: A Case Study", working paper.

Bielecki, T., and M. Rutkowski, 2002, *Credit Risk: Modelling, Valuation and Hedging*, (Berlin: Springer-Verlag; New York: Heidelberg).

Bielecki, T., and M. Rutkowski, 2003, "Dependent Defaults and Credit Migrations", *Applicationes Mathematicae*, 30, pp. 121–45.

Black, F., and J.C. Cox, 1976, "Valuing Corporate Securities: Some Effects of Bond Indenture Provisions", *Journal of Finance*, 31, pp. 351–67.

Black, F., and M. Scholes, 1973, "The Pricing of Options and Corporate Liabilities", *J. Political Economy*, 81, pp. 637–54.

Blanchet-Scalliet, C., and M. Jeanblanc, 2000, "Hazard Rate for Credit Risk and Hedging Defaultable Contingent Claims", to appear in *Finance and Stochastics*.

Collin-Dufresne, P., and J.-N. Hugonnier, 1999, "On the Pricing and Hedging Of Contingent Claims in the Presence of Extraneous Risks", working paper, Carnegie Mellon University.

Duffie, D., and D. Lando, 2001, "The Term Structure of Credit Spreads with Incomplete Accounting Information", *Econometrica*, 69, pp. 633–64.

Elliott, R.J., M. Jeanblanc, and M. Yor, 2000, "On models of Default Risk", *Mathematical Finance*, 10, pp. 179–195.

Greenfield, Y., 2000, "Hedging of Credit Risk Embedded in Derivative Transactions", Thesis, Carnegie Mellon University.

Jamshidian, F., 2002, "Valuation of Credit Default Swap and Swaptions", working paper.

Jeanblanc, M., and M. Rutkowski, 2002, "Default Risk and Hazard Process", *Bachelier Congress 2000*, (Berlin: Springer-Verlag; New York: Heidelberg).

Jeanblanc, M., and M. Rutkowski, 2003, "Hedging of Credit Derivatives within the Reduced-Form Framework", working paper.

Kusuoka, S., 1999, "A Remark on Default Risk Models", *Adv. Math. Econom.* 1, pp. 69–82.

Lando, D., 1998, "On Cox Processes and Credit-Risky Securities", *Rev. Derivatives Res.* 2, pp. 99–120.

Leland, H.E., 1994, "Corporate Debt Value, Bond Covenants, and Optimal Capital Structure", *Journal of Finance*, 49, pp. 1213–52.

Lotz, C., 1998, "Locally Minimizing the Credit Risk", working paper, University of Bonn.

Lukas, S., 2001, "On Pricing and Hedging Defaultable Contingent Claims", thesis, Humboldt University, Berlin.

Merton, R., 1974, "On the pricing of Corporate Debt: the Risk Structure of Interest Rates", *Journal of Finance*, 29, pp. 449–70.

Schönbucher, P.J., 1998, "Pricing Credit Risk Derivatives", working paper, University of Bonn.

Vaillant, N., 2001, "A Beginner's Guide to Credit Derivatives", working paper, Nomura International.

Wong, D., 1998, "A Unifying Credit Model", working paper, Research Advisory Services, Capital Markes Group, Scotia Capital Markets.

Zhou, C., 1996, "A Jump-Diffusion Approach to Modeling Credit Risk and Valuing Defaultable Securities", – working paper, Federal Reserve Board, Washington.

Section 5

Regulatory, Documentation and Legal Aspects

Introduction

Jon Gregory

BNP Paribas

In a market where information is freely accessible, risk will be transferred from risk-averse institutions to less risk-averse protection sellers. Access to such information is an important component in the growth of a market such as credit derivatives. One problem that can exist is that of asymmetric information. For example, a protection buyer and seller may not have access to the same information as to a probability of default, and this may prevent some otherwise beneficial transfer of risk. Another potential problem is moral hazard, which is a classic problem in insurance and can occur if one party changes its behaviour to the detriment of another party. For example, one party in a CDS can influence the probability of a credit event indirectly, such as refusing to extend credit. Indeed, this occurred with the Conseco restructuring example, as some of the protection buyers were among the company's lenders who, presumably, could "influence" the restructuring. In a CDO transaction, the manager may hold some or all of the equity tranche to limit moral hazard. This may assure note holders that management will be for the benefit of maximising the return and/or minimising the risk on the structure. That said, the tranche risk profiles differ, so, given that the manager is at the bottom of the capital structure, there may be incentive to take above-average risks with the aim of achieving a high level of equity returns.

The rapid growth of the credit derivatives market has created many operational risks. It has been hard for back and middle offices of banks to keep pace with the developments on the trading desk. Furthermore, the required legal structure has not developed at the same pace as the products themselves. There is a clear need for effective systems and controls so as to avoid documentation errors, especially for portfolio transactions for which the documentation can be rather complex. This final section aims to deal with some of the important regulatory, documentation and legal aspects, whose development is crucial in supporting the continuing progression of the credit derivatives market. All of the relevant topics, including standardisation of documentation, rating-agency approaches and portfolio credit risk modelling, are covered.

A derivatives market will obviously suffer if there is a lack of consensus on the underlying documentation and the development and use of standardised documentation has been crucial to the growth of the CDS market. For example, this limits the possibility that buyers or sellers of protection may be exposed to unforeseen basis risk due to credit-event definitions, settlement procedures, reference assets or deliverable obligations. **Louise Marshall** from the **ISDA** highlights the issues that the market has faced and will continue to face in order to sustain its growth, including a summary of the changes in the ISDA 2003 Credit Derivatives Definitions. This chapter covers the problems regarding credit-event definitions (most derivatives payoffs are quite easy to define, whereas those coming from credit events are not so), which need to be continually updated after such events as the Conseco restructuring or the UK energy company National Power demerger. This chapter also discusses accounting and taxation issues, in the former case, the "fair value" accounting due to be introduced in 2005 via IAS39 could have a significant effect on the CDO market since it suggests that they must be "marked-to-market", although these issues are still currently under debate.[1]

In the next chapter in this section, **Rodanthy Tzani** and **Maria Leibholz** of **Moody's Investor Services** discuss credit-linked notes, covering in detail the structure of these products in relation to funding considerations and collateral, definition of credit events and payment structures. They also give details of the role of an SPV in such a transaction. Finally, the authors then give an overview of the rationale in rating these structures and the quantitative methodology used by Moody's to calculate ratings. Such a methodology should give (via a rating) an accurate summary of the relative strength of a given structure, which will clearly represent all possible elements ranging from individual default probabilities and diversification to potential legal issues. As I discussed in Section 3, it is clearly important that these methodologies be improved both in terms of the estimation of parameters and underlying model, so as to give investors the best possible idea of the underlying risk in portfolio products that are becoming increasingly sophisticated. It is equally important that investors seek to better understand the complex products and risks they are taking on.

An important motivation for banks involved in the credit derivatives market has been regulatory. The 1988 Basel Accord (Basel I) defines an 8% regulatory capital charge on corporate exposures. In particular, since the capital charge does not recognise credit quality, so a short-term investment-grade loan carries the same capital charge as a longer-maturity sub-investment-grade asset. This has led to regulatory capital arbitrages and given banks the incentive to transfer risk either using single-name protection or via a balance-sheet CDO. Basel I gives a strong incentive for high-quality assets to be transferred, the resulting decrease in capital being out of line with any actual gain in terms of risk reduction. Such misalignments of capital requirements and real economic risk should be improved with the new Basel capital accord (Basel II). Furthermore, as banks have implemented internal economic capital models, the differences between economic capital and regulatory capital charges are much more apparent. In the final chapter, **Erik Heitfield** of the **Federal Reserve Board** discusses the use of credit derivatives to manage credit risk under Basel II. This will allow use of a one-year probability of default (PD), which will mean that lower-risk assets will attract a lower capital charge than more risky ones. However, in contrast with market risk, credit risk modelling is not sufficiently well advanced to recognise directly default correlations in calculating capital requirements. Under Basel I, protection buyers may replace the risk weighing of an asset with that of an eligible protection seller. In Basel II, the range of eligible protection sellers has been widely expanded but the author argues that this proposed substitution approach will be still rather conservative in most cases.

1   The US equivalent of IAS39, FAS 133, is already in place.

19

ISDA's role in the credit derivatives marketplace

Louise Marshall

International Swaps and Derivatives Association

As is typical across the range of asset classes underlying privately negotiated derivatives, the role of the International Swaps and Derivatives Association (ISDA) in the credit derivatives market is diverse. As one would expect, ISDA has played a significant role in establishing the underlying documentation for credit derivatives, this being the area of expertise for which the Association is most widely known. However, the Association has also been extremely active in lobbying for appropriate capital treatment under the new Basel rules, and also in regional regulatory, tax and accounting jurisdictions. Not least, ISDA has served as a forum for market practitioners to address issues relating to the trading conventions best suited to this marketplace.

ISDA also monitors the continued development of the credit default swap (CDS) market. CDSs have become commoditised derivative products to much the same effect as plain vanilla interest rate swaps,

---

Panel 1
ABOUT ISDA

ISDA is the global trade association representing leading participants in the privately negotiated derivatives industry. ISDA was chartered in 1985, and today has more than 600 member institutions from 46 countries on six continents. These members include most of the world's major institutions that deal in privately negotiated derivatives, as well as many of the businesses, governmental entities and other end users that rely on over-the-counter (OTC) derivatives to manage efficiently the financial market risks inherent in their core economic activities.

---

accounting for the larger part of the credit derivatives market. In its sampling for the first six months of 2002, ISDA estimated the market size for CDS notional volume at US$1.6 trillion, an increase of 44% for that period. In the following six months to year-end 2002, statistics for the same product set showed an increase of 37% to US$2.15trillion. These figures represent outstanding notional volumes in single name default swaps, baskets of ten or fewer default swaps, and portfolio swaps of ten credits or more.

DOCUMENTATION AND THE ROLE OF ISDA

It is unlikely that the market could have accelerated at this pace without a sound infrastructure. One of the Association's principal undertakings in relation to the CDS market has been, and continues to be, that of establishing a secure framework of robust documentation and legal certainty. These and other privately negotiated derivatives products benefit from the existing documentation platform provided by the ISDA's Master Agreement and credit support documentation, supported by the legal certainty of enforceability through the netting and collateral opinions commissioned by the Association. In terms of the CDS market itself, this foundation supports the product-specific work that led to the 1998 publication of the ISDA Long-Form Confirmation for CDSs and, in 1999, the ISDA Credit Derivatives Definitions. The latter has become the cornerstone of default swap documentation, enabling smooth functioning and standardisation in the market.

As with all nascent markets, development is defined in part by tests of the infrastructure. In 2001, ISDA addressed such tests by publishing three supplements to the 1999 Definitions. The first of these responded to one of the more significant tests the credit derivatives market has faced: the so-called restructuring issue. Its inclusion as one of the credit events in default swap documentation is intended to guard against the eventuality of the debt of a reference entity losing economic value after the restructuring of its debt. Discussions around the nature of corporate restructuring were triggered by the Conseco case in the United States. In September 2000, the restructuring of Conseco's bank loan debt resulted in some market participants availing themselves of a so-called 'cheapest-to-deliver option', whereby buyers of protection were able to deliver lesser value securities than the bank loans being hedged (see Chapter 4 for more detail).

This created a lot of unrest in the default swap market, as participants endeavoured to close the documentation loophole that had permitted this to happen. But the market was at odds over how the documentation should be amended to avoid similar occurrences in the future. ISDA hosted numerous discussions around the issue of a new restructuring clause, and in January 2001 formed the Credit Derivatives Market Practice

Committee, which enabled traders in the CDS market to exchange views on issues of business practice. Tackling the restructuring issue was the committee's first challenge. Subcommittees were formed with members of the market's three main constituencies – protection sellers, protection buyers, and dealers – and were established in London and New York, the two main centres for the credit derivatives market. A representative for each of the constituencies in each location was appointed as the primary interlocutor to the working group, which became known as the Group of Six (the G6).

The G6 set to work on revising the restructuring clause, aiming to provide an acceptable documentation solution through the members' respective business input. Between January and May of 2001, the working group operated via the six constituencies/subcommittees of the G6 and alongside ISDA's Documentation Committee to draft an appropriate solution to the cheapest-to-deliver option.

Published in May 2001, the new version of the restructuring credit event became known as 'Modified Restructuring' in the market. Modified Restructuring was widely adopted by the North American market, and is now one of four choices offered in the 2003 Definitions. Under this revised definition, the deliverable obligation must be fully transferable with no consent required. Ultimately, the European market chose not to trade with this version due to issues associated with regulations on transferability of obligations. The ISDA Credit Derivatives Market Practice Committee and the ISDA Documentation Committee therefore set to work on a third version, commonly referred to as Modified Modified Restructuring ('Mod Mod R'), which was developed over the course of 2002 and published in the new 2003 Definitions.

Under Mod Mod R, the maturity of the restructured bond or loan may be up to 60 months after the restructuring date, but for all other deliverable obligations, the maturity may be only up to 30 months. Perhaps more significantly, the deliverable obligation must be 'conditionally transferable'; therefore consent may not be unreasonably withheld. By consensus, participants in the European market agreed to implement this version on the recommended global implementation date for the 2003 ISDA Credit Derivatives Definitions, which was set for 20 June, 2003.

FOUR CHOICES

The 2003 Definitions offer parties four choices relating to restructuring:

1. To trade with 'full' or 'old' restructuring, with no modification to the deliverable obligations aspect;
2. To trade with Modified Restructuring, as has been market practice in North America since the publication of the Restructuring Supplement in May 2001;

3. To trade with Mod Mod R, the new provision, which generally aims to address issues raised in the European market; or

4. To trade without restructuring.

The latter approach has gained support in several areas, and while it is not strictly speaking a documentation solution, it does demonstrate that the new Definitions reflect another stage in the development of a relatively new market. It has been a significant development amidst many attempts to fit the infrastructure to user requirements.

At an early stage in the ISDA discussions, it became clear that end-user protection sellers wanted to limit the amount of exposure to restructuring risk they could attract through use of CDSs to the extent that, in some cases, they decided to eliminate it from the list of credit events they would sell protection on. An argument presented in favour of doing so was that many banks only want to buy protection against restructuring because it is a requirement under Basel.

Many market participants – most vociferously protection sellers, but also some dealers and banks – have argued that there is no economic necessity for the restructuring clause in a default swap contract. The current requirement under the Basel capital rules, however, means that it must be included in order for banks to obtain full capital relief on loans hedged with these products. Many participants argue that it is this requirement that has perpetuated its inclusion in many standard contracts; others favour a more conservative approach and say they would prefer to have the option to purchase restructuring protection regardless of capital requirements. Some firms have dropped restructuring from their standard trades, but the market at large is awaiting final confirmation on this point from Basel before adopting it as standard across the board.

These proponents believe it is possible to consider a loan as being fully hedged if the contract by which it is hedged does not contain a restructuring clause. They argue that, in effect, the risk of economic loss arising from restructuring is significantly mitigated by the other main credit events under ISDA documentation. One consideration offered up in discussions with the Basel Committee was to offer capital relief on CDSs lacking a restructuring clause, as long as the maturity of the swap matched the maturity of the underlying loan. Banks' reaction to this was that it was not only a specious argument, but it was also very easy to arbitrage.

Ultimately, ISDA and its fellow associations seem to have successfully defended the view that capital relief is warranted in most cases without the need for the derivative to hedge restructuring risk. Early indications have been that the requirement will be dropped, but it now remains to be seen how closely the Basel Committee's new Accord will reflect this.

KEY CHANGES

In addition to the new restructuring clause, key changes represented in the 2003 ISDA Credit Derivatives Definitions versus the 1999 Definitions include the following.

A new test for identifying the successor to a reference entity

In a new approach, the 2003 Definitions offer a new numerical threshold test. Under the 1999 Definitions, the test was whether the new entity had assumed 'all or substantially all' of the assets of the reference entity. However, this test proved to be problematic in circumstances where the quantitative split between the obligations and assets of the old and new entity were fairly close. Thus, a series of quantitative thresholds are set forth in the 2003 Definitions.

Amendments to various credit events, including bankruptcy, repudiation/ moratorium

Besides restructuring, the other credit events amended in the 2003 Definitions were bankruptcy and repudiation/moratorium. In the context of sovereign CDSs, the repudiation/moratorium credit event was amended following discussions among members after the Argentina debt crisis in 2001 and 2002. Under the 2003 Definitions, a more specific trigger for the credit event is offered.

Alternative procedures for non-deliverable bonds and loans

A binding notice of Physical Settlement was introduced. Under the 2003 Definitions, the buyer is required to notify the seller of the deliverable obligations it will deliver. The buyer may send the seller multiple notices until the physical settlement date, with the last notice being binding.

Guarantees

The 2003 Definitions clarify that the obligations of a reference entity can be its direct obligations. These include an obligation of a 'Downstream Affiliate', called a 'Qualifying Affiliate Guarantee', or an obligation of a third party guaranteed by the reference entity, called a 'Qualifying Guarantee'. This last category of third party guarantees is only included if the parties specify as such in their confirmation.

Novation provisions

A new article was introduced to address the novation or assignment of credit derivative transactions. A Novation Agreement and a Novation Confirmation are also offered to assist parties in documenting and obtaining the requisite consents to the assignment of such transactions.

Many of ISDA's efforts in the area of documentation for credit derivatives have focused on the deliverable assets in the event of a restructuring clause being included in a default swap. Looking to the future, ISDA has undertaken to review the trigger events that precipitate a settlement, as well as issues surrounding the bankruptcy trigger in relation to a CDS.

OTHER AREAS OF CONSIDERATION
Accounting

A further area of ISDA involvement in the CDS market is that of accounting across many jurisdictions. Under IAS 39, the International Accounting Standards Board's standard for fair value accounting, credit derivatives reporting will come onto the balance sheet. This means they will be marked to market, unlike underlying loan books, which are accounted for on an accrual basis.

Under existing accounting standards outside the United States, derivatives and other hedges have qualified for hedge accounting treatment, which does not require marking to market (and can therefore be marked-to-model). A key concern now is that in order to qualify for hedge accounting treatment, a derivative must exactly match the underlying transaction, thus presenting a significant issue in respect of CDSs used to hedge loan portfolios.

This standard, which is set for implementation in 2005, mirrors that of the Financial Accounting Standards Board's (FASB) FAS 133 in the United States, which has been in effect for several years. While the issues are of concern to ISDA's European members, firms that report both inside and outside the United States do not want to cloud the issue further by reporting on a different basis in different centres. They are continuing to do so through ISDA while independently working towards acceptable standards for reporting practices.

Taxation

Credit derivatives market participants are also attempting to rationalise a layer of complexity relating to the treatment of these instruments for taxation purposes. In the United States, the Internal Revenue Service (IRS) has sought industry guidance on the nature of these instruments as compared to both guarantees and insurance contracts. While credit derivatives are neither of these things, the industry view is that in order to qualify for treatment as financial instruments, they must fit a series of criteria. They must be documented under an ISDA Master Agreement, to which one party must be a dealer under Rule 475, and the reference obligation must not be related to the credit protection buyer or the credit protection seller. Should the IRS choose to determine that credit derivatives constitute *insurance*, they would fall subject to excise tax at 4% on each transaction. Should CDSs be deemed to be *guarantees* for taxation purposes, they would be subject to withholding tax at 30% on each transaction.

ISDA and its members provided the comments requested by the

IRS (in a letter dated 2 May, 2003, available from ISDA's Website: www.isda.org), and continue to seek certainty for these products in North America. In a reversal of the situation in the accounting arena, Europe has already achieved certainty on CDSs, where they are subject to derivatives taxation treatment.

Regulation and risk management

For regulatory purposes, there are efforts and initiatives underway to address certainty of treatment in many jurisdictions. These instruments have attracted regulatory attention in the United Kingdom, for example, where the regulatory framework for insurance and securities is contained within the same body, the Financial Services Authority (FSA). Consequently, ISDA and its membership have been keen to distinguish these products from insurance products.

ISDA's Risk Management Committee, through its Credit Risk Mitigation Working Group, has been particularly active in its discussions with regulators on the issue of capital relief attained through use of CDSs. ISDA has received encouraging news from the Credit Risk Mitigation Sub-Group of the Basel Committee, which is chaired by Norah Barger of the Federal Reserve Board. Working with this sub-group, ISDA has often joined forces with the London Investment Banking Association (LIBA), the Bond Market Association (BMA), and the Risk Management Association (RMA) on issues of capital adequacy.

Practices for handling non-public information in credit portfolio risk management

In response to concerns expressed by the investor community, ISDA – along with the International Association of Credit Portfolio Managers, the Loan Syndications and Trading Association, and the Bond Market Association – has been actively working towards standards and practices for the handling and use of material non-public information when financial institutions engage in credit portfolio risk management activities. This is an issue of common interest to the various constituent memberships, and to other credit market participants.

Through an *ad hoc* working group known as the Joint Market Practice Forum, the associations have published a document for industry review and comment entitled *Statement of Principles and Recommendations Regarding the Handling of Material Non-public Information by Credit Market Participants*.[1] The associations anticipate that this document will be helpful in raising awareness within the industry on important issues arising from the management of credit portfolio risk. The document suggests controls and procedures that firms may wish to consider employing to ensure compliance with applicable law and sound business practice. It also addresses the applicability of securities laws in the United States, along with related practices that credit market participants may wish to consider with respect to trading credit derivatives. Initial responses to the document from regulators and end investors alike have been favourable, and the Joint Market Practice Forum anticipates a move to publish the document in final form in July 2003.

Effective collaboration has taken place between members from all constituencies of the marketplace, fellow trade associations, regulators, and rating agencies. It is only within the context of a secure and supportive legal and regulatory framework that a market the size of the credit derivatives market can continue to flourish. As the market continues to develop and mature, ISDA and its documentation will continue to adapt to its needs.

SUMMARY

In this area of the market more than any other, the development of sound market practice is inexorably intertwined with that of documentation, regulation, risk management, accounting, and taxation. The smooth functioning of the product and its usefulness as a risk management tool are contingent upon the appropriate treatment in respect of all of these issues. Through its membership, ISDA continues to work for as much flexibility as the marketplace requires, in order that it may flourish.

---

1   *Statement of Principles and Recommendations Regarding the Handling of Material Nonpublic Information by Credit Market Participants.*

20

Credit linked notes

Rodanthy Tzani and Maria Leibholz*

Moody's Investors Service

WHAT ARE CREDIT LINKED NOTES AND WHO USES THEM?

Credit linked notes (CLNs) are debt instruments whose payments are tied to the performance of the debt obligations of selected entities or "reference entities" – ie, they are linked to the credit quality of the reference entities' obligations. The cashflow promised to the holder of the CLN note depends on the occurrence of pre-specified events ("credit events") in the reference entities, specifically default within the asset pool. Depending on the transaction, the underlying portfolio can consist of a single reference entity or many.

The performance of the reference entity obligations is linked to the CLNs through a simple bilateral agreement in which one party agrees to absorb losses beyond a specified level, or through a derivative contract known as a credit default swap (CDS).[1] We explain both arrangements below. The opposite party to the swap (or agreement) is referred to as the swap counterparty or simply the counterparty.

The CLN structure is meant to transfer the credit risk associated with the underlying reference entities to the CLN holder and away from the counterparty. The note holder agrees to "pay" the counterparty on the occurrence of the specified events. Essentially, the CLN structure provides the counterparty with protection (ie, credit protection) to help them hedge against specific risk factors beyond a specified threshold in a particular sector.

* The authors wish to acknowledge the following colleagues, each of whom have contributed valuable analytical perspective and experience: Moody's managing director William May and Moody's senior vice president, David Teicher, Derivatives-Structured Finance as well as Professor Alexios Polychronakos, physics department, City College of CUNY. The authors also wish to acknowledge senior editor and financial writer Dale Wagner, Moody's Rating Communications.

The CLN note holder, who is "selling" credit protection, is motivated by the opportunity to invest in the credit performance of a specified sector, without direct ownership of the underlying assets. The structures have become popular with investors because they allow access to previously unavailable markets. They also allow investors to take advantage of tax arbitrage opportunities. CLNs are sometimes referred to as "synthetic" transactions because they enable the note holder to re-create (ie, to synthe-sise) the credit risk exposure of specified industries or entities without purchasing the assets.

For example, a counterparty that is exposed to the credit risk of a number of entities enters into a CLN and buys credit protection on these entities. The holders of the CLN agree to pay for losses stemming from defaults on the obligations of these entities – in this way, they sell credit protection.[2] In another example, the counterparty uses a reference port-folio to arbitrage (ie, they take a short position) and gets paid for defaults occurring in a specific selection of reference entities.

CLNs have also been used extensively in securitisations of banks' port-folios. Regulatory capital requirements imposed by the Basel Committee Capital Accord encourage lending institutions to use securitisation tech-niques to free-up their lines of credit by moving loan portfolios off their balance sheets. By allowing a special purpose vehicle (SPV) to have full exposure to the credit risk of the loan portfolio without the full transfer of a legal title, banks are able to decrease capital requirements without obtaining requisite consents and incurring the expense associated with a loan sale. Additionally, the volatility of a high-yield market can be miti-gated, marginally, by the instant diversification provided by a note linked to the credit of a basket of underlying securities.

There are two basic CLN transaction types.

❏ In the *counterparty-funded* structure, the CLNs are issued directly by the counterparty, who receives the proceeds from the issuance and sale of the CLNs, and promises to make the interest and principal payments to the CLN holders.
❐ In the *SPV-funded* structure, the CLNs are issued by a special purpose vehicle (SPV),[3] typically a trust, which holds the proceeds from the issuance and sale of the CLNs and enters into a swap agreement with the counterparty.

In each case, however, the payments on the CLNs are ultimately tied to the performance of the reference entity obligations.

In this chapter, we describe the two different types of CLN: counter-party-funded and SPV-funded. We explain the CLNs' structural elements, payments and economics, reference pools, and their definitions of credit events. We continue by explaining Moody's rating methodology, including the modelling approach and legal analysis. We end by presenting our conclusions.

UNDERSTANDING COUNTERPARTY-FUNDED CREDIT LINKED NOTES

As we have already explained, a counterparty-funded CLN is issued directly by the counterparty to the investors, usually through a specific note program. The payments on the note are linked to a number of pre-defined credit events in the pool of reference entities. The investors (ie, note holders) pay the note's face value to the issuer, who is then obliged to pay periodic interest ("coupon") and the invested principal at maturity, if no credit events occur in the reference pool. Because the transactions are "structured", there may be several notes written against a given pool, each bearing different levels of risk.[4]

If credit events occur during the life of the transaction, the promised cashflow (either interest or principal) may be reduced by an amount equal to the losses occurring due to the agreed on credit events.

The clear difference between CLN and cashflow CBO transactions is that, in cashflow transactions, the reference entities' obligations are held directly by the issuer and the losses in the transaction are associated with defaults on a specific obligation. In a CLN, however, the issuer doesn't typically own the assets of the pool and the note holder is exposed to the reference entity's risk across all of the entities' outstanding obligations.

Thus, the scope of the applicable credit risk depends on how the specific credit events are defined. Clearly, a broad definition of credit events introduces more risk into the transaction than a narrow and very precise definition.

Definition of credit events

A credit event is typically defined as the occurrence of one of the following events with respect to underlying obligors in the reference pool.

1. *Bankruptcy* is defined in the ISDA[5] credit derivatives definitions and refers to the underlying obligors of the reference entities of the reference pool.
2. A *failure to pay* event is defined as missed or delayed payments of interest or principal under any obligations of the reference entity. A minimum amount, usually US$1 million, is required to define a meaningful failure to pay event.
3. *Restructuring* of a specified obligation of a reference entity in the pool triggers a credit event for the purpose of the CLN transaction. The meaning of restructuring is broad and somewhat ill-defined, but, as discussed in the previous chapter, the industry has been working on narrowing this definition within the standard ISDA credit derivatives definitions.[6] There are three standard versions of the restructuring

definition that are used globally: the "old restructuring", the "modified restructuring" and the "modified-modified restructuring". The first one is typically used in Europe, the second in the US and the third in Asia. ISDA is still working to reach consensus on a global structure for trading on restructuring. A minimum amount of US$10 million is usually required for the obligation that is restructured to qualify for a credit event.[7]

The typical reference portfolio

The reference portfolio can consist of just one reference entity or a number of reference entities. Each of the entities is assigned a reference amount (the "notional"), which is a percentage of the total value of the pool.

The pool can be *static*, which means that it does not allow changes or replacements throughout the life of the transaction, which is usually five years. Alternatively, it can be *managed*, allowing the substitution of individual reference entities or replacements according to specific guidelines.

For example, a typical portfolio for a static synthetic transaction could include a pool of 100 corporate US, Canadian or European entities with a US$1 billion total notional. However, the different pools can vary substantially in number and selection of reference entities. CLNs that include asset backed securities (ABS) in the underlying portfolio or even other structured derivative products are also common.

Structure of counterparty-funded credit linked notes

The basic structure of a CLN that is funded via the counterparty is illustrated in Figure 1. In this example, the value of the reference portfolio is US$1 billion and the value of the note equals 10% of the value of the portfolio.

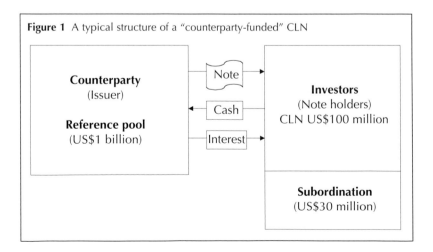

Figure 1 A typical structure of a "counterparty-funded" CLN

If credit events occur in this pool, the first losses up to US$30 million will be covered by the subordinated piece ("equity"). Losses that exceed US$30 million will be borne by the note holders, in order of subordination. The note holder in this example bears the "second loss" piece of the credit risk of the pool.

The point at which the losses start affecting a specific note holder is called the *attachment* point or *threshold*. Losses cannot exceed the total value of the note (ie, US$100 million) and this maximum loss is called the *tranche size* or simply the *notional* of the note.

Settling payments: cash versus physical settlement

A CLN transaction can be structured to provide for *cash settlement* or *physical settlement*. Cash settlement requires a monetary compensation based on the value lost. Physical settlement requires the delivery of an actual debt instrument.

In most cases, settlement of losses occurs immediately after the occurrence of a credit event, (following the procedure of valuation and settlement as specified by the documents) or on the next payment date, although some do settle losses at maturity.

In the case of cash settlement, the principal paid to the note holder is reduced by an amount equal to the calculated losses which is the cash settlement amount paid to the counterparty.

In the case of physical settlement, the principal is reduced by the full amount of the notional of the reference entity whose obligation defaulted. In exchange, the note holder receives an obligation of the defaulted entity.

The losses are calculated to address the *severity* of loss – ie, the percentage loss – on the reference entity's debt multiplied by the reference entity's notional amount. After a credit event occurs, the debt obligation (or deliverable obligation) of the reference entity that suffered the event is evaluated according to a pre-established valuation procedure to determine the severity of the event. The transaction documents define which of the reference entity's debt obligations would serve as an acceptable deliverable obligation for use in valuation in the case of cash settlement, or which would be acceptable for delivery in the case of physical settlement.

The losses thus equal the difference between the amount of credit exposure the issuer has to the related underlying obligor and the value (ie, final price) of the deliverable obligation at settlement. Losses on the entire reference portfolio that exceed the threshold of the CLN are paid by the note holders up to the notional of the notes. In other words, the amount of principal that the note holders will receive at maturity will be reduced by an amount equal to the losses. On the other hand, the outstanding notional of the notes is also reduced ("written down") by an amount equal to the losses.

UNDERSTANDING SPECIAL PURPOSE VEHICLE FUNDED CREDIT LINKED NOTES

An alternative and structurally more complicated CLN is the SPV-funded CLN. In this case the note is issued through an SPV, and the SPV, instead of the investor, plays the role of the seller of protection.

The main structural difference between this and the counterparty-funded CLN is the fact that there is a swap agreement (CDS) between the SPV and the counterparty. Under the terms of the swap, the SPV is obligated to pay the counterparty for losses occurring attributable to credit events in the reference pool. In turn, the counterparty pays the SPV a periodic fee ("premium") for such protection. Under the terms of the swap, credit events similar to those established for a counterparty-funded CLN are specified.

Collateral

An SPV-funded CLN also differs from a counterparty-funded CLN in that the SPV often enters into an investment agreement using the proceeds of the notes.

The proceeds of the notes received by the SPV can be invested in a number of different ways. The type of investment and the credit quality of the chosen collateral depends on the rating of the note that the issuer is attempting to achieve. The collateral assets generally have high ratings relative to the desired rating of the note. The investments are also very liquid, so they can provide for the payments to the counterparty on the occurrence of credit events.

The most common investments are as follows.

1. *Aaa-rated assets*, such as credit card ABS, which are typically issued by a third party unrelated to the buyer. This assures independence from the risk of the swap counterparty.
2. *Aaa-rated guaranteed investment contracts (GICs)* issued by an Aaa-rated entity. When the issuer of the GIC program is not rated a guarantee from another Aaa-rated entity is usually provided.
3. Another approach involves a *repurchase (Repo) Agreement or Securities Lending Agreement (SLA)*. Here, the SPV can use the cash proceeds from the sale of the note to purchase securities, but puts these securities in a collateral account to be used if the SPV is unable to provide cash for the payments on the occurrence of credit events. The assets of the Repo or the SLA account are relatively highly rated securities, often issued or guaranteed by the US Government. On the other hand their value is decreased accordingly relative to the cash held by the counterparty.

Structure of a special purpose vehicle-funded credit linked note

The basic structural elements of an SPV-funded CLN are illustrated in Figure 2.

Prior to maturity, the SPV collects interest payments on the investments it makes with the note proceeds (usually Libor plus a small percentage) and also receives a fixed periodic fee (the premium) from the counterparty under the CDS. These are the two sources of income for the SPV that provide for the interest payments (coupon) due to investors on the note.

The note holder buys the note from the SPV in an amount equal to the face value of the note (notional), but unlike counterparty-funded CLNs, in which the investors buy the note directly from the counterparty, in this case the SPV serves as middleman. The SPV pays the coupons due to the note holders and is also responsible, under the CDS, for paying the swap counterparty for losses experienced as a result of credit events on the reference pool.

The *losses* equal the *severity* of loss on the reference entity's debt, multiplied by the reference entity's notional amount. The CDS underlying the CLN transaction may provide for either *physical settlement* or *cash settlement*. In this case, the cash settlement mechanism works in a similar way to that used for counterparty-funded CLNs. However, while counterparty-funded CLNs subtract an amount equal to the losses directly

Figure 2   A Typical Structure of an SPV-funded CLN Transaction

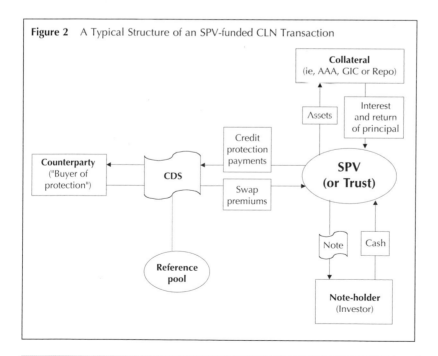

from the outstanding principal of the notes, within the SPV-funded structure, it is the SPV that delivers cash equal to the losses to the counterparty.

Similarly, where the CDS calls for physical settlement, the seller (SPV) will pay the buyer the full amount of the notional of the reference entity and receive a defaulted obligation of the reference entity from the buyer. The transaction documents – ie, swap confirmation – will define what constitutes an acceptable deliverable obligation for delivery in the case of physical settlement, or valuation in the case of cash settlement.

If a credit event occurs under the swap and after the valuation of the loss, the SPV *liquidates* the appropriate amount of collateral. This amount is equal to either the SPV's credit exposure to the reference entity in respect to which the credit event has occurred, or to the amount of loss, depending on the specifics of the transaction.

Usually, for static transactions, an amount equal to the credit exposure to the reference entity that has sustained a credit event is liquidated. This entity is then excluded from the portfolio. For managed transactions, a collateral amount equal to the losses is liquidated. The amount liquidated – ie, the credit protection payment – is paid to the swap counterparty under the CDS.

On the maturity date of the notes – which coincides with the *termination date* of the swap – the remaining collateral is liquidated and the proceeds are paid to the note holders up to the amount due on the note. Shortfall on this payment can result from either principal loss payments associated with credit events under the CDS, or losses on the collateral.

If the swap terminates before the scheduled maturity date because of a termination event – eg, default of the swap counterparty, default of the collateral securities or the occurence of certain other events such as illegality or force majeur – there are usually termination payments. These payments are determined according to the swap agreement – ie, ISDA Master Agreement and Schedule to the ISDA Master Agreement. These payments can increase or decrease the losses to the note holders.

Summary: role of the special purpose vehicle

To summarise, the purposes and activities of the SPV in this CLN structure are limited to:

❑ entering into a CDS with the buyer of protection;
❑ issuing notes to be sold to the investors and paying the periodic interest and principal to the investors;
❑ taking the proceeds from the sale of the notes and investing them in appropriate collateral (ie, GIC or Repo);
❑ collecting the interest from the collateral and the swap premium from the swap counterparty;
❑ liquidating, in the case of a credit event, all or part of the collateral and

Panel 1
CLN LOSSES

The following recreates a possible loss scenario for a CLN transaction. Assume that in a cash settlement CLN transaction with the structure of that shown in Figure 1 all reference entities have a notional amount of US$10 million each.

If a reference entity has a credit event (ie, failure to pay) six months into the transaction and the final price on the debt obligation used for the valuation is 27%, the losses on the transaction are calculated as 73% × US$10 million = US$7.3 million.

Because this amount is below the threshold of the CLN note (which is US$30 million), no losses will be borne by the investors.

Three months later a second credit event occurs in the reference pool. This time one of the reference entities suffers a restructuring event in one of its obligations. The obligation delivered for valuation has a value of 40%. Therefore, the losses are now calculated as 60% × US$10 million = US$6 million. Still there are no losses affecting the investors of the note.

A year later two more credit events occur where two reference entities file for bankruptcy. The losses are now 87% and 90% correspondingly. The losses to the investors are 87% × US$10 million = US$8.7 million and 90% × US$10 million = US$9 million. The total cumulative losses in the transaction are now US$31 million. These exceed the threshold amount for the CLN note by US$1 million and therefore these losses are borne by the investors of this CLN. Any subsequent losses up to US$100 million are also allocated to the note holders.

passing funds equal to the losses to the buyer of protection according to the swap agreement; and

❑ liquidating, at maturity, the remainder of the collateral and giving the principal of the notes (if no credit event occurs) or the principal minus the losses (in the case of credit events) to the investors.

MOODY'S ANALYSIS OF CREDIT LINKED NOTES: GAUGING EXPECTED LOSS

The quantitative component of Moody's rating of CLNs is based on our estimation of expected loss (EL) to the investor. The concept of EL incorporates both the likelihood of default and the level of loss (the "severity") that the note holder may sustain if a default occurs.

Essentially, EL is the level of loss (if any) that Moody's believes investors are likely to sustain on their original investment during the life of the CLN, relative to the promise made to the holders of the note. For the purpose of assigning a credit rating, loss is viewed as the shortfall in the present value of payments received, relative to the present value of the cashflow promised to the note holder. This is dependent on the likelihood of defaults occurring within the reference pool and their severity.

To determine the likelihood of default, Moody's uses quantitative models that test or "stress" the performance of the note – in particular, the reference entities and the collateral – across a wide range of interdependent economic conditions.

In the case of CLN transactions, losses occur primarily because of credit events in the reference pool. The risk associated with the CLN transactions depends on the transaction's definition of credit events as well and the definitions of defaults on the other parts of the transaction. Once these are known, Moody's will assess the risk and likelihood of the specified credit events occurring in the reference pool. Any other credit risk linked to the transaction, that decreases or increases specific stress scenarios to accommodate the particulars of the transaction, are also assessed. Moody's rating will reflect these observations.

Moody's process for rating CLNs entails:

1. identifying the promise made to the holders of the CLN;
2. isolating and quantifying the sources of credit risk in the transaction; and
3. calculating the EL on the CLN relative to the promise made.

Identifying promised cashflows
The promised cashflow is usually well-defined: the transaction pays a fixed (or floating) coupon and the principal at maturity.

CLN transactions that promise only the principal or coupon do exist and their ratings differ accordingly. For example, a CLN that promises only the principal at maturity can usually earn a higher rating than would a similar CLN that promises principal at maturity with a periodic coupon during its lifetime.

Sources of credit risk
The second step in Moody's rating methodology for CLNs is the identification of the different sources of risk. The main sources of risk in a CLN are derived from the underlying portfolio of reference entities, the swap counterparty, the collateral and the risk introduced by the structural features of the transaction. Depending on the type of the CLN, whether counterparty-funded or SPV-funded, some or all of these may be sources of risk.

Underlying portfolio as source of risk
Moody's assesses the credit quality of the entities in the reference pool based on the creditworthiness of the individual entities as reflected by their ratings.[8] A typical reference portfolio consists of entities that are in

the Baa range (at the low end of Moody's investment grade spectrum), although CLNs with reference portfolios both lower and higher than Baa also exist.

Credit events as source of risk

Default can mean different things to different people and thus must be defined clearly in the documentation. We all agree that a missing payment is a default, but each transaction may have a different threshold for what constitutes "missed", particularly when the entity is "pickable", meaning that the payment can be delayed.

Moody's definition of default includes:

❑ missing or delayed payment of interest and/or principal;
❑ bankruptcy; and
❑ distressed exchange.

Moody's opinion of the risk of default as defined by these criteria is reflected in Moody's credit ratings. In the CLN transaction, the criteria for determining the events that constitute default are specified in the credit event definitions.

Because the transactions are structured specifically to address credit risk – as opposed to other types of risk, such as market risk – the credit rating on the transaction is a critical risk determinant. For a Moody's-rated CLN to transfer the actual risk of default, as defined by Moody's, to the note holder, the transaction's default definitions should coincide with Moody's definitions. If not, Moody's will adjust stress factors accordingly, as noted below.

If the definition of credit events is too broad, events that are not likely to result in a default can trigger payments and, therefore, loss for the note holders. In general, the lower the number of allowable credit events in the structure, the less risk the transaction poses to the investors.

Moody's rating assessment for CLNs seeks an exact definition of credit events. By identifying credit events, we are better able to identify and separate the credit risk – ie, the risk of loss following default – from other types of risk.[9]

For CLN transactions that include extra credit events (the so-called "soft" credit events), Moody's increases (adds extra stresses) the default probability, while modelling the likelihood of those events.

Valuation procedure as a source of risk

For cash settlement CLN transactions, risk can also be introduced by the valuation procedure for calculating the severity of a loss after a credit event. For example, one element of this process is determining how soon after a credit event the valuation should take place.

Moody's data shows that, on average, the value of debt is lower shortly after a credit event than after the market settles, translating into higher losses for note holders.

Ideally, the defaulted security should be valued at maturity to obtain the maximum recovery. However, both parties, the counterparty and the note holder, usually favour early settlement. Consequently, the valuation procedure usually takes place within the second month after the credit event.

Moody's decreases – ie, adds extra stresses to – the assumed recoveries on the defaulted entities in the modelling process if the valuation procedure described in the documents fails to:

1. allow for the market to settle, usually at least 30 days after the event;
2. permit a second valuation date, usually 15 days after the first, in the event that there are no successful bids during the first one; and
3. obtain bids for the deliverable obligations from at least five dealers that are active in the relevant market and are unaffiliated with the buyer.

Deliverable obligation as a source of risk

An extra risk can also be introduced in the CLN through the definition of "deliverable obligation".

On the occurrence of a credit event, the calculation agent, who is usually the counterparty, chooses a debt obligation of the reference entity to be valued for determining the losses attributable to the credit event. The obligation that can be delivered – ie, the deliverable obligation – for the valuation procedure should satisfy, among other characteristics defined in the documents of the transaction, the requirement of being of the same seniority (*pari-passu*) as originally specified.

Moody's data, however, show that within the same seniority, some obligations can have a lower value – ie, recover less – than others. These obligations are referred to as "cheapest-to-deliver".

An example of a cheapest-to-deliver obligation is a "convertible", which, generally speaking, can be a debt obligation that can be converted to equity. Again, Moody's data shows that these obligations recover less than on average other pari-passu obligations.[10]

If these options are not removed from the structure in the documents, Moody's decreases (stresses) the recoveries on the defaulted securities when modelling the transaction for ratings purposes.

Counterparty as a source of risk

In addition, assessing the risks associated with valuation and delivery definitions, Moody's reviews the risk associated with exposure to a potential counterparty default.

SPV-funded CLN transactions are usually structured in such a way that only the periodic spread is at risk upon default of the swap counterparty. This, and the fact that the swap counterparty is typically a highly rated entity, means that these losses are usually small. There are several possible remedies if the rating of the counterparty is not high enough relative to the desired rating on the note. Among these, the counterparty can post all premium payments in advance, if only the premium is at risk. Alternatively, the documents can include provisions for posting collateral on downgrades of the counterparty below a specified threshold level.

In the case, however, of counterparty-funded CLNs, the risk associated with the counterparty can be higher and may include the potential loss of note principal. In these cases, the counterparty risk is incorporated into our model, and the EL associated with this risk may have an impact in the rating of the note.

Collateral as a source of risk

The re-investment of investors' proceeds may be another source of risk to the SPV-funded CLN. Ideally, this part of the structure does not introduce any extra risk into the CLN transaction. To avoid such risk being introduced through the investment of the proceeds, Moody's will conduct a separate evaluation using Moody's market value model to gauge market risk in repo or securities lending accounts.[11] Depending on the desired rating on the note, the equivalent rating to the collateral account is such that the extra credit risk introduced in the CLN is relatively small.

There may also be some collateral risk in counterparty-funded CLN transactions for which note proceeds are invested in Aaa-rated ABS securities issued by the counterparty itself. This investment mechanism does not effectively separate the collateral from the risk of the counterparty. In these instances, Moody's analyses the volatility of the market value of the collateral and, based on the volatility and probability of counterparty default, calculates the expected loss.

Early termination as a source of risk

In the case of the SPV-funded CLNs, the swap can terminate early, based on specified events. These usually include default of the swap counterparty and additional termination events, as defined in the documents – these may be broad and may not capture default under Moody's definition of default. Additional early termination risk can be introduced via overbroad definitions of counterparty default.

Early termination is significant because there are typically required payments on early termination under a swap, potentially increasing losses to investors.

Moody's rating analysis favours CLNs where the events of counterparty default coincide with Moody's definition of default, together with CLNs that restrict other additional termination events. Moreover, provisions that require the payments on early termination to be subordinated to the payments on the notes will better protect the investors.

Expected loss (EL)

The primary losses in a CLN transaction typically occur when there are credit events in the underlying portfolio. To model the likelihood of these losses, Moody's reviews a very wide range of possible credit event scenarios, specifically, the likelihood of defaults of the reference entities.

The default probability is reflected in Moody's ratings on each reference entity. Default probabilities (DPs) are published in Moody's idealised DP tables. For each of the possible credit event scenarios, Moody's computes the present value of the realised cashflow. We assume that the CLN will sustain losses in a particular scenario when the realised cashflow is less than the promised cashflow.

The EL is defined as the average over losses for all possible default scenarios, expressed as a percentage of the promised cashflow.

To assign a rating, Moody's compares the EL of CLN to that of conventional bullet corporate bonds of equal duration, which is computed using Moody's idealised default tables.

Quantitative analysis-modelling[12]

Moody's uses the multi-binomial method to calculate the EL for CLN transactions.[13] This method is based on Moody's Binomial Expansion Technique (BET).[14]

The idea behind the BET method is to map the original pool of entities to a "fictitious" pool that contains D independent and homogeneous entities. The entities in the new pool have the same notional (N), coupon and rating, but the probability of default of each is independent of the others. The total notional amount of the original and new pools are the same – that is, $ND = \sum_{i=1}^{n} N_i$. Therefore, the losses of the original pool can be modelled using the new, simplified pool. The default probability of j entities out of a pool of D independent entities is given by the binomial formula:

$$P_j = \frac{D!}{j!(D-j)!}\, p^j\,(1-p)^{(D-j)} \tag{1}$$

where p is the weighted average probability of default of the pool, and represents the default probability of each of the entities in the new pool.

The number of independent entities in the fictitious binomial pool is determined by the requirement that the variance of the values of the original and the new pools be the same. This number is called "diversity score" and is given by the formula[15]

$$D = \frac{\left(\sum_{i=1}^{n} p_i N_i\right)\left(\sum_{j=1}^{n} q_i N_i\right)}{\sum_i \sum_j \rho_{ij}\, \sqrt{p_i q_i p_j q_j}\, N_i N_j} \tag{2}$$

where n is the number of reference entities in the original pool, N_i denotes the notional amount of the reference entity i, p_i is the probability of default of the entity i, $q_i = 1 - p_i$, and ρ_{ij} denotes the correlation between i and j.

There are $D + 1$ possible default scenarios in the pool. The EL is then calculated as the sum over all possible default scenarios of the products of the probability of default times the loss for each of the scenarios. It is given by

$$EL = \sum_{j=0}^{D} P_i L_j \qquad (3)$$

where L_j denotes the loss of the note given the default scenario and j is the number of defaults. The loss L_j for a given scenario is calculated by computing the present value of the cashflow received given that j entities defaulted.

Given their thin subordination, CLNs are very sensitive to defaults in the reference pool. Moody's uses the multi-binomial method to capture the default behaviour of a CLN's reference pool. The multi-binomial method consists of separating the reference pool into k independent sub-pools, usually according to their ratings, and mapping each sub-pool to a number of independent credits (D_α, where $\alpha = 1, ..., k$). The default probability of each scenario within the same sub-pool is given by Equation (1) and the total EL for the CLN is given by

$$EL = \sum_{(j_1,...,j_k)} P_{j_1} ... P_{j_k} L_{j_1...j_k} \qquad (4)$$

where $P_{j_1} ... P_{j_k}$ denotes the probabilities of j entities defaulting out of the pools $1, ..., k$ and $L_{j_1...j_k}$ gives the loss in the scenario that $j_1, ..., j_k$ entities defaulted from each of the sub-pools $1, ..., k$.

The diversity score of the sub-pools, D_α, can be calculated using the same formula (see Equation 2) for each sub-pool. If, however, there are correlations between the entities of different pools, this choice does not guarantee that the variance of the value of the new (multi-binomial) pool will be the same as that of the original portfolio. To account for this we choose re-scaled diversity scores $D'_\alpha = \lambda D_\alpha$, where the scaling factor λ is given by:

$$\lambda = \frac{1}{N^2 Dpq} \sum_{\alpha=1}^{k} N_\alpha^2 D_\alpha p_\alpha q_\alpha \qquad (5)$$

where N_α and p_α are the new notional and probability of default of entities in the new sub-pool α.

To better capture the default behaviour of the reference pool, Moody's often uses a simulation approach to generate the defaults of the underlying sub-pools.[16] This can be described as follows. One throws a die with probability equal to the marginal default probability for each specific sub-pool of entities in a specific time period (usually annually or semi-annually). The model records the defaults that occur in each sub-pool during the specified period and calculates the losses in the CLN under that default scenario. This process is repeated approximately 100,000 to 200,000 times. At the end, the model averages the losses for all default scenarios and gives the final EL number for the CLN.

In the calculation of losses, Moody's also incorporates the CLN's cashflow. In most CLN transactions, the cashflow waterfall is very simple, especially for the cases where the pool is static.

Managed CLNs, however, may utilise over-collateralisation (OC) – a surplus of expected cashflow used to help protect the transaction from losses- or they may use interest coverage (IC) tests or other more elaborate features to gauge default likelihood. Moody's will assess the format and efficiency of the required tests.

For each default scenario modelled, the cashflows are reduced accordingly. The interest payments as well as the principal due to note holders reflect these losses. The losses are first allocated to the equity portion (which is usually at the bottom of the waterfall and is typically not rated) and then to the CLN notional which is senior. Losses will affect the CLN investor dependant on the severity of the event and the number of total defaults.

Legal analysis/legal opinions
Most investors are not equipped to determine whether an SPV, which is meant to shield investors from direct exposure to the bankruptcy risk of the counterparty, is bankruptcy remote, and whether it will be subject to US entity level tax, US withholding tax, or local withholding tax.

These issues are addressed in the opinions of legal counsels, as are issues of valid incorporation, good standing, ability of an SPV to enter into the transaction, and validity of the exemption of the offering from the securities laws. Moody's analysis of the transaction relies on these opinions.

Taxation of an SPV
An SPV incorporated in the US must organise itself as a partnership or a limited liability company to achieve pass-through tax treatment for US federal income tax purposes.

Non-US domiciled SPVs are operated in such a way that they qualify for a statutory exemption. One of these operational guidelines requires that SPVs invest proceeds from the issuance of notes in high quality instruments maturing no later than the maturity of the CLNs. If an SPV acquires commercial paper or other similar investments that are rolled over during the lifetime of the CLNs, the owners of the notes must make specified representations regarding their ownership of the notes and agree to certain covenants.

Subject to satisfaction of certain conditions, the issuer can avoid US federal income tax withholdings on payments made under the CDS or the notes.

Often, CLNs with a single tranche structure are issued as a single class of certificates and are treated as equity, rather than indebtedness, of the SPV for US federal income tax purposes. The notes that are considered equity are not eligible for purchase by benefit plan investors, unless investment by such investors in any class of notes considered equity is maintained at less than 25%.

Bankruptcy remoteness

In a typical transaction, CLNs are issued out of a newly created SPV that is bankruptcy remote. The only assets of the SPV are the CDS and the collateral purchased with the proceeds of the notes.

If a bankruptcy proceeding commences with respect to an SPV, the holders of the CLNs, as secured creditors of an SPV who have a perfected security interest in the assets of an SPV, should ultimately be able to realise on the assets. However, if an SPV becomes the subject of another entity's bankruptcy or insolvency proceedings, it could cause delays in payments to the holders of the notes (a result of "automatic stay" provisions of the US Bankruptcy Code).

An SPV's bankruptcy risk is minimised by organising it as an entity that is separate from the counterparty with no operations history that could give rise to any liabilities. The SPV's activities must be limited to those necessary to fulfil its purpose, which is issuing the notes, entering into CDS, and holding certain types of collateral.

Usually, the organisational documents of an SPV have safeguards to prevent voluntary bankruptcy filings. Other parties to the transaction (eg, the trustee and CDS counterparty) will typically covenant not to file a bankruptcy petition against an SPV for a statutorily applicable preference period (usually one year and one day) after all the CLNs have been repaid in full.

Securities law implications

CLNs are usually offered and sold pursuant to exemptions from securities laws to institutional investors. Since most of these securities are placed privately, they are not offered for sale to individuals within the US. In some instances, the number of persons who can own outstanding securities of an SPV is limited to 100 to comply with the Investment Company Act of 1940. This can have implications for the minimum denominations of the CLNs increasing to 1/100th of the total issuance.

CONCLUSION

In conclusion, CLNs are valuable financial instruments based on their flexibility and ability to redistribute credit risk among investors. Properly used, they can provide hedging, investment opportunities and liquidity to the credit market.

Structurally, CLNs can be quite complicated and expose the investor to a variety of risks, some readily apparent and some hidden. Investors complement the risk assessment of these instruments with the opinion of independent evaluators, such as rating agencies, as part of their investment and evaluation procedures. The role of such agencies in rating CLNs is, therefore, very important to investors.

Moody's rating methodology for CLNs is based on the concept of EL on the notes. Moody's identifies, analyses and evaluates all explicit and implicit credit related risks, and incorporates them in a sophisticated mathematical model for the transaction.

Moody's also makes a full assessment of the actual and potential legal issues in the notes' structure and, when deemed appropriate, makes suggestions for modifications that would make the notes conform to standard assumptions or market expectations. The final Moody's rating assigned to the notes represents a distillation of the exhaustive evaluation procedure described above, and constitutes a valuable indicator for note holders.

1   CLNs that use derivative contracts known as "total return swaps" also exist, but in this chapter we will only analyse the CLNs that use "credit default swaps" as underlying contracts.

2   In the most common CLN transactions, the investor is the seller of credit protection. In principle, however, the situation can be reversed and the investor can *buy* credit protection through a CLN transaction. For the purposes of this chapter, we think of the investor as the ultimate seller of protection.

3   The SPV is a structural entity meant to segregate the notes from the potential bankruptcy risk of the counterparty. For a more complete explanation, please see *Legal Analysis/Legal Opinion* in this chapter.

4   A structured finance transaction usually involves several levels or "tranches" of notes, ranging in credit risk, with the senior-most rated Aaa (lowest risk). The riskiest piece (usually unrated) is subordinated to the others. In other words, the cashflows from this piece will be delegated to the other notes, if needed. The next riskiest piece is the second-most subordinated and so on. For the purposes of this discussion, we will assume that a transaction has only one note issued at the more senior level (higher rating) and one at the junior level (the subordinated level).

5   The International Swaps and Derivatives Associations, Inc. (ISDA) is the major trade association for participants in the privately negotiated derivatives markets. ISDA's published standards for swap structures set the standard for swaps definitions and documentation around the world.

6   See Tolk S. J., (2001).

7   Additional credit events are defined in the ISDA credit derivatives definitions, but only the events listed here can be associated directly with credit risk.

8   See Hamilton, D.T. *et al*, (2003).

9   See Tolk S. J, (2001) and Yoshizawa Y., (2003).

10 See Hamilton, D.T *et al*, (2001).

11 See Crousillat C., (2002).

12 In this section, we present the basic modelling approach. There are, however, many "variations on the theme", with each structure and each analyst using different techniques.

13 In principle, however, Monte Carlo or other simulation techniques can be used in rating CLNs with more exotic portfolios or portfolios with only a small number of credits. During this process, one generates the default scenarios of each of the credits in the portfolio and calculates the losses occurring in each of the scenarios.

14 See Remeza, H., and J. Gluck (2000).

15 See Cifuentes A., *et al* (2000).

16 The usual binomial technique is also used, wherein one allows all entities of each pool to default one by one, all with the same weighted average probability. In such a case, the EL is calculated using different default profiles where the defaults are distributed during the lifetime of the CLN.

BIBLIOGRAPHY

Cifuentes A., I. Efrat, J. Gluck and E. Murphy, 1998, "Buying and Selling Credit Risk: A Perspective on Credit-Linked Obligations", *Credit Derivatives* (London: Risk Books).

Cifuentes, A. and G. O'Connor, 1996, "The Binomial Expansion Method Applied to CBO/CLO Analysis", Moody's Special Report

Cifuentes A. and C. Wilcox, 1998, "The Double Binomial Method and its Application to a Special Case of CBO Structures", Moody's Special Report.

Crousillat C., 2002, "Moody's Rating Methodology: An Alternative Approach to Evaluating Market Value CDOs", Moody's Special Report.

Hamilton D. T., *et al*, 2003, "Default and Recovery Rates of Corporate Bond Issuers: A Statistical Review of Moody's Ratings Performance, 1920–2002", Moody's Special Comment.

Hamilton, D.T., P.M. Stumpp and R. Cantor, 2001, "Default and Recovery Rates of Convertible Bond Issuers: 1970–2000", Moody's Special Comment.

Remeza, H., and J. Gluck, 2000, "Moody's Approach to Rating Multisector CDO's" Moody's Special Report.

Tolk S. J., 2001, "Understanding The Risks In Credit Default Swaps", Moody's Special Report.

Yoshizawa Y., 2003, "Moody's Approach to Rating Synthetic Collateralized Debt Obligations", Moody's Special Report.

21

Using guarantees and credit derivatives to reduce credit risk capital requirements under the New Basel Capital Accord

Erik Heitfield*

Federal Reserve Board

INTRODUCTION

New bank capital adequacy standards being developed by the Basel Committee on Banking Supervision are intended to align minimum regulatory capital requirements more closely with the underlying economic risks faced by banks. Since financial guarantees and credit derivatives are designed to provide protection against credit risk, the Basel Committee has proposed allowing banks to use these instruments to reduce regulatory capital requirements. This chapter examines the Basel Committee's proposed capital treatment for hedged credit exposures under the new Capital Accord (Basel II) and compares this treatment with a stylised portfolio credit risk model.

The next section of this chapter provides a brief overview of the development and objectives of Basel II. At the new Accord's core is a simple portfolio credit risk model that we call the ASRF/Merton model. Basel II uses this model to set regulatory capital charges for unhedged credit exposures that take into account cross-exposure differences in credit risk parameters measuring default probabilities and recovery rates. The section entitled "The Advanced Internal Ratings Based Approach" describes the ASRF/Merton model in detail. The Basel Committee proposes to account for the credit risk mitigating effects of guarantees and credit derivatives by allowing a bank that obtains credit protection for a loan to substitute risk parameters associated with the protection provider for those associated

---

* The views expressed here are solely those of the author, and do not reflect the opinions of the board of governors of the Federal Reserve System or its staff.

with the reference obligor. Unlike the capital treatment for unhedged exposures, this substitution approach is not derived from an underlying portfolio credit risk model. The section headed "A Capital Model for Hedged Exposures" shows how the Basel Committee's ASRF/Merton model can be extended to assess internally consistent regulatory capital charges for hedged exposures.

The section headed "Model Calibrations" compares the regulatory capital charges produced by the ASRF/Merton model for hedged exposures with those arising from the substitution approach. The substitution approach produces capital charges that are much higher than those generated by the ASRF/Merton model when credit protection provided by high credit quality guarantors is used to hedge risks for exposures to high credit quality obligors. When the risks arising from exposures to low credit quality obligors are hedged, differences between the substitution approach and the ASRF/Merton model depend on the extent to which defaults by protection providers are sensitive to systematic risk. The final section of this chapter draws conclusions from this analysis and discusses some caveats.

BACKGROUND: THE BASEL CAPITAL ACCORDS

In 1988, members of the Basel Committee on Banking Supervision signed the Basel Capital Accord (Basel I), establishing a uniform framework for setting minimum regulatory capital requirements for banks operating in industrialised countries. While the Accord does not have the force of law, its recommendations have been adopted by bank regulatory authorities in all G10 countries and in most other countries where internationally active banks are chartered.

Basel I established an 8% regulatory minimum for a measure of bank capital adequacy that has come to be called the risk based capital ratio (RBCR). The RBCR is similar to a standard leverage ratio, but relies on more sophisticated definitions of capital and assets than are commonly used. The capital figure used in the numerator of the RBCR includes equity capital as well as loan loss reserves and certain types of equity like debt instruments such as convertible bonds. More importantly from a risk management perspective, the denominator – termed risk-weighted assets – is calculated by taking a weighted sum of both on- and off-balance-sheet exposures. In opting to weight assets by risk, the Basel Committee (1988, Paragraph 28) hoped:

1. to reduce regulatory incentives for banks to shed low-risk assets,
2. to provide a means for assessing regulatory capital against off-balance-sheet exposures, and
3. to establish a measure of capital adequacy that would facilitate comparisons across banks operating in different countries.

In a rudimentary way, the weights used in calculating risk weighted assets are intended to reflect the underlying risks associated with different types of exposures. For example, most commercial loans are given a risk weight of 100%, but residential mortgages, which are believed to entail less credit risk, are given a risk weight of 50%. Thus the marginal Basel I capital requirement for a C&I loan is 8%, while the marginal requirement for a residential mortgage is only 4%. Though the Basel I risk weights allow for a course positive relationship between risk and regulatory capital charges, they do not take into account the finer distinctions among risks that can be identified using modern risk-management techniques. For example, under Basel I, all performing C&I loans are given risk weights of 100%, regardless of differences in credit quality. A one-year maturity AAA-rated loan is assessed at exactly the same marginal regulatory capital charge (8%) as a five-year maturity BB-rated loan.

Over the 15 years since the Basel Capital Accord was negotiated, the limitations of its course risk-weighting approach have become increasingly apparent. As best practice risk management techniques have continued to advance, bankers and their regulators have observed significant and systematic differences between the regulatory capital charges imposed by Basel I, and the economic capital charges generated by banks' internal models. Such discrepancies give banks strong economic incentives to shift lending or to engage in regulatory capital arbitrages in order to bring regulatory and economic capital requirements closer together. When regulatory capital requirements do not reflect differences in risk, banks may choose to shift lending away from those low-risk assets that are assigned excessively high regulatory capital charges. Alternatively, sophisticated banks have found ways to reduce overall regulatory capital requirements by engaging in arbitrages to shift assets off their balance sheets where they are given low risk weights. Needless to say, these sorts of activities undermine the spirit and stated objectives of Basel I.

The limitations of Basel I led regulators to begin work on a new Basel Capital Accord (Basel II) in 1999. Over the past five years a number of technical working groups under the direction of the Basel Committee secretariat have engaged in an aggressive programme of theoretical and empirical research, augmented by extensive dialogue with industry participants, to design a more risk-sensitive framework of bank capital adequacy standards. In May 2003, the Basel Committee released its third consultative paper (CP3) for public comment. This document proposes language for the new Accord and should provide a good indication of what will appear in the final Accord. Work on Basel II is currently scheduled for completion by the end of 2003, and the new Accord is expected to be implemented in G10 countries starting in 2007.

The Basel Committee's objectives in developing Basel II are articulated in CP3 (Paragraph 3):

[Basel II] is intended to foster a strong emphasis on risk management and to encourage ongoing improvements in banks' risk assessment capabilities. The Committee believes that this can be accomplished by closely aligning banks' capital requirements with prevailing modern risk management practices, and by ensuring that this emphasis on risk makes its way into supervisory practices and into market discipline through enhanced risk- and capital-related disclosures.

Basel II consists of three mutually reinforcing pillars. Pillar I establishes minimum risk-based capital requirements intended to cover the credit and operational risks faced by well-diversified financial institutions. Pillar II establishes guidelines for supervising banks' internal risk-management processes and empowers regulators to require that banks hold capital buffers to mitigate those economic risks not explicitly addressed under Pillar I. Pillar III imposes new public-disclosure requirements on banks with an eye towards increasing transparency and facilitating more effective market discipline of bank capital adequacy.

In order to accommodate differences in sophistication among banks and cross-country differences in approaches to bank supervision, Basel II proposes three procedures for calculating credit risk capital charges under Pillar I. Though the three approaches differ in terms of their complexity, they are all extensions of the simple asset-weighting scheme introduced in Basel I. The analysis in this chapter will focus on the most sophisticated of these approaches: the Advanced Internal Ratings Based (A-IRB) approach. This is the approach that will most likely be applied to those large, internationally active banks that tend to make significant use of derivatives to hedge credit risk.[1]

Under the A-IRB approach, the risk weights used for calculating a bank's risk-based capital ratio are generated using a stylised portfolio credit risk model that incorporates bank-supplied data on the characteristics of individual credit-risk exposures as well as "hard-wired" parameters set by the Basel Committee. Banks are required to report estimates of the one-year-ahead probability of default (PD), the percentage loss given default (LGD), and the average maturity (M) associated with each of their credit exposures. These parameters are plugged into supervisory formulae to derive exposure risk weights. The A-IRB approach accounts for the credit risk mitigating effects of collateral requirements, eligible financial guarantees and credit derivatives by allowing banks to modify the PD and LGD parameters associated with some risk exposures. The next section summarises the derivation of the supervisory formulas used in the A-IRB approach.

THE ADVANCED INTERNAL RATINGS BASED APPROACH

In developing risk-weight functions for the A-IRB approach, the Basel Committee set out to ensure that each exposure's regulatory capital charge would reflect its contribution to portfolio credit risk, and that the aggregate capital held by a bank would be sufficient to satisfy a 99.9% portfolio value-at-risk (VAR) target. In general, these two objectives cannot both be satisfied at the same time. However, Gordy (2003) has shown that under a particular set of stylised assumptions a decentralised approach establishing portfolio-wide capital requirements is possible. If one assumes that:

1. the portfolio is well diversified so that no single exposure can have a meaningful effect on overall portfolio risk;
2. a single risk factor is the sole source of systematic risk in the portfolio; and
3. realisations of the systematic risk factor are negatively related with the conditional expected losses associated with most risk exposures,

then one can assess capital on an exposure by exposure basis that, in aggregate, satisfies a portfolio VAR target.

Specifically, capital for an individual exposure is derived by plugging the 0.1th percentile of the systematic risk factor into the conditional expected loss function for that exposure. This asymptotic-single-risk-factor (ASRF) framework serves as the theoretical foundation for the A-IRB risk-weight formulas used in Basel II.

To operationalise the ASRF framework, one must specify a probabilistic model of the losses associated with each credit-risk exposure. The A-IRB approach relies on a simple one-factor Merton model, similar to that underlying the popular CreditMetrics risk management tools (Gupton, Finger, and Phatia, 1997) described in Chapter 6. Under this model, an obligor defaults when the value of its assets falls below a critical fixed threshold. Because future asset values are uncertain, defaults occur randomly. Common shocks to future asset values produce cross-obligor correlations in defaults.

Let Y denote the appropriately normalised asset value for an obligor at a one-year assessment horizon, and assume

$$Y = X \sqrt{\rho} + U \sqrt{1 - \rho}$$

where X is a systematic risk factor that affects all obligors and U is an idiosyncratic obligor specific risk factor that is uncorrelated with X. The obligor defaults if Y falls below a fixed threshold γ. The asset correlation parameter ρ measures the relative importance of systematic risk in determining the obligors' likelihood of default. By assumption, X and U are both standard normal random variables, so Y is also standard normal. The marginal probability of default for the obligor is

$$PD = \Phi(\gamma)$$

where $\Phi(x)$ is the standard normal cumulative distribution function (CDF). Since the normal CDF has a well-defined inverse function, if the obligor's PD is known, γ can be calculated using the transformation $\gamma = \Phi^{-1}(PD)$.

By assumption, the loss given default (LGD) of an exposure is independent of the systematic risk factor. Therefore, the conditional expected loss function for an unhedged exposure given X is

$$c(X) = Pr\left[X\sqrt{\rho} + U\sqrt{1-\rho} \le \gamma \,|\, X \right] \cdot LGD$$

$$= \Phi\left(\frac{\Phi^{-1}(PD) - X\sqrt{\rho}}{\sqrt{1-\rho}} \right) \cdot LGD$$

Since X is a standard normal random variable, its 0.1th percentile is $X_q \equiv -\Phi^{-1}(0.999)$. Plugging X_q into c(X) yields the ASRF capital formula for an unhedged risk exposure to the obligor:

$$k_u = \Phi\left(\frac{\Phi^{-1}(PD) + \Phi^{-1}(0.999)\sqrt{\rho}}{\sqrt{1-\rho}} \right) \cdot LGD \qquad (1)$$

Equation (1) depends on three risk parameters: the PD and LGD associated with the credit exposure, and the asset correlation parameter ρ. In the course of developing Basel II, the Basel Committee determined that it would be feasible for bank supervisors to validate PD and LGD parameters provided by banks, but that practical constraints would make it very difficult for supervisors to validate asset correlation parameters effectively. For this reason the A-IRB approach allows banks to supply their own estimates of the PD and LGD associated with each exposure, but makes use of "hard-wired" assumptions about asset correlation parameters. The value of the asset correlation parameter depends on the particular type of exposure (commercial and industrial, residential mortgage, revolving retail credit etc) and in some cases the PD of the exposure. For C&I loans to large corporate obligors, the asset correlation parameter ranges from a high of 24% for low-PD obligors, to 12% for high-PD obligors according to the formula

$$\rho(PD) = \frac{1 - \exp(-50 \cdot PD)}{1 - \exp(-50)}\,0.12 + \frac{\exp(-50 \cdot PD)}{1 - \exp(-50)}\,0.24 \qquad (2)$$

Taken together Equations (1) and (2) determine the A-IRB capital charge per unit exposure for unhedged C&I loans (CP3, paragraph 241). The risk weight for an exposure is calculated by dividing equation (1) by 8%. The total regulatory capital charge assessed against an exposure is equal to the product of (1) and a forecast of the value of the exposure at default.[2] The

A-IRB formula produces regulatory capital charges for unhedged C&I exposures that rise smoothly with PD and are proportional to LGD. According to CP3, the PD should reflect an unbiased forecast of the obligor's probability of default over the next year, and the LGD should reflect an estimate of the expected loss per unit exposure in the event that the obligor defaults.

If a loan is guaranteed by a third party or the bank holding that loan hedges its credit risk by purchasing a credit-default swap on a bond issued by the reference obligor, then the credit loss to the bank flowing from a default by the reference obligor may be greatly reduced or even eliminated entirely. A bank that hedges credit risk in this way can adjust the PD and LGD of a hedged loan to reflect the risks associated with a loan to the credit protection provider (hereafter called the guarantor) rather than the reference obligor. Thus if the guarantor has a lower PD than the reference obligor and an exposure to that guarantor has a comparable or lower LGD than an exposure to the reference obligor, the bank can receive a lower risk weight on the hedged exposure. However, the proposed capital rules place a bound on this adjustment. According to paragraph 270 of CP3,

> [T]o the extent that the [credit risk mitigation] is recognised by the bank, the adjusted risk weight will not be less than that of a comparable direct exposure to the protection provider ... [B]anks may choose not to recognise credit protection if doing so would result in a higher capital requirement.

The practical implication of this rule is that the bank can choose to apply either the risk weight for an unhedged exposure to the reference obligor, or the risk weight for an unhedged exposure to the guarantor, whichever is lower.

This "substitution approach" to recognising the risk-mitigating effects of credit hedges has been criticised by some banks and industry associations, particularly the International Swaps and Derivatives Association (ISDA). In comment letters to the Basel Committee, ISDA (2001, 2002) has argued repeatedly that the substitution approach is too conservative because it fails to account properly for the fact that both the reference obligor and the guarantor must default at the same time for a bank to incur a default related loss on a hedged exposure. To examine this argument in detail, we next extend the ASRF/Merton model to derive explicit capital charges for hedged exposures.

A CAPITAL MODEL FOR HEDGED EXPOSURES

To use the ASRF framework to derive capital for a hedged exposure, one must calculate the conditional probability that both the reference obligor (denoted o) and the guarantor (denoted g) default, given a realisation of the systematic risk factor X. To accomplish this, this section extends the simple one-factor Merton model presented in the previous section by introducing a separate risk factor that affects only the obligor and the guarantor. Because this extra risk factor does not influence other exposures in the bank portfolio, it does not violate the ASRF assumptions.[3] However, it allows for the possibility that an obligor and a guarantor may have more in common than a corresponding pair of unrelated obligors.

Since systematic risk can affect both the obligor and the guarantor, defaults by these two counterparties will not generally be independent. Furthermore, in some circumstances it is reasonable to expect that a common risk factor may influence the credit quality of the obligor and the guarantor that does not directly affect most other exposures. For example, if a manufacturer guarantees a loan to an upstream parts supplier, both the guarantor and the obligor may be subject to common shocks above and beyond those macroeconomic shocks that affect other obligors. Similarly, if the seller of a credit default swap (CDS) tends to specialise in providing credit protection on exposures to a particular industry sector, it may be subject to the same sector-specific shocks as the reference obligor. To account for both systematic risk and common risks facing the obligor and the guarantor, we model the normalised assets of the obligor and the guarantor using the following equation system:

$$Y_o = X \sqrt{\rho_o} + (Z_{og} \sqrt{\psi_{og}} + E_o \sqrt{1 - \psi_{og}}) \sqrt{1 - \rho_o}$$
$$Y_g = X \sqrt{\rho_g} + (Z_{og} \sqrt{\psi_{og}} + E_g \sqrt{1 - \psi_{og}}) \sqrt{1 - \rho_g}$$

X is the same systematic risk factor defined earlier. Z_{og} is a risk factor that is specific to the obligor–guarantor pair, but affects no other risk exposures. E_o and E_g are idiosyncratic risk factors that affect only the obligor and the guarantor respectively. X, Z_{og}, E_o and E_g are all uncorrelated with each other and each is assumed to have a standard normal distribution.[4]

The obligor asset correlation parameter ρ_o measures the relative importance of the systematic risk factor in determining whether or not the obligor will default. It has exactly the same economic interpretation as the asset correlation parameter introduced in the previous section. The guarantor asset correlation parameter ρ_g measures the relative importance of systematic risk in determining whether the guarantor will default. ψ_{og} measures the relative contribution of the obligor–guarantor risk factor Z_{og}. Correlations in the assets of the obligor and the guarantor are driven by both the systematic risk factor and the obligor–guarantor risk factor. The obligor–guarantor asset correlation ρ_{og}, is defined as

$$\rho_{og} \equiv Cor\ [Y_o,\ Y_g] = \sqrt{\rho_o \rho_g} + \psi_{og} \sqrt{(1 - \rho_o)(1 - \rho_g)}$$

As in the previous section, we assume that the obligor defaults if Y_o falls below a critical threshold γ_o, so that $PD_o = \Phi(\gamma_o)$. Similarly, the guarantor defaults if its asset value falls below γ_g, so $PD_g = \Phi(\gamma_g)$. The unconditional joint probability that both the obligor and the guarantor will default is

$$JPD_{og} = \Phi_2(\Phi^{-1}(PD_o), \Phi^{-1}(PD_g); \rho_{og})$$

where $F(x_1, x_2; r)$ is the bivariate CDF for a pair of standard normal random variables with correlation r. In general JPD_{og} is much smaller than either PD_o or PD_g. The difference between joint and marginal default probabilities, often called the "double default" effect, is the primary focus of industry criticisms of the Basel Committee's substitution-approach capital treatment for hedged exposures.

The conditional expected loss function for a hedged exposure is

$$c_{og}(X) = Pr\left[Y_o < \gamma_o \cap Y_g < \gamma_g \mid X\right] \cdot LGD_{og}$$

$$= F\left(\frac{\Phi^{-1}(PD_o) - X\sqrt{\rho_o}}{\sqrt{1 - \rho_o}}, \frac{\Phi^{-1}(PD_g) - X\sqrt{\rho_g}}{\sqrt{1 - \rho_g}}; \psi_{og}\right) \cdot LGD_{og}$$

where LGD_{og} is a measure of loss given default that accounts for the bank's ability potentially to pursue recoveries from both the obligor and the guarantor in the event that both counterparties default. Using the definition of ρ_{og} given above, we can rewrite $c_{og}(X)$ in terms of the three asset correlation parameters ρ_o, ρ_g, and ρ_{og}. Plugging X_q into this function yields the ASRF capital charge for a hedged exposure:

$$k_H = F\left(\frac{\Phi^{-1}(PD_o) + \Phi^{-1}(0.999)\sqrt{\rho_o}}{\sqrt{1 - \rho_o}}, \frac{\Phi^{-1}(PD_g) + \Phi^{-1}(0.999)\sqrt{\rho_g}}{\sqrt{1 - \rho_g}};\right.$$

$$\left.\frac{\rho_{og} - \sqrt{\rho_o \rho_g}}{\sqrt{(1 - \rho_o)(1 - \rho_g)}}\right) \cdot LGD_{og} \tag{3}$$

This capital formula is quite a bit more complicated than the capital formula for unhedged exposures derived in the last section. It depends on the PDs of both the obligor and the guarantor as well as a joint LGD parameter, and it relies on three – rather than one – asset correlation parameters.

Two special cases are of particular interest. First, if one is willing to assume that there is no "extra" correlation between the assets of the obligor and the guarantor beyond that generated by both counterparties' exposures to the systematic risk factor, then calculating the ASRF capital charge for hedged transactions becomes much easier. When $\psi_{og} = 0$, defaults by the obligor and the guarantor are conditionally independent given X, so Equation (3) simplifies to

$$k_H = \Phi\left(\frac{\Phi^{-1}(PD_g) + \Phi^{-1}(0.999)\sqrt{\rho_g}}{\sqrt{1 - \rho_g}}\right)$$

$$\cdot\left[\Phi\left(\frac{\Phi^{-1}(PD_o) + \Phi^{-1}(0.999)\sqrt{\rho_o}}{\sqrt{1 - \rho_o}}\right) \cdot\right] LGD_{og} \tag{4}$$

Except for the fact that LGD_{og} should reflect recoveries from both the obligor and the guarantor, the bracketed term in Equation (4) is identical to Equation (1). Thus when $\psi_{og} = 0$ capital for a hedged exposure can be approximated by applying a discount (that depends on the guarantor PD) to the capital charge for an unhedged exposure to the guarantor.

If we assume that $\rho_o = \rho_g = \rho$, then Y_o and Y_g collapse to the single random variable $Y_{og} = X \sqrt{\rho} + Z_{og} \sqrt{1 - \rho}$. In this case the conditional expected loss function is

$$c_{og}(X) = Pr[Y_{og} < \gamma_o \cap Y_{og} < \gamma_g \mid X] \cdot LGD_{og}$$

$$= Pr[X \sqrt{\rho} + Z_{og} \sqrt{1 - \rho} < \min \{\gamma_o, \gamma_g\} \mid X] \, LGD_{og}$$

$$= \Phi \left(\frac{\Phi^{-1}(\min\{PD_o, PD_g\}) - X\sqrt{\rho}}{\sqrt{1 - \rho}} \right) \cdot LGD_{og}$$

If we further assume that $LGD_{og} = LGD$, then plugging X_q into the equation above yields

$$k_H = \Phi \left(\frac{\Phi^{-1}(\min\{PD_o, PD_g\}) + \Phi^{-1}(0.999)\sqrt{\rho}}{\sqrt{1 - \rho}} \right) \cdot LGD$$

which is exactly the capital charge implied by Basel II's substitution approach. Thus, the substitution approach can be viewed as a special case of the ASRF/Merton model for hedged exposures in which:

1. the credit quality of the obligor and the guarantor move in lock-step with one another (that is, their normalised asset values are perfectly correlated); and
2. the LGD of the hedged exposure is the same as that of the unhedged exposures (that is, there are no opportunities to obtain additional recoveries if the guarantor defaults).

MODEL CALIBRATIONS
How different are capital charges produced by the substitution approach proposed in CP3 from those produced by the extended ASRF/Merton model derived in the last section? The answer depends on what is assumed about obligor asset correlations and obligor–guarantor asset correlations, and on whether LGDs are lower for hedged exposures than for comparable unhedged exposures. The last section showed that the ASRF/Merton model and the substitution approach produce identical results when the risks to obligors and guarantors are perfectly correlated and there are no double-recovery effects. This section compares the two approaches to assessing capital charges for hedged exposures under a broader range of assumptions about asset correlations. Throughout the

analysis that follows we abstract from possible double-recovery effects by assuming that the LGD of an exposure is equal to 45%, whether that exposure is to the obligor, the guarantor or both counterparties. All calibrations assume a one-year-maturity C&I loan, so the obligor asset correlation parameter is determined by Equation (2). Each capital charge is expressed as a percentage of the value of an exposure prior to default.

Substitution approach

Table 1 reports substitution approach capital charges for a range of obligor and guarantor PDs. For each PD combination, the capital charge for a hedged exposure is calculated by first computing the charges associated with unhedged exposures to both the obligor and the guarantor, and then taking the lesser of these two values. By comparing the substitution approach capital charges with the capital charges for an unhedged exposure shown in the last row of the table, one can see that, when there are no double-recovery effects, the substitution approach provides no regulatory capital relief for hedged exposures in cases where the PD of the guarantor exceeds that of the obligor.

Base case

As a base case for the ASRF/Merton model, we first consider what capital charges look like when both the obligor and the guarantor asset correlations are determined by Equation (2), and the obligor–guarantor asset correlation is equal to $\rho_{og} = \sqrt{(\rho_o \rho_g)}$ (that is, $\Psi_{og} = 0$). These parameter assumptions treat guarantors in a manner symmetric with corporate obligors. They imply that guarantors have the same sensitivity to systematic risk as corporate obligors, and that there are no additional sources of common risk between obligors and guarantors.

Base case ASRF/Merton capital charges are reported in Table 2. A comparison of Tables 2 and 1 reveals that the ASRF/Merton model produces dramatically lower capital charges for hedged exposures, partic-

Table 1. Substitution approach capital charges

| Guarantor PD (%) | Obligor PD (%) | | | | | | | |
	0.03	0.10	0.50	1.00	2.00	5.00	10.00	50.00
0.03	0.62	0.62	0.62	0.62	0.62	0.62	0.62	0.62
0.10	0.62	1.54	1.54	1.54	1.54	1.54	1.54	1.54
0.50	0.62	1.54	4.40	4.40	4.40	4.40	4.40	4.40
1.00	0.62	1.54	4.40	6.31	6.31	6.31	6.31	6.31
Unhedged exposure	0.62	1.54	4.40	6.31	8.56	12.80	18.56	39.29

Table 2. ASRF/Merton base-case capital charges

Guarantor PD (%)	Obligor PD (%)							
	0.03	0.10	0.50	1.00	2.00	5.00	10.00	50.00
0.03	0.01	0.02	0.06	0.09	0.12	0.18	0.26	0.54
0.10	0.02	0.05	0.15	0.22	0.29	0.44	0.63	1.34
0.50	0.06	0.15	0.43	0.62	0.84	1.25	1.81	3.84
1.00	0.09	0.22	0.62	0.89	1.20	1.80	2.60	5.51
Unhedged exposure	0.62	1.54	4.40	6.31	8.56	12.80	18.56	39.29

ularly when low PD guarantors provide credit protection for loans to low-PD obligors. Under the base case assumptions, obligor and guarantor defaults are conditionally independent given X, so double-default effects on capital charges are particularly large. The base case calibrations provide something of a lower bound on the capital charges generated by the ASRF/Merton model. Increasing the assumed values of the obligor–guarantor asset correlation and the guarantor asset correlation leads to higher capital charges.

High obligor–guarantor asset correlation

Under the base case assumptions, the obligor–guarantor asset correlation parameter ranges from 12% to 24% depending on the PDs of the counter-parties. As noted in the last section, it is possible that defaults by obligors may be affected by common factors, above and beyond the systematic risk factor that affects all counterparties. Table 3 reports ASRF/Merton capital charges that assume a high obligor–guarantor asset correlation (50%). Like the base case calibrations, the figures reported in Table 3 assume that the guarantor asset correlation parameter is given by Equation (2).

Comparing Tables 3 and 2 shows that, as expected, increasing the value of ρ_{og} leads to higher ASRF/Merton capital charges for hedged exposures. Greater correlation between the assets of an obligor and a guarantor implies that all else equal the two counterparties are more likely to default together, attenuating double-default effects. As demonstrated in the last section, as the obligor–guarantor asset correlation parameter approaches 100%, the ASRF/Merton capital charges for hedged exposures will tend to approach those generated by the substitution approach.

High guarantor asset correlation

According to Fitch, Inc (2003), credit guarantees are most commonly sold by large banks and insurance companies. These types of institutions tend to do a good job diversifying away idiosyncratic risk, so we might expect protec-

Table 3. ASRF/Merton capital charges given high obligor–guarantor asset correlation ($\rho_{og} = 0.50$)

Guarantor PD (%)	Obligor PD (%)							
	0.03	0.10	0.50	1.00	2.00	5.00	10.00	50.00
0.03	0.05	0.10	0.21	0.27	0.33	0.42	0.50	0.61
0.10	0.10	0.20	0.46	0.60	0.75	0.97	1.18	1.52
0.50	0.21	0.46	1.08	1.44	1.83	2.46	3.10	4.40
1.00	0.27	0.60	1.44	1.93	2.48	3.36	4.29	6.15
Unhedged exposure	0.62	1.54	4.40	6.31	8.56	12.80	18.56	39.29

tion sellers to have low overall risk (low PDs) but relatively high exposure to systematic risk (high ρ_g). Table 4 reports capital charges for the same obligor–guarantor asset correlation parameter assumption used in the base case, but with a high guarantor asset correlation parameter (50%).[5]

For high PD obligors, the ASRF/Merton capital charges are much more sensitive to assumptions about the guarantor asset correlation parameter than they are to assumptions about the obligor–guarantor asset correlation parameter. This can be seen by comparing Table 4 with Table 3. Increasing the assumed exposure of guarantors to systematic risk implies that guarantors are more likely to default during times of systemic stress, reducing the utility of the credit protection they provide.

Comparing Tables 4 and 1 shows that when the assumed guarantor asset correlation and the obligor PD are both relatively high, the ASRF/Merton model can generate capital charges that exceed those produced by the substitution approach. To understand why, it is helpful to think about what happens in the limiting case in which the obligor's PD

Table 4. ASRF/Merton capital charges given high guarantor asset correlation ($\rho_g = 0.50$)

Guarantor PD (%)	Obligor PD (%)							
	0.03	0.10	0.50	1.00	2.00	5.00	10.00	50.00
0.03	0.02	0.06	0.17	0.25	0.33	0.50	0.72	1.53
0.10	0.06	0.15	0.44	0.63	0.86	1.28	1.86	3.94
0.50	0.18	0.45	1.28	1.83	2.49	3.72	5.39	11.41
1.00	0.26	0.65	1.85	2.66	3.60	5.39	7.81	16.53
Unhedged exposure	0.62	1.54	4.40	6.31	8.56	12.80	18.56	39.29

is 100%. In this setting, all payments to the bank come from the guarantor, so the ASRF/Merton capital charge for the hedged exposure is equal to the A-IRB capital charge given the guarantor's PD and asset correlation. In contrast, the substitution approach calculates capital using the guarantor's PD but the CP3 asset correlation formula. Thus, if the guarantor asset correlation exceeds that given in Equation (2) the ASRF/Merton capital charges for hedged exposures will be larger than the substitution approach when obligor PDs are high.

High obligor–guarantor asset correlation and high guarantor asset correlation

Table 5 shows ASRF/Merton capital charges under the assumption that both the obligor–guarantor asset correlation and the guarantor asset correlation are 50%. This calibration shows that, even under a combination of rather conservative asset correlation assumptions, the ASRF/Merton model produces significantly lower capital charged than the substitution approach when obligor PDs are low. However, the ASRF/Merton model produces higher capital charges than the substitution approach when obligor PDs are high.

CONCLUSIONS

Under Basel II, A-IRB capital charges for unhedged exposures are derived from a stylised portfolio credit-risk model that accounts for cross-exposure differences in default probabilities, loss rates, and sensitivities to systematic risk. In contrast, the Basel Committee's proposed capital treatment for hedged exposures is not derived from an underlying credit-risk model. Instead, it relies on simple, but to some extent *ad hoc*, adjustments to the PDs and LGDs associated with unhedged exposures. Earlier in this

Table 5. ASRF/Merton capital charges given high obligor–guarantor asset correlation (ρ_{og} = 0.50) and high guarantor asset correlation (ρ_g = 0.50)

Guarantor	Obligor PD (%)							
PD (%)	0.03	0.10	0.50	1.00	2.00	5.00	10.00	50.00
0.03	0.08	0.17	0.41	0.57	0.76	1.05	1.30	1.72
0.10	0.16	0.36	0.91	1.27	1.70	2.41	3.09	4.39
0.50	0.33	0.78	2.08	2.95	3.99	5.81	7.79	12.47
1.00	0.42	1.00	2.71	3.86	5.24	7.69	10.53	17.86
Unhedged Exposure	0.62	1.54	4.40	6.31	8.56	12.80	18.56	39.29

chapter we were able to show that the very same economic assumptions used by the Basel Committee to develop a regulatory capital model for unhedged exposures can be used to derive a regulatory capital model for hedged exposures.

Calibrations presented in the last section indicate that the ASRF/Merton model for hedged exposures is sensitive to assumptions about the interdependence among risks faced by obligors and guarantors. Not surprisingly, when the risks facing a guarantor are highly correlated with those facing a reference obligor, a credit hedge provides less protection and hence receives a higher capital charge. Similarly, when a guarantor's credit quality is exceptionally sensitive to systematic risk it cannot provide effective protection against systematic shocks.

The calibrations presented in this chapter abstract from the possibility that LGDs for hedged exposures might be lower than those for unhedged exposures. Generally, when a lender uses a CDS to hedge credit risk, it has the opportunity to pursue recoveries from both the seller of the CDS and the reference obligor in the event that both counterparties default. All else equal, accounting for these sorts of double-recovery effects would tend to lower the capital charges produced by the ASRF/Merton model.

Comparisons between the ASRF/Merton model for hedged exposures and the Basel Committee's proposed substitution approach suggest that, when high quality guarantors provide credit protection for exposures to high quality obligors, the substitution approach produces much higher regulatory capital charges than would arise from a more internally consistent regulatory capital treatment. When exposures to obligors with poor credit quality (high PDs) are hedged, the story is more complicated. The substitution approach may lead to either higher or lower regulatory capital charges depending on the extent to which defaults by credit-protection sellers are sensitive to systematic risk.

When we ask the narrow question, "Does the substitution approach produce credit risk capital charges that are consistent with the regulatory capital model applied to unhedged exposures?" the answer appears to be "No." If the Basel Committee were to consider implementing a capital treatment for hedged exposures along the lines developed in this chapter, two important practical challenges would need to be addressed. First, the Basel Committee's prior experience in developing a capital treatment for unhedged exposures has shown that it is exceptionally difficult to pin down asset correlation parameters using data that are currently available. Hence, implementing an ASRF/Merton model for hedged exposures would almost certainly require a degree of supervisory judgment. Second, applying the ASRF/Merton model for hedged exposures would add considerable complexity to an already very complex set of regulatory standards.[6] The Basel Committee would therefore have to weigh the benefits of greater internal consistency against the costs of additional regulatory complexity. As is often the case when there are trade-offs, a compromise between competing objectives may be warranted.

1 Regulators in the US have indicated their intention to implement only the A-IRB approach, and to mandate Basel II treatment for only the largest, internationally active US banks (Ferguson, 2003).

2 For C&I loans, the A-IRB capital formula includes a multiplicative adjustment for loan maturity. For simplicity, we restrict attention to one-year maturity loans where this adjustment drops out.

3 See Pykhtin and Dev (2002) for a similar application to ASRF capital charges for loan-backed securities.

4 The ASRF/Merton model for hedged exposures is derived under the assumption that assets for the obligor and the guarantor are jointly normally distributed, but richer joint probability specification using alpha-stable models could also be used. See Chapter 15 of this book or Embrechts, Klüppelberg and Mikosch (1997) for a discussion of this broader class of models.

5 If we assume that systematic risk is the only driver of correlation between an obligor and a guarantor, then ρ_{og} is the geometric mean of ρ_o and ρ_g, so increasing the value of ρ_g has the effect of increasing ρ_{og}. For this reason, when the guarantor asset correlation is 50% and ψ_{og} = 0, the obligor–guarantor asset correlation ranges from 24–35% depending on the obligor PD.

6 The third consultative paper is 216 pages long.

BIBLIOGRAPHY

Basel Committee on Banking Supervision, 1988, "International Convergence of Capital Measurement and Capital Standards", URL: http://www.bis.org/publ/bcbs04a.htm (1988). Basel: Bank for International Settlements.

BIS, 2003, "Third Consultative Paper", URL http://www.bis.org/bcbs/bcbscp3.htm (29 April 2003). Basel: Bank for International Settlements.

Embrechts, P., C. Klüppelberg and T. Mikosch, 1997, *Modelling Extremal Events for Insurance and Finance*, corrected second printing, 1999 (New York: Springer-Verlag).

Ferguson, R. W., 2003, "Testimony before the United States Senate Committee on Banking, Housing, and Urban Affairs", 18 June 2003 (Washington, DC: Federal Reserve Board).

Fitch Inc, 2003, "Global Credit Derivatives: Risk Management or Risk?", Fitch Ratings, *Credit Policy*, special report, 10 March.

Gordy, M. B., 2003, "A Risk-Factor Model Foundation for Ratings-Based Bank Capital Rules", *Journal of Financial Intermediation* 12(3) July 2003 pp. 199–232.

Gupton, G. M., C. C. Finger and M. Bhatia, 1997, *CreditMetrics: Technical Document* (New York: J P Morgan).

ISDA (International Swaps and Derivatives Association), 2002, letter from E. Sebton, ISDA, to D. Hendricks, BIS Working Group on Overall Capital, 20 December.

ISDA, 2001, letter from E. Sebton, ISDA, to O. Page, chair, Capital Group, Basel Committee on Banking Supervision, 3 October.

Pykhtin, M., and A. Dev, 2002, "Credit Risk in Asset Securitisations: An Analytical Model", *Risk* May 2002, pp S16–S20.

Glossary

arbitrage pricing theory (APT) an alternative asset-pricing model to the capital asset-pricing model (CAPM). Unlike CAPM, which specifies returns as a linear function of only **systematic risk**, arbitrage pricing theory may specify returns as a linear function of more than a single factor.

asset-backed security (ABS) asset whose value is based on the right it gives the owner to receive distributions from the proceeds of financial assets that provide collateral for the security.

asset correlation correlation of returns from two risky assets.

asset securitisation process whereby loans, receivables and other illiquid assets with similar characteristics in the balance sheet are packaged into interest-bearing securities that offer attractive investment opportunities.

asset swap consists of a defaultable coupon bond and an interest-rate swap that swaps the bond's coupon into a default-free Libor plus the asset-swap rate.

back-testing the validation of a model by feeding it historical data and comparing the model's results with the historical reality.

balance sheet a document detailing a company's assets and liabilities. The two quantities that have to "balance" are (1) assets and (2) the sum of liabilities and shareholders' equity.

bankers paradox arises since the counterparties to whom a financial institution is most exposed are likely to be those with whom they have the best relationships. Traditional methods of managing credit risk, like imposing credit limits, therefore imply that the financial institution should stop transacting with the counterparties with whom it has good relationships.

banking book *see* **trading book**.

bankruptcy the liquidation of a firm's assets when it is unable to meet its financial obligations; distinct from **default**.

Basel or Basle I Capital Accord, originally published in 1988, that sets down the agreement among the G10 central banks to apply common minimum capital standards to their banking industries. A target ratio of capital to weighted risk assets is set at 8%.

Basel II New Basel Capital Accord, due for completion in the fourth quarter of 2003, will replace the **Basel** Capital Accord. The new Accord focuses on:

❏ Minimum capital requirements, which seek to refine the measurement framework set out in the Basel Capital Accord. In particular, the new measurements are designed to make the capital requirements more sensitive to the actual risk of the assets and to take operational risk into account.
❏ Supervisory review of an institution's capital adequacy and internal assessment process.
❏ Market discipline through disclosure requirements and recommendations.

Beta a measure of the systemic risk of an asset. It is the correlation coefficient between the expected return on the asset and that of the market.

beta distribution a family of parametric probability distributions with two degrees of freedom defined on the interval [0,1]. One of the Weibull class of distributions.

Brownian motion a type of **Markov process** that is used to specify the stochastic process of asset prices – also known as the Wiener process.

calibration (of a model) see **parameterisation**.

capital allocation/attribution the allocation of capital to the business lines in a financial institution.

capital asset pricing model (CAPM) model giving the expected return for an asset as linearly dependent on its beta.

capital charge the required regulatory capital imposed on banks by the supervisory bodies.

capital relief banks can obtain regulatory capital relief by transferring lower-yield corporate credit risk off their balance sheet. **Basel I** rules all corporate debt carries an identical 100% risk weighting, which requires assignment of 8% of capital. A bank may wish to transfer higher-rated, lower-yield assets from its balance sheet, to obtain lower regulatory capital requirements, which can be achieved via a **CDO** transaction.

collateralised debt obligation (CDO) a securitisation in which an **SPV** issues bonds or notes against an investment in a diversified pool of assets.

The CDO structure allocates interest and principal repayments from the cashflow generated from the assets to a prioritised collection of **tranches**. Senior notes are paid before mezzanine and lower-rated notes. Any residual cashflow is paid to the equity piece. This makes the senior CDO notes significantly less risky then the collateral.

Cholesky decomposition can be applied to a square matrix A, if it is symmetric ($a_{ij} = a_{ji}$) and positive definite (all positive eigenvalues). There is then a special, more efficient, triangular decomposition: $L.L^T = A$, where L is a lower triangular matrix. Using this method is about a factor of two faster than alternative methods for solving linear equations.

collateralisation the backing of a security by an asset.

commitment normally means a loan and is composed of two portions: drawn and undrawn. A commitment is an amount the bank has agreed to lend, at a borrower's request, up to the full amount of the commitment.

concentration risk see **credit risk concentration**.

correlation of credit quality the correlation of the *credit ratings* or rating changes of entities in a portfolio.

correlation of default *see* **default correlation**.

counterparty risk the risk that the counterparty in a transaction will default and not be able to meet the transaction obligations.

counterparty risk weighting see **risk weighting**.

country risk the risk that borrowers within a country will not be able to repay their obligations to foreign creditors because of negative political or general economic factors. Also known as sovereign risk.

credit concentration see **credit risk concentration**; see also **credit paradox**.

credit curve analogous to the yield curve, a series of default swap (or asset swap or bond) prices for a given underlying credit used to define the forward default probability curve for pricing purposes.

credit derivative a specific class of financial instrument whose value is derived from an underlying market instrument driven primarily by the **credit risk** of private or government entities. The underlying instruments of credit derivatives are generally in the form of corporate debt and securities issued by sovereign entities.

credit enhancement any method or technique that reduces the credit exposure of a transaction with a counterparty.

CreditMetrics the framework used by JP Morgan for quantifying credit risk in portfolios of credit products, fixed-income instruments and financial instruments subject to counterparty default.

credit migration short of a default, the extent to which the **credit quality** of an obligor or counterparty improves or deteriorates.

credit paradox the dramatic rise in the loan spreads required as exposure to the same obligor increases. The phenomenon forces many banks to take on larger amounts of credit exposure in search of larger spreads, thereby exposing themselves to an even larger probability of suffering from default. *See also* **credit risk concentration**.

credit quality the credit quality of a firm at a specific point in time is measured by the probability that it will be able to pay off its contractual obligations. The first instance of failure to do so is defined as default.

credit repo credit repurchase agreement.

credit (or default) risk the risk that a loss will be incurred if a counterparty to a transaction does not fulfil its financial obligations in a timely manner.

credit risk concentration (concentration risk) if a loan portfolio is highly concentrated in terms of exposure to a specific industry or country, it is highly susceptible to correlated **default** and **credit migration** events. The opposite of *diversification*.

credit risk models models that attempt to quantify credit risk – eg, value-of-the-firm models; recovery-of-promised-payoff models; instantaneous-risk-of-default models.

credit swaps agreement between two counterparties to exchange disparate cashflows, at least one of which must be tied to the performance of a credit-sensitive asset or to a portfolio or index of such assets. The other cashflow is usually tied to a floating-rate index (such as Libor) or a fixed rate, or is linked to another credit-sensitive asset.

credit spread difference between the yield on a risky debt and the **risk-free rate**.

creditVAR value-at-risk due to default (to a given confidence level and time-horizon).

default failure of a firm to make a payment on a coupon or reimburse its debt.

default correlation the degree to which the default of one obligor is related to the default of another. The quantity that ties the **risk contribution** of a risky asset to the portfolio.

default payment leg the payments that occur due to credit events.

default point critical threshold for defaulting posited by KMV Corporation on the basis of the observation that a firm is more likely to default when its asset value reaches a certain critical level somewhere between the value of total liabilities and that of short-term debt. Defined by KMV as the "book value" of the firm's liabilities – roughly approximated by the sum of the short-term debt and one-half of the long-term debt.

default probability *see* **expected default frequency**.

default process in most cases of default there are transitions between credit ratings (**credit migration**) before the default state is reached; this is known as a multi-state default process. A two-state default process consists of the two possible events "no default" and "default" at the analysis horizon.

density function (of a distribution) the area under the density curve across an interval represents the probability over that interval.

distance to default an index defined by KMV Corporation as the distance between the expected asset value of a firm at the analysis horizon and the **default point**, normalised by the standard deviation of the future asset returns.

diversification putting your eggs in more than one basket as a way of reducing risk.

drift mathematically, the deterministic component of a Brownian motion indicating the general slope and direction of the random motion.

economic capital capital necessary for the bank to remain solvent in the event of **extreme loss**. Economic capital is the number of standard deviations away from the **expected loss** that is necessary to protect the bank from insolvency in the event of extreme losses in the bank's portfolio due to default risk. Also known as "risk capital". *See also* **value-at-risk**.

EDF see **expected default frequency**.

EL see **expected loss**.

event risk a risk defined as a change in value of an asset or position due to occurrences such as a merger or acquisition, changes in market conditions, political upheavals or other unforeseen circumstances.

expected default frequency (EDF) the probability that an obligor will default before the maturity of the contracted obligation to pay. Such probabilities can be estimated from historical data or analytically using options theory. Same as probability of default.

expected exposure the amount the bank can expect to lose, on average, over the period of time in which it extends credits.

expected loss (EL) the average loss the bank can expect to incur on an asset over the period up to a specified horizon. *See also* **unexpected loss**.

exposure vulnerability to loss from unanticipated events.

extreme loss loss arising from defaults of catastrophic magnitude, which tend to occur more frequently when market conditions deteriorate beyond a certain point.

extreme value theory an actuarial science that focuses on extreme events and their associated tail probabilities; it looks explicitly at extreme outcomes and provides a series of natural models for them. The tail of an empirically observed loss distribution, however incomplete, can be fitted to some analytical "extreme distribution", facilitating the analysis of tail or extreme events.

factor models dependency, typically between asset values, through driving factors. Each firm's assets will be given by a weighted linear combination of the random driving factors. This technique reduces the dimensionality of modelling dependency.

fat tails describes that the distribution implies a large probability of extreme movements.

first loss describes the first loss(es) to be sustained on a **reference portfolio**.

first-passage time mathematically, the first instantaneous occurrence of an event, such as default.

forward (transaction) agreement to exchange a predetermined amount of currency, commodity or other financial instrument at a specified future date and at a predetermined rate.

Gaussian describes that a random variable has a **normal distribution**, or that multiple random variables have a multi-variate Normal distribution.

game theory a theory of individual rational decisions taken under conditions of less than full information concerning the outcomes of those decisions.

Group of Ten (G10) countries Belgium, Canada, France, Germany, Italy, Japan, the Netherlands, Sweden, the United Kingdom and the United States.

Group of Six (G6) countries France, Germany, Italy, Japan, the United Kingdom and the United States.

hedge a strategy to reduce exposure by effecting a transaction that offsets an existing position.

hedge fund private investment partnerships that seek above-average returns through aggressive portfolio management. Due to their private nature, hedge funds are allowed to use leverage, short sales and other non-traditional techniques to enhance returns.

high-yield (bond) a bond that offers a high yield due to compensate for a relatively high probability of default.

idiosyncratic risk risk due to factors originating from the firm itself.

illiquid asset essentially, a lack of liquidity in an asset or in a portfolio of assets held by a transactor. The condition is always relative, since almost all assets vary in degree of liquidity. A corporate loan is less liquid than, say, a US Treasury security.

internal (credit) risk rating a bank's own assessment of the risk associated with an entity as opposed to the ratings issued by credit rating agencies. Essentially, it is the bank's primary indicator of risk for individual credit exposures and is used to provide guidance for setting *loan loss reserves*, profitability analysis and loan pricing analysis.

intrinsic value the amount by which an option is in-the-money, that is, its value relative to the current forward market price. Option premiums comprise intrinsic value and time value.

investment grade (bond) a bond which has a high bond rating (BBB and above for S&P).

ISDA International Swaps and Derivatives Association.

joint distribution a multi-variate distribution that depends on two or more variables.

joint probability of default the probability that one obligor will default if another defaults.

kurtosis a measure of how fast the tails or wings of a probability distribution approach zero, evaluated relative to a **normal distribution**. The tails are either fat-tailed (leptokurtic) or thin-tailed (platykurtic). Markets are generally leptokurtic. The fatter the tails, the greater the chance a variable will reach an extreme value, implying that models such as Black-Scholes – which assumes a perfect normal distribution – produce pricing biases for deep in- or out-of-the-money options.

leptokurtosis phenomenon when the probability distribution has a larger mass on the tail and a sharper hump than is consistent with the assumption of a normal distribution. *See also* **kurtosis**.

leverage the ability to control large amounts of an underlying variable for a small initial investment. Futures and options are regarded as leveraged products because the initial premium paid by the purchaser is generally much smaller than the nominal amount of the underlying. Leverage is usually measured as a quantity called *lambda*. Many structured notes are said to be leveraged because their coupon is governed by a multiple of a reference interest rate (such as Libor). It is also possible to deleverage a note by linking its coupon to a fraction of the reference rate.

leverage ratio the ratio between a firm's equity and debt.

LGD see **loss given default**.

liquidity risk the risk associated with transactions made in illiquid markets. Such markets are characterised by wide bid-offer spreads, lack of transparency and large movements in price after a deal of any size. A firm wishing to unwind a portfolio of illiquid instruments (eg, highly tailored structured notes) may find it has to sell them at prices far below their fair values, exacerbating the problems that prompted the decision to unwind.

loan an agreement whereby one party provides monies to another party for a set period in return for regular payment of interest and principal.

loan portfolio a collection of illiquid assets, eg loans, held by an institution in its banking book.

loss given default (LGD) the fraction of the exposure amount that will be lost on default or, more appropriately, the fraction of the debt the bank is not likely to recover from the obligor once it has defaulted.

loss probability distribution the probability distribution of loss in portfolio value.

loss severity degree of loss in the event of default. *See also* **loss given default**.

model risk the risk arising from the misuse of financial models, including miscalibration and incorrect specification.

market risk exposure to a change in the value of some market variable, such as interest rates or foreign exchange rates, equity or commodity prices. For holders of a derivatives position, market risk may be passed through from a change in the value of the underlying to the price of the derivative, or it may arise from other sources, such as implied volatility or time decay.

marking-to-market to mark-to-market is to calculate the value of a financial instrument (or portfolio of such instruments) on the basis of the current market rates or prices of the underlying. Marking-to-market on a daily (or more frequent) basis is often recommended in risk management guidelines.

Markov process an ordered set of discrete random variables, each of which has at any time a given state or value dependent only on the state of the variable immediately before it. It assumes that only the current value of a stochastic (random) variable is important in predicting future values of that variable.

Markov property (condition/process) of a system, that its evolution in time depends only on the state that preceded it.

martingale a probabilistic interpretation of the payout of a "fair game". The expected gain at any point in the future is equal to the actual gain now.

maximum likelihood estimator a technique that estimates model parameters, by maximising the probability that the model could have produced the observed data.

mean-reversion the phenomenon by which interest rates and volatility appear to move back to a long-run average level. Interest rates' mean-reverting tendency is one explanation for the behaviour of the volatility term structure. Some interest-rate models incorporate mean-reversion, such as Vasicek and Cox-Ingersoll-Ross, in which high interest rates tend to go down and low ones up.

modified modified restructuring CDS provides protection against defaults and restructuring events. In a default event the buyer of protection may deliver any transferable obligation of the reference entity. In a restructuring event the buyer of protection may deliver any transferable obligation of the reference entity, provided the obligation matures before the later of 60 months after the restructuring date and the CDS maturity. *See also* **modified restructuring**, which has more restrictive date restrictions.

modified restructuring CDS provides protection against defaults and restructuring events. In a default event the buyer of protection may deliver any transferable obligation of the reference entity. In a restructuring event the buyer of protection may deliver any transferable obligation of the reference entity, provided the obligation matures before the earlier of 30 months after the restructuring date and the latest maturity date of all restructured obligations. However, this date restriction can't be earlier than the CDS maturity or later than 30 months after the CDS maturity. See also **modified modified restructuring**, which has less restrictive date restrictions.

Monte Carlo simulation a method of determining the value of a derivative by simulating the evolution of the underlying variable(s) many times over. The discounted average outcome of the simulation gives an approximation of the derivative's value. This method may be used to value complex derivatives, particularly path-dependent options, for which closed-form solutions have not been or cannot be found. Monte Carlo simulation can also be used to estimate the **value-at-risk** (VAR) of a portfolio. In this case, a simulation of many correlated market movements is generated for the markets to which the portfolio is exposed, and the positions in the portfolio are revalued repeatedly in accordance with the simulated scenarios. The result of this calculation is a probability distribution of portfolio gains and losses from which the VAR can be determined. The principal difficulty with Monte Carlo VAR analysis is that it can be very computationally intensive.

multi-factor model any model in which there are two or more uncertain parameters in the option price (one-factor models incorporate only one cause of uncertainty: the future price). There are two main reasons for using multi-factor models. The first is that they permit more realistic modelling, particularly of interest rates, although they are very difficult to compute. The second is that multi-factor options (for example, spread options) have several parameters whose volatilities need to be treated independently and in which the degree of correlation between the underlyings has to be treated separately.

net present value (NPV) a technique for assessing the worth of future payments by looking at the present value of those future cashflows discounted at today's cost of capital.

netting refers to the offsetting of transactions between two parties with settlement of the net difference.

non-systematic risk *see* **specific risk**.

normal distribution a symmetric distribution described by two parameters, the mean and the standard deviation.

notional amount the quantity of an underlier (the primary instrument or variable) to which a derivative contract applies.

obligor-specific risk risk associated with a particular client; tends to increase with diminishing company asset size.

one-factor model a model or description of a system where the model incorporates only one variable, or uncertainty: the future price. These are simple models, usually leading to closed-form solutions, such as the Black-Scholes model or the Vasicek model.

operational risk the risk run by a firm that its internal practices, policies and systems are not sufficiently rigorous or sophisticated to cope with adverse market conditions or human or technological errors. Although operational risk is not as easy to identify or quantify as market or credit risk, it has been implicated as a major factor in many of the highly publicised derivatives losses of recent years. Sources of operational risk include: failure to correctly measure or report risk; lack of controls to prevent unauthorised or inappropriate transactions (the so-called "rogue trader" syndrome); and lack of understanding among key staff.

option a contract that gives the purchaser the right, but not the obligation, to buy or sell an underlying at a certain price (the exercise or strike price) on or before an agreed date (the exercise period). For this right, the purchaser pays a premium to the seller. The seller (writer) of an option has a duty to buy or sell at the strike price should the purchaser exercise this right. With European-style options, purchasers may take delivery of the underlying only at the end of the option's life. American-style options may be exercised, for immediate delivery, at any time over the life of the option. Options can be bought on commodities, stocks, stock indexes, interest rates, bonds, currencies.

outstandings generic term referring to the portion of the bank's asset that has already been extended to a borrower (in the case of loans and bonds) and also to other receivables in the form of contractual payments that are due from its customers. If on default a borrower is unable to fulfil its contractual obligations or the receivables fail to come in, the bank is exposed to the entire amount of the outstandings. Examples of outstandings are term loans, credit cards, bonds and receivables.

over the counter an over-the-counter (OTC) security or instrument is one that is traded by private negotiation rather than in a supervised environment such as a derivatives exchange. The range of instruments available OTC is typically wider and more tailored than in organised markets.

pairwise correlation of default the correlation between the defaults of two assets. See **joint probability of default**.

parameterisation the subjective choice of parameters used as inputs to a risk model; also known as "calibration".

parametric distribution a probability distribution whose shape and form are specified by certain parameters.

par yield curve a yield curve constructed by calculating the coupons necessary for bonds of various maturities to be priced at par.

path-dependent option a path-dependent option has a payout that is directly related to movements in the price of the underlying during the option's life. By contrast, the payout of a standard European-style option is determined solely by the price at expiry.

payoff the return from an instrument or position.

portfolio expected loss the simple sum of individual expected losses from all the risky assets in a portfolio.

portfolio unexpected loss unexpected loss at portfolio level. Unlike **portfolio expected loss**, this loss is *not* equal to the linear sum of the individual unexpected losses of the risky assets making up the aggregate portfolio. Because of diversification effects, the portfolio unexpected loss is very much smaller than the sum of the individual unexpected losses.

portfolio variance the square of the standard deviation of the portfolio's return from the mean.

premium leg payments arising from premium payments.

prepayment risk the risk that the value of a mortgage-backed security will change due to a change in the prepayment behaviour of the mortgages on which it is based. If a mortgage is prepaid, the principal of the security declines, as does its average life, although its final maturity remains unchanged. This will in turn affect the duration of the security and its value. Prepayment risk also occurs with callable bonds and cancellable swaps, in which case it refers to the reinvestment risk that an investment repaid early may have to be reinvested at a lower rate of return.

principal-guaranteed product any investment vehicle that allows investors to gain exposure to an asset while guaranteeing the return of their principal. Such products are normally constructed by buying a deep-discount bond (often a zero-coupon bond) and using the rest of the money to buy embedded call or put options to gain exposure to a second asset, often a stock index.

priority of payment see **waterfall**.

put-call parity the relationship between a European-style put option and a European-style call option on the same underlying with the same exercise price and maturity. Put-call parity states that the payout profile of a portfolio containing an asset plus a put option is identical to that of a portfolio containing a call option of the same strike on that same asset (with the rest of the money earning the risk-free rate of return). In practice, therefore, a put option on, say, a stock index can be constructed by shorting the stock and buying a call option. The relationship means that traders can arbitrage mispriced options.

quanto product an asset or liability denominated in a currency other than that in which it is usually traded.

random walk the series of values taken by a random variable with the progress of some parameter such as time. Each new value (each new step in the walk) is selected randomly and describes the path taken by the underlying variable. *See also* **stochastic process**.

RAROC see **risk-adjusted return on capital**.

rating the evaluation of an issuer's investment quality by a rating agency.

recovery rate the extent to which the face value of an obligation can be recovered once the obligor has defaulted.

reduced-form model is a credit risk model with its underlying assumptions imposed on the prices of the firm's traded liabilities. This type of model is "reduced-form" compared with a **structural model**, which needs to deduce the prices of the firm's traded liabilities from structural assumptions.

reference portfolio a portfolio of obligations whose credit events will trigger default payments in the credit derivative.

regulatory capital sufficient capital imposed by regulators on banks that must be maintained to provide a cushion to absorb losses that would otherwise cause a bank to fail.

replacement cost often used in terms of credit exposure, the replacement cost of a financial instrument is its current value in the market – in other words, what it would cost to replace a given contract if the counterparty to the contract defaulted. Aside from bid-ask conventions, it is synonymous with market value.

replication replicating the payout of an option by buying or selling other instruments. Creating a synthetic option in this way is always possible in a complete market. In the case of dynamic replication this involves dynamically buying or selling the underlying (or normally, because of cheaper transaction costs, futures) in proportion to an option's delta. In the case of static replication, the option is hedged with a basket of standard options whose composition does not change with time.

repo agreement to buy (sell) a security while at the same time agreeing to sell (buy) the same security at a predetermined future date. The price at which the reverse transaction takes place sets the interest rate over the period (the repo rate). The most active repo market is in the US, where the Federal Reserve sets short-term interest rates by lending securities. In a reverse repo, the buyer sells cash in exchange for a security. Repos can benefit both parties. Buyers of repos often receive a better return than that available on equivalent money-market instruments, and financial institutions, particularly dealers, are able to get sub-Libor funding. A variation on the repo is the buy-/sell-back. The buy-/sell-back's coupon becomes the property of the purchaser for the duration of the agreement. It is preferred by credit-sensitive investors such as central banks.

required spread the spread the bank needs to charge given a particular level of return.

restructuring is an event that causes the terms of the relevant obligation to become less favourable to the holders. These events include a reduction in the principal amount or interest payable, a postponement of payment, a change in ranking in priority of payment or other composition of payment. The ISDA consider restructuring a credit event.

risk-adjusted return on capital (RAROC) the expected spread over economic capital, calculated for individual assets or portfolios.

risk adjustment the process whereby returns from dissimilar business lines are measured on a comparable basis according to their riskiness.

risk-based capital standard/adequacy generally referred to as the BIS capital rules.

risk capital see **economic capital.**

risk contribution the incremental risk that the exposure of a single asset contributes to the portfolio's total risk.

risk-free rate a theoretical interest rate at which an investment may earn interest without incurring any risk.

risk management control and limitation of the risks faced by an organisation arising from its exposure to changes in financial market variables, such as foreign exchange and interest rates, equity and commodity prices or counterparty creditworthiness. This may be because of the financial impact of an adverse move in the market variable (market risk), because the organisation is ill prepared to respond to such a move (operational risk), because a counterparty defaults (credit risk) or because a specific contract is not enforceable (legal risk). Market risks are usually managed by hedging with financial instruments, although a firm may also reduce risk by adjusting its business practices. While financial derivatives lend themselves to this purpose, risk can also be reduced through judicious use of the underlying assets, eg, by diversifying portfolios.

risk measurement assessment of a firm's exposure to risk. *See also* **value-at-risk**.

risk-neutral a theoretical condition whereby investors require no compensation for taking risk.

risk-weighted assets (RWA) assets weighted in accordance with their relative credit-riskiness.

risk weighting when calculating the amount of capital that the Bank for International Settlements (BIS) advises should be set aside to cover the credit risk generated by derivative transactions, banks first calculate a "credit equivalent amount" and then multiply this figure by the appropriate counterparty risk weighting (eg, 20% for OECD incorporated banks). The product of this calculation is the final risk-weighted amount.

R2 coefficient the linear correlation coefficient indicates the degree of linear correlation between two quantities. This can be interpreted as measuring the quality of a straight-line fit to the pairs of values. The value of R2 lies between 0 and 1, inclusive, where a value of 1 indicates perfect correlation and values near 0 indicate that the variables are uncorrelated.

securitisation the conversion of assets (usually forms of debt) into securities that can be traded more freely and cheaply than the underlying assets and generate better returns than if the assets were used as collateral for a loan. One example is the mortgage-backed security, which pools illiquid individual mortgages into a single tradable asset.

senior tranche/super-senior tranche the **tranche** of a **collateralised debt obligation** (CDO) with very low probability of default. The senior tranche is funded with notes of rating typically AA or above. A super-senior tranche arises when the CDO is only partially funded by notes. The collateral not guaranteed by the **SPV** will have an extremely low probability of default (typically rated AAA) and is known as the super-senior tranche. This can be most cheaply protected by the issuer using a CDS to transfer the risk rather than funding with issue of notes.

skew a skewed distribution is one that is asymmetric. Skew is a measure of this asymmetry. A perfectly symmetrical distribution has zero skew, whereas a distribution with positive (negative) skew is one where outliers above (below) the mean are more probable. An example of an asymmetric distribution in the financial markets is the distribution implied by the presence of a volatility skew between out-of-the-money call and put options.

solvency ratio the formula for setting down the size of the balance-sheet credit run by a financial institution based on the riskiness and size of the capital; also known as a capital ratio.

sovereign debt when the obligor is a state or government.

special-purpose vehicle (SPV) is a trust, corporation, partnership, or a limited-liability company that is set up to buy assets and issue debt and equity tranches.

specific risk also known as non-systematic risk, this represents the price variability of a security that is due to factors unique to that security, as opposed to that portion due to systematic risk, the generalised price variability of the related interest rate or equity market.

stochastic process formally, a process that can be described by the evolution of some random variable over some parameter, which may be either discrete or continuous. Geometric Brownian motion is an example of a stochastic process parameterised by time. Stochastic processes are used in finance to develop models of the future price of an instrument in terms of the spot price and some random variable; or, analogously, the future value of an interest rate or foreign exchange rate. See also **martingale.**

stochastic volatility one of the key assumptions of the Black–Scholes model is that the stock price follows geometric Brownian motion with constant volatility and interest rates. However, in real markets, volatility is far from constant (see trading volatility). If volatility is assumed to be driven by some stochastic process, however, the Black–Scholes model no longer describes a complete market because there is now another source of uncertainty in the option-pricing model. Since the mid-1980s a variety of approaches have been attempted to resolve this difficulty, most notably the Heath–Jarrow–Morton framework.

stress-testing analysis that gives the value of a portfolio under a range of worst-case scenarios.

structural model is a credit risk model with underlying assumptions imposed on the firm's balance sheet or structure. This contrasts to a **reduced-form model.**

student-t distribution a symmetrical distribution if the population is normally distributed with unknown standard deviation.

subordinated debt a debt that is ranked lower than another security in the priority of its claim on the issuer's assets.

super-senior tranche see **senior tranche.**

synthetic CDO a type of **CDO** structure that uses credit derivatives to transfer risk from a referenced portfolio of credit exposures. This may be preferable to transferring the actual assets into the SPV.

systemic risk the risk that the financial system as a whole may not withstand the effects of a market crisis. Banking regulators have been concerned by the concentration of derivative risk among a relatively small number of market participants, with the concomitant risk that the failure of a major dealer could have serious knock-on effects for many other market participants.

term loan a loan with a payment of interest where the principal is usually paid out some years later.

term structure of interest rates relationship between interest rates on the same securities with different maturities.

time value the value of an option other than its intrinsic value. The time value therefore includes cost of carry and the probability that the option will be exercised (which in turn depends on its volatility).

total return swap (TRS) swap agreement in which the total return of bank loans or credit-sensitive securities is exchanged for some other cashflow, usually tied to Libor, or other loans or credit-sensitive securities. It allows participants effectively to go long or short the credit risk of the underlying asset.

trading book bank portfolio containing securities that are actively bought and sold for the purpose of making short-term profit, in contrast to the banking book, which generally consists of loans.

transition matrix an array of transition or migration probabilities from one credit rating to another.

transition probability the probability that the **credit quality** of a firm will improve or deteriorate; quantifies **credit migration**; *see* **transition matrix**.

tranche a class of an asset-backed security (eg, a **collateralised debt obligation**).

UL *see* **unexpected loss.**

underlying the variable on which a contract is based.

undiversifiable risk the amount of credit risk that cannot be diversified away by placing or removing an asset in a portfolio; also called **systematic risk**.

unexpected loss (UL) uncertainty in the amount of loss in portfolio value caused by market conditions. This uncertainty, or more appropriately the *volatility* of loss, is the so-called *unexpected loss*. Unexpected losses are triggered by the occurrence of **default** and unexpected **credit migrations**.

value-at-risk (VAR) formally, the probabilistic bound of market losses over a given period of time (the holding period) expressed in terms of a specified degree of certainty (the confidence interval). Put more simply, the VAR is the worst-case loss expected over the holding period within the probability set out by the confidence interval. Larger losses are possible but with a low probability. For instance, a portfolio whose VAR is US$20 million over a one-day holding period, with a 95% confidence interval, would have only a 5% chance of suffering an overnight loss greater than US$20 million.

value-of-the-firm models propose that the underlying process driving a firm's default (or credit rating change) is the firm's asset value (after Merton), a structural model.

volatility measure of the variability (but not the direction) of prices or interest rates.

waterfall (or cashflow waterfall) refers to the ordering of payments by tranche seniority in a **CDO**.

Wiener process see **Brownian motion**.

worst-case (credit risk) exposure estimate of the highest positive market value a derivative contract or portfolio is likely to attain at a given moment or period in the future, with a given level of confidence.

worst-case (credit risk) loss estimate of the largest amount a derivatives counterparty is likely to lose, with a given level of probability, as a result of default from a derivatives contract or portfolio.

yield the interest rate that will make the net present value of the cashflows from an investment equal to the price (or cost) of the investment. Also called the internal rate of return. The current yield relates the annual coupon yield to the market price by dividing the coupon by the price divided by 100 and ignores the **time value** of money or potential capital gains or losses. Simple yield to maturity takes into account the effect of the capital gain or loss on maturity of a bond in addition to the current yield.

yield curve the yield curve is a graphical representation of the term structure of interest rates. It is usually depicted as the spot yields on bonds with different maturities but the same risk factors (such as creditworthiness of issuer) plotted against maturity. The usual features of a spot-yield curve are higher long-term yields than short-term yields and a curve for default-free bonds that is lower at each point than the equivalent curve for riskier debt. It is possible to construct variants of the yield curve from this basic form. The par-yield curve is found by calculating the coupons that would be necessary for bonds of each maturity to be priced at par; the forward-yield curve is found by extrapolating the spot-yield curve point by point, based on the implied forward interest rates.

zero-coupon bond a debt instrument issued at below-par value. The bond pays no coupons; instead, it is redeemed at face value at maturity.

Index